Donald Davidson

Donald Davidson

Meaning, Truth, Language, and Reality

Ernie Lepore
Kirk Ludwig

CLARENDON PRESS · OXFORD

OXFORD

UNIVERSITY PRESS

Great Clarendon Street, Oxford OX2 6DP

Oxford University Press is a department of the University of Oxford.
It furthers the University's objective of excellence in research, scholarship,
and education by publishing worldwide in

Oxford New York

Auckland Cape Town Dar es Salaam Hong Kong Karachi Kuala Lumpur
Madrid Melbourne Mexico City Nairobi New Delhi Shanghai Taipei
Toronto

With offices in

Argentina Austria Brazil Chile Czech Republic France Greece
Guatemala Hungary Italy Japan South Korea Poland Portugal
Singapore Switzerland Thailand Turkey Ukraine Vietnam

Oxford is a registered trade mark of Oxford University Press
in the UK and in certain other countries

Published in the United States
by Oxford University Press Inc., New York

© Ernie Lepore and Kirk Ludwig 2005

The moral rights of the authors have been asserted
Database right Oxford University Press (maker)

First published 2005

British Library Cataloguing in Publication Data

Data available

Library of Congress Cataloging in Publication Data

Lepore, Ernest, 1950–
   Donald Davidson: meaning, truth, language, and reality / Ernie Lepore and Kirk
Ludwig.
      p. cm.
   Summary: "Ernest Lepore and Kirk Ludwig present a critical exposition of the
philosophical system of Donald Davidson (1917–2003)"—Provided by publisher.
   Includes bibliographical references and index.
   1. Davidson, Donald, 1917– I. Ludwig, Kirk, 1959– II. Title.
   B945.D384L47 2005   191—dc22   2004024979

ISBN 0–19–925134–7

1 3 5 7 9 10 8 6 4 2

Typeset by Newgen Imaging Systems (P) Ltd., Chennai, India
Printed in Great Britain
on acid-free paper by
Biddles Ltd, King's Lynn, Norfolk

For John and Julia Ludwig

In memory of
Irma Santangello and Ernest Lepore

Preface

Since the publication of "Actions, Reasons and Causes" in 1963, when he was 46 years old, Donald Davidson's work in the philosophy of action, mind, and language has been at the center of the stage of analytic philosophy. His work has also been influential in linguistics and cognitive science, and in the last decade and a half has begun to be discussed widely both in the continental tradition, through his work on larger themes in the philosophical tradition, and in literary criticism, through his work on language. There has been a steady stream of seminal articles over the years, making fundamental and influential contributions to action theory, philosophical psychology, metaphysics, the philosophy of language, the theory of meaning, and even ethics. Each field to which Davidson has contributed has been fundamentally altered by his writings. Not all analytic philosophers have agreed with his conclusions, but it is a measure of the depth and importance of his work that nearly all who deal with topics Davidson has treated feel compelled to address what he has had to say about them. Davidson's influence is all the more remarkable because his corpus of work consists mainly of short, extremely condensed, sometimes programmatic articles, difficult even by the standards of analytic philosophy. In addition, most of these articles were widely scattered and hard to obtain prior to the collection of the bulk of those written in the 1960s and 1970s into *Essays on Actions and Events* and *Inquiries into Truth and Interpretation*, published in 1980 and 1984 respectively by Oxford University Press. Since then, two further volumes of essays have been published by Oxford University Press, *Subjective, Intersubjective, Objective* (2001) and *Problems of Rationality* (2004). A final collection of essays from Oxford, *Truth, Language and History*, and a book, *Truth and Predication,* are in press. Despite the obstacles raised by the difficulty of the work and its relative inaccessibility, Davidson ranks among the most influential writers in analytic philosophy in the twentieth century, writers who have transformed the way we think about the subject.

It is characteristic of Davidson's work that what apparently began as two relatively distinct projects, one with the aim of understanding the nature of rational action, the other with the aim of understanding what it is to speak a language, became significantly interrelated, each drawing on results of the other. This ability to synthesize the results of work in different areas, and to see the relevance of a result or solution to a problem in one area to problems in another, is one of the most striking features of Davidson's work. It was an insight of this kind which led to Davidson's proposal to use a Tarski-style truth theory as the core of a theory of meaning for natural languages, which in turn sparked a revolution in philosophical semantics. This ability to set old problems in a new light has been an important source of Davidson's influence. Another source of his influence has been a systematic vision of the connections between fundamental issues in philosophy, centered around understanding the relations between language, thought, and the world. The centerpiece and nexus of Davidson's philosophy is the project of the radical interpreter, who interprets another on the basis of evidence that does not presuppose any detailed knowledge of his thoughts or any knowledge of the meanings of his words. The radical interpreter's stance is fundamentally third person. The choice of this as the stance from which to investigate language and thought and their relation to the world is motivated by the thought that language is essentially and centrally a social phenomenon, and so must be understood from the public stance. Davidson attributes the basic point to Quine: he "revolutionized our understanding of verbal communication by taking seriously the fact... that there can be no more to meaning than an adequately equipped person can learn and observe; the interpreter's point of view is therefore the revealing one to bring to the subject." Study of the project of radical interpretation aims to make us respect this insight:

the third-person approach to language is not a mere philosophical exercise. The point of the study of radical interpretation is to grasp how it is possible for one person to come to understand the speech and thoughts of another, for this ability is basic to our sense of a world independent of ourselves, and hence to the possibility of thought itself. The third-person approach is yours and mine.   (Davidson 2004 (2001): 143)

The radical interpreter must construct his picture of another's thoughts and words and his connection with reality all at once out of the public resources available to any objective knower. Out of the investigation of the constraints on radical interpretation and the assumptions needed for success emerges a unified picture of human beings as rational animals, whose knowledge of the world, of their own minds, and the meanings and minds of others, is as essential a part of their nature as is the power of thought and speech.

Unlike other systematic thinkers, such as Quine, Davidson never attempted a book-length treatment of his views to put them into a canonical form and to identify important changes to and developments in the original project.

The task of elaborating his program, identifying changes in it, and relating it to contemporary developments has been left largely in the hands of other philosophers, both sympathetic and unsympathetic, and has taken place largely in technical journals. While many books have been written under the inspiration or influence of Davidson's work, there have been relatively few attempts to give a book-length treatment to either significant parts, or most of Davidson's philosophy. Much of what is available presents a misleading picture of Davidson's central project, and all fail to do justice to the interconnections between his work in various areas.

The present book, undertaken against this background, is the first of two on Davidson's central philosophical project. It aims to provide a critical exposition and assessment of the broader themes of Davidson's work. The second, *Donald Davidson: Truth-Theoretic Semantics* (OUP, 2005; henceforth *Truth-Theoretic Semantics*), is devoted to a more detailed and thorough development of his work within the truth-theoretic framework introduced in Part I of this book. We will make reference to this second book at various points where themes and topics discussed or mentioned are taken up at greater length.

This work has been long in preparation, far longer than the authors anticipated when setting out to write it. We hope this has resulted in a better book than we would otherwise have written. We know it has resulted in a longer book. We hope, at any rate, that it has resulted in a good book, but this we must leave to others to judge. We have had a lot of help in the course of writing and preparing the manuscript. It would be impossible to thank everyone individually who has contributed to our thinking about the subjects of this book, and we apologize now to all of those we should mention but do not. We should like however to make special mention of the following people who have made helpful comments and provided important advice: Ana Maria Andrei, Emil Badici, Daniel Boisvert, Kent Johnson, Peter Klein, Sarah-Jane Leslie, Christopher Lubbers, Robert May, Paul Pietroski, Dugald Owen, Greg Ray, Charles Siewert, Barry Smith, Robert Stainton, and several anonymous readers for Oxford University Press. We also extend thanks to our students in seminars over the years at Rutgers University and the University of Florida, and to Elka Shortsleeve for preparing the index. We owe a special debt of gratitude to Donald Davidson, both for providing the subject-matter of the book, and for much of inspiration in this and many other projects. It is one of our great regrets that this work was not completed before his unexpected death on 30 August 2003.

Contents

Contents

Detailed Table of Contents

Detailed Table of Contents

Detailed Table of Contents

Note on In-Text Citations

The author–date citation method is used in the text. When the citation is to a reprinted essay, the format of the citation is as follows, where 'n' is a place-holder for the page or pages cited, if any.

(Author Date-of-Collection (Original-Publication-Date): n)

This allows readers to keep track of the original publication date of material cited, which is relevant to understanding the development of Davidson's work and many interpretive issues. In the bibliography, the references are ordered by author, date of collection, and then original publication date. Where further distinctions are required, '*a*', '*b*', '*c*', etc. are appended to the date of collection, and works are further ordered alphabetically by title. For example, the following citation

(Davidson 2001*c* (1973): 138)

would be sorted first by the author's last name, 'Davidson', then by the date of publication of collection from which page numbers are cited, 2001, and then by the original date of publication. The '*c*' appended to '2001' indicates that there are at least three entries which share these features. They will be listed in order in the bibliography. Original publication information follows the main entry. Thus, for example, the portion of the bibliography corresponding to the above is:

Davidson, D. (2001*a* (1973)). In Defence of Convention T. *Inquiries into Truth and Interpretation* (2nd edn.), pp. 65–75. New York: Clarendon Press. Originally published in H. Leblanc (ed.), *Truth, Syntax and Modality*. Dordrecht: North-Holland Publishing Company.

——(2001*b* (1973)). The Material Mind. *Essays on Actions and Events* (2nd edn.), pp. 245–60. New York: Clarendon Press. Originally published in P. Suppes, L. Henken, G. C. Moisil, and A. Joja (eds.), *Proceedings of the Fourth International Congress for Logic, Methodology, and Philosophy of Science*. Amsterdam: North Holland Publishing Co.

——(2001*c* (1973)). Radical Interpretation. *Inquiries into Truth and Interpretation* (2nd edn.), pp. 125–39. New York: Clarendon Press. Originally published in *Dialectica*, 27 (1973), 314–28.

1

Introduction

What is it for words to mean what they do?

(Davidson 2001*a*, p. xiii)

1. Synoptic Overview of Davidson's Philosophy

P. F. Strawson—borrowing a phrase from Virginia Woolf—once described Donald Davidson as a man "of thoroughbred intelligence who rides his mind at a gallop across country in pursuit of an idea" (Strawson 1984). This wonderful image captures better than a more prosaic description would the excitement of Davidson's work, which has ranged across almost the entire field of philosophy and has had a profound influence on the development of analytic philosophy in the last half of the twentieth century.

The two central projects of Davidson's philosophy are those of understanding the nature of human agency and the nature of language. The first is represented by Davidson's work in the philosophy of action. The second is represented by his work in the philosophy of language, and especially in the theory of meaning. The two projects are interconnected. Human beings, on the one hand, are linguistic agents. Therefore, understanding human agency requires understanding what it is to be able to speak a language, and the ways that is bound up with our capacities for reasoning and acting. Possessing a language, on the other, is having the capacity to interpret, and to speak so as to be interpretable, by other speakers, and, thus, is having a capacity for a specialized form of agency. Understanding the nature of agency, then, is essential for understanding our capacity for speech, just as understanding our capacity for speech is essential for understanding the nature of specifically human agency.

Our main concern is with Davidson's work in the theory of meaning and the philosophy of language, and with conclusions he has reached in the philosophy of mind, metaphysics, and epistemology, which rest directly on work in the philosophy of language. His work in the philosophy of action forms part of the foundation for his work in the philosophy of language, and we will note where it has a role to play, but we will not give it detailed critical attention.

There are two central themes in Davidson's program in the philosophy of language. One is his famous proposal to employ the structure of a Tarski-style (absolute) truth theory, which assigns truth conditions to each sentence of the language from a finite set of axioms, in pursuit of providing a compositional meaning theory for a natural language, that is, an account of how we understand semantically complex expressions on the basis of understanding semantically primitive ones and their combinations. The truth theory aims to fulfill this role in virtue of meeting constraints that are supposed to guarantee that the assignment of truth conditions to sentences of the language can be used to interpret them. This gives the concept of truth a central role in the project of understanding language and meaning, a role which has been the source of a great deal of confusion about the nature of Davidson's concerns and proposals, confusions which will be cleared up in the sequel.

The other central theme is the adoption of the stance of the radical interpreter of another speaker as methodologically basic in understanding language and connected matters. In this, the principal influence on Davidson was Quine's project of radical translation (Quine 1960). However, unlike Quine, who conceived of himself as providing a scientifically respectable reconstruction of the notion of meaning, Davidson aims rather to illuminate our ordinary concept. The radical interpreter is confined to evidence that bears on interpretation of another that includes what can be observed and described neutrally with respect to the intention or meaning of the other's behavior, and which specifically excludes any information about the meanings of any of his expressions and any detailed knowledge of the contents of his beliefs, desires, intentions, and other propositional attitudes. Adopting the position of the radical interpreter as methodologically basic is motivated by the principle that what matters to meaning, and thoughts bound up with meaning, must be in principle available to another speaker. As Davidson puts it at one point, "The semantic features of language are public features. What no one can, in the nature of the case,

figure out from the totality of the relevant evidence cannot be part of meaning"
(Davidson 2001*a* (1979): 235). Or, again:

As Ludwig Wittgenstein, not to mention Dewey, G. H. Mead, Quine, and many
others have insisted, language is intrinsically social. This does not entail that truth
and meaning can be *defined* in terms of observable behavior, or that it is "nothing but"
observable behavior; but it does imply that meaning is entirely determined by observable
behavior, even readily observable behavior. That meanings are decipherable is not a
matter of luck; public availability is a constitutive aspect of language.   (Davidson
1990*b*: 314)

The two themes, framing the project of giving a compositional meaning theory
in terms of constructing a suitable truth theory for the language, on the one
hand, and seeing the basic standpoint for investigating constitutive features
of language as being that of the radical interpreter, on the other, are straightforwardly connected. The project of the radical interpreter is cast in the form
of confirming a truth theory for a speaker's language that can be used to
interpret correctly the speaker's utterances.

The project of radical interpretation aims to shed light on the concept of
meaning and those of the propositional attitudes by relating them to more basic
concepts, not through providing analyses of the target concepts in terms of
more basic concepts, but through showing how evidence described in terms of
those more basic concepts can be marshaled in support of a theory of interpretation for a speaker (see Chapters 11–12). The inspiration for this approach to the
theory of meaning lies in Davidson's early work at Stanford on testing axiomatic decision theory, the formal theory of choice behavior (see Chapter 12).
From that work, Davidson drew two morals: first, that by "putting formal
conditions on simple concepts and their relations to one another, a powerful
structure could be defined"; and, second, that the formal theory itself "says
nothing about the world," and that its content is given in its interpretation by
the data to which it is applied (Davidson 1999: 32). Applied to the theory of
meaning, the aim is to illuminate the concepts of the theory by introducing a
powerful formal structure in the form of a formal truth theory for a language,
which we then seek to show that we can confirm on a relatively thin evidential base, in a way that suffices for it to be used to interpret speakers of the
language. As Davidson puts it:

In philosophy we are used to definitions, analyses, reductions. Typically these are
intended to carry us from concepts better understood, or clear, or more basic epi-
stemologically or ontologically, to others we want to understand. The method I have

suggested fits none of these categories. I have proposed a looser relation between concepts to be illuminated and the relatively more basic. At the centre stands a formal theory, a theory of truth, which imposes a complex structure on sentences containing the primitive notions of truth and satisfaction. These notions are given application by the form of the theory and the nature of the evidence. The result is a partially interpreted theory. The advantage of the method lies not in its free-style appeal to the notion of evidential support but in the idea of a powerful theory interpreted at the most advantageous point. This allows us to reconcile the need for a semantically articulated structure with a theory testable only at the sentential level. The more subtle gain is that very thin evidence in support of each of a potential infinity of points can yield rich results, even with respect to the points. (Davidson 2001c (1973): 137)

Thus, Davidson offers one central standpoint from which to investigate the foundations of thought and language. In this lies one of the features of Davidson's program which has most excited philosophers, namely, that it offers the hope of replacing our reliance on what David Wiggins has called "the miscellaneous anecdotal materials out of which we have so garrulously attempted to construct a philosophy of language" (Wiggins 1980: 334) with a principled framework for investigating language, meaning, and related linguistic and psychological concepts.

The picture that emerges has implications far beyond the philosophy of language, and suggests a radical revision to the traditional Cartesian conception of our relation to the world and to each other. Most significant, perhaps, is the idea that the third person point of view is basic to understanding meaning, and so thought in turn, since it is bound up with meaning. When we then investigate what must be so for interpretation to proceed from this standpoint, two points of great significance emerge. The first is that we must see others not only as largely rational agents, but as having largely true beliefs, including largely true empirical beliefs. This is expressed in the famous Principle of Charity. The second is the observation that very different interpretation schemes, from the point of view of the interpreter, can make equally good sense of a speaker's behavior.

The first supports directly the thesis of the impossibility of massive error in our beliefs, particularly our empirical beliefs, and the relational determination of thought content. Since Charity also requires us to find others largely in agreement with us, and so forces us to find others sharing with us, by and large, the same concepts, it also plays a crucial role in Davidson's argument for the impossibility of conceptual relativism, understood as the claim that it is possible for there to be radically different, i.e. non-overlapping, conceptual schemes. It emerges also as an unavoidable assumption of interpretation that we can know the thoughts of others, and that there is a presumption that speakers know their own thoughts and meanings.

The second leads to some surprising conclusions about meaning and reference. Namely, since different interpretation and reference schemes may account for all the data equally well, and the content of the theory is exhausted by its account of the data, schemes which intuitively seem to assign different referents or truth conditions to the same sentences capture the facts equally well. These are the theses of the inscrutability of reference and indeterminacy of translation—the former being a special case of the latter. With additional premises, Davidson argues from this standpoint also that language is necessary for thought, and that thought can emerge only in the general context of communication with other speakers. Taken together, these theses amount to a fundamental rejection of empiricism and the epistemic priority of experience in our knowledge of the external world. We elaborate these and some additional themes below.[1]

2. Goals

Our topic in this book, as we have said, is that portion of Davidson's philosophy which is grounded in his work in the theory of meaning and philosophy of language. We have two main goals.

The first is to provide a systematic exposition of Davidson's influential work in the philosophy of language, particularly in the theory of meaning, and of his work in philosophy of mind, metaphysics, and epistemology based upon it. Davidson's work is scattered through a large number of articles, published over a period of more than forty years, and Davidson himself has never attempted a systematic exposition of his program or philosophy. While the program has retained its basic methodology, at the heart of which lies the aim to construct a recursive truth theory for natural languages meeting certain constraints, there have been many modifications and revisions to it as it has been developed by Davidson and his followers. There is consequently no one place the student, interpreter, critic, or developer of Davidson's work can look to find its canonical formulation. Davidson's articles together form a kind of mosaic, which one must view all at once to see the overall pattern and the many interconnections. This, together with a certain enigmatic (at times, even oracular) quality to Davidson's articles, whose subtleties, complexity, and cross references often cannot be fully appreciated except against the background of his other articles,

---

[1] For a fuller discussion of Davidson's life and intellectual development see Davidson 1999; Ludwig 2003; Lepore 2004.

makes access to his thought difficult, despite its evident importance. There is therefore a need for an account of Davidson's program in the philosophy of language which lays out its historical development, assesses the motivations and arguments for it, identifies modifications and revisions, and the reasons for them, and gives a systematic account of the current state of the program.

Our purpose is not assentation, however. The second aim is to critically assess Davidson's program, to mark its successes, but also to identify where its accomplishments fall short of its ambitions, and, since it is an ongoing research program, to assess its prospects for the future, and to contribute to the expansion of that program.

We address this book to two audiences. The first is those who are coming to Davidson's work for the first time. While we presuppose a certain amount of philosophical sophistication and training, it should be accessible both to serious upper division undergraduate majors in philosophy, and to beginning graduate students. We have aimed to provide enough background in our discussions of various philosophical issues that arise for readers not yet full-fledged members of the profession to follow the discussion, and to be in a position to think about it on their own. The second is professional philosophers and others who work in the philosophy of language and who have an interest in sorting out and assessing Davidson's program. Thus, we have not hesitated to extend or to criticize Davidson's work, or to reformulate it in ways that help to clarify its foundations, while also providing an introduction and assessment of it.

This is the first of two books on Davidson's central philosophical project. We develop here the philosophical foundation of truth-theoretic semantics, which underlies Davidson's discussion of radical interpretation and the theses he develops on that basis. But we have reserved for another book detailed discussion of Davidson's contributions to work within truth-theoretic semantics, and our own contributions to work within that program (Lepore and Ludwig 2005; henceforth *Truth-Theoretic Semantics*). This companion to the present volume takes up the story about truth-theoretic semantics where this one leaves it at the end of Part I. The present book concentrates on the broader philosophical themes of Davidson's project.

3. Keynotes

It will be useful to provide a summary of some of the major themes of Davidson's work in the philosophy of language and their interconnections. The following list is not intended to be exhaustive, but rather to identify broad themes which structure Davidson's project and give it its distinctive character. Each of them will be explained and elaborated.

(a) Compositionality

Natural languages contain an infinite number of nonsynonymous sentences. Given the finite capacities of speakers, competence in speaking a language must be based on grasp of a finite portion of it which suffices to put one in a position to understand the rest (see Chapter 2 for extended discussion). Natural languages are then perforce compositional, in the sense that their expressions admit of a division into primitive and complex expressions, the relation between which is that the complex expressions are understood on the basis of grasp of the primitives and their arrangement in the complexes. The observation that natural languages are compositional is at the foundation of Davidson's program in the theory of meaning. Davidson has had a central role in bringing to prominence the importance of the requirement that a meaning theory for a natural language exhibit it as compositional. The requirement focuses our attention on the need to uncover structure in natural languages. While this is clearly something which philosophers from time immemorial have been engaged in, it had not been, until Davidson's work, always clearly separated from the project of conceptual analysis of primitive terms. Placing these two projects in the light of one another helps to illuminate both. To understand any range of talk in natural languages, it is important to know both the application conditions for primitive expressions, and to know what entailment relations hold among sentences in the range of discourse on the basis of structure. This can only be done by placing the sentences of interest in the context of a complete theory for the language (or at least that portion of it which appears in the range of discourse of interest). Understanding structure in terms of a compositional meaning theory for a language helps to put into sharp focus questions about logical form, as opposed to analysis, and to provide a criterion for correctness of proposals about the logical form of a sentence or range of sentences. Roughly, the logical form of a sentence is revealed by how the theory exhibits our understanding of it as resting on our understanding of its significant parts and their mode of combination (see chapter 13 of *Truth-Theoretic Semantics* for discussion).

(b) Meaning

The requirement that a meaning theory for natural languages be compositional is one of the engines that drives Davidson's work in the theory of meaning. This helps to make clear something which many commentators on Davidson have been confused about.[2] Davidson's interest in the theory of meaning has always been in the ordinary notion of meaning. In particular, it has not been his aim to reject as unintelligible, or incoherent, the ordinary notion of meaning, but instead to provide an explication of it. That is, his project has been to provide a description of natural languages and the semantic properties of expressions—not to provide a reconstruction of them, or the ordinary categories in terms of which we understand our talk. As Davidson puts it, "the task of a theory of meaning as I conceive it is not to change, improve, or reform a language, but to describe and understand it" (Davidson 2001c (1967): 29).[3] This is, as noted, in contrast to Quine, who rejects the ordinary concept of meaning as unclear and inadequately explicated, and offers in its place a concept intended to be of greater scientific respectability.[4] This point is of great importance in understanding and assessing Davidson's program, and we will return to its elaboration and defense below (Chapter 6).

(c) The Inutility of Reifying Meanings

A central theme of Davidson's approach to the theory of meaning has been that reifying meanings plays no useful role. Davidson's rejection of meanings as entities is not due to a rejection of Platonism in general in favor of nominalism. It is rather based on two sorts of arguments. The first sort seeks to show that introducing meanings as entities leads to disastrous consequences (see the discussion of "the slingshot argument" in Chapter 3, §4). The second sort urges that, in any case, the work that a meaning theory needs to do can be done without them. No properties, no senses, no propositions, no relations, no semantic universals of any kind are required to carry out the project of providing an adequate compositional meaning theory for natural languages for sentences which do not explicitly refer to them (see chapter 11 of *Truth-Theoretic Semantics* for a discussion of attempts to make good on this claim for so-called opaque contexts). If correct, this is an important point for two reasons. First, it undermines arguments for Platonism based on the indispensability of appeal to meanings as entities for the purposes of understanding the semantics of natural languages. Second, and more importantly in the context of the meaning theory, it shows that appeal to such entities, rather than contributing to an understanding of our linguistic abilities, is a distraction, because

[2] See e.g. Ramberg 1989; Stich 1976.　[3] See also Davidson 2001b (1983): 203.
[4] See in particular Quine 1953, 1960.

8

it introduces concepts and an ontology which are represented as necessary for understanding, when they are not. We gain the clearest view of a subject when we understand it in terms of the simplest set of concepts required for that purpose. There is, however, a deeper point to be made about the inutility of reifying meanings. The point just elaborated is that meanings (treated as entities) are not *necessary* in order to carry out the project of giving a compositional semantics for a natural language; but they are not *sufficient* either, and why this is so highlights one of Davidson's central insights, and helps to explain why they are not necessary. They are not sufficient for two reasons. The first is that assignments of entities of any kind to expressions alone cannot provide rules which explain how to understand complex expressions in terms of their significant parts, which is necessary for an adequate account of any language which has a compositional structure. The second is that knowing the referent of an expression, whether or not it is a meaning, is not itself sufficient to understand it. (See Chapter 3 for discussion of these points.)

(d) Truth

A deep appreciation of the difficulty in making meanings, construed as entities, pay their way in the theory of meaning motivates what is most distinctive about Davidson's approach to providing a compositional meaning theory for natural languages. That is his suggestion that the recursive structure of a Tarski-style truth theory (Tarski 1983 (1935)), modified for a natural language, which meets certain constraints, can play a central role in the project of constructing a compositional meaning theory for natural languages. The explanation of what this comes to in detail is the aim of Part I. But several general features of the proposal can be noted now. First, if successful, it promises to illuminate the concept of meaning by linking it with that of truth, and in particular to that of providing truth conditions. This connection between meaning and truth is one of the central themes of Davidson's work in the philosophy of language. Second, by using the recursive structure of a truth theory to provide a compositional meaning theory, the proposal aims to provide an account of our understanding of natural languages without having to appeal to meanings as entities (see Chapters 2 and 3 especially). Third, employing a truth theory of Tarski's style promises to provide a meaning theory which employs only an extensional logic. This constraint, if it can be met, simplifies the logic of the theory, but also places fairly severe requirements on the regimentation of the logical form of sentences in natural languages.

(e) Truth and Ontology

Connected with the employment of a truth theory at the core of a compositional meaning theory for natural languages is what Davidson has called 'the method of truth in metaphysics'.[5] In its basic form, the method of truth in metaphysics aims to investigate questions about ontological commitment by investigating what we are committed to by our commitment to the truth of what we say. Some of our commitments lie on the surface of our talk. If we commit ourselves to the truth of the sentences 'there are volcanoes in Iceland' and 'bandicoots are beyond the pale' we incur commitments to the existence of Iceland, to there being entities which are volcanoes, and to there being things which satisfy the open sentence 'if x is a bandicoot, then x is beyond the pale', that is, to things of which it would be at least intelligible to predicate (even if falsely) 'is a bandicoot' or 'is beyond the pale'. But some of our commitments are not so easy to read off from the surface structure of our sentences. Commitment to the truth of the sentence, 'Galileo said that the earth moves', for example, clearly does not commit one to the existence of the earth or to the existence of moving objects. On the other hand, it has been urged that commitment to the truth of such sentences commits us to the existence of propositions or sentence meanings named by the complement clause of such sentences, in this case, 'that the earth moves'. We are said to be committed to propositions by commitment to the truth of such sentences on the grounds that the only way to give a compositional account of the meaning of sentences of the form

$$\text{Noun phrase} + \text{verb} + \text{'that'} + \text{sentence}$$

is to treat so-called that-clauses as expressions which refer to the meanings of the contained sentences. (See chapter 11 of *Truth-Theoretic Semantics* for our discussion of this issue in particular.) The method of truth in metaphysics enjoins us to put questions about what ontological commitments we have in virtue of the structure of the sentences whose truth we commit ourselves to in the framework of a truth theory for the language. For it is only in the context of a systematic theory for the language that we can be confident that we have uncovered what ontology the truth of various sentences in the language requires.

[5] See Davidson 2001*b* (1967), 2001 (1968), 2001*b* (1974), 2001*a* (1977).

(f) Interpretation

Davidson treats compositional meaning theories as empirical theories, theories of particular speakers or natural languages, which must be confirmed on the basis of public evidence. By treating the theory as an empirical theory of this kind, we treat it as a theory of interpretation. This helps to illuminate the meanings of primitive expressions by showing how to link systematically concepts employed in the theory to concepts employed in describing the evidence available to the interpreter of another speaker. Since speakers are rational agents, this locates the concept of meaning in the context of a theory of rational agency and communication, and is one of the most distinctive features of Davidson's general approach. (As Davidson acknowledges, Quine is the pathbreaker here, despite his different aims.) Importantly, the project aims to illuminate the concept of meaning by tracing out the connections between it and a broad range of other concepts with which it is allied in our descriptions of ourselves and our interactions with one another, rather than by giving necessary and sufficient conditions for the application of the predicate 'is meaningful'. It is also by placing the theory of meaning in the context of a theory of the interpretation of human action in general, as we have noted, that Davidson hopes to arrive at some of his more ambitious metaphysical and epistemological theses. These issues are discussed in Part III.

(g) Anti-Cartesianism

A central feature of what we will call the Cartesian tradition, though its pedigree is older, is that at the foundation of the structure of our justified beliefs about the world are our beliefs about our own mental states, our attitudes, experiences, and sensations. Davidson's approach to the theory of meaning and interpretation, and to central issues in epistemology, is anti-Cartesian in the sense that he rejects this assumption. This emerges in a variety of ways in the development of his project, but most clearly in assumptions Davidson makes about radical interpretation. The radical interpreter (see Chapter 11) is restricted ultimately to behavioral evidence in formulating a theory of interpretation for another speaker. From this standpoint, Davidson treats the central concepts of the theory of interpretation of another speaker as theoretical concepts, whose function is to keep track of behavior. Viewed from this perspective, the role of a theory of interpretation is to identify and systematize patterns in the behavior of speakers in relation to their environment. If this is right, then we do not have access first to facts about speakers' meanings

11

and attitudes, including our own. A number of the most important theses Davidson has argued for flow from this. How Davidson aims to reconcile the treatment of the central concepts of interpretation as theoretical concepts with first person authority, that is, the fact that speakers are necessarily more authoritative in general about their own attitudes and sensations, is discussed in Chapter 20.

(h) The Rejection of Empiricism

A consequence of Davidson's taking the third person position of the radical interpreter as methodologically fundamental is his rejection of all forms of traditional empiricism, which attempt to give an account of our knowledge of the world by appeal to sensory experience. What is distinctive about empiricism is not the thought that sensory experience can play a role in justifying our beliefs about the world around us, but that it plays the role of a foundation for our empirical knowledge. This in turn entails that the first person point of view is fundamental, since each person's experience is treated as being his own foundation for his empirical knowledge. In adopting the third person point of view as fundamental, then, Davidson rejects a central tenet of all forms of empiricism, and the traditional project associated with it of explaining our empirical knowledge by appeal to experience. Rather, in Davidson's view, our knowledge of the world around us, of other minds, and of our own minds, has a unified source in our nature as rational beings capable of communicating with one another (see Chapters 19 and 22 especially).[6]

We have identified these as major themes because they underlie and structure the program in the philosophy of language, philosophy of mind, epistemology, and metaphysics. The requirement that an account of how we understand natural languages exhibit them as compositional is what gives rise to the suggestion that meaning theories for natural languages be cast in the form of a Tarski-style truth theory. This in turn links in an interesting and novel way the concepts of truth and meaning. Treating the structure of sentences in the context of a comprehensive theory for a language leads to the proposal for how to uncover logical form and to the method of truth in metaphysics. The aim to provide a comprehensive understanding of natural languages leads to the treatment of the truth theory for a language as an empirical theory, and to the adoption of the stance of the radical interpreter as the

---

[6] See Davidson 2001 (1975), 2001*a* (1982), 2001*b* (1982), 2001*a* (1983), 2001 (1984), 2001*a* (1987), 2001*b* (1987), 2001*a* (1988), 2001 (1989), 2001 (1991), 2001 (1992).

standpoint for confirmation, linking the structure of a rich theory with its basic evidence, and placing the theory of meaning in the context of a theory of rational agency. Adopting this stance as fundamental is tantamount to the rejection of Cartesianism and empiricism.

4. Methodology

Since our aim is to provide a historically oriented exposition of Davidson's program, we will be tracing its development from its beginnings in "Theories of Meaning and Learnable Languages" through to recent work. One of the reasons this is important is that if we do not trace out the development of Davidson's work, we are apt to treat different expressions of his views as if they were expressions of a single view. Since his views have changed in some significant ways, this can only lead to confusion. Davidson's work is unified by the proposal that a truth theory meeting certain constraints can serve as a meaning theory. Thus, we will be developing that proposal in parallel with its historical development. Although Davidson does not present in his writings a formal truth theory, the philosophical project he articulates is centered around the project of providing such a theory. Many of the technical and philosophical issues cannot be discussed or even formulated clearly without an actual theory with respect to which they can be raised. For this reason, we will introduce informally a truth theory for a simple language in Chapter 4, and some modifications in subsequent chapters. This will then serve also as the background for the discussion of the project of radical interpretation, and the various modifications of that project.

At each stage of our development of the project, we will be evaluating the arguments Davidson advances for his views. Sometimes we will decide that the arguments do not achieve their aims. If we find alternative means for doing so within the framework of the theory, we advance them. If we do not offer such an alternative, we assess the relevance of the (alleged) failure for the project as a whole. In addition, we will discuss many of the major criticisms which have been leveled against Davidson's project, and discuss alternatives to our interpretation of it.

5. Overview

This book is divided into three parts. Part I provides a historical introduction to the project of providing a compositional meaning theory in the form of a truth theory. This part is divided into nine chapters. These discuss, in turn, (i) the compositionality requirement on meaning theories for natural languages (Chapter 2); (ii) difficulties for trying to meet the requirement by appeal to meanings as entities or to meaning axioms (Chapter 3); (iii) the introduction of a truth theory to perform the compositional work of a meaning theory, together with a truth theory of a simple language modeled on English (Chapter 4); (iv) an initial discussion of the sort of modifications which must be made to a truth theory to adapt it to the context sensitivity of many natural language expressions (Chapter 5); (v) Davidson's initial proposal that a merely extensionally adequate truth theory suffices for all that is wanted out of a compositional meaning theory (Chapter 6); (vi) the extensionality and determination problems, which have to do with selecting from among the true truth theories the one that can be used in a compositional meaning theory, and selecting which of its theorems are to serve to give the meaning of target natural language sentences, respectively (Chapter 7); (vii) the objection, initially introduced by John Foster, that what Davidson specifies a speaker should know is not adequate for him to interpret a natural language (Chapter 8); (viii) the exact relation of the right truth theory (which we call an "interpretive truth theory") to a compositional meaning theory (Chapter 9); and, finally, (ix) the difficulties presented for the approach by the unboundedness of natural languages, the presence of surface level ambiguities, vague expressions, and the semantic paradoxes (Chapter 10). This constitutes the basic introduction to Davidson's semantic program.

In order to keep attention focused on foundational issues, we do not attempt to work out in detail in Part I all the technical issues that attend formulating an adequate truth theory for natural languages. We turn to this task in this book's companion volume, *Truth-Theoretic Semantics*, which is the more technical of the two. We discuss its contents below.

Part II takes up the project of radical interpretation. The project of radical interpretation links up Davidson's proposal about the form of a compositional meaning theory for a natural language with broader questions about the interrelations between and grounding of our use of the family of concepts we employ in making sense of linguistic beings. Radical interpretation is interpretation of another speaker from the standpoint of a speaker who does not know anything about the language of the speaker or any details of his attitudes. By seeing how to marshal evidence about a speaker's interactions with his environment in support of a theory of interpretation built around an interpretive truth theory, we see how the concepts of the theory are related to the concepts deployed in its evidential base, and the concepts we employ in attempting to describe the speaker as a rational agent. Our examination of Davidson's description of the project of the radical interpreter aims both to clarify it and its role in his overall philosophical position, and to critically evaluate it and the conclusions Davidson has drawn from reflection on it. This part is divided into seven chapters. These discuss (i) how to frame the project of radical interpretation (Chapter 11); (ii) the radical interpreter's procedure and the role of a Tarski-style truth theory in it (Chapter 12); (iii) the nature of and the justification for the Principle of Charity, which Davidson famously invokes on behalf of the radical interpreter (Chapter 13); (iii) the role of the theory of agency and additional constraints on theory formation (Chapter 14); (iv) the famous claim that interpretation leads to objective indeterminacy of interpretation theories (Chapter 15); (v) Davidson's development of a unified theory of meaning and action (Chapter 16); and, finally, (vi) Davidson's well-known, and, at first face, shocking, claim that "there is no such thing as a language, not if a language is anything like what many philosophers and linguists have supposed" (Davidson 1986: 446), and how this could be compatible with his basic program in the theory of meaning (Chapter 17). Our main critical conclusion is that there is considerable doubt that Davidson can justify a priori, as he needs to, the assumption that radical interpretation can succeed for any speaker. The discussion of this central issue is continued in the next part where additional arguments for the assumption are considered.

Part III considers in detail a number of well-known specific conclusions, and the arguments for them, that Davidson has advanced on the basis of reflection on the project of radical interpretation. We take up in turn (i) the argument for the impossibility of radically different conceptual schemes (Chapter 18); (ii) the impossibility of massive error about our environments and the concomitant thesis of externalism about thought content (Chapter 19); (iii) the grounding of first person authority and knowledge in reflection on radical interpretation (Chapter 20); (iv) the inscrutability of reference (Chapter 21); and (v) an argument for the necessity of speakers being radically interpretable, and, indeed, radically interpreted, based on requirements on our having the concept of objectivity, that is, the concept of the difference between truth and error (Chapter 22). Our conclusions in this part are largely negative. We argue that Davidson has not successfully show that there cannot be radically different conceptual schemes, though we also suggest some reasons to think that more straightforward arguments show that the most radical suggestions along these lines cannot be correct; that Davidson does not successfully show how first person authority and knowledge can be explained from the standpoint of the radical interpreter; that Davidson has not justified the claim of the inscrutability of reference; and that he has not shown that a requirement on having the concept of objectivity is that we be radically interpretable or radically interpreted.

Since we make, in Part I, many references to more detailed discussions of issues in truth-theoretics in this book's companion volume, *Donald Davidson: Truth-Theoretic Semantics*, we provide a brief overview of its contents here. *Truth-Theoretic Semantics* discusses some of the influential suggestions which Davidson has himself made about the logical form of natural language constructions, but also refines, clarifies, and extends Davidson's semantic program. We apply the framework systematically to a wide range of important natural language constructions, not all of which Davidson has himself explicitly addressed, and we do not hesitate, on critical evaluation, to amend or discard Davidson's proposals in favor of others. We do not provide a comprehensive treatment of the semantics of English, a task larger than any pair of individuals could undertake with success. Our aim is rather to discuss the application of the program of truth-theoretic semantics to some central features of natural languages and to some potential problem areas. *Truth-Theoretic Semantics* contains some original extensions of the semantic program drawn from work of the authors, and comprises fourteen chapters. It lays out in a condensed form the philosophical foundations of truth-theoretic semantics in Chapter 1, which are covered in Part I of the present book. Chapter 2 takes up the modifications to a truth theory needed to enable it to handle quantifiers, and discusses the extension of standard techniques to restricted quantifiers. Chapter 3 implements these techniques for a simple artificial language, which extends the simple language introduced in this book in Part I. Chapter 4 discusses the proper treatment of singular terms and related matters, proper names, indexicals and simple demonstratives. Chapter 5 takes up complex demonstratives, that is, noun phrases such as 'that awful man who ate the burrito in the elevator'. Chapter 6 turns to quotation devices. Chapter 7 discusses adjectives and adverbs, and, in particular, how to handle topic dependent adjectives and adverbs, such as 'slow' and 'slowly', whose contribution to the truth conditions of a sentence are understood relative to the noun or verb that they modify. The book then takes up, in three chapters, the semantics of tense and temporal modifiers in English. Chapter 8 discusses the simple tenses of state and event verbs, past, present, and future. Chapter 9 discusses the interaction of tense with temporal adverbials and quantifiers. Chapter 10 discusses tense in sentential complements, as in attitude and indirect discourse reports, and provides an analysis of the perfect tenses. Chapter 11 discusses indirect discourse and attitude sentences, including, of course, Davidson's own paratactic analysis. Chapter 12 then considers how non-declarative sentences, imperatives, and interrogatives can be brought into the fold of a truth-theoretic semantics. Chapters 13 and 14 address two more general issues. Chapter 13 discusses what light Davidson's program sheds on the question of how to understand and reveal logical form in natural languages. Chapter 14 discusses Davidson's views on the concept of truth, which plays so central a role in his philosophy of language.

Part 1

Historical Introduction to Truth-Theoretic Semantics

... a satisfactory theory of meaning must give an account of how the meanings of sentences depend upon the meanings of words.

(Davidson 2001c (1967): 17)

1. Introduction

In Part I, in Chapters 2–10, we begin our introduction to Davidson's program in the philosophy of language. We have two aims. One is to expound in some detail the early history of the program and its dialectical background. Without an adequate understanding here, one cannot adequately understand the development of Davidson's philosophy as a whole, or adequately assess it. Our other aim is to explain against this background how a truth theory may be used in pursuit of a compositional meaning theory. This will help us to appreciate the philosophical importance, in addition to the technical merits, of the proposal, and pave the way for a fuller understanding of the role of reflection on the project of the radical interpreter in Davidson's philosophy of language, the topic of Part II.

Chapter 2 begins with the requirement, which Davidson famously introduced in "Theories of Meaning and Learnable Languages," that a meaning theory[7] for a natural language be compositional, that it exhibit how complex

---

[7] A word about terminology is in order. To avoid confusion, when referring to a theory about meaning or truth (or the concepts of meaning or truth), we will use the phrases 'theory of meaning'

expressions can be understood on the basis of an understanding of their significant parts and structure. We will clarify this requirement, discuss Davidson's learnability argument and our own arguments for it, as well as its relation to linguistic competence; finally, we will respond to some objections based on misunderstandings of the compositionality requirement.

Chapters 3 and 4 take up Davidson's equally famous suggestion that we find ready-made in a Tarski-style truth theory a theoretical structure that can discharge the task of providing a compositional meaning theory.

Chapter 3 is concerned with the historical and dialectical background of this suggestion, and, in particular, with Davidson's criticisms of traditional approaches to a theory of linguistic understanding in which meanings conceived of as abstract entities play a pivotal theoretical role. The central thrust of his criticisms is that postulating meanings as entities has no utility. We identify as key to his conclusion a point implicit in the shape of his discussion, though not explicitly articulated, namely, that to the extent to which a theory quantifying over meaning serves its purpose, it does so *not* by dint of referring to meanings, but by implementing a mechanism that fortuitously, relative to the assignment of meanings to terms, matches sentences of the object language (the language the theory is about) with sentences in use in our metalanguage (the language of our theory) which are the same in meaning. Meeting this condition is both necessary, and sufficient, for a meaning theory to enable its possessor to understand object language sentences. This discussion will set the stage for Davidson's suggestion that a truth theory meeting suitable constraints can serve this purpose with no more ontological resources than are required for the theory of reference.

Davidson's central insight is that a suitable analog for natural languages of Convention T, which Tarski introduced as a requirement on a materially adequate definition[8] of a truth predicate for a formal language, is what a truth theory should satisfy to be usable as a theory for interpreting the sentences

---

or 'theory of truth', as appropriate. When referring to a theory which aims to specify for each sentence of a language what it means or what its truth conditions are (in a sense to be made precise), we will use the expressions 'meaning theory' and 'truth theory', respectively. The distinction is important. A truth or meaning theory is not a theory of truth or of meaning, though the latter might make reference to the former. Davidson often uses 'theory of meaning' and 'theory of truth' in the sense in which we use 'meaning theory' and 'truth theory'. Though he is guilty of no confusion here, there is evidence that some commentators have been misled by his usage.

[8] For the purposes of our discussion we are using 'truth theory' and 'truth definition' interchangeably. A recursive truth theory can be treated as an implicit definition of the truth predicate for which it fixes an extension (i.e. the set of things it is true of). This implicit definition can, in turn, be turned into an explicit one (of sorts) by appeal to set theory. See the appendix to Chapter 4.

for which it provides truth conditions. Tarski's Convention T holds that an extensionally adequate definition of a truth predicate 'is T' for a language L must entail all sentences of the form $[T]$,

  $[T]$ s is T if and only if p,

where s is a sentence of L and 'p' is replaced by a sentence of the theory which translates s (henceforth, 'a T-sentence'). If the sentence replacing 'p' translates s, clearly it is true just in case s is. Thus, 'is T' is guaranteed to have s in its extension if, and only if, s is true. Davidson reasoned that if one knew a truth theory that one knew satisfied Convention T (and a bit more), one would know something sufficient to interpret its object language sentences. Thus, if one could specify a condition on a truth theory which, if met, would guarantee it had among its theorems all of the T-sentences for its object language, one would be in a position to construct truth theories that could be used to interpret these object language sentences. We elaborate and defend this interpretation of the central idea of Davidson's truth-theoretic semantics in Chapter 4, illustrating in detail how a truth theory for a simple context insensitive language meeting appropriate constraints can be used to specify the meanings of its object language sentences. Our illustration will enable us to elicit all the central conceptual issues without the complications attendant upon formulating a truth theory for a language more closely resembling a natural language.

Our development of this proposal differs in some respects from its development in Davidson's hands. In particular, our constraint that a truth theory qua compositional meaning theory must have interpretive axioms (see Chapter 4, §3) appears to violate Davidson's constraint that one not make use of any semantical concepts beyond those available in the theory of reference in saying what is required of a truth theory for it to meet Convention T. The explanation of this requirement is connected with an important interpretive issue, namely, whether Davidson intended, as we claim, to exploit the connection between truth and meaning expressed in Convention T to use a truth theory to do the work of a compositional meaning theory, or, as some commentators have claimed, to abandon, as confused, the traditional concept of meaning altogether, in favor of a more austere conception. We call this latter interpretation the Replacement Theory. According to it, Davidson aims to replace the theory of meaning with the theory of reference on the grounds that the concept of meaning is hopelessly confused. If we are right, the Replacement Theory embodies a deep misunderstanding of Davidson's program and concerns.

We offer an account of why Davidson's discussion takes the turn it does, which has given the impression to many readers (the Replacement Theory, or something like it, appears to be widely held) that he intends to *abandon* the pursuit of a meaning theory *in favor of* a truth theory. Our account hinges on distinguishing two different, though related, projects. "Truth and Meaning" opens announcing that its concern will be with the question of what it is to give an "account of how the meanings of sentences depend upon the meanings of words." We will call this 'the initial project' (without prejudice as to whether Davidson from the outset intended to pursue a more ambitious project). We argue that any appearance that he abandons the initial project arises because he combines it with a more ambitious one, which we call 'the extended project', at precisely the point he introduces his suggestion for how to circumvent the difficulties of traditional approaches. The extended project involves not only explaining the meanings of complex expressions on the basis of their structure and the meanings of their significant parts, but also illuminating what it is for any words, including semantical primitives, to mean what they do. The initial project is subsumed by, but not identical with, the extended project, in the sense that it can be pursued independently.

We argue that Davidson, observing that a truth theory meeting (an appropriate analog of) Convention T would serve the purpose of a meaning theory, and also having the extended project in mind, had hoped to find, in adapting a truth theory to accommodate context sensitive elements in natural language, enough constraints to ensure that an extensionally adequate truth theory could be used as a meaning theory as well. That is, we argue that the appearance that Davidson has abandoned the traditional project comes from misreading the intent of his proposal that an extensionally adequate truth theory for a natural language is all we need in the way of a meaning theory. His proposal is not that we should abandon meaning, but rather that an extensionally adequate truth theory for a natural language *ipso facto* satisfies (an appropriate analog of) Convention T, and thereby reveals a deep connection *between* truth and the traditional target of the theory of meaning.

The discussion of these issues spans Chapters 4–6. Chapter 5 is mainly concerned to articulate the modifications to a truth theory required to adapt it to a language with context sensitive elements. We illustrate these modifications with extensions and revisions to the simple language introduced in Chapter 4. This will enable us to appreciate why it would seem promising to think that a merely extensionally adequate truth theory would suffice for interpretation. We discuss Davidson's extensionalist proposal and defend our interpretation of its role and force in Chapter 6, as well as explain why the proposal fails.

That it fails is something Davidson came to recognize,[9] and aimed to improve upon in his later suggestion that a truth theory confirmed from the standpoint of the radical interpreter *ipso facto* suffices for interpretation, a topic we take up in Part II.

Conditions introduced in Chapter 4 on a truth theory intended to serve in pursuit of a meaning theory address the initial project only. Separating the projects in this way, and specifying an uncontroversial and clear sufficient condition for a truth theory to meet the needs of a compositional meaning theory helps us to evaluate proposals for more informative constraints on truth theories designed to yield theories adequate for interpretation. Clarifying this, and the early proposal in "Truth and Meaning" for an informative constraint, will benefit us immensely when we consider his later suggestion that a truth theory confirmable by radical interpretation is interpretive.

Chapters 7 and 8 take up some prominent objections to truth-theoretic semantics. They are, we argue, easily met, once we become clear about the distinction between the initial and extended projects, and about how a truth theory can serve in pursuit of a meaning theory. Of particular importance is distinguishing between what we know when we know a truth theory of an appropriate sort, and what we have to know about the truth theory to use it for interpretation. In Chapter 9, we put to use our earlier discussion to formulate explicitly a meaning theory by reference to a truth theory, which clearly shows the relation between them, and then briefly discuss the relation between the truth theory and an account of speakers' semantic competence. Finally, Chapter 10 takes up several objections to the project of truth-theoretic semantics based on claims about the semantic defectiveness of natural languages, in particular, ambiguity, an ill-defined syntax, the semantic paradoxes, and vagueness. We argue that the gap between natural languages and ideal languages that these 'defects' reveal raises no obstacle to pursuing the project of formulating a meaning theory for natural languages by way of the vehicle of an interpretive truth theory.

---

[9] See Davidson's retrospective remarks in the introduction to *Inquiries into Truth and Interpretation* (Davidson 2001*b*: p. xiv).

2

Learnable Languages and the Compositionality Requirement

> When we can regard the meaning of each sentence as a function of a finite
> number of features of the sentence, we have an insight not only into what
> there is to be learned; we also understand how an infinite aptitude can be
> encompassed by finite accomplishments.
>
> (Davidson 2001 (1966): 8)

This chapter concerns Davidson's compositionality requirement on adequate
meaning theories for natural languages. We discuss what specifically the
requirement is in §1, Davidson's learnability argument for it in §2, and additional considerations in favor of its conclusion in §3. We consider the relation
of the requirement to linguistic competence in §4, answer some objections
based on misunderstandings in §5, and consider briefly its importance and historical influence in §6. This will set the stage for our discussion in Chapter 3
of what form of theory could satisfy the compositionality requirement.

1. The Compositionality Requirement

The compositionality requirement is introduced in "Theories of Meaning and
Learnable Languages," published in 1965, though Davidson had been presenting earlier versions for several years prior to its initial publication (along with
"Truth and Meaning," originally published in 1967). "Theories of Meaning and Learnable Languages" is primarily critical. Davidson identifies as
a criterion of adequacy for semantic theories of natural languages that they
exhibit these languages as compositional, and he applies it to a number of

then prominent analyses, for example, of quotation and belief sentences.[10] "Truth and Meaning" continues and extends the criticism of traditional theories, and sketches an alternative program (briefly mentioned in the first article, Davidson 2001 (1966): 8), in which a Tarski-style truth theory is to play the role of a meaning theory which meets the criterion first articulated in "Theories of Meaning and Learnable Languages."

The compositionality requirement is initially stated in quotation [a] from "Theories of Meaning and Learnable Languages."

[a] I propose what seems to me clearly to be a necessary feature of a learnable language: it must be possible to give a constructive account of the meaning of the sentences in the language. Such an account I call a theory of meaning for the language, and I suggest that a theory of meaning that conflicts with this condition, whether put forward by philosopher, linguist, or psychologist, cannot be a theory of a natural language; and if it ignores this condition, it fails to deal with something central to the concept of a language. (Davidson 2001 (1966): 3)

What does Davidson mean by a "constructive account of the meaning of the sentences in a language," and why should offering one be required of an account of meaning for natural languages?

A constructive account of the meanings of sentences in a natural language requires defining a predicate that applies to all and only grammatical sentences of the language, and enables us, as Davidson puts it, "to specify, in a way that depends effectively and solely on formal considerations, what every sentence means" (Davidson 2001 (1966): 8). In fact, his requirement is stronger, for he requires that we specify what each sentence means in a way that enables us to understand it on the basis of understanding its significant parts. By 'specifying the meaning of a sentence' it is clear that Davidson intends the specification to enable anyone who understands the specifying language to understand the sentence. This competence feature of his requirement is important, and we will have occasion to return to it in this and other chapters. Let us call any theory for a language that meets this requirement a *compositional meaning theory* for that language. More formally,

> [CM] A compositional meaning theory for a language *L* is a formal theory that enables anyone who understands the language in which

---

[10] It should be said that the analyses of the sorts of devices or locutions Davidson criticizes were not intended to be answers to his question. His point is rather that, whether or not so intended, it is a legitimate constraint on analyses that they not render unintelligible how a finite speaker could understand the infinity of sentences in which the constructions in question appear.

> the theory is stated to understand the primitive expressions of *L*
> and the complex expressions of *L* on the basis of understanding
> the primitive ones.[11]

Note that something stronger is meant by 'compositionality' in [*CM*] than
that the meaning of a complex expression is a *function* of the meanings of
its parts. Since functions are mappings, which can be represented as sets of
ordered n-tuples, they are easy to come by. But simply guaranteeing that there
is a function from the meanings of a complex expression's parts to its meaning doesn't ensure that its meaning is scrutable on the basis of knowledge
of the meanings of its parts and their mode of combination. Davidson specifically requires that a compositional meaning theory provide information
about the meanings of the parts of a complex expression and their mode of
combination sufficient to come to understand the complex. This is captured
by [*CM*].

That we have a compositional meaning theory is supposed to be a requirement on a theory for any *natural* language. For natural languages are spoken
by finite creatures who lack magical abilities. But natural languages have
indefinitely many nonsynonymous meaningful sentences, each of which their
speakers could understand—given world enough and time, but no increase
in their competence. What this seems to require is that our ability to speak
a language be based on our understanding of a finite number of semantical
primitives and rules for their combination. We will call any such language
compositional. We will consider the argument in detail in the next section.
According to Davidson, an expression is a 'semantical primitive' if the "rules
which give the meaning for the sentences in which it does not appear do not
suffice to determine the meaning of the sentences in which it does appear"
(2001 (1966): 9). It is unclear what he means by 'give the meaning' and 'do
not suffice to determine'. However, it is natural to suppose he had in mind
initially that a set of rules *gives the meaning* of a sentence provided that *someone
who knows them can come to understand the sentence*; and that if someone who
knows the rules for a range of expressions is not thereby in a position to
understand some expression, then they *do not suffice to determine* the meaning of the expression. In effect, Davidson's characterization of a semantical
primitive treats an expression as a primitive provided that it cannot be

---

[11] This does not mean that in knowing the theory we *ipso facto* understand every object language
sentence, but, rather, that in knowing the theory we are in a position to do so.

understood on the basis of understanding other expressions and rules for their combination.

If Davidson is right, then his requirement on a learnable language (a language which finite beings like ourselves could come to understand) extends beyond eliminating false theories, for if natural languages are compositional, then in accounting for what it is for the expressions of natural languages to mean what they do, we must explain how we understand complex expressions on the basis of understanding their parts. Thus, offering a compositional meaning theory for natural languages becomes central in the study of meaning.[12]

2. The Learnability Argument

Davidson represents the requirement that an adequate meaning theory for a natural language be compositional as resting on several empirical assumptions. In "Theories of Meaning and Learnable Languages" (Davidson 2001 (1966)) the argument is represented as follows (p. 9).

(1) Natural languages have an infinite number of nonsynonymous expressions, and, in particular, an infinite number of nonsynonymous sentences.
(2) We can (fixing our cognitive capacities and life spans) learn natural languages (since we have done so).
(3) "...we do not at some point suddenly acquire an ability to intuit the meanings of sentences on no rule at all."
(4) "...each new item of vocabulary, or new grammatical rule, takes some [minimum][13] finite time to be learned."
(5) "...man is mortal."
(6) Thus, natural languages have "a finite number of semantical primitives" [1–5].
(7) Thus, it must be possible to account for how an infinite number of nonprimitive expressions in natural languages can be understood in terms of a finite vocabulary of semantical primitives [1, 6].

---

[12] Some insight into the development of Davidson's philosophy of language can be gleaned from an early paper of his, "The Method of Extension and Intension" (Davidson 1963). This paper, for the *Library of Living Philosophers* volume on Carnap, was written in the 1950s, although the volume did not appear until 1963. Davidson criticized Carnap's method of intension and extension in part on the grounds that its account of belief sentences did not show how such sentences were understood on the basis of their semantically significant elements. Thus, this early work on belief sentences can be seen as leading naturally to questions about learnability, which figure so prominently in "Theories of Meaning and Learnable Languages."

[13] It is possible, of course, for an infinite sum of time intervals to be finite if they form a series that decreases rapidly enough. Here we must assume that there is a lower limit on the length of a time interval in which a new item of vocabulary may be acquired—an entirely reasonable assumption.

Argument (1)–(7) assumes that we learn natural languages, and it seems clear that Davidson has in mind that we learn our first languages.[14] His argument, then, is that each semantical primitive in the vocabulary must be learned independently, and that learning each requires a (minimum) finite amount of time. If the language had an infinite number of semantical primitives, it would take an infinite amount of time to learn them all. Until one had learned each primitive expression, one would not have learned the language. We learn natural languages in a finite amount of time. Therefore, natural languages lack an infinite number of primitive expressions. Natural languages have infinitely many nonsynonymous sentences. Therefore, our understanding of at least many sentences depends on our understanding of semantically primitive expressions—by way of rules providing, from the meaning of primitives and their mode of combination, a specification of the meaning of the complex expressions.[15]

3. Other Considerations in Favor of Compositionality

(1)–(7) is more vulnerable to empirical refutation than it need be, for Davidson assumes that first languages are learned. If 'learning' means acquiring a competence in the use of each semantic primitive by a process independent of acquiring one for others, then our having learned a natural language does not follow from the fact that we speak one, nor does it follow from our speaking a language that we once did not, for acquiring the ability to speak a language and learning it are distinct. It is conceptually possible that one could become competent in Mandarin by a lucky blow to the head. But that would not count as learning Mandarin, nor would it have involved separate steps corresponding to the learning of each of the semantic primitives of Mandarin. Of course, this is not how we acquire our first languages, but it is not clear that the process by which we do acquire our first language, or an infinite fragment of our first

---

[14] In a more recent paper, Davidson glosses his early argument: "A learnable (or interpretable) language must have a finite primitive vocabulary. The argument is that we are not born knowing the languages we come to speak, so we must learn the meaning (interpretation) of each independent item in the vocabulary. Given that it takes a finite length of time to learn each item, and that men and women are mortal—well, you see how it goes. The point may be trivial, but a number of semantic theories have failed to observe it" (Davidson 1993: 79).

[15] In what sense are we supposed to know or have learned languages with an infinite number of nonsynonymous sentences? Of course, we never entertain every sentence of the language, and could not, given our limitations. So we have not in fact explicitly understood every sentence of our languages. Our understanding of some of the expressions of our languages then must consist simply in our independent understanding of others and our knowing rules which suffice to understand those built from them, abstracting from our cognitive limitations and finite life spans.

language, is a matter of independent mastery of each of a range of semantically primitive expressions.[16]

The argument need not, however, rely on the assumption that first language acquisition is a matter of learning. First, we can observe that any natural language can be learned as a second language so that, whether or not we learn our first language, it is learnable. Second, the reason why we think natural languages have an infinite number of nonsynonymous sentences rests on the observation that there are recursive devices[17] in natural languages for constructing sentences out of simpler elements we understand, and on the basis of which we understand the sentences we construct from them.[18] For example, competent speakers of English know that if ϕ and ψ are English sentences, then $\ulcorner\phi$ and $\psi\urcorner$[19] is as well, and that it is true just in case ϕ is true and ψ is true. Even apart from the presence of such readily recognizable recursive devices in the language, it is clear that there is structure even in the simplest sentences of the language: thus, any competent speaker of English knows that for any proper name α and English predicate $\ulcorner$is $\psi\urcorner$, $\ulcorner\alpha$ is $\psi\urcorner$ is an English

---

[16] Some of Davidson's own remarks support this point. In summarizing a discussion of the conceptual interdependence of demonstratives and predicates, he says, "The lesson for theories of language learning is wholly negative, but not perhaps without importance: in so far as we take the 'organic' character of language seriously, we cannot accurately describe the first steps towards its conquest as learning part of the language; rather it is a matter of partly learning" (Davidson 2001 (1966): 7). His suggestion seems to be that in acquiring a first language we acquire at once a set of interconnected capacities. Is this supported also by the view that sentences are conceptually fundamental in understanding language? The idea would be, if to learn a language is to acquire sentence understanding, we get sets of capacities for applying words when we learn. But, of course, this is compatible with acquiring discrete small packages, each of which takes a certain minimum finite time.

[17] By a recursive device we mean one that can be used to form a complex from simpler elements, and which can then be reapplied to that result, and so on. A recursive truth theory is one that specifies truth conditions by means of recursive devices.

[18] There are hints at other reasons for requiring a semantic theory for natural languages to be finitely specifiable. At the beginning of "Semantics for Natural Languages," Davidson says, "Since there seems to be no clear limit to the number of meaningful expressions [of natural languages], a workable theory must account for the meaning of each expression on the basis of the patterned exhibition of a finite number of features" (Davidson 2001*d* (1970): 55). His suggestion seems to be that it is a requirement on us as theorizers that we have a finitely specifiable theory. But only in part, for this passage also presupposes implicitly that natural languages are in fact compositional, since it assumes there is in natural languages a patterned exhibition in sentences of a finite number of features. This is also hinted at in "Radical Interpretation": "If we are to state explicitly what the interpreter might know that would enable him to do this, we must put it in finite form" (Davidson 2001*c* (1973): 127–8). However, it is not clear Davidson intends a different motivation here, since a footnote he attaches to this sentence cites "Theories of Meaning and Learnable Languages."

[19] The corner quotation marks are used throughout to abbreviate a description of an expression. For any symbols, $\phi_1, \phi_2, \phi_3, \ldots$, $\ulcorner\phi_1\phi_2\phi_3\ldots\urcorner = \phi_1\widehat{}\phi_2\widehat{}\phi_3\ldots$ = the concatenation of ϕ_1 with ϕ_2 with $\phi_3\ldots$ Thus, $\ulcorner\phi$ and $\psi\urcorner = \phi\widehat{}$ 'and' $\widehat{}\psi$.

sentence, and that it is true iff (if and only if) ψ is true of the referent[20] of α. If we understand the component expressions in sentences of this form, we can understand complex expressions built up from them.

Finally, we can note that mastery of the use of each semantical primitive in a language must be encoded in our nervous systems separately from each other, and that our capacities for encoding uses of semantical primitives are finite. It follows that our mastery of a language with infinite expressive resources must rest on mastery of a finite number of semantical primitives and rules that enable us to understand complex expressions on the basis of the primitives they comprise. The moral is that the observation that we as finite speakers can be said to have a competence that extends over an infinite number of sentences is just a way of making salient what we know from more mundane observations, that our languages are, and are understood to be, compositional. The conclusion that Davidson reached should be neither controversial nor surprising; the importance of his argument is that it made salient to philosophers and semanticists the need to think of understanding words and expressions in the context of a comprehensive theory for the language which exhibits the language as compositional.

4. Relation to Knowledge of a Language

It is worthwhile isolating a feature of argument (1)–(7) that raises questions about Davidson's commitments when he eventually suggests a truth theory can "do duty as" a meaning theory. We argued that an adequate account of a natural language must provide a compositional meaning theory for the language, on the grounds that only a language with a compositional meaning theory could be the language of a finite being, given that the language contains infinitely many nonsynonymous sentences. It looks, then, as if the motivation for his requirement is that a compositional meaning theory should represent how finite speakers of a natural language can understand a potential infinity of sentences, that is, it looks as if the aim of a compositional meaning theory is to explain or exhibit somehow what such speakers know that enables them to understand potentially any sentence of their language. Furthermore, it looks as if to apply this requirement to analyses of particular expressions of natural language, a theorist must assume his analyses capture in part what speakers know in understanding such expressions as a part of their language. Thus,

---

[20] When speaking of the object to which an expression refers, we will use the term 'referent' rather than 'reference', to avoid the ambiguity of the latter expression between act, relation, and object.

it appears that the theory Davidson produces must explain or exhibit what enables speakers to understand a potential infinity of sentences. Strong support for this interpretation is provided by quotations [*b*]–[*d*] from "Theories of Meaning and Learnable Languages" and "Truth and Meaning":

[b]   It is not appropriate to expect logical considerations to dictate the route or mechanism of language acquisition, but we are entitled to consider in advance of empirical study what we shall count as knowing a language, how we shall describe the skill or ability of a person who has learned to speak a language.   (Davidson 2001 (1966): 7–8)

[c]   Guided by an adequate theory, we see how the actions and dispositions of speakers induce on the sentences of the language a semantic structure.   (Ibid. 8)

[d]   The work of the theory is in relating the known truth conditions[21] of each sentence to those aspects ('words') of the sentence that recur in other sentences, and can be assigned identical roles in other sentences. Empirical power in such a theory depends on success in recovering the structure of a very complicated ability—the ability to speak and understand a language.   (Davidson 2001*c* (1967): 25)

If this interpretation is right, then providing a finitely specifiable theory of a natural language that correctly assigns meanings to all of its sentences is a necessary, but not a sufficient, condition for providing an adequate theory. To be adequate, it must also recover the structure of our ability to speak and understand our language(s).[22,23] However, passages in later writings, for example,

[21] This anticipates Davidson's own proposal for how to give a compositional meaning theory, which we review in detail below. For the moment, a caution is in order about the expression 'truth conditions'. The expression is not intended to introduce a new kind of entity assigned to sentences, but rather to be a compendious way of talking about a theorem in a truth theory for a language which says that a sentence *s* is true iff such and such. Talk about *s*'s truth conditions is talk about the correct theorem for it in the truth theory. For authors who use 'truth conditions' in a quite different way, see Field 1977, 1994; Fodor 1990*b*. A particularly egregious misunderstanding of Davidson, which represents him as treating truth conditions or satisfaction conditions as entities which are identified as meanings, can be found in Cummins 2002.

[22] As Dummett has put it aptly, the aim is to provide "a theoretical representation of a practical ability" (1993: 36). This need not, however, as Dummett sometimes suggests, be taken to mean that the speaker is to be represented as having propositional knowledge (implicit or otherwise) of the theory that represents his practical ability to speak and understand his language.

[23] This places more constraints on the theory than that it be finitely formulable, for it requires that it reveal as much structure in a language as is present in the mastery of its speakers. Thus, e.g. a language with a finite number of sentences, say, 100 subject-predicate sentences, could be given a finite meaning theory by providing for each an axiom of the form '*s* in *L* means that *p*'. But if speakers of the language recognize structure in these sentences, inasmuch as their mastery of the language relies on recognition of structure, then the theory would not be adequate: a compositional theory would still be called for. The requirement of a compositional meaning theory is not primarily motivated by the infinitude of sentences formulable in our languages. It is motivated by the fact that our languages are compositional, i.e. by the fact that we understand utterances of sentences in

in "Radical Interpretation" (Davidson 2001c (1973): 126), suggest that it is *no* part of Davidson's aim to account for how speakers actually understand a potential infinity of sentences.[24] We return to the question about the relationship between a semantic theory for a language and this goal in Chapter 9.

5. Objections to the Compositionality Requirement

There are a number of objections to the compositionality requirement in the philosophical literature. Some authors claim natural languages are demonstrably not compositional. We will not consider those arguments here.[25] However, a number of arguments purporting to show that Davidson's argument is flawed, or that his conclusion is too strong, rest on mistakes about what his project and commitments are, and so it will be useful to examine them briefly.

First, some critics object that Davidson is committed to saying one cannot learn a theory that is not finitely axiomatizable.[26] We suspect critics who advance this objection have confused the conclusion of Davidson's argument for a compositional meaning theory in "Theories of Meaning and Learnable Languages" with his suggestion in "Truth and Meaning" that any such theory could take the form of a finitely axiomatized Tarski-style truth theory in a first-order formal language. His suggestion in "Truth and Meaning" is about how to meet the requirement argued for in his earlier article. The argument, however, clearly does not require a finitely axiomatized theory. It requires that the meanings of all elements of the language be exhibited as constructible from

our language on the basis of mastering how their elements can be used systematically to produce sentences with different meanings. Our finitude and the infinitude of meaningful sentences in our languages simply highlight this fact.

[24] See Davidson 1990*b*: 312, "There must, of course, be *some* sense in which speaker and interpreter have internalized a theory; but this comes to no more than the fact that the speaker is able to speak as if he believed the interpreter would interpret him in the way the theory describes, and the fact that the interpreter is prepared so to interpret him. All we should require of a theory of truth for a speaker is that it be such that, *if* an interpreter had explicit propositional knowledge of the theory, he would know the truth conditions of utterances of the speaker."

[25] We do not foresee serious disagreement about whether natural languages are compositional in the sense that words make similar contributions to different sentences, and are understood to do so. It would, as our examples make clear, be absurd to deny one can give a compositional account e.g. of much of English. Disputes arise, rather, over whether we might not be able to make sense of there being in natural languages an infinite number of semantic primitives which we nonetheless are able to grasp in a way that avoids considerations advanced in the text. We cannot address these concerns here. We discuss in *Truth-Theoretic Semantics* how to accommodate alleged problematic constructions for giving a compositional semantic theory for natural language. If the accounts there are successful, this will serve to establish that natural languages are (or can be) compositional. (See Schiffer 1987, 1992.)   [26] See e.g. Haack 1978; Chihara 1975; Tennant 1977.

a finite number of semantical primitives and a finite number of primitive rules. An instance of the kind of theory offered as a counterexample to Davidson's claim is (first-order) Peano Arithmetic. Peano Arithmetic is supposed to count as a counterexample to Davidson's claim that a theory is learnable only if it has a finite number of axioms, because Peano Arithmetic introduces an axiom schema that generates infinitely many axioms.[27]

In reply, two points need to be made. The first is minor. Davidson's requirement is on a learnable language, not a learnable theory.[28] Learning a language is not learning a theory. Thus, it is a mistake to recast it as a requirement on a learnable theory. Second, the connection between a finitely formulable theory and the compositionality requirement is that, if a language has a compositional meaning theory, then it is possible to provide a constructive theory of the language, in the sense discussed above. While this condition can be satisfied by a theory with a finite number of axioms which correctly assign meanings to every element of the language, satisfying this requirement doesn't require providing such a theory, if it conveys the same information through finitely graspable axiom schemata.[29]

A second mistake about the import of Davidson's argument is that it commits him to speakers having propositional knowledge of a correct semantic theory for their natural language.[30] Although in the passages quoted above, Davidson requires a semantic theory for a particular natural language to represent in some sense a speaker's ability to speak his language, this is weaker than requiring the speaker to have propositional knowledge of a correct semantic theory for his language. Davidson does not claim that a speaker must have propositional knowledge of a correct semantic theory for his language in order to speak it.[31] While one might seek to explain a speaker's ability to speak

---

[27] In particular, the induction axiom for first-order Peano Arithmetic is an axiom schema: every instance of the following schema is an axiom, where '$F(\ldots)$' is replaced by a formula and '$S(x)$' denotes the successor of x : $((F(0)\&(x)(F(x) \supset F(S(x)))) \supset (x)(F(x)))$.

[28] See Chomsky 1969.

[29] It is worth adding that those theories formulated using an axiom schema can be formulated without it. For example, since every axiom schema can be converted into an inference rule that allows one to put on a line in a proof an instance of the schema with the empty set as premises, for any theory T with an infinite number of axioms introduced by axiom schemata, one can formulate a theory T' which eliminates the axiom schemata in favor of rules. This will result in a theory which has the same theorems as the original, but a finite number of axioms. Seen from this point of view, the distinction between rules and axiom schemata is simply a matter of bookkeeping.

[30] This mistake may well be connected with the mistake identified in the first of the two points in the previous paragraph, for there would be no point in distinguishing learning a language and learning a meaning theory for the language, were the former an instance of the latter.

[31] For example, in "Radical Interpretation," Davidson says, of the motivation for asking the question "What could we know that would enable us to understand any potential utterance of a

and understand a language by attributing to him propositional knowledge of a finite theory for his language, this is not being suggested in the above passages.

An example of this kind of interpretive error is found in Matthews,[32] who argues that Davidson is proposing that in first language learning a learner is inducing from a finite data sequence consisting of sentences heard on different occasions a finitely axiomatized theory. His mistake is to suppose Davidson aims to characterize how we acquire our languages, rather than what that language mastery amounts to. If one thought both that Davidson aimed to account for how language mastery was acquired, and that a compositional semantic theory of the sort Davidson proposed was supposed to do this work, it would be natural, perhaps, to suppose Davidson thought the process was one in which a child learning a language was like a proto-scientist postulating an interpretation theory on the basis of evidence available to him about the verbal behavior of others in his environment.[33] But Davidson proposes nothing like this. Although he does appeal to empirical facts about language learning to argue that a semantic theory for a natural language must be compositional, these appeals do not presuppose that language learning is a matter of a prelinguistic theorizer inducing a theory on the basis of evidence. Nor is there anything in his position, as we have remarked, to suggest he thinks mastery of a language consists in propositional knowledge of a theory of the language. While a semantic theory for a language would enable someone who knew it to interpret any sentence in the language, it is not clear that knowing

speaker?" "... it is not altogether obvious that there is anything we actually know which plays an essential role in interpretation" (Davidson 2001*c* (1973): 125). In Davidson 1986: 438, he says, "To say that an explicit theory for interpreting a speaker is a model of the interpreter's linguistic competence is not to suggest that the interpreter knows any such theory. ...They are rather claims about what must be said to give a satisfactory description of the competence of the interpreter." In "The Structure and Content of Truth" (Davidson 1990*b*: 311–12), Davidson says the aim of the theory is, *inter alia*, to "describe a certain complex ability": "it at once describes the linguistic abilities and practices of the speaker and gives the substance of what a knowledgeable interpreter knows which enables him to grasp the meaning of the speaker's utterances. This is not to say that either speaker or interpreter is aware of or has propositional knowledge of the contents of such a theory." In Davidson 1994*b*: 3, he writes, "let me say (not for the first time): I do not think we normally understand what others say by consciously reflecting on the question what they mean, by appealing to some theory of interpretation, or by summoning up what we take to be the relevant evidence."

[32] For example, in Matthews 1986: 52: "The suggestion is that we learn the semantics of a language by inducing a semantic theory for that language from this finite number of sentences which constitutes the data for the learning task." See also Hacking 1975: 143, who seems to think Davidson holds that what people *actually* know in knowing what a sentence means is a *T*-sentence plus its proof from a truth theory.

[33] One way to see that this cannot be right is to note Davidson's commitment to the dependence of thought on possession of a language. See Davidson 2001 (1975).

any such theory is required for speaking the language, for we may not know one.[34] And simply knowing such a theory (having propositional knowledge of its axioms) would not in itself suffice for mastery of the language, because mastery consists in having the ability to speak and understand the language. Propositional knowledge of a language of the sort acquired from a phrase book or language text is a far cry from being able to speak and understand it.[35]

6. The Influence of the Compositionality Requirement

Before proceeding, it is crucial to note how *influential* Davidson's suggestion for reorienting the theory of meaning was at the time.[36] The source of his influence rests, as we have noted, not so much on uncovering something surprising and previously unnoticed, as in his rendering salient for semanticists and philosophers of language the importance of the compositional requirement for understanding what it is for expressions to mean what they do, and for thinking through how to give natural language semantics and provide analyses of natural language expressions. It is a measure of Davidson's influence that the discussion of compositionality, and, indeed, of the relation between truth theories and meaning theories, has taken center stage in current philosophical discussions of meaning. A sense of the distance between the conception of the task of semantics at the time of the publication of "Truth and Meaning" and the present one can be gleaned by a cursory glance at a number of then popular texts. William Alston's then widely used primer *Philosophy of Language* (1964) will serve as an example.

Alston's first chapter, on "Theories of Meaning," describes the 'problem of meaning' as that of answering the question, "What are we saying about a linguistic expression when we specify its meaning?," that is, "we are," he says, "trying to give an adequate characterization of one of the uses of

[34] For an alternative view, see Lepore 1997.

[35] Since Davidson is not claiming that speakers represent the semantic knowledge the theorist would have which describes their abilities to understand and speak their languages, recent debates about whether representations of semantic knowledge are necessary for language understanding are not pertinent to Davidson's claims here. (See Schiffer 1987; Fodor 1989; Lepore 1997.) What Davidson's views are not compatible with is the view that natural languages lack a fully compositional semantics and a finite number of semantical primitives.

[36] Here is a retrospective remark by Davidson made in 1993: "Like many others, I wanted answers to such questions as 'What is meaning?', and became frustrated with the fatuity of the attempts at answers I found in Ogden and Richards, Charles Morris, Skinner and others. So I substituted another question which I thought might be less intractable: What would it suffice an interpreter to know in order to understand the speaker of an alien language, and how could he come to know it?" (Davidson 1993: 83).

'mean' and its cognates" (Alston 1964: 10). Alston discusses the 'referential', 'ideational', and 'behavioral' theories of meaning, theories not about the semantic structure of languages, but rather about how to analyze the word 'meaning'. Current philosophy of language is still interested in how to analyze 'meaning', or at least in how to shed light on what it is for words and sentences to have meanings,[37] but it is now recognized that an essential part of any complete answer to this question must involve an account of the semantic structure of a language, and, in particular, a compositional account of the meanings of complex expressions in terms of the meanings of their significant parts. One virtue of recognizing this is that it isolates a problem within the theory of meaning (broadly construed) that can be attacked and which promises illumination on the nature of meaning without requiring a full analysis of the concept of meaning.

[37] e.g. Searle 1983.

3

The Form of a Meaning Theory and Difficulties for Traditional Approaches

> Paradoxically, the one thing meanings do not seem to do is oil the wheels of a theory of meaning—at least as long as we require of such a theory that it non-trivially give the meaning of every sentence in the language.
>
> (Davidson 2001c (1967): 20–1)

"Truth and Meaning" is justly Davidson's most famous paper in the philosophy of language. It was first published in 1967, but, as we have mentioned, he had been presenting it for several years before along with "Theories of Meaning and Learnable Languages." "Truth and Meaning" has, perhaps unfortunately, tended to overshadow its companion piece. They should be read in sequence. As the opening paragraph makes clear, "Truth and Meaning" is intended to take up the story where "Theories of Meaning and Learnable Languages" leaves off.

[e] It is conceded by most philosophers of language, and recently by some linguists, that a satisfactory theory of meaning must give an account of how the meanings of sentences depend upon the meanings of words. Unless such an account could be supplied for a particular language, it is argued, there would be no explaining the fact that we can learn the language: no explaining the fact that, on mastering a finite vocabulary and a finitely stated set of rules, we are prepared to produce and to understand any of a potential infinitude of sentences. I do not dispute these vague claims, in which I sense more than a kernel of truth. Instead I want to ask what it is for a theory to give an account of the kind adumbrated. (Davidson 2001c (1967): 17)

What this shows is important for our overarching interpretive aim in Part I, namely, that Davidson's project does *not* involve a rejection of the ordinary notion of meaning as *unintelligible*—even if that notion should need in some ways to be made more precise, and clarified for the purposes of theory.[38] "Truth and Meaning" does not abandon the pursuit of compositional meaning theories in favor of something else, but rather considers how their aims are best pursued. We will consider first the further defense of this claim, and then, in Chapter 6, why things might have appeared otherwise, at least to some readers.

For now, our concern will be with the first part of Davidson's argument for truth-theoretic semantics, his criticisms of attempts to pursue the aim of a compositional meaning theory by apparently more direct means. We begin in §1 by considering the most straightforward way of trying to conceive of what work a compositional meaning theory would do. We will present two proposals for the form of meaning specification to be sought as the output of the theory, and then identify two strategies for pursuing each, one of which requires developing a logic for intensional contexts, and the other of which requires an ontology of meanings to serve as the referents of terms in the theory of meaning. Most of Davidson's discussion is directed at the second— which was then by far the most popular—of these two approaches. We explain Davidson's variant on Plato's Third Man argument against the utility of meanings in pursuing a meaning theory in §2, and draw some morals from a simple example drawn from the theory of reference. The lessons to be drawn here have not been adequately appreciated in the semantics community, and, in our view, point to the fundamental difficulty with an appeal to abstract entities in meaning theory. We take up in §3 a Fregean (though not Frege's) pro- posal for generating meaning theorems by treating open sentences as denoting functions from arguments to sentence meanings, suggested, ironically, by the preceding critique of meaning entities. This leads us to discuss Davidson's famous slingshot argument in §4, which we clarify, and then argue is unlikely to be persuasive to its opponents. However, we argue in §5 that the lessons of §2 apply to the Fregean proposal as well, and show why the appeal to meanings as entities is neither necessary nor sufficient for the work of a the- ory of meaning. Finally, in §6, we survey difficulties for fallback positions, in particular, the prospects for pursuing a meaning theory while treating the

---

[38] Davidson remarks explicitly on this contrast between his aims and Quine's in 1985*b*: 172: "Like Quine, I am interested in how English and languages like it (i.e. all languages) work, but, unlike Quine, I am not concerned to improve on it or change it. (I am the conservative and he is the Marxist here.)" Among the reviewers of Davidson's work who explicitly note this is Guttenplan 1985.

contexts following 'means' or 'means that' as inaccessible to quantification, and by using substitutional quantification. Chapter 4 begins the discussion of Davidson's positive proposal.

1. The Form of a Theory of Meaning

A compositional meaning theory in the sense in which Davidson seeks one is (i) a formal theory with (ii) a finite number of rules for (iii) a finite number of semantical primitives, which (iv) enables its knower to specify the meaning of (to come to understand) every sentence of his language. We will consider two natural proposals for what form the theory's theorems should take, and in subsequent sections consider what obstacles face attempts to provide a theory that generates theorems of the right sort.

The most straightforward suggestion is that the desired theory must meet constraints (i)–(iii) and entail for each sentence of the object language L a sentence in the metalanguage of the form [M],

> [M] s in L means p,

where 's' is replaced by a structural description of a sentence of the object language (a description of the sentence as a concatenation of primitives of the language[39]) and 'p' is replaced by a sentence of the metalanguage which means the same as the object language sentence denoted by the structural description that replaces 's'. The suggestion is that we would have the right theory provided that it entailed for L only true theorems of the form [M].

Notice that in this sort of construction whatever expressions follow 'means' do not function in their usual way. We cannot freely intersubstitute terms alike in referent, extension, or truth value and be guaranteed to preserve truth value (we cannot intersubstitute *salva veritate*). To preserve truth under substitution, the substituted term must be synonymous with the term substituted for. Likewise, terms in the context following 'means' do not contribute in the usual way to the conditions under which the containing sentence is true. The truth value of the contained sentence does not matter to the truth of the whole, nor does what lies in the extensions of its predicates, and, further, the speaker incurs

---

[39] For example, adopting a convention to read in spaces between any word and a succeeding word connected by the concatenation sign, we would describe the sentence 'I have taken all knowledge to be my province' as follows: 'I'⌢'have'⌢'taken'⌢'all'⌢'knowledge'⌢'to be'⌢'my'⌢'province'. We require a certain kind of structural description of the sentence rather than simply a name of it because the theory needs to be able to specify the meanings of sentences on the basis of their structure and specifications of meaning for their significant parts.

40

no commitment to the truth or referent of any of the terms. Indexicals and deitic elements do not function relative to context and speaker's intentions in their usual way. When a speaker uses 'I', or 'that', for example, in the context following 'means', he is not understood to have referred to himself or to anything. Thus, for example, in saying [1] in English, the sentence 'I am tired' is not being used by a speaker[40] to say anything about himself at the time of utterance.

[1]   'Je'⌢'suis'⌢'fatigué' in French means *I am tired*.

A theory which issued in theorems of this sort, if workable, would extend straightforwardly to nondeclarative sentences, as illustrated in [2].

[2]   'Ça'⌢'va'⌢'?' in French means *how are you?*

The theorem forms we want a theory to entail accommodate directly sentences in any mood.

Essentially, such theorems simply match object language sentences with sentences in the metalanguage that translate them, which are in some sense used (though not with the usual commitments) in the sentence. We do not, on this approach, articulate anything about what these sentences mean as used on particular occasions. We preserve, of course, context sensitive features by matching sentences with translating sentences; but that they are context sensitive remains implicit.

If we wish to articulate the role of context sensitive elements in a language, and thereby say something not about what sentences mean considered apart from their uses, but what we mean by a use of them, then we need to move to a second approach which employs a slightly different construction, substituting for 'means' in [M] 'means that', as in [M'], where ϕ may be an open sentence containing bound instances of 'S' and 't'. This will allow us to quantify over speakers and times in specifying what a sentence means as used by a speaker at a time.

[M']   For all speakers S, and times t, s as uttered by S at t in L means that ϕ.

As noted, the difference between [M] and [M'] is that in [M'] we use 'means that...' in place of 'means...' in [M]. These constructions are not equivalent, as can be seen from the fact that in [M'] the ellipsis must be replaced

---

[40] We will use throughout 'utterance' to cover all forms of speech acts and 'speaker' to refer to anyone who makes an utterance.

by a declarative sentence or sentence form, whereas there are no restrictions on what form of expression can replace the ellipsis in [*M*]. We use 'means that . . .' when we want to talk about what is traditionally called propositional meaning, either of a sentence, or of an utterance of a sentence, if it contains context sensitive elements. Obviously, there is no such restriction on 'means . . .', as [1] and [2] show. The difference in meaning shows up also in the possibility of quantifying into the complement of 'means that . . .' as in [*M'*], something we cannot do in [*M*], and this is the feature of this context we aim to exploit. (Where no confusion threatens, we will label indifferently sentences of the form of [*M*] and [*M'*] *M*-sentences.)

An example will clarify the approach. Consider the treatment of 'Je suis fatigué' in [3].

[3] For all speakers *S*, and times *t*, 'Je'⁀'suis'⁀'fatigué' as uttered by *S* at *t* in French means that *S* is tired at *t*.[41]

This treatment specifies the meanings of sentences with context sensitive elements by appeal to rules that determine their referents relative to context (speaker and time above). Thus, [3] embodies the rule that the first person pronoun as used by a speaker at a time refers, then, to the speaker, and the rule that the present tense of a verb is interpreted as about the time of utterance. An advantage of this second approach is that it provides a way of specifying the meanings of utterances of sentences as opposed to just the sentences themselves, that is, it looks to be able to tell us what a sentence would mean on an occasion of use. (To extend it to sentences in other sentential moods, however, may require introducing into the semantics verbs in addition to 'means'.[42])

Of the two suggestions, we favor the second, precisely because (i) it yields explicit information about the role of context sensitive elements in the language, rather than leaving it implicit as the first approach does, and, consequently, (ii) enables us to state using the theory what an utterance by a speaker on an occasion means, which the first approach does not. It will also become apparent, as we proceed, that the second approach lends itself more naturally to elaboration in terms of a truth theory meeting certain desirable constraints.

---

[41] It should be noted that [3] treats the context following 'means that' as taking directly referring terms. We will pass over here issues about how to understand properly the relativization of the semantic predicate to speaker and time. See Ch. 5 for discussion.

[42] See our discussion in *Truth-Theoretic Semantics*, ch. 12, of the extension of the truth-theoretic approach to nondeclaratives for elaboration.

On this second approach, as on the first, however, the contexts following our semantic verbs, even though we quantify into them, do not permit inter-substitution of general terms *salva veritate*, and the truth value of an instance of a theorem is not a function of that of the sentence following 'means that'. In the case of both proposals, this gives rise to the question of how to produce appropriate theorems from axioms that specify in the same way meanings of primitive elements and structures in the target sentence.

There appear to be two basic options available on either approach to formulating a meaning theory. One would be to try to formulate a logic for intensional contexts. Intensional contexts are those that fail one or another test of extensionality, such as existential generalization on singular terms, or intersubstitutability *salva veritate* on the basis of co-reference, co-extensionality, or sameness of truth value. So, the logic for such contexts treats them as opaque to the usual apparatus of quantification theory. Its aim would be to enable us to derive appropriate M-sentences from intensional axioms about primitive expressions. It is by no means easy to see how this could be done, and we regard this as a fallback position rather than an initial line of defense. We review the difficulties in §6 below. The other, more popular option is to follow Frege in what we will call the 'extensional strategy'. This strategy treats 'means' or 'means that' as relational, and permits quantification theory access to expressions in the apparently intensional contexts following them, but treats those expressions as referring to entities of a different sort than they refer to in other contexts, in particular, to entities as finely individuated as the meanings of the expressions denoting them, that is, it treats them as referring to their own meanings. Axioms of the theory would assign entities to primitive expressions, and use quantification theory to generate appropriate M-sentences.

This latter approach can seem quite natural. We are encouraged by ordinary language to think that there are such things as meanings. Questions such as, 'What is the meaning of "naufrage" in French?', look to have the same form as questions such as, 'What did you put in your pocket?', whose answer involves referring to something. These questions have the form, 'What x is such that x is F'. A complete answer would be expressed by a sentence in which 'x' in 'x is F' is replaced by a referring term. With this encouragement, it is almost irresistible to appeal to meanings in theoretical work in the philosophy of language, and there is a long history in philosophy of reifying meanings. Locke's theory of meaning, and later Frege's and Russell's, though very different in kind and sophistication, are alike in treating meanings as entities, and in supposing that in saying what the meaning of an expression is, we aim to be talking about some sort of thing. But it is by no means necessary for everyday purposes to suppose that meanings are entities to communicate what we want to. For example, instead of 'What is the meaning of "naufrage" in French?', we can as well ask, 'What does "naufrage" mean in French?', the answer to which—' "naufrage" means shipwreck'—does not commit us, on its face, to an entity which is the meaning of 'naufrage'. The question whether in this construction 'shipwreck' is to be treated as referring to its meaning is theoretical, of a piece with the question of the utility of referring to meanings in the theory of meaning. When we turn from asking, 'What is it for a word to have a meaning', to 'How do the meanings of complex expressions depend on the meanings of their parts?', assigning meanings as entities to expressions begins to look considerably less promising.

The main burden of the rest of this chapter is to explain and evaluate Davidson's reasons for not availing himself of quantification over meanings or appealing to an intensional logic in pursuing meaning theories for natural languages. His principal reason for rejecting quantification over meanings is skepticism about its utility. His principal reason for not pursuing a nonextensional logic of intensional contexts was despair of seeing how it was to go, and, importantly, the prospect for achieving the right result by indirection. In the following discussion, we follow more or less the progress of Davidson's argument in "Truth and Meaning," elaborating where appropriate.

2. The Third Man Argument and Morals Drawn from an Example

The general problem facing theories that assign meanings to expressions is to explain how to arrive at the meanings assigned to complexes on the basis of those assigned to their significant parts. The first difficulty Davidson raises for any effort to do so is a variant of Plato's Third Man argument, and it brings out an important limitation of the appeal to meanings.

Suppose we set out to explain how to understand complex expressions in terms of their significant parts by assigning reified meanings to these parts. Take, as an example, the sentence 'Bertrand Russell kissed Ottoline Morrell'. Assign, just for the purposes of discussion, Bertrand Russell as the meaning of 'Bertrand Russell', Ottoline Morrell as the meaning of 'Ottoline Morrell', and the relation of kissing to 'kissed'. These assignments alone do not enable us to understand 'Bertrand Russell kissed Ottoline Morrell', for the exact same assignments are involved in 'Ottoline Morrell kissed Bertrand Russell', which differs in meaning. Merely assigning meanings to the parts, therefore, could not in general suffice for understanding complexes built up out of them. A natural response is to add that *concatenating* 'Bertrand Russell' with 'kissed' and 'Ottoline Morrell' *in that order* is itself a bit of syntax with meaning which combines the meanings of 'Bertrand Russell', 'kissed', and 'Ottoline Morrell' in just the right way. But if the order in which expressions are tokened is semantically significant, then we should, in order to apply the current explanatory scheme consistently, assign it a meaning as well. Instead of three meanings, four are in play, and we must ask, again, how to *combine* them to understand the whole. We could try to make this explicit by representing the additional meaning as the referent of a word which we can add explicitly to our list, say, 'so-combined', so that we now have,

Bertrand Russell kissed Ottoline Morrell so-combined.

But we seem no further along in understanding how these four meanings are to be combined to yield the meaning of the whole. We may be inclined to say we know, because the order does tell us how to understand the complex expression. But this is independent of our having assigned the individual expressions and their order individual meanings as their referents. If the meanings alone sufficed, then the order in which the expressions occur would make no difference. But it clearly does. Further moves along the same lines are equally hopeless. The difficulty this highlights is independent of the *sort* of entity meaning is, or the *relation* one takes them to bear to expressions.

The moral is that assigning meanings to expressions cannot suffice all *by itself* to provide a compositional meaning theory. Appealing only to assignments of meanings to expressions will never by itself enable us to understand complexes built up out of them. It is this shortcoming that ultimately explains the inutility of appealing to meanings as entities for providing a compositional meaning theory.[43] What we need in addition are *rules* attaching to the forms of complex expressions. The emerging point is that, once we have such rules for combining primitive expressions which enable us to understand

---

[43] Early evidence that it is the inutility of meanings that motivates Davidson's rejection of them, rather than more general ontological scruples, is found in "The Method of Intension and Extension" (Davidson 1963: 319–20): "One may well ask what it adds to our understanding of an expression (or ability to 'grasp its meaning') to be told it corresponds to an entity when all we are told of the entity, in effect, is that it is the meaning of the expression. When this is the only function served by an entity within the theory then those who wish to be parsimonious may simply reject the entity in question without serious consequences for Carnap's theory." This attitude toward meanings as entities, that they must pay their way in a theory by doing some work, is, as noted in Ch. 1, a prominent theme in Davidson's writings.

complexes built out of them, assigning meanings to the elements of complex expressions has no role to play in explaining how we understand those complexes.

Davidson illustrates these points in an example drawn from the theory of reference. Consider a language L consisting of 'the father of' (which, for present purposes, we treat as unstructured) and several proper names (say, those of Virginia Woolf and other members of the Bloomsbury group). Proper names are referring terms, and, we will suppose, the concatenation of 'the father of' with a proper name or referring term is also a referring term. A theory for L must account for the referent of any arbitrary referring term. Let's see how far assigning meanings (thought of as entities) to each primitive expression in our simple language advances this task. Suppose the entity we assign to 'the father of' is a *function* which maps persons to their fathers. Can this assignment help determine that the concatenation of 'the father of' and 'Virginia Woolf' refers to the father of Virginia Woolf? The answer is 'no'. For it fails to tell us how to determine what 'the father of Virginia Woolf' refers to on the basis of knowing what 'the father of' and 'Virginia Woolf' refer to. That is, it does not yield instructions for determining the referent of 'the father of Virginia Woolf' on the basis of knowing that 'the father of' refers to a certain function and that 'Virginia Woolf' refers to Virginia Woolf.

We need to be told how to determine the value of the function given an arbitrary argument. In particular, we need a rule that specifies the referent of 'the father of Virginia Woolf' given the referent of 'Virginia Woolf' as argument. More generally, we need a rule that specifies for any argument expression for 'the father of', which object the resulting expression denotes, as in [R]:

> [R]   For all referring terms α, the concatenation of 'the father of' with α
> refers to the father of what α refers to.

We could complete the characterization of reference for expressions like this by adding a list of axioms for each proper name in the language of the form: $\ulcorner \alpha$ refers to $\ldots \urcorner$, where we replace '$\ldots$' by what α refers to, as in,

> 'Virginia Woolf' refers to Virginia Woolf.
> 'James Strachey' refers to James Strachey.

[R] provides a rule for determining the referent of the complex expression on the basis of knowing the referent of a concatenated referring term. But notice that once we have this rule, there is no point to assigning an entity to 'the father of', which plays no role in [R].

It would obviously be fatuous to amend [R] to [R']:

> [R'] For all referring terms α, the concatenation of 'the father of' with α refers to the value of the function denoted by 'the father of' with the referent of α as argument.

Not only is reference to the function in [R'] otiose, but since reference to it is secured by reference to an expression not *used* but *only mentioned*, knowledge of [R'] does not suffice for understanding that the referent is the father of what α refers to. Though [R'] *plus* the observation that 'the father of' refers to a function that maps objects onto their fathers suffices, this suggestion makes evident that all the work is being done by the *use* of 'the father of . . .'. Assigning an entity to 'the father of' is superfluous: it is neither necessary nor sufficient for understanding expressions of the form ⌜the father of α⌝. What's doing the work is the *rule* that *uses* an expression *synonymous with* the one in the object language for which reference conditions are being given.

Since this simple example is a harbinger of what is to come, it is worth while pausing and reflecting on its chief features. First, this way of specifying the referent of expressions of the form ⌜the father of α⌝ in *L* employs *the concept of reference*. Second, this way of specifying the referent of the complex expression *uses* the expression 'the father of' (and our specification of the referents of individual proper names uses those proper names themselves). It is an important feature of the project that Davidson initiates here that neither employing the concept of reference nor using the expressions which form the complexes whose referents we want to determine controverts this way of specifying the referents of expressions in *L*.

With respect to the first point, Davidson's aim is not to analyze the concept of reference, but to explain how the referents of complex expressions can be understood on the basis of their significant parts. With respect to the second point, since, again, his aim is to explain how the referents of the complex referring terms depend on those of their parts, we need no prior account of how the simple referring expressions refer. (This point, which applies to a recursive truth theory for a language, should be kept in mind in thinking about the relation between Davidson's program in the theory of meaning and more recent discussions about descriptivist and causal theories of proper names. See *Truth-Theoretic Semantics*, chapter 4, for further discussion.) The sense in which we explain how the referents of complex referring expressions depend on those of their significant parts is that the rule we provide for determining the referent of the complex expression in terms of that of its parts enables anyone who knows what the parts refer to, and understands the rule, to determine what the referent of the complex expression is. Third, we can give a precise way of specifying success conditions for a theory of reference which the above theory meets, but which itself does not require assignment of a referent to every single expression (e.g. 'the father of'), namely, that the theory entail all instances of the schema,

$$t \text{ refers to } r$$

with 't' replaced by a description of a referring term as a concatenation of a finite number of the primitive symbols of the language, and 'r' replaced by a co-referring term. (Looking ahead, this is the parallel for this simple theory of Convention T for a truth theory.)

3. A Fregean Proposal

The lessons of the preceding discussion counsel abandoning an appeal to (reified) meanings on the grounds that they fail to "oil the wheels of a theory of meaning" (Davidson 2001c (1967): 20). However, the success of this theory suggests, ironically, extending the strategy further in a way that brings meanings back to center stage. Seeing why this particular move ultimately fails to rehabilitate the utility of meanings will help to drive home the lesson with greater force and clarity.

The suggestion is to adopt Frege's[44] proposal to treat predicate expressions, and incomplete sentential expressions more generally (expressions obtainable from sentences by replacing one or more significant expressions with a variable), as functional in character, like 'the father of x'. Consider, for an example, the sentence 'Caesar thrice refused the crown'. We obtain the open sentence 'x thrice refused the crown' by removing its subject term. If we treat the result as a functional expression, we may hope to isolate a rule for understanding such a sentence. To take an example, we would want to say that a sentence formed by concatenating a singular term such as 'Caesar' with 'thrice refused the crown' is itself a referring term. It refers to the value of the function 'x thrice refused the crown', whatever that may be, given the referent of 'Caesar', namely, Caesar, as argument. Generalizing yields the following rule (for convenience

---

[44] Frege 1997.

we italicize the sentence in a referring position, that is, the sentence after 'refers to', which, on this proposal, is to be taken as a referring term):

> [*S*]   For any referring term α, the concatenation of α with 'thrice refused the crown' refers to *the referent of α thrice refused the crown*.[45]

Provided that we can treat sentences such as 'the referent of "Caesar" thrice refused the crown' as referring to *meanings*, we may thereby, in a suitably enriched theory, hope to extend our success with a fragment of the language involving referring terms to the entire language. The connection with the original project of providing a meaning theory that generates theorems of the form [*M*] would be made transparent by replacing 'refers to' by 'means' in our theorems.[46] Thus, ironically, the model we have advanced for how to eliminate reified meanings from a theory for the language *L* appears to show how to use reified meanings of sentences in giving a compositional meaning theory for a natural language.

4. The Slingshot Argument

Whatever other worries one might have, it is clear that this sketch of a meaning theory must be considerably developed in order to see whether it could serve generally as a meaning theory. Davidson's objection, however, is based not on any skepticism about the possibility of implementing it in detail, but on a famous argument dubbed 'the slingshot' by Barwise and Perry in an

[45] This could be rewritten as follows to make it clearer how this is supposed to be read: "For any referring term α, the concatenation of α with 'thrice refused the crown' refers to thrice-refused-the-crown (the referent of α)", where we understand 'thrice-refused-the-crown (x)' as a functional expression.

[46] Frege himself did not identify the referents of sentences with their meanings, but instead with their truth values (the circumstance of their being true or of their being false). The project Davidson aims to stop here is one which would employ Frege's treatment of incomplete expressions in a way Frege did not intend. Frege's reason for not taking sentences to refer to their meanings (or *senses*) was that if open sentences such as 'x is a body illuminated by the Sun' are treated as functional expressions, sentences formed from them by replacing the variable with singular terms alike in what they refer to (e.g. 'The Morning Star' and 'The Evening Star') should not change the referent of the whole (Frege 1997: 156). But, arguably, sentences so alike need not be alike in meaning, as in 'The Morning Star is a body illuminated by the Sun' and 'The Evening Star is a body illuminated by the Sun'. If so, then 'x is a body illuminated by the Sun' cannot refer to a function from things to sentence meanings, for it would have to yield the same meaning for the same argument. Someone who pursues the line sketched in the text would have to argue that these examples do not meet all the conditions necessary for Frege's argument to go through. There would be two main theses to uphold: first, that definite descriptions are not true singular terms but quantified noun phrases, and, second, that our intuitions about differences in what is meant by utterances of sentences containing true singular terms can be accounted for pragmatically.

important critical discussion.[47] The slingshot argument aims to show that any compositional meaning theory in which sentences refer to their meanings is unworkable, because once we assume sentences are singular referring terms, we are forced to the patently false conclusion that all sentences alike in truth value are synonymous. We will suggest that the argument is not likely to be effective against its intended opponents, but argue, just the same, in the next section, that the utility of the appeal to meanings as entities is illusory.

Davidson's argument relies on two explicit assumptions: (i) "logically equivalent singular terms have the same reference," and (ii) "a singular term does not change its reference if a contained singular term is replaced by another with the same reference" (Davidson 2001c (1967): 19).[48] Since the slingshot argument has had considerable influence, and its basic strategy is repeated in Davidson's writings in different contexts (e.g. to show that appeal to facts, or states of affairs, cannot do the explanatory work required of them), it will be worth while to present it relatively carefully before assessing it.[49]

The argument (schema) is as follows.

(1) "[L]ogically equivalent singular terms have the same reference."

(2) "[A] singular term does not change its reference[50] if a contained singular term is replaced by another with the same reference."

(3) Sentences are singular terms and refer to their meanings.

(4) Sentences 'S' and 'R' are alike in truth value.

(5) 'R' is logically equivalent to '$\{x: x = x \ \& \ R\} = \{x: x = x\}$'.

(6) Thus, 'R' and '$\{x: x = x \ \& \ R\} = \{x: x = x\}$' have the same referent (by 1, 3, and 5).

(7) '$\{x: x = x \ \& \ R\}$' and '$\{x: x = x \ \& \ S\}$' are co-referring singular terms (by 4).

---

[47] So-called because this tiny argument is intended to slay the Fregean Giant (Barwise and Perry 1981a, 1981b, 1983; Neale 1995).

[48] Davidson, following Quine, Church, and Gödel, attributes the argument to Frege, but cites a version of it from Church 1956. Church 1943 also used a version of the argument in a critical review of Carnap 1942. A slightly different version of the argument is in Gödel 1966. It is not easy, however, to find the argument in Frege's writings.

[49] Variants of the argument appear in other contexts, in an argument against the correspondence theory in "True to the Facts" Davidson 2001 (1969): 42, and in an argument against taking facts to be the relata of the causal relation in "Causal Relations" Davidson 2001a (1967): 153. See also Davidson 2001a (1967), 2001b (1967).

[50] This is not quite the right way to put things, since e.g. 'the father of Samuel Clemens' and 'the father of Mark Twain' are not the same singular terms. But it is easy to reformulate it, and the intention is clear enough. If one singular term t is obtainable from another t' by substituting for a singular term appearing in t' a co-referring singular term, then t and t' are co-referring.

(8) '$\{x: x = x \ \& \ R\} = \{x: x = x\}$' and '$\{x: x = x \ \& \ S\} = \{x: x = x\}$' have the same referent (by 2, 7).

(9) 'S' and '$\{x: x = x \ \& \ S\} = \{x: x = x\}$' are logically equivalent.

(10) 'S' and '$\{x: x = x \ \& \ S\} = \{x: x = x\}$' have the same referent (1, 3, and 9).

(11) Thus, 'R' and 'S' have the same referent (by 6, 8, 10).

(12) Thus, 'R' and 'S' have the same meaning (by 3, 11).

(Read '$\{x: Fx\}$' as 'the set of all x such that Fx'.) (1) and (2) are Davidson's main assumptions. (3) is the target for a *reductio*. (4) is a schema where 'R' and 'S' stand in for any sentences alike in truth value. The argument proceeds in (5) by noting the logical equivalence of 'R' with an identity statement whose truth or falsity hinges entirely on the truth or falsity of 'R' itself. (1), (3), and (5) are supposed to entail (6), and likewise (1), (3), and (9) are supposed to entail (10). Expressions of the form '$\{x: x = x \ \& \ P\}$' are treated as singular terms. Any such expression denotes the universal set if the sentence that replaces 'P' is true; otherwise, the empty set. Thus, '$\{x: x = x \ \& \ R\}$' and '$\{x: x = x \ \& \ S\}$' co-refer because either they both refer to the empty set or to the universal set (7), given that 'R' and 'S' are alike in truth value (4). By (2), they can be substituted for one another in singular terms, preserving the referent of the original term. Thus, (2) and (7) entail (8). We have then a chain of identities of referents starting from (6) moving through (8) and (10), arriving at (11), from which (12) follows together with the assumption (3) that sentences refer to their meanings.

The slingshot begins with the assumption that logically equivalent singular terms co-refer. Logical equivalence is usually applied to sentences rather than to singular terms. Two sentences are logically equivalent iff they agree in truth value on all reinterpretations of their nonlogical terms, or, equivalently, under all models. When are two singular terms logically equivalent? Davidson doesn't say. However, it is natural to extend the model-theoretic characterization for sentences to singular terms by saying that singular terms are logically equivalent iff they co-refer in all models, or under all reinterpretation of their nonlogical terms. Thus, for example, 'Mark Twain' and 'Samuel Clemens' are not logically equivalent, but 'Mark Twain' and 'Mark Twain' are, and, if definite descriptions are singular terms, 'Mark Twain' and 'the x such that $x =$ Mark Twain' are logically equivalent as well. For treating the definite article, 'the', and '$=$' as logical terms, but not the proper name, it is clear that the denotation of the definite description varies with the assignment to the name. There may be other characterizations of logically equivalent singular terms, for example, in terms of preserving all logical truths containing them under substitution, but it looks as if plausible alternative characterizations will isolate the same set of pairs of logically equivalent singular terms. In what follows, then, we will assume singular terms are logically equivalent iff they co-refer in all models.

If the slingshot is sound, then two sentences are synonymous just in case they are alike in truth value—an intolerable result. Davidson's solution, as we noted, is to reject premise (3), the claim that sentences refer to their meanings, thus scotching the Fregean proposal of the previous section. However, for the argument to refute its intended opponent, that is, the semantic theorist who introduces for theoretical purposes the hypothesis that sentences refer to their meanings, it must rely only on assumptions this theorist could not avoid, or which would seem reasonable in the light of what he holds. For otherwise someone committed to treating sentences as referring to their meanings will be unmoved by the argument; he will simply reject one of its assumptions.

The argument appears vulnerable at only three places, premises (1) and (2), and an assumption presupposed in moving from (4) to (7), that is, that expressions of the form '$\{x: Fx\}$' are singular terms. Rejecting (2) is unpromising. It is forced on anyone who adopts the Fregean view under discussion, namely, that removing a significant expression from a singular term and replacing it with a variable yields a functional expression.[51] For then, since what the term denotes depends only on the arguments of the function the incomplete expression denotes, substituting one co-referring singular term for another in an argument place could not yield a different value of the function, since the function takes the same argument for both argument terms.

This leaves premise (1), and the presupposition that terms such as '$\{x: Fx\}$' are singular terms. We begin with the latter. The problem with this presupposition is that there are powerful reasons to regard the definite description '$\{x: x = x \ \& \ R\}$' as a quantifier expression and not as a singular term.[52] If so, then premise (2) has no application in (8). We would need an argument to

[51] Fregeans are forced by their adherence to this principle to deny semantic innocence for the complement clauses of sentences of indirect discourse, modal sentences, and psychological attitude sentences. Thus, e.g. it is often maintained that, although the referent of 'Mark Twain' and 'Samuel Clemens' is the same, the sentence 'Frege believed that Mark Twain wrote *The Adventures of Tom Sawyer*' may be true while 'Frege believed that Samuel Clemens wrote *The Adventures of Tom Sawyer*' is false. If so, to maintain the Fregean view, one must maintain that in complement clauses of such sentences 'Mark Twain' and 'Samuel Clemens' do not have the referents they have in other contexts, but refer to different things.

[52] See Russell 1905, 1919, for the *locus classicus*, and Neale 1990 for a recent defense and elaboration of Russell's theory.

show that the following premise is true: a singular term does not change its referent if a constituent definite description is replaced by another with the same denotation. This might be thought unproblematic, since it is provable that in extensional contexts definite descriptions are interchangeable *salva veritate*.[53] However, this falls short of what is needed. For this would not show that the referent of the containing singular term (granting that sentences are singular terms) does not change, unless one had already committed oneself to the claim that all sentences alike in truth value refer to the same thing.[54] That is, letting S('the F') be a sentence containing 'the F' in an extensional context, if 'the F' and 'the G' co-denote, then it is provable that,

$$\text{S('the } F\text{') is true iff S('the } G\text{') is true.}$$

But *this* does not establish that,

$$\text{S('the } F\text{') and S('the } G\text{') co-denote,}$$

unless we assume sentences *alike in truth value* co-denote. But that is what the argument is supposed to *establish*.

Let us set this difficulty aside, however. It may be that we can circumvent it by reinterpreting premise (1). Let us understand (1) as a claim about what we will call singular denoting expressions, which by stipulation include both singular terms and definite descriptions. The denotation of a definite description, 'The F', is the unique object, if any, of which 'F' is true. We will say also that a singular term's referent is its denotation (to have a term that covers both the denotation of a description and the referent of a singular term). We now understand (1) as the claim that logically equivalent singular denoting expressions co-denote. Two singular denoting expressions are logically equivalent iff they co-denote in all models. It looks as if this version of the argument will go through, barring further difficulties.

However, as remarked above, the argument can be persuasive for its target audience only if it is non-question-begging. And it may seem that someone already committed to the assumption that sentences refer to their meanings is thereby committed to *rejecting* the claim that logically equivalent singular denoting expressions co-refer. For neither sentences alike in truth value nor even logically equivalent sentences would ordinarily be thought to be thereby synonymous. For example, 'Roses are red' and 'Roses are red and violets are blue or not blue', though logically equivalent, are not synonymous. Hence,

---

[53] See Russell and Whitehead 1962: *14.15.   [54] See Hochberg 1975.

anyone who holds that sentences refer to their meanings must deny that logically equivalent sentences co-refer. And, hence, it seems that one must also deny that logically equivalent singular denoting expressions must co-denote.[55]

This response is too quick, however. For it is not clear *how it could make sense* to deny that logically equivalent singular denoting expressions co-refer. Haven't we simply defined 'logically equivalent denoting expressions' so that they co-refer? (And how else could one reasonably extend the notion of logical equivalence to singular denoting expressions?) (1) is not negotiable; it expresses a stipulative definition. If this is right, there appears to be a shorter argument to rejecting the thesis that sentences are singular terms that refer to their meanings, namely,

(1)   Logically equivalent sentences can differ in meaning.
(2)   Logically equivalent singular terms (or singular denoting expressions) cannot differ in referent.
(3)   Therefore, by (1) and (2), sentences are not singular terms that refer to their meanings.

But this argument is not, as it stands, sound. For it to go through, we need to add another assumption, which we will call the 'Hidden Assumption', namely,

> If two sentences are logically equivalent, in the sense that
> both are true in every model, then if they are singular
> terms, they are logically equivalent singular terms.

If the Hidden Assumption is true, then we can legitimately infer (3) given (1) and (2). But not otherwise! Is it true? We cannot treat it as true *by definition*, since being true in all models and co-referring in all models are not equivalent, that is, the sense in which two sentences are said to be logically equivalent in the antecedent is not the same as that in which they are said to be logically equivalent in the consequent, given that they are singular terms. It is then open to Davidson's opponent to deny the Hidden Assumption, and thereby deflect the slingshot argument. The Hidden Assumption would be warranted if one had reason to hold that what is preserved in all models in pairs of logically equivalent sentences in the first sense of 'logical equivalence' is the same as what is preserved in all models in the second sense of 'logical equivalence'. That is, we need a reason to hold that sameness of truth value *entails* sameness of referent. But, once again, to support this argument we must already

---

[55] See Barwise and Perry 1981*a* for essentially the same criticism in the context of their own semantic theory in terms of what they call 'situations'.

have established what we set out to *show*. What we need is an argument for the assumption that logically equivalent sentences co-refer—if sentences are singular referring terms[56]—which starts from assumptions that the proponent of the view that sentences refer to their meanings could not reject as question begging.

Returning to the original argument, we can see that the Hidden Assumption is at work in the move from (5) to (6). For we can infer that 'R' and '$\{x: x = x \ \& \ R\}$' are co-referring singular terms from (1), (3), and (5) only if their having the same truth value in all models suffices for them to co-refer in all models. Without the Hidden Assumption, the argument equivocates on 'logically equivalent'. The Hidden Assumption seems, however, to be question begging. Baldly claiming that 'R' and '$\{x: x = x \ \& \ R\}$' are *logically equivalent singular terms* also looks question begging.

We wish to emphasize that we do not hold that sentences are referring terms that denote their meanings. Whatever one's reservations about the slingshot argument, it is hard to see how not to agree with Davidson that sentences should not be treated as referring to their meanings.

5. The Inutility of Meanings

Apart from considerations about the soundness of the slingshot argument, however, it is doubtful that the suggestion represented in [S] from §3, repeated here, is viable (where, recall, 'the referent of α thrice refused the crown' is treated as a term that refers to a meaning, namely, the value of the function denoted by 'x thrice refused the crown', given the referent of α as argument).

[S]   For any referring term α, the concatenation of α with 'thrice refused the crown' refers to *the referent of α thrice refused the crown.*

The reason goes back to observations of §2. What aids us in [S] to understand object language sentences is *not* that it treats sentences as referring terms. Rather, it is that *a sentence in the metalanguage is paired with an object language sentence which translates it*. This is the deep reason for the inutility of meanings in pursuit of a compositional meaning theory. To see that this is so, we consider

---

[56] One could also aim to replace this assumption, required for the inference from (1), (3), and (5) to (6) in the original argument, with a weaker premise which can still do the work needed in the argument, and try to show that it can be supported in a non-question-begging way even if the original assumption cannot. Neale 1995 e.g. interprets Gödel's corresponding argument about sentences referring to facts as relying on a weaker assumption analogous to the assumption required here. We will not discuss Neale's argument here.

substitutions of co-referring terms for the referring term on the right in [S]. On the current proposal, the expression '⟨the referent of "Caesar"⟩ thrice refused the crown' (the brackets are to aid in parsing) co-denotes with 'the meaning of "Caesar thrice refused the crown"'. Correspondingly, for any referring term α, ⌜⟨the referent of α⟩ thrice refused the crown⌝ co-denotes with ⌜the meaning of α⌒'thrice refused the crown'⌝. If we substitute accordingly in [S] we get [S']:

> [S'] For any referring term α, the concatenation of α with 'thrice refused the crown' refers to the meaning of α⌒'thrice refused the crown'.

But one could understand [S'] and fail to understand any sentence consisting of the concatenation of a referring term with 'thrice refused the crown'. Yet, if understanding a sentence is knowing its referent, then [S] and [S'] should both suffice, if either does. What has gone wrong?

We must conclude that it is not through *knowing its referent* (if any) that we understand a sentence. If it were, then it should make no difference whatsoever how the referent is picked out, and [S] and [S'] should convey the meaning of the sentence equally well. In fact, [S] does not *state* anything sufficient for understanding sentences of the form ⌜α thrice refused the crown⌝. It gives the illusion of so doing, because it employs the expression 'thrice refused the crown' in its complement, an expression we already understand. Thus, what's doing the work here is the fact that [S] employs a predicate in its complement synonymous with the predicate mentioned in its subject, and that we know this fact, so that in understanding [S] we are well placed to understand the predicate mentioned in the subject term. That we have assigned entities as the referents of sentences is doing no work.

If we apply [S] to an instance, we see even more clearly that the idea that sentences are referring terms does no work. For instantiating [S] to a referring term such as 'Caesar', and then applying a reference axiom for 'Caesar' yields:

> The concatenation of 'Caesar' with 'thrice refused the crown'
> refers to *Caesar thrice refused the crown*.

That the complement sentence is used in its usual sense, if not with its usual commitments, enables us to understand the sentence described in understanding the complement sentence; that it has a referent is irrelevant. All that talk of referents allows us to do is pair mentioned sentences with used sentences. If we could achieve the same effect without talk of referents, clearly it would be preferable to do so. In effect, as we will see, this is exactly what Davidson's proposal to use a Tarski-style truth theory as the core of a meaning theory accomplishes.

6. Fallback Positions

Before we take up Davidson's positive proposal in Chapter 4, we want to consider and dismiss other suggestions about more straightforward ways of pursuing the object of a compositional meaning theory.

It is no refuge from the argument of the preceding section to abandon talk about the referents of sentences and their parts and appeal directly to talk about their meanings. This either comes to the same thing put in a slightly different vocabulary, or it leaves us with no means of advancement. It might be suggested that we adopt the following proposal: given the meaning of 'Virginia Woolf' as argument, the meaning of 'is the author of *A Room of One's Own*' yields the meaning of 'Virginia Woolf is the author of *A Room of One's Own*'. But, as Davidson notes, this is vacuous. It describes what the extensionalist wants, but fails to provide a compositional meaning theory in Davidson's sense, since it does not specify, in the sense articulated above, the meaning of the sentence on the basis of the meanings of its parts: no one would understand 'Virginia Woolf is the author of *A Room of One's Own*' by being given this account of how its meaning is generated from the meanings of its subject term and predicate. This complaint exactly parallels our objection to the utility of saying that the referent of 'the father of Virginia Woolf' is the value of the function denoted by 'the father of' with the referent of 'Virginia Woolf' as argument.

It is no help to appeal to a recursive account of syntax and a dictionary, for this produces no insight into how the recursive syntax helps to provide from the meanings of the semantical primitives a specification of the meanings of complex expressions. A simple example from the theory of reference will suffice to make the point. Suppose one is given the following recursive syntactic rule for forming well-formed referring terms,

If ϕ is an expression, then $\ulcorner$'ϕ'$\urcorner$ is an expression.

Suppose then one's lexicon contains the following entry:

'Virginia Woolf' refers to Virginia Woolf.

Clearly, these do not help us understand the referent of "Virginia Woolf" (i.e. the quotation name of 'Virginia Woolf'). What is needed is an explanation of the semantic role of the recursive syntactic device of quotation.[57]

---

[57] This issue will receive further discussion in *Truth-Theoretic Semantics*, especially ch. 13 on logical form.

There are two further suggestions Davidson considers briefly and rejects in the following compressed passage:

[*f*] ... having found no more help in meanings of sentences than in meanings of words, let us ask whether we can get rid of the troublesome singular terms supposed to replace '*m*' and to refer to meanings. In a way, nothing could be easier: just write '*s* means that *p*', and imagine '*p*' replaced by a sentence. Sentences, as we have seen, cannot name meanings, and sentences with 'that' prefixed are not names at all, unless we decide so. It looks as though we are in trouble on another count, however, for it is reasonable to expect that in wrestling with the logic of the apparently nonextensional 'means that' we will encounter problems as hard as, or perhaps identical with, the problems our theory is out to solve. (Davidson 2001*c* (1967): 22)

The first suggestion he hints at is that we treat not sentences but expressions of the form 'that *p*' (where '*p*' is replaced by a sentence) as terms referring to meanings. Although he dismisses this suggestion, it is not clear why. There is his suggestion that expressions of the form 'that *p*' are not names. This would suffice to scotch the proposal only if it meant that such expressions either were not, or could not be treated as, referring expressions. It is not clear, however, why that should be so.[58] He may have in mind that an argument like the slingshot, to show that all sentences alike in truth value co-denote, if we assume they are singular referring terms, could be devised to show that any two expressions of the form ⌜that *R*⌝ and ⌜that *S*⌝ co-refer just in case *R* is true iff *S* is true. The assumptions required are: (i) if *S* is logically equivalent to *R*, ⌜that *R*⌝ co-refers with ⌜that *S*⌝, and (ii) singular terms *t* and *t'* co-refer if *t* is obtained from term *t'* by substituting for a contained singular term a co-referring singular term. We can then, assuming that expressions of the form 'that *p*' are singular referring terms, construct an argument parallel to that above to show that the expression on each of the lines below co-refers with the one on the previous line:

(1) That *R*
(2) That $\{x: x = x\} = \{x: x = x \,\&\, R\}$
(3) That $\{x: x = x\} = \{x: x = x \,\&\, S\}$
(4) That *S*

We invoke (i) to infer (2) from (1), and (4) from (3), and (ii) for the move from (2) to (3), substituting '$\{x: x = x \,\&\, S\}$' for '$\{x: x = x \,\&\, R\}$'. Concerns similar

---

[58] Indeed, one suggestion we will consider about indirect discourse treats that-clauses as referring terms. They seem to be referring terms grammatically, as in 'That John is tall is true'.

to those raised earlier could be raised again here, but if the earlier argument is successful, it would be difficult to resist its parallel here.

We saw above that the slingshot argument is not necessary to show that treating sentences as terms referring to their meanings does no real work in a meaning theory, and the same point carries over to treating that-clauses as terms referring to the meanings of the contained sentences. Clearly, if we generate theorems of the form [4],

[4]   *s* means that *p*

we cannot replace 'that *p*' with any co-referring term, and retain the utility of the theory as a means of conveying the meaning of *s*. For example, [5],

[5]   *s* means the meaning of '*p*'

should convey the same thing as [4], but it is useless for conveying the meaning of any sentence, because the supposed referent of 'that *p*' in [4] is not what does the work, rather it is that '*p*' is used. This observation is a generalization of our earlier criticism of [*S*]. No appeal to meanings as the referents of expressions (apart possibly from singular referring terms whose only contribution to a sentence may be their referents) will in itself provide us with a way of exhibiting how we understand complex expressions on the basis of their significant parts. Where it appears that such an appeal helps, we must tacitly be supposing the use of expressions the same in meaning as those for which referents are being specified. It would be hard to overemphasize the importance of this point for semantics.

The final suggestion Davidson entertains is to provide a compositional meaning theory which treats the context following 'means' or 'means that' in '*s* means that *p*' as intensional, and then try to provide a compositional meaning theory by employing a system of proof for intensional contexts. This is the first of the two options we mentioned in §1. Davidson's remark that "it is reasonable to expect that in wrestling with the logic of the apparently nonextensional 'means that' we will encounter problems as hard as, or perhaps identical with, the problems our theory is out to solve" (see [*f*]) is too brief to be convincing. However, an initial survey of what it might be like to carry out this project can help to elicit some of the difficulties. The advantage of adopting the extensionalist approach is that by using the usual apparatus of quantificational logic we can prove theorems by means of replacement principles. We are deprived of these devices if we treat the context following 'means that' as intensional. We cannot always intersubstitute terms if they are co-denoting, and we cannot intersubstitute sentences solely on the basis of their being the same in truth value, or even necessarily co-denoting, or necessarily the same in truth value. In fact, in a context such as that following 'means that' we know that we can intersubstitute expressions only if they are synonymous. Perhaps this is why Davidson says that in wrestling with the logic of 'means that' "we will encounter problems as hard as, or perhaps identical with, the problems the theory is out to solve." For this makes it look as if whatever principle we identify must presuppose we can identify synonymous expressions. The difficulty that this presents is that it presupposes that we already have a specification of the meanings of every complex expression of the language, which is just what the compositional meaning theory itself is supposed to deliver.

To appreciate these difficulties, consider how we might try to devise a theory of the appropriate sort for a simple language, consisting of the (English) sentences 'Roses are red' and 'Violets are blue', and the connective 'and', and any sentence $\phi^\frown$'and'$^\frown\psi$, where ϕ and ψ are sentences. We want a finite theory that entails every true M-sentence for the language. What should the axioms of this theory be? A first suggestion might be:

(1) 'Roses are red' means that roses are red.
(2) 'Violets are blue' means that violets are blue.
(3) 'and' means *and*.

But how do we derive from (1)–(3), say, (4)?

(4) 'Roses are red and violets are blue' means that roses are red and violets are blue.

(1)–(3) are mute, since none provides a rule that determines the meaning of a complex expression (in this case, expressions of the form $\ulcorner\phi$ and $\psi\urcorner$) on the basis of its parts. We need a recursive rule that determines the meaning of any conjunction in the language. The difficulty this raises is that we must relate a description of a sentence in terms of contained sentences to an intensional context following 'means that'. That is, we need to add an axiom of the form:

(5) $(\phi)(\psi)(\ulcorner\phi$ and $\psi\urcorner$ means that p)

But since the context following 'means that' is intensional, the initial quantifiers can't range over variables in any sentence replacing 'p'. So, it is mysterious how we could relate the structure of a sentence of the form $\ulcorner\phi$ and $\psi\urcorner$ to meaning conditions specified in nonrecursive axioms. It is hard to see what would work, since we need to employ quantification over expressions in order to talk about the contributions of expressions like 'and' to any sentence in which they might appear, and, given that, we must link their use with whatever follows 'means that'. This makes the straightforward approach seem hopeless, and explains why it is so natural to try to treat either sentences or sentences prefaced with 'that' as referring expressions.

Another approach Davidson does not consider, but which might be thought to provide an alternative to the extensional approach, is to employ substitutional quantification. We will use $\ulcorner (\Pi p)\phi \urcorner$ to symbolize the universal substitutional quantifier, understood as follows:

> (Def) $\ulcorner (\Pi p)\phi \urcorner$ is true iff for all terms t in the substitution class of 'p', the sentence that results from replacing all free occurrences of 'p' in ϕ with t is true.[59]

(It is important to note that this is a *meaning giving* biconditional, i.e. this characterization of the truth conditions for $\ulcorner (\Pi p)\phi \urcorner$ exhausts our understanding of it.) Using substitutional quantification, the axiom for 'and' is (6),

(6) $(\Pi p)(\Pi q)$('p and q' means that p and q)

where variables 'p' and 'q' range over sentences in the language.[60]

The main difficulty with this approach, from our current perspective, is not that it is technically unfeasible, but that it will not satisfy one of our desiderata, namely, that someone who understands the theory understands the meanings of complex expressions on the basis of the meanings of their significant parts. The reason can be found in our understanding of substitutional quantification. If we understand substitutional quantification as above, in understanding (6) we need not understand any of the expressions in the sentence form ' 'p and q' means that p and q'. In particular, we need not understand 'and' or 'means that'. But then one can know this theory without knowing the meaning of any conjunctions in the language. This is reflected in the fact that (6) is completely independent of any axioms attaching to the components of the sentence such as (1)–(3).

This point can be seen more clearly by noting that we understand (7) just as well as (6), even if we do not understand French. For (7) means no more than (8), given our explanation of substitutional quantification. Then instantiating

---

[59] We omit explicit relativization to a language but appropriate relativization is to be understood throughout (alternatively, the truth predicate is to be understood as specifically a predicate for the language to which it is applied).

[60] Davies 1981*a*: ch. 2, sketches a substitutional approach to providing a compositional meaning theory. He does not discuss the objection we raise here.

to, say, 'le temps est perdu' and 'la mémoire est regagnée', for 'p' and 'q', respectively, we get (9).

(7) $(\Pi p)(\Pi q)$('p et q' signifie que p et q).

(8) for all terms t in the substitution class of 'p', for all terms t' in the substitution class of 'q', the sentence that results from replacing all free occurrences of 'p' with t and all free occurrences of 'q' with t' in "p et q' signifie que p et q' is true.

(9) "le temps est perdu et la mémoire est regagnée' signifie que le temps est perdu et la mémoire est regagnée' is true.

One can understand (9) perfectly well without knowing a word of French, and it is clear then that knowing what (9) states is not sufficient to come to know what 'le temps est perdu et la mémoire est regagnée' means.

A fortiori, no insight is gained into the role of 'and' in the language by understanding (6). So, no understanding is provided of how understanding the parts of the complex sentence contributes to understanding the whole. One can see that something has gone wrong by reflecting that if we avail ourselves of substitutional quantification, we can apply it directly to Schema [M^*],

$[M^*]$ $(\Pi\phi)$('ϕ' means ϕ)

where the substitution class for 'ϕ' are well-formed sentences of the language. This, however, reveals no structure in the object language. Applying the same strategy to subsets of sentences of the language is no advance, since if we identify these syntactically, we have revealed nothing about the semantic role of the recursive devices in them, and if we identify them by the semantic roles of the recursive devices in them, we have done the work we wanted in some other way.[61]

---

[61] For further discussion of substitutional quantification and compositional meaning theories, see Lepore 1983: 433–47.

4

The Introduction of a Truth Theory as the Vehicle of a Meaning Theory

> The path to this point has been tortuous, but the conclusion may be stated simply: a theory of meaning for a language *L* shows 'how the meanings of sentences depend upon the meanings of words' if it contains a (recursive) definition of truth-in-*L*.
>
> (Davidson 2001*c*: 23)

In this chapter we explore Davidson's positive proposal to use a truth theory to do the work of a compositional meaning theory. Reviewing the difficulties attending the attempt to accomplish this end by quantifying over meanings helps to highlight how the truth theory can achieve what is wanted, without the same commitments. That this aim is Davidson's is not uncontroversial, and we will discuss at length in Chapter 6 why it may appear that he offers a replacement for a meaning theory rather than a novel way of pursuing its aims. The principal aim of this chapter, however, is to explain, as we see it, how a truth theory can be pressed into service as the recursive core of a compositional meaning theory. This will involve the discussion of a sample truth theory for a very simple language in illustration. We begin with a brief overview of the proposal in §1, and then, since a detailed understanding of it requires reflection on the actual mechanics of a truth theory, we introduce a truth theory for a version of a language we call Simple English in §2. In §3, we show how appropriate constraints on the theory enable it to do the work of a compositional meaning theory. In §4, we lay the groundwork for the discussion of why Davidson does not avail himself of the constraint we introduce. In Chapter 5, we introduce modifications to Simple English to illustrate the modifications to a truth theory required to accommodate context sensitive elements; this is necessary for an adequate understanding of the motivation for the constraint Davidson initially introduces, which is discussed further in Chapter 6.

1. The Proposal

Davidson's positive proposal is expressed in the notoriously cryptic passage [g], which marks the transition from the criticisms of traditional approaches discussed in the last chapter to the positive project ([g] follows immediately on [f]).

[g]   The only way I know to deal with this difficulty [that of dealing with the "logic of the apparently non-extensional 'means that'"] is simple, and radical. Anxiety that we are enmeshed in the intensional springs from using the words 'means that' as filling between description of sentence and sentence, but it may be that the success of our venture depends not on the filling but on what it fills. The theory will have done its work if it provides, for every sentence *s* in the language under study, a matching sentence (to replace '*p*') that, in some way yet to be made clear, 'gives the meaning' of *s*. One obvious candidate for matching sentence is just *s* itself, if the object language is contained in the metalanguage; otherwise a translation of *s* in the metalanguage. As a final bold step, let us try treating the position occupied by '*p*' extensionally: to implement this, sweep away the obscure 'means that', provide the sentence that replaces '*p*' with a proper sentential connective, and supply the description that replaces '*s*' with its own predicate. The plausible result is

(T)   *s* is *T* if and only if *p*.

What we require of a theory of meaning for a language *L* is that without appeal to any (further) semantical notions it place enough restrictions on the predicate 'is *T*' to entail all sentences got from schema *T* when '*s*' is replaced by a structural description of a sentence of *L* and '*p*' by that sentence.

Any two predicates satisfying this condition have the same extension, so if the metalanguage is rich enough, nothing stands in the way of putting what I am calling a theory of meaning into the form of an explicit definition of a predicate 'is *T*'. But whether explicitly defined or recursively characterized, it is clear that the sentences to which the predicate 'is *T*' applies will be just the true sentences of *L*, for the condition we placed on satisfactory theories of meaning is in essence Tarski's Convention *T* that tests the adequacy of a formal semantical definition of truth.   (Davidson 2001*c* (1967): 22–3)

We quote this famous passage in full because understanding what is going on here is crucial to understanding the relation between Davidson's announced project of providing a compositional semantics for a natural language and his later project of *radical interpretation* (already foreshadowed here, and in "Theories of Meaning and Learnable Languages"), and because it is genuinely puzzling what exactly *is* going on here. The rest of this chapter will be concerned with explaining and elaborating the suggestion in this passage.

We note a few points at the outset, to which we will return. In the previous chapter, we remarked that the utility of referring to meanings in a compositional meaning theory is lost as soon as we pick out the meaning of an expression e with an expression e' which differs in meaning from e. What seemed crucial was not that we referred to a meaning, but that we *used* (even if without its usual commitments) a sentence in our metalanguage the same in meaning as the object language sentence we aim to understand. This is in essence the feature which Davidson seeks to preserve in the above transition. "The theory will have done its work if it provides, for every sentence s in the language under study, a matching sentence (to replace 'p') that, in some way yet to be made clear, 'gives the meaning' of s." When we choose as the matching sentence s itself (assuming the metalanguage embeds the object language), the sense in which the meaning is given is straightforward: we are *using* on one side of the connective a sentence synonymous with the sentence of which 'is T' is predicated on the other. If we knew this, we would be in a position to understand the object language sentence. (We will elaborate on all of this below.) We can generalize by requiring that the sentence that replaces 'p' in our schema translate (or interpret) the object language sentence, to allow for cases in which the object language is not embedded in the metalanguage. This is, as Davidson notes, to place on our theory a requirement which Tarski placed on a materially adequate definition of a truth predicate for a language, and, hence, the proposal that a truth theory meeting Tarski's Convention T (above, p. 21)—or a suitably modified Convention for natural languages to accommodate context sensitive elements—can do all the work of a meaning theory. This is the suggestion we elaborate below.

It looks as if we would get at least close to our goal, then, if we had a truth theory for a language we knew met Tarski's Convention T. However, Davidson does not simply say that a truth theory meeting Tarski's Convention T is a meaning theory. He says, rather, that "What we require of a theory of meaning for a language L is that *without appeal to any (further) semantical notions* [our emphasis] it place enough restrictions on the predicate 'is T' to entail all sentences got from schema T when 's' is replaced by a structural description of a sentence of L and 'p' by that sentence" (or, in the general case, a translation (or interpretation) of it). This requirement, if we are right, is motivated by the desire to pursue *not* the initial, but the extended project (see the introduction to Part I), that is, by a desire to provide insight into not just how the meanings of complexes depend on the meanings of their significant parts, but also what it is for their primitive parts to have the meanings they do. It is also one of the sources, given Davidson's subsequent suggestion about which constraints will do the job, for the view that his aim is not to pursue meaning theory through the vehicle of a truth theory, but to replace the former with the latter, in much the same spirit in which Quine suggests replacing traditional epistemology with naturalized epistemology.[62]

However, it is impossible to discuss in further detail the nature and adequacy of Davidson's proposal without at least considering the actual form of a simple recursive truth theory. Therefore, before continuing our discussion of the inter-pretive and philosophical issues, we must introduce an informal truth theory for a simple language modeled on a fragment of English. We will call this simple language and its successors 'Simple English', indicating where appro-priate different versions with subscripts, starting with '0'. In §2, we begin by describing the syntax of Simple English$_0$, and then formulate an (axiomatic) truth theory for it, and, finally, show how to apply the axioms to determine the truth conditions for a sample sentence from Simple English$_0$. This will enable us in §3 to answer whether, and if so how, a truth theory can aid the project of formulating a compositional meaning theory for a language, and in §4 to raise some questions about the particular way in which Davidson pursues this project, and, in particular, why he imposes the restriction noted above.

2. A Truth Theory for Simple English$_0$

Simple symbols include predicates, names, and logical constants. Simple English$_0$ does not have quantifiers or variables. Including these would intro-duce additional complications in the formulation of the truth theory (the introduction of the satisfaction relation and either sequences or functions from variables to objects as satisfiers) which are irrelevant to understanding the role a truth theory can play in pursuing the goal of a compositional meaning theory. (We discuss these complications in *Truth-Theoretic Semantics*, chapter 3.) To keep clear the distinction between the symbols of Simple English$_0$ and our informal metalanguage, Simple English$_0$ appears in a different typeface. Simple English$_0$ has one (untensed) predicate, 'is ambitious', two names, 'Brutus' and 'Caesar', which we will also call singular terms, three logical

[62] Quine 1969*a*.

constants, 'and', 'or' and 'Not :', left and right parentheses, ' (' and ') ', and the space 'θ'. *Expressions* in Simple English$_0$ are finite strings of the above symbols. *Atomic formulas* are expressions consisting of a name followed by a space followed by a predicate. For example:

```
Caesar is ambitious
Brutus is ambitious
```

Molecular formulas are built up out of atomic formulas using the logical connectives in accordance with rules (i)–(ii) below (illustrations are provided after each). A formula is an expression that is either atomic or molecular.

(i) If ϕ is a formula, then its negation, $\ulcorner$ Not :$\phi\urcorner$, is a formula.

```
Not: Caesar is ambitious
```

(ii) If ϕ and ψ are formulas, then their conjunction, $\ulcorner(\phi$ and $\psi)\urcorner$, and disjunction, $\ulcorner(\phi$ or $\psi)\urcorner$, are formulas.

```
(Caesar is ambitious and Brutus is ambitious)
(Brutus is ambitious or Caesar is ambitious)
```

All formulas of Simple English$_0$ are sentences; atomic formulas are atomic sentences and molecular formulas are molecular sentences.

Our informal truth theory for Simple English$_0$, TRUTH$_0$, will exploit what we know about the intended meanings of its terms. They are intended to mean what they would in English, but for the elimination of any context sensitive features. That Simple English$_0$ is context insensitive requires that our metalanguage be as well. Thus, we will treat the metalanguage predicates used in the axioms as tenseless. We will suppose, for the purposes of discussion, that an untensed predicate is true of an individual iff the corresponding tensed predicate in English is true of the individual at some time. Thus, for example, 'x is ambitious' in the metalanguage used below will be interpreted to be true of an object iff for some time t, that object is ambitious. In another departure from English, we will introduce parentheses in the metalanguage to indicate the scope of the sentential connectives, where appropriate.

That the axioms we provide for Simple English$_0$ use expressions which translate the object language expressions is, as we will see, the condition we will impose below on its serving as an appropriate vehicle for a compositional meaning theory.

The axioms of TRUTH$_0$ divide into different categories, according to their different functions. Base axioms assign reference conditions to names, and truth conditions to atomic sentences. Recursive axioms assign truth conditions to molecular sentences in terms of the truth conditions of their constituent sentences. By this device, the truth conditions of molecular sentences are ultimately reduced to those of atomic sentences. Explanatory remarks follow the axioms in each category.

1. Base axioms

1 Reference$_0$ axioms

For any singular referring term α, we treat $\ulcorner\text{Ref}_0(\alpha)\urcorner$ as an abbreviation for $\ulcorner$the referent of α in Simple English$_0\urcorner$.

    R1. $\text{Ref}_0(\text{‘Caesar’}) = \text{Caesar}$
    R2. $\text{Ref}_0(\text{‘Brutus’}) = \text{Brutus}$

Reference axioms assign referents to names; they tell us what each proper name refers to.

2 Truth$_0$ axioms for atomic formulas

We will abbreviate ‘is true in Simple English$_0$’ as ‘is true$_0$’.

    B1.   For all names α, $\ulcorner\alpha$ is ambitious$\urcorner$ is true$_0$ iff $\text{Ref}_0(\alpha)$ is ambitious.

The base axioms R1–R2, and B1 assign reference and truth conditions to expressions of the language which do not function recursively to generate more complex expressions out of simpler ones. What this contrast comes to is best understood by comparing the axioms with the recursive axioms below.

11. Recursive axioms for truth$_0$ for molecular formulas[63]

    RC1.   For all formula ϕ, $\ulcorner\text{Not}:\phi\urcorner$ is true$_0$ iff it is not the case that ϕ is true$_0$.
    RC2.   For all formulas ϕ, ψ, $\ulcorner(\phi$ and $\psi)\urcorner$ is true$_0$ iff (ϕ is true$_0$ and ψ is true$_0$).
    RC3.   For all formulas ϕ, ψ, $\ulcorner(\phi$ or $\psi)\urcorner$ is true$_0$ iff (ϕ is true$_0$ or ψ is true$_0$).

---

[63] These are called ‘recursive axioms’ because, in giving truth conditions for formulas, they employ the predicate ‘truth$_0$’ as applied to simpler formulas out of which the complex one is constructed.

The recursive axioms give truth$_0$ conditions for formulas devised from simpler formulas by the syntactical rules (i) and (ii) above. They do this for the infinitely many expressions devisable using them by giving truth$_0$ conditions of complex terms in terms of truth$_0$ conditions of the parts from which they are constructed. By continued application of the recursive axioms, one reaches parts whose truth$_0$ conditions issue from the base axioms, which eliminate the truth predicate. (Although we have presented TRUTH$_0$ as a series of axioms, it can be transformed into a closed form recursive definition of 'true$_0$', and with the help of a little set theory, into (a kind of) explicit nonrecursive set-theoretic definition. These techniques are illustrated in the appendix to this chapter.)

Now let us consider an illustration of applying the axioms of TRUTH$_0$ to spell out informally the conditions under which 'is true$_0$' applies to some sentence of Simple English$_0$, for example, ⌜(Brutus is ambitious or Not:Caesar is ambitious)⌝. We want to apply the axioms to this sample sentence to yield a biconditional which reveals in the metalanguage under just what conditions this sentence is true$_0$, according to TRUTH$_0$. We do this by constructing an informal proof (1)–(7). The proof does this by appealing to axioms at each point which provide reference$_0$ or truth$_0$ conditions in the metalanguage for object language names or sentences which use terms which translate the object language terms.

(1) ⌜(Brutus is ambitious or Not:Caesar is ambitious)⌝ is true$_0$
  if and only if
  ⌜Brutus is ambitious⌝ is true$_0$ or ⌜Not:Caesar is ambitious⌝ is true$_0$. [From RC3 by two applications of Universal Quantifier Instantiation[64]]

(2) ⌜Not: Caesar is ambitious⌝ is true$_0$ iff it is not the case that ⌜Caesar is ambitious⌝ is true$_0$. [From RC1 by Universal Quantifier Instantiation]

---

[64] To state the three rules of inference we employ here, we introduce some notation. 'UQuant(ϕ, v)' means 'the universal quantification of ϕ with respect to v'. 'Inst(ϕ, v, β)' means 'the result of replacing all instances of the free variable v in ϕ with the singular term β'. Note that we count structural descriptions of object language terms as singular terms. 'Eq(ϕ, ψ)' means 'the biconditional linking ϕ with ψ (in that order)'. 'S(x)' stands for a sentence containing the grammatical unit x, which may be a word, phrase, or sentence. 'Ident(α, β)' means 'the identity sentence linking α with β (in that order)'. This allows us to state the rules of inference as applying to sentences in certain categories without having to define the syntax precisely. *Universal Quantifier Instantiation*: For any sentence ϕ, variable v, singular term β: Inst(ϕ, v, β) may be inferred from UQuant(ϕ, v). *Replacement*: For any sentences ϕ, ψ, S(ϕ): S(ψ) may be inferred from Eq(ϕ, ψ) and S(ϕ). *Substitution*: For any singular terms α, β, sentence S(α): S(β) may be inferred from S(α) and Ident(α, β).

(3) ⌜(Brutus is ambitious or Not:Caesar is ambitious)⌝ is true_0
if and only if
⌜Brutus is ambitious⌝ is true_0 or it is not the case that ⌜Caesar is ambitious ⌝ is true_0. [From (1) and (2) by Replacement]

(4) ⌜Brutus is ambitious⌝ is true_0 iff Ref_0('Brutus') is ambitious. [From B1 by Universal Quantifier Instantiation]

(5) ⌜Caesar is ambitious⌝ is true_0 iff Ref_0('Caesar') is ambitious. [From B1 by Universal Quantifier Instantiation]

(6) ⌜(Brutus is ambitious or Not:Caesar is ambitious)⌝ is true_0
if and only if
Ref_0('Brutus') is ambitious or it is not the case that Ref_0('Caesar') is ambitious. [From (3) and (4) and (5) by two applications of Replacement]

(7) ⌜(Brutus is ambitious or Not:Caesar is ambitious)⌝ is true_0
if and only if
Brutus is ambitious or it is not the case that Caesar is ambitious. [From (6), R1, and R2 by two applications of Substitution]

Note that our (informal) proof (1)–(7) is a string of biconditionals. We invoked only three rules of inference, Universal Quantifier Instantiation, Replacement Schema, and Substitution of Identicals (see n. 64 for definitions). The proof proceeds by applying these rules to the axioms of the theory and previous lines of the proof.

We have so far laid out the form of what we have called a truth theory of Simple English_0, but we have not said much about why one should consider the predicate 'true_0', whose extension is characterized by TRUTH_0, to have anything to do with the truth, or to have all and only true object language sentences in its extension. TRUTH_0 may be said to be a truth theory in virtue of its form, but this does not yet guarantee that its "truth predicate" has anything to do with the intuitive notion of truth. It is at this point that Tarski's Convention *T* enters the picture. One of Tarski's great insights was to see how to provide a criterion for determining what he called the *material adequacy* of a recursive definition like that above, a criterion which if met guarantees that 'is true_0' has all and only the true sentences of the object language in its extension.

70

The criterion in application to $TRUE_0$ is that the theory has as theorems all sentences of the form $[T]$ (a T-form sentence),

$[T]$ s is true$_0$ iff p,

in which 's' is replaced by a structural description of an object language sentence, and 'p' is replaced by a sentence of the metalanguage which translates the object language sentence.[65] We call such instances of $[T]$ 'T-sentences'.[66] Material adequacy guarantees that any sentence to which 'is true$_0$' applies is true iff the sentence used in the metalanguage is true, because the meaning of a sentence determines (relative to the world) its truth value, that is, whether it is true or false. Two sentences alike in meaning, then, must be alike in truth value. Thus, the sentence used on the right hand side of a T-sentence must agree in truth value with the sentence mentioned on the left, of which it is a translation. Thus, if $TRUE_0$ meets Tarski's Convention T, then 'is true$_0$' has in its extension all and only true sentences of Simple English$_0$. In light of the intention that the truth theory should meet Tarski's Convention T in characterizing the extension of true$_0$, we may plausibly say that it expresses a restriction of the intuitive concept of truth to Simple English$_0$.

3. A Solution to the Problem of Providing a Compositional Meaning Theory without Quantifying over Meanings

We return now to the discussion of how a truth theory may serve in the pursuit of the goal of a compositional meaning theory. Knowledge of a compositional meaning theory is supposed to put us in a position to understand complex expressions of a language by providing us with understanding of their significant parts and the significance of their mode of combination. We have observed that a truth theory which issues in T-sentences will *ipso facto* provide a pairing of object language sentences with sentences used in the metalanguage which translate them (restricting our attention to context insensitive languages for the moment). It looks then as if certain knowledge about a truth theory will place us right where we want to be. It is not quite enough, however, just to require that we know that $\mathfrak{I}$ is a truth theory for L and that we know

---

[65] See Tarski 1983 (1939): 187–8.

[66] That is, we distinguish a T-form sentence from a T-sentence. The latter on our use is a T-form sentence in which the right hand side translates or interprets the sentence mentioned on the left hand side. This use of 'T-sentence' corresponds to Tarski's use of 'equivalence of the form (T)' in Tarski 1944: 344.

what $\Im$ expresses and that we know that $\Im$ meets Convention T. For we want
to know something which enables us to understand the complexes on the basis
of understanding their parts and the modes of combination of these parts. So,
we seek a condition on a truth theory for a language which ensures that,
with knowledge expressed by the theory and knowledge that it is a theory that
expresses this knowledge, we can understand complex expressions on the basis
of understanding their significant components and mode of combination.

In light of the sample truth theory for Simple English$_0$ in the preceding
section, we can lay down a condition which will meet our requirement. In
providing our truth theory, we exploited what we knew about the intended
interpretations of the primitives of Simple English$_0$ by using translations of
them in the metalanguage to provide reference and truth conditions for them.
We will call such axioms *interpretive*.

Consider the effect of this first for the truth$_0$ conditions for an atomic sentence. If we prove a T-sentence using just applications of Universal Quantifier
Instantiation and Substitution, the expressions being substituted on the right
hand side of the biconditional translate those on the left, and we preserve the
semantic form of the sentence. This ensures that the sentence used to give
truth conditions (i) translates the object language sentence and (ii) is constructed from parts which translate the parts of the object language sentence, and
are used in the same way in the metalanguage sentence as the corresponding
object language terms are used in it. We see in the proof, then, relative to the
knowledge that the axioms provide translations of the singular term and predicate in the object language sentence, how the meaning of the whole depends
on the meanings of the parts and their mode of combination.

This point carries over to the proofs of T-sentences for molecular sentences.
For example, when we apply Universal Quantifier Instantiation to RC2, the
effect is to specify truth conditions of the object language sentence in terms of a
metalanguage sentence whose main connective translates the main connective
of the object language sentence. Further applications of the axioms to the
two conjuncts on the right hand side will by stages provide translations of
them, until the final result is a metalanguage sentence that translates the object
language sentence whose truth conditions it specifies, derived from axioms that
translate the object language terms they apply to, and reproduce the structure
of the object language sentence at each step. Thus, the proof of the T-sentence
from interpretive axioms which relies only on their content will show how
our understanding of the sentence depends on our understanding of the parts
and their mode of combination. We will call a truth theory with interpretive
axioms an *interpretive truth theory*.

72

The form of the proof by which we generate a T-sentence is important to the question whether it shows how its components combine to determine the meaning of the object language sentence. If we restrict inference rules in such proofs to those employed above, and require that they be employed in application to the axioms and sentences derived from them, then it is intuitively clear that any proof ending in a T-form sentence that has eliminated the semantic vocabulary introduced by the theory will be a T-sentence, and that the structure of the proof will reveal how the component words combine to determine the meaning of the object language sentence. Formalizing our truth theory would then enable us to provide a strictly syntactic criterion for a T-form sentence being a T-sentence. Let us call a 'canonical proof' a proof characterized formally which is designed intuitively to draw only on the content of the axioms of the theory to prove T-form sentences in which we have eliminated the semantic vocabulary introduced by the theory (see Chapter 7, §3, for more on canonical proofs). This will result in T-form sentences which assign truth conditions to sentences, which appeal only to conditions specifying the role of the constituent expressions using terms synonymous with those for which they fix truth conditions. Let us call any T-form sentence resulting from a canonical proof a *canonical theorem* of the theory. We can be confident that any canonical theorem of the theory is a T-sentence, provided that the axioms of the theory are interpretive. If we can specify a canonical procedure for proving T-form sentences, we can show how the meanings of complex expressions are understood on the basis of the meanings of their parts, if we have an interpretive truth theory. We can make explicit this connection between a truth theory and our original project in the following way:

[1] For every sentence s, language L, s in L means that p iff a canonical theorem of an interpretive truth theory for L uses a sentence that translates 'p' on its right hand side.

As exhibited, [1] is a schema with respect to 'p'. Thus, an interpretive truth theory, plus a procedure for identifying the T-sentences among its theorems, seems to provide all we need to be able to say what every sentence in the object language means, ignoring for the moment difficulties associated with applying Tarski's method to natural languages instead of the more circumscribed language given in illustration above.[67] What we wanted was a (formal) theory which, from a finite number of rules and semantical primitives, issued in a

---

[67] Church 1951: 102, seems to have had essentially this insight. This was brought to our attention by Wallace 1978: 54.

specification of the meaning of every sentence of the language. It was not part of the "bargain also to give the meanings of the atomic parts," as Davidson says (2001c (1967): 18). Thus, it looks as if we have all the resources we need in TRUTH$_0$ *if* the axioms of TRUTH$_0$ are interpretive.[68]

4. The Extended Project

Is our work done? Interestingly, Davidson does not pursue this line, and that is part of what is so puzzling about [g] above, and succeeding passages in "Truth and Meaning." Recall what he says:

What we require of a theory of meaning for a language L is that without appeal to any (further) semantical notions it place enough restrictions on the predicate 'is T' to entail all sentences got from schema T when 's' is replaced by a structural description of a sentence of L and 'p' by that sentence [or a translation of it into the metalanguage]. (Davidson 2001c (1967): 23)

When he says that we want further restrictions which suffice to yield a truth theory that satisfies Convention T, he excludes, he says, "any (further) semantical notions." It is clear he has in mind by '(further) semantical notions' anything other than truth, and, perhaps, satisfaction and reference. For the proposal Davidson goes on to consider appeals simply to the truth of the theory. So construed he would exclude any appeal to the claim that the truth theory's axioms be interpretive, in the above sense.

Why should Davidson add this restriction? For the solution adumbrated in §3 seems sufficient to meet the goals of the initial project (assuming an otherwise acceptable truth theory for a natural language). The answer, we think, is that at precisely the point where Davidson suggests introducing a truth theory to do the work of a compositional meaning theory, he aims also to show how this proposal can simultaneously illuminate what it is for primitive expressions in the language to mean what they do, that is, he pursues what in the Introduction we called the extended project, which would prohibit helping ourselves to knowledge of the meanings of primitive expressions in the language. This would have been a very natural ambition.

While Davidson's insistence on the importance of constraining theorizing about natural languages by attending to its compositional structure represents an important departure from the traditional focus of the philosophy of language, given the philosophical climate in which he was writing, a question

---

[68] It is instructive to compare this account with the skepticism expressed in Harman 1974.

which surely interested him was how to shed light on the notion of meaning in general.[69] Against the background of the project of providing a compositional meaning theory, this question takes the form of asking how the primitive expressions in the language, or, more generally, any expressions in the language, get their meanings. Thus, we suggest, when Davidson conceived of the possibility of making a recursive truth theory do the work required of a compositional meaning theory, the idea naturally occurred to him that the move to truth might also illuminate the concept of meaning itself in essentially the terms of the theory of reference. That is, it may have begun to look to him as if to have a true truth theory for a *natural* language would be *ipso facto* to have an *interpretive* truth theory. This suggestion does not seem very promising, if we are thinking of context insensitive languages, for merely matching sentences alike in truth value does not look to be adequate to match sentences alike in meaning. The thought, though, is that for a language with context sensitive elements we would have to capture in the truth theory the systematic connections between the use of words, and events, objects, and states of affairs, and that this would place enough additional constraints on the theory to ensure it would *ipso facto* issue in *T*-sentences.

As we see it, the extended project develops through two stages. In the first stage, Davidson proposes that a merely extensionally adequate truth theory for a natural language (i.e. one that is simply true) would thereby meet Tarski's Convention *T* or an analog for natural languages. In the second stage, when it became apparent that this condition was too weak, he appeals to confirmation by the procedures of a radical interpreter as an additional constraint. The project of the radical interpreter and its relation to the extended project will be our focus in Part II. The remainder of this part is devoted to developing the framework of a truth theory to accommodate context sensitive elements, assessing the prospects for satisfying Convention *T* (or an appropriate analog) by a merely extensionally adequate truth theory for such a language, and to responding to various objections that have been leveled against the possibility of employing a truth theory to meet the goals of a compositional meaning theory. We begin these tasks in the next chapter by considering in a preliminary fashion what modifications must be made to a truth theory to deal with context sensitive elements in a language. We must consider these modifications before we consider in detail why a merely extensionally adequate theory

---

[69] We cite again (see n. 36) his retrospective remark (Davidson 1993: 83): "Like many others, I wanted answers to such questions as 'What is meaning?', and became frustrated by the fatuity of the attempts at answers I found in Ogden and Richards, Charles Morris, Skinner and others."

for such a language might be thought to issue in T-sentences. We take up that topic in the following chapter and explain both why it seemed promising, and why it cannot be achieved; we provide there also a defense of our reading of Davidson's intentions in passage [g] and subsequent discussion in "Truth and Meaning."

Appendix: A Closed Form Recursive Definition of 'true$_0$'

This appendix presents a closed form recursive definition of 'is true$_0$' based on TRUTH$_0$, and then, with the help of some set theory, a related nonrecursive set-theoretic definition of 'is true$_0$'.

To produce a closed form recursive definition, one combines the separate clauses of the axiomatic truth theory into one clause by giving truth conditions on the right hand side of a quantified biconditional of the form,

For all s, s is true iff . . . ,

which gives the appropriate form of the truth condition, conditional on the sentence being of an appropriate form.

(Def.) For all sentences γ of Simple English$_0$,
  γ is true$_0$ iff

  (a) if γ='Caesar is ambitious', then Caesar is ambitious;
  (b) if γ='Brutus is ambitious', then Brutus is ambitious;
  (c) if there is a ϕ such that $\gamma = \ulcorner \text{Not} : \phi \urcorner$, then it is not the case that ϕ is true$_0$;
  (d) if there are ϕ, ψ, such that $\gamma = \ulcorner (\phi \text{ and } \psi) \urcorner$, then ϕ is true$_0$ and ψ is true$_0$;
  (e) if there are ϕ, ψ, such that $\gamma = \ulcorner (\phi \text{ or } \psi) \urcorner$, then ϕ is true$_0$ or ψ is true$_0$.

Since in (a)–(e) we test for all the possible forms of Simple English$_0$ sentences, we are guaranteed to have specified for any sentence of Simple English$_0$ truth conditions. The recursive clause, then, can be unpacked further by reapplication of the definition, to yield finally a determination of truth conditions which contains no semantic terms.

76

We can transform this in turn into an explicit set-theoretic definition in which 'is true$_0$' appears only on the left hand side of 'iff'. First, we define the set **T** as follows.

(Def.) **T** = the set Σ such that for any x, $x \in \Sigma$ iff x is a sentence of Simple English$_0$ and

[(*a*) $x =$ 'Caesar is ambitious' and Caesar is ambitious or

(*b*) $x =$ 'Brutus is ambitious' and Brutus is ambitious or

(*c*) there is a ϕ such that $x = \ulcorner \text{Not} : \phi \urcorner$ and it is not the case that $\phi \in \Sigma$ or

(*d*) there are ϕ, ψ, such that $x = \ulcorner (\phi \text{ and } \psi) \urcorner$ and $\phi \in \Sigma$ and $\psi \in \Sigma$ or

(*e*) there are ϕ, ψ, such that $x = \ulcorner (\phi \text{ or } \psi) \urcorner$ and $\phi \in \Sigma$ or $\psi \in \Sigma$].

The conditions to the right of 'iff' recursively specify membership in Σ in just the way required to ensure that all and only sentences of Simple English$_0$ in the extension of 'true$_0$', as defined above, are members of Σ. Then, we define 'is true$_0$' as follows.

(Def.) For any sentences s of Simple English$_0$,
s is true$_0$ iff $s \in$ **T**.

A note of caution is in order here. This provides a definition of 'is true$_0$' that is the same in extension as the recursive definition. If we wish to treat the definitions as concept giving, that is, if we think of what follows 'iff' as meaning giving (synonymous except for perhaps extra complexity), it is not clear that the set-theoretic definition, if it is concept giving at all, provides the same definition as the recursive definition.

These techniques are readily extended to more complicated truth theories.

5

Truth and Context Sensitivity

> I turn now to one more, and very large, fly in the ointment: the fact that
> the same sentence may at one time or in one mouth be true and at another
> time or in another mouth be false.

(Davidson 2001c (1967): 33)

In this chapter, we introduce some of the modifications required of a truth theory in order for it to be applicable to languages with context sensitive elements.
These modifications need to be revised to respond to certain complexities; we
take these up in *Truth-Theoretic Semantics*. The treatments here will suffice to
illustrate points relevant for the immediate discussion, which will not be undermined by subsequent refinements. This discussion will serve to illustrate more
clearly how the framework of a truth theory can be used to pursue the aim of a
compositional meaning theory, and sets the stage for a discussion in Chapter 6
of Davidson's initial suggestion that an extensionally adequate truth theory
for a natural language would *ipso facto* meet an appropriate modification of
Tarski's Convention T. In §1, we consider which modifications must be made
to the truth predicate to accommodate context sensitive linguistic elements.
We modify Convention T to apply to a truth theory appropriately modified in
§2. Finally, in §3, we show which modifications must be made to the axioms
of a truth theory for a language with context sensitive elements by modifying
Simple English$_0$ to include context sensitive features, and accordingly revise
our characterization of an interpretive truth theory.

1. Adapting the Truth Predicate

Unlike the sentences in the formal languages Tarski discussed, natural language sentences need not be true or false independently of use, for example,
the sentences 'I am hungry' and 'This is hot'. The former may be true as used

by Ludwig on one occasion, but false on another, or false as used by Lepore on the same occasion. This is because such sentences include expressions whose contributions to what is said using them are determined only relative to contextual factors. In these sentences, the expressions are 'I' and 'this' and their main verbs, which are in the present tense. To adapt Tarski's techniques to natural languages, we must modify both the form of T-sentences and Tarski's Convention T in order to accommodate this aspect of natural language sentences.

To illustrate, consider applying Tarski's Convention T to 'Je suis le roi de France'.

[1]   'Je suis le roi de France' is true in French iff I am the king of France.

[1] incorrectly represents the truth conditions of its target sentence for at least three connected reasons. First, a semantic theory for a language should be *interpersonal* in the sense that it can be stated by anyone indifferently without changing what it states. A theory with indexicals or other context sensitive referring terms that can shift their referents between different speakers cannot meet this condition, since two people in relevantly different contexts would fail to state the same thing. Thus, applying Convention T to natural languages will not yield the sort of theory we seek. A second, related point is that, in stating a theory with [1], we omit an important feature of the meaning of the object language sentence. For [1] represents the object language as having context *independent* truth conditions, which it clearly does not, and so it gives a flawed picture of the truth conditions of the object language sentence. This flaw emerges in noticing that, were an interpreter to employ [1] in interpreting someone who uttered 'Je suis le roi de France', she would suppose he was referring to her. Finally, both of these points show that we want our theory to issue in *general* statements of truth conditions. If the truth conditions of sentences are relative to contexts of use, then the theory must be stated in a way that relativizes truth conditions to contexts of use. These points, of course, hold for all sentences whose truth conditions are relativized to context, not just for [1].

In [1], we must accommodate both the relativization to time implied by the tense of the verb and the relativization of the referent of 'Je' to the speaker uttering it. We may hope, in fact, that relativizing to a speaker and a time of use will fix generally the features of the context that are relevant for evaluating the truth or falsity of sentences relative to contexts of use. (For present purposes, it will not matter if we assume this is so; we take up this question in

79

Truth-Theoretic Semantics.) The question is how to exhibit the relativization by appeal to the speaker and time.

Two basic approaches are available. One adds argument places to the truth predicate (and other semantic predicates, such as 'means that'), which are then used to exhibit the relativization of the evaluation of sentences as true or false to contextual parameters represented by these extra argument places. The other approach retains a one- or two-place predicate (one-place if truth predicates restricted to a single language are used, as in Simple English$_0$, and two-place predicates if a truth predicate with an argument place for language is used), but applies these predicates not to sentences, but to speech acts using sentences. We will pursue the first approach in this chapter, following out Davidson's initial proposal.[70] (We will sketch the alternative approach, and discuss the relation between the two proposals, in the appendix.)

In "Truth and Meaning" (Davidson 2001*c* (1967): 34), Davidson suggests the treatment illustrated in [2]:

> [2] For all speakers *S*, times *t*, 'Je suis le roi de France' is true in French
> *as (potentially) spoken by* S *at* t iff *S* is the king of France at *t*.[71]

[2] introduces a truth predicate with argument places for sentences, languages, speakers, and times. The idea is to shift to talking about the truth of a sentence as *spoken* in order to fix what is contributed by a context to determining truth conditions. How does this shift affect our understanding of the adequacy condition that a truth theory should meet, and what is the relation of a truth theory so modified to a compositional meaning theory for the language? Before we answer these questions, we need to consider how to understand 'is true as (potentially) spoken by *S* at *t*'.

The parenthetical 'potentially' is included in [2], because, otherwise, [3] will be false if someone has been king of France, but has never uttered 'Je suis le roi de France'.[72]

---

[70] In a footnote in a later paper Davidson seems to indicate that he regards either approach as acceptable: "I assume that a theory of truth for a language containing demonstratives must apply strictly to utterances and not to sentences, or will treat truth as a relation between sentences, speakers, and times" (Davidson 2001 (1968): 106 n. 16).

[71] When we discuss tense in *Truth-Theoretic Semantics*, this relatively simple approach to the present tense will give way to a more complicated picture. The complications will not affect the present discussion.

[72] Davidson has suggested that his original worries about [3] were misplaced, in light of his later suggestion that the theorems of a truth theory for a natural language be treated as laws (Davidson 2001*b* (1976). This, in effect, treats the theorems of the theory as prefaced by an operator 'it is a law that'. This has an effect similar to treating 'potentially' as a sentential modifier. It is not clear this avoids the problem, however. Suppose for argument's sake at least one king of France never

[3]   For all speakers S, times t, 'Je suis le roi de France' is true in French as spoken by S at t iff S is the king of France at t.

We are trying minimally to specify conditions under which a sentence is true in virtue of what it means, so we cannot admit false theorems or even possibly false theorems if we are to succeed.[73] However, as Evans (1985: 359–60) points out, we cannot succeed by reading [2] as [4], instead of [3].

[4]   For all speakers S, times t, if 'Je suis le roi de France' were used by S at t in French, then, as spoken by S at t, 'Je suis le roi de France' would be true in French iff S is king of France at t.

since, aside from worries about how to evaluate counterfactuals, this strategy for interpretation would assign sentences such as 'I am not speaking'[74] false T-theorems. For substituting 'I am not speaking' for 'Je suis le roi de France' in [4] and relativizing to English instead of French yields [5].

[5]   For all speakers S, times t, if 'I am not speaking' were used by S at t in English, then, as spoken by S at t, 'I am not speaking' would be true in English iff S is not speaking at t.

Now instantiate the quantifiers in [5] to some particular S^* who is not speaking at some particular time t^*. This yields [5'].

[5']   If 'I am not speaking' were used by S^* at t^* in English, then as spoken by S^* at t^*, 'I am not speaking' would be true in English iff S^* is not speaking at t^*.

If 'I am not speaking' were used by S^* at t^* in English, then as used by S^* at t^*, 'I am not speaking' would not be true in English because anyone who utters 'I am not speaking' is *thereby* speaking. Yet, the right hand side

---

thought it worth while to say that he was king of France. An instantiation of the left hand side of [3] entails that the referent of the singular term that the variable 'S' is instantiated to is the person who uttered 'Je suis le roi de France'. By hypothesis, our modest French king never did so. Yet, he was king of France. Thus, [3] instantiated to this king and a time at which he was king yields a false biconditional. No instance of a true law statement, however, is false. Thus, if there was such a king, [3] does not express a law. But even if there has been no such king, if it is not nomically impossible that there be one, as it surely is not, [3] still cannot express a law. Thus, this maneuver does not meet our difficulty.

[73] In Chapter 10, we will briefly explore whether a meaning theory based on a truth theory is necessarily threatened by there being sentences of the theory that are not truth valued. To the extent to which there are exceptions, it will not undermine the point being made here.

[74] We take 'speak' here in the sense of perform an utterance act, where this includes e.g. producing inscriptions, hand signaling, and so on.

of [5'] is about the actual situation, rather than the counterfactual situation in which we imagine S^* is using 'I am not speaking' (note the 'is' in contrast to 'were'); and in the actual situation, S^*, recall, is not speaking at t^*. So, if 'I am not speaking' were used by S^* at t^*, as spoken by S^* at t^*, 'I am not speaking' would be false in English, but 'S^* is not speaking at t^*' would be true, and so the biconditional in the consequent would be false for any counterfactual situation in which 'I am not speaking' were used by S^* at t^* in English.

Replacing 'is' after 'iff' in [5] with 'were' provides a remedy, for in those counterfactual circumstances in which 'I am not speaking' is uttered, the speaker would be speaking, and so his utterance would be false in English, preserving the truth of our modified [5]. However, this still does not capture the intended interpretation.

We want to understand the object language sentence as it would be understood in whatever circumstances the speaker utters it, and then ask what must be the case *as things stand* in order for it, so understood, to be true or false. This prompts Evans's suggestion that we read $\ulcorner \phi$ is true as (potentially) spoken by S at t in L iff ... $\urcorner$ as $\ulcorner$if ϕ were used by S at t in L, as things actually stand, ϕ would be true iff ... $\urcorner$. This suggestion gets at the idea that we want to understand the object language sentence as we would if it were uttered by a speaker S at a time t. Another way of putting this point is to say that what we want is a specification of what has to be the case for the sentence to be true, when we understand it relative to the speaker and time as input to whatever rules determine the contribution of the context sensitive elements to fixing its interpretive truth conditions. We will adopt a less laborious way of expressing this idea, interpreting the relevant predicate as $\ulcorner \phi$ *understood as if spoken by s* at t is true in L iff ... $\urcorner$.[75] Thus, we rewrite [2] as [2']:

> [2'] For all speakers S, times t, 'Je suis le roi de France' understood as if spoken by S at t is true in French iff S is the king of France at t.

For notational convenience, we will abbreviate 'understood as if spoken by S at t' as 'for S at t'.

---

[75] Another worry that might arise is whether Davidson can appeal to a modifier which is understood implicitly in terms of a subjunctive conditional. Davidson clearly aims to provide a truth theory for natural languages in a purely extensional logic. This need not be a difficulty at this point, however, since the argument places for sentence, speaker, and time in our semantic predicates are fully extensional, as is indicated by the fact that we are quantifying into them.

2. Revising Convention *T*

We now take up the question of modifying Tarski's Convention *T* to apply to a truth theory with a truth predicate relativized as above. '*S* is the king of France at *t*' is not synonymous with 'Je suis le roi de France'. As we have seen, this is not what we want in the case of a sentence with context sensitive elements. We want something that tells us relative to a speaker and time what the sentence means.[76] In [2'], relative to a speaker and time, the right hand side expresses what the object language sentence would express as used by that speaker at that time, which is what we want. Let us say that when the right hand side of a biconditional provides this kind of explanation of the meaning of the sentence denoted on the left, it *interprets* the object language sentence.[77]

We can make this precise, and show how to formulate our analog of Convention *T* for natural languages, in the following way. Recall that with a context *in*sensitive language, such as Simple English$_0$, the connection between a truth theory meeting Tarski's Convention *T* and a specification of the meanings of sentences of the object language is made by observing that, when Convention *T* is met, that is, when what replaces '*p*' in [*T*] translates *s*, the corresponding *M*-sentence is true.

[*T*] *s* is *T* iff *p*

[*M*] *s* means that *p*

We can restate Convention *T*, then, by saying it requires the sentences that replace '*p*' be so related to *s* in [*T*] that the corresponding instances of [*M*] are true. When we turn to a context sensitive language, and relativize the truth predicate to a speaker and time, we must likewise relativize our meaning predicate to a speaker and time (recall the second approach of Chapter 3, §1). Thus, the target of our meaning theory would be theorems of the form:

[*M'*] For any speaker *S*, time *t*, *s* for *S* at *t* means in *L* that *p*.

---

[76] In a traditional vocabulary, what we want to know is what proposition is expressed by a *use* of the sentence in the language by a speaker at a time. We will express this idea, however, without appeal to propositions. We note also here that this story will have to be complicated ultimately in the case of demonstrative elements. See the discussion in *Truth-Theoretic Semantics*, ch. 4.

[77] It might be thought that, because we have modified Tarski's Convention *T* so that the desired relation between the object and metalanguage sentences is weaker than translation, we are offering a revisionist account of meaning. The ordinary concept of meaning, however, is still in use; the method of explicating the meaning of a given expression only travels a more indirect route than providing a synonym. We provide instead a way of saying what the meaning of the sentence is, as used by a speaker at a time. See the discussion below of the relativization of the meaning predicate also to contextual parameters.

What we want out of our truth theory is that among its theorems should be all instances of [T'],

> [T']   For any speaker S, time t, s for S at t is true in L iff p.

whose corresponding M'-sentences are true. A T'-form sentence is interpretive, then, just in case its corresponding M'-sentence is true. We will call such sentences, as for context insensitive languages, T-sentences (thus, a T-sentence for a context insensitive object language is a sentence of the form [T] for which the corresponding instance of [M] is true, and for a context sensitive object language one of the form [T'] for which the corresponding instance of [M'] is true). The right hand side of the embedded biconditional in a [T']-form sentence interprets the object language sentence, then, just in case it is a T-sentence. Our analog of Convention T for natural languages, which we will call *Davidson's* Convention T, can be stated as follows:

> (D)   An adequate truth theory for a context sensitive language L must entail every instance of [T'] for which the corresponding instance of [M'] is true.[78]

3. Adapting the Axioms of the Truth Theory

We now consider how to incorporate the current suggestion about how to adapt a truth theory to a natural language into a sample (informal) truth theory. We will also discuss what it is for axioms of a truth theory for a context sensitive language to be interpretive in the light of our sample theory.

We start with the vocabulary of Simple English$_0$. To this we add the singular terms 'I' and 'that', which we will suppose are synonymous with 'I' and 'that' in English. We will group names, indexicals, and demonstratives together under the heading 'singular referring terms'. We will treat predicates of the form $\ulcorner$is $\phi\urcorner$ as present tense predicates, and suppose that, for each present tense predicate in the language, there is a past tense predicate of the form $\ulcorner$was $\phi\urcorner$ in the simple past. The new language we will call Simple English$_1$. We will give a fuller treatment of context sensitive singular terms

---

[78] Note also the condition Davidson gives in "Semantics for Natural Languages": "A third condition is that the statements of truth conditions for individual sentences entailed by the theory should, in some way yet to be made precise, draw upon the same concepts as the sentences whose truth conditions they state" (Davidson 2001*d* (1970): 56). This restriction is a way of limiting the sentence that specifies truth conditions to one which will not fail to interpret the sentence for which it provides truth conditions. See the discussion of the extensionality problem below. Note that for different theories we will want of course different schemas where their syntax differs.

in *Truth-Theoretic Semantics*, chapter 4, as well as accommodate problems that arise for modifications suggested here when we consider the ramifications throughout the fragment treated; we give a fuller treatment of tense there also, in chapters 8–10.

The suggestion Davidson makes in [2], which we are following, does not directly dictate how to modify the axioms of the theory. One suggestion would be to modify the truth predicate by adding two places, one for speakers and one for times, and then have axioms for each predicate that give truth conditions for the concatenation of the predicate with 'that' and 'I'. However, because, aside from tense, the context sensitivity so far considered in sentences with terms like 'I' and 'that' attaches to referring terms, it is more natural, and, as it will turn out, more economical, to incorporate context sensitivity into the reference axioms for these and other context sensitive singular terms.

Since 'I' and 'that' have referents only on those occasions on which they are used, reference axioms for these terms are universally quantified over speakers and times. For convenience, we will abbreviate 'the referent of α for S at t in Simple English$_1$' as '$\mathrm{Ref}_1(S, t, \alpha)$'. The rule that governs the referent of 'I' in English is that it refers to the person using it. The rule that governs 'that' in English (to a first approximation) is that it refers to the object the speaker demonstrates when using it.[79] Our Simple English$_1$ terms are to mean the same, so we give the following axioms for 'I' and 'that':

I1. For any speaker S, any time t, $\mathrm{Ref}_1(S, t, \text{'I'}) = S$.
I2. For any speaker S, any time t, $\mathrm{Ref}_1(S, t, \text{'that'}) = $ the object demonstrated by S at t.[80]

Having introduced a reference relation relativized to a speaker and a time, it will be convenient to revise the original reference axioms R1–2 using the new reference relation; though with a proper name the same referent is assigned for each speaker and time. It is not necessary to do so for technical reasons, as long as we use the appropriate reference relations in the corresponding predicate

[79] This treatment is inadequate as a general treatment because, as a moment's thought will make evident, it will not always yield the correct results for two-place predicates whose argument places are both occupied by the same demonstrative, e.g. 'That is bigger than that'. A similar difficulty arises when one traces through the consequences of molecular sentences in general. We take up this problem and other refinements needed to accommodate the truth theory to all the complexities demonstratives introduce in natural language in *Truth-Theoretic Semantics*.

[80] The use of the definite description on the right hand side of the identity sign will be abandoned in our treatment in *Truth-Theoretic Semantics*, ch. 4, since (*a*) there will not be a denotation for every speaker and time pair, and (*b*) we want a variable in the place it occupies, so that the demonstrative is represented as a directly referring term.

axioms for proper names or indexicals. Thus, for example, we could employ two distinct reference relations as in the following:

$$\text{Ref}_1(\text{‘Caesar’)}=\text{Caesar}.$$
$$\text{For any speaker } S, \text{ time } t, \text{Ref}_1(S, t, \text{‘I’}) = S.$$

But then we would need separate axioms relating the unrelativized reference axioms and relativized reference axioms to each predicate, in the following way (for notational convenience, we will write 'ϕ is true$_1$ in Simple English$_1$ for S at t' as 'ϕ is true$_1(S, t)$') :

> For all names α, $\ulcorner\alpha$ is ambitious$\urcorner$ is true$_1(S, t)$ iff Ref$_1(\alpha)$ is ambitious at t.
>
> For all indexicals or demonstratives β, $\ulcorner\beta$ is ambitious$\urcorner$ is true$_1(S, t)$ iff Ref$_1(S, t, \beta)$ is ambitious at t.

The advantage of using the same reference relation is that it allows us to state more economically the truth conditions for singular terms concatenated with predicates. For this reason, we will rewrite R1–2 using the reference relation relativized to a speaker and time.

R1. For any speaker S, time t, Ref$_1(S, t, \text{‘Caesar’}) = $ Caesar
R2. For any speaker S, time t, Ref$_1(S, t, \text{‘Brutus’}) = $ Brutus

Now we turn to axioms for sentences of Simple English$_1$. We relativize the truth predicate to a speaker and time, as discussed in §1. We now rewrite B1 and add an axiom for 'was ambitious'.

B1. For any speaker S, time t, singular term α, $\ulcorner\alpha$ is ambitious$\urcorner$ is true$_1(S, t)$ iff Ref$_1(S, t, \alpha)$ is ambitious at t.
B2. For any speaker S, time t, singular term α, $\ulcorner\alpha$ was ambitious$\urcorner$ is true$_1(S, t)$ iff Ref$_1(S, t, \alpha)$ is ambitious at some $t' < t$.

The modifications illustrated above distribute throughout the theory initially introduced. We would rewrite RC1 as follows:

RC1. For any speaker S, time t, formula ϕ, $\ulcorner$Not$:\phi\urcorner$ is true$_1(S, t)$ iff it is not the case that ϕ is true$_1(S, t)$.

And similarly for RC2 and RC3.

In addition, our understanding of what it is for axioms to be interpretive must be modified slightly when moving to a language with context sensitive expressions, in a way similar to the way Tarski's Convention T must be modified for truth theories for natural languages. We want to say that an axiom for a referring term or predicate is interpretive if—in the context of the axiom—it *interprets* the object language term. For a referring term, we require that the axiom give the right referent relative to the contextual parameters. For a predicate such as 'is ambitious', what we want of its axiom B1 is that every sentence B1* derived from it by instantiating the metalinguistic variable to a singular term a, and replacing '$\text{Ref}_1(S, t, a)$' with a metalanguage functional term '$A(S, t)$', such that for any S, t, $\text{Ref}(S, t, a) = A(S, t)$ (and note here that '$A(S, t)$' would be a constant function when the object language singular term is a proper name, so that, for example, the value of the appropriate function for the singular term 'Caesar' would be Caesar for every speaker and time), be such that the corresponding sentence M1 is true:[81]

> B1*.   For any speaker S, time t, $\ulcorner a$ is ambitious$\urcorner$ is true$_1(S, t)$ iff $A(S, t)$ is ambitious at t,
>
> M1.   For any speaker S, time t, $\ulcorner a$ is ambitious$\urcorner$ means$_1(S, t)$ that $A(S, t)$ is ambitious at t.

Suppose, for example, that 'a' is replaced by 'I'; then we require that M1^a be true as a condition on B1 being interpretive, where for any $S, t, A_I(S, t) = S$:

> M1^a.   For any speaker S, time t, $\ulcorner$I am ambitious$\urcorner$ means$_1(S, t)$ that $A_I(S, t)$ is ambitious at t.

This is equivalent to M1^b.

> M1^b.   For any speaker S, time t, $\ulcorner$I am ambitious$\urcorner$ means$_1(S, t)$ that S is ambitious at t.

Now take the case of a proper name. Suppose 'a' is 'Caesar'. Then we have for M1, M1^c, where for any $S, t, A_c(S, t) =$ Caesar.

---

[81] We treat '$A(S, t)$' as a directly referring term, so that when we instantiate 'S' and 't' to a particular speaker and time, the contribution of '$A(S, t)$' to what is meant by a sentence is just the value of the function for those arguments. This is to assume that names and other referring terms in our simple language are directly referring terms, that is, that their only contribution to what we understand by an utterance of a sentence in which they are used is what they refer to, relative to the speaker and time. If more is required for other languages, such as matching of a Fregean sense of a name in the object language with a Fregean sense of a name in the metalanguage, this can be incorporated into the requirement on the axioms. As we have mentioned, there are additional complications in the case of demonstratives. See *Truth-Theoretic Semantics*, ch. 4 for discussion of these issues.

M1^c. For any speaker S, time t, $\ulcorner$Caesar is ambitious$\urcorner$ means$_1$(S, t) that $A_c(S, t)$ is ambitious at t.

'$A_c(S, t)$' is a directly referring term, so we may replace it with 'Caesar'. So, the effect of this is to require that M1^d be true as a condition on B1 being interpretive:

M1^d. For any speaker S, time t, $\ulcorner$Caesar is ambitious$\urcorner$ means$_1$(S, t) that Caesar is ambitious at t.

This requirement is readily generalizable by replacing object and metalanguage predicates in B1* and M1 with schematic letters. Modifying the requirement for recursive axioms is not necessary, since the connectives we have introduced are not context sensitive.

We are now ready to return to the question whether these modifications to a Tarski-style truth theory ensure that an extensionally adequate truth theory for a natural language will *ipso facto* meet what we are calling Davidson's Convention T. The hope that it will is encouraged by the observation that, particularly through the need to correctly represent truth conditions for sentences containing demonstratives, we add a very powerful constraint on the class of acceptable theories. How this helps, and whether it is adequate, will be the topic of the next chapter.

Appendix: Formulating a Truth Theory for Natural Languages which Predicates Truth of Utterances of Sentences

In this appendix, we take up the alternative suggestion mentioned in the text for extending Tarski's work to natural languages. This suggestion was made originally by Weinstein 1974, and at one point endorsed by Davidson (see Davidson 2001c (1967): 34, n. 17). The suggestion is to conditionalize on the speaker's utterance of an object language sentence as in [6]:

[6]   For all speakers S, times t, utterances u,
    if u is an utterance of 'Je suis le roi de France' by S at t,
    then u is true in French iff S is the king of France at t.

(Our development of this idea does not follow the details of Weinstein's.) This will ensure that our theory does not entail falsehoods just because some sentences never get uttered. A theory for L will be adequate provided that it entails all instances of the schema [U],

[U]   For all speakers S, times t, utterances u,
    if u is an utterance of s by S at t
    then u is true in L iff p.

where the following relation holds between 's' and the metalanguage formula
that replaces 'p': (i) 's' is replaced by a structural description of a sentence of
L; (ii) if ϕ is a metalanguage formula, perhaps containing the variables 'S' and
't', that replaces 'p', then for any S^*, t^* if u is an utterance of s by S^* at t^*, then
u means the same as the result of replacing the variables, if any, 'S' and 't' in
ϕ with metalanguage names of S^* and t^*.[82] This says that the theory is correct
if its theorems give truth conditions for utterances of the sentences of L by
way of sentences in the metalanguage which mean the same as the utterances
of those L-sentences understood relative to L. Alternatively, we can state the
condition of adequacy in terms of the corresponding modification of our [M']
theorems:

[M'']   For all speaker S, times t, utterances u,
    if u is an utterance of s by S at t
    then u means in L that p.

The condition of adequacy may be stated as follows: a truth theory (in the
style sketched) is adequate iff it entails all instances of [U] for which the
corresponding instances of [M''] are true.

What are the ramifications of this approach for the axioms of our truth
theory? We need to modify them so that the truth predicate applies to an
utterance of the relevant sentences. No change is needed for the reference
axioms. To write the axioms succinctly, let '$U(u,\ \gamma,\ S,\ t)$' mean 'u is an
utterance of γ by S at t'. Consider axiom B1 for a predicate of Simple English$_1$,
repeated here.

B1.   For any speaker S, time t, singular term α, ⌜α is ambitious⌝ is
    true $_1(S, t)$ iff Ref $_1(S, t, \alpha)$ is ambitious at t.

---

[82] For full generality, we would have to talk of translation in a language which is an extension
of the metalanguage at most in that it includes names of S' and t', since the metalanguage may not
have enough names for all the speakers and times in the domain of quantification.

To modify B1 for a theory which predicates truth of utterances, we replace
'$\ulcorner\alpha$ is ambitious$\urcorner$ is $\text{true}_1(S,\ t)$' with 'utterance u, if $U(u,\ \ulcorner\alpha$ is
ambitious$\urcorner$, S, t), then u is true_1', to get:

> B1′. For any speaker S, time t, singular term α, utterance u,
>
> $\quad$ if $\quad$ $U(u, \ulcorner\alpha$ is ambitious$\urcorner, S, t)$
>
> $\quad$ then $\quad$ (u is true_1 iff $\text{Ref}_1(S, t, \alpha)$ is ambitious at t).

For a recursive axiom, say RC1, repeated here,

> RC1. For any speaker S, time t, formula ϕ, $\ulcorner\text{Not}:\phi\urcorner$ is $\text{true}_1(S, t)$ iff it is
> not the case that ϕ is $\text{true}_1(S, t)$,

the modification is more complicated. We want an utterance of a sen-
tence $\ulcorner\text{Not}:\phi\urcorner$ to be true_1 iff it is not the case that its contained utterance of ϕ is true_1. Thus, we need to attend both to the utterance
of the whole of a complex sentence and of its component sentences.
Let '$C(u,\ u_1,\ u_2,\ldots)$' mean 'u contains u_1 and u_2 and... '. We can
revise RC1 for a truth theory that applies to utterances of sentences as
follows:

> RC1′. For any speaker S, time t, formula ϕ, utterances u, u_1,
>
> $\quad$ if $\quad$ $C(u, u_1)$ and $U(u, \ulcorner\text{Not}: \phi\urcorner, S, t)$ and $U(u_1, \phi, S, t)$
>
> $\quad$ then $\quad$ (u is true_1 iff it is not the case that u_1 is true_1).

If we instantiate RC1′ to a speaker, time, formula, and utterances that don't
satisfy the antecedent, the whole is true. Suppose we instantiate RC1′ to
a speaker, time, formula, and utterances that make the antecedent true.
In particular, suppose ϕ is 'Caesar is ambitious', u^* is an utterance
of 'Not:Caesar is ambitious' by S^* at t^*, and u_1^* is the contained
utterance of 'Caesar is ambitious'. In this case we can detach the
consequent of the instantiation of RC1′ to get:

> u^* is true_1 iff it is not the case that u_1^* is true_1.

We can derive from B1′

> if $U(u_1^*, \ulcorner\text{Caesar is ambitious}\urcorner, S^*, t^*)$, then ($u_1^*$ is
> true_1 iff Caesar is ambitious at t^*).

By hypothesis, the antecedent is true, so from these two results we can derive,

> u^* is true_1 iff it is not the case that Caesar is ambitious at t^*,

which is the correct result. We can modify RC2 similarly to arrive at RC2′.

RC2′. For any speaker S, time t, formulas ϕ, ψ, utterances u, u_1, u_2,
   if $C(u, u_1, u_2)$ and $U(u, \ulcorner \phi \text{ and } \psi \urcorner, S, t)$ and
       $U(u_1, \phi, S, t)$ and $U(u_2, \psi, S, t)$
   then (u is true$_1$ iff (u_1 is true$_1$ and u_2 is true$_1$)).

From this it is clear what the general pattern of modification is in moving from a theory in the style presented in the main text of this chapter to a theory which predicates truth of utterances, and vice versa. The same information can be extracted from either sort of theory. (These remarks extend to theories for languages which include quantifiers, though obviously the approach sketched here needs to be revised to accommodate a satisfaction relation, which will have to be defined for open formulas of the object language; see Weinstein 1974 for details.) The relation between a T-sentence for a truth theory with a truth predicate relativized to contextual parameters such as speaker and time, and a T-sentence for a truth theory that applies the truth predicate to utterances, is illustrated in the following schema:

   For all speakers S, times t, s is true(S, t) in L iff p

   iff
   for all speakers S, times t, utterances u,
   if u is an utterance of s by S at t
   then (u is true in L iff p)

Thus, the truth conditions for a sentence in a theory using a relativized truth predicate are just the conditions under which an utterance of the sentence is true (suitably instantiated to speaker and time). In light of this, differences in the formulations involve no substantive difference of approach, and are more a matter of bookkeeping. The choice between these formulations may be viewed as a matter of convenience. A truth theory that applies a truth predicate to utterances makes more perspicuous the fact that, for natural languages, the utterance act is the locus of semantic interpretation, but the apparatus involved in formulating it is considerably more cumbersome than for a theory which employs a relativized truth predicate. We therefore choose to develop truth theories for natural languages using a relativized truth predicate.

6

Davidson's Extensionalist Proposal

> What appears to the right of the biconditional in sentences of the form '*s* is true if and only if *p*' when such sentences are consequences of a theory of truth plays its role in determining the meaning of *s* not by pretending synonymy but by adding one more brush-stroke to the picture which, taken as a whole, tells what there is to know of the meaning of *s*.
>
> (Davidson 2001*c* (1967): 26)

We have discussed the modifications to a truth theory necessary to apply it to natural languages with context sensitive elements, and we have illustrated these techniques with respect to Simple English$_1$. We are now ready to consider the restrictions Davidson wished, at least in "Truth and Meaning," to impose on a theory which entails sentences of the form [*T*], in order for it to satisfy his Convention *T*, and his *motivation* for these restrictions.

[*T*] For all speakers *S*, and times *t*, *s* is *T* for *S* at *t* iff *p*.

Our concern in this chapter is to survey the evidence for the Replacement Theory, according to which Davidson is proposing that we abandon the traditional pursuit of the theory of meaning in favor of the more austere but coherent theory of reference, and to argue for our alternative interpretation, according to which he merely hopes to find, in an extensionally adequate truth theory for a natural language, modified to accommodate context sensitive elements, a theory that *ipso facto* is interpretive. In Chapter 7, we take up two related objections to this proposal.

In deciding the exegetical issue, it is important to attend closely to what Davidson actually says. The project he sets for himself is to provide "for every sentence *s* in the language under study, a matching sentence ... that, in some way yet to be made clear, 'gives the meaning' of *s*" (Davidson 2001*c* (1967): 23). The function of the predicate 'is *T* for *S* at *t*' in [*T*] is to apply to object language sentences such that the metalanguage sentences used on the right hand side of the biconditional give their meaning, in some sense. At the end of quotation [*g*] in Chapter 4, Davidson offers a grammatical criterion for meeting the constraint on an adequate meaning theory for a language. This fails for a truth theory adapted for a natural language, because *T*-sentences will have the form of [*T*] above, and what replaces '*p*' may be an open sentence, and even with a context insensitive language, the criterion works only if the metalanguage includes the object language. So, this criterion will not ensure success in the general case. This is why we need the more general characterization given, first with Tarksi's, and then with Davidson's, Convention *T*. After offering the syntactic criterion, Davidson notes that satisfying it will *ipso facto* satisfy Tarski's Convention *T*. He then remarks that "a theory of meaning for a language *L* shows 'how the meanings of sentences depend upon the meanings of words' if it contains a (recursive) definition of truth-in-*L*" (Davidson 2001*c* (1967): 23). His claim seems misleading, however, for here we have an unarticulated predicate 'true-in-*L*', and apparently only the requirement that it be extensionally adequate (a definition in general is extensionally adequate if it captures the extension of the concept to be defined). Satisfying this requirement by itself will suffice to satisfy neither Tarski's nor Davidson's Convention *T*, for, though a truth definition meeting either convention will thereby be extensionally adequate, not every extensionally adequate definition of a predicate 'true-in-*L*' for a language *L* will satisfy the appropriate convention.

There are passages in "Truth and Meaning," however, which read as if extensional adequacy is all that Davidson requires for the project he is engaged in. Consider, for example, [*h*].

[*h*] ... the definition works by giving necessary and sufficient conditions for the truth of every sentence, and to give truth conditions is a way of giving the meaning of a sentence. To know the semantic concept of truth for a language is to know what it is for a sentence—any sentence—to be true, and this amounts, in one good sense we can give to the phrase, to understanding the language.   (Davidson 2001*c* (1967): 24)

In [h], it *looks* as if he is saying that to know extensionally adequate conditions for the truth of a sentence is to know its meaning, at least in the sense that it allows one to understand it. Some commentators took this to indicate that Davidson is not pursuing the project of providing an account of sentence meaning in the traditional sense, but is instead replacing it with a different project.[83]

The record in "Truth and Meaning" appears genuinely equivocal. It is not obvious that Davidson was completely clear in his own mind about exactly how to employ a truth theory as a meaning theory. He suggests as much himself in retrospective remarks.[84] We are confident, however, that he is *not* committing himself here to rejecting, in essence, the application of Davidson's Convention *T*, which is how passage [*h*], and similar ones have been read (quite widely, in fact), but is just unclear about what *in toto* is required to satisfy it.[85]

After passage [*h*] above, Davidson goes on to discuss devising a truth theory for one's own language. In this case (barring complications due to indexical expressions and the need to regiment natural language expressions so that the apparatus of a truth theory will apply to them—see Truth-Theoretic Semantics, chapter 4 for further discussion), the syntactic criterion suffices. This is because the sentence mentioned on the left hand side of [*T*] is the sentence used on the right. This identity guarantees that the sentence used interprets the sentence mentioned. So, with a recursive definition of a predicate meeting this criterion, one would have a theory which successfully paired each sentence of the language with a sentence which gives its meaning (in a quite straightforward

---

[83] Stich 1976, having read only early Davidson papers, adopts this line. In surveying the first wave of papers on Davidson's program in semantics, one senses that many authors saw the project as related to, but not identical with, the project of providing a compositional meaning theory. One dissenter who adopts our line is Guttenplan 1985.

[84] See e.g. fn. 11 in "Truth and Meaning" in *Inquiries into Truth and Interpretation*, added for its publication in that collection (Davidson 2001*c* (1967): 26); also Davidson 2001*b*: xiv, 2001*b*: 171–2), and fn. 20 in Davidson 1990*b*: 286.

[85] It is clear enough in later work that satisfying Davidson's Convention *T* is the aim of constructing a truth theory that is a meaning theory. See Davidson 2001*c*: 175) e.g. "Someone who can interpret English knows, for example, that an utterance of the sentence 'Snow is white' is true if and only if snow is white; he knows in addition that this fact is entailed by a translational theory—that it is not an accidental fact about that English sentence, but a fact that *interprets* the sentence. Once the point of putting things this way is clear, I see no harm in rephrasing what the interpreter knows in this case in a more familiar vein: he knows that 'Snow is white' in English *means that* snow is white." See also this passage in Davidson 2001*a* (1974): 150, "A theory of truth will yield interpretations only if its *T*-sentences state truth conditions in terms that may be treated as 'giving the meaning' of object language sentences. Our problem is to find constraints on a theory strong enough to guarantee that it can be used for interpretation." Could anything be clearer? Furthermore, Davidson says, on the next page (151): "If the metalanguage predicates translate the object language predicates, things will obviously come out right; if they have the same extensions, this might be enough." Clearly the aim is an interpretive truth theory. From Davidson 2001*b* (1974): 224 we have: "How can a theory of absolute truth give an account of communication, or be considered a theory of meaning? It doesn't provide us with the materials for defining or analysing such phrases as 'means', 'means the same as', 'is a translation of', etc. It is wrong to think that we can *automatically* construe *T*-sentences as 'giving the meaning' of sentences if we put no more constraint on them than that they come out true."

sense—as we have shown). Davidson was fully aware of this, and no one could ask for more.

If this is right, the expression 'truth conditions' in passage [*h*] must be read as something more than what is expressed by a sentence extensionally equivalent to the sentence for which it is used to give what we may call merely extensionally adequate truth conditions (henceforth, 'extensionally adequate truth conditions'). Instead, we must understand the expression 'truth conditions' so that a *T*-form sentence does not give truth conditions of a sentence unless the sentence used on the right hand side of the biconditional interprets the sentence mentioned on the left, or the sentence form in the context of the sentence provides an interpretation of the sentence mentioned on the left. (It is worth reiterating that, despite its grammatical form, 'truth conditions' is not being used to talk about a thing or things, but derives its sense rather from its use in 'to give the truth conditions of', which is spelled out as above. So, talk about the truth conditions of a sentence is shorthand for talk about giving the truth conditions of a sentence.)

Nonetheless, some passages in "Truth and Meaning" seem to suggest that extensionally adequate truth conditions alone suffice, for example, in Davidson's discussion of whether a correct theory could have as a consequence [*S*]:

[*S*]   'Snow is white' is true iff grass is green.

He suggests that no extensionally adequate theory could issue in [*S*], but that "if . . . [*S*] followed from a characterization of the predicate 'is true' that led to the invariable paring of truths with truths and falsehoods with falsehoods— then there would not . . . be anything essential to the idea of meaning that remained to be captured" (Davidson 2001*c* (1967): 26). One way to read him is as rejecting the aim of providing a truth theory that meets Davidson's Convention *T*, and so as rejecting the traditional project of giving a meaning theory, as in some way illegitimate. However, this is scarcely compatible with how he opens his essay, and incompatible with his later attempts to improve upon the adequacy conditions (Davidson 2001*c* (1973): 138–9, 2001*b* (1973): 150–3, 2001*b* (1976): 171–2). If he were aiming only to replace the ordinary notion of meaning with one more tractable, then placing additional constraints on the theory would not be required. The search for such constraints presupposes a target that has not been hit. A more adequate interpretation is that Davidson genuinely hoped that the nontrivial task of providing an extensionally adequate truth theory of a *natural* language, which must accommodate, in particular, indexicals and demonstratives, would *in itself* suffice to satisfy his Convention T.[86] In particular, he assumed that, once we realized that the theory must get the right results for the truth of sentences with indexicals and demonstratives, we would see that powerful additional constraints are being placed on the theory. Consider our spurious T-sentence, [S], reformulated with a relativized truth predicate,

[1]   'Snow is white' is true for S at t iff grass is green at t.

If we required that the theory must also achieve the right results for sentences such as 'That is snow' and 'That is white', then it may appear that we have enough additional resolving power to eliminate [1]. Suppose that a speaker S^* demonstrates an object d at time t^* in uttering 'That is snow'. Instantiating a T-theorem, in a theory which generates [1], for 'That is snow' and employing an appropriate reference axiom for 'that' will yield [2]:

[2]   'That is snow' is true for S^* at t^* iff d is grass.

---

[86] See fn. 10 of "Truth and Meaning," in particular, and his remark, "Sentences with demonstratives obviously yield a very sensitive test of the correctness of a theory of meaning, and constitute the most direct link between language and the recurrent macroscopic objects of human interest and attention" (Davidson 2001c (1967): 35). Unfortunately for our effort to get an unequivocal statement on this out of Davidson's work, we have apparently contrary passages. First, there is his claim in "Theories of Meaning and Learnable Languages" that: "I do not mean to argue here that it is necessary that we be able to extract a truth definition from an adequate theory ..., but a theory meets the conditions I have in mind if we can extract a truth definition; in particular, no stronger notion of meaning is called for" (Davidson 2001: 8). Second, there is this passage at the beginning of "Moods and Performances," published in 1979: "I have argued that a theory of truth patterned after a Tarski-type truth definition tells us all we need to know about sense. Counting truth in the domain of reference, as Frege did, the study of sense thus comes down to the study of reference." (Davidson 2001b (1979): 109). This passage might be taken to suggest that the most we can make out of sense is what we learn about a language through constructing a correct truth theory for it. This impression is reinforced in his "Reply to Cargile" in Davidson 2001c (1970): 143–4: "A theory of truth entails, for each sentence s of the object language, a theorem of the form 's is true if and only if p'. Since the sentence that replaces 'p' must be true (in the metalanguage) if and only if s is true (in the object language), there is a sense in which the sentence that replaces 'p' may be called a translation of s; and if the metalanguage contains the object language, it may be called a paraphrase. (These claims must be modified in important ways in a theory of truth for a natural language.) But it should be emphasized that paraphrase or translation serves no purpose here except that of giving a systematic account of truth-conditions. There is no further claim to synonymy, nor interest in regimentation or improvement. A theory of truth gives a point to such concepts as meaning, translation, and logical form; it does not depend on them." This passage also suggests that we are not to think of ourselves as operating with an independent conception of meaning, and aiming to show that placing constraints on a truth theory can help us achieve our goal of specifying meanings in that sense for all sentences in an infinitary language. We feel here the frustration many readers have felt with Davidson's papers, and we confess that it is just not obvious to us that Davidson had clearly in mind the connection between a truth theory and a meaning theory we have identified. It is, however, there to be identified in Davidson's suggestion, and it is a quite natural observation. If it is not what Davidson had in mind, *it should have been.*

But if 'snow' means *snow* in S^*'s idiolect, [2] will be false. So, we can see why Davidson thought that the changes needed to adapt a truth theory to natural languages might, in and of themselves, sufficiently constrain an extensionally adequate theory so as to ensure that it is interpretive.[87]

Further support for this interpretation is to be found in Davidson's essays roughly contemporaneous with "Truth and Meaning," in which there is no suggestion he has changed his mind about his aims, but in which it is clear that a theory's meeting Tarski's or Davidson's Convention T is a condition of adequacy. For example,[88] in "Semantics for Natural Languages," first presented in 1968 and published in 1970, Davidson says that,

[i] A theory of truth entails, for each sentence s, a statement of the form 's is true if and only if p' where in the simplest case 'p' is replaced by s. Since the words 'is true if and only if' are invariant, we may interpret them if we please as meaning 'means that'. So construed, a sample might then read ' "Socrates is wise" means that Socrates is wise'. (Davidson 2001*d* (1970): 60)

Davidson describes a truth theory of the sort he has in mind as *empirical*, as we have already assumed above. This is because he intends it to function as a theory for a natural language; we do not, and could not, know *a priori* how to interpret the expressions of a natural language, or how to assign them interpretive truth conditions. For one's own language, though one's knowledge is not *a priori*, there is no difficulty in identifying which T-form sentences satisfy Davidson's Convention T. The difficulty arises in figuring out what the axioms of the theory ought to be in order to construct canonical proofs of them. It is altogether different for another's language (even to some degree for other speakers of one's own language, a theme emphasized more in Davidson's later work). Here the task of verifying the theory is nontrivial, and we find in "Truth and Meaning," though not emphasized there, the first descriptions of

[87] It is worth noting briefly that a similar response to the problem is available if we have a name in the object language, say, 'Frosty', which refers to something that is snow. For if we are allowed to assume that we can identify the right reference axioms, then the axioms required to generate [1] will generate an incorrect T-theorem for 'Frosty is snow', namely: 'Frosty is snow' is true for S at t iff Frosty is grass. One might protest that we could have a mistaken reference axiom for 'Frosty' which treats it as referring to something which is grass (a bale, e.g.), which would then yield a true T-theorem for 'Frosty is snow'. (This would not be so easy, since we have to make adjustments for all the other things we might say truly of Frosty.) But the same objection can be lodged against the appeal to demonstratives: for that works straightforwardly only if we can assume that we get the right reference axioms for them. Still, demonstratives do give us the power to refer to anything at any time, and so give us effectively the resolving power of having very many more names in the language than we in fact do.

[88] Consider also: "Making a systematic account of truth central in empirical semantics is in a way merely a matter of stating old goals more sharply" (Davidson 2001*d* (1970): 62).

radical interpretation, with many of its central themes: the idea that our data will consist in part in what sentences the speaker holds true, the requirements that we find the other mostly right and mostly rational, and the emergence of indeterminacy (Davidson 2001c (1967): 27). Radical interpretation will be addressed more fully in Part II, but here it is worth noting that, at this point, Davidson does not suggest that empirically verifying a theory is itself one of the restrictions to be imposed on an adequate truth theory for the purposes of a meaning theory, though this will later become a major theme.

We return now to a question we postponed answering earlier. We said that if Davidson's goal were merely, as he announces in his opening paragraph ([e] in Chapter 3), to provide a compositional meaning theory for a language, it would seem that he has all he needs in a truth theory, provided that the axioms of the theory are interpretive, and that we had a characterization of *canonical* proofs for deriving *T*-sentences. As already noted, this is not what Davidson does. Rather, he initially aims to get everything he needs out of a truth theory (i.e. satisfaction of Davidson's Convention *T*) by settling on an extensionally adequate theory. In later work, the extra restriction imposed (see below and fn. 11 of "Truth and Meaning") is that the theory be empirically verified. The motivation for this is introduced at the end of passage [*g*]:

What we require of a theory of meaning for a language *L* is that *without appeal to any (further) semantical notions* [our emphasis] it place enough restrictions on the predicate 'is *T*' to entail all sentences got from schema *T* when '*s*' is replaced by a structural description of a sentence of *L* and '*p*' by that sentence.

When Davidson requires that the restrictions placed on the definition of a predicate for a language not appeal to any further semantical notions, he appears to exclude any semantic notion not needed for defining 'is *T*'. In particular, he would exclude 'means', 'synonymous', 'interpretive', and so on (unless an object language sentence employs terms that mean the same as these). This may explain why he fails to take our route, namely, why he doesn't simply require the axioms to be interpretive. What is left unexplained is *why* Davidson should at this point place this severe restriction on his project.[89] One reason, as we have suggested, is that he has changed his focus of Investigation *from the relatively narrow question* of how we can understand the meanings of complex expressions in terms of understanding the meanings of their parts—what we

---

[89] It is worth noting that adopting the interpretation of 'is true for *S* at *t*' we urged above shows this is hard to do. For this is an abbreviation for 'understood as if spoken by S at t'. Still, one could aim to place constraints on a truth theory without invoking semantic predicates other than those explicitly occurring in the theory.

are calling the initial project—*to the more ambitious question* of what it is for any expression, complex *or* primitive, in a language to have the meaning it does—what we are calling the extended project. If restrictions could be placed on the definition of a predicate applying to the sentences of a language L sufficient to pick out all of the T-sentences of L, without using semantical notions beyond truth, reference (and satisfaction), one would illuminate in a important way what it is for the sentences of a language to have their meanings. In particular, if, as Davidson seemed initially to hope, any extensionally adequate truth theory were *ipso facto* interpretive, it would seem that sentence meaning in a language would have been fixed essentially by a structure required merely for extensionally adequate truth conditions, thus revealing an important and unnoticed connection between meaning, truth as relativized to a speaker and time, and the recursive structure of natural languages. This would simultaneously fix the meanings of the primitive expressions of the language, according to Davidson, because the meaning of a word is exhausted by its contribution to the meanings of the sentences in which it appears. Indeed, this idea seems in part to have suggested to Davidson that there might be enough structure in an extensionally adequate truth theory to satisfy Davidson's Convention T; consider passage [*j*] in this light.

[*j*] If sentences depend for their meaning on their structure, and we understand the meaning of each item in the structure only as an abstraction from the totality of sentences in which it features, then we can give the meaning of any sentence (or word) only by giving the meaning of every sentence (and word) in the language.[90] Frege said that only in the context of a sentence does a word have a meaning; in the same vein he might have added that only in the context of the language does a sentence (and therefore a word) have meaning.   (Davidson 2001*c* (1967): 22)

We will return below to the question whether this shift in focus in Davidson's investigation unnecessarily complicates some parts of his development of the extended project, when he returns to the question of what restrictions must be placed on the definition of a truth predicate for a language if it is to serve

[90] This must be an exaggeration, or a loose expression. An account of the meaning of a sentence would involve an account of what its words mean and their mode of combination, and an account of that, in turn, would involve an account of the meanings of many other sentences that could be constructed from them; but this does not imply, as Davidson's passage suggests, that for any relatively rich language, to determine the meaning of a sentence is to determine the meanings of *every other* sentence in the language. Sentences disjoint in vocabulary are counterexamples, and Davidson's definition of a semantical primitive in "Theories of Meaning and Learnable Languages" presupposes you can't construct the meaning of every expression of the language from knowing the meanings of those in any given sentence. (See also Davidson 1993: 80 n. 3.)

as a meaning theory. The danger arises that, in the initial and controversial suggestion that a merely extensionally adequate truth definition would suffice as a meaning theory, we lose sight of what is an uncontentious additional restriction on the definition of a truth predicate which will do the job. When Davidson rejects his early suggestion, what he replaces it with is not what is given above, but instead the requirement (see Chapter 11) that the theory be verified by the procedures of a radical interpreter. 'Radical interpretation' is a term of art in Davidson's philosophy and it will be the focus of our attention in Part II. We will argue there that Davidson's requirement raises difficulties for getting a clear view of the job he sets for the radical interpreter.

7

The Extensionality and Determination Problems

> ... a *T*-sentence does not give the meaning of the sentence it concerns: the
> *T*-sentence does fix the truth value relative to certain conditions, but it does
> not say the object language sentence is true *because* the conditions hold.
>
> (Davidson 2001*c* (1973): 138)

So far, we have discussed how Davidson lays out his basic strategy, and how to
interpret his project in "Truth and Meaning." Now we turn to a constellation
of difficulties, each of which is alleged to undercut the possibility of using
a truth theory as the core of a meaning theory. We have assembled all the
materials needed to deal with them, and it remains only to apply them here.
The interest in doing so lies in the utility that responding to these objections
has in clarifying how a truth theory can be employed in pursuit of a meaning
theory, and in showing that objections that many philosophers think cripple
Davidson's project rest mostly on a failure to elucidate correctly how a truth
theory can relate to a meaning theory. We consider two objections in this
chapter, the *extensionality* and the *determination* problems. In Chapter 8, we
take up Foster's problem, according to which any statement of knowledge of
a truth theory suitable for interpretation will violate Davidson's constraints
on his program. Reviewing these objections and responses to them will clarify
further the criteria a truth theory must satisfy to serve a meaning theorist, and
the role it plays in providing a compositional meaning theory for a natural
language. In Chapter 9, we outline the form the meaning theory proper will
take, making explicit the role of a truth theory, and the criteria it must meet to
perform its role; we consider the relation between a compositional meaning
theory in this form, and a theory of semantic competence in a language. In

Chapter 10, we consider briefly four defects of natural languages which might be thought to pose difficulties for any effort to provide a *formal* theory for natural languages.

The first major objection, the *extensionality problem*, charges that an extensionally adequate truth theory is not *ipso facto* interpretive. This problem is *inter*-theoretic, inasmuch as it involves gleaning from among a variety of extensionally adequate theories only one which is interpretive. This objection is correct, as far as it goes, and it shows Davidson's initial hope that an extensionally adequate truth theory would *ipso facto* be interpretive fails. But it is not fatal to the initial project of pursuing a compositional meaning theory by way of an appropriately constrained truth theory. We consider the problem and explain why Davidson's initial hope was ill-founded in §1. In §2, we consider various attempts to remedy this difficulty, arguing that none of them suffices. We then explain why, as we are utilizing truth theories in pursuit of compositional meaning theories, we do not have an extensionality problem.

The second objection, the *determination problem*, is that, since any truth theory will have among its theorems noninterpretive *T*-form sentences, knowing an interpretive truth theory, and even knowing that it is interpretive, is insufficient for interpretation. This problem is *intra*-theoretic, inasmuch as it is about identifying interpretive theorems, even when they issue from an interpretive theory. Once separated from the extensionality problem, the determination problem is easy to solve by way of appeal to appropriately constrained proofs, *canonical proofs*, as we have called them. This objection is taken up in §3.

1. The Extensionality Problem

Recall that Davidson's initial constraint on a definition of the predicate 'is *T*' was that the *T*-form sentences we proved on its basis must be true.[91] His hope was that by demanding this for every sentence of a natural language, including those with indexicals and demonstratives, sufficient structure would be imposed to ensure that all the *T*-sentences for the language would be among the *T*-form sentences provable from the recursive definition of 'is *T*'. The difficulty is that the requirement that every *T*-form sentence be an extensionally adequate biconditional requires only that every axiom be an extensionally adequate biconditional, and not that it be interpretive as well.

---

[91] The problem raised in this section has been widely discussed, notably by Davidson 2001*d* (1970); Foster 1976; Loar 1976.

But requiring only extensionally adequate biconditional axioms will not guarantee that among the consequences of our theory will be any T-sentences for the language. This can be demonstrated with the following fragment of a truth theory. For convenience, we will elucidate this point for a language L without context sensitive elements—the point extends straightforwardly to truth theories modified to accommodate such elements.

Suppose in L, 'dog' means 'canine with a heart', and L has one proper name, 'Fido'. Suppose, as a matter of fact, something is a canine with a heart iff it is a canine with a liver (these predicates being tenseless). Then axioms a1 and a2 provide an extensionally adequate truth theory $\mathcal{T}$ for L:

> a1. 'Fido is a dog' is T in L iff Ref('Fido') is a canine with a liver.
> a2. Ref('Fido') = Fido.

From $\mathcal{T}$ we can prove T-form sentence [1], but not T-sentence [2].

> [1] 'Fido is a dog' is T in L iff Fido is a canine with a liver.
> [2] 'Fido is a dog' is T in L iff Fido is a canine with a heart.

Since the T-sentence is [2], and not the mere T-form sentence [1], locating a predicate in the metalanguage to devise an extensionally adequate axiom for a predicate in the object language L fails to guarantee that the axiom is interpretive. Thus, nothing guarantees that an extensionally adequate truth theory is *ipso facto* interpretive.

The problem can arise even if we have no simple predicate in the metalanguage co-extensive with a primitive object language predicate. So, consider the axioms b1 and b2 for a truth theory $\mathcal{T}'$.

> b1. For all names α, $\ulcorner\alpha$ is red$\urcorner$ is T iff Ref(α) is red.
> b2. Ref('A') = A.

We can derive from $\mathcal{T}'$ the T-sentence [3].

> [3] 'A is red' is T iff A is red.

Now let us modify b1 as in b1'.

> b1'. For all names α, $\ulcorner\alpha$ is red$\urcorner$ is T iff Ref(α) is red and the earth moves.

Since 'the earth moves' is true, b1' is true if b1 is. Carrying out our proof as before, we derive the T-form sentence [4].

> [4] 'A is red' is T iff A is red and the earth moves.

[4] will be true if b1 of our unmodified theory is true. Since '*A* is red' and '*A* is red and the earth moves' are not synonymous, both extensionally adequate truth theories cannot be interpretive.

This result obtains, regardless of how much we enrich our language, provided that the right hand sides of our biconditionals are extensional. For in that case, suppose we can prove [5] from our axioms, where $\ulcorner\phi(\alpha)\urcorner$ represents a sentence with a term α. Then for any term β co-extensive, but not synonymous, with α, we can replace α with β in the theory's axioms and prove a true biconditional of the form [6]. For, since α and β are co-extensive, [7] and so [8] obtain.

> [5] s is T iff $\phi(\alpha)$
> [6] s is T iff $\phi(\beta)$
> [7] $\phi(\alpha)$ iff $\phi(\beta)$
> [8]   (s is T iff $\phi(\alpha)$) iff (s is T iff $\phi(\beta)$)

[7] expresses the condition that α and β are co-extensive; from this [8] follows. So, replacing α with β in the axiom, which allows one to derive [6] instead of [5], results in a true theorem if the original was true. Given that α and β are not synonymous, it follows that at most one of these theories is interpretive, though both are extensionally adequate.

In "Truth and Meaning," as we have remarked, Davidson apparently hoped that because the truth theory must produce correct results for every sentence in the object language, and because the object language contained demonstratives and indexicals, this would suffice to rule out noninterpretive truth theories. This reflects a general strategy of locating features of the object language sensitive to differences in meaning among object language expressions to adjudicate between distinct truth theories. Demonstratives remove some bad theories, as we have noted.[92] Any theory that issues in the extensionally correct, but noninterpretive, [9], on the basis of using 'is grass' and 'is green' in the metalanguage in the standard way in axioms for 'is snow' and 'is white' in the object language, would plausibly be ruled out because English contains demonstratives. Treating demonstratives as we have illustrated above, with standard axioms for predicates, would yield as theorems [10] and [11].

> [9]   'Snow is white' is T for S at t in English iff grass is green.
> [10] For all speakers S, times t, 'That is snow' is T for S at t in English iff what is demonstrated by S at t is grass.

---

[92] On the assumption that we have the right axioms for the demonstratives, see n. 87.

[11] For all speakers S, times t, 'That is white' is T for S at t in English iff what is demonstrated by S at t is green.

Any theory with these theorems, however, assigns the wrong extension to 'is true for S at t in English'. 'That is snow', for example, is not true in English for a speaker at a time iff what the speaker demonstrates at that time is grass. On the contrary, when English speakers truly utter 'That is snow', what they demonstrate is snow, not grass.

However, this test fails to rule out extensionally adequate but noninterpretive axioms for object language predicates. For if an object language predicate ϕ is co-extensive with a metalanguage predicate ψ, then an axiom for ϕ which uses ψ will be extensionally adequate, whether or not it is interpretive, and the T-form sentence we prove on its basis together with our axioms for object language demonstratives will still be extensionally adequate.

2. Counter Moves, Problems, and Solution

This strategy for producing theories equivalent with respect to truth, but not with respect to meeting Convention T, fails if there are contexts on the right hand side of our biconditionals in which two terms can be intersubstituted only if they are synonymous. For in that case, it will be possible for a context, say, $\psi(\alpha)$, to be such that its truth value changes when a co-extensional, but nonsynonymous term β is substituted for α. These are what we shall call strongly intensional contexts. Modal contexts are not strongly intensional, for they allow terms to be intersubstituted freely as long as they are necessarily co-extensive. Likewise, nomological contexts, for example, contexts created by 'it is a law that', are not strongly intensional, for they allow intersubstitution of predicates in these contexts if they are nomically co-extensive. Strongly intensional contexts in English include those following propositional attitude verbs, such as 'believes', 'hopes', and the like. Consider the following axiom c1 and its modification c1', obtained by adding to the right hand side of c1 as a conjunct a logical truth LT.

c1.　For all names α, ⌜α snores⌝ is T iff Ref(α) snores.
c1'.　For all names α, ⌜α snores⌝ is T iff Ref(α) snores and LT.

Abbreviate 'Ref(α) snores and LT' as 'Ref(α) znores'. Necessarily, something snores iff it znores. If there are no strongly intensional contexts in our language, our truth theory cannot distinguish between these axioms on the basis of the truth values of the theorems they yield. Suppose, however, L includes a verb 'believes' which means in *L* what it does in English, and suppose *L* contains the proper names 'John' and 'Albert'. Then the first and second theories (ignoring technical difficulties!) will have as theorems [12] and [13], respectively.

[12]   'John believes that Albert snores' is *T* iff John believes that Albert snores.

[13]   'John believes that Albert snores' is *T* iff John believes that Albert znores.

Since nothing guarantees that [13] is true if [12] is, we no longer have a proof that from any extensionally adequate truth theory we can generate another extensionally adequate truth theory. Since both still *might* be true, we have no guarantee there won't be two extensionally adequate truth theories for the language. However, it might be plausibly thought that for any natural language, for any two nonsynonymous co-extensive simple predicates φ and ψ, there will be a pair of sentences θ and Δ such that φ occurs in θ where ψ occurs in Δ, and which are such that for some believer, θ can be correctly used after 'believes' to correctly attribute a belief to him, while Δ cannot.[93] In this case, extensional adequacy would be an adequate test for interpretiveness.[94]

[93] The response to the extensionality problem depends on supposing that the only axioms to change are base ones. However, one might think that by modifying recursive clauses or clauses dealing with proper names, adjustments could be made which would produce a noninterpretative truth theory with true theorems. The axiom for 'believes', however it is handled, might have an exception clause built into it to accommodate the predicate in the modified axiom, with the result that the truth conditions are as follows: " 'John believes that Albert snores' is *T* iff LT and John believes that Albert snores." That is, the effect of the special clause might be to export the extra conjunct outside the scope of 'believes' on the right hand side of the biconditional. Two points can be made. First, this maneuver can be blocked by requiring that all terms in a given semantic category be treated in the same way by the recursive clauses of the theory. Thus, there can be no special clauses to deal with particular predicates on the basis of what they mean in recursive clauses, and likewise for proper names and terms in other semantic categories. The motivation is that recursive clauses in a truth theory are sensitive to the semantic category of terms they cover, but not to the meanings of these terms. This enables us to grasp the meanings of an indefinitely large range of new sentences by knowing the meanings of the recursive terms in a language, and learning the meaning of a new primitive expression. Second, the problem may arise for simple predicates, in which case there is no possibility of recourse to special rules that look at the structure of the complement sentence.

[94] What if we considered sentences in the object language which state what object language expressions mean, such as, for example, ' 'Albert snores' means in *L* that Albert snores'? In this case, we would have theorems for our first and second theories such as (i) ' 'Albert snores' means in *L* that Albert snores' is *T* iff 'Albert snores' means in *L* that Albert snores; and (ii) ' 'Albert snores' means in *L* that Albert snores' is *T* iff 'Albert snores' means in *L* that Albert znores. Clearly only one of these would be true, and this doesn't depend on any contingent facts about believers. Thus, one could argue that an extensionally adequate theory for a language with a predicate meaning '*y* means in *x* that *p*' will *ipso facto* be correct. This does render the thesis, though, considerably less interesting, even trivial. In addition, it would require stating the criterion in reference to a class of theories

A number of problems remain for this defense of Davidson's original suggestion. Two are generated by his own commitments; the other two are independent of those commitments.

The first difficulty for pursuing this strategy on Davidson's behalf is that he is committed to giving an entirely extensional truth theory for natural languages (i.e. that there are no nonextensional contexts inside the truth theory). In particular, Davidson sketches an account of how to give extensional truth conditions for apparently intensional contexts (see *Truth-Theoretic Semantics*, chapter 11). With this commitment, he cannot accept the solution we sketched above. In addition, if he is right that the semantics for apparently intensional contexts is after all extensional, then the putative fact on which the above response depends will not obtain.

The second difficulty is that it may seem that, in saying for which languages extensional adequacy plausibly suffices for interpretiveness, we must characterize them as those which include strongly intensional contexts. But these contexts we have characterized as those in which substitutions preserve truth only if the term substituted is synonymous with the term for which it is substituted. Plausibly, this violates the spirit at least of Davidson's constraint that one say what suffices for interpretiveness without an appeal to any semantic notions like synonymy. One might respond that the relevant class of verbs could be described without making reference to their strong intensionality, but aside from this seeming a superficial dodge, we must still talk of languages having terms in them that mean what verbs in the relevant class mean, so we seem again to have invoked a forbidden semantical notion in saying under what conditions extensional adequacy suffices for interpretiveness.

A third difficulty we have ignored is how to construct a truth theory for strongly intensional contexts. Recall that the difficulties here are in part motivated by Davidson's move to an extensional truth theory in the first place. Until this problem is solved—we have offered no solution to it—the above sketch of a solution to the extensionality problem cannot be executed. (Moreover, certain solutions to the problem of incorporating (what we have identified as) strongly intensional contexts into a truth theory would render them useless for the above purpose. We will discuss these problems in *Truth-Theoretic Semantics*; in particular, we will discuss in Chapter 11 a natural extension of Davidson's account of indirect discourse to belief sentences which treats 'John believes that' as a stand alone sentence, and 'that' as a singular referring term, which

which are characterized partly using a semantic term, which appears to violate Davidson's constraint. A similar difficulty arises for appeal to strong intensionality, as we note below.

when used with 'Albert snores' following it, refers to its utterance. On this view, there is strictly speaking no strongly intensional context at all, and a proof of the *T*-sentence for 'John believes that' does not employ any of the terms usually thought of as appearing in its complement.[95])

Finally, since, as we have observed, it is at least possible for there to be two extensionally adequate truth theories for any language not equally interpretive, it follows that there is a sense in which the claim that an extensionally adequate truth theory for a natural language is interpretative does not provide the kind of illumination of meaning we are seeking. For the claim that extensional adequacy suffices, if true, is true for no principled reasons but only contingently so. That is, all we will have shown is the extensional equivalence of 'is interpretive' and 'is an extensionally adequate truth theory'. But in seeking to understand what it is for words to mean what they do, we want conditions on a truth theory that conceptually guarantee the theory is interpretive. Even if the above strategy succeeded, it wouldn't achieve this end.

If we despair of appealing solely to extensional adequacy to secure the right result, we might try to strengthen the requirement, while still not invoking any of the forbidden notions. In particular, as Davidson suggested in later work, it would be natural to require that the theory's relevant *T*-theorems express natural laws, that is, they hold as a matter of nomic necessity. This would require the axioms of the theory to be treated as laws, and so, too, the *T*-form sentences that are derivable from them. We could make this explicit, as we have noted, by prefacing 'it is a law that' to the axioms. However, while this would enable us to distinguish between predicates only accidentally co-extensive, it would not be adequate, because it would not distinguish between predicates nomically (or metaphysically) co-extensive, such as 'is water' and 'is H_2O'.

We could strengthen the operator to 'it is analytic that', or 'it is a matter of meaning alone that', but doing so is still inadequate. First, there is a sense in which this proposal fails to meet the initial constraint, since it invokes the notion of analyticity, truth in virtue of meaning, which is a semantic notion. Second, though, even waiving this objection, it will not enable us to distinguish between logically or conceptually necessarily co-extensive predicates, such as 'is a cube' and 'is a regular polyhedron with six faces', though they are not synonymous. Since for any predicate ϕ, we can introduce a predicate χ,

---

[95] Similarly, a metalinguistic account will not be useful, because it will give a clause for 'believes' such as: 'John believes that Albert snores' is *T* iff Believes(John, 'Albert snores'). Here the axioms for 'snores' in the object language play no role.

understood to apply to something as a matter of meaning iff ϕ applies to it and LT, where LT is a logical or conceptual truth, it is clear that this is still not strong enough.

However, there is another solution to the extensionality problem, one already invoked in Chapter 4, which seeks not to force the truth theory to say anything stronger than what its words mean, but instead says something about a condition the axioms must meet for the theory to do its job. Namely, the interpretive theory, the theory issuing in T-sentences in the right way, is that truth theory whose *axioms* are *interpretive*. We want the axioms of the truth theory to pair metalanguage terms used in specifying truth conditions with the object language terms that they translate. These translations are what we require of a truth theory for it to serve in pursuit of a meaning theory. But it is not something we require the truth theory to *state*. It is by virtue of stating a condition *on* the truth theory that the theory itself does not state that we can use an extensional logic in proving T-sentences, which then provide us with the means of understanding the object language sentences for which they specify truth conditions. And they do this not by stating what those sentences mean, but rather by stating truth conditions for them, which we know likewise provide their interpretations, because we know the theory is interpretive.

This solution is not, as we noted before, Davidson's. His own suggestion, after the first hope faded, is to be found in his writings on radical interpretation. It is to require the truth theory to be empirically verified. This is likewise a strategy which does not seek to make the truth theory say anything strong enough to ensure it issues in T-sentences, but rather to say something about it that suffices. It is motivated by pursuit of the extended project; for appeal to the constraint that the axioms be interpretive violates the constraint that we say what is required without an appeal to semantical notions. The success of Davidson's later proposal depends on whether the imposed condition ensures that the axioms of the theory are interpretive. We take up Davidson's solution in Part II, and evaluate it in the light of the requirement given here.

3. The Determination Problem and Canonical Proofs

A second difficulty remains even if we know that a truth theory is interpretive, and that it generates every T-sentence for the object language. For if the logic for the metalanguage is reasonably rich, not only will T-sentences be provable, but so too will many T-form sentences which are not T-sentences. For example, if we can prove a T-form sentence like [14], we can prove in any standard logic a sentence of form [15], where LT is any tautology.

> [14] s is T iff p.
> [15] s is T iff p and LT.

[14] and [15] cannot both be interpretive. The problem is to determine which provable T-form sentences are in fact T-sentences. So, we need a way of identifying, on the basis of formal considerations alone, the right T-form sentences. In general, when the object language is not embedded in the metalanguage, we cannot rely on the test that the used sentence replace the mentioned one (and even when the object language is embedded, a problem arises for this test with respect to sentences that contain indexicals or other context sensitive terms). A formal criterion, then, must take the form of a syntactically specified proof procedure by which all and only T-sentences are provable.

We have already indicated how to accommodate this problem. We return to it here, because it is important to distinguish the determination problem from the extensionality problem, with which it has been confused, and because a more explicit treatment will aid in our response to Foster's problem in Chapter 8.

Intuitively, we want the T-form sentences derived solely on the basis of the content of the axioms of the theory, and whose derivations rely on no additional resources of the logic of the truth theory. A T-form sentence whose proof draws only upon the content of interpretive axioms will itself give truth conditions for its object language sentence in terms which interpret this sentence. How the proof procedure is formulated in detail will depend on the details of the logical system in which the theory is formulated. Our aim in general is to require that only certain sorts of inference are sanctioned, and (perhaps) that they be drawn in a certain order, on the basis of the kind of sentence we face at each stage of the proof procedure, with the aim of preventing spurious material, such as tautologies, from being introduced gratuitously in the proof. One potential strategy is to restrict the logic so that only those T-form sentences which are T-sentences can be derived from the axioms. If this is possible, then even when our logic enables us to derive T-form sentences which are not T-sentences, we can characterize some proofs, those which rely only on those rules which, when the logic is restricted to them, allow us to prove only those T-form sentences which are T-sentences, as canonical proofs; and we can then characterize the T-form theorems they enable us to prove as canonical theorems.

Let us now illustrate relatively informally how to effect this sort of strategy for characterizing a canonical proof for the theory $TRUTH_0$. The T-sentences for $TRUTH_0$ will be easily identified if the axioms are interpretive, as we will assume they are. The T-sentences are all and only the instances of the schema [16], where 'p' is replaced by an English sentence with the same string of symbols that constitute the sentence denoted by the structural description replacing 's'.

[16] s is true$_0$ iff p.

It is easy enough to characterize the constraints on a proof that guarantee that it draws solely on the content of the axioms, and so yields all and only the T-sentences for the theory. A *canonical proof* for $TRUTH_0$ is, we suggest:

(*a*) a finite sequence of sentences of our metalanguage for $TRUTH_0$ the last of which is a T-form sentence (as above) containing no semantic vocabulary introduced by the theory on the right hand side;

(*b*) each member of which is either (i) an axiom, or (ii) derived from earlier members by *Universal Quantifier Instantiation*, *Substitution*, or *Replacement* as defined in n. 64 in Chapter 4, repeated here for reference.

> *Universal Quantifier Instantiation*: For any sentence ϕ, variable v, singular term β: Inst(ϕ, v, β) may be inferred from Uquant(ϕ, v).
> *Substitution*: For any singular terms α, β, sentence $S(\alpha)$: $S(\beta)$ may be inferred from $S(\alpha)$ and Ident(α, β).
> *Replacement*: For any sentences ϕ, ψ, $S(\phi)$: $S(\psi)$ may be inferred from Eq(ϕ, ψ) and $S(\phi)$.

A canonical theorem of $TRUTH_0$ is a canonically provable T-form theorem of $TRUTH_0$. The T-sentences will be all and only the canonical theorems of $TRUTH_0$. All that stands in the way of a completely formal characterization is a formal characterization of our metalanguage.

Why should we be so confident that proofs proceeding in accordance with (*a*) and (*b*) yield all and only T-sentences? $TRUTH_0$ is by hypothesis interpretive. It is evident that the rules we can appeal to prohibit the introduction of logical truths at any stage in a proof. They can operate only on earlier members of the proof. The only sentences that can enter into a proof without being derived from earlier members are axioms. All the axioms are universally quantified, and to derive anything from them one must first use Universal Quantifier Instantiation on object language expressions. This yields sentences from which further sentences can be derived only by replacement either of singular terms in the sentences on the right hand sides, if appropriate, or of the sentence on the right hand side by another which appears on the right hand side of a biconditional with the first sentence on the left. Arriving at an appropriate T-form sentence requires eliminating the semantic vocabulary from the right hand side of a sentence derived from one of the sentential axioms. The only means of doing so results in the replacement of semantic predicates of object language expressions by metalanguage expressions, which by hypothesis translate their object language counterparts. The end result is a T-form sentence whose right hand side translates the object language sentence denoted on the left, that is, the end result is a T-sentence.

We illustrated this here for the very simple truth theory TRUTH$_0$, but there is no reason to doubt that we can formulate acceptable characterizations of canonical proofs which meet our intuitive requirement for more complex theories. This problem is technical, rather than conceptual.

A syntactical characterization of the class of canonical proofs gives us a syntactical characterization of the class of canonical theorems, and so, relative to the assumption that a theory is interpretive, of the theory's T-sentences. The importance of this emerges when we ask what it is that a theorist is required to know in order to be in a position to use the theory for interpretation. We take this up more fully in the next chapter.

8

Foster's Objection

The trouble is, the theory does not state that it has the character it does.

(Davidson 2001c (1973): 174)

This chapter faces the last of the three objections generally held, in the history of the reception of Davidson's proposal, to present the most serious principled obstacles to carrying out his project. This particular objection has come to be known in the literature as Foster's problem (Foster 1976). It is seen by many philosophers to present an intractable difficulty for Davidson's use of a formal truth theory as a meaning theory.[96] We will pose it in two stages. In the first, the charge is that what Davidson initially claims will suffice to put one in a position to understand any sentence in a language L is insufficient. In the second, the claim is that what needs to be added to remedy the first difficulty is unavailable to Davidson, given his own self-imposed constraints. Thus, the objection goes, the project cannot be carried out successfully within the confines of Davidson's constraints. We will not here be especially concerned with the first stage of the problem. Davidson denied ever having held the view Foster attributes to him.[97] The more important question is whether there is any reason to think that the knowledge of a truth theory required for interpretation violates constraints Davidson himself places on the project, or constraints anyone else following in his footsteps in pursuit of a compositional meaning theory by way of a truth theory must adopt. We will show that what is required doesn't violate any of these constraints.

---

[96] See Foster 1976; Loar 1976; Evans and McDowell 1976: introduction; Davidson 2001b (1976); Wallace 1978: 51. More recent discussions include Soames 1989, 1992, 2003: 297–311; Higginbotham 1992; Richard 1992.   [97] Davidson 2001 (1976): 174.

The initial problem is supposed to arise from Davidson's original claim that:

> [1] Knowing that $\mathcal{T}$ is a truth theory for L, and knowing the facts $\mathcal{T}$ states suffices to understand L.

Foster objected that one could know that $\mathcal{T}$ is a truth theory for L, and know the facts it states, yet still not know that $\mathcal{T}$ states those facts (for the truth theory is here a syntactic object, fixed by a set of sentences which are its axioms). For example, we might know that the theory lately spoken of by so and so is a truth theory for L, and we might know that, so described, the truth theory is true. We might also know the propositions expressed by its axioms (maybe we have been told independently all the things expressed by its axioms). Still, we don't know what the theory's axioms are, and we don't know its axioms express anything we know. So, we are not in a position to use that theory to derive truth conditions for sentences of L, even though we meet the conditions specified in [1] with respect to it. Even adding what its axioms are to what we know about the theory would not be enough. We still need minimally to know what propositions the axioms express (what they meant or stated). We could know what the axioms were without knowing what they meant. (The axioms might be presented to us e.g. in German, by an authority, so that we correctly take ourselves to have been presented with a correct truth theory.) The trouble with [1], then, is that knowing that $\mathcal{T}$ is a truth theory for L, and knowing what it states is not knowing what its axioms are, or what they express. For the theory is a syntactic object, and knowing it is true, and knowing even what its axioms are, and that they are true, does not suffice to know what its axioms express, even if what they express is something we also know. And we do need to know minimally what the theory says in order to use it to interpret another (though even this, we will remark, is not enough).

Foster suggests replacing [1] with [2],

> [2] Knowing that some truth theory for L states that ... suffices to understand L.

where we replace '...' with sentences in the speaker's language which express the axioms (now in the sense of propositions) of a truth theory for L. [2] suffices to put one in a position to understand the sentences of L, Foster argues, because if one knew that some truth theory for L states that ..., where '...' is filled in as above, one could argue from the knowledge one has to a statement of the meaning of any sentence of L. So, consider a sentence D of L. If one knows what the axioms of some truth theory for L state, Foster claims one knows that,

(1)   Some truth theory for L states that D is true iff every x is F.

From this he claims one can infer successively,

(2)   Some truth theory for L has as a logical consequence a sentence which states that D is true iff every x is F.

(3)   Some truth theory for L has a T-sentence whose left hand side designates D, and whose right hand side states that every x is F.

(4)   A sentence which states that every x is F translates D.

(5) D means that every x is F.

This information, however, is not quite sufficient. First, one needs to know that the theory has among its theorems all the T-sentences for the language, something Foster does not state explicitly. Second, one must know something sufficient to enable one to isolate from among those theorems those which are the T-sentences. This is the determination problem discussed in Chapter 7. In particular, because the theory will have sentences of the right form as logical consequences which are not T-sentences, (4) does not follow from (3).

These difficulties can be remedied, as we will show below. However, remedying them will be of no help unless Davidson can avail himself of this strategy and, as we have noted, Foster argues that he cannot. The reason he offers is twofold. First, what is known is not (Foster alleges) expressed extensionally. Second, in consequence, we are not using an extensional logic. Both of these points, Foster claims, conflict with Davidson's *own* constraints on his project. Foster's objection, however, fails, on both counts.

First, he is mistaken about Davidson's commitments. It is not part of Davidson's project, as Davidson responds to Foster, to describe in purely extensional terms what someone could know that would suffice for interpreting another.[98] The truth theory can be stated in a purely extensional language. But what we know about it that enables us to use it for interpretation need not be stateable in a purely extensional language. This point is connected with the one we made in Chapter 7 at the end of §2, that his aim is not to make a truth theory state everything one needs to know to use it for interpretation, but rather to

---

[98] Soames 1992: 21 has repeated the very same charge, which threatens to stick despite Davidson's having previously corrected the record in print.

state something about it that suffices for interpretation. Davidson's own way of putting what is required is as follows:

someone is in a position to interpret the utterances of speakers of a language L if he has a certain body of knowledge entailed by a theory of truth for L—a theory that meets specified empirical and formal constraints—and he knows that this knowledge is entailed by such a theory. (Davidson 2001*b* (1976): 172)

Davidson does wish to show that apparently intensional constructions in English are extensional, but that is an independent thesis. If he succeeds, what one could know that would suffice to interpret a language would be extensional; otherwise, it would not. But he is not laying down a blanket objection against stating what one could know that would suffice for interpretation using sentences traditionally regarded as harboring intensional contexts.

What about the charge that, if in stating what someone knows we must use intensional idioms, then we are committed to relinquishing extensional logic, the sort of logic to which Davidson is committed? The answer is that the extensional logic is to be employed in the truth theory in deriving T-sentences. Since a statement of what is known that suffices for interpreting another is not intended to be expressed by the truth theory alone, the fact that one may use intensional idioms in stating what one would have to know does not mean any sentences in the truth theory itself must contain such constructions. So, nothing immediately follows from the use of intensional idioms in stating what one needs to know to use a truth theory to interpret a language about the logic of the theory being nonextensional. This consequence would arise only if the language the theory is about contains intensional constructions on which the theory needs to operate to generate T-sentences.

Any problem that exists in this area arises independently of the question of what one needs to know to use a truth theory to interpret a speaker of a language. If difficulties arise in pursuing the aim of using an extensional logic in a truth theory of a natural language, they will have their source in intensional contexts in the language on which the theory must operate to generate T-sentences. Davidson is committed, as we have said, to treating natural languages as fully extensional in an interpretive truth theory. We will return to whether this can be done in *Truth-Theoretic Semantics*, chapter 11. For present purposes, what is important is that these problems having to do with intensional contexts are not generated by any claim about what it is one has to know to use a truth theory for interpretation.

While Foster's objection fails, what Davidson claims in the above passage suffices to put one in a position to interpret another falls short of what *is* needed for interpretation, in roughly the same way that what Foster claims suffices falls short. In the rest of this chapter, we say why and what needs to be added, and then give an explicit statement of what is needed for TRUTH$_0$ for Simple English$_0$.

Davidson says that if one knows that a truth theory $\mathcal{T}$ for L, meeting certain empirical and formal constraints, entails a certain body of knowledge (expressed by the theory), then one can interpret an utterance of any sentence of L. In a number of respects his proposal fails to specify all that one needs to know. First, Davidson evidently assumes that meeting whatever empirical and formal constraints are intended suffices for the theory to be interpretive (in the sense defined previously). That is itself something else one would have to know together with the fact that the theory met those constraints. Second, since, as we have observed, the consequences of the theory will include a plethora of true biconditionals of the right form for each object language sentence, merely knowing what the theory entails is insufficient. One needs a way of identifying those consequences of the theory which are T-sentences, and one also needs to know what those consequences express.

There is no great difficulty in saying what one needs to know.[99] The reader who recalls our discussion of Simple English$_0$ will recognize he was himself in possession of knowledge which enabled him to interpret all of its sentences on the basis of what he knew about the theory. This includes what the axioms of the theory are, what they mean or state, that the theory is interpretive, and a procedure for constructing a proof the last line of which is a T-sentence, relative to the assumption that the theory is interpretive. That is to say, in general, what a speaker needs to know, in Davidson's framework, to interpret another, can be put as follows,

1. that theory $\mathcal{T}$, with axioms ..., is an interpretive truth theory for L;
2. that ... is a canonical proof procedure for $\mathcal{T}$ (i.e. a procedure that, relative to the assumption that the axioms of $\mathcal{T}$ are interpretive, produces all and only T-sentences as theorems); and
3. that axiom A1 of T means that ..., axiom A2 of $\mathcal{T}$ means that ..., ...,

---

[99] Wallace 1978 suggests an alternative solution, mentioned in passing in Ch. 7, which involves prefacing the axioms of the truth theory with an operator, 'it is a matter of meaning alone that', which he claims suffices for the knowledge of the modified theorems prefaced by the operator to ground one's understanding of object language sentences. His aim in prefacing axioms with this operator is to insure that they are interpretive. However, as we noted then, this fails if we interpret the operator in its most natural way. For an axiom could be true as a matter of meaning alone, and not be interpretive. For example, "For all names α, $\ulcorner \alpha$ is a triangle$\urcorner$ is true iff Ref(α) is a trilateral." In any case, it is not necessary, as we have shown, to make the truth theory say something stronger for it to serve its role in enabling a theorist to interpret the object language.

where what fills in '...' in (1) is a list of axioms of $\mathcal{T}$, and in (2) a description of a canonical proof procedure. One could articulate this a bit more by putting certain constraints in for 'interpretive', and then adding that the speaker knows that those constraints suffice for the theory to be interpretive. This would accord with what we said above must be added to Davidson's account. Is the knowledge outlined in (1)–(3) sufficient? (1) and (3) guarantee that the theorist understands an interpretive truth theory for L, and knows that he does. This closes the gap that Foster thought that Davidson left open. (2) guarantees, physical and mental limitations aside, that the theorist can use this knowledge to select just those theorems of $\mathcal{T}$ which are T-sentences. To be able to produce (knowingly) a T-sentence one understands for any utterance of a sentence of L is sufficient to be able to interpret that sentence.[100]

We can illustrate this proposal using TRUTH_0, for which we have already formulated a canonical proof procedure. What one would need to know in order to know how to interpret the sentences of Simple English$_0$ is [1]–[3] (we forbear from rewriting all of the clauses):

[1] TRUTH_0 is an interpretive truth theory for Simple English$_0$, whose axioms are

   R1. $\text{Ref}_0(\text{'Caesar'}) = \text{Caesar}$.
   R2. $\text{Ref}_0(\text{'Brutus'}) = \text{Brutus}$.
   A1.   For all names α, $\ulcorner\alpha$ is ambitious$\urcorner$ is true$_0$ iff $\text{Ref}_0(\alpha)$ is ambitious.

   . . .

[2]   Axiom R1 means that $\text{Ref}_0(\text{'Caesar'}) = \text{Caesar}$.
   Axiom R2 means that $\text{Ref}_0(\text{'Brutus'}) = \text{Brutus}$.
   Axiom A1 means that for all names α, $\ulcorner\alpha$ is ambitious$\urcorner$ is true$_0$ iff $\text{Ref}_0(\alpha)$ is ambitious.

   . . .

[3]   A canonical proof for TRUTH_0 is a finite sequence of sentences of Simple English$_0$ the last sentence of which is a T-form sentence, and each of which is an axiom or is derived from an axiom on an earlier line by *Universal Quantifier Instantiation*, *Substitution*, or *Replacement*.

We can put this observation to use immediately in pursuit of an explicit meaning theory, the topic of the next chapter.

---

[100] This meets a criticism Soames 1992: 28, 2003: 308 makes against Foster's suggestion, a version of which Davidson endorses in the above quotation.

9

Relation to an Explicit Meaning Theory and to Semantic Competence

I see no harm in rephrasing what the interpreter knows in this case in a more familiar vein: he knows that 'Snow is white' in English *means that* snow is white.

(Davidson 2001*b* (1976): 175)

Our discussion of Foster's problem raises the question of whether we can employ the explicit characterization of what one needs to know to use a truth theory for interpretation to formulate, likewise, an explicit meaning theory of a language by reference to a truth theory, and in this way render precise the relation between an interpretive truth theory and a meaning theory. In this chapter, we take up this task in §1. This paves the way for us to take up in §2 the question of the relation of an interpretive truth theory to linguistic competence.

1. Relation to an Explicit Meaning Theory

A truth theory is not itself a meaning theory. To insist that it be one would be to insist that the truth theory itself state everything one would need to know to interpret the language for which it is a theory. As we have seen, supposing that the theory itself has to do this is the root of a number of spurious objections to Davidson's program. Davidson himself is on record denying that the truth theory states everything someone needs to know to use it to interpret utterances of sentences in a language. The utility of a truth theory lies partly in its *not* stating what we want a compositional meaning theory to state. His claim is that a truth theory *meeting certain constraints* can be *used* for the purposes of a compositional meaning theory for a speaker's language. These constraints are intended to ensure that the theory is interpretive. Appropriate knowledge *about* an interpretive truth theory for a language, as outlined above, empowers its possessor to interpret any sentence in the object language, and constitutes knowledge equivalent to that required by a compositional meaning theory.

But if knowledge about a truth theory is equivalent to the knowledge of what is expressed by a compositional meaning theory, then this should enable us to state, in terms of the knowledge we must have about a truth theory, an explicit compositional meaning theory that allows us to derive for each sentence of the object language an appropriate M-sentence, $[M]$.

> [M]   For all speakers S, times t, s means for S at t in L that p.

To do this, we need only make explicit the connection between an interpretive truth theory and a meaning theory. The connection is that if we have an interpretive truth theory, then the right hand sides of its canonical theorems provide *interpretations* of the sentences denoted on the left. And this we have *defined* in terms of their corresponding M-sentences being true. Thus, if we know this for a particular T-sentence of the form,

> [T]   For all speakers S, times t, s for S at t is true in L iff p.

we know that the sentence that replaces 'p' in [T] can be substituted for 'p' in [M] to yield a true sentence. Thus, our explicit meaning theory—what a speaker can know that will enable him to infer for each sentence of L a theorem of the form of [M]—can be expressed by an explicit statement of what someone has to know about a truth theory to use it for the purposes of a compositional meaning theory, namely, to interpret each object language sentence, and the explicit connection noted above between an interpretive truth theory's canonical theorems and the target theorems of a compositional meaning theory. That is, for a language L, the following constitutes the outline of an explicit compositional meaning theory stated in terms of knowledge of an interpretive truth theory, and the connection noted between its canonical theorems and M-theorems.

> [1]   Every instance of the following schema is true:
>   For all speakers S, times t, s for S at t in L means that p iff it is
>   canonically provable on the basis of the axioms of an interpretive

truth theory T for L that for all speakers S, times t, s for S at t is true in L iff p.

[2] $\mathcal{T}$ is an interpretive truth theory for L whose axioms are . . .

[3]   Axiom . . . of $\mathcal{T}$ means that . . .
     Axiom . . . of $\mathcal{T}$ means that . . .

    . . .

[4]   A canonical proof in $\mathcal{T}$ is . . .

[1] simply states Davidson's Convention T, making precise the role a truth theory is to play in a compositional meaning theory for a natural language.[101]

2. Relation to Semantic Competence

We now address briefly the question of what relation Davidson sees between a Tarski-style truth theory used as above in a compositional meaning theory for a language L and speaker competence with L. As noted earlier (Chapter 2), many authors assume Davidson supposed that the theory so formulated would be one that speakers had explicit or implicit *propositional* knowledge of, and one which they deployed in understanding others. Davidson explicitly says he does not suppose that speakers know any such theory. An interpretive theory for L is supposed to suffice for anyone who knows it to interpret utterances of L. This condition of adequacy is imposed on the theory by the theorist's goal of providing a theory sufficient to determine interpretations for every sentence of the target language on the basis of knowing a finite number of semantical primitives and rules. But it is no condition of adequacy that Davidson places on the theory that speakers of L know the theory.

Still, we might wonder what connection, if any, Davidson might see between the truth theory used in a compositional meaning theory for L and speaker competence with L. Minimally, if the structure of the theory correctly represents the semantic properties of sentences of L, as it must if it is to capture how the meanings of complexes depend on meanings of their parts, that structure must be mirrored in the structure of the ability of speakers of L to speak and understand it. This is in fact how Davidson put it in early papers.

---

[101] At the end of "Reply to Foster," Davidson gives a reason for thinking, given his paratactic account of intensional contexts, that this would not be a theory in the formal sense. For on the paratactic account, the axioms stating what axioms of the truth theory mean would contain a demonstrative element, and so would not have a content apart from context. We postpone further discussion until ch. 11 of *Truth-Theoretic Semantics*.

In "Theories of Meaning and Learnable Languages" and in "Truth and Meaning," he seems to hold that a compositional meaning theory for a language aims to capture "the structure of a very complicated ability—the ability to speak and understand a language" (Davidson 2001*c* (1967): 25). There is some evidence, though inconclusive, that Davidson's views about the relation between a meaning theory meeting the compositionality requirement and the competence of speakers of *L* changed from what he expressed in these early papers. For the claim that the theory is supposed to capture the structure of speakers' ability to speak and understand the language appears to drop in and out in later writings, suggesting greater circumspection on his part about whether to endorse it as a constraint on an appropriate theory. For example, at the beginning of "Belief and the Basis of Meaning," he characterizes the theory as capturing something about speakers that sounds weaker:

The theory may be used to describe an aspect of the interpreter's competence at understanding what is said. We may, if we please, also maintain that there is a mechanism in the interpreter that corresponds to the theory. If this means only that there is some mechanism or other that performs that task, it is hard to see how the claim can be false. (Davidson 2001*a* (1974): 141)

The connection endorsed here appears weaker than that the theory capture the structure of the interpreter's ability, for it seems merely to claim that the theory and the interpreter's ability issue in the same interpretations, nothing more. Note also on the next page,

... the theory can be used to describe what every interpreter knows, namely a specifiable infinite subset of the truths of the theory.   (Ibid. 142)

This says that the theory issues in theorems which in some sense the native interpreter can be said to know. However, these passages need not be in conflict with the earlier ones, for the idea that different mechanisms could subserve the same competence is compatible with the idea that, at an appropriate level of description, they all express the same dispositional structure.[102]

Irrespective of whether Davidson has continued to endorse the requirement that the truth theory capture in some more robust sense the structure of a speaker's ability to speak and understand his language, we believe it is both defensible and important for Davidson's program.

---

[102] For example, in a later paper, Davidson again says that the truth theory "is a model of the interpreter's linguistic competence" (1986: 438), but follows this up with the remark that some mechanism "must correspond to the theory." This supports the interpretation just given. See also in this connection Davidson 1994*b*: 3–5.

The requirement itself, though, requires elucidation. What does it mean to say that a truth theory for a language *L*, one which is to serve as a component in a meaning theory for *L*, captures the structure of a speaker's ability to speak and understand sentences of *L*? The connection Davidson intended between truth theories and speakers' abilities doesn't seem to be that speakers know an appropriate truth theory and have appropriate knowledge about it, so that what they say and how they understand others can be represented as the result of inferences from the theory. His thought, rather, seems to be that the ability itself is constituted out of distinct but interlocking abilities or dispositions of various types which attach to semantical primitives of the language. We can see this at work in the acquisition of new vocabulary. What we acquire is the ability to use a new word. Part of what is involved in that ability is knowledge of how to use it in conjunction with other words of various types whose use we already know. For example, when we acquire a new predicate, 'is *F*', of a type that applies to physical objects, we acquire the ability to use it in conjunction with noun phrases we already understand that apply to, or are about, physical objects. We know what we would say using it with these other words. Since our competence with words involves knowledge of how to use them to say things in conjunction with others, given their types, having one such ability involves having others. But the abilities are nonetheless distinct, since, in general, they can be lost or acquired independently of one another. It may be that to have any language one needs to have a certain critical mass of such interwoven abilities, but they are still independent in the sense that any one of them may be lost without the agent ceasing to possess the ability to speak a language.

There may be more than one way to articulate how the structure of an interpretive truth theory for a language *L* aims to represent the structure of the ability to speak *L*. We describe here a simple minimal way of setting out the correspondence between the structure of the theory for *L* and the structure of the ability to speak *L*. We want to be able to set up correspondences between elements of the theory and the distinct abilities of the speaker which constitute the speaker's ability to speak *L*. The most straightforward way to do this is to require for each distinct ability, each distinct competence in the use of a word, a distinct axiom in the theory. Thus, with each semantical primitive of the language, there will be associated a distinct ability, knowledge of how to use that semantical primitive, and for each semantical primitive, there will correspond an axiom in the theory. This condition should be met if we have interpretive axioms. For this requires that the axioms correctly reflect both the semantical category of the word, predicate, sentential connective, or quantifier, and its

Historical Introduction

specific meaning. Thus, an interpretive truth theory represents the structure of the ability to speak a language by having an axiom for each primitive which correctly encodes its semantical role, and referent or application conditions. This corresponds to a disposition in a competent speaker to use the word in accordance with its semantic role and reference or application conditions.[103]

This connection is in fact the basis for our evidence in formulating truth theories for our own language. The interlocking dispositions we have to use words, which involve both knowledge of how to combine a word of a certain sort with other words given their types, and what its specific reference or application conditions are, enable us to recognize when distinct constructions have common elements, and so to arrive at a list of primitives and a characterization of their combinatorial role. We recognize when entailment relations hold between sentences on the basis of their forms, and these data then must be accommodated in an adequate interpretive truth theory for the language. We also recognize when a complex structure is understood on the basis of a rule for decomposing it into simpler parts, to which the same or different decomposition rules can be applied. All these data play a role in arriving at correct axioms representing the compositional structure of sentences of the language. Hence, speaker intuitions of this sort are a primary (though not inviolable) source of data about logical form in natural language. (See *Truth-Theoretic Semantics*, chapter 13, for a full discussion of this notion of logical form.)

It is important to note that the requirement that the theory capture the structure of a speaker's ability to speak and understand his language, and that it be interpretive, come to the same thing. That it be interpretive is the requirement that its axioms be interpretive. Thus, not any theory that issues in *T*-sentences is adequate. It must issue in them from the right axioms. And there is a fact of the matter about which axioms are correct, because there is a fact of the matter about the structure of speakers' dispositions to use words. For our own language, we have relatively easy access to those facts, though it is not transparent and requires reflection on how we would use words, abstracting from nonsemantic considerations, in various circumstances. For speakers of other languages, we confront a greater epistemic challenge, but we cannot doubt that they are in the same position with respect to their own languages.

---

[103] See Davies 1981*b*; Evans 1981, for a similar line. Both Evans and Davies suggest that the constraint is that the derivations in the theory correspond to a causal explanation of the speaker's comprehension of a sentence given in terms of his dispositions. See also Soames 1984, 1989, 1992.

124

10

The Problem of Semantic Defects in Natural Languages

... the task of a theory of meaning as I conceive it is not to change, improve, or reform a language, but to describe and understand it.

(Davidson 2001*c* (1967): 29)

In this final chapter of Part I, we consider briefly some of the difficulties facing attempts to give a formal compositional meaning theory due to various sorts of defects in natural language. This will complete our discussion of the foundations of the truth-theoretic approach to compositional semantics for natural languages, and set the stage for our discussion of its integration with the project of radical interpretation in Part II.

In this chapter, we will consider four particular difficulties posed for the program of truth-theoretic semantics, which have their source in defects in natural languages from the standpoint of an ideal language. The first is the presence of structural and lexical ambiguity (§1). The second is that natural languages do not have a precisely specified syntax (§2). The third is the problem of the semantic paradoxes (§3). And the fourth is the problem of semantic vagueness, the fact that many terms in natural languages, even most, have not had their meanings fully and precisely fixed, in particular, in a way that leaves no precise boundary between acceptable and unacceptable uses (§4).[104]

---

[104] For the latter two problems, see also Ludwig and Ray 2002.

1. Ambiguity

The fact that some sentences in natural language are ambiguous means that an interpretive truth theory in the style we have been sketching cannot be directly formulated for a natural language. Ambiguity can be lexical, that is, it can attach to individual words, such as 'pen' or 'bank' or 'troll'. Or it can be structural, that is, it can attach to complex expressions, as in 'Most men love some woman' or 'Bud and Pearl saw the Rocky Mountains while they were flying to California', each of which has two possible readings, though one tends to be dominant.[105] While this can be a boon to the poet (Blake: "Never seek to tell thy love, love that never told can be"), or the comedian (Groucho Marx: "One morning, I shot an elephant in my pajamas. How he got into my pajamas I don't know"), it is a hindrance to giving a formal compositional meaning theory for the language.

Our aim is to have a formal theory that issues in M-sentences, knowledge of which suffices to interpret any utterance of an object language sentence. For this purpose, our axioms must be interpretive. What are we to do with an ambiguous word like 'pen'? Should it receive a different axiom for each of its alleged senses (the *Oxford English Dictionary* has five entries for 'pen' as a noun and three as a verb, and gives thirty-four distinct senses)? The difficulty with this proposal is that it will issue in a theory which assigns incompatible truth conditions to sentences. Take the axioms we would get for two of the senses of 'pen' (ignoring tense for the moment), P1 and P2.

P1. For any name α, $\ulcorner \alpha$ is a pen$\urcorner$ is true in English iff Ref(α) is a nib.[106]

P2. For any name α, $\ulcorner \alpha$ is a pen$\urcorner$ is true in English iff Ref(α) is a female swan.

Supposing a reference axiom for 'Ned' assigns Ned as its referent in English, we could derive the following two canonical theorems, T1 and T2, from P1 and P2:

T1. 'Ned'⌢'is a pen' is true in English iff Ned is a nib.

---

[105] We concentrate here on inscriptions of words, which helps to simplify things. However, words which are written differently may be spoken in the same way, e.g. 'fowl' and 'foul', and words which are written the same may be spoken differently, as in 'Does the buck see the does?' Thus, some tokens of sentences may be ambiguous in the relevant sense while others are not. To run the truth theory, we would have to settle on a standard syntactic representation of the vocabulary of the language (for purposes of a formal theory characterized in terms of "shape") in the face of these discrepancies in how words are represented in different media.

[106] 'Nib' is ambiguous, but we use it here by stipulation in the sense of 'detachable metal pen point'.

T2. 'Ned'⌢'is a pen' is true in English iff Ned is a female swan.

From T1 and T2 it follows that Ned is a nib iff Ned is a female swan, but if Ned is one it is not the other. The same problem will arise for structural ambiguity. The problem is exacerbated when we consider *M*-sentences, for then the mere fact that each axiom we give for a single word or structure uses words which differ in meaning will result in incompatible *M*-sentences, even though their T-form sentences might both be true. 'Sanguine', for example, has the sense of 'ruddy', as well as 'cheerful', and these are not mutually exclusive. So, it might be that anyone who was ruddy was also cheerful, and in this case we would not be committed to a falsehood by our truth theory. But we would still arrive at incompatible *M*-sentences, since it can't both be that 'Ned is sanguine' means in English that Ned is ruddy and that he is cheerful. (We can say truthfully that '*x* is sanguine' is *used* in English to mean either *ruddy* or *cheerful*, but this is a way of saying that it is ambiguous, and that it is disambiguated in use by the speaker's intentions; we do not flatly say it means two different things, *unrelativized* to anything else.)

An alternative suggestion (made by Davidson in "Truth and Meaning") is to give axioms in the metalanguage that use metalanguage terms ambiguous in precisely the same way as object language terms. Davidson puts it this way: "As long as ambiguity does not affect grammatical form, and can be translated, ambiguity for ambiguity, into the metalanguage, a truth definition will not tell us any lies" (Davidson 2001*c* (1967): 30). For an ambiguous word like 'pen', we give a single axiom using a word in the metalanguage ambiguous in precisely the same way: for any name α, ⌜α is a pen⌝ is true in English iff Ref(α) is a pen. The caveat that the ambiguity does not affect grammatical form is important, though. Structural ambiguity cannot be dealt with by repeating it in the metalanguage, because we want to be able to formalize our theory so that we can describe a syntactic criterion that, relative to certain assumptions, picks out the theorems that are *T*-sentences. This requires that its sentences not be structurally ambiguous, because the rules of inference must operate over sentences described purely syntactically, and they must also be truth preserving. We cannot admit an inference rule that takes us from a sentence described purely syntactically to another which on one interpretation preserves truth but on another does not.[107] So, this

---

[107] For example, consider an argument from 'John loves Sue or John loves Betty and John loves Jane' to 'If John does not love Sue, then John loves Betty and John loves Jane'. On one possible reading of the premise this preserves truth (i.e. '(John loves Sue or (John loves Betty and John loves Jane))', but on the other it does not (i.e. '((John loves Sue or John loves Betty) and John loves Jane)'.

suggestion does not represent a general solution to the problem of ambiguity, even if it is adequate for primitive terms whose ambiguity does not affect structure.

Even with a primitive term whose ambiguity does not affect structure, it is not clear this response is acceptable. It yields ambiguous T-theorems and ambiguous M-theorems. What are these theorems telling us about the object language? They tell us nothing until we decide to interpret their ambiguous terms in one way rather than another. But once we disambiguate them, the trouble is that they do not tell us that the object language sentences have more than one interpretation. Indeed, they misrepresent the facts, once we disambiguate them by interpreting them in one way rather than another, for they represent the object language sentences as having just one set of truth conditions, or meaning just one thing. This is a mistake akin to giving unrelativized truth conditions for sentences containing context sensitive elements. And this is true regardless of how we disambiguate them. The problem is that if we do not disambiguate them, the theories tell us nothing, but when we do, they tell us the wrong thing.

Is this the death knell, then, for the project of giving a compositional meaning theory for a natural language? No. At least two routes are open to us in responding to ambiguity in natural languages. We will describe them here, but leave for *Truth-Theoretic Semantics*, chapter 3, §8, a more detailed discussion. The first is to formulate the truth theory (and, correspondingly, the meaning theory) not for the natural language in the first instance, but for a regimented cousin which disambiguates syntactically both primitive terms (e.g. by appending subscripts to the natural language term for each distinct meaning) and structures (e.g. by introducing explicit variables and parentheses to indicate scope relations among quantifiers). As an adjunct to the theory for this regimented cousin, we would catalog possible interpretations of primitive terms and structures of the language into the regimented language. Then, to apply the theory in interpretation would require mapping a sentence in use onto one of its interpretations in the regimented language, and then interpreting the sentence in use in accordance with the interpretation assigned by the theory to the regimented sentence it is mapped onto. The truth-*cum*-meaning theory itself would not tell us which sentence of the regimented language the natural language sentence was to be mapped onto. But we should not expect it to. In general, disambiguating ambiguous sentences depends on general knowledge about the conversational context that we could not expect to be captured in a meaning theory for the language. At most, we could provide the instruction to interpret the sentence in accord with the speaker's intentions.

128

But telling us what a speaker intends on an occasion of use is not within the purview of the meaning theory.

The second route would treat the object language in the theory directly, but would also further relativize the assignment of truth conditions to speaker's intentions. That is, each axiom could be formulated so that the right hand side of the biconditional is a conjunction of conditionals the antecedents of which are statements to the effect that the speaker intended the object language word or structure in question to be interpreted in a certain way, one for each way in which it could be interpreted.

While this latter technique has the advantage over the former in that it applies directly to the object language and represents in the theory itself the additional step required in interpretation, namely, disambiguation in context, it is considerably more cumbersome. Either of these two approaches looks to preserve the same information about the object language. The choice between them, then, can be dictated by which approach is more convenient and, on that score, working with a regimented language derived from the natural language of study will be the preferred approach.[108]

2. The Lack of a Precise Syntax for Natural Languages

A second difficulty is that natural languages lack a precisely defined syntax. While this point is worth mentioning, we will not spend much time on it, since it is no threat to accomplishing the main aims of formulating compositional meaning theories for natural languages. A formal theory for an object language

[108] A third possibility, which is standard among linguists, is that ambiguity is homophony: 'pen' is homophonous, as between two words, just like 'foul'/'fowl'; and similarly, 'I shot an elephant in my pajamas' is homophonous as between two sentences with different structures. On this view, subscripting 'pen' and including brackets in 'I shot an elephant in my pajamas' is not a regimentation of natural language; it's a way of describing natural language expressions, which have properties (and structure) that go beyond their phonological (or inscriptional) properties. What one thinks of this alternative depends on what is meant by 'sentence' and 'word'. The logician's and linguist's uses of 'expression' and correlative terms like 'word' and 'sentence' need to be distinguished. The logician's is the one we need to start with, because, for one, we need a formal theory, which operates over objects which are specified in a way that does not presuppose even that they are meaningful. A second reason we need the thinner notion is that we are also concerned with the project of coming to know what language someone speaks without presupposing anything about its semantics. And the way Davidson does this, via hold true attitudes toward sentences (see Ch. 11), requires that the notion of sentence be one which does not build in anything about its semantic features, and which is available to a radical interpreter: this will include actual sounds and inscriptions, which do not, however, encode in their structure all the features relevant to individuation of sentences and words in the linguist's sense.

requires a recursive characterization of the grammatical expressions of the language, for we wish to be able to describe each sentence of the language purely syntactically as composed out of its simple components in a way that allows us to assign it truth conditions on the basis of axioms attaching to its primitive terms and their modes of combination. Natural languages can be defective in this regard in two ways. First, it can be unclear exactly what the vocabulary of a natural language is, even at a given time, and even in the idiolect of a given speaker.[109] Second, it can be unclear exactly what is to count as an acceptable grammatical construction. This problem is exacerbated if we think about natural languages as spoken by linguistic communities over periods of time. Many words and constructions of Elizabethan English, for example, no longer are in common use. Do they still fall into the class of grammatical expressions of English? And much leeway is allowed in English constructions for various purposes (e.g. inverting the usual order of sentence construction, NP + copula + adjective, 'Heart of oak are our ships, Jolly tars are our men'). Poets distort English syntax regularly in novel ways, and yet are well enough understood, and aren't taken to be speaking a foreign tongue. The difficulty here need not be just epistemic. It may be that its source lies in our terms 'idiolect' and 'language' not being precisely definable given current usage. Does this make the prospect of developing a formal theory for a natural language hopeless? Where it is unclear whether a word or construction should count as part of a language, a theory of the language cannot pronounce definitely on it, and must skirt the question. But this hardly constitutes an obstacle to formulating for large parts of natural language an adequate lexicon and grammar, and applying our theory to it. Arbitrary decisions sometimes must be made for the sake of getting on with the business, but the insight we seek from an explicit compositional meaning theory for a language will not be diminished by overlooking some vocabulary or omitting some constructions which are arguably variants of acceptable ones, for with a workable theory, we know how to include what we leave out, if we should choose to do so.

3. Semantic Paradoxes

A more serious problem for a Tarski-style truth theory for a natural language is posed by the semantic paradoxes. Natural languages appear to be universal in

---

[109] Difficulty in determining how many senses a word has obviously will cause difficulties here as well, for it will then be unclear in the regimented language for which we actually give the theory how many terms it has on this count as well.

that anything we can meaningfully say we can say in natural language. If so, natural languages include all the apparatus required to have their own truth predicate and to refer to their own sentences. These two features enable us to construct semantic paradoxes.

A simple example is [*L*], which we can call 'The Liar', where Ref('The Liar') = 'The Liar is not true in English'.

[*L*]   The Liar is not true in English,

The *T*-sentence for [*L*] using English as its own metalanguage is [*TL*] (ignoring tense):

[*TL*]   'The Liar is not true in English' is true in English iff The Liar is not true in English.

We get [*TL*] just by disquotation. But since Ref('The Liar') = 'The Liar is not true in English', we can deduce [*TL*$^+$]:

[*TL*$^+$]   'The Liar is not true in English' is true in English iff 'The Liar is not true in English' is not true in English.

[*TL*$^+$] is a formal contradiction. (Indeed, if 'The Liar' and 'The Liar is not true in English' are both directly referring terms, then [*TL*] and [*TL*$^+$] are equally interpretive.) No formal contradiction is true, and to escape the conclusion that it is false, we must deny it has a truth value at all. Thus, any truth theory that generates [*TL*] cannot be true. The semantic paradoxes look to present a serious difficulty for pursuing natural language semantics through the vehicle of a truth theory, at least if that requires, as it seems natural to assume, that the truth theory be *true*.

The difficulty survives if we move to a truth theory that introduces an unstructured predicate in a metalanguage distinct from the object language to cover object language sentences, say, 'true-in-English'. This may look like it helps, because it enables us to block the derivation of a formal contradiction. The *T*-sentence for [*L*] (representing the metalanguage in a different font) would be:

[*TL**]   'The Liar is not true in English' is `true-in-English` iff `The Liar is not true in English`.

From [*TL**] we can derive [*TL**$^+$].

[*TL**+] ‘The Liar is not true in English' is true-in-English
iff 'The Liar is not true in English' is not true in
English.

However, in contrast to [*TL*+], [*TL**+] is not a formal contradiction, because
the predicates 'is true-in-English' and 'true in English' are distinct (the
former being *one-place*, the latter *two-place*). However, that we have blocked the
derivation of a formal contradiction does not show that [*TL**] is acceptable.
For [*TL**] to be interpretive, 'true' as used in our metalanguage on the right
hand side of [*TL**] must translate 'true' in the object language. On the assumption that the object language predicate is coherent and has an extension, so that
the metalanguage predicate 'true' has an extension when relativized likewise
to English, 'true-in-English' must have the same extension as 'true in
English'. From this it will follow that [*TL**] is necessarily false. If we deny that
the object language truth predicate has an extension after all, to avoid this conclusion, and suppose it to be semantically defective, then we must still admit
that at least some sentences containing it are without truth value. This defect is
then transmitted to the metalanguage by the requirement that the truth theory
meet Convention T (for, minimally, we want to say that, where it looks like
we have a necessary falsehood derived from semantic principles, the sentence
in fact lacks a truth value altogether). And we must then acknowledge that
some theorems of the truth theory are not true (even if not false either). Thus,
the assumptions that give rise to the difficulties that the semantic paradoxes
involve us in are not avoided by appeal to a metalanguage with an object
language specific truth predicate, if we allow the object language to have an
unrestricted truth predicate and the resources to formulate liar-like sentences.

Tarski avoided these problems by defining truth only for object languages
that lack their own truth predicates. This restriction prevents sentences like [*L*]
from being formulated in the object language. However, if we attempt to define
truth in Tarski's style for natural languages, which do contain their own truth
predicate, we can generate formal contradictions, as in [*TL*] or theorems which
involve us in incoherence as in [*TL**].

No consensus prevails on what to say about the semantic paradoxes in
natural languages, and it would be impossible to survey the vast literature on
the subject here. In the remainder of this discussion, we concentrate on two
things. First, we consider what Davidson has to say in response to the threat
of the semantic paradoxes. If our interpretation of his remarks is correct, his
suggestion is that the semantic paradoxes, contrary to appearance, do not
arise in natural languages. Second, we consider whether, even if Davidson is

mistaken, and the semantic paradoxes are a feature of natural languages, they present an insuperable obstacle to pursuing compositional semantics *via* an interpretive truth theory. We will suggest that even if the semantic paradoxes are irremediable features of natural languages, they need not be an insuperable obstacle to the project of truth-theoretic semantics, as we have characterized it.

Davidson's own remarks on the challenge are perfunctory, if suggestive. In "Truth and Meaning," he remarks,

The semantic paradoxes arise when the range of the quantifiers in the object language is too generous in certain ways. But it is not really clear how unfair to Urdu or to Wendish it would be to view the range of their quantifiers as insufficient to yield an explicit definition of 'true-in-Urdu' or 'true-in-Wendish'. Or, to put the matter in another, if not more serious, way, there may in the nature of the case always be something we grasp in understanding the language of another (the concept of truth) that we cannot communicate to him. In any case, most of the problems of general philosophical interest arise within a fragment of the relevant natural language that may be conceived as containing very little set theory. Of course these comments do not meet the claim that natural languages are universal. But it seems to me that this claim, now that we know such universality leads to paradox, is suspect. (Davidson 2001*c* (1967): 28–9)

There are two suggestions in this passage. One is that little is lost if we ignore the semantic vocabulary. We return to this below. The other, the motivation for which is not made clear, is that natural languages should not be regarded as having the expressive resources required to generate the paradoxes, despite appearances to the contrary. We begin with this second suggestion.

The semantic paradoxes are said to arise when the range of a language's quantifiers is too generous, and so the corresponding suggestion that natural languages are not subject to the paradoxes may be taken to be that the range of natural language quantifiers is to be restricted to avoid the paradoxes. Why is this expressed in terms of the range of the quantifiers in the language? Recall that a closed form definition of a truth predicate for a language *L* would have the form,

> For all sentences *s* of *L*, if … *s* …, then *s* is *T* iff …; if
> … *s* …, then *s* is *T* iff …,

where each antecedent is a condition on the form of *s* (see the appendix to Chapter 4). If the quantifiers of the object language do not include within their scope every sentence of the object language, particularly those with 'is *T*', we could not generate the semantic paradoxes from a sentence of the above form stated in the language, nor could we define a truth predicate for the language

133

as a whole. In order to block the paradoxes, we would also have to insist either that singular terms in the language not refer to sentences with 'is T', or at least that if such terms are in the language, they not be allowed to occur in argument position with the predicate 'is T'.

These restrictions, if they held for natural languages, would obviate the problem. But why would Davidson suppose that, once we know that the claim that natural languages are universal leads to paradox, we should find it suspect? He does not elaborate on his thought. But his saying that we should think that the quantifiers of natural languages will not allow the occurrence of paradoxical sentences suggests that he had in mind that each natural language predicate should be understood to have typed argument places, that is, argument places that can take grammatically only referring terms or variables which refer to, or take on as values, entities of a sort that is appropriate for that predicate. This would mean that when quantifiers appear with these predicates, the variables would be understood to range over only appropriate sorts of entities, given the type of the predicate in question. If we combine this idea with the view that our predicates are always understood so that they respect something like Russell's vicious circle principle, we can infer that our semantic predicates can take only argument terms which refer to sentences which do not contain those predicates.

Russell's vicious circle principle prohibited the definition of a totality in terms of members which presupposed the totality. The intuitive idea is that, since a totality is defined by what its members are, if a definition (putatively) introduces as a member of a totality one which presupposes that the totality is already defined, no coherent definition can be given. Without going into the details of how Russell would have applied this principle to the present case, we can just consider the intuitive application to a truth predicate. A truth predicate applies to meaningful declarative sentences. The meaning of the truth predicate may be said intuitively to be given by the conditions required for a sentence to fall under it, given the sentence's meaning. But now consider a sentence which includes the truth predicate. If the meaning of the truth predicate is given by the conditions required for a sentence, given its meaning, to fall under it, then any attempt to specify the meaning of a truth predicate by asking after the conditions required for a sentence *containing it* to fall under *it* will already presuppose the meaning we are trying to fix. Thus, we find ourselves inside a vicious circle of just the sort that Russell sought to bar with the vicious circle principle. On the assumption that our uses of truth predicates in natural languages are coherent, and that these predicates are fully meaningful, we should infer that they do not take as argument terms any terms which refer to sentences containing those truth predicates understood in the same sense, or any variables which can take on as values sentences containing those truth predicates understood in the same sense. The suggestion, in a nutshell, then, is that natural language sentences are interpreted by their speakers so as to avoid vicious definitional circles.

The obvious reply is that natural languages contain sentences in which a term referring to a sentence containing a truth predicate has a truth predicate predicated of it. For example, "'Snow is white' is true' is true" appears to be a sentence of English. This need not be an obstacle to the proposal, for there is a way to render this compatible with the general form of the suggestion. We could allow sentences containing 'is true' to have 'is true' predicated of them, provided that we interpret these truth predicates differently. In particular, on the current suggestion, the second occurrence of 'is true' in "'Snow is white' is true' is true" will have a different, broader application range than the first, but will not include within its range any sentence in which it itself occurs with that same interpretation.[110] This induces an infinite hierarchy of interpretations of truth predicates, and correspondingly of quantifiers, which are understood differently depending on the restrictions on the values of their variables, imposed by what predicates they are used with.[111]

This idea, we speculate, is what Davidson had in mind in the suggestion, in the passage above, that the claim that natural languages are universal is suspect once we see it leads to paradox. If this view is correct, the semantical paradoxes don't present a problem for truth-theoretic semantics, because natural languages are not subject to them. We do not, however, wish to rest the defense of truth-theoretic semantics on the claim that natural languages are not subject to the semantic paradoxes. It is at least tendentious to claim that speakers of natural languages have the sophistication this response to the problem presupposes. And it does not seem *impossible* for a natural language

---

[110] We still must exclude some sentences containing a truth predicate which do not have coherent interpretations, The Liar, for instance, since we cannot assign any interpretation in the hierarchy to the predicate and have the change of references generated by the subject ground out in a sentence not containing a truth predicate.

[111] This suggestion might be thought to raise worries about the learnability of the language. Whether it does hinges on whether the concept of truth expressed by the $n + 1$st predicate in the hierarchy is derivable from that expressed by the nth. Plausibly, this is so, for given a method of fixing the meaning of a truth predicate at the nth level in terms of a class C of meaningful sentences which do not presuppose it, to introduce a new predicate at the next highest level requires only that we reapply the same method to C augmented by the meaningful sentences containing the nth level truth predicate.

to be semantically defective in the way that would give rise to the semantic paradoxes. We therefore want to ask whether, on the assumption that natural languages are subject to the paradoxes, this presents an insuperable obstacle to pursuing truth-theoretic semantics.

We think the answer is 'no'. The first point to make is that, even if some sentences in natural languages, that is, those with semantic predicates, pose difficulties, this need not infect the rest of the theory. That is, the infection is localizable, and can be excised by excluding from the theory axioms for semantical predicates in the object language. This is Davidson's other suggestion.[112]

Imagine a universal language with its own truth predicate and referential apparatus sufficient to construct liar-like sentences. Imagine that we self-consciously construct a language from the universal language by omitting its semantic terms. In so doing, we do not change the meanings of the rest of the vocabulary.[113] If we succeed in constructing a truth theory for this language that meets Davidson's Convention T, and we can identify the T-sentences of the theory, then we can interpret every nonsemantic sentence of the language, and see how our understanding of those sentences rests on our understanding of their significant parts and mode of combination. If this is correct, we need not despair of providing a meaning theory for virtually all of another's language (as far as its basic vocabulary goes) by way of a truth theory, while avoiding paradox in virtue of our theoretical commitments.

The same point applies to our own language. First, we excise from our own language all semantic terms that have application to its own expressions. The resultant language will be less rich than the one we speak, in that it will lack the resources to talk about the semantic properties of its expressions, but otherwise will be the same. Then, we can construct a truth theory for this language which meets Davidson's Convention T, and employ it as above to serve as a meaning theory, and in particular to show how the meanings of complex

---

[112] We take it that this is also Davidson's main suggestion in the following passage from "In Defense of Convention T" (2001*a* (1973): 72): "Once [we allow resources for referring to sentences and their truth] into the language, semantic antinomies result. The ideal of a theory of truth for a natural language in a natural language is therefore unattainable if we restrict ourselves to Tarski's methods. The question then arises, how to give up as little as possible, and here theories allowed by Convention T seem in important respects optimal ... It is only the truth predicate itself (and the satisfaction predicate) that cannot be in the object language."

[113] It is worth noting that this maneuver provides some reason for thinking Davidson should not see himself as a radical meaning holist, for then, according to popular accounts, to drop even the semantic predicates would result in a change of meaning of all the terms in the language, but then the maneuver here, endorsed by Davidson, would be unavailable.

expressions depend on those of their parts. What this strategy omits, from our own and other languages, is an account of the meanings of sentences with semantic terms. To this extent, our ambition to provide a meaning theory for natural languages would not be fully achieved. But even so, this is no obstacle to constructing an illuminating theory for vast reaches of natural language, and this seems sufficient reason to conclude that the semantical paradoxes present no serious threat to delivering much of what is interesting about a compositional meaning theory for a natural language.

Our discussion so far has been predicated on the assumption that we wish to avoid formulating a truth theory for a natural language which engenders paradox. If what we have said is right, even wishing to avoid this consequence, there is no serious obstacle to carrying out most of the project. But it might be worth considering briefly whether we must insist that the truth theory not have theorems of the sort that generate troubles. It may seem obvious we don't want our truth theory to have consequences that cannot be true, because it is supposed to serve in pursuit of a meaning theory, and we wish to possess true theories. But this sort of reasoning embodies a mistake about the relation between a truth theory for a natural language and a meaning theory that we have encountered elsewhere. Recall it is not the truth theory *per se*, as we have emphasized, that is the meaning theory. The truth theory says nothing about what expressions in the object language mean. This mistake has been the basis of a number of criticisms of using a truth theory in a meaning theory, but these criticisms err by supposing that the truth theory *is* the meaning theory. It is not. Rather, an interpretive truth theory matches sentences in the object language with translations in the metalanguage. As we saw in Chapter 4, to generate statements about the meanings of the object language sentences, we need to employ [1], repeated here,

[1] For every sentence s, language L, s in L means that p iff a canonical theorem of an interpretive truth theory for L uses a sentence that translates 'p' on its right hand side.

Seen in this light, in order to derive M-sentences for each sentence in the object language, the theorist need not be committed to the truth of the truth theory for L, but rather only to the truth of [1].[114] The interpretive truth theory, then, provides the recursive machinery necessary to generate

---

[114] One of us (Ludwig) is more optimistic about this strategy for accommodating semantic para-doxes, and vagueness—to which we extend it in the next section—than the other (Lepore), who has reservations about the strategy in both cases.

interpretive T-sentences, and these in turn with [1] can be used to generate correct M-sentences. So, even if the truth theory is formally inconsistent, adherence to [1] and to the theory's being interpretive will not commit one to any inconsistencies. The truth theory together with a canonical proof procedure will operate on the Liar as it does on every other sentence to produce an interpretive T-sentence [2]. [2] can't be true, as we've observed. However, applying [1] to it yields [3].

> [2] 'The Liar is not true in L' is true-in-L iff The Liar is not true in L.
>
> [3] 'The Liar is not true in L' means in L that The Liar is not true in L.

And [3] is both true and exactly what we want a compositional meaning theory to say about the target sentence! From this perspective, fear of admitting a universal truth predicate in the object language is needlessly timid.

4. Vagueness

A predicate is vague when its usage does not always dictate whether it applies or fails to apply,[115] and dictates no precise border line between paradigm cases and others.[116] A referring term is vague when usage does not dictate to which among a range of possible items the term refers. Color predicates are paradigms of vague predicates. There is no precise borderline between cases in which usage clearly licenses applying 'is red' to something, and clearly licenses applying 'is orange', for example. But many, even most, predicates in common use admit of vagueness along one or more dimensions. Most ordinary referring terms are likewise vague, since usage unsurprisingly fails to guide us about which collections of molecules, among many, for example, we are referring to.

---

[115] 'Applies' and 'fails to apply', as we are using these terms, are semantic relations. The latter is not the same as 'does not apply'. For example, 'is meaningful' applies to the pair $<$'$2+2 = 4$', English$>$, and fails to apply to $<$'All mimsy were the borgroves', English$>$ but neither applies nor fails to apply to $<$Brutus, Caesar$>$.

[116] Some authors deny that ordinary terms are vague, and claim instead that we are simply irremediably ignorant of their boundary lines. If this is true, then, of course, there would be no difficulty presented for truth-theoretic semantics. In this section we will not be concerned to adjudicate between so-called epistemic and semantic theories of vagueness. We are more concerned about whether semantic vagueness, granting there can be such a thing, would undermine truth-theoretic semantics for natural languages.

138

When we take up the task of providing a compositional meaning theory for natural language, we naturally bring to it the same idealizations that inform our use of terms in natural languages. When we speak, we speak as if all terms had fully specified application and reference conditions. For the most part this presents no difficulties, since usually our purposes and circumstances do not call upon us to make decisions about problematic cases, and we know enough to avoid using vague terms where our usage provides us with inadequate guidance. But this insouciance, however innocent in the practicalities of everyday life, cannot be extended into theoretical work.

In particular, we wish to look at two kinds of concern which the prevalence of vague terms in natural languages raises about the prospects for the project of formulating compositional meaning theories for them by way of interpretive truth theories. The first concern is that if the object language contains vague expressions, we are faced with a dilemma. Either we use precise terms in the metalanguage to specify their truth conditions, or we use vague terms. If we use precise terms, we misrepresent the semantic facts about the object language terms. If we use vague terms, we only vaguely specify the truth conditions for object language sentences. The second concern is that, on the assumption that we must use vague terms in our theory to provide a truth theory for an object language containing vague terms, our truth theory will issue in theorems which are neither true nor false.

The first of these worries rests on a confusion. If an object language term is vague, then that is a fact about the degree to which community usage has fixed its application conditions, or, perhaps more appropriately, the degree to which community usage has failed to fix its application conditions. The way and degree to which a term is vague is a semantic fact about it, in the way in which a term's being meaningful or meaningless is. If the goal of a meaning theory is to match in an *M*-sentence an object language sentence with a metalanguage sentence that interprets it, then the metalanguage sentence will do its job precisely only if its terms have the same semantic properties, including semantic defects, as those of the object language sentence it is interpreting. To specify the meaning of a vague term, we must use a term that is vague in the same way and to the same degree. The metalanguage must include predicates that match those in the object language, in Quine's words, "umbra for umbra, penumbra for penumbra" (1960: 41). For the aim of a compositional meaning theory—to put us in a position to understand any sentence in the object language on the basis of understanding its elements and their arrangement—requires, in the case of a sentence containing a vague term, that the understanding match precisely the degree to which usage in the object language fails to fill out the application conditions of the object language term.

The second concern is more serious, and is akin to the difficulty raised by the semantic paradoxes. Ludwig and Ray 2002 argue that if vague predicates have no first or higher order boundaries between fully acceptable uses along a relevant dimension of variation (numbers of hairs, e.g. in the case of 'is bald') and uses which are not fully acceptable, then no sentences using vague predicates are either true or false. If this is so, then a truth theory that uses vague terms in the metalanguage, which we have just argued is necessary if the theory is to issue in interpretive canonical theorems, would issue in theorems which are not truth evaluable. Thus, for example, the T-sentence for 'Caesar is bald' (again ignoring tense) would be [4].

[4]   'Caesar is bald' is true-in-English iff Caesar is bald.

But if sentences containing vague predicates are neither true nor false, since [4] uses the vague predicate 'is bald', it too is without truth value. Even if one does not accept this view that every sentence containing a vague term is without truth value, there is still a difficulty as long as applications of vague predicates to borderline cases fail to be truth evaluable, for our truth theory will contain axioms that generalize over referring positions. The objection, then, would be that, since we cannot formulate a truth theory for a language with vague predicates which is both interpretive and true, we must abandon the project of pursuing a truth-theoretic semantics for natural languages.

This conclusion, though, is too hasty. As with the semantic paradoxes, the truth or truth evaluability of the truth theory appears not to be required to reveal the compositional semantic structure of a sentence through the proof of a T-sentence for it, or to establish the truth of the meaning theory we formulate by reference to it. On the second point specifically, if what we must endorse is [1] above, which tells us that we may infer an M-sentence from an interpretive T-sentence, then a T-theorem can qualify as a T-sentence without being true or even truth evaluable. If a truth theory is interpretive, then from an interpretive T-sentence, such as that above for 'Caesar is bald', we can infer a true M-sentence, [5], which is after all our ultimate target (along with exhibiting compositional structure through the proof of the T-sentence).

[5]   'Caesar is bald' means in English that Caesar is bald,

If [5] is truth evaluable, then the non-truth-evaluability of some sentences of the truth theory need not present an obstacle to our project. The predicate 'is bald' is used in the above M-sentence, in the sense that to understand the sentence we must understand it. But using a vague predicate in itself need not pose a difficulty for the view that the *M*-sentence is true. It would do so only if the predicate were used in a way that undermined the M-sentence's truth evaluability. However, on the face of it, the contribution of 'is bald' to the truth conditions of [5] does not require it to have a precise extension. [5] is true just in case the sentence in the complement means what the mentioned sentence does. In this case, this requires that the vague predicate 'is bald' in the object language and the vague predicate 'is bald' in the metalanguage, used in the complement, be vague in exactly the same way, that is, that the meaning giving practices associated with each are relevantly the same. In the present case, where the metalanguage embeds the object language, that is, where our theory is homophonic, there can scarcely be any doubt that this condition is met. And if it can be met in this case, it can be met in principle in the case in which the metalanguage and object language are distinct. Consequently, our meaning theory is not endangered by the use of vague terms in the metalanguage of the truth theory used as the vehicle for producing *M*-sentences.

The view of vagueness just discussed holds that it is a variety of semantic incompleteness. It has been maintained that the problem with vague terms is not that they are semantically incomplete, but rather than they are semantically over-complete in a certain respect that renders them inconsistent, in the sense that one can derive contradictions by using the terms in accordance with the rules abstractable from our practice for their use.[117] Without endorsing this view, if the remarks we have made already are correct, then this view need not threaten the project of truth-theoretic semantics, since commitment to the truth of the relevant axioms in addition to their interpretiveness is what generates difficulties, and the purposes of the meaning theory would appear to be served by commitment to interpretiveness.

There is another worry that sometimes arises about the pursuit of the project of developing a compositional meaning theory for natural languages, since there are vague terms in natural languages.[118] That worry is that since the aim of a meaning theory for a natural language is to abstract from whatever practices govern our use of terms in that language, for any language with terms to which no complete and consistent set of rules abstractable from our behavior attaches, we must give up the project. It does seem correct that a project which presupposes that all the terms of natural languages were semantically complete could not be carried out, given that this presupposition is false. But we hope to have shown already that the presence of semantically incomplete expressions

---

[117] See Dummett 1975 and Unger 1979 for examples.   [118] See Wright 1976, 1987.

in a natural language need not be a barrier to providing a compositional meaning theory which aims to produce true M-theorems, and to exhibit how the meanings, partial, complete, or inconsistent, of the components of complex expressions contribute to the meanings, partial, complete, or inconsistent, of the complexes. In other words, it is not, and should not be, a presupposition of a meaning theory as we have described it that the expressions in a language for which such a theory can be given are semantically complete and consistent.[119]

It should be emphasized that these remarks are not intended to minimize the importance of the role of a truth theory in giving a compositional meaning theory. We are not saying that the truth theory is merely a convenient method of deriving M-theorems. The truth theory, as we have said, plays a crucial role in exhibiting the compositional semantic structure of sentences of the object language through the vehicle of a canonical proof. The truth theory is indispensable for this purpose. And it should be emphasized also that the requirement imposed on the axioms of an interpretive truth theory, that they be interpretive, will guarantee the truth of the axioms in all cases in which the semantic practices associated with the object language terms render them semantically complete. So we are not saying that the truth of the theory is irrelevant. The point is rather that the properties of the truth theory relevant to our interests in pursuing a compositional meaning theory are preserved by the requirement of interpretiveness even when a language has semantic defects which affect the usual connection between interpretiveness and truth.

---

[119] The compositional meaning theory avoids the difficulties of vague predicates, because the rules it is concerned to codify in a truth theory concern the categories of terms, not their specific content. A theory which aimed to provide rules for the application of predicates would of course be frustrated in the case of semantically incomplete predicates. Likewise, the attempt to explain linguistic competence by attributing a theory to a speaker would run aground when it came to vague predicates, for there could be no such theory. Competence could not be correctly so represented.

Summary of Part 1

Part I has largely been concerned to lay the foundations for our discussions in later chapters. We have examined the early development of Davidson's program in the theory of meaning, drawing primarily on his twin papers "Theories of Meaning and Learnable Languages" and "Truth and Meaning." The former introduced the project of constructing a compositional meaning theory for natural languages, the initial project. The latter introduced the suggestion that a Tarski-style truth theory can fulfill this function, while arguing that it is dubious that quantification over meanings serves any useful purpose; at the same time, we have argued, Davidson introduces what we have labeled the extended project.

The initial project of constructing a compositional meaning theory can be pursued independently of asking how to understand what it is for any expression in a language—primitive or complex—to mean what it does in the mouths of its speakers, for our concern *vis-à-vis* this project is not with what primitive expressions mean, or how they come to mean what they do, but rather with understanding their systematic contributions to the meanings of the sentences in which they occur.

The extended project, however, aims to illuminate simultaneously the meanings of complex expressions and the primitives from which they are constructed. We have argued that in "Truth and Meaning," Davidson had hoped that the extensional adequacy of a truth theory for a natural language would suffice for it to meet an analog of Tarski's Convention T (Davidson's Convention T, as we have been calling it). We defended this interpretation of his aim in "Truth and Meaning" against the so-called Replacement Theory, an alternative interpretation that some of his writings have suggested, according to which his aim is not to present an old project in new dress, but rather to replace it with another one. This interpretation, we argued, is not tenable when we consider the context in which his proposal was initially made, and subsequent developments in the light of difficulties that arise for the first proposal. The shift from the initial to the extended project (or the combination of the two) makes it seem as if Davidson aimed to replace, rather than illuminate, the notion of meaning. The shift to the extended project, and, consequently, the search for a non-question-begging constraint that enables a truth theory to satisfy Davidson's Convention T, has important implications for the formulation of Davidson's project of radical interpretation, which we will discuss in Part II, and the relation of that project to finding non-question-begging constraints on a truth theory that suffice for it to be used as a meaning theory.

We have also made a start in this part on illustrating what modifications might be made to a Tarski-style truth theory in order to adapt it to natural languages. What we have done so far is incomplete and, as we have remarked, the proposals for how to handle demonstratives and tense in particular will require significant revision. We discuss these issues further in *Truth-Theoretic Semantics*. We also will examine there some of Davidson's work in the program in application to problems of logical form, and treat a variety of other problematic constructions within the confines of the program as well.

We have been concerned to respond to prominent objections to Davidson's project, and to clarify, in the course of so doing, the role of a truth theory in providing a compositional meaning theory for a natural language. We have argued that the objections can be met, at least for the purposes of giving a compositional meaning theory. Objections to Davidson's choice of a recursive truth theory are met by observing that the constraints on the project require more than just meeting Tarski's or Davidson's Convention T. The aim from the beginning has been to provide a compositional meaning theory, which requires exhibiting how the meanings of complexes depend on those of their significant parts. The extensionality problem can be solved by the requirement identified in Chapter 4 that the theory be interpretive. However, this is no solution to the worry that one must not appeal to semantical notions other than those required for the truth theory to ensure interpretiveness. Further discussion of this issue is postponed until Part II. But it should be noted that this problem is generated not solely by the aim to provide a compositional meaning theory for a natural language, but also by the requirement that one do it in a way that illuminates how primitive expressions in the language get their meanings. For the purposes of explaining how a compositional meaning theory can be provided by using the resources of a recursive truth theory, it is perfectly acceptable to require that the theory be interpretive.

The determination problem is solvable by appeal to a canonical proof procedure. The guiding idea is to construct in a given formal theory a procedure that draws only on the content of the axioms of the theory in proving appropriate T-form theorems. That the axioms are interpretive will guarantee that the canonically provable T-form theorems are T-sentences. Foster's problem turns out to rest on a misunderstanding about what can be invoked in saying what one can know that would enable one to interpret another. The mistake is to think that everything that one must know must be stated within the truth theory, or, if not, at least without using semantic vocabulary aside from that drawn from the theory of reference. We formulated explicitly in Chapter 8 what a theorist must know about a truth theory in order to use it for interpretation. This led us to the formulation of an explicit compositional meaning theory in Chapter 9, and a discussion of the relation of the theory to a representation of linguistic competence. We tentatively suggested the truth theory be treated as corresponding in its interpretive axioms to the interlocking dispositions which constitute a speaker's practical ability to speak and understand the language.

We have also responded to worries about the prospects of truth-theoretic semantics that have their source in various defects in natural languages: ambiguity, the lack of a precise syntax, semantic paradoxes, and vagueness. While these difficulties must be recognized, none of them, we believe, proves fatal for the project. Ambiguity can be handled either by conditionalizing on speaker intentions, or by formulating the theory for a disambiguated regimented cousin of the language and indicating which range of terms in the regimented language represents the various interpretations of the original language's terms, relying on information about context of utterance to decide onto which of the regimented sentences to map the natural language sentence for the purpose of interpretation. The lack of a precise syntax just means that some arbitrary decisions must be made when we construct formal theories for natural languages, but it does not lessen the interest or utility of the project. The semantic paradoxes and the presence of vague terms in natural languages can engender defects within the truth theory that we formulate for those languages. One way out, as suggested by our explicit formulation of a meaning theory in Chapter 9, is to see the meaning theory as committed primarily to the truth theory being interpretive, so that it issues in interpretive canonical theorems, by proofs which exhibit compositional semantic structure. This is weaker than the requirement that the truth theory be true, though for a language which is semantically complete and free from predicates with inconsistent rules of application, interpretiveness will guarantee that the truth theory is true. But for a compositional meaning theory, the truth theory serves by being a vehicle for deriving interpretive *T*-sentences from axioms which are interpretive, in a way that shows how understanding complexes depends on understanding of their parts and their mode of combination. And it can do this irrespective of defects which lead to paradox or failure of truth evaluability in the truth theory itself. The meaning theory, since it talks about rather than asserts the truth theory, is insulated from the difficulties semantic defects give rise to for the truth theory.

Part II

Radical Interpretation

All understanding of the speech of another involves radical interpretation.

(Davidson 2001*c* (1973): 125)

1. Introduction

We identified in Part I two interrelated projects Davidson undertakes in his seminal article "Truth and Meaning"—providing a compositional meaning theory for a natural language and illuminating what it is for words to mean what they do. The former, which is also the project of assigning logical forms to natural language sentences, is subsumed by the latter, since any general account of what it is for words to mean what they do must account for both their logical roles in the language, and how we understand complex expressions on the basis of their significant parts. We argued that initially, at least, Davidson hoped a merely extensionally adequate truth theory would satisfy Davidson's Convention *T*, thereby enabling it to be the core of a meaning theory. That hope proved to be ill-founded. However, we argued, if one sets aside the extended project, one can give sufficient conditions for a truth theory to serve in pursuit of a compositional meaning theory, namely, that it be interpretive (Chapter 4). This suggestion is not Davidson's in "Truth and Meaning." The reason why lies in his pursuit of the extended project, to which the project of providing a compositional meaning theory becomes subordinated. Once he abandoned hope that an extensionally adequate truth theory would *ipso facto* meet his Convention *T*, a theme sounded already in "Truth and Meaning" takes center stage, namely, that a truth theory for a natural language should be empirical. We are to view the theory as about a speaker's or community's *actual* language, which an interpreter aims to confirm or disconfirm by appeal to relevant evidence. Understanding of its central concepts is then sought in exhibiting how they are to be applied in the theory on the basis of evidence which does not already presuppose their application.[120] In this part, we examine this further and central development in Davidson's work—the project of *radical interpretation.*

Chapter 11 discusses the project, as initially presented in "Radical Interpretation," in the form of two questions: what could one know that would suffice for interpreting another, and how could one come to know it? We will clarify what these questions are asking in light of constraints that Davidson places on acceptable answers, and then consider his answers in light of our discussion in Part I. Davidson proposes that if we know a truth theory for a speaker's language, and also know it has been confirmed empirically, from the standpoint of what he calls a radical interpreter, then we know something that enables us to interpret that speaker. His answer as to how we could come to know it is by means of radical interpretation. The radical interpreter's position is characterized by constraints on the sorts of evidence to which he can appeal. We argue that Davidson's answer to the first question must be modified if the radical interpreter's goal is to have an independent characterization. We then distinguish two projects, the ambitious one—according to which speakers are by their nature radically interpretable—and the modest one—according to which whether speakers are radically interpretable is an empirical claim about the speakers we encounter. Seeing Davidson as engaged in the ambitious project, we suggest, makes better sense of the more ambitious philosophical theses that he has argued for on the basis of reflection on the conditions under which speakers are interpretable. But we also discuss evidence against taking him to be engaged in this project. Our discussion necessarily extends through the rest of the chapters of this part and into Part III, since it is tied up with the questions of how we are to understand Davidson's arguments

---

[120] See e.g. "Radical Interpretation" Davidson 2001*c* (1973): 137: "I have proposed a looser relation between concepts to be illuminated and the relatively more basic. At the centre stands a formal theory, a theory of truth, which imposes a complex structure on sentences containing the primitive notions of truth and satisfaction. These notions are given application by the form of the theory and the nature of the evidence. The result is a partially interpreted theory." See also Davidson 2001*a* (1974): 142: "The problem is salient because uninterpreted utterances seem the appropriate evidential base for a theory of meaning. If an acceptable theory could be supported by such evidence, that would constitute conceptual progress, for the theory would be specifically semantical in nature, while the evidence would be described in non-semantical terms. An attempt to build on even more elementary evidence, say behaviouristic evidence, could only make the task of theory construction harder, though it might make it more satisfying. In any case, we can without embarrassment undertake the lesser enterprise."

for such theses as the necessity of charity in interpretation, the indeterminacy of interpretation, the impossibility of radically different conceptual schemes, the impossibility of massive error, the grounding of first person authority, and the inscrutability of reference, theses which "may be described as philosophical fallout" of Davidson's approach to truth and interpretation (Davidson 2001*b*: p. xviii).

Chapter 12 details the procedures of the radical interpreter. Chapter 13 discusses the content and justification of the principle of charity. Chapter 14 discusses additional constraints on interpretation derived from a background a priori theory of agency, and constraints not derived directly from the assumption the radical interpreter can succeed. Chapter 15 addresses the question of the nature, extent, and justification of indeterminacy of interpretation. Chapter 16 addresses a development in Davidson's work which involves taking the attitude of preferring one sentence true to another as a basic form of data in interpretation. Chapter 17, finally, takes up the question of the implications of adopting the standpoint of the radical interpreter as methodologically basic in investigating meaning for traditional philosophical conceptions of the nature of language.

11

Clarifying the Project

> That meanings are decipherable is not a matter of luck; public availability
> is a constitutive aspect of language.
>
> (Davidson 1990*b*: 314)

The project of radical interpretation, in outline, is the project of interpreting
another speaker from evidence that does not presuppose any knowledge of the
meanings of his terms or any detailed knowledge of his propositional attitudes.
The aim of this chapter is to lay out Davidson's initial way of rendering the
extended project in terms of radical interpretation in his eponymous seminal
article, and to discuss some important issues about how to understand the force
of the account he there develops. Specifically, in §1, we discuss the questions
Davidson begins with, which frame the project, clarifying them in light of the
constraints he wishes to impose on their possible answers. We then argue that
the answers to these questions which emerge in "Radical Interpretation" must
be modified if we are to have an independent criterion of success in radical
interpretation. This plays an important role when we come later to evaluating
the possibility of success in radical interpretation. In §2, we distinguish between
two ways of understanding the project, a modest and an ambitious version,
depending on whether or not we are to take it as part of the project to establish
that speakers are by their very nature radically interpretable. We consider
evidence for, and against, Davidson's being engaged in the ambitious rather
than the modest project, and argue that it makes best sense of his overall
philosophical project to take Davidson to be engaged in the ambitious project.
In the next chapter, we take up a detailed discussion of the procedures of the
radical interpreter, as understood by Davidson.

1. Initial Questions and Answers

At the beginning of "Radical Interpretation," Davidson poses two questions:

(Q1)   What could we know that would enable us to interpret another speaker's utterances?

(Q2)   How could we come to know it (on the basis of evidence that does not presuppose any knowledge of it)?

As Davidson says, this is not to ask what we do know that we rely on in interpreting others, nor how we come to know what (if anything) we do know that we rely on in interpreting others. The purpose of asking (Q1) and (Q2) is not to investigate how human beings actually acquire knowledge of natural languages, or how they manage to arrive at correct interpretations of others. The questions aim, rather, at conceptual illumination, by showing how the central concepts of a theory of interpretation can be empirically applied on the basis of evidence that does not presuppose anything about their application.[121,122] (As David Lewis has put it, the question is "how do *the facts* [in the sense of basic facts] determine these facts [the facts about the speaker's attitudes and meanings]?" (1974: 333).) This is a pursuit of the extended project of "Truth and Meaning" by a means other than arguing that an extensionally adequate theory suffices to fix correctly the interpretations of object language sentences.[123] It is in connection with this strategy for investigating the central

[121] For an explicit statement of Davidson's methodological stance see Davidson 2001*c* (1973): 137. In a retrospective remark about his choice of these questions, Davidson has said: "Like many others, I wanted answers to such questions as 'What is meaning?', and became frustrated by the fatuity of the attempts at answers I found in Ogden and Richards, Charles Morris, Skinner and others. So I substituted another question which I thought might be less intractable: What would it suffice an interpreter to know in order to understand a speaker of an alien language, and how could he come to know it?"(Davidson 1994*a*: 126). Motivation for the substitution lies partly in his aim to avoid the fruitless search for substantive necessary and sufficient conditions for the application of a predicate such as 'is meaningful' in favor of articulating "a looser relation between concepts to be illuminated and the relatively more basic" (Davidson 2001*c* (1973): 137).

[122] This should serve as a caution to those who have interpreted Davidson as aiming to "explicate" talk of meaning "in terms of truth" (Horwich 1999: 250). While Davidson takes the concept of truth to be basic and primitive, "[w]ithout grasp of the concept of truth, not only language, but thought itself, is impossible" (Davidson 2000: 72), and so not amenable to analysis in other terms, he also takes it to be a concept possession of which is coordinate with other concepts we use in describing our ability to speak and understand others. Davidson puts it this way at one point: "All these concepts [intention, belief, desire] (and more) ... are essential to thought, and cannot be reduced to anything simpler or more fundamental" (Davidson 2000: 73).

[123] As Davidson says, "In a paper first read in Biel, Switzerland, in May 1973 ["Radical Interpretation"], I criticized my own earlier attempts to say exactly what the relation is between a theory of truth and a theory of meaning, and I tried to do better" (2001*b* (1976): 171).

concepts of a theory of interpretation that many of Davidson's most celebrated conclusions about the nature of meaning, language, reference, and the propositional attitudes are developed.

In answer to question (Q1), we want a theory knowledge of which would suffice to interpret any of the utterances of a speaker of a natural language.[124] In light of Chapter 8, a natural answer to (Q1) would take the form of [K].

[K]   [1] T is a truth theory for L whose axioms are ..., and which is interpretive,
     [2]   Axiom ... of T means that ...
           Axiom ... of T means that ...

        ...

     [3]   ... is a canonical proof procedure for T.

Knowing that T is interpretive, [1], tells us that its canonical theorems provide interpretations of the sentences for which they provide truth conditions. [2] guarantees that one is in a position to understand T's theorems, and [3] guarantees that one is in a position to identify its canonical (and, given [1], therefore, its interpretive) theorems. In this light, an answer to (Q2) would include an account of how to confirm for an appropriate theory (whose axioms one knew, and which one had a canonical proof procedure for) that it is interpretive, that is, its axioms are interpretive in the sense of §2 of Chapter 5.

However, this is not Davidson's answer. While [2] and [3] are implicit in his account, he does not appeal to knowledge of an interpretive truth theory. Instead, he appears to want an answer to (Q1) which would have in the place of 'is interpretive' in [K] a substantive condition on a truth theory that suffices for it to be interpretive. It is not altogether clear why this should be so, given the character of the project, and how it is supposed to illuminate the concepts of interpretation theory, though we will make some suggestions.

In the rest of this section, we will first elucidate what condition Davidson wants to impose on a truth theory (in addition to its being simply true), so that knowing that it meets that condition would suffice, with [2] and [3], for interpreting L. We will then turn briefly to a clarification of question (Q2), and consider next whether the condition that Davidson apparently wishes to impose on a truth theory for it to serve for interpretation is one we should think gives us any confidence that the theory can in fact be so used. We will argue

---

[124] See Davidson's remark on p. 128 of "Radical Interpretation": "what is wanted of the theory ... [is]: someone who knows the theory can interpret the utterances to which the theory applies" (Davidson 2001c (1973)).

that it does not, and consider alternative suggestions, finding each inadequate as well. Finally, we will argue that in light of the new project, it makes no sense to seek to replace 'is interpretive' in [K] with something substantive, that being a holdover from "Truth and Meaning" of a different way of thinking about how we are to illuminate the concepts of interpretation theory.

What constraint Davidson would put in the place of 'is interpretive' in [K] emerges only slowly in his development of the project. Davidson poses three questions in "Radical Interpretation" in his "defence of the claim that a theory of truth, modified to apply to a natural language, can be used as a theory of interpretation" (2001c (1973): 131).

1. Is it reasonable to think a theory of truth of the sort described can be given for a natural language?
2. Would it be possible to tell that such a theory was correct on the basis of evidence plausibly available to an interpreter with no prior knowledge of the language to be interpreted?
3. If the theory were known to be true, would it be possible to interpret utterances of speakers of the language?

(2) and (3) are central to our current interest. In the course of addressing (2), Davidson argues that "we cannot assume in advance that correct translation can be recognized without preempting the point of radical interpretation; in empirical applications, we must abandon the assumption" (Davidson 2001c (1973): 134). This means that we must try to confirm an empirical truth theory which can be used as a theory of interpretation for a natural language L without assuming anything about what the expressions of L mean.

It is apparently this, at least in part, that motivates Davidson to seek a way of saying what we could know that would enable us to interpret a speaker without appealing to any semantical notions. He does not invoke what we have been calling Davidson's Convention T, or anything like the requirement that the truth theory be interpretive, *apparently,* at least in part, because he thinks doing so would *violate* the constraint that *we start with evidence that does not presuppose anything about the meanings of object language expressions.* He says, instead, "an acceptable theory of truth must entail, for every sentence s of the object language, a sentence of the form: s is true if and only if p, where 'p' is replaced by any sentence that is true if and only if s is" (2001c (1973): 134). The idea, it seems, is that this restriction allows the theory to be tested without a prior understanding of any sentence in the object language.

It seems doubtful to us that the restriction on the evidence we can invoke does supply an adequate motivation for stating what we could know without appeal to the notion of translation or other semantical notions. We will return to this, but for now, let us consider further how to understand the restriction to be imposed.

We should first ask why we should suppose that the confirmation of a theory that meets the constraint would enable us to interpret any object language sentence? As Davidson notes:

[*a*] a *T*-sentence[125] does not give the meaning of the sentence it concerns: the *T*-sentence does fix the truth value relative to certain conditions, but it does not say the object language sentence is true because the conditions hold [and, because the sentence means that those conditions hold]. (Davidson 2001*c* (1973): 138)

Thus, Davidson accepts that knowing the theory is true *does not* enable us to use it for interpretation. Nor, he says (ibid.), would knowing a canonical proof of a *T*-sentence suffice.[126] What, then, would? Davidson notes the challenge and adumbrates his solution in [*b*].

[*b*] It might seem that there is no chance that if we demand so little of *T*-sentences, a theory of interpretation will emerge. And of course this would be so if we took the *T*-sentences in isolation. But the hope is that by putting appropriate formal and *empirical* restrictions on the theory as a whole, individual *T*-sentences will in fact serve to yield interpretations. (Davidson 2001*c* (1973): 134, italics added)

The formal constraints are that the theory entail, from a finite base, a *T*-form sentence for every object language sentence (and that there be a mechanical procedure for identifying a privileged class of *T*-form sentences which draw only on the content of the axioms). What are the empirical restrictions? The answer appears to be that *the theory be empirically confirmed or confirmable from the standpoint of the radical interpreter*, as indicated in [*c*].

[*c*] If we knew that a *T*-sentence satisfied Tarski's Convention *T*, we would know that it was true, and we could use it to interpret a sentence because we would know that the right branch of the biconditional translated the sentence to be interpreted. Our present trouble springs from the fact that in radical interpretation we cannot assume

---

[125] Note here that Davidson does not use '*T*-sentence', as is our convention in this book, to mean a *T*-theorem that is interpretive, but to mean what we mean by '*T*-form theorem'. See n. 66 in Part I.

[126] See also "Belief and the Basis of Meaning," "For the purposes of interpretation, however, truth in a *T*-sentence is not enough. A theory of truth will yield interpretations only if its *T*-sentences state truth conditions in terms that may be treated as 'giving the meaning' of object language sentences. Our problem is to find constraints on a theory strong enough to guarantee that it can be used for interpretation" (2001*a* (1974): 150), and "Reality Without Reference," "I do think that reasonable empirical constraints on the interpretation of *T*-sentences (the conditions under which we find them true), plus the formal constraints, will leave enough invariant as between theories to allow us to say that a theory of truth captures the essential role of each sentence" (Davidson 2001*b* (1977): 224).

that a T-sentence satisfies the translation criterion. What we have been overlooking, however, is that we have supplied an alternative criterion: *this criterion is that the totality of T-sentences should (in the sense described above) optimally fit evidence about sentences held true by native speakers.* The present idea is that what Tarski assumed outright for each T-sentence can be indirectly elicited by a holistic constraint. If that constraint is adequate, each T-sentence will in fact yield an acceptable interpretation.

A T-sentence of an empirical theory of truth can be used to interpret a sentence, then, provided we also know the theory that entails it, and know that it is a theory that meets the formal and empirical criteria. (Davidson 2001c (1973): 139, emphasis added)

It appears, then, that Davidson's answer to (Q1), what could one know that would enable one to interpret another speaker's sentences, can be put as in [K^*].

> [K^*]   [1] T is a truth theory for L whose axioms are ... , and which is confirmable from the standpoint of the radical interpreter.
>
>   [2]   Axiom ... of T means that ...
>   Axiom ... of T means that ...
>
>   ...
>
>   [3]   ... is a canonical proof procedure for T.

The difference between [K] and [K^*] consists in substituting for 'interpretive' in [K] a substantive condition on a theory being interpretive, namely, being confirmable from the standpoint of the radical interpreter.

If this is his answer, certain difficulties arise, independently of our even saying what radical interpretation is, in seeing how it can play the role it is supposed to, difficulties which have consequences for evaluating the possibility of radical interpretation in later chapters. Before we explain why, however, we turn to (Q2).

Davidson's answer to how we could come to confirm something knowledge of which would suffice for interpreting another speaker is provided by his description of the procedures of the radical interpreter. We will consider these procedures in detail in Chapter 12. To understand what kind of answer Davidson intends, we do not need to know what radical interpretation is, but it is important to understand the epistemic position of the radical interpreter. Understanding this position will also clarify what question Davidson intends to be asking, since the constraint initially given in answering (Q2) is insufficient to determine his answer.

What defines the radical interpreter's epistemic position is the evidence he has available in interpreting another. We characterize this in two stages, saying what the radical interpreter (A) can and (B) cannot appeal to.

> (A) What the radical interpreter can appeal to: (i) knowledge of the speaker's attitudes toward the truth of sentences in his language, such as what sentences the speaker believes true, hopes true, fears true, desires true, as well as the speaker's preference for the truth of one sentence over another; (ii) knowledge of the speaker's interactions with his environment described in a way that does not entail anything about his attitudes or the meanings of his words; we can in addition, allow the interpreter as much knowledge of the physical world as he likes, as long as it is not described in a way that entails anything about the speaker's attitudes or meanings, though most of it will be irrelevant.

Of the knowledge allowed by (ii), most of it will not be relevant to interpretation. What will be is the speaker's behavior and causal interactions with his environment.[127]

> (B) What the radical interpreter cannot appeal to: (i) knowledge of the meanings of any of the expressions of the object language; (ii) knowledge of "the complex and delicately discriminated intentions with which the sentence is typically uttered" (Davidson 2001c (1973): 127), or, more generally, knowledge of any of the speaker's propositional attitudes other than what is allowed in (A).

A question might arise about whether the knowledge described in A(i), for example, is independent of, or, rather, rests upon the knowledge described in A(ii). In "Radical Interpretation," Davidson is noncommittal,[128] but in other places he seems to suppose that ultimately knowledge of hold true attitudes

---

[127] Throughout our discussion, talk about a speaker's behavior and causal or physical interactions with his environment assumes they are described so as not to entail anything about his attitudes or the meanings of any of his words or sentences.

[128] He does, however, say this: holding true "is an attitude an interpreter may plausibly be taken to be able to identify before he can interpret, since he may know that a person intends to express a truth in uttering a sentence without having any idea *what* truth" (Davidson 2001c (1973): 135). Here the suggestion appears to be that we can plausibly arrive at knowledge of hold true attitudes on the basis of more primitive evidence, and so can profitably investigate what is required to interpret another by helping ourselves to hold true attitudes in describing how we could justify an interpretation.

rests on more primitive behavioral evidence. For example, in "Thought and Talk," Davidson says (emphasis added):

The interlocking of the theory of action with interpretation will emerge in another way if we ask how a method of interpretation is tested. *In the end, the answer must be that it helps bring order into our understanding of behaviour.* But *at an intermediate stage,* we can see that the attitude of holding true or accepting as true, as directed towards sentences, must play a central role in giving form to a theory.   (Davidson 2001 (1975): 161)

And in "Belief and the Basis of Meaning," he writes: "Everyday linguistic and semantic concepts are part of an intuitive theory for organizing more primitive data, so only confusion can result from treating these concepts and their supposed objects as if they had a life of their own." (Davidson 2001*a* (1974): 143).

This suggests strongly that Davidson takes up the description of the project as it starts with hold true attitudes as a matter of convenience, regarding the interpreter's knowledge of these attitudes as grounded ultimately on more primitive behavioral evidence. This way of understanding the status of knowledge of hold true attitudes also seems to fit with both Davidson's general attitude toward the kind of evidence relevant to determining facts about meaning and with the kinds of results he hopes to get out of reflection on radical interpretation. In any case, whether Davidson is committed to the evidence he helps himself to in A(i) resting on that in A(ii) is important for our understanding of the force of reflections on radical interpretation. We will explain how in detail as we go along. In addition to the passage we just quoted, Davidson seems to be so committed, when he remarks at the beginning of "The Inscrutability of Reference" (Davidson 2001*a* (1979): 227), that "the totality of behavioral evidence, actual and potential ... is all that matters to questions of meaning and communication." Here he seems quite explicit. (See also passage [*d*] below from "The Structure and Content of Truth".) However, there is contrary evidence too. Some we will discuss later in this chapter. One passage which seems to flat out deny the aspiration to ground interpretation ultimately on observable behavior of speakers is in a reply to a paper of David Lewis's, in which Davidson denies that a complete physical description of a person gives enough information to enable one to interpret a speaker. He says, "This I think is false" (Davidson 1974: 345). How to reconcile this with such passages as those above and the ambitious claims he hopes to found on reflection on the procedure of radical interpretation is unclear to us. But it will be enough for our evaluative purposes here to say what the consequences are of grounding interpretation ultimately on information available in A(ii), or, instead, denying that one can do so.

All of the restrictions on the evidence available to the radical interpreter in (A) and (B) are not motivated directly by the requirement that one come to know an answer to (Q1) in a way that does not presuppose already knowing that answer. For detailed knowledge of a speaker's attitude contents, for example, would not, except possibly in the case of knowledge of a speaker's beliefs about what his sentences mean, constitute even partial knowledge of the content of the theory to be confirmed. (There might be doubt about whether one needs to exclude knowledge of what the speaker believes his words mean. For if he can err about what his words mean, then knowing what he believes need not in itself suffice to know what his words mean. However, if he must know, by and large, what his words mean, and we knew this, then if we knew what he believed his words to mean, we would know too much.) Davidson rejects an appeal to knowledge of a speaker's attitudes, because "we cannot hope to attach a sense to the attribution of finely discriminated intentions independently of interpreting speech" (Davidson 2001*c* (1973): 127). This expresses the idea that our knowledge of the finely discriminated contents of others' propositional attitudes is based ultimately on evidence which is at the same time evidence for what others mean by what they say. Since Davidson hopes to confirm a theory of interpretation for another on the basis of evidence that does not presuppose interpretation, and, it seems, ultimately, on purely behavioral evidence, this suggests that he thinks that, ultimately, evidence for the contents of others' attitudes and the meanings of their words is behavioral evidence that does not presuppose any knowledge of their attitudes, including what sentences they hold true. By 'ultimately' here we mean that in an account of one's justification for attributing both attitudes to others and interpretations to their sentences, knowledge of their behavior and interaction with their environment would be prior, in the order of justification, to knowledge of their attitudes and of the meanings of their sentences.[129]

If this is, as it were, the 'original' epistemic position for interpreting others, then the point of adopting this position as the one from which an interpretation theory is to be confirmed is that in this way we relate the concepts of the theory to the most fundamental evidence we have for applying them.[130] This shows that Davidson's interest is not primarily in answering (Q2), how could

---

[129] In "The Social Aspect of Language," Davidson remarks, "I do not think I have ever conflated the (empirical) question how we actually go about understanding a speaker with the (philosophical) question what is necessary and sufficient for such understanding" (1994*b*: 3).

[130] While this represents Davidson as holding that behavioral evidence is fundamental for attributions of attitudes to others and interpretations of their sentences, it does not commit him to anything like traditional Cartesian foundationalism, which, as we noted in Ch. 1, he rejects.

we come to know something sufficient to interpret any potential utterance of another speaker (on the basis of evidence that does not presuppose knowledge of it), but rather in answering a more specific question, namely, (Q2′).

(Q2′)   How could we come to know something knowledge of which would suffice to interpret another speaker *from the standpoint of the radical interpreter*?

We return now to Davidson's *apparent* answer to (Q1), raising two objections. We will also consider whether there might be another way of understanding the appeal to empirical confirmability that does not encounter these two difficulties. Finally, we will suggest that [K] is after all the only proper answer to (Q1).

(Q1) asks what we could know that would enable us to interpret the words of another speaker. If [K*] is the answer, then it is what we are to confirm from the standpoint of the radical interpreter. To confirm [K*] from the standpoint of the radical interpreter is to confirm that a certain truth theory can be confirmed to be true from the standpoint of the radical interpreter. Now, a first oddity with this answer is that Davidson apparently wants the description of the radical interpreter's procedure for confirming a truth theory to be his answer to (Q2′). But this would require as an answer to (Q1), *not* [K*], but, rather, the result of replacing 'interpretive' in [K] with 'true'. We have, however, already established that knowledge that a truth theory for a speaker's language is true is insufficient to interpret him. So, there appears to be a mismatch between the answers Davidson wants, and needs, to give to (Q1) and (Q2′).

Let us put this aside though. Suppose we answered (Q2′) by describing a procedure which was supposed not to confirm that a truth theory is true, but that it is confirmable from the standpoint of the radical interpreter. Given that what we confirm is merely that the theory can be confirmed from certain evidence, what confidence should we have that this theory is interpretive? For what magical properties could being confirmable add to the theory's being true which would transform it from something *in*adequate for interpretation into something adequate? On the face of it, the best way to confirm that a truth theory is confirmable is to confirm it. Suppose we do so, and remark that we have done so. Then what have we added that ensures it is interpretive? If something sufficient has been added, as a by-product, so to speak, of confirmation, it must be stateable independently of saying that the theory has been confirmed, for that alone cannot guarantee that it has any properties relevant to interpretation other than those we have confirmed that it has, which are admittedly inadequate. So it looks as if the deeper problem with [K*] is that it should give us no confidence that knowing what it specifies suffices for interpretation.

Are we being uncharitable to Davidson? We have summed up his idea that the theory meets certain empirical constraints, that it "(in the sense described above) optimally fit evidence about sentences held true by native speakers" (Davidson 2001c (1973)), by saying that it is confirmable by the radical interpreter. This captures what the evidence in question is, and certainly the sense in which the theory is to optimally fit the evidence, and, thus, seems a fair summary of the requirement. But could it help, in any case, to put instead that the theory optimally fit evidence about sentences held true by native speakers? For this tells us *only* that we have good reason to think the theory is true: but, as we have observed, that is *not enough*, and if some other property is a by-product of its being confirmable, it can be stated independently, and included in an explicit statement of what it is we are trying to confirm, so that we can see that confirming this would result in something sufficient for interpretation. So, neither appeal to confirmability nor optimally fitting evidence, if that is different, should increase our confidence that the theory confirmed is usable for interpretation.

It might be suggested, with textual support, that what Davidson says in "Radical Interpretation," quoted in [c], *mis*characterizes (or misleads us about) which empirical constraint he really has in mind. We have already seen that simply remarking that the theory is extensionally adequate is not enough. However, in "Reply to Foster," and in a retrospective footnote to "Truth and Meaning," Davidson says his appeal to empirical confirmation was intended to render salient that the theorems of an empirically confirmed theory would be laws,[131] and so support counterfactual statements.[132] This would remove

---

[131] We will avoid throughout any commitment to an analysis of the concept of (natural) law. We will take laws to be expressed by sentences, and we will take it to be appropriate, when a sentence expresses a law, to preface it with 'it is a law that'; we will sometimes express this by saying the sentence or what the sentence expresses is nomically necessary. We take laws to support appropriately related counterfactual statements and predictions and to be supported by their instances; we will sometimes express this by saying that a generalization which expresses a law is projectible. When we speak of a law of a certain form or speak directly of a sentence as a law, this should be understood as shorthand for talking about laws expressed by sentences of that form or by that sentence. Cf. Davidson 2001a: 217.

[132] See n. 11 of "Truth and Meaning," in Davidson 2001c (1967). In "Reply to Foster" Davidson says, "it still seems to me right, as far as it goes, to hold that someone is in a position to interpret the utterances of speakers of a language L if he has a certain body of knowledge entailed by a theory of truth for L—a theory that meets specified empirical and formal constraints—and he knows that this knowledge is entailed by such a theory" (Davidson 2001b (1976): 172). And again (ibid. 172–3): "But in *radical* interpretation, this [translation] is just what cannot be assumed. So I have proposed instead some empirical constraints on accepting a theory of truth that can be stated without appeal to such

161

the difficulty we have noted above for the criterion Davidson appears to give in "Radical Interpretation." And this would avoid the counterexample discussed in Chapter 7 in which from one extensionally adequate theory we generated another by adding a contingently true sentence as a conjunction to the truth conditions for a predicate. For example, consider the T-form sentence (1) generated by adding 'and Tallahassee is the capital of Florida' to the right hand side of the axiom for the predicate 'is white' (we stipulate these expressions have the interpretations they have in English).

(1) 'Stone Mountain is white' is true(S, t) iff Stone Mountain is white at t and Tallahassee is the capital of Florida at t.

The problem is that, while (1) is true, and generated by an extensionally adequate theory, it is not interpretive. We avoid this sort of counterexample if we require our theorems to be laws.[133] For (1) to be a law, it must be that

concepts as those of meaning, translation, or synonymy, though not without a certain understanding of the notion of truth. By a course of reasoning, I have tried to show that if the constraints are met by a theory, then the T-sentences that flow from that theory will in fact have translations of s replacing 'p'." What are those empirical constraints? Not just that it is true, but that it be confirmed to be true for the actual speaker of the language. This seems to suggest that it is the process of confirming the theory to be true that will of necessity zero in on the right theory, i.e. an interpretive one. This is suggested in the following passage (ibid. 173). "That empirical restrictions must be added to the formal restrictions if acceptable theories of truth are to include only those that would serve for interpretation was clear to me even when I wrote 'Truth and Meaning'. My mistake was not, as Foster seems to suggest, to suppose that *any* theory that correctly gave truth conditions would serve for interpretation; my mistake was to overlook the fact that someone might know a sufficiently unique theory without knowing that it was sufficiently unique. The distinction was easy for me to neglect because I imagined the theory to be known by someone who had constructed it from the evidence, and such a person could not fail to realize that his theory satisfied the constraints." However, a page later (p. 174) Davidson says, "A theory that passes the empirical tests is one that in fact can be projected to unobserved and counterfactual cases, and this is apparent to anyone who knows what the evidence is and how it is used to support the theory. The trouble is, the theory does not state that it has the character it does." This passage suggests that the point of empirical confirmability is to yield T-theorems which can be treated as laws. What Davidson says does not make clear enough, however, what he intends. It may well be that he did not at this point distinguish very clearly in his own mind what it was about empirical confirmability which was supposed to yield interpretability. More recently he has summed up his view as follows, which seems clearly to indicate that his view is that the simplest law-like theory is interpretive: "I think this worry can be overcome by reflecting on the fact that when such a theory is treated as an empirical theory, T-sentences are laws which state the truth conditions not only of actual utterances but also of unspoken sentences. Laws formulated as universally quantified biconditionals convey far more than identity of truth value. This consideration, and the constraints that follow from the logical relations among sentences should, when coupled with the usual pressure for simplicity, ensure that contrived, gerrymandered theories are weeded out" ("Reply to Higginbotham," in Hahn 1999: 688).

[133] What does it mean to say that the theorems of the theory are laws? If we are thinking of theorems which relativize truth to a language characterized as an abstract object, it does not make any clear sense, except in so far as we interpret it as the claim that the theorems hold in all nomically

there is no nomically possible world in which Stone Mountain is white, and Tallahassee is not the capital of Florida. But Stone Mountain, which is white, would have been white even if Jacksonville had been chosen as the capital of Florida instead of Tallahassee. It might be suggested, then, that the right answer to (Q1) (and even the answer Davidson intended) is $[K^{**}]$.

$[K^{**}]$ [1] T is a truth theory for L whose axioms are ... and whose axioms are (*ceteris paribus*) laws.[134]

[2]   Axiom ... of T means that ...

Axiom ... of T means that ...

. . .

[3]   ... is a canonical proof procedure for T.

However, as we also noted in Chapter 7, an appeal to even the nomic necessity of *T*-form sentences does not suffice for their being interpretive. There are nonsynonymous predicates nonetheless co-extensive in all nomically possible worlds (at least), such as plausibly 'is a golden element' and 'has atomic number 79'. Thus, knowledge that $[K^{**}]$ would not be sufficient to interpret sentences of the object language. It would be only if the following were true:

(2)   Every instance of the following schema is true:

For all speakers S, times t, s in L means(S, t) that p

iff

it is canonically provable on the basis of the true *law-like* axioms of a truth theory for L that for all speakers S, times t, s is true(S, t) in L iff p.

But since there are counterexamples to (2), it is not true.

At this point it might be suggested that the intent of appealing to empirical confirmation is not just that it will yield a theory whose theorems can be treated

---

possible worlds. But if we think of the theorems as relativizing truth to a speaker, we can suppose that the theorems represent empirical claims about the speaker's dispositions, that is, they can be seen as representing the fact that sentences as uttered by the speaker are true in all nomically possible worlds in which we keep the dispositions of the speaker relevant to fixing their meaning the same in just the conditions specified in the theorem.

[134] We modify 'laws' with *ceteris paribus* ('all other things being equal'), because these laws are rough laws which can be assumed to hold only relative to certain conditions obtaining—conditions which cannot be spelled out exhaustively without changing to a different vocabulary. As Davidson says at one point, "With an ample sprinkling of 'other things being equal' and 'under normal conditions' clauses, we constantly utilize generalizations that relate the mental and the physical in everyday life. But here nothing like the laws of physics is in the cards" (Davidson 2004 (2001): 148). See also centrally Davidson 2001*b* (1970).

as laws supporting counterfactuals, but that if it is empirically confirmed, then all the general constraints on theory building will apply, and the fact that the theory has passed this test makes it interpretive. It might be urged, for example, that certain potential counterexamples will be eliminated by this constraint, because we will seek the simplest theory, and this theory will be *ipso facto* interpretive.

This is of no help, however, even if we were guaranteed that there is a simplest theory. We know we need to do more than just confirm a true, and even true counterfactual supporting, truth theory for a speaker. We need to know not just under which conditions a speaker's sentences are, or would in all physically possible worlds be, true, but also conditions under which his sentences are true, and which at the same time provide an interpretation of those sentences (as used). We cannot assume without argument that the *simplest* true counterfactual supporting theory achieves this aim. *M* may be the simplest mapping of terms in an object language onto the vocabulary of the metalanguage that yields a true counterfactual supporting theory. But this *in itself* is no reason to think that the resulting theory *is* interpretive. We have no reason to expect that every language we might encounter will have lexical primitives that mean what ours mean, and so we may have to use a complex predicate in our language to specify in our language interpretive truth conditions for another's, or even to extend our language. The same point extends to any general constraint on theory confirmation. In general, if our explicit goal is to confirm *a true counterfactual supporting truth theory* for a speaker's language, since such a theory *is not ipso facto* interpretive, we need an argument that the general constraints met in arriving at *that sort* of theory will yield an *interpretive* truth theory. Therefore, we cannot *at the outset* treat the empirical confirmability of a truth theory as sufficient for interpretiveness. That would beg the question.

Perhaps it will be suggested that, after all, confirmability by a radical interpreter is sufficient, if we suppose we have described radical interpretation so that it guarantees success. Perhaps confirmability by the radical interpreter is to be understood to include adherence to the principle of charity (see the next chapter for more on this), which holds that most of a speaker's beliefs about his environment are true, and that, given this detail, we can in fact see that the theories confirmed by radical interpreters are indeed interpretive. In general, first, it is not clear that the procedure so described does guarantee that the theory is interpretive (see Chapters 13 and 15 for further discussion). Second, the principle of charity itself stands in need of justification. And, finally, we still need an independent characterization of the goal in order to ask whether the procedure described is adequate to it.

It seems clear what our goal should be: it should be to come to know the sort of thing stated by [K]. And why should we not adopt this as our answer to (Q1)? Knowledge expressed by something of the form of [K] would suffice, and, in stating what knowledge would suffice in this way, we do not sacrifice the aim of illuminating the concepts of the theory by confirming it on an evidential base (if we can) that does not presuppose any of the content of the theory. Perhaps Davidson did not give this answer because he was thinking still of the aim of the extended project in "Truth and Meaning." The extended project hopes to find a substantive condition on a truth theory that will ensure it is interpretive. Davidson's first suggestion appeared to be that extensional adequacy suffices. But it is inadequate. Before proposing that, however, Davidson did not pause to formulate an adequacy condition on a compositional meaning theory that takes for granted knowledge of the meanings of primitive expressions, the basis for [K]. Upon finding extensional adequacy insufficient, it would be natural to seek another substantive condition rather than to retreat to something uncontroversial; the thought that placing the theory in the context of radical interpretation might be what is needed would lead naturally to [K*], bypassing [K] altogether. Second, the pull of the requirement that the evidence with which the interpreter starts not include any of the content of the theory to be confirmed may suggest that the answer to (Q1) should not include the requirement that the theory generate canonical theorems that meet Davidson's Convention *T*, or anything which would entail that the theory did.[135] (See the transition in [c] above in particular.) However, neither of these is a good reason. On the first point, as we have noted, if the point of radical interpretation is to illuminate the concepts of the theory of interpretation by relating them to evidence that does not presuppose their detailed application to a subject, the illumination is achieved not by placing a substantive condition on a theory of truth which by itself suffices for its being interpretive.

---

[135] In "Belief and the Basis of Meaning," Davidson says (2001*a* (1974): 151): "There remain the further primitive expressions to be interpreted [after questions of logical form have been determined]. The main problem is to find a systematic way of matching predicates of the metalanguage to the primitive predicates of the object language so as to produce acceptable *T*-sentences. If the metalanguage predicates translate the object language predicates, things will obviously come out right [this is our suggestion in Ch. 4]; if they have the same extensions, this might be enough. But it would be foreign to our programme to use these concepts in stating the constraints: the constraints must deal only with sentence and truth." Clearly a desire not to infect the evidential base with such concepts as interpretation or translation has influenced not just how Davidson describes the interpreter's procedure, but also how he thinks about what it is that the interpreter aims to confirm.

To try to hold on to that requirement, while at the same time shifting to this alternative way of illuminating the concepts of the theory of interpretation, is to conflate two quite different projects. On the second point, it is a confusion to suppose that a restriction on what counts as evidence one can invoke, in order to illuminate the concepts in the theory we are seeking to confirm, places restrictions on how we state what it is we want to confirm from that evidential base. Indeed, this way of thinking about how we can provide illumination of the concepts of the theory presupposes that we have stated what we want to come to know using the concepts we want to illuminate.

The only condition that clearly serves for a truth theory to be interpretive is that it be interpretive. This, then, is the aim of the radical interpreter: to confirm a truth theory for a speaker's language that meets appropriate formal constraints, *and* to confirm that it is interpretive.[136]

2. A Modest Project and an Ambitious Project

We turn now to a more general question about the investigation of the procedures of the radical interpreter: what is the force of the results we can draw from reflection upon what the radical interpreter must assume about his subject-matter? In particular, question (Q2′) has an important presupposition (P) in terms of which we can characterize two ways of thinking about the role of an analysis of the project of radical interpretation in investigating meaning and related matters.

(P)   One can come to know something sufficient to interpret a speaker from the evidential position of the radical interpreter.

---

[136] It should be clear from this discussion, whether or not our final conclusion about how one should specify the goal of the radical interpreter is correct, that it has not been Davidson's aim, certainly since "Radical Interpretation," to explain meaning in terms of some suitably strong notion of 'truth conditions'. Despite this, there appears to be a consistent misunderstanding of Davidson's project on this point, as expressed, for example, in this passage from a paper by Paul Horwich, listing difficulties for Davidson's project of truth-theoretic semantics: "After thirty years there still remains the notorious unsolved problem of how to articulate a conception of truth conditions ('u is true *iff* p') that is strong enough to constitute the corresponding attribution of meaning ('u means that p')" (Horwich 1999: 250). There is no problem, notorious or not, of this sort for Davidson's project because it has never been an aim of his project to do what it is charged here with being unable to do. The object has been to place constraints on a truth theory that enable us to use it for interpretation, that is, that suffice for the theory to meet Davidson's Convention T. It is confused to think of this as a matter of introducing a strong enough notion of 'truth conditions' to do the job, as if the project were that of analyzing meaning in terms of some antecedent notion of truth condition.

If (P) is true, we will say radical interpretation is possible. If not, we will say radical interpretation is impossible. But one can adopt either of two positions on (P). On the one hand, (P) can be accepted as an unargued for assumption, in which case any conclusions reached about the nature of the radical interpreter's subject-matter, on the basis of uncovering what the radical interpreter must assume to carry out his project, are conditional on the truth of (P). Suppose the radical interpreter can succeed only if *p*. If (P) is taken as an unargued assumption, then at best we would be able to infer from this condition on the radical interpreter's succeeding that:

If radical interpretation is possible, then *p*.

On the other hand, we can argue for (P). If we established (P), then we would be in a position to affirm anything we discover that the radical interpreter must assume to be successful. An argument for (P) would be either a posteriori or a priori. An a posteriori argument, however, would presuppose that we can identify a correct interpretation for another's language independently of the procedures of the radical interpreter, since to argue for an interpretation by employing the procedures of the radical interpreter is to presuppose (P). If, however, as we suggested in §1, Davidson sees the epistemic position of the radical interpreter as our 'original' position with respect to the thoughts of others and the meanings of their sentences, he will not suppose that there is a prospect for an independent confirmation of an interpretation theory, that is, an account of how we are justified in believing an interpretation theory which would not ultimately satisfy a radical interpreter. If we are right, Davidson will, instead, suppose that unless a radical interpreter could be justified in believing a true interpretation theory for a speaker, no one could. (However, see below for some contrary evidence.) Thus, given this assumption, if we are not to take (P) on faith, we must argue for it a priori. This would also ensure that anything we discovered the radical interpreter must assume to succeed at interpretation would be not just true, but necessarily true.[137] In contrast, if we argued only a posteriori for the possibility of radical interpretation, we could conclude only that what the interpreter must assume for success is true, or at best perhaps a matter of physical necessity. We will call the project that

---

[137] We are assuming here that if one can know (P) a priori, it is necessary. This need not involve a general commitment to a priori truths being necessary. All that is required for this claim is that, even if there are cases of synthetic a priori truths (see Kripke 1980), they involve special features not present in this case (e.g. one clear case of a synthetic a priori truth, 'All actual philosophers are philosophers', clearly depends on the special logical features of 'actual').

takes (P) on faith *the modest project,* and the one that aims to provide an a priori argument for (P) *the ambitious project.*

An interesting parallel can be drawn between the ambitious project and at least one interpretation of Kant's strategy in the transcendental deduction. Kant is sometimes interpreted in the transcendental deduction as assuming that we have knowledge of things in space, and asking what must be so if this is possible. For Kant, we can also distinguish two projects, one more and one less ambitious. The more ambitious project seeks to show that we do have knowledge of things in space, so that we can conclude positively that what must be so, *if* this is possible, *is* so; the modest project takes for granted the starting assumption, so that our conclusions are left conditional in nature. Much of the interest of both Kant's and Davidson's projects, we believe, lies in the possibility of discharging the antecedents of the conditionals for which they argue.

Whether Davidson is engaged in the modest or ambitious project is a matter of great significance. Support for the view that he is engaged in the ambitious project is provided by the following passage from "The Structure and Content of Truth" (Davidson 1990*b*: 314).[138]

[*d*] What we *should* demand ... is that the evidence for the theory be in principle publicly accessible, and that it not assume in advance the concepts to be illuminated. The requirement that the evidence be publicly accessible is not due to an atavistic yearning for behavioristic or verificationist foundations, but to the fact that what is to be explained is a social phenomenon. Mental phenomena in general may or may not be private, but the correct interpretation of one person's speech by another must *in principle* be possible. A speaker's intention that her words be understood in a certain way may of course remain opaque to the most skilled and knowledgeable listener, but what has to do with correct interpretation, meaning, and truth conditions is necessarily based on available evidence. As Ludwig Wittgenstein, not to mention Dewey, G. H. Mead, Quine, and many others have insisted, language is intrinsically social. This does not entail that truth and meaning can be *defined* in terms of observable behavior, or that it is "nothing but" observable behavior; but it does imply that meaning is entirely

---

[138] This thought is expressed in many other passages as well. For example, "It should be emphasized that these maxims of interpretation are not mere pieces of useful or friendly advice; rather they are intended to externalize and formulate (no doubt very crudely) essential aspects of the common concepts of thought, affect, reasoning and action. *What could not be arrived at by these methods is not thought, talk, or action*" (Davidson 1985*a*: 92, emphasis added). See also Davidson 2001*a* (1983): 147–8: "As a matter of principle, ... meaning, and by its connection with meaning, belief also, are open to public determination ... What a fully informed interpreter could learn about what a speaker means is all there is to learn; the same goes for what the speaker believes."

determined by observable behavior, even readily observable behavior. That meanings are decipherable is not a matter of luck; public availability is a constitutive aspect of language.

By saying that "meaning is entirely determined by observable behavior," Davidson means one can in principle confirm an interpretation theory for another on the basis of only observable behavior. And this claim is grounded on the observation that "language is intrinsically social" (as Quine puts it in the first sentence of the preface of *Word and Object*, "Language is a social art"). Presumably, this observation is meant as an a priori truth.[139] Thus, the argument in the passage seems to be precisely for presupposition (P). Furthermore, if we are right, unless Davidson is engaged in the ambitious project, and can support (P) with an a priori argument, many of his conclusions about the *nature* of thought, language, meaning, truth, and knowledge, will be unattainable.

There is also evidence that Davidson does not see himself as engaged in the ambitious project, as witnessed in his remarks responding to criticism on the role of radical interpretation in his account of language and thought. In "Radical Interpretation Interpreted,"[140] he writes,

---

[139] Or as near as one can get. Quine, of course, would not endorse characterizing this as an a priori truth, as opposed to one near the center of the web of belief. Davidson, however, despite remarks about the futility of traditional analysis aimed at coming up with informative necessary and sufficient conditions for the application of concepts central to our conceptual scheme, and some animadversions on traditional distinctions such as that between the analytic and synthetic, and necessary and contingent (e.g. 2001*b* (1970): 272–3), is clearly more sympathetic to the distinction between a priori and a posteriori truths, or conceptual and non-conceptual truths, than Quine is. Davidson often speaks of there being truths constitutive of a subject-matter e.g. (ibid. 273 and Davidson 2001*a* (1970): 220 ff.), and he seems to have in mind conceptual connections in these contexts. Sometimes this is explicit, as in this passage, "There are conceptual ties between the attitudes and behavior which are sufficient, given enough information about actual and potential behavior, to allow correct inference to the attitudes" (Davidson 2001*b* (1982): 100). There are many other passages of a similar sort e.g. "I have been engaged in a conceptual exercise aimed at revealing the dependencies among our basic propositional attitudes at a level fundamental enough to avoid the assumption that we can come to grasp them—or intelligibly attribute them to others—one at a time" (Davidson 1990*b*: 325). We will, in our discussion of the distinction between the modest and ambitious programs, continue to employ the traditional terms 'a priori' and 'a posteriori'. However, for our purposes, these terms could be replaced with *any* pair that captures the difference between the kind of grounding involved in establishing truths constitutive of a subject-matter, and in establishing truths which are not. It is clear enough that that distinction is at work, and *plays the role* in Davidson's work of the traditional distinction between knowledge of conceptual and non-conceptual truths.

[140] Davidson 1994*a*. This is a response to Fodor and Lepore 1994. The present account of the structure and point of Davidson's discussion of radical interpretation differs in important respects from that in this article.

[*e*]   [i] I do not think I have ever argued for the claim that radical interpretability[141] is a condition of interpretability. [ii] Not only have I never argued that every language is radically interpretable; I have not even argued that every language can be understood by someone other than its employer, since it would be possible to have a private code no one else could break. [iii] I do not think, and have not argued, that radical interpretation of natural languages *must* be possible; I have argued only that it *is* possible. [iv] The point of the "epistemic position" of the radical interpreter is not that it exhausts the evidence available to an actual interpreter, but that it arguably provides sufficient evidence for interpretation. (Davidson 1994*a*: 121, roman numerals added)

[iv] is compatible with the ambitious program. [ii] is not clearly incompatible with it. In the next paragraph, Davidson says, "I have maintained that anyone with any language must have a non-private language" (ibid. 122). From this vantage, [ii] need not mean that there are, or could be, *speakers* not radically interpretable. However, [i] and [iii] seem to reject any ambition to show on a priori grounds that, for any speaker, it is possible to interpret him from the standpoint of the radical interpreter (assuming this would support a claim of necessity).[142]

Why then be interested in radical interpretation? Davidson says in this article that the interest in the project lies entirely in showing one way interpretation can proceed. He says that whatever general truths he has maintained about the nature of language and speakers, he has argued for independently of his claim that radical interpretation is possible.

It is not so easy to see that all of Davidson's well-known theses about the nature of language, meaning, and belief can be established independently of the claim that radical interpretation is possible. We will be concerned with the details of his arguments in subsequent chapters in this part and the next. In the

---

[141] In a note, Davidson 1994*a*: 128 n. 2, Davidson distinguishes between two ways in which he has used the expression 'radical interpretation'. On the first, it refers "to any interpretation from scratch, that is, without the aid of bilingual speakers or dictionaries." This is the wide reading. In the second, it refers "to the special enterprise of interpreting on the basis of a limited and specified data base." This is the narrow reading. In [*e*] he intends the narrow reading, the sense in which we have characterized radical interpretation in this chapter. It is not clear to us in what way Davidson imagines the evidential base for the interpreter "from scratch" to be richer than that for the radical interpreter in the narrower sense. It may be that the only difference he has in mind has to do with whether we start with just observations of behavior, or with attitudes toward the truth of sentences and behavior. This, however, would not involve the interpreter from scratch having a richer, but rather a poorer, initial starting point.

[142] It is possible that Davidson has in mind to deny simply the claim that any *language* must be radically interpretable, on the grounds cited in [ii], but not to deny that any *speaker* must be radically interpretable. This would render [i] and [iii] compatible with pursuit of the ambitious project. But, in the context, this would be disingenuous.

present article, he mentions only four theses, (A1) that natural languages are compositional, (A2) that a speaker's attitudes must be attributed in patterns appropriate to their contents and the assignments of meanings we make to the speaker's words (we will discuss this further in Chapter 14), (A3) that "many basic sentences must be true at those times when they are held true by a speaker" (Davidson 1994a: 123), and, finally, (A4) that the meanings of sentences in a speaker's language depend on the meanings of other sentences in the language, which he characterizes as following from (A2). (A1) and (A2) do not depend on the possibility of radical interpretation for support. We reviewed in Chapter 2 the argument for (A1). We will discuss (A2) in Chapter 14, and (A4) is one aspect of (A2). (A3) expresses one aspect of what Davidson has called 'the principle of charity'. He does not say why he thinks his argument for the principle of charity does not rest in part on the possibility of radical interpretation.[143] We will examine the justification of the principle of charity in detail in Chapter 13. We will argue there is good reason to think that if the principle of charity is to be justified in a form which will do the work required of it, it looks as if that justification must rest on the assumption that the radical interpreter can correctly interpret a speaker, and that charity is required for this.[144] Furthermore, there are conclusions Davidson has reached not listed here, which we will discuss below, and which also look as if their support derives from the requirement that a speaker can be correctly interpreted from the standpoint of radical interpretation. There are also passages in which it certainly appears as if Davidson is making claims in conflict with passage [*e*]. Consider this passage from which we have taken the epigraph for Part II.

The problem of interpretation is domestic as well as foreign: it surfaces for speakers of the same language in the form of the question, how can it be determined that the

---

[143] Could it be that he has in mind arguments for externalism such as that involving the Swampman in "Knowing One's Own Mind" (Davidson 2001b (1987))? Yet the principle of charity was introduced long before this discussion, and long before Davidson makes any explicit reference to externalism. Indeed, it is natural to see his considered arguments for externalism as resting on the principle of charity, or that part of it that involves assuming that most of a speaker's beliefs directed at his environment are true, rather than the other way around, and to see the principle of charity (that aspect of it) as resting on the need to assume it to succeed in interpretation (see Ch. 19). If there are independent arguments for this principle in Davidson's work, they are well hidden.

[144] This is a typical remark (emphasis added): "Since charity is not an option, but a condition of *having a workable theory*, it is meaningless to suggest that we might fall into massive error by endorsing it ... Charity is forced on us; whether we like it or not, if we want to understand others, we must count them right in most matters" (Davidson 2001c (1974): 197). This follows on a discussion of what is required for a radical interpreter to come to interpret another successfully. Charity is introduced (in one use) to solve the problem of the interaction of meaning and belief. See Chs. 12 and 13 for further discussion.

171

language is the same? Speakers of the same language can go on the assumption that for them the same expressions are to be interpreted in the same way, but this does not indicate what justifies the assumption. All understanding of the speech of another involves radical interpretation.   (Davidson 2001*c* (1973): 125)

Admittedly, the last, striking sentence in this passage does not assert necessity. But it is hard to read it without thinking that the reasons urged for it are thought to support it in virtue of the very nature of the subject-matter, that is, that the features of language being appealed to are not thought to be contingent, but rather constitutive.[145]

   That is, there is evidence that Davidson does aim to establish general truths about speakers on the grounds that they could not otherwise be interpreted, but must be interpretable since they are speakers. One might try to reconcile the remarks in [*e*] with this evidence by supposing Davidson means only to claim above that radical interpretation, as he describes it, may not work, but for reasons independent of observations about the assumptions the radical interpreter must make to succeed, assumptions which would have to be made by any interpreter of another. In this case, he could claim he has an argument for the various theses he has apparently argued for by reflection on radical interpretation which does not commit him to saying speakers must be radically interpretable. Rather, the argument would be that speakers must be interpretable, and that, no matter how it is done, it will require the assumptions identified in the discussion of radical interpretation. If this were right, there would be no need to argue a priori that radical interpretation of a speaker is possible to get the results desired.

   However, since Davidson's detailed discussions of what must be assumed about our subject in interpretation occurs in his discussion of radical interpretation, if he aims to establish such claims as (A3) a priori, he owes us a reason to think that the truth of (A3) is required not only for success at radical interpretation (if that is possible at all), but for success in interpretation in general, by whatever method, or using whatever evidence, we might avail ourselves of. If reflection on radical interpretation is to enable us to see this, then a

---

[145] Other passages reinforce the impression, e.g. "The fact that radical interpretation is so commonplace—the fact, that is, that we use our standard method of interpretation only as a useful starting point in understanding a speaker—is hidden from us by many things, foremost among them being that syntax is so much more social than semantics" (Davidson 2001*c* (1974): 279). See also: "The point of the theory is not to describe how we actually interpret, but to speculate on what it is about thought and language that makes them interpretable. If we can tell a story like the official story about how it is possible, we can conclude that the constraints the theory places on the attitude may articulate some of their philosophically significant features" (Davidson 2004*a* (1995): 128).

case must be made for seeing such claims as (A3) being required by features which radical interpretation must share with any method of interpretation. We have not identified anything that looks like an explicit argument for this in Davidson's work.[146] None of the interpretive options is comfortable, leaving us with an exegetical puzzle we are not sure how to resolve. We find Davidson's investigation of radical interpretation philosophically most interesting when it is taken to reveal constitutive features of its subject-matter. If we are to take what the radical interpreter has to assume about his subject-matter to reveal constitutive features of language and thought, then we need an a priori argument for the possibility of success of radical interpretation for any speaker. Or, at least, we require, in line with the previous paragraph, an a priori argument for what drives the need to make the relevant assumptions about the subject-matter being something that would be required no matter the kind of interpretation in question. Our considered position is that despite [*e*], Davidson should be taken as committed to there being an a priori argument for (P), on some interpretation which will support the various theses he has argued for about the nature of linguistic agents by reflection on what we must do to interpret them. This makes the best sense of his overall philosophical project. We have already said much in support of this; and further support will emerge in our discussion of the details of the arguments Davidson gives for the results he aims to found on reflection on the procedures for interpreting a speaker from behavioral evidence, and whatever we can know a priori about speakers. In subsequent discussion, we will therefore continue to be interested in whether we can find in Davidson's writings an a priori argument for the assumptions needed, and interested also in what conclusions we can legitimately draw from reflection on the project of radical interpretation, depending on whether such an a priori argument is available. For the moment, we turn to an examination of the procedure of the radical interpreter.

---

[146] Recall the distinction between the narrow and wide reading of 'radical interpretation' drawn in n. 141. One might try to reconcile Davidson's apparently conflicting remarks by taking him, in passages where he seems to suggest or argue radical interpretation is a condition on interpretability, to be intending to use 'radical interpretation' in the broad rather than narrow sense. This still leaves the task of disentangling from his discussions what he thinks is special about radical interpretation in its narrow sense, and what is not.

12

The Procedure of the Radical Interpreter

> Since we cannot hope to interpret linguistic activity without knowing what a speaker believes, and cannot found a theory of what he means on a priori discovery of his beliefs and intentions, I conclude that in interpreting utterances from scratch—in *radical* interpretation—we must somehow deliver simultaneously a theory of belief and a theory of meaning. How is this possible?
>
> (Davidson 2001*a* (1974): 144)

In this chapter, we present the basic form of the radical interpreter's procedure and the role the principle of charity plays in it. In §1, we discuss the motivation for isolating hold true attitudes for special attention in radical interpretation. In §2, we discuss an important analogy Davidson has drawn between empirical decision theory and confirming an interpretation theory. In §3, we discuss the central role of the principle of charity in connecting the interpreter's initial evidence with something that could be used to project an interpretive truth theory. §4 considers three interpretations of the principle of charity intimated by various passages in Davidson's work, which we shall call 'Veracity', 'Charity', and 'Agreement', and argue that the correct interpretation is Charity. §5 argues that Charity is insufficient, however, for the task it is assigned. A stronger principle is required, which we shall call 'Grace', which we introduce in §6. §7 summarizes the discussion by laying out as a series of stages the procedure of the radical interpreter.

Davidson's account of the procedure of the radical interpreter has changed and been enriched during the course of its development. In this chapter, we focus on its first stage of development. The most important subsequent development has been the introduction of a method to identify the logical constants by appeal to patterns among subjects' attitudes of preferring one sentence true to another. We will consider this development in Chapter 16. Since the later procedure incorporates rather than replaces the earlier, conclusions arrived at by consideration of the features of radical interpretation we discuss here are not undermined by these later developments.

1. From Behavior to Holding True

Radical interpretation can be viewed as directed either toward a language community or a single speaker. Interpreting a single speaker is conceptually prior to interpreting a language for a community, since the latter requires identifying a group of speakers each of whom speaks (nearly) the same language.[147] This does not mean, however, that we can arrive at an adequate account of a speaker's language without considering how the words he uses would be interpreted in the mouth of any speaker of the language. Consider, for example, the case of the first person pronoun, 'I', in English. If we did not consider its interpretation in the mouth of an arbitrary speaker of English, we would miss an important aspect of its meaning, namely, that it refers to whoever uses it. In fact, a general feature of context sensitive terms in English is that they are interpreted relative to their use by a particular speaker. This means that a radical interpreter must gather evidence for the interpretation of individual speakers, but also gather evidence relevant to the interpretation of sentences of a given speaker's language as used by an arbitrary speaker of it. In what follows we will assume that the radical interpreter has identified a community of speakers who speak the same language, and is considering how to interpret their language. (In Chapter 17, we will consider the claim that some interpreters of Davidson have advanced that he has rejected the conception of a language we are appealing to here.)

As we noted in Chapter 11, ultimately (it seems), the radical interpreter relies only on behavioral evidence in confirming for a community of speakers an interpretive truth theory that meets appropriate formal constraints (henceforth, this qualification about appropriate formal constraints will be presupposed).

---

[147] When Davidson introduced the project of radical interpretation, he represented the project as issuing in a truth theory for the language of a community, that is, as having theorems of the form, "(T) 'Es Regnet' is true-in-German when spoken by x at time t if and only if it is raining near x at t" (Davidson 2001c (1973): 135). He goes on to say, however (ibid.), "The appeal to a speech community cuts a corner but begs no question: speakers belong to the same speech community if the same theories of interpretation work for them."

Radical Interpretation

To confirm a truth theory for a language, we must have a grammar for it, since the theory relies on structurally describing sentences of the object language on the basis of their parts. So, one task for the radical interpreter is to identify the syntactic structure of the object language on the basis of behavioral evidence. It is not clear how confident we should be that this can be done on the basis of the evidence we allow the radical interpreter, but for the sake of argument we will allow that it can be done.

Even with a grammar for the object language, however, it is far from clear how behavioral evidence can combine with it to yield evidence employable in confirming a truth theory for the language. Davidson makes a brilliant suggestion. From the standpoint of the radical interpreter, we cannot assume we know in advance what speakers believe, or what their sentences mean. However, knowledge of which sentences speakers *hold true* (that is, which sentences they believe to be true) presupposes neither knowledge of the detailed contents of their beliefs, nor of the meanings of the sentences they hold true.[148] And what sentences speakers hold true can be seen, by and large, to be the result of what they believe about the world generally, and what they believe about what their sentences mean (relativized to a context). For if one believes that p, and thinks that s means that p, then given that if it is true that p, and s means that p, then s is true, one can rationally infer that s is true. If we knew that at a time t a speaker S held true a sentence s, and if we knew either what s means relative to S and t, or the belief on the basis of which he held s true (assuming he knows the meaning of s, and arrives at his belief that s is true at t on the basis of that and his other beliefs), we could solve for the other element of the pair. If we begin only with knowledge of which sentences speakers hold true, we may hope yet to break into the circle of meaning and belief by finding a further constraint that would allow us to hold one element of the pair fixed while solving for the other (see esp. Davidson 2001a (1974): 145–8.). As Davidson puts it at one point, "behavioral or dispositional facts that can be described in ways that do not assume interpretations, but on which a theory of interpretation can be based, will necessarily be a vector of meaning and

---

[148] It might be objected that knowledge of a speaker's hold true attitudes is as suspect as knowledge of his other attitudes. Is the thought that the sentence 'Caesar conquered Gaul' is true as spoken in English at t less sophisticated than the thought that blood is red? Furthermore, if, by and large, for any belief, a speaker holds true a sentence that expresses its content on the basis of knowing the meaning of the sentence, it seems that by allowing the interpreter knowledge of the contents of a speaker's hold true attitudes, one gives him information sufficient to interpret at least some of the speaker's sentences, i.e. sentences about sentences being true. We do not ourselves see that Davidson has a good reason to think we are in any better position to identify hold true attitudes without interpreting speech than we are to identify other sorts of attitudes, but we will not press the point.

belief" (ibid. 148). Thus, Davidson suggests that we suppose the interpreter can arrive at knowledge of speakers' hold true attitudes[149] on the basis of purely behavioral evidence, and that this, suitably constrained, can provide the appropriate basis for confirming a theory of truth for their language.[150] We will return to the question of which additional constraints are required below.

Ultimately, as we already remarked, we will expect our identification of hold true attitudes (not to be confused with assertions) to be based on behavioral evidence. If this evidence enables us to determine that someone has performed an assertion, that will reveal directly, if we judge it sincere, that the speaker holds the asserted sentence true. Other speech acts, however, if we can identify them, may also reveal which sentences a speaker holds true.[151] A command or request indicates that the speaker holds true the negation of a sentence closely related to the sentence uttered. For instance, if, in English, a speaker issues

---

[149] It is a presupposition of this procedure that speakers have hold true attitudes directed toward most or all of their belief expressing sentences. This might be thought to be rather doubtful, since many speakers are not very reflective. This would certainly require some sort of reworking of the project, if so (as seems likely). But perhaps this idealization is not too damaging, since the information about what sentences speakers would hold true in various circumstances presumably could be extracted from a complete account of their dispositions (if information about what hold true attitudes they actually had could be), and used in place of information about actual hold true attitudes as evidence for the next stage of interpretation. For we may suppose speakers do, or are already disposed to, have beliefs about what their words and sentences mean, and are capable of inferring from this and what they believe to the truth of sentences expressing their beliefs.

[150] In "Belief and the Basis of Meaning," Davidson says (2001*a* (1974): 144): "I hope it will be granted that it is plausible to say we can tell when a speaker holds a sentence to be true without knowing what he means by the sentence, or what beliefs he holds about its unknown subject matter, or what detailed intentions do or might prompt him to utter it." The same theme is echoed in "Thought and Talk" (2001 (1975): 161): "The interlocking of the theory of action with interpretation will emerge in another way if we ask how a method of interpretation is tested. In the end, the answer must be that it helps bring order into our understanding of behavior. But at an intermediate stage, we can see that the attitude of *holding true* or *accepting as true*, as directed towards sentences, must play a central role in giving form to a theory." Finally, Davidson says, in "The Structure and Content of Truth," that "meaning is entirely determined by observable behavior, even readily observable behavior" (1990*b*: 314). Of course, initial identifications of hold true attitudes are subject to revision in the light of further evidence and how well the theory one arrives at on the basis of an initial assignment of hold true attitudes fits all of one's evidence. There is therefore no commitment here to seeing hold true attitudes as reducible one by one to behavior. The choice of knowledge of hold true attitudes as a salient intermediate stage of interpretation echoes Quine's appeal to assents to sentences as basic evidence in radical translation (see Quine 1960: ch. 2).

[151] This point is made in "Thought and Talk" (2001 (1975): 161–2): "most uses of language tell us directly, or shed light on the question, whether a speaker holds a sentence to be true. If a speaker's purpose is to give information, or to make an honest assertion, then normally the speaker believes he is uttering a sentence true under the circumstances. If he utters a command, we may usually take this as showing that he holds a certain sentence (closely related to the sentence uttered) to be false; similarly for many cases of deceit. When a question is asked, it generally indicates that the questioner does not know whether a certain sentence is true; and so on."

a command by uttering "Close the door!", we can usually infer that he holds true the negation of "The door is closed" (or, perhaps better, simply holds false "The door is closed"). This inference requires our having already identified syntactically the different moods, and the relation of the form of a sentence in the imperative to what we can call its propositional core, that is, the sentence which the speaker wants the person to whom the command is directed to make true; for a speaker may also issue a command by using an indicative sentence, such as "You will polish my boots, then put out the trash."[152] But granting this, we could infer from the sincere use of either sentence the speaker held true the negation of a closely related sentence, without knowing the meanings of any sentence. Similarly, a question, if asked in search of information, reveals that the speaker suspends belief about the truth of a pair of sentences or a range of sentences (any of which would answer the question); a promise, if delivered sincerely, indicates the speaker holds true a sentence about the future involving himself. In these and other ways, identification of speech acts on the basis of behavioral evidence, if possible, will lead to the identification of a speaker's hold true attitudes; though we may also hope to be able to infer that a speaker has certain hold true attitudes on the basis of non-linguistic evidence.[153]

2. The Analogy with Empirical Decision Theory

If we know what a speaker's hold true attitudes are, we can identify his beliefs or meanings, if we can fix the other member of the pair. This way of formulating the problem was suggested to Davidson by a parallel with the empirical testing of decision theory. The parallel, which he draws explicitly (e.g. "Belief and the Basis of Meaning," 2001a (1974): 145–8),[154] can be deployed at various points

---

[152] The independence of the mood of a sentence and the force with which it is uttered (statement, command, question, and so on), as this example illustrates, may elicit doubt that we would be in a position to use information of this sort prior to progress in interpretation, since it requires us to have identified the differences between moods and logical constants such as negation. If we can settle questions of logical form prior to interpreting predicates, as Davidson sometimes assumes (see 2001c (1973): 136), this will present no problem; otherwise, the availability of the sorts of evidence here discussed must await independent access to what a speaker's sentences mean, perhaps through more direct inferences to a speaker's hold true attitudes. In any case, since Davidson restricts his attention mostly to hold true attitudes, we will do so as well.

[153] We will consider a sophistication of this picture by the addition of degrees of belief or confidence in the truth of a sentence, and correspondingly degrees of desirability of sentences, in Ch. 16.

[154] Davidson's early work on decision theory with Patrick Suppes and J. C. C. McKenzie played an important formative role in his thinking both about interpretation theory and the philosophy of action (Davidson *et al.* 1957). Davidson recounts some of this early work and the morals he drew from it in "Hempel on Explaining Action" (2001a (1976): 269–73). There is a sense in which one can see all of Davidson's work as extensions of the early work on decision theory.

to illuminate his conception of interpretation theory, and is worth considering in some detail. We describe the parallel briefly here.

Decision theory, or rational choice theory, is concerned with examining the conditions under which it is rational to prefer, or to adopt, one or another of available actions. If we call choice the manifestation of preference in action, one's rational choices are determined by one's preferences among the options one believes to be open to oneself. One's preferences are determined in turn by two factors: the *relative desirability* of outcomes of actions open to one to undertake, and what one believes the chances of each outcome are (i.e. the *subjective probability* one assigns to each possible outcome). For example, imagine one is faced with the choice of whether to accept a bet on the winner of a race, that is, the choice of whether to agree, or not, to *pay* a certain amount *if* one's choice of a winner is *incorrect*, in order to *get* a payoff *if* one's choice is *correct*. In this case, the rational choice, between accepting the bet or not, will depend on the relative desirability assigned to the outcomes of winning and losing the bet, and on what one estimates the probability of each, and on the relative desirability of not accepting the bet.

Suppose one is considering a bet on Long Shot's winning a race that pays off twice what one must pay if one loses, and that (improbably) one values money in proportion to its amount, no matter the amount. Suppose also that whether Long Shot wins or loses is otherwise an event that one is indifferent to, that is, that otherwise there is neither cost nor benefit to one in Long Shot's winning or losing. Then, using numbers to track relative desirabilities and subjective probabilities, if one estimates the chances of Long Shot winning at .8 (and so of not winning at $1 - .8 = .2$, all probabilities summing to 1), one can evaluate the options of betting versus not betting by summing the relative desirability of each possible outcome weighted by its subjective probability as follows,

$$\text{Value of betting} = .8 \times 2N + .2 \times -N = 1.4N$$
$$\text{Value of not betting} = .8 \times 0 + .2 \times 0 = 0$$

where 'N' represents the value of the money bet. Since the value of betting is greater than that of not betting, for someone with these relative desirabilities and subjective probabilities, the rational choice is to bet. If, on the other hand, the probabilities had been reversed, that is, if one estimated Long Shot's chance of winning at .2, then the value of betting would have been $-.4N$, and the rational choice would be to abstain from betting.

Decision theory is normative. Its prescriptions, like those above, are meant to show what it is to act rationally in choice situations. But it is not just normative, for its axioms are usually treated as more or less constitutive of what it is to be an agent—at least this is Davidson's position. We say 'more or less', because there can be varying degrees of falling off from perfect rationality without throwing into complete disarray our picture of someone as an agent. But constitutive, because too much departure from decision theoretic norms of rationality threatens to undermine our conception of someone as an agent at all. Thus, the structure of a theory about the preferences of a particular agent, like that of a Tarski-style truth theory for a particular speaker's language, can be laid out to some extent prior to its application. What is left unspecified in a Tarski-style theory is which particular assignments of satisfaction conditions are to be made to which particular expressions in the object language; whereas what is left unspecified in a decision theory prior to its empirical application is the assignments of subjective probabilities and relative desirabilities. In the case of decision theory, empirical application requires determining from the actual choices a person makes what his preferences are, and then assigning relative desirabilities and subjective probabilities in conformity with these preferences. Since his preferences are determined jointly by his relative desirabilities and subjective probabilities, if we knew what his preferences were and either his relative desirabilities or his subjective probabilities, we could solve for the other.

However, if we seek to confirm a particular assignment of subjective probabilities and ranking of options for an agent without presupposing we know either, then we must attempt to find a way of constraining one of the two degrees of freedom in interpreting an agent's actual choices. A solution to this problem was originally provided by Frank Ramsey.[155] What we need to find are certain sorts of patterns among an agent's preferences that suffice to fix one of their two independent determiners, given how preferences are the resultant of desirabilities and subjective probabilities. So, suppose an agent is *indifferent* between two bets on an event E, the occurrence or non-occurrence of which itself he is indifferent to. Let us suppose the agent thinks there is no difference, for example, between the Republicans and the Democrats, and the event E in question is a Republican's winning the next presidential election. On the first bet he receives something ($10, e.g.) on which he places a value V, if E occurs, and something ($20, e.g.) on which he places a value V^*, if E does not. On the second bet this is *reversed*: he receives something on which he places a value V^* if E occurs, and something on which he places a value V if E does not. Letting 'p' stand for the probability he assigns to E's occurring, and 'v' and 'v^*' stand for numbers assigned to the values he assigns to the outcomes to

---

[155] Ramsey 1990 (1931).

keep track of their ranking,[156] his *indifference* between the two bets, that is, his placing equal (expected) value on the outcome of either bet, can be represented as follows:

$$pv + (1 - p)v^* = pv^* + (1 - p)v$$

This is equivalent to

$$2pv - 2pv^* = v - v^*$$

which yields

$$p = \tfrac{1}{2}.$$

Thus, by identifying a special pattern among the agent's preferences, one can solve for subjective probability by just using data in the form, ultimately, of the agent's choice behavior. After identifying the subjective probability the agent assigns to one sort of event, one can use it in turn to investigate his rankings among others on the basis of the relative desirability he assigns to them, and use this information in turn to investigate the subjective probabilities he assigns.[157]

Davidson conceives of the task facing the radical interpreter, who wants to confirm a truth theory for a speaker's language, as analogous to the task of someone who wishes to confirm a particular assignment of relative values and subjective probabilities to an agent: " Broadly stated, my theme is that we should think of meanings and beliefs as interrelated constructs of a single theory just as we already view subjective values and probabilities as interrelated constructs of decision theory" (2001*a* (1974): 146). Corresponding to preferences are hold true attitudes, and to choices, speech acts. The radical interpreter's problem parallels that of the decision theorist. The former has to determine from preferences an assignment of relative values and subjective probabilities; the latter has to determine from sentences held true an assignment of meanings to sentences and contents to beliefs. As with decision theory, we may hope that some pattern among sentences held true will help to reveal their meanings. The patterns among sentences held true we could expect to find would be due to dependencies between the truth values of sentences that the speaker takes there to be because of beliefs about sentence meanings (entailment relations,

---

[156] It is important not to confuse the numbers we use to keep track of the desirabilities and subjective probabilities with the desirabilities and subjective probabilities. We do calculations on numbers representing desirabilities and subjective probabilities in order to represent the relative ranking among preferences: the legitimacy of doing this requires that we be able to show that there is a structure in the phenomenon we correctly keep track of with the relations between the numbers we assign to the different desirabilities and subjective probabilities.

[157] The interested reader can find a method of this sort described in Jeffrey 1983: ch. 3

necessary truth) or beliefs about natural laws. For example, if the speaker thinks 'bachelor' means 'unmarried man', then he will think that 'Abe is a bachelor' entails 'Abe is unmarried' and 'Abe is a man'. If he thinks it is a law of nature that unsupported objects close to the earth's surface fall, then he will think that if 'X is an unsupported object near the earth's surface' is true at t, then 'X will fall' is true at t. This will provide important clues to such things as logical form and semantic entailments.[158] However, it would still leave open the empirical conditions for the application of most predicates. To make further progress, then, we must ask how our evidence in the form of sentences held true by a speaker can be combined with our other evidence to break into the circle of belief and meaning. As Davidson puts it, "[i]n order to sort things out, what is needed is a method for holding one factor steady while the other is studied" (Davidson 2001 (1975): 167).

3. The Introduction of the Principle of Charity

The principle of charity is introduced to do this work. To understand its role, however, we must first consider what the interpreter can learn about a speaker's hold true attitudes by observing the speaker in his environment.

The hold true attitudes which will provide the first entry into someone's language, according to Davidson, will be those directed toward sentences a speaker sometimes holds true and sometimes does not hold true (or holds false) in response to events or conditions in his environment. These we will call occasion sentences; these sentences *generally* contain a context sensitive element ('indexical sentences', for short). Thus, for example, for us, 'You are standing on my foot' is an occasion sentence. But not all *indexical* sentences will be *occasion* sentences. 'My favorite color is red', for example, may be held true constantly by someone regardless of events and conditions in his environment, and 'I exist' is held true all the time for everyone who speaks English (assuming all our beliefs are represented by hold true attitudes). Occasion sentences need not be just sentences held true for relatively short periods of time. In practice, as we will see, what matters is how well one can correlate hold true attitudes with what is going on in the speaker's environment. 'It is day' and 'It is night' are held true for relatively long periods each day and night by English speakers,

---

[158] For example, if we have in hand a syntactic analysis of the object language, and we find a rough pattern of the following sort among the speaker's hold true attitudes, "*Ceteris paribus*, whenever the speaker holds true a sentence of the form $\ulcorner \boxtimes \phi \psi \urcorner$, he holds true ϕ, and he holds true ψ, and whenever he holds true ϕ, and he holds true ψ, he holds true $\ulcorner \boxtimes \phi \psi \urcorner$ but not otherwise," then we have evidence that '$\boxtimes$' expresses conjunction. We do not say this is conclusive evidence.

but one could easily imagine noticing a salient correlation between conditions in the environment and English speakers holding these sentences true which would help in their interpretation. Similarly, 'It is winter' and 'It is summer' could be correlated with the seasons, and even, for example, 'The economy is in a recession' with economic conditions. The empirical interpretation of predicates will rely on occasion sentences, since in these sentences words in the object language are applied to what is going on around the speaker, in a way that allows us to correlate what is going on in his environment with what his words mean.

Note that as we have characterized occasion sentences, they may differ from speaker to speaker; they are identified not as some class of sentences containing special terms, but relative to speakers' dispositions to hold them true in response to conditions in their environment.

If we consider occasion sentences, the principal evidence we have relating to their interpretation consists of the conditions under which speakers hold them true. This is the point at which our observations bear most importantly on the interpretations we wish to assign to speakers' sentences. Given our identification of speakers' hold true attitudes, and the conditions under which they hold true occasion sentences, we can inductively establish (*ceteris paribus*) laws[159] of the form,

(L)   For all speakers S, times t, *ceteris paribus*, S holds true s at t iff p.[160]

where 'S' ranges over members of the target linguistic community,[161] 'p' is replaced by an open sentence that specifies relative to time, and perhaps other contextual features, conditions under which speakers hold the sentence

---

[159] We take no stand on the analysis of *ceteris paribus* ('other things being equal') laws and will simply assume a common-sense understanding of the sort of rough *ceteris paribus* laws invoked in everyday causal explanations.

[160] Guttenplan 1985 raises the question of how Davidson can treat T-form sentences as laws given his anomalous monism, i.e. the position according to which while every token mental event is a token physical event, there are no *strict* psychophysical laws. In this connection, it is important to note that L-sentences are *ceteris paribus*, not strict, laws. Thus, Davidson's position here prima facie does not commit him to strict psychophysical laws. Commitment to strict psychophysical laws would follow only if he were committed to it being possible to eliminate in principle the *ceteris paribus* clause without shifting to a different family of concepts than those expressed in the *ceteris paribus* law. See "Mental Events" (Davidson 2001*b* (1970)).

[161] Restricting the quantifier to range over members of a linguistic community C (at a time period t) has the same effect for the truth theory as relativizing the truth predicate to a language. To transform the truth theory into a theory for the language spoken by members of C at t, we would introduce a name for the language by way of a description, the language spoken by such and such a linguistic community during such and such a period, and replace the truth predicate with one relativized to the language, and drop the restriction on the quantifier to members of C.

true,[162] and '*s*' denotes an *occasion sentence*. We will call such sentences *L*-sentences. Note that *L*-sentences are inductively confirmed, and are about the conditions under which occasion sentences are held true by a speaker. The law must be a *ceteris paribus* law, because we cannot expect speakers always to hold true a sentence in appropriate circumstances. Though there is a rabbit in the vicinity, a speaker may not hold true 'There is a rabbit', even if it means that *there is a rabbit*, because he fails to notice it, or he thinks he is suffering from a hallucination, or the like. Similarly, a speaker may on occasion mistake a muskrat he sees in the reeds for a rabbit.

L-sentences express the interpreter's evidence at the point at which it bears most directly on the interpretation of speakers' sentences. We want to move from this to something relevant to confirming a truth theory, namely, a state-ment not of the conditions under which members of a language community *hold true* sentences, but rather a statement of the conditions under which those sentences *are* true. Since *L*-sentences obviously do not entail sentences that state such conditions, we must augment our theory with a principle that will allow us to bridge the gap, that is, a principle which warrants inferring from *L*-sentences corresponding *T*-form sentences (henceforth, '*TF*-sentences') that can be used to project an interpretive truth theory for the entire language.

(TF)   For all speakers S, times t, s is true for S at t iff p.

We treat this principle, for now, as an assumption to be added to what the interpreter knows which enables him to infer from *L*-sentences corresponding *TF*-sentences. The principle Davidson famously proposes for bridging this gap he has called, following Quine, 'the principle of charity'.[163] The ambition that this represents should not be underestimated. It is on the face of it amazing to think that, just from noticing correlations of the sorts summed up by *L*-sentences, we could arrive with confidence at any view about whether the sentences held true are true, let alone at an assignment of meanings to them, without any assumptions about the speakers other than that they are speakers (and, in particular, without assumptions about their thoughts, which we are forbidden on Davidson's conception of the project). Yet, that is Davidson's ambition, through his surrogate, the radical interpreter.

---

[162] This locution, as we have noted before, is not intended to introduce a new kind of entity, a condition, but rather is a way of talking about which sentence goes in for '*p*' in (L) in order for it to be true.

[163] Quine credits the phrase to Wilson 1959. See Quine's comment on "Belief and the Basis of Meaning" (Quine 1974: 328).

It should be noted at the outset, in the light of the analogy we have drawn explicitly with decision theory, that there is no analog of the principle of charity in Ramsey's solution to the supposed parallel problem in the case of breaking into the circle of desirabilities and subjective probabilities. The principle of charity, on which we elaborate below, is introduced because patterns among hold true attitudes, as we have just noted, are not sufficient to fix one of the two factors which determine hold true attitudes (belief and meaning), to solve for the other. The principle of charity, in its role in fixing one of belief or meaning so that we can solve for the other, given hold true attitudes, requires support *beyond* any provided by abstract considerations governing coherent patterns of beliefs, meanings, and hold true (and other) attitudes. It will be, of course, crucial, then, to see what sort of justification can be provided for the principle introduced to do the job. Before we come to that, however, we must clarify exactly what that principle is.

4. Three Interpretations

Stating the principle of charity is not as straightforward as it might be, since Davidson gives it what appear to be at least three importantly different formulations. Which formulation one takes as basic has important consequences for the status of the theory reached on its basis. Furthermore, its distinct formulations have not been generally acknowledged in the secondary literature, and so different commentators have come to different conclusions about the tenability of the principle on the basis of its different formulations. For these reasons, each formulation deserves close attention, though it will become clear in the light of how Davidson frames the problem that one must be taken as basic.

Before we proceed, we want to limit discussion of the principle of charity to just that aspect of it which is relevant to moving specifically from *L*-sentences to *TF*-sentences. Davidson usually treats under the heading of 'the principle of charity' a family of principles, not all of which are directly relevant to providing a warrant from inferring *TF*-sentences from *L*-sentences. We will return to the question of what else is included under this heading in Chapter 13.

With this qualification in hand, we can state each of the three formulations suggested by the text, and examine them in turn. The first is that, *ceteris paribus*, a speaker's *hold true attitudes directed toward occasion sentences are* true. The second is that, *ceteris paribus*, a speaker's *beliefs about his environment* are in fact true. The third is that, *ceteris paribus*, the speaker and interpreter *agree* about the speaker's environment. We take the second as basic. The first and third transparently fail to achieve all that Davidson wants from the principle of charity (restricted to its application to the transition from *L*-sentences to *TF*-sentence).

The first interpretation is suggested in the following passages (there are others as well[164]):

> The general policy . . . is to choose truth conditions that do as well as possible in making speakers hold sentences true when (according to the theory and the theory builder's view of the facts) those sentences are true.   (Davidson 2001*a* (1974): 152)

> I propose that we take the fact that speakers of a language hold a sentence to be true (under observed circumstances) as prima-facie evidence that the sentence is true under those circumstances.   (Ibid.)

This proposal is, in short, to treat *L*-sentences as (defeasible) evidence for the corresponding *TF*-sentences; the relevant principle, which we will call 'Veracity', is, with '*s*' restricted to occasion sentences:

> (Veracity) For all speakers S, times t, sentences s, *ceteris paribus*: S holds true s at t iff s is true(S, t).

Davidson needs a quantified *bi*conditional here rather than just the left to right quantified conditional, because he wants to infer from *L*-sentences to *TF*-sentences, which are quantified biconditionals. The *ceteris paribus* clause pre-empts absurdity in both directions (speakers are not omniscient, and they make mistakes). Veracity says, in effect, that for each sentence s, there are conditions such that, if they hold, a speaker holds true s just in case it is true relative to the speaker at the time at which he holds it true.

---

[164] A passage with elements of both the first and third interpretations is this passage from "Truth and Meaning," Davidson's earliest mention of the principle of charity: "What [the linguist] must do is find out, however he can, what sentences the alien holds true in his own tongue (or better, to what degree he holds them true). The linguist then will attempt to construct a characterization of truth-for-the-alien which yields, so far as possible, a mapping of sentences held true (or false) by the alien on to sentences held true (or false) by the linguist" (2001*c* (1967): 27). Attention here is focused only on the other's hold true attitudes, but the requirement is not that they be true, but that they be paired with sentences the linguist holds true. Consider also, "It would be possible to generate a correct theory simply by considering sentences to be true when held true . . ." (Davidson 2001 (1975): 168), followed immediately by a statement of the principle which corresponds to the second interpretation, "provided, that is, all beliefs, at least as far as they could be expressed, were correct." Though Davidson does not distinguish these different formulations, as we will see, they are importantly different. Another expression of the first form is "We get a first approximation to a finished theory by assigning to sentences of a speaker conditions of truth that actually obtain (in our own opinion) just when the speaker holds those sentences true" (Davidson 2001*c* (1974): 196).

186

To see what's wrong with Veracity, it will be helpful first to work through how the interpreter will proceed from this point to confirm an interpretive truth theory for a speaker. (We remind the reader that we have adjusted the goal of the interpreter's project explicitly to that of confirming an interpretive truth theory.) The procedure described will be the same regardless of which formulation of the principle of charity we consider, but considering it here will help to highlight what kind of assumption is needed to bridge the gap between *L*-sentences and corresponding *TF*-sentences *in the right way*.

With Veracity and a range of *L*-sentences in hand, we would accept (tentatively) a range *R* of *TF*-sentences. We then construct a truth theory by postulating a set of axioms for the vocabulary of the object language sentences for which there are *TF*-sentences in *R*, which have those *TF*-sentences as canonical theorems. Thus, *TF*-sentences we arrive at play the role of target canonical theorems. They are therefore evidence at an intermediate stage for the truth theory that the radical interpreter constructs for members of a linguistic community, to serve as the core of an interpretation theory for them.

L-sentences are inductively confirmed laws. An interpretation theory, of which a truth theory is the core, is a theory for the language of a speaker or group of speakers, any of whose potential utterances we want to be able to interpret. We therefore seek an interpretation theory which will give the right results not just for those occasions on which we have observed speakers, but also for the future, and for a range of relevantly similar counterfactual situations. Thus, we want our truth theory, which generalizes at least over times, to be projectible and counterfactual supporting. Since the axioms of the theory are projected to entail the *TF*-sentences that we derive from *L*-sentences, if the derived theory is to be projectible, the *TF*-sentences must be as well. This requires Veracity to be at least as strong as the *L*-sentences to which it applies, that is, that Veracity must be at least nomically necessary. We will come below to the question of what support might be adduced for bridge principles like Veracity, but it is important for now to recognize that they must be at least nomically necessary, if *TF*-sentences derived from them and *L*-sentences are to be nomically necessary, and so, capable of supporting predictions and counterfactual statements. If the *TF*-sentences so derived are nomically necessary, the axioms postulated on their basis will be as well.

Now we can state what the problem is with Veracity. The radical interpreter aims to confirm an interpretive truth theory for the speaker he is interpreting. Since the axioms of the truth theory are projected to entail the *TF*-sentences derived from *L*-sentences, for the theory arrived at to be interpretive, those

TF-sentences must be interpretive, that is, they must be *T*-sentences (in our terminology). In Chapter 7, we argued that in order for *TF*-sentences to be interpretive, it was not enough that they be nomically necessary; that is, their having the status of laws, and so being counterfactual supporting, is insufficient to establish that they are interpretive. Thus, if *all* we know about them is that they are law-like, we do not yet know enough to know that the theory we project on their basis is interpretive. Therefore, the principle used to move from *L*-sentences to *TF*-sentences must license the latter as interpretive, that is, what we must assume is that *L*-sentences are (defeasible) evidence that corresponding *TF*-sentences are true *and* interpretive. Veracity, however, is too weak to meet this requirement. For Veracity, even assuming it is nomically necessary, gives us at most that *TF*-sentences derived from *L*-sentences are nomically necessary. But we need something sufficient to entail that, *ceteris paribus*, if *s* is an inductively confirmed *L*-sentence, its corresponding *TF*-sentence is interpretive. That is, we need something sufficient to entail what we will call 'Interpretiveness'.

> (Interpretiveness) For any sentences s_1, s_2, by and large,
> if s_1 is an inductively confirmed *L*-sentence and s_2 is its
> corresponding *TF*-sentence, then s_2 is interpretive.

We said above that, although some passages in Davidson's corpus suggest Veracity is what he understands by the principle of charity, these passages do not express his intention fully. He has in mind a principle which is closely related to, and entails, Veracity, and which is also supposed to suffice for Interpretiveness. This is the second interpretation we mentioned above, according to which the principle of charity is that most of a speaker's beliefs about his environment are true. This is different from saying that most of the speaker's hold true attitudes directed toward occasion sentences are true, since his hold true attitudes are not beliefs about his environment, but about the truth of sentences about his environment. This assumption is stronger than Veracity, which, when we recall the analogy Davidson draws with decision theory, we can see could not be the fundamental assumption. In that analogy, hold true attitudes were treated as analogous to preferences. Preferences are the resultant of two factors, an agent's relative values and subjective probabilities. In order to solve for either, we need to hold the other fixed. The idea is to employ a similar strategy with respect to interpretation theory.

Hold true attitudes are the result of two factors, what the speaker believes, on the one hand, and what his sentences mean, on the other. The connection is made by the *assumption* that the speaker knows, by and large, what his sentences mean, and infers from his knowledge of what his sentences mean, and his beliefs, that sentences that express his beliefs are true. In the case of occasion sentences, the causal chain that produces his hold true attitudes toward such sentences starts with some event or condition in his environment, which causes him to form a belief, which in turn causes him, given his knowledge of the meanings of sentences in his language, to hold true the sentence (or sentences) of his language which at that time expresses that belief. Given this assumption about the etiology of most of a speaker's hold true attitudes, the suggestion is that we can arrive at an interpretation of a speaker's sentences, in the light of correlations between his hold true attitudes and conditions in his environment, by assuming that, *ceteris paribus*, those beliefs about his environment prompted by it (his beliefs whose contents are expressed by occasion sentences) are true, that is, what we will call 'Charity'.

> (Charity) For any speaker S, time t, belief b, *ceteris paribus*: b is a belief of S's at t about and prompted by S's environment iff b is true.

(Again, the biconditional formulation is needed because we aim to derive biconditional *TF*-sentences.)

Evidence that Charity is Davidson's considered position on this aspect of the principle of charity is easy to find. In "Radical Interpretation," the idea that we are holding beliefs about the environment fixed in order to solve for the meaning of sentences held true comes out clearly in the following passage,

This method is intended to solve the problem of the interdependence of belief and meaning by holding belief constant as far as possible while solving for meaning. This is accomplished by assigning truth conditions to alien sentences that make native speakers right when plausibly possible, according, of course, to our own view of what is right. (Davidson 2001c (1973): 137)

This conception of the task emerges also in "Thought and Talk":

The attitude of holding a sentence true (under specified conditions) relates belief and interpretation in a fundamental way. We can know that a speaker holds a sentence to be true without knowing what he means by it or what belief it expresses for him. But if we know he holds the sentence true *and* we know how to interpret it, then we can make a correct attribution of belief. Symmetrically, if we know what belief a sentence held true expresses, we know how to interpret it. The methodological problem of interpretation is to see how, given the sentences a man accepts as true under given circumstances, to work out what his beliefs are and what his words mean.   (Davidson 2001 (1975): 162)

And, as we have mentioned, the analogy with the problem of determining desirabilities and subjective probabilities from preferences in decision theory shows that Davidson intends the principle of charity to play the role of holding fixed one of the two factors that result in hold true attitudes, namely, belief, in order to "solve for meaning."[165]

A third way Davidson sometimes puts the principle of charity (and a way in which the principle is often interpreted) merits discussion, namely, as we said above, as the assumption that the speaker agrees with the interpreter about the nature of their shared environment (explicable error aside). That is, as what we will call 'Agreement', when, as above, the content of the beliefs involve events or conditions in the environment shared by interpreter and speaker:

> (Agreement) *Ceteris paribus*: the interpreter believes p iff the speaker believes p.

This interpretation too receives support from passages in Davidson's work, such as the following:[166]

We want a theory that satisfies the formal constraints on a theory of truth, and that maximizes agreement, in the sense of making Kurt (and others) right, as far as we can tell, as often as possible. (Davidson 2001*c* (1973): 136)

So in the end what must be counted in favor of a method of interpretation is that it puts the interpreter in general agreement with the speaker: according to the method, the speaker holds a sentence true under specified conditions, and these conditions obtain, in the opinion of the interpreter, just when the speaker holds the sentence to be true. (Davidson 2001 (1975): 169)

One result of the interpreter's applying Charity will be that he finds the speaker largely in agreement with him about their shared environment, at least in the sense that the beliefs attributed to the speaker will be shared by the interpreter. (Of course, the interpreter may believe things about the environment

---

[165] Even if the textual evidence underdetermines whether it's Veracity or Charity Davidson explicitly holds, it's clear he must have had at least Charity in mind, for it alone can make sense of the vector metaphor, that held true attitudes are a vector of meaning and belief. We hold true the sentences we do on the basis of what we believe about the world and what we think our sentences mean, i.e. we hold true those sentences whose meanings on the occasion express our beliefs then. With that in mind, the right thing to say is that Charity comes in at the level of beliefs about the world, and not about sentences.

[166] Other examples are, "Torn between the need to make sense of a speaker's words and the need to make sense of the pattern of his beliefs, the best we can do is choose a theory of translation that maximizes agreement" (Davidson 2001 (1968): 101), and, "I apply the Principle of Charity across the board. So applied, it counsels us quite generally to prefer theories of interpretation that minimize disagreement" (Davidson 2001*b*: p. xvii).

190

the speaker has no beliefs about, compatibly with the interpreter interpreting the speaker.) Thus, Charity requires Agreement. However, Agreement and Charity are distinct. The difference turns out to be important, as we will see when we come to Davidson's arguments against the possibility of massive error in our empirical beliefs in Chapter 19. If only Agreement were required for interpretation, we would require an additional assumption to move from agreement between speaker and interpreter to a shared *true* picture of the world. Charity requires assuming a speaker's beliefs are true, and Agreement does not. We can squeeze Charity out of Agreement only by assuming the interpreter's beliefs are mostly true. It is clear, we think, in light of the quotations above, that Davidson's intention is that the principle of charity, as applied to occasion sentences, should be interpreted as Charity, and not as Agreement. Not to trespass too far on matters we will discuss in detail later, we will set aside for now further discussion of the importance of this particular distinction.

Before turning to the question of whether Charity is up to its assigned job, we should discuss the role of the *ceteris paribus* clause in these principles. The reason it is needed is that the interpreter must be free to reject an *L*-sentence as providing adequate support for a corresponding *TF*-sentence if, in light of every *L*-sentence he has assembled as evidence, he achieves a better overall theory of the speaker by dropping some of the corresponding *TF*-sentences. Thus, the principle that takes us from *L*-sentences to interpretive *TF*-sentences must itself be *ceteris paribus*. The interpreter needs that, by and large, *L*-sentences license corresponding interpretive *TF*-sentences. But it may be that, in the end, certain *L*-sentences have their truth explained without sanctioning corresponding *TF*-sentences as interpretive. Perhaps all the rabbits in a speaker's environment, unbeknownst to him, have been replaced by mechanical replicas, to preserve the charm of seeing leporiforms upon the grass in the evening, without the danger of uncontrolled reproduction in the absence of natural predators. As a result, *ceteris paribus*, he holds true 'That's a rabbit' when and only when he sees a mechanical replica of a rabbit. In light of our overall theory, we may want to attribute to him systematic error rather than a belief that mechanical replicas of rabbits populate his environment.[167]

---

[167] Some critics have ignored Davidson's cautions about this, supposing him to require that speakers be found in conformity with one's own views even when their circumstances would make us expect them to be led to mistaken beliefs. For example, "Speakers can be allowed to differ more often and more radically with respect to some sentences than others, and there is no reason not to take into account the observed or inferred individual differences that may be thought to have caused anomalies (as seen by the theory)" (Davidson 2001*a* (1974): 152). Note also that in a footnote to

Finally, it is important to recall that our discussion here has focused on what is needed to get, in particular, from *L*-sentences to *TF*-sentences. The principle of charity is often, however, stated by Davidson more broadly than in Charity, namely, as the principle that we are to assume the speaker we are to interpret has largely true beliefs, *and* is largely rational (according to our lights, as Davidson says, though if we are right, this really should go without saying). Charity represents only the first part of this more general principle. We treat them separately, because, on the face of it, each part is differently motivated. Charity is motivated by the need to bridge the gap between *L*-sentences and *TF*-sentences. The requirement that speakers in general have mostly true beliefs is motivated, as we will discuss in Chapter 14, by two considerations, only one of which is Charity. The requirement that we find the other largely rational, which we return to below, is motivated by an a priori theory of agency—the subject of Davidson's work in the philosophy of action. It should also be noted that, in more recent work, he has distinguished two aspects of the principle of charity, which he calls 'the Principle of Coherence' and 'the Principle of Correspondence'.[168] The former is the requirement that the speaker's beliefs be found to be largely consistent, and thus is a part of the broader requirement that the speaker be identified as a rational agent. The latter corresponds to the requirement that the interpreter find the speaker largely right in his beliefs, which subsumes Charity.

5. Is Charity Sufficient?

We have argued that Charity is the right way to interpret Davidson's principle of charity, as it applies to bridging the gap between *L*-sentences and *TF*-sentences. We said, though, that whatever principle is used must suffice to warrant Interpretiveness. Interestingly, Charity is insufficient, and we need an even stronger assumption. The problem is that Charity requires *only*

this passage Davidson refers the reader to David Lewis's "Radical Interpretation," in which Lewis advises assigning beliefs to the speaker on the basis of what one would expect someone with his constitution and history to come to believe in his circumstances. Davidson also says, pointedly, "the fact that a theory does not make speakers universal holders of truths is not an inadequacy of the theory; the aim is not the absurd one of making disagreement and error disappear. The point is rather that widespread agreement is the only possible background against which disputes and mistakes can be interpreted" (2001a (1974): 153). This is also of importance in announcing the theme of holism and the global constraint of rationality on attitude attributions. Davidson's conception of how the principle of charity is supposed to be applied is much more like what Grandy (1973) has called the 'principle of humanity' than his critics have supposed.

[168] See e.g. Davidson 1985a: 92; 2001b (1988): 211.

that a speaker's beliefs about his environment are true, and, consequently, it does not secure his true beliefs being correlated with conditions that prompt them in a way that ensures that any statement of such conditions specifies the contents of his beliefs. Minimally, this assurance is needed to infer that *TF*-sentences derived using Charity are interpretive. For it is conditions which prompt a speaker's hold true attitudes which figure in *L*-sentences for them. If no such conditions give the contents of the speaker's beliefs, they do not provide interpretations of the sentences he holds true on that basis, relative to the context.

To see this, consider a particular speaker S^* and some sentence s_0. Suppose we know that (L1) is an *L*-sentence for S^* for s_0. Instantiate (L1) to some particular time t^*, as represented in (L2), and suppose that the *ceteris paribus* conditions are met.

(L1) For all times t, *ceteris paribus*, S^* holds true s_0 at t iff p.

(L2) *Ceteris paribus*, S^* holds true s_0 at t^* iff p^*.

'p^*' is the result of instantiating any instance of 't' in 'p' to t^*. What we want is that 'p^*' should inform us about what s_0 means relative to S^* and t^*. The question is whether Charity guarantees that it does, or, at least, gives us reason to suppose it does, barring further complications in fitting theory to evidence.

We can infer S^* has some belief at t^* whose content is expressed by s_0 for S^* at t^* solely on the basis of assumptions about why S^* comes to hold s_0 true at t^*. For we know that S^* holds s_0 true because he believes that q (for some replacement here of 'q'), and he believes that s_0 means that q, and that if s_0 means that q, then s_0 is true iff q. Given that s_0 expresses, for S^* at t^*, S^*'s belief that q, it follows that s_0 is true for S^* at t^* iff S^*'s belief that q is true.

Let us bring Charity onto the stage. Charity tells us that this environmentally prompted belief that q of S^*'s is true (*ceteris paribus*, but we ignore this for now). So, we can infer that s_0 is in fact true also for S^* at t^* *since* it expresses this true belief. Since S^* holds true s_0 at t^* iff p^*, (L2), and holds true s_0 iff S^* believes that q (from the explanation of why S^* holds true any sentence), we can infer (TF*).

(TF*) s_0 is true for S^* at t^* iff p^*.

But can we now infer (other things being equal) that s_0 means for S^* at t^* that p^*? We can only if the principles we have assembled license inferring that what replaces 'p^*' and what replaces 'q' mean the same. But Charity does not, as we have seen, guarantee this, for it does not say that the conditions we identify as prompting the belief are the ones the belief is about. To secure this, an additional assumption is needed.

6. The Assumption of Grace

It may seem that, given our account of why a speaker typically holds true a sentence, and our knowledge that in light of this the speaker holds true the sentence in just the conditions in which he believes what the sentence expresses, we could simply cull from those conditions what the sentence means for the speaker at that time. But, to repeat, we cannot do this because all that Charity licenses is that the speaker's beliefs are true under those conditions, and not that those conditions specify the contents of the speaker's beliefs. The principle needed, then, is not Charity, but the assumption that, by and large, a speaker's beliefs about his environment are about conditions prompting his having those beliefs, that is, the interpreter needs to assume what we will call 'Grace',

> (Grace) *Ceteris paribus*, when we replace '*p*' in (S)
> (S) *S* believes at *t* that *p*
> with a sentence that expresses the content of an environ-
> mentally prompted belief of *S*'s, the sentence expresses
> also a condition in *S*'s environment that prompts that
> belief.[169]

We may say, if we like, that speakers must be in a state of Grace to be interpretable from the standpoint of the radical interpreter. Grace is sufficient for Charity, since it guarantees that, *ceteris paribus*, for any environmentally prompted belief that *p* of *S*'s , *S* believes that *p* iff *p*. It secures therefore also Agreement and Veracity, whenever a speaker is interpretable by a radical interpreter.

Relative to certain assumptions, Grace also suffices for Interpretiveness. Let us assume (1).

(1) *Ceteris paribus*, the *L*-sentences that the interpreter confirms identify conditions under which a speaker holds true sentences and these conditions are also the prompting conditions, if any, which those beliefs, that are the basis on which the speaker holds those sentences true, are about.

---

[169] Note in particular that we do not assume here that the speaker is omniscient: this only says that if a belief of his is prompted by the environment, then it is about a prompting condition, so that in identifying the right prompting condition, one reads off the content of the belief.

To be explicit, we add (2), which we have already introduced.

(2) *Ceteris paribus*, a speaker S holds true s at time t because, and only because, he knows that s means(S, t) that p and believes that p, and knows that if s means(S, t) that p, then s is true(S, t) iff p.[170]

If we say, as in (1), that a speaker holds true s on the basis of a belief that p, it is to be understood in the sense of (2). Consider an L-sentence for a speaker and sentence instantiated to a time, say (L2) again.

(L2) *Ceteris paribus*, S^* holds true s_0 at t^* iff p^*.

We know that some belief is the basis of S^*'s holding true s_0 at t^*. Grace tells us the belief on the basis of which S^* holds true s_0 is about a prompting condition; (1) tells us that 'p^*' expresses the right condition. (2) tells us that s_0 expresses the content of that belief relative to S^* at t^*. So, we can infer, *ceteris paribus*, S^* holds true s_0 at t^* iff s_0 means(S^*, t^*) that p^*. But then, *ceteris paribus*, (3) is also true, where (and because) the sentence on the right interprets the one on the left.

(3) s_0 is true(S^*, t^*) iff p^*.

That is just what we need for Interpretiveness.

Charity is inadequate for its assigned job. The stronger principle Grace is needed. In what follows, we will substitute Grace for Charity in describing the radical interpreter's procedure, though the reader should keep in mind that Grace is a substitute for the principle Davidson actually invokes. In work after *Inquiries*, Davidson has argued it is the upshot of reflection on the radical interpreter's procedures that a speaker's beliefs are about conditions in his environment they are nomically correlated with (see, "A Coherence Theory of Truth and Knowledge," Davidson 2001a (1983)). This is, in effect, an appeal to Grace. It is not clear, however, whether Davidson realizes Grace does not follow from Charity, and is essentially stronger. (See our discussion of Davidson's arguments about the impossibility of massive error in Chapter 19.)

The fact that Grace is a *ceteris paribus* principle means that the inference from L-sentences to the claim that the corresponding TF-sentences are interpretive is itself subject to revision in the light of further evidence, if this is needed to

---

[170] We add the 'ceteris paribus' clause to allow that speakers may hold true sentences which do not express the content of any belief, e.g. because they think it true on authority but do not understand it.

achieve a better overall theory. What we require of the theory for an initial set of *L*-sentences is that it entail corresponding *TF*-sentences. As evidence accumulates, the interpreter can adjust the range of *TF*-sentences he chooses to accommodate. When enough evidence is in (it is to be hoped that) the interpreter can be confident his theory is, by and large, correct.[171]

7. Stages of Interpretation

To sum up this part of the discussion, then, the procedure outlined so far can be represented as having the following main stages.

Stage 1

Justify *L*-sentences on the basis of behavioral evidence. (Sub-stages will involve identifying logical form and hold true attitudes of speakers.)

Stage 2

From *L*-sentences together with Grace and (1)–(2) infer *TF*-sentences as, other things being equal, appropriate target canonical theorems for an interpretive truth theory for the language:

(TF)   For all speakers S, times t, s is true for S at t iff p.

Stage 3

Formulate a (formal) truth theory that has as canonical theorems the *TF*-sentences arrived at in stage 2.

Stage 4

Derive so far untested *TF*-sentences for occasion sentences, and test them against predictions that their corresponding *L*-sentences are true; make partial assignments of contents to attitudes on the basis of corresponding attitudes

---

[171] It has been suggested that the principle of charity can be interpreted not as a principle the interpreter must accept, but rather as a *ceteris paribus* inference rule which licenses moves from *L*-sentences to interpretive *TF*-sentences. But this does not represent a substantively different interpretation. For the inference rule to serve the purpose for which it is introduced, it would have to guarantee that, *ceteris paribus*, the *TF*-sentences inferred from *L*-sentences were interpretive. And this will be so just in case Grace is true.

toward sentences and check the assignments against predictions of behavior using the a priori theory of rational agency, in so far as possible.

Stage 5

Repeat stages 1–4, throwing out *L*-sentences in the initial data as needed, until theory and observation coincide.

We will comment below on ways to elaborate various of these stages, but this forms the main outline of the procedure of the radical interpreter.[172]

We have laid out our account of the relation of evidence to theory as an outline of the procedure an actual interpreter might follow. Alternatively, one could imagine assembling first all of the relevant behavioral facts and considering the best overall fit of theory with evidence given our assumptions about the connection between prompting conditions and belief contents.

We now turn to two important issues. The first is the question what justifies the principle of charity (Chapter 13). The second is the issue of the nature and role of additional constraints on getting an adequate theory of interpretation (Chapter 14).

---

[172] Will this procedure net us all of the vocabulary of the object language? Perhaps some of the object language vocabulary never appears in any occasion sentence! But in principle it looks as if any bit of vocabulary can appear in an occasion sentence ('I am thinking of an odd number', 'That rainbow is not a proposition', 'The photons traveling through this piece of fiber optic cable are carrying digitally encoded information'); in addition, once we have a working theory for that portion of the language dealing with concrete objects and their properties, the interpreter will be as well placed to learn from an informant the theoretical vocabulary of the language as a native speaker first learning those terms.

13

The Justification of the Principle of Charity

> Since charity is not an option, but a condition of having a workable theory,
> it is meaningless to suggest that we might fall into error by endorsing it . . . If
> we can produce a theory that reconciles charity and the formal conditions
> for a theory, we have done all that could be done to ensure communication.
> Nothing more is possible, and nothing more is needed.
>
> (Davidson 2001c (1974): 197)

We argued in Chapter 12 that Charity is the correct interpretation of
Davidson's principle of charity, but also that it is inadequate for justifying
the claim that the *TF*-sentences corresponding to *L*-sentences are interpretive,
and that a principle at least as strong as Grace is needed. In this chapter, our
concern is with how to justify either Charity or Grace. Of the three arguments
we will consider, the second and third will apply equally to either Charity or
Grace, and so there will be no need to distinguish between them. The first, if
successful, would at most support Charity, though we will argue it is unsuccessful. With this in mind, we will use 'the principle of charity' to stand in for
Charity, Grace, or either indifferently, as appropriate.

To understand the force of requiring that the principle of charity be justified, recall the analogy with empirical decision theory. There the parallel
problem was to use empirical data to fix one of two factors that jointly determine preference, namely, subjective probability and desirability. In that case,
there is a pattern among preferences, expressible in choices, which together
with the formal features of the theory suffice to determine the subjective probability an agent assigns to a particular event. This provides initial entry into an
assignment of probabilities and desirabilities. Recall, we said that if an agent

is indifferent between receiving something of value V upon event E (to which he is indifferent) or V^* otherwise, and something of value V^* upon event E or V otherwise, then he assigns probability $1/2$ to E. We did not need an *additional* assumption about agents to ensure that we could break into the circle of degrees of probability and desirability. In this respect, as we have noted, the parallel between decision theory and interpretation theory is not exact. For while patterns among preferences suffice to fix in a crucial case one of the two facts that determine preferences, patterns among hold true attitudes do not by themselves fix the empirical content of beliefs, or the meanings of a speaker's sentences. We must, in the case of interpretation theory, bring to bear an additional assumption, namely, the principle of charity. For nothing in a theory of rational agency and belief requires that most of our beliefs about our environment be true. The motivation and justification of this additional principle then must lie elsewhere.

As we have said, there are two attitudes to take toward the principle of charity. According to the first, it is an assumption we take on board in exploring what must be assumed if radical interpretation is to be possible. Without it, radical interpretation fails. With it, it looks to be successful. To adopt this attitude toward the principle is to pursue what we called the modest project in Chapter 11. According to the second, we do not merely assume the principle of charity, but argue for it. It is clear, however, that an inductive argument for the principle of charity is out of the question in the context of radical interpretation. For any inductive argument would have to identify a speaker's beliefs independently of relying on the principle itself. The radical interpreter's access to the speaker's beliefs, however, relies crucially *on that assumption*. The justification of the principle of charity must proceed independently of comparing *what* the speaker believes *with* his environment. The radical interpreter needs, it would seem, an a priori justification for the principle, if it is not simply to be taken on faith. To adopt this attitude toward the principle is to pursue what we called the ambitious project in Chapter 11. In many places it seems clear that Davidson takes the application of charity to be constitutive of the nature of speakers, as, for example, in the epigraph to this chapter, and so, is committed to arguing for it a priori.

We will examine three possible a priori arguments for the principle of charity. The first, which we call the argument from the (moderate) holism of attitude content, and which Davidson gives explicitly, we discuss in §1. The second, a form of argument to the best explanation, which Davidson does not give explicitly, we discuss because it might be thought that Davidson has the resources to justify the principle of charity on the basis of such an argument, and there are reasons to think Davidson would find it congenial. We discuss this in §2. The third, the argument from the necessity of radical interpretation, we discuss in §3. There is considerable evidence that Davidson argues in this fashion, though, as we have noted, there is also textual evidence against it (see §2 of Chapter 11). We think, however, that attributing to him the intention to argue in this fashion makes the best sense of his overall philosophical project. Whether this is so or not, it makes the project potentially more interesting and important than it would otherwise be. We take stock in §4.

1. The Argument from the (Partial) Holism of Attitude Content

The first argument, the argument from the holism of attitude content, Davidson advances explicitly in the following passage.

[a]   We can ... take it as given that *most* beliefs are correct. The reason is that a belief is identified by its location in a pattern of beliefs; it is this pattern that determines the subject matter of the belief, what the belief is about. Before some object in, or aspect of, the world can become part of the subject matter of a belief (true or false) there must be endless true beliefs about the subject matter. False beliefs tend to undermine the identification of the subject matter; to undermine, therefore the validity of a description of the belief as being about the subject. And so, in turn, false beliefs undermine the claim that a connected belief is false ... It isn't that any one false belief necessarily destroys our ability to identify further beliefs, but that the intelligibility of such identifications must depend on a background of largely unmentioned and unquestioned true beliefs. To put it another way: the more things a believer is right about, the sharper his errors are. Too much mistake simply blurs the focus.

   What makes interpretation possible, then, is the fact that we can dismiss a priori the chance of massive error. A theory of interpretation cannot be correct that makes a man assent to very many false sentences: it must generally be the case that a sentence is true when a speaker holds it true. So far as it goes, it is in favor of a method of interpretation that it counts a sentence true just when speakers hold it to be true ... according to the method, the speaker holds a sentence true under specified conditions, and these conditions obtain, in the opinion of the interpreter, just when the speaker holds the sentence to be true.   (Davidson 2001 (1975): 168–9)[173]

In this passage Davidson intends to support the principle of charity a priori. However, his argument, even granting its premises, fails to establish the principle on either interpretation.

---

[173] The argument appears also in Davidson 2001*a* (1977).

The main premise of the argument is that for a belief to be about a particular kind of thing, even if false, it must have a place in a pattern of largely true beliefs which fix its subject-matter. The examples Davidson provides make clear what he has in mind. Thus, he says, to believe or wonder or speculate whether a gun is loaded, one needs to believe *such things as* that "a gun is a weapon, that it is a more or less enduring physical object, and so on" (Davidson 2001 (1975): 157). The point is familiar. Using concept talk, his point is that to have one concept, and so, a belief involving it, one must understand or grasp the concept. Grasping a concept, on this view, consists in turn in having a set of general beliefs about things of the kind to which the concept applies, which express truths about it in virtue of the kind specified by the concept. Perhaps, as Davidson suggests (see Chapter 14), no particular set of beliefs is required. Nonetheless, unless one has a suitably large set of connected a priori beliefs about things of the kind to which the concept applies, one does not grasp the concept; and grasping it is a condition on possessing it, and possessing it is a condition on having beliefs which involve the concept.

Even if this view were enough to establish that to have any beliefs, one must have a great number of true beliefs, it fails to establish what Davidson needs for the success of radical interpretation. The argument establishes at most that one must have a great many true *general* beliefs (beliefs about what is true of everything of a certain kind) involving the concepts which figure in one's beliefs. This is apparent in Davidson's examples. One must believe that a gun is a weapon, that is, that if anything is a gun, it is a weapon, that guns are more or less enduring physical objects, that is, if anything is a gun, it is a more or less enduring physical object, and so on. However, the principle of charity (on either interpretation), as employed in the procedure of the radical interpreter, must be applied specifically to a speaker's beliefs about his immediate environment—not to general beliefs, but beliefs about particulars ('particular beliefs').[174] That is, the radical interpreter needs not just the assumption that most of our general beliefs are true, but also, minimally, the assumption that beliefs prompted by environmental conditions

---

[174] Of course, if one believes that Charles is a squirrel, then one must believe a number of related things about Charles such as that he is a physical object, that he is alive, that he eats nuts, and so on: however, to attribute the concept of a squirrel to you, it is not necessary that one suppose these beliefs of yours are true. Rather, you must believe such things as these of Charles if you believe he is a squirrel, because they are consequences of the general truths about squirrels you believe. It is only the general beliefs which we must count as true to see you as possessing the concept: we may have to see you as having many related particular beliefs if you have one, but seeing them as true is not a condition on seeing you as possessing the concepts expressed in them.

are also, by and large, true. A Cartesian skeptic would find no comfort in an argument based on what is required for concept possession, for he could grant everything it entailed without having been given a reason to suppose correct any of his beliefs about the way things actually were in his environment (if any).

Could it be argued that an accurate attribution of a concept to another required seeing him as correctly deploying it in relation to particular things in his environment? Suppose that we found someone who systematically applied 'red', in good light, to things which are green. Would it not be reasonable to think he means by 'red' what we mean by 'green'? There are reasons to doubt we would be *forced* to take him to mean *green* by 'red'. For example, if we could find a systematic explanation for his misapplication that made sense of him having the concept of red and attaching it to the word 'red' in the first place, then we could take him now to mean what we mean by 'red', but just to be getting it wrong. Perhaps he correctly acquired the concept of red, and associated it with the word 'red', attaching it to red things in his environment initially, but afterwards suffered from a physiological condition that made green things look red to him. Yet, even in the case described by this story, we must presuppose he did correctly apply the concept in the past.

The real trouble with the suggestion is that the pressure we feel to take him to be expressing the concept green with his word 'red' comes from our tacitly taking him to have by and large correct perceptual representations of his environment and correct perceptual beliefs. If we thought he had very different beliefs about his environment than we did, and, in particular, that he was massively mistaken about it, we could not take what he applies his terms to as a reliable guide to which concepts he expresses by them. Thus, these sorts of reflection cannot be used to support the principle of charity. Rather, we can suppose that what someone applies, or appears to apply, words to is necessarily a guide to what concepts he expresses only if we have reason to think the principle of charity is a constitutive principle governing interpretation. This leaves us no further along then.

2. The Argument to the Best Explanation

It is not clear that the second argument we wish to consider, a form of argument often advanced in support of comprehensive philosophical theories for some domain, is one Davidson has ever explicitly endorsed, though it is one which we have reason to think he would find congenial, for reasons we give below. The argument has the following form:

(1) If the assumption that *p* is required in the best overall theory of the nature of human beings and their place in the natural world, then *p*.

(2) The principle of charity is required in the best overall theory of the nature of human beings and their place in the natural world.

(3) Therefore, the principle of charity is true.

(1) is taken to be true for any grammatical substitution for '*p*'. This will yield a valid argument for (3) substituting a statement of the principle of charity for '*p*' in (1). The following questions can be raised about it. First, what is the status of the claim that instances of (1) are true? We have urged that Davidson needs an a priori argument for the principle of charity; therefore, if (1)–(3) is to serve his purposes, then that instances of (1) are true must be treated as knowable a priori. Clearly, 'best' cannot be taken here to mean simply *true*, since (2) would then be question begging. So, the best theory must be identified by its ability to account for, in a sense characterizable independently of establishing the truth of the theory, what the theory takes as its data. We have in mind a theory which sanctions, by and large, our pre-reflective beliefs about ourselves and our relation to each other and our environment, where relinquishing those beliefs threatens our world view with incoherence. Thus, for example, the belief that we have knowledge of things in space and time would be a belief that should be accounted for by the theory. The status of assumption (1) as a priori, then, depends on the status of the claim that the beliefs it would have to accommodate can be known to be true a priori as well. It is hard to see how to show this. However, it should also be acknowledged that there is a long tradition in philosophy of treating the assumption that instances of (1) are true as a basic methodological presupposition. And it must be admitted that if (2) were true, conditionalizing on (1) would still yield an important and interesting philosophical result.

The main burden on the argument then should be that of showing that (2) is true. This is not, however, a question that can be answered in a short space, and is of a piece with an overall evaluation of the account of language and mind which Davidson offers. Our evaluation of it must therefore emerge in the details of our analysis of Davidson's overall position. It is important to consider this form of argument, however, since support for a particular part of a theory may come from the explanatory work the theory as a whole is able to do. Even if we do not find satisfactory support for the principle of charity in any direct argument for it, we should not overlook the possibility of this more indirect source of support. (This point can be made, *mutatis mutandis*, about presupposition (P), namely, that radical interpretation is possible.)

3. The Argument from the Necessity of Radical Interpretability

The third argument appeals to presupposition (P), as having been established independently and a priori. The argument is:

(1) Interpretation from the standpoint of the radical interpreter is possible.
(2) If interpretation from the standpoint of the radical interpreter is possible, then the principle of charity is true.
(3) Therefore, the principle of charity is true.

If the premises are knowable a priori, so is the conclusion. Davidson holds, we believe, (2) to be an a priori truth, and, if we are right, he should hold also that (1) is an a priori truth.[175] (Notice, a point we will come back to at greater length in Chapter 19, that this argument has as a conclusion that most of our empirical beliefs are true.) We leave aside for now the question what reason we have to believe (1) is true and knowable a priori (one reason to believe it true would be an independent argument for the principle of charity, but that is obviously not available if we here invoke (1) in an argument for the principle of charity). We will return to this issue in Chapter 22. What about (2)? Radical interpretation is possible only if an interpreter can come to justify an interpretation theory for a speaker on the basis of behavioral evidence. (2) then requires that unless the radical interpreter assumes the principle of charity, he will be unable to justify an interpretive truth theory for the speaker. But why must the interpreter assume the principle of charity to justify an interpretive truth theory for the speaker? Why is it crucial for the success of radical interpretation? Why must the radical interpreter assume that most of a speaker's beliefs about his environment are true, or that the contents of his environment-directed beliefs are given by conditions that prompt them?

The answer in outline must be that there is no other reasonable assumption for the interpreter to adopt to solve the problem of finding a way to employ his evidence in the form of *L*-sentences to arrive at interpretive *TF*-sentences.

---

[175] See our discussion in §2 of Ch. 11.

The problem can be represented in the following way. The interpreter must move from *L*-sentences, as in (L), to *TF*-sentences, as in (TF).

(L)   For all times t, *ceteris paribus*, S holds true s at t iff p.
(TF) For all times t, s is true (S, t) iff q.

The difficulty is to figure out what sort of systematic relation should obtain between the conditions determined by what goes in for 'p' and by what goes in for 'q'. In the place of 'q' we want a sentence that interprets s for S at t. The simplest solution to the problem is to suppose that what replaces 'p' and 'q' should be the same sentence. What assumption about the nature of the speaker would justify this? *The assumption that the speaker's environment-directed beliefs are mostly true and about conditions that prompt them.* So the argument goes. This would explain, prima facie, why it is reasonable to infer from an *L*-sentence to the conclusion that the corresponding *TF*-sentence is interpretive. If we had independent grounds for thinking radical interpretation must be possible, we would have an explanation of why it is possible on this assumption, and that provides indirect support for it.

Is there a better, or at least equally good, alternative? This would require an account of a systematic relation between the conditions under which a speaker holds true a sentence and the interpretation of the sentence, and an explanation of this relation in terms of the nature of the speaker *qua* speaker. While there are many ways we could imagine relating the conditions under which a speaker holds a sentence true to interpretations of the sentence, it is not easy to see what plausible explanations might be given of the relation in terms of the nature of the speaker. If it is correct that no competing account of the relation and explanation of it is both as simple and plausible as that Grace is true, then this will justify (2).

This is not a proof of (2). It is rather a sketch of an argument for (2). To be completed, more would have to be said about why there are no plausible alternatives. It looks as if the grounds for urging this would have to be largely considerations of simplicity. We are looking for explanations of what constitutive features of a speaker would explain a systematic connection between the conditions under which speakers hold occasion sentences true and the interpretations of those sentences. The simplest connection and explanation is provided by the principle of charity, or, specifically, by Grace. If we take simplicity here to be a prima facie guide to truth, then barring any other considerations (and it is hard to see what else to bring to bear), we have a reason to endorse the principle of charity as the correct explanation of why it is an a priori truth that radical interpretation is possible. This in turn will justify (2).

(2) is justified by the assumption that (1) can be established a priori, and by the claim that the principle of charity provides the simplest account of how to bridge the gap between (L) and (TF) by appeal to constitutive features of speakers.

We will mention two concerns about this argument, though we will not pursue them. The first is that there is no good reason to think the simplest theory is more likely to be true than a more complicated one. However, in defense of Davidson, we can note that this principle is widely assumed both in philosophy and the sciences. Its defense, therefore, is not his special charge. The second is a more general concern about the strategy. The argument requires us to suppose constitutive features of agents determine that speakers are necessarily radically interpretable. It looks then as if we ought to be able to advance independent reasons for thinking that the required features of agents are their constitutive features, that is, it should fall out of our concept of a speaker that his beliefs are about the conditions that prompt them, independently of this being the simplest explanation for the possibility of radical interpretation. This is not to say that the argument does not provide support for its conclusion if the premises are correct. Rather, we will have some reason to think that the second premise is not correct if there is no other reason to believe that Grace is true other than that it is needed in order for it to be true that necessarily speakers are radically interpretable. There is some reason to be suspicious of this, for prima facie it does not seem impossible for most of one's beliefs about one's environment to be false. It might be thought that to be a speaker requires communicating with others, and that this would be impossible without knowledge of one's environment, and so, largely true beliefs about it. But this is not the sense in which we are interested in whether most of a linguistic being's beliefs about his environment must be true. Someone is a speaker in virtue of having the capacity to speak a language, to communicate with others. Even Robinson Crusoe is a linguistic being, though he has no opportunity of communication with others. Could a linguistic being, someone with the capacity to speak a language, to communicate with others in favorable circumstances, fail to have a mostly correct view of the nature of his world? We can grant for the sake of argument that if he were in a position to communicate with others, he would have to have mostly correct beliefs about his environment. But why could he not be unfavorably placed, in part because he has mostly false beliefs? Traditional skeptical scenarios employed by philosophers in raising the problem of radical skepticism about the external world will serve as models of how someone could be so unfavorably placed. So, there is no direct route from the characterization of someone as a speaker to the conclusion that he is mostly right about his environment. On the only characterization that *would* secure this, namely, that someone is not just a linguistic being, but is so situated that he is in communication with others at least now and again, we *secure* the result only by rendering it *uninteresting*. For it then has no consequences for what must be so about linguistic beings as such, beings capable of speaking to others if the opportunity arises.

4. Taking Stock

It will be helpful to pause at this point to take stock of our discussion so far. The initial project of "Truth and Meaning" was to show how to provide a compositional meaning theory for a natural language. The extended project was to provide at the same time insight into what it was for any of the terms of a language to have the meanings they do. When the constraint that a truth theory be extensionally adequate failed to suffice for it to serve as a meaning theory, we entertained a number of additional suggestions. We concluded that the only constraint that clearly suffices is that the theory's axioms be interpretive. When we turned to considering the project of the radical interpreter, which aims to shed light on the concepts deployed in a theory of interpretation for a speaker by showing how evidence can be marshaled in its support, we argued that the interpreter must aim to confirm that a specific truth theory for the speaker's language which he knows, and for which he knows how to specify canonical theorems, be interpretive. Against this background, we have examined how a radical interpreter, ultimately restricted to appealing to behavioral evidence, could confirm something sufficient to interpret any potential utterance of a speaker of a natural language. Patterns among hold true attitudes provide a partial picture of logical form for the language, but to interpret primitive predicates we must, if we are to succeed, in basic cases, relate them to events and conditions in the speaker's environment. Thus, of special importance for the project is the confirmation of *L*-sentences, relating conditions in the speaker's environment to his hold true attitudes toward occasion sentences. The identification of hold true attitudes is supposed to proceed, ultimately, on the basis of purely behavioral evidence. But, assuming it is possible, identifying hold true attitudes does not itself beg the question of what the speaker's sentences mean (for the most part). However, to move from evidence of this form to interpretive *TF*-sentences (i.e. *T*-sentences) which could be used to project the axioms of a truth theory for the speaker's language, we needed a principle which takes us (*ceteris paribus*) from *L*-sentences to *T*-sentences.

The principle Davidson invokes, Charity, holds that a speaker's beliefs about his environment are, by and large, correct. We argued that a stronger assumption is needed, which we called 'Grace', which entails Charity. Grace emerges as an essential assumption of radical interpretation. How Grace is to be supported therefore becomes a matter of central importance, and is connected with the question whether the project of radical interpretation is to be conceived of as modest or as ambitious. We have argued that it should be conceived as ambitious. But this means that Grace must be supported by an a priori argument, either directly, or indirectly by an a priori argument directly for the possibility of radical interpretation. This central issue is one to which we will return again and again. In the next chapter, Chapter 14, we first consider additional constraints on a correct interpretation theory for a speaker and their sources, and discuss their relevance to the distinction between the modest and ambitious projects. This will complete the basic account of the procedure of the radical interpreter. We then turn in Chapter 15 to a discussion of the important issue of the extent to which these constraints underdetermine the choice of interpretation theory, and the extent to which interpretation can be said to be indeterminate. In the penultimate chapter of Part II, Chapter 16, we discuss the integration of the basic procedure of the radical interpreter into a broader theory of meaning and action which Davidson has called 'The Unified Theory of Meaning and Action'. Chapter 17 discusses the consequences of taking the standpoint of the radical interpreter as methodologically fundamental for our understanding of linguistic communities and public languages.

14

The Theory of Agency and Additional Constraints

> Each interpretation and attribution of attitude is a move within a holistic theory, a theory necessarily governed by concern for consistency and general coherence with the truth, and it is this that sets these theories forever apart from those that describe mindless objects, or describe objects as mindless.
>
> (Davidson 2001*a* (1974): 154)

In this chapter, we consider in more detail the constraints on an adequate theory discussed above, and additional constraints, as well as their sources, and their relation to the ambitious and modest projects. In §1, we discuss the role and source of the a priori theory of agency that the radical interpreter brings to bear in interpretation. This provides a framework within which behavior can be interpreted as an expression of agency. In §2, we discuss the role of holism about attitude content as a constraint on interpretation. This is properly subsumed by the constraints provided by the theory of agency, but the attention it has received justifies a separate discussion. We explain what holism about attitude content comes to in Davidson's view, distinguishing it from other forms of holism attributed to him. In §3, we discuss what constraints he says we can expect to be able to impose on the logical form of object language sentences and on what grounds these constraints. In §4, we discuss the constraints that arise from seeing a speaker as a member of a particular linguistic community. Finally, in §5, we discuss whether the radical interpreter can bring to bear empirically obtained knowledge of speakers' psychologies in narrowing down interpretation theories for speakers, arguing that this is incompatible with the philosophical aims of reflection on radical interpretation.

1. The A Priori Theory of Rational Agency

One of the most important constraints Davidson imposes on an adequate theory of interpretation is that its interpretations of sentences and corresponding assignments of contents to beliefs and other attitudes make speakers out to be *rational agents*. According to Davidson, this requires that speakers' actions, including speech acts, be represented as minimally rational in the sense that each be rationalized by a belief–desire pair, that is, that the action be caused by, and made to seem desirable in the light of, some end of the agent, and some belief of the agent's about how to obtain the end.[176] This is a condition on speakers acting at all. But there are additional, holistic constraints, as well. Thus, speakers' beliefs must be made out, on the whole, to be consistent, and their preferences sensible, and, more particularly, their beliefs and preferences must, on the whole, be rational in the sense of conforming to the axioms of decision theory. Davidson says, "We weaken the intelligibility of attributions of thoughts of any kind to the extent that we fail to uncover a consistent pattern of beliefs and, finally, of actions, for it is only against a background of such a pattern that we can identify thoughts" (2001 (1975): 159). The thought here is not that we know as a matter of empirical psychology that speakers conform to the axioms of decision theory and the norms of rational agency. Rather, the norms of rational agency describe a pattern such that too great a departure from them would prevent our describing someone or something as an agent, and, consequently, as a believer or speaker. The theory of rational agency places a priori constraints on the patterns of attitudes, contents, subjective probabilities, and preference orderings that we can assign to speakers, and thus represents a powerful constraint on interpretation. The constraints are holistic in the sense that they must be imposed on the whole system of a speaker's attitudes; while the whole system, however, must closely conform to the norms of rationality, local deviations are possible, and the requirement that speakers be made out as a whole to be rational does not determine where to locate these deviations.[177]

The source of the theory of rational agency is to be found in Davidson's work in action theory, and, importantly, it is not motivated by what is required for the radical interpreter to succeed. That is, unlike the case of the principle of

---

[176] See Davidson 2001 (1963).

[177] This theme has been elaborated with great subtlety by Davidson in a series of papers on the nature and limits of irrationality, esp. Davidson 2001*a* (1970), 2004 (1982), 2004 (1985), 2004 (1986).

charity, in justifying the use of the theory of rational agency in interpretation, it is not necessary to assume that radical interpretation is possible.

What we have said so far underdescribes the constraints. In general, we can appeal to whatever can be shown to be a pattern in the attitudes of a rational agent, and, more particularly, a linguistic agent, on a priori grounds; this may include a complex series of interlocking attitudes, beliefs, desires, and intentions in the production of action, as well as norms for marshaling what an agent takes to be evidence in support of belief (e.g. Bayesianism). Importantly, there is potentially more to appeal to here than just general constraints on rational agency, for we are committed to taking subjects to be linguistic agents, agents whose repertoire includes speech acts. If we can specify general constraints on patterns of attitudes that speakers must exhibit in performing speech acts in particular, then these patterns should be sought in subjects in any circumstances where it looks apt to treat them as performing a speech act. Thus, for example, we could bring to bear a theory that relates whatever intentions speakers have to the speech acts they perform, in something of the style of Grice's attempt to reduce utterance meaning to speaker's intentions (Grice 1989: chs. 5 and 6).

An attempt at a complete inventory would be out of place here, where the aim is to detail the *kinds* of constraints available to the radical interpreter. What the constraints drawn from the a priori theory of rational agency help us elicit are the interconnections between our concepts of meaning, truth, reference, and the rest of the family of linguistic concepts, and the range of concepts deployed in our thinking about agency and the propositional attitudes. The project of the radical interpreter serves as a methodological tool for investigating their interconnections, and, thereby, as a way of illuminating them.[178]

2. Holism about Attitude Content

A second important constraint already touched on in our discussion of arguments for the principle of charity is what we call, somewhat misleadingly, 'holism about attitude content'. This is, properly, a part of the theory of agency, but the discussion it has received in the literature justifies its separate treatment. Holism about attitude content, as the phrase is used here, means that in attributing any given attitude to a speaker, one is thereby committed to

---

[178] Again, see Davidson's remarks on philosophical method in "Radical Interpretation" (2001*c* (1973): 137).

attributing a perhaps endless range of related attitudes, though, importantly, not any specific set of additional attitudes.[179]

There are two different ways in which an attribution of a given attitude constrains attributions of others, according to Davidson.[180] First, there are what we will call cross-modal constraints, that is, constraints on attributions of attitudes in different psychological modes (belief, desire, hope, fear, intention, etc.). Thus, according to Davidson, to attribute a desire to an agent requires attributing beliefs, and vice versa; attitudes come only in patterns of interlocking kinds whose contents are related. Second, to attribute any attitude requires attributing beliefs, and attributing any belief requires attributing an endless range of other beliefs with related contents. The pattern of related contents in part supports attributing to the subject concepts involved in the belief attributed; in part, the pattern is derived from the content of the particular belief, for one would expect, for example, someone who believed that he was sitting down to believe that his legs were bent, and that he would have to stand before walking, and so on. According to Davidson, it may be pointless to insist on a particular list of beliefs (there may always be special explanations available for why one or another expected belief does not show up), but without some such appropriate pattern, we cannot sustain our attribution.

His constraint is holistic in two senses. First, it requires attitudes to be attributed in patterns of interconnected attitudes, rather than individually. Second, the constraint that a pattern be found is applied at the level of the whole system of beliefs, so that no particular attributions of contents to particular beliefs is dictated, only that whatever contents are attributed fit into one or another appropriate pattern. Of two patterns, one chooses the one which makes the agent out to be more rational, other things being equal. It is important also to note in what senses this constraint is not holistic. It is not an instance of what we will call *rigid holism*, the view that to have a particular attitude with a particular content there are other specific attitudes with specific contents you

---

[179] By saying one is committed to the one in virtue of the other, we mean no more than would be said by saying that someone who says that a number is even is committed to saying it is divisible by 2.

[180] This theme is expressed in the following passage from "Rational Animals": "The propositional attitudes provide an interesting criterion of rationality because they come only as a matched set. It may sound trivial to say that a rich pattern of beliefs, desires and intentions suffices for rationality; and it may seem far too stringent to make this a necessary condition. But in fact the stringency lies in the nature of the propositional attitudes, since to have one is to have a full complement. One belief demands many beliefs, and beliefs demand other basic attitudes such as intentions, desires . . . . This does not mean that there are not borderline cases. Nevertheless, the intrinsically holistic character of the propositional attitudes makes the distinction between having any and having none dramatic" Davidson 2001*b* (1982): 96. See also Davidson 2004*b* (1995): 12–17.

must have. Nor is it an instance of what we will call *extreme holism*, the view that one can have a particular attitude with a particular content iff one has all the other attitudes one in fact has, so that any change in the content of one attitude would entail a change in the contents of every other attitude. Davidson's position, at least as described here, is incompatible with the latter, and what he says here leaves open whether he endorses the former.[181]

We return in this context to a passage in "Truth and Meaning," which we have mentioned before ([*j*] in Chapter 6). Davidson says,

If sentences depend for their meaning on their structure, and we understand the meaning of each item in the structure only as an abstraction from the totality of sentences in which it features, then we can give the meaning of any sentence (or word) only by giving the meaning of every sentence (and word) in the language. Frege said that only in the context of a sentence does a word have meaning; in the same vein he might have added that only in the context of the language does a sentence (and therefore a word) have meaning.   (Davidson 2001 (1967): 22)

This passage has been taken by many authors to commit Davidson to radical meaning holism, according to which the meaning of every expression depends on the meaning of every other in a language. Davidson has explicitly denied he is committed to radical meaning holism: "I am not an unbuttoned holist in that I do not say the meaning of a sentence depends on the meanings of all sentences" (1994*a*: 124). In a note attached to this sentence, he quotes the last part of the passage above and says of it, "I have subsequently been more restrained on this topic." Perhaps, then, this passage is hyperbole, its point being only to emphasize that to understand a single sentence is to be in a position to understand an indefinitely large range of other sentences.

3. Constraints on Logical Form in the Object Language

Davidson also holds that the recursive structure of a Tarski-style theory of truth will impose a constraint on the interpretation of the object language. Davidson says,

There are constraints of a formal nature that flow from the demand that the theory be finitely axiomatized, and that it satisfy Convention *T* (as appropriately modified). If

---

[181] Thus e.g. he says, in a passage quoted previously: "There are good reasons for not insisting on any particular list of beliefs that are needed if a creature is to wonder whether a gun is loaded. Nevertheless, it is necessary that there be endless interlocked beliefs. The system of such beliefs identifies a thought by locating it in a logical and epistemic space" (2001 (1975): 157).

the metalanguage is taken to contain ordinary quantification theory, it is difficult, if not impossible, to discover anything other than standard quantificational structures in the object language ... We must expect the theory to rely on something very like Tarski's sort of recursive characterization of satisfaction, and to describe sentences of the object language in terms of familiar patterns created by quantification and cross-reference, predication, truth-functional connections, and so on ... The result of applying the formal constraints is, then, to fit the object language as a whole to the Procrustean bed of quantification theory ... The identification of the semantic features of a sentence will then be essentially invariant: correct theories will agree on the whole about the quantificational structure to be assigned to a given sentence. (Davidson 2001*a* (1974): 150–1)

The requirement that the theory be finitely specifiable, itself motivated by a view about the nature of natural languages, will force us to find recursive semantic structure in the object language, but this leaves open what sort of structure we will find. Davidson here also holds that in using a Tarski-style truth theory as the core of an interpretation theory for the speaker, we will find the object language to have an underlying logic of the sort that the metalanguage (i.e. our language) has. This marks, incidentally, an important difference between Quine's and Davidson's approaches to the interpreter's task (see Chapter 15). While surface grammar may mislead about logical form,[182] according to Davidson, one would expect to find familiar recursive devices in the object language.

The force of this constraint is not entirely clear. It is too strong, if interpreted as requiring that the object language has the same recursive devices as the metalanguage. We can imagine, for example, a spoken language more impoverished than ours, one without, for instance, quantification. In that case, of course, 'finding' quantification structure in the object language would be a mistake, and it is difficult to see why having quantification structure in the language of the theory would *ipso facto* force us to find quantification structure in the object language. In addition, we can imagine perhaps recursive devices in an object language without any echo in standard quantification theory—at least it is hard to see how to rule this out a priori. In that case, it would seem appropriate to enrich the metalanguage. Moreover, since we can clearly imagine metalanguages with different logical resources, it could not be generally true that whatever logic is available in the metalanguage is *ipso facto* available in the object language.

---

[182] We take the notion of logical form and semantic form to be the same. See *Truth-Theoretic Semantics*, ch. 13 for a fuller discussion.

What is true is that, by limiting the logical resources of the metalanguage, we constrain ourselves in interpreting object language sentences. We will find ourselves attempting to make sense of all of the structure of the object language in terms of the structures available in the metalanguage. There are four familiar kinds of axioms dealing with object language expressions in standard Tarski-style theories: reference axioms (if the object language has singular terms), satisfaction clauses for primitive predicates (of one or more places), satisfaction clauses for truth-functional connectives, and satisfaction clauses for quantifiers. If we adopt a standard Tarski-style theory, these will form our basic repertoire for providing an extensional recursive semantics, and in adopting such a form for a truth theory, we will be committing ourselves to finding object language sentences to be analyzable for the most part in terms of them, with perhaps some variation on the basic themes to accommodate the language's native apparatus.

It is not clear, however, what reason could be mustered for holding a priori that any language we wish to interpret will be correctly interpretable with the recursive resources of standard quantification theory. Unless we can produce some such reason, we will have no reason to think the constraints imposed on a theorist by adopting a standard Tarski-style truth theory will lead to an adequate interpretation of the object language. An a priori argument for the constraint would amount to an argument that no natural language could have recursive semantic devices not representable in standard quantification theory.

There is something that does follow from the use of a truth theory, however. For any truth theory we recognize as such will represent sentences as containing predicates and either singular referring terms or quantifiers. This basic structure is imposed on anything we would recognize as a language in which truths can be stated. This is properly a constraint on interpretation forced on us not by any contingent restriction on the resources of the metalanguage, but by our concept of language and truth.

The actual sorting of sentences into various categories of logical form will depend on identifying entailment relations among sentences based on form, rather than on conceptual connections between primitive predicates. If we can identify negation and either disjunction or conjunction, or a connective that functions like the Sheffer stroke, we can identify a complex connective which functions as the material conditional, and then identify potential entailments by identifying sentences (or translations of sentences) of the form $\ulcorner C(\phi, \psi)\urcorner$, where '$C$' represents the connective in the object language that functions like the material conditional, which are held true, more or less, come what may. We may then hope that trial and error in parsing the sentences into recursive and non-recursive features, and assigning satisfaction conditions so that the *TF*-sentences arrived at by the methods of the radical interpreter are entailed by the axioms of our nascent theory, will accommodate all of the entailments we identify, in a way that makes plausible that we have appropriately apportioned them between form, on the one hand, and conceptual connections among predicates (semantic entailment), on the other. It should be noted that in the case of the task of identifying the logical forms of a language other than our own, we lack (initially, anyway) a resource that we have in the case of our own language, which Davidson helps himself to in giving accounts of the logical forms of English sentences. This is our own intuition about entailment relations, and, in particular, about whether or not an entailment is a matter of form: for we already begin with an intuitive knowledge of how to sort terms into different logical categories, for example, we know 'all' and 'and' and 'there is a' are not predicates, and we can judge whether a form of inference is correct (such as that from something of the form $\ulcorner \alpha\phi\text{-ed at } t\urcorner$ one can infer something of the form $\ulcorner \alpha\Phi\text{-ed}\urcorner$). This resource is unavailable for another language until we already have a working interpretation theory (at least, if we are restricted to the position of the radical interpreter). But to arrive at a working interpretation theory, we will already have had to make many decisions about logical form, and so cannot treat what we at some point identify as our subject's intuitions about logical form independently of judgments about the logical forms of his sentences.

4. Conformity in a Linguistic Community

Another important constraint is provided by locating the subject of interpretation as a member of a (like-minded) linguistic community. We can expect that the members of the community use words *more or less* in the same way.

The interpreter who assumes his method can be made to work for a language community will strive for a theory that optimizes agreement throughout the community. Since easy communication has survival value, he may expect usage within a community to favor simple common theories of interpretation. (Davidson 2001 (1975): 169)

Given a community of speakers with apparently the same linguistic repertoire ... the theorist will strive for a single theory of interpretation: this will greatly narrow his practical choice of preliminary theories for each individual speaker. (In a prolonged dialogue, one starts perforce with a socially applicable theory, and refines it as evidence peculiar to the other speaker accumulates.) (Davidson 2001*a* (1974): 153)

This gives us an additional check on our attributions of meanings and beliefs to a particular speaker. We will still face a trade-off between belief, meaning, and truth. But if there is a strong enough presumption that a speaker is using his words in conformity with others, we will suppose that those of his hold true attitudes which conflict with those of others in his community, and which are not to be explained as due to context sensitive features of the sentence (such as the presence of a referring term such as 'I'—see below), express false rather than true beliefs, and should not be used to generate a T-sentence for the purpose of projecting a truth theory. Likewise, we will assume that members of the community are in general agreement, and we can use this information to select those TF-sentences we wish to use to begin our formulation of a community-wide interpretation theory. In addition, making sense of the detailed linguistic and non-linguistic interactions among members of the linguistic community should provide a rich source of evidence on which to fit a pattern of attitudes, meanings, and contents that renders the evidence intelligible. The interpreter must make sense of conversations as well as reports about speakers' environs, and of grapplings with the social interaction in addition to the physical. Thinking about the speaker as a member of a linguistic community is important in another way for successful interpretation, as noted before (Chapter 12, §1). This comes out in reflecting on how we would correctly interpret indexical terms whose semantic values depend upon who uses them. Suppose a speaker uses a word ω, on our best evidence, to refer to himself. This evidence is compatible with interpreting ω as a name for the speaker, or as an indexical term like 'I'. To distinguish between these hypotheses, it is essential to know what the word would refer to in the mouths of other speakers of the language. This point extends to other demonstrative and indexical terms, 'you', 'they', 'we', 'this', 'that', etc., and even tense, since we need to distinguish between interpreting tense as making reference to the time at which any speaker of a sentence utters the sentence or the time at which a particular speaker utters it. An easy way to see the importance of gathering evidence across members of the linguistic community is to note the need to arrive at T-sentences which generalize over speakers. This is needed precisely because there will be many semantic devices whose semantic values in a context depend on who the speaker is. It is clear that to confirm such sentences we must pay attention to how the truth conditions of utterances vary across speakers.

It does not quite follow that we cannot gather enough evidence to decide how to correctly interpret an isolated speaker. What follows is that we need to know how to interpret utterances of his sentences across speakers. If he is identified as a member of a linguistic community, we can collect the kind of needed evidence by seeing how interpretations of utterances should differ by varying the speaker and time. Without this aid, we need information about how our speaker would interpret another who used the sentences he uses. Given complete information about his dispositions, non-intentionally described, we would be in a position to do this (if we can do it by appeal to evidence across a community of speakers). As a practical matter, the interpreter could himself go proxy for the speaker's linguistic community by using a preliminary interpretation in attempting to speak with his subject. The aim would be to settle on that interpretation which yields the best overall account of the speaker's hold true attitudes, and his hold true attitudes acquired as a result of the interpreter's attempt to engage him in conversation, in particular.[183]

It might be thought that the attempt to locate a speaker as a member of a linguistic community will drop the interpreter into a vicious circle. For to know that a group of speakers share a language, it looks as if he must be in a position to interpret each speaker's language. But if, in order to interpret each speaker's language, he must locate the speaker in a community of speakers who share a language, he will be unable to break into the circle of meaning. The previous paragraph shows that the difficulty is not insuperable by showing how an interpreter might hope to interpret in principle an isolated speaker. But the interpreter may aim for a more direct method of confirmation as well by testing various community-wide interpretation schemes against disparate interpretation theories for individuals in the supposed community, and choosing that scheme or set of schemes which provides the best overall fit with the data.

5. The Role of Empirical Constraints

A final topic to discuss here is not a particular constraint, but the role of a class of constraints in radical interpretation, namely, empirically derived constraints, where this means contingent a posteriori truths about the speakers

---

[183] There have been cases in which an individual isolated from his linguistic community has been interpreted. For a poignant telling of one such case, see *Ishi in Two Worlds* (Kroeber 1961). This does not settle any philosophical issues about radical interpretation, of course, since anthropologists and linguists do not operate under the constraints imposed on the radical interpreter.

we wish to interpret. In practice, no doubt, we make many empirical assumptions about speakers. We assume, most importantly, we and our subjects are very much alike in our basic and recurring desires, what we find salient in our environments, what we are apt to notice, what we find interesting or insignificant, kind or hateful, dangerous or comforting, and so on, always with a caveat about explicable differences, whose explanation would be grounded in an account of how we would, or might, have reacted to their history and situation.[184] Can the radical interpreter help himself to these sorts of assumptions? There are two reasons to think he cannot.

First, if, as we have argued, the radical interpreter is ultimately to start from purely behavioral evidence, then all assumptions about what a speaker is apt to find interesting, what his desires are, what he finds dangerous, attractive, and so on, must themselves ultimately be based upon behavioral evidence. Therefore, empirical assumptions of these sorts cannot be among the basic constraints on radical interpretation. They could at best be derived constraints, which arise from the basic evidence plus the application of the fundamental constraints.

Second, as we conceive it, the project of radical interpretation aims to be a completely general account of interpretation, and, hence, of meaning, communication, and whatever is essentially connected with these. To take on board as fundamental constraints contingent assumptions about the psychology of particular speakers, or groups of speakers, would undermine the generality of the results we would hope to obtain from reflection on the nature of radical interpretation. For this reason also, we should reject bringing to bear in the basic description of radical interpretation contingent assumptions about the psychology of speakers whom we wish to interpret. This will secure that the conclusions we reach about meaning and language on the basis of reflection on radical interpretation will be conclusions about meaning and language as such, and not about the meaning or language of this or that particular group of speakers or kind of speaker.

This concludes our discussion of the constraints which can be brought to bear on the task of correctly interpreting another from the standpoint of the radical interpreter. There are three classes of constraints in total. Some are imposed because without them we cannot connect our evidence with what it is supposed to be evidence for (mainly the principle of charity, interpreted as Grace). Some are a priori constraints dictated by the nature of the subject-matter, principles constitutive of what it is to be an agent or a speaker. Finally,

---

[184] See Lewis 1974.

some are empirically derived constraints, such as contingent principles about the psychologies of the speakers the interpreter wishes to interpret. The third of these, we have argued, the radical interpreter cannot help himself to, if his conclusions about the nature of thought and language are to have the degree of generality which Davidson evidently aims for. In the next chapter, we turn to the question whether the remaining constraints are sufficient to enable a radical interpreter to justify a theory of interpretation for a speaker. We take this up in the context of a discussion of the degree to which the evidence the interpreter has underdetermines the theory he reaches, and the relation between underdetermination of theory by evidence and permissible variations between theories all of which may in some sense be said to capture the same facts, that is, indeterminacy of interpretation.

15

Indeterminacy

> ... belief and meaning cannot be uniquely reconstructed from speech behaviour. The remaining indeterminacy should not be judged as a failure of interpretation, but rather as a logical consequence of the nature of theories of meaning (just as it is not a sign of some failure in our ability to measure temperature that the choice of an origin and a unit is arbitrary).
>
> (Davidson 2001*b* (1973): 257)

Davidson has claimed that, after all the facts are in, "significantly different theories of truth" will "fit the evidence equally well,"[185] and, hence, that there will be equally acceptable but different theories of interpretation, theories which capture equally well the speaker's dispositions. In the first instance, this appears to be the underdetermination of theory by (all the possible) evidence. Davidson claims also that these equivalent theories capture equally well all the facts about what the speaker's sentences mean, and that the content assignments to his attitudes made on the basis of these different theories capture equally well what he believes, wants, and so on. This is so despite the fact that equally acceptable theories may "differ in assigning clearly non-synonymous sentences"[186] of the metalanguage, even ones which differ in truth value,[187] to an object language sentence. The ground for his claim is that the facts about the speaker's dispositions fix completely the facts about his meanings and attitudes. Davidson calls this, echoing Quine, the *indeterminacy* of interpretation.[188]

In this chapter, we address the important questions of what the indeterminacy of interpretation is, how much of it to expect, and how much is allowable. The argument of this chapter is central to our evaluation of the project of

[185] Davidson 2001*d* (1970): 62.   [186] Davidson 2001 (1968): 100.
[187] Davidson 2001*a* (1979): 228.   [188] Quine's phrase is the 'indeterminacy of translation'.

radical interpretation. At the end, we conclude that the evidence available to the radical interpreter, together with the constraints he can legitimately bring to bear on his task, genuinely underdetermine the theories he can confirm, and that the appearance of underdetermination cannot be accounted for by appeal to the indeterminacy of interpretation, to whatever extent it is indeterminate. If this is correct, radical interpretation is not possible, that is, presupposition (P) (see Chapter 11, §2) of Davidson's initial question is false. We cannot confirm anything knowledge of which (we would be justified in believing) would suffice for interpretation from the radical interpreter's standpoint. However, our argument is still hostage to the possibility of providing an a priori argument for (P). We consider what arguments might be advanced for (P) in Chapter 22.

We will first give a brief overview, in §1, of the context in which talk of the indeterminacy of a theory for a given domain arises, and its relation to underdetermination. This discussion is not intended to be exhaustive, but only to sketch in as much background as is needed to understand the context of Davidson's claims about indeterminacy.[189] Then, in §2, we identify what we believe is the central assumption of Davidson's approach to radical interpretation. This is the assumption that the central concepts of the theory of interpretation—the concepts of meaning, belief, desire, intention, and the like—have their contents exhausted by their roles in accounting for the behavior of a speaker in a way that results in empirically equivalent theories of speakers, after all the evidence is in, that state the same facts.[190] In §3, we review two challenges to this assumption, which, if correct, would ensure that radical interpretation is not possible. The first has to do with whether or not our having access to our own mental states independently of observing our behavior can be reconciled with Davidson's position on the central concepts of interpretation theory. We postpone an extended discussion of this until Chapter 20, where we take up Davidson's most direct response.

---

[189] Quine introduced the term 'indeterminacy' (1960: ch. 2) in the phrase 'the indeterminacy of translation'. What exactly Quine meant by the phrase there and elsewhere has been a matter of considerable debate. We do not intend to undertake an exegesis of the debate, but instead to say something general enough about the conditions under which indeterminacy is said to arise to provide a framework for our discussion of Davidson's use of the term. Davidson clearly intends to be advancing a doctrine similar to Quine's. Fortunately, we will not have to answer the question whether he and Quine understand the term in the same way in order to discuss Davidson's use.

[190] e.g. "Quine revolutionized our understanding of verbal communication by taking seriously the fact, obvious enough in itself, that there can be no more to meaning than an adequately equipped person can learn and observe; the interpreter's point of view is therefore the revealing one to bring to the subject" (Davidson 1990a: 78).

The second challenge has to do with whether, from the interpreter's point of view, there are empirically equivalent but incompatible starting points for projecting interpretation theories. If there are, then the radical interpreter is not in a position to justify an interpretation theory for a speaker. We argue in §4 that there are empirically equivalent but incompatible starting points for projecting interpretation theories. In §5, we consider responses which seek to show either that we can bring to bear additional constraints to solve the problem, or that the constraints in place are likely to be adequate taken as a whole. We argue that these responses are unconvincing. In §6, we argue that the problem cannot be removed by insisting that this is just a matter of the indeterminacy of interpretation. Finally, in §7, we show that Davidson's attempt to show that indeterminacy is innocuous by appeal to an analogy with measurement theory cannot be used to undermine the conclusion that the radical interpreter is not in a position to know he has confirmed an interpretive theory.

1. Underdetermination and Indeterminacy

It is evidently crucial to understanding the role and nature of indeterminacy in interpretation theory to begin with an account of what is meant by 'indeterminacy' and the conditions under which it is appropriate to say translation, interpretation, meaning, or the like is indeterminate. Indeterminacy is said to arise for a range of theories only when choice among that range is underdetermined by the range of their available evidence. Since indeterminacy so-understood is characterized in relation to underdetermination, we begin with a brief characterization of the latter.

Consider two theories, T_1 and T_2, that we will suppose initially, in some intuitive sense, say (or seem to say) incompatible things about their respective domain. We can leave it open exactly how to understand what the incompatibility comes to. The sense in which what the two theories say is incompatible is a free parameter in characterizing indeterminacy. In this case, we will say T_1 and T_2 are alternatives of one another. Suppose further that E is a statement of evidence each theory accounts for equally well. In this case, we will say E *underdetermines* each of T_1 and T_2. A theory is underdetermined by a statement of evidence E iff the theory accounts for E, but it is possible that an alternative theory accounts for E equally well. Underdetermination is always relative to a certain body of evidence. Though T_1 and T_2 may be underdetermined relative to E, further evidence E^+ may show, for example, that T_1 is superior to T_2, since T_1 may account for E^+, while T_2 does not, or is incompatible with it. So, relative to E, T_1 and T_2 may be underdetermined, but relative to E and E^+, T_1 and T_2 may not be underdetermined.

Indeterminacy is not just underdetermination. Two theories might be underdetermined relative to some evidence E, but one might be correct and the other incorrect. If we have not just underdetermination, but indeterminacy, then each theory is said to capture equally well the facts of the matter.

Indeterminacy arises from underdetermination for a range of theories when two further conditions are met.[191] The first is a condition on evidence.

(i) Evidence marshaled for the theories is all the possible relevant evidence.

The second condition is the crucial one, but it is not easy to state clearly. It is intended to capture the idea that what the theories say about the world is exhausted by their implications for facts in the domain of evidence. If we want to allow that there can be underdetermination in the light of all possible relevant evidence in some domains without indeterminacy, then, where there is indeterminacy, it will have to be due to special features of the theories concerned. Presumably, it will be due to special features of the concepts deployed in the theory—something special about how we understand their role and content. We will therefore express the second requirement as a constraint on the concepts employed in the theory. Intuitively, the idea is that the concepts in the theory are understood in the light of their empirical interpretation, that is, the conditions under which they are to be applied or withheld from an object. In decision theory, for example, the concept of degree of belief and desirability (how strongly someone believes something, and how much he desires it) receive empirical interpretations in terms of an agent's choice behavior, that is, the pattern of the agent's choice behavior wholly determines what his degrees of belief and desirabilities are: there can be no further hidden facts about them (see Chapter 16 for further discussion). Thus, two apparently differing theories about degrees of belief and desirabilities (in this case they may appear to differ because we use different systematic assignments of numbers to keep track of relations among degrees of belief and desirabilities) which account for the same choice behavior, that is, correctly predict it, will not actually be stating different facts about the agents. So the idea we are after is that what is special

[191] The two conditions are jointly sufficient, but they are not both necessary. There is no reason to suppose indeterminacy may not arise if the first condition is not met, as long as the second one is, even if two theories make different empirical predictions, for some of the differences, or apparent differences, between them may not make a difference in their implications for the evidence.

about alternative theories which admit of the possibility of indeterminacy is that the content of their concepts, which are not just observational concepts, is exhausted by their application in the domain of evidence in a way that results in the content of the theories' theoretical claims not transcending their predications about facts in the domain of evidence. We will call such concepts, for want of a better phrase, 'purely theoretical concepts'. We can state the second condition in terms of this notion.

(ii)   The concepts of the theories are purely theoretical concepts.

Two theories meeting conditions (i) and (ii) state the same facts.

Suppose, then, that E is a statement of all possible evidence about a certain domain, and that T_1 and T_2 are two intuitively *incompatible* theories that optimally account for E, and that the *content* of the theoretical claims of T_1 and T_2 is exhausted by their use in accounting for E; then we will say that there is no fact of the matter about which of T_1 or T_2 is correct, that is, that it is *indeterminate*. Suppose T_1 and T_2 share their central theoretical terms— let us call these 'F-terms', and facts stated using them '*F*-facts'—but account for E using different axioms, axioms which (apparently) differ, for example, in what properties and relations they invoke and what objects they refer to. Then we can say that F-facts are indeterminate, or, alternatively, assert the *indeterminacy of F-facts*.

2. Indeterminacy of Interpretation

We turn now to the application of these notions to the case of theories for interpreting the speech of another. For interpretation to be indeterminate, first, there must be at least two possible interpretation theories for a speaker, I_1 and I_2, both of which account for all the possible relevant evidence for interpretation, and, yet, are alternatives of one another; and, second, their central concepts, the concepts of meaning, reference, truth, belief, desire, preference, intention, and so on, must be purely theoretical, that is, have their content exhausted by their role in accounting for the relevant evidence in such a way that alternative theories accounting for all the relevant evidence represent the same facts. The evidence available for the radical interpreter is a speaker's behavior, and, more generally, his behavioral dispositions in his environment (described in a way that does not presuppose anything about the speaker's thoughts and meanings). From this standpoint, it is clear that whether, and if so to what extent, interpretation is indeterminate, given the results of radical interpretation, depends, first, on whether the concept of meaning and related concepts are purely theoretical concepts, second, on whether the evidence available from the standpoint of the radical interpreter exhausts the relevant evidence, and, third, on whether, and to what extent, the evidence available to the radical interpreter leaves open (intuitively) incompatible interpretation theories.

The question of whether, and if so to what extent, the thesis of the indeterminacy of interpretation is true is connected with one raised but put aside earlier, namely, whether radical interpretation is possible. To maintain a priori that radical interpretation is possible is to maintain that *the evidence available to the radical interpreter* exhausts the content of the central concepts (particularly meaning) deployed in interpretation, in a way that guarantees empirically equivalent theories state the same facts after all the evidence is in. Since the radical interpreter is restricted, ultimately, to behavioral evidence (even though, for convenience, Davidson describes the procedure from the point of having identified sentential attitudes), this would be to hold that the concepts deployed in interpretation theory, from belief to meaning, are to be conceived as systematizing and tracking complex patterns—ultimately of behavior—in relation to a speaker's environment.[192] This does not amount to behaviorism, because there is no claim that the concepts of the theory are reducible one by one to behavioral concepts, or that sentences about meaning or belief, and so on, are synonymous with sentences about behavior. (Compare the role of theoretical terms in physics.) However, it is to hold that the point of the concepts of the theory is to track behavior non-intentionally and non-semantically described, and that what content a theory of a speaker couched in such terms has is exhausted by its systematizing that behavior. As Davidson has put it at some points, intentional descriptions supervene on behavioral descriptions.[193]

[192] That Davidson so regards the central concepts of the theory of interpretation is clear: "Broadly stated, my theme is that we should think of meanings and beliefs as interrelated constructs of a single theory just as we already view subjective values and probabilities as interrelated constructs of decision theory" (2001*a* (1974): 146). Again: "Everyday linguistic and semantic concepts are part of an intuitive theory for organizing more primitive data, so only confusion can result from treating these concepts and their supposed objects as if they had a life of their own" (ibid. 143).

[193] Thus, in "Thought and Talk": "Adverting to beliefs and desires to explain action is . . . a way of fitting an action into a pattern of behavior made coherent by the theory. This does not mean, of course, that beliefs are nothing but patterns of behaviour, or that the relevant patterns can be defined without using the concepts of belief and desire. Nevertheless, there is a clear sense in which attributions of belief and desire, and hence teleological explanations of beliefs and desire, are supervenient on behaviour more broadly described" (Davidson 2001 (1975): 159). Correct attributions of attitudes supervene on behavior iff there can be no two objects alike with respect to behavior, but differing

Indeterminacy requires more, however. It requires that the evidence, together with all legitimate constraints, permit different and intuitively incompatible theories. Suppose the evidence available to the radical interpreter exhausts all relevant evidence. And suppose the evidence plus the constraints Davidson describes leave open different (intuitively) incompatible theories. It is still open to deny indeterminacy by arguing for additional, overlooked constraints.

At this point we can begin to see how profoundly anti-Cartesian Davidson's approach to interpretation is. This is most transparent in his treatment of the concepts of interpretation theory as purely theoretical in the way described above. He adopts a certain view of the epistemic status of applications of such concepts, namely, that we lack prior access to facts of the sort that these concepts are deployed in stating; our purchase on such facts is based, ultimately, on evidence of another sort, evidence that is epistemically prior to facts about interpretation and belief. His position requires rejecting the Cartesian assumption that at the foundation of justified beliefs about the world are beliefs about mental states, attitudes, experiences and sensations; moreover, it apparently requires rejecting the assumption that, whether our beliefs about our own mental states lie at the foundation of our justified beliefs about the external world, we have non-inferential knowledge of them. The status of this claim is of the greatest possible importance for understanding the mind–world relation.

Of course, this picture of the role and status of the central concepts deployed in a theory of interpretation for another person cannot be taken for granted. And the question of the range of acceptable theories, given the constraints on, and evidence available to, the radical interpreter, is relevant to whether or not it is plausible to suppose that the constraints on the theory are adequate, and that the central concepts and claims of the theory should be treated as having their content exhausted by their role in accounting for evidence available to the radical interpreter. Too much apparent indeterminacy may well persuade us that we have overlooked constraints, or mistaken the status of the concepts deployed in the theory, or overlooked relevant evidence.[194]

---

with respect to correct attributions. See e.g. Davidson 2001*b* (1970): 214 and 1974: 345. See also Davidson 1990*b*: 314.

[194] Thus, David Lewis: "*Credo*: if ever you prove to me that all the constraints we have yet found could permit two perfect solutions ... you will have proved that we have not yet found all the constraints" (1974: 343).

3. Two Challenges

We raise two specific questions about the adequacy of the assumptions about interpretation theory, and its relevant evidence, that are required to support the indeterminacy of interpretation. The first question is about the intelligibility of the required picture of our epistemic position. The second question is about whether the thesis of indeterminacy can plausibly be maintained given the *extent* of underdetermination of theory by evidence, and whether the *source* of the underdetermination can intelligibly be understood as giving rise to indeterminacy.

(1) If concepts such as those of meaning, belief, intention, and so on, are treated as purely theoretical, relative to some source of evidence, the interpreter's application of these concepts to himself must be treated in the same way. The difficulty with this is twofold.

First, it requires an account of the interpreter's knowledge of evidence for the application of such concepts (for the moment we focus on their attribution to others) which does not presuppose he knows independently whether such concepts apply, not only to others, but to himself. For otherwise the content of the concepts would prima facie not be exhausted by their role in accounting for such evidence. But whether or not one accepts the assumption of the Cartesian skeptic that, globally, knowledge of one's experiences and conscious mental states is epistemically prior to one's knowledge of events in one's environment, it is very difficult to account for our knowledge of particular events in our environment without presupposing knowledge of representational perceptual experiences. If someone knows that a tree is in front of him, or that a cat is on his lap, it is (special circumstances aside) at least in part on the basis of his present perceptual experiences. Since attributions of representational perceptual experiences cannot be made apart from treating their subject as a believer, knowledge of such experiences (that one has one and what it represents) would seem to presuppose knowledge of the application of concepts in the proscribed range in our access to what is treated as ultimate evidence for their correct application. If, as seems correct, all knowledge of the occurrence of particular events in our environment rests in part on knowledge of perceptual experience, then we cannot represent the concepts in question as purely theoretical concepts relative to such evidence, at least if we can know the concepts apply to anything. If this is right, then if we are in an epistemic position to apply these concepts to anything, they cannot be treated as purely theoretical concepts introduced fundamentally to help us systematize behavior.

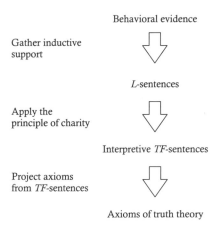

Figure 1

The second, and, of course, connected difficulty arises from the observation that we typically take ourselves to know what we think and experience independently of any observations of our behavior or interactions with our environment, and we likewise suppose others to be similarly so positioned with respect to their own thoughts and experiences; this is reflected in the phenomenon of first person authority, namely, in according to another's sincere first person assertions about his own mental states the presumption of truth, while no such presumption attaches to our claims about his mental life independently of support by behavioral evidence. (Indeed, we assumed in our account of the relevance of identifying hold true attitudes, in order to discover meaning and belief content, that speakers are authoritative about their beliefs and meanings.) On the face of it, this is incompatible with the view that the point of these concepts is to enable us to systematize observed behavior in others. We will not consider this difficulty in detail here, since Davidson addresses it specifically, and we consider his account in Chapter 20.

(2) To pursue the second question, we need to turn to the details of the procedure of radical interpretation. This procedure is represented in Figure 1. In the stage represented by the first arrow, we assume that we can identify hold true attitudes; Davidson assumes no indeterminacy arises at this stage. *L*-sentences, which are generalizations about the conditions under which speakers hold true sentences, are universally quantified inductively supported generalizations, which employ no more concepts than those already at play in the evidence for them. *L*-sentences provide the evidence for the next stage in the process.

However, this stage is not as innocent as it may at first appear, and, we will argue, a difficulty arises here which proves fatal to the project of radical interpretation. We develop the point in the rest of this section and the next.

The interpreter aims to find, for each object language occasion sentence s, an L-sentence, abbreviated as 'L_s'. Ultimately, the evidential base for the truth theory consists of a complete set of L-sentences, in the sense that, for each object language occasion sentence s, there is (ambiguity aside) a unique L_s sentence in the set.[195] Some may ultimately be discarded. But we must have a great many for there to be an adequate evidential base for projecting an interpretive truth theory at the next stage. Let us call the culled set of L-sentences used to yield TF-sentences from which we project the truth theory the *data set*. We will say that two different data sets are equivalent if, and only if, for each s, if L_s^1 is the L-sentence for s in the first set, and L_s^2 is the L-sentence for s in the second, then L_s^1 is equivalent to L_s^2. Two L-sentences are equivalent iff the sentences (open or closed) on their right hand sides *translate* one another.

This so far merely states a condition on the equivalence (from the point of view of interpretation theory) of classes of L-sentences which serve as the primary data for arriving at a set of TF-sentences, which in turn serve as the evidential base for projecting the axioms of a truth theory. No danger threatens unless the interpreter's evidence can support non-equivalent (in the above sense) data sets equally well. Suppose it can. Then we will be able to confirm inductively two different and non-equivalent data sets, D_1 and D_2. Minimally, there will be an L-sentence L_s^1 in D_1 and an L-sentence L_s^2 in D_2 for a sentence s of the object language which will be used to project TF-sentences, TF_s^1 from L_s^1, and TF_s^2 from L_s^2, which represent s as having *differing interpretive truth conditions*. This will require the axioms of the generated theories which have these TF-sentences as canonical theorems to represent some of the contained terms as differing in meaning. It will then be impossible to avoid the conclusion that *at least one* of the theories is incorrect. If, compatibly with the rest of the constraints on interpretation, an interpreter starting from either D_1 or D_2 could construct an empirically adequate theory of interpretation, we would have to conclude that, since both theories could not be correct, the interpreter is not in a position to confirm, within the constraints available, a correct interpretation theory for the speaker's language. Whether there might still be a sense in which both theories could be treated as adequate and equally good we will return to shortly.

---

[195] For the remainder of the current discussion, we ignore ambiguity; if radical interpretation is not possible for an unambiguous language, it is not possible for an ambiguous one.

In Chapter 12, we outlined reasoning which could lead us, *ceteris paribus*, from *L*-sentences to interpretive *TF*-sentences. What difficulty does the possibility of equally well-supported but non-equivalent data sets pose for that line of reasoning? If the conclusion of the previous paragraph is correct then it follows that, if there can be such non-equivalent data sets, some assumption in the outlined reasoning must be mistaken. The reasoning depended crucially on (Grace), (1), and (2), repeated here.

> (Grace) *Ceteris paribus*, when we replace '*p*' in (S)
> (S) *S* believes at *t* that *p*
> with a sentence that expresses the content of an environmentally prompted belief of *S*'s, the sentence expresses also a condition in *S*'s environment that prompts that belief.

(1) *Ceteris paribus, the L-sentences* that the interpreter confirms *identify* conditions under which a speaker holds true sentences that are also *the prompting conditions*, if any, which *those beliefs*, that are the basis of the speaker's holding those sentences true, *are about*.

(2) *Ceteris paribus*, a speaker *S* holds true *s* at time *t* because, and only because, he knows that *s* means(*S, t*) that *p* and believes that *p*, and knows that if *s* means(*S, t*) that *p*, then *s* is true(*S, t*) iff *p*.

What is interesting about this is the role of (1) in particular. If the interpreter finds, or has reason to believe that there are, non-equivalent equally well-confirmed data sets for a speaker's language, he has reason to reject (1). For that would show that the interpreter's confirming an *L*-sentence is not *ipso facto* sufficient to identify, even *ceteris paribus*, the content of the belief on the basis of which the speaker holds true the relevant sentence. Without (1), even granting Grace and (2), he cannot justify a selection of *TF*-sentences as an appropriate base on which to project an interpretive truth theory.

4. Non–Equivalent Sets of *L*-Sentences

We argue now that there are non-equivalent data sets confirmable from the interpreter's evidence. A sufficient condition for this is that there be two law-like sentences for an occasion sentence *s* of form (L) expressing different laws that can appear in data sets.

(L) *Ceteris paribus*: *S* holds true *s* at *t* iff *p*.

First, it is obvious that for any confirmable *L*-sentence, other true ones that state different laws will be confirmable if there are true counterfactual supporting biconditionals of form (EQ), with identical *ceteris paribus* conditions, where what replaces '*p*' and '*q*' in (L) and (EQ) are nonsynonymous.

> (EQ)   *Ceteris paribus*: *p* iff *q*

Will there be appropriate true law-like sentences of the form (EQ)? Yes.

(*a*) We can always form a conjunction of '*p*' and a sentence which expresses a nomically necessary truth or one nomically necessary relative to (i.e. holding fixed) the *ceteris paribus* conditions. It might be thought that this could be ruled out in principle by appeal to simplicity as a constraint on theory formation. This response is open to the objection that we have no a priori reason to think the simplest laws will be ones that lead to interpretive truth conditions; in fact, we have no very good reason to think we know what the simplest laws are that account for our own hold true attitudes. In any case, this response cannot be made to the considerations advanced immediately below in (*b*) and (*c*).

(*b*) We can substitute for a predicate in '*p*' a nomically co-extensive nonsynonymous predicate, at least relative to the *ceteris paribus* conditions (plausible examples are 'watery stuff' and 'H_2O', 'golden element' and 'element with atomic number 79', etc., where 'watery stuff' and 'golden mineral' express the phenomenal concepts of water and gold).[196]

(*c*) We can substitute for '*p*' any sentence nomically equivalent (but nonsynonymous) relative to the *ceteris paribus* conditions. Thus, for example, if relative to conditions *C*, a distal event expressed by '*p*' suffices for a speaker to hold true a certain sentence, it will also suffice for the truth of sentences about intermediate conditions necessary for the transmission of the causal efficacy of the distal event to the speaker (e.g. a certain kind of pattern of irradiation of one or the other or both of the speaker's retinas).

In addition to these sources of alternative *L*-sentences, we can also observe that, since *L*-sentences must be *ceteris paribus* laws, there are likely to be many different *L*-sentences for each sentence of the object language. This can arise in either of two ways:

(*d*) Given an *L*-sentence for *s*, which is a *ceteris paribus* law, there will always be another *ceteris paribus* law which differs from it in that the condition expressed by '*p*' in the first is a part of the background conditions in the new one, while one of the background conditions in the original plays

---

[196] Note that these are metalanguage expressions, not object language ones, so even if we had a syntax for the object language, we could not decide between them on that basis.

the role in the new law of the condition expressed by 'p' in the original. This would yield a non-equivalent L-sentence for s. Why think this is so? We have a sentence of the form:

$$\text{If } C, \text{ then } x \text{ holds true } s \text{ iff } p.$$

Represent 'C' as 'C_1 & C_2 & ... C_n'. The claim is that we can find a conjunct of 'C', which we represent with the schematic letter 'C_i', which meets the following condition. Represent the condition expressed by 'C' minus that expressed by 'C_i' as 'C^-'. The conditions expressed by 'p' and by 'C^-' are together nomically sufficient for that expressed by 'C_i'. In this case, if our original conditional was a law, so will be

$$\text{If } p \,\&\, C^-, \text{ then } x \text{ holds true } s \text{ iff } C_i.$$

For if the condition expressed by 'p & C^-' obtains, so will that expressed by 'C_i'. This is sufficient for 'C' to obtain. But then by the original conditional, that suffices, given the condition expressed by 'p', for it to be true that x holds true s. As a matter of nomic necessity then, the consequent is true if the antecedent is.

Why suppose there is such a condition? We get something like our original sentence when we consider the past light cone[197] relevant to x holding true s for some representative class of cases. We consider some part of the background conditions in the light cone as specially relevant, and select it out as p. The rest of the light cone is sufficient for both x holds true s and p. But many conditions in the light cone could have been selected.

(*e*) The *ceteris paribus* condition functions to conditionalize the biconditional in L-sentences. This is necessary, because we can be confident that no plausible interpretive condition obtains when and only when we hold a sentence true, since sometimes we make mistakes, or are just ignorant about what is in our environment, or do not believe things truly. The aim is to arrive at *ceteris paribus* conditions which fail to obtain on those occasions on which we have false beliefs or hold true false sentences. It is overwhelmingly plausible that if

---

[197] The past light cone of an event is fixed by the region of space around it for each past time from which a light signal could have reached it in the time interval between it and the event. No signal can travel faster than the speed of light, so this represents the space–time region within which events occur which can causally affect the given event. We can visualize a light cone in three dimensions by taking the vertical axis as the temporal axis, and the horizontal axes as spatial dimensions. A cone is described by the boundary of the two-dimensional region from the limit of which a light signal can reach the location of the event given the time between it and the event. If space is measured in light seconds, and time in seconds, then the past light cone will have a slope of $45°$. The light cone for three spatial dimensions is represented by a time ordered series of spheres centered on the location of the event.

there is one way to conditionalize on causal conditions to secure the nomic necessity of a biconditional of the right form, then there are many. Thus, for example, if there are conditions in the distal environment relative to which a speaker holds true a sentence *s* iff *p*, there will be more proximal conditions relative to which the speaker will hold true *s* iff *q*, where *that p* and *that q* are non-equivalent conditions.

(*a*)–(*e*) show that the interpreter's evidence suffices to confirm many different non-equivalent sets of *L*-sentences for typical speakers. Indeed, it seems clear that, given one complete set of *L*-sentences, we could generate an equally well-confirmed set none of whose members were equivalent with any *L*-sentence in the original. This suffices for there to be non-equivalent data sets for interpretation. Is this enough to show radical interpretation is impossible? We think 'yes', but before establishing this, we want to consider a number of ways in which the conclusion might be resisted.

5. Responses and Replies

The prima facie difficulty is that, inasmuch as different non-equivalent data sets can be confirmed from the standpoint of the radical interpreter, he has a choice among different non-equivalent sets of putatively interpretive *TF*-sentences from which to project a truth theory. These sets will lead to non-equivalent theories, between which the interpreter's evidence is unable to decide. Thus, since they cannot all be right, the interpreter is in no position to confirm a correct theory.

What the argument shows, if correct, is that there are not enough constraints on our project. A natural suggestion is to rule out many of the *L*-sentences for any given occasion sentence *s* of the object language, because the conditions they isolate *we know the speaker is unlikely to be thinking or talking about*, such as, for example, events at his retinas or vibrations on his eardrums. We know what people are likely to find salient in their environments, what interests them, what they have an interest in pursuing, and so on, and this will significantly limit the range of acceptable *L*-sentences. We might call this the *principle of saliency*: *ceteris paribus*, take the speaker to find salient in his environment what you find salient, and to be thinking about or noticing what you would in his place.

Assumptions of just this sort (and many more) play a crucial role in justifying our interpretations of others' utterances in everyday life. However, this sort of information is *not* available to the radical interpreter, as we remarked in §5 of Chapter 14. We cannot suppose he is informed about contingent features of a speaker's psychology on pain of undermining the generality of the results we wish to reach on the basis of consideration of his procedure. And it is certainly not conceptually necessary that a thinking being find salient or notice or think about the same things in its environment that *we* do. While what is salient to dogs and owls overlaps what is salient to us, there are clearly many things salient to them that are not salient to us. And it is easy to imagine a being whose sensory apparatus is different enough from ours that there is very little or no overlap in the ranges of things we each find salient in the same environment. In addition, if we are to take seriously the claim that the concepts employed in the theory of interpretation are purely theoretical ones, used to track and systematize patterns in behavior non-intentionally and non-semantically described, then any such assumptions would themselves ultimately have to be justified on the basis of behavioral evidence alone.

A more promising approach would be to insist that although different sets of non-equivalent *L*-sentences are confirmable from the interpreter's initial data, in the process of trying to arrive at a holistically acceptable theory—a theory that accommodates all of one's data within the constraints imposed by the a priori theory of agency and of speakers, and the formal constraints imposed by the form of a truth theory—the interpreter will be able to converge on a unique set of *L*-sentences. The hopeful thought is that the "richness of the structure of thought and meaning will necessarily tease out a workable interpretation" (Davidson 2004 (2001): 149). This would be the best sort of response to our challenge, because it would meet it head on. And it is plausible to suppose that holistic constraints would result in the rejection of many sets of *L*-sentences as inappropriate. However, it is difficult to see how to establish that, for any speaker, the additional constraints would narrow down the acceptable sets of *L*-sentences to one, or even to a small range of sets fairly similar to one another. A thought experiment will help to illustrate these difficulties.

Let us suppose we have created a virtual reality suit, a device to be worn like a space suit, capable of manipulating input to one's sensory surfaces with great flexibility and sensitivity. While presently over the technical horizon, it is no great stretch to suppose such suits one day being produced, and taking the danger of sunburn out of a day at the beach. (To allow for wearers to move in ways required by their trips, we can suppose them suspended in a tank of water.) Imagine now the point of such suits being perverted by equipping their exteriors with sensory receptors which simply transmit the stimulus of the environment by way of the suit's mechanism to the sensory surfaces of its wearer. The image of the suit as a transmitter of the causal impact of the environment on a speaker makes vivid the possibility of seeing the speaker as responding to two different causal environments, one the distal environment, one the proximal environment created by the suit. If we suppose a suit equipped with a speaker (in another sense of the word), so that we can, as it were, hear what its wearer is saying, we could attempt to interpret his speech. It is not implausible to think that if we find someone ensuited moving and speaking in a way that seemed inappropriate for his environment (a large featureless tank of water), we could interpret him as responding to what is going on in the proximal environment provided by the suit. If so, then clearly in the case in which someone is in a suit which merely transmits the causal influence of the environment, he could be interpreted as discussing either the proximal or distal environment. It is wildly implausible, however, to suppose there is no fact of the matter about what he is thinking. And that this is so is relevant evidence in thinking about the nature of the concepts we are concerned with. Someone does not get to reject this possibility because his *theoretical* position rules it out: we are concerned now with whether such a position is well-founded. The point of the thought experiment is not undermined by its hypothetical nature. We are, in any case, all ensuited, as it is, for our bodies are transmitters of the causal influence of distal events, and only lack of familiarity and ingenuity prevent us from perversely interpreting others as talking not just mostly about themselves.

The issue cannot be left here. It is possible to add further a priori constraints to those surveyed already. For example, one might require that speakers be interpreted as talking only about what can form the topic of a conversation among a community of speakers, and argue that this will at least rule out interpretations which treat speakers as talking about events at or near their sensory surfaces. It will, however, be more appropriate to consider this issue in another context (see Chapter 22).

6. Is This Just More Indeterminacy?

It is time to consider the response that our objection to the possibility of radical interpretation ignores the indeterminacy of interpretation. This response is important but needs to be examined carefully. We note first that a blanket appeal to indeterminacy in the face of unintuitive consequences of possible interpretations will be unconvincing, unless backed up by further argument and an attempt to explain away the appearance that unacceptable results may be obtained by pursuing the procedures of the radical interpreter. Otherwise, appeal to indeterminacy will appear *ad hoc* and question begging. We will consider below both what motivation might be given for insisting on indeterminacy, and what diagnosis might be offered for the appearance that the interpreter cannot justify a correct theory. However, first it is crucial to detail how indeterminacy is supposed to arise. For we want the account to make sense from the theoretical position of the interpreter, that is, it must be possible to make sense of the claim that despite differences in the theories to which he may be led by his evidence, they represent the same facts.

Reconsider Figure 1 above. There are three stages in the procedure for arriving at a truth theory for the object language. In the first, from behavioral evidence we identify hold true attitudes, and then on the basis of observations of the conditions under which a speaker holds true sentences, we arrive at a set of *L*-sentences which form the evidence for the next step. At the second stage, we employ the principle of charity to arrive at (what we hope are), *ceteris paribus*, *T*-sentences (again, in our sense). In the final stage, we use these as evidence to project the axioms of a truth theory which entails them. At the last stage, when projecting a truth theory which is to entail our *TF*-sentences, there may be scope for indeterminacy.[198] But indeterminacy at this stage could not help with our challenge to the possibility of radical interpretation. The problem arises because we can arrive at different sets of non-equivalent *TF*-sentences from which to project a truth theory. Since the different theories we thereby project will entail *TF*-sentences which (in the full theory) yield different representations of how sentences are to be interpreted in the object language, whatever indeterminacy is involved in providing interpretations of primitive expressions will not yield indeterminacy in the interpretations yielded by *TF*-sentences. To make a case for a response to the challenge by appeal to indeterminacy, then, one must make a case that it arises appropriately in the first two stages.

The *L*-sentences used as the data for the second stage of radical interpretation (as represented in Figure 1) are to be conceived of as explained by the following facts. First, the subject is so constituted and situated that, *ceteris paribus* (the same *ceteris paribus* conditions as those intended in the *L*-sentence to be explained), his beliefs about his environment are true. Second, he knows

---

[198] There may be cases in which the way a device functions in a language underdetermines its translation into another language in the sense that two ways of doing it seem to capture the facts of usage equally well (as far as the resources of the interpreter's language are able to). Quine gives as an example translation of certain complex determiners in Japanese into English, which has no syntactic equivalent (Quine 1969*b*: 30–9). Whether Quine's description of the case is correct will not concern us; the underdetermination we are concerned with arises in a different place.

what his sentences mean. Third, he holds true those sentences which express his beliefs about his environment on the basis of his beliefs and his knowledge of sentence meaning, that is, when he believes that p and believes that s means that p, he holds true s. By supposing that this explains his holding the subject sentence true in the conditions specified in an L-sentence, we can infer that the conditions specified in the L-sentence interpret the sentence held true.

Davidson links indeterminacy to the possibility of trade-offs between belief and meaning in explaining a speaker's hold true attitudes.[199] We suppose generally a speaker holds true occasion sentences based on what he believes about his environment and knows about the meanings of the sentences he holds true. The trade-off he has in mind is between the conditions under which we choose to regard a speaker's beliefs about his environment as true and the meanings we attribute to his sentences. If we assign a certain meaning to a sentence s, then in certain conditions in which the speaker holds it true, we will have to suppose he has a false belief. If we choose to attribute to him in those circumstances a true belief, then the meaning assigned to the sentence will have to be different. Notice that what is being explained here is not a bit of behavior non-intentionally and non-semantically described, but rather beliefs, even if only about the truth of sentences and not their meanings. Thus, indeterminacy is supposed to arise because there are different ways of explaining this—that is, different assignments of meanings to sentences and contents to beliefs, all of which do equally well given the rest of the allowable constraints, in accounting for sentences held true.

According to Davidson, this trade-off is a principal source of indeterminacy in interpretation. The data consist of the circumstances in which speakers hold true sentences. There are different ways of distributing truth values to sentences in these circumstances so as to preserve the principle that the speaker be treated as largely right about his environment. The aim is to distribute truth values so that the speaker is largely right about his environment, and so that we can specify conditions in which he is consistently right. In the formulation of L-sentences to serve as the basis for the next stage of interpretation, distributing truth values to his sentences so as to make him consistently right about his environment is mostly a matter of choosing *ceteris paribus* conditions in the

[199] "When all the evidence is in, there will remain, as Quine has emphasized, the trade-offs between the beliefs we attribute to a speaker and the interpretations we give his words. But the resulting indeterminacy cannot be so great but that any theory that passes the tests will serve to yield interpretations" (Davidson 2001c (1973): 139). See also Davidson 2001c (1974): 196 and 2001 (1975): 153.

L-sentences, though there will also be the option of supposing in some cases that a speaker's beliefs are typically or always mistaken.

Does appeal to the indeterminacy of interpretation meet the objection that there are a large number of different potential starting points for the radical interpreter at the second stage of his procedure which can be justified on the basis of his evidence? The answer, we think, is 'no'.

First of all, there is too wide a range of possible interpretations for it to be plausible that what is going on is merely a matter of indeterminacy. This is therefore a count against holding (given our constraints) both that behavioral evidence (and hold true attitudes) exhausts our evidence and that the concepts deployed in interpretation theory are purely theoretical concepts (consider our thought experiment in the previous section in this connection).

Second, it is not clear from the point of view of the radical interpreter that *he* can treat different theories he could confirm as *stating the same facts*, which is required in order to treat the resulting range of theories as an expression of the indeterminacy of interpretation, rather than simply underdetermination by all the possible conceptually relevant evidence. Here is the difficulty. From the point of view of the interpreter, the different *L*-sentences he can confirm are non-equivalent in the sense that they state different laws. This guarantees that the sentences (open or closed) on their right hand sides are not synonymous, for otherwise, since their left hand sides are the same, they would express the same proposition, and so could not express different laws. By hypothesis they do express different laws. Thus, starting with different *L*-sentences at the second stage of the procedure, however they are arrived at, will generate corresponding *TF*-sentences which from the interpreter's perspective must be treated as assigning different interpretations to the speaker's sentences. Thus, the interpreter must regard the different theories he can confirm as *strictly* incompatible with one another (not just apparently or intuitively). According to the two theories, sentences of the object language will mean different things. In other words, it is incoherent for the interpreter to regard the different theories which he could confirm as both true. For suppose he confirms two theories for a language *L*, designated as the language of a particular speaker, according to one of which (1) is true, and according to the other of which (2) is true. The interpreter also knows that (3) is true, and therefore that (4) is.

(1) 'Alpha is a gavagai' means in *L* that Alpha is a rabbit.
(2) 'Alpha is a gavagai' means in *L* that Alpha is a squirrel.
(3) 'rabbit' is not synonymous in English with 'squirrel'.

239

(4) 'Alpha is a rabbit' does not mean in English the same as 'Alpha is a squirrel'.

However, from (4) it follows that (1) and (2) cannot both be true, and, since they are consequences of the different meaning theories he can confirm, at least one theory must be incorrect. Although in our example we chose translations into sentences that differ in truth value (something which we have noted Davidson allows as possible), this point holds even if two interpretations take sentences into sentences of the metalanguage necessarily equivalent, provided they still differ in meaning.

It is no response to insist assignments of meanings to sentences should be relativized to an interpretation theory. This would remove the formal inconsistency noted above, but is *ad hoc* and unexplained. Claims about the meanings of sentences must be relativized only to languages or speakers. Nothing else is or could be relevant. Davidson himself has noted that *truth* is relativized only to a language (plus contextual parameters determined by speaker and time), for example, "there is, then, a reasonable way to relativize truth and reference: sentences are true, and words refer, relative to a language" (Davidson 2001*a* (1979): 240). Moreover, it is clear why on Davidson's view the truth of sentences in a language, or relative to a linguistic community, cannot be seen as relative to a truth theory, since facts about the truth conditions of sentences are used as evidence for the theory. The identification of the evidence must be independent of identification of the correct truth theory for the language. Since truth conditions for sentences are determined by what they mean, if meaning were relative to more than a language, truth would be also. It follows that meaning is relative only to a language.[200]

---

[200] Davidson once gave the following response to the objection (put by Ian Hacking) that two theories of interpretation that take the same object language sentence into a true and false metalanguage sentence could not both be true: "It is not a contradiction if the theories are relativized to a language, as all theories of truth are. Our mistake was to suppose there is a unique language to which a given utterance belongs. But we can without paradox take that utterance to belong to one or another language, provided we make allowance for a shift in other parts of our total theory of a person" (Davidson 2001*a* (1979): 239–40). It is not easy to see how his response can get a purchase on the objection in the text, since we identified L as the language of the speaker. Both theories are of L, and the truth predicate in each is relativized to L. Indeed, we could formulate a theory for an individual speaker without reference to a language at all. But let us waive this objection. Suppose our two theories are relativized to different languages. Then if each is just as good a theory of the speaker's language, but they are different languages, we are committed to saying that his language is identical to each of two distinct ones not identical with each other, which is a contradiction. In the next section, we consider whether Davidson's way of explaining what indeterminacy of interpretation comes to by appeal to an analogy with the use of numbers in measurement theory provides any relief.

Even if we waive this objection, however, relativization to an interpretation theory helps less than might be thought. A falsehood might still be derived, if meanings assigned to terms resulted in their having different extensions, provided that all instances of the following schema are true:

(5)   If ϕ means in L according to T that p and T is true, then ϕ is true in L iff p

(where 'according to T' marks the relativization of claims about meaning to a theory). For in this case, we can derive (6) from (appropriately relativized versions of) (1) and (2), on the assumption that each interpretation theory is true,

(6)   Alpha is a rabbit iff Alpha is a squirrel,

which is false. We cannot see any grounds for denying (5), which seems to express a basic conceptual truth about the connection between truth and meaning, one implicit in Tarski's Convention T (and one which Davidson endorses). With the choices the interpreter has about what to treat as a part of the *ceteris paribus* clause, it seems clearly open to him to assign meanings in a way that will assign different extensions to the same predicate. Thus, the interpreter cannot treat all the theories he can confirm as stating the same facts. To avoid this objection, the class of theories compatible with the evidence would have to be narrowed to one in which each theory assigned to each predicate the same extension.

It might be thought that appropriately revising assignments of referents to terms would enable one to maintain the same distribution of truth values over sentences. Thus, on one scheme we would interpret the pair 'Alpha' and 'is a rabbit' as *Alpha* and *is a rabbit*, where in our view Alpha is a rabbit, and on the other, as *Beta* and *is a squirrel*, where in our view Beta is a squirrel. However, we must also take into account demonstratives and quantifiers, which will complicate things. If we want our demonstratives to have as their referents what people demonstrate using them, then this will constrain different schemes to assign the same referents to uses of demonstratives, and we will get a result similar to (6) when we consider uses of 'This is a rabbit' in which either a rabbit or a squirrel is demonstrated. If we have predicates which differ in the number of things in their extensions, numerical quantifiers, often treated as logical terms, and *definable in first order logic*, if interpreted in the same way on both schemes, will give rise to troubles, for from our two schemes we would be able to derive sentences of the form, for example, 'There are n rabbits iff there are n squirrels'; for some replacement for 'n', one side will be true and the other false, if the number of rabbits is not the number of squirrels.[201] Thus, the logic of the object language, determined by *which* terms are *which logical terms*, would have to be indeterminate as well, in a way that allowed different interpretations without disturbing the distribution of truth values over sentences. But it is not easy to see how to do this, unless it is not even determinate which terms are referring terms and which are predicates, for the meanings of different quantifiers force different logical relations with other sentences based on their forms alone. For example, from 'For all x, x is F' each sentence of the form 'a is F' follows, where 'a' is a proper name.[202]

There is no refuge in appealing to an a priori argument for the possibility of radical interpretation, that is, for the presupposition of (Q2′), namely,

(P) One can come to know something sufficient to interpret another speaker from the evidential position of the radical interpreter.

If we had such an argument, we could maintain that since interpretation is possible, and more than one theory was confirmable from the radical interpreter's standpoint, and the radical interpreter had no evidence which could be brought to bear in favor of one theory over the other, there could be no difference in content between them. However, a proof that among the allowable theories are ones which cannot be jointly true would suffice to show that they are different in content, and consequently that there is no sound a priori argument for the possibility of radical interpretation.

---

[201] One might insist that the numerals could be reinterpreted on the two schemes as well, but this misses the point of the remark that the numerical quantifiers are definable in first order logic. We could rewrite 'There are 2 rabbits' e.g. using only logical terms, when we include, as is standard, the identity sign, '=', as a logical term, 'There is an x and there is a y such that (it is not the case that $x = y$ and (x is a rabbit and y is a rabbit))', and so on. Even if one denied that the first order paraphrase captured the meaning and form of the original, it would give rise to the problem independently.

[202] We will return to these matters in Ch. 21 on the inscrutability of reference. Davidson has suggested that "two satisfactory theories may differ in what they count as singular terms or quantifiers or predicates, or even with respect to the underlying logic itself" (2001a (1979): 228). It is not clear how much variation he thinks is possible, since he does say that such indeterminacy is "put under greater control if one insists, as I do, on a Tarski-style theory of truth as the basis of an acceptable translation manual" (ibid.). In any case, as we have noted, Davidson's own position commits him to rejecting relativization of truth and meaning to anything except languages, and also to theories which assign sentences with different truth values to the same object language sentence being equally well confirmed.

7. Does the Analogy with Measurement Theory Save the Position?

We have not yet considered Davidson's explanation of what indeterminacy of interpretation comes to, and why indeterminacy of interpretation is not a matter of concern. Davidson employs an analogy which draws on measurement theory to explain the relation between the different theories of a speaker's attitudes and meanings which are confirmable from the standpoint of the radical interpreter.[203] We will argue that the analogy cannot be used to blunt the force of the objection we are considering.

In measurement theory, one is concerned with how numbers are assigned to quantities or properties to keep track of relations among them. This requires first having a theory of the phenomena we wish to measure. The theory will state relations between the properties or quantities in terms of which we characterize the phenomena of interest. For example, the theory of thermodynamic temperature will state that for any systems, s_1, s_2, s_3, if the temperature of s_1 is more than that of s_2 and that of s_2 more than that of s_3, then that of s_1 is more than that of s_3, that is, temperatures are transitive. And here the 'more than' relation is given physical sense by a measurement technique that tells us when the temperature of one system is more than, less than, or the same as that of another (there need not, of course, be a single technique). The theory itself, or an auxiliary theory, will tell us what observations, under what conditions, tell us what properties or quantities, of the sort the theory is about, systems have, and what observations, under what conditions, establish that the properties or quantities stand in the relations the theory specifies, for example, by relating relative temperature to the height of a mercury column in a glass tube, or relative mass to the behavior of objects on a balance. The task then is to show how a systematic assignment of numbers to quantities or properties, anchored in observational conditions, can be used to mirror, or keep track of, in relations between the numbers assigned, the relations between the quantities or properties in terms of which we characterize the phenomena of interest. Measurement of thermodynamic temperature provides a simple example. To assign numbers to temperatures for the purpose of keeping track of the relations among them requires that we assign numbers that capture all of the distinctions in the phenomenon which we can draw on the basis of measurement techniques. Temperatures admit of an ordering on the basis of measurement techniques

---

[203] See Davidson 2001*a* (1974): 154, 2001*b* (1977): 224–5, 2001 (1989): 59–65.

on a linear scale; moreover, we can make sense physically of intervals between temperatures. Thus, we can make sense of the difference between the high and low temperatures on the winter solstice being the same as that between the high and low temperatures on the summer solstice. We can also make sense of a lowest temperature in physical terms (least molecular motion), which enables us to make physical sense of assigning an origin (the origin point of the Kelvin scale, $-273.15\,°C$). However, we cannot make sense of an absolute interval between temperatures that would support, for example, the claim that the temperature of boiling water was exactly *n* degrees more than that of freezing water. Thus, assigning zero to the minimum temperature, we assign numbers in ascending order on the basis of techniques for ordering temperatures. For this purpose we can choose arbitrarily the result of a measurement on some material in certain standard conditions as the temperature to which, for example, 100 will be assigned. Whether we assign 100 or 1,000 to the result of that measurement *x*, we will be able to keep track of the relations among temperatures equally well as long as we assign numbers consistently with the scale we have settled on. (The same point could be made using the more complicated example of decision theory.) Thus, numbers can be assigned to temperatures on what is called a ratio scale.[204] All scales measuring thermodynamic temperature assign the same physical state zero, but their choice of unit of temperature is arbitrary, and each can be obtained from each other by a simple multiplier, $t_1 = n \times t_2$.

Now consider two scales for assigning numbers to temperatures, ignoring absolute zero—the Fahrenheit and Centigrade scales. Clearly, there is no incompatibility between saying that the freezing point of water is 32 degrees Fahrenheit and 0 degrees Centigrade. These are just two ways of stating the same facts. Similarly, Davidson suggests, two different interpretation theories

---

[204] Common scales are nominal, ordinal, interval, ratio, and absolute. A *nominal* scale keeps track only of numerical differences between individuals or attributes, as in numbered jerseys worn by football players. An *ordinal* scale keeps track of an ordering relation on individuals or attributes. Examples are grades for academic performance and the Moh's scale for hardness, determined by which minerals scratch which. *Interval* scales assign numbers so that differences between numbers reflect differences of the attribute being measured, that is, using '$A(x)$' to represent the value of the attribute for x, and '$N(x)$' to represent the number assigned to x on an interval scale, if $\mathrm{diff}(A(x), A(y)) > \mathrm{diff}(A(s), A(t))$, then $N(x) - N(y) > N(s) - N(t)$. A *ratio* scale keeps track of both differences and ratios of quantities, adding to an interval scale an absolute origin, as in the case of thermodynamic temperature measured in degrees Kelvin, or measurement of length in feet or meters. An *absolute* scale assigns numbers to things so that all properties of the numbers reflect analogous properties of the attribute, as in using numbers to keep track of votes for candidates.

can state the same facts about a speaker.[205] The Fahrenheit and Centigrade scales are linear transformations of one another; the assignment of numbers to temperatures is unique up to a linear transformation ($ax + b$). Each acceptable assignment of numbers captures the same empirical pattern in the phenomenon of temperature. "In much the same way," Davidson says, "I suggest that what is invariant as between different acceptable theories of truth is meaning" (Davidson 2001*b* (1977): 225).

We have already seen that the analogy *must break down*, since unlike statements of temperature in Fahrenheit and in Centigrade, statements of meaning according to theories equally well confirmed from the radical interpreter's standpoint cannot all be true (they can, as we saw, entail what are clearly falsehoods). There is, however, another way to understand the analogy which might be of help. It is clear that a sentence of the form ⌜α is 5⌝ and of the form ⌜α is 7⌝ are incompatible. Someone who uses different assignments of numbers to keep track of temperatures does not do so because he thinks 'is 5' and 'is 7' mean the same. Rather, what he recognizes is that the structure of the relations among numbers can be used to keep track of an empirical pattern among temperatures. The possibility of doing this in different ways shows that the pattern of relations among numbers is richer than that among the states that the numbers are used to keep track of. Certain distinctions we draw among numbers lack empirical application; with temperature scales, there is no application of the concept of an absolute interval (the distance between 0 and 1, e.g.). Thus, we can say that the structure he uses to keep track of the phenomenon of temperature is essentially richer than the phenomenon itself.[206]

Likewise, we may say that the interpreter does not suppose that (1) and (2) mean the same, or are in any sense equivalent. Nonetheless, we may regard him as using either one, in the context of appropriate systems of assignments of

---

[205] Thus: "Indeterminacy of meaning or translation does not represent a failure to capture significant distinctions; it marks the fact that certain apparent distinctions are not significant. If there is indeterminacy, it is because when all the evidence is in, alternative ways of stating the facts remain open. An analogy from decision theory has already been noted: if the numbers 1, 2, 3 capture the meaningful relations in subjective value between three alternatives, then the numbers −17, −2, and +13 do as well. Indeterminacy of this kind cannot be of genuine concern" (Davidson 2001*a* (1974): 154). See also Davidson 2001*b* (1977): 224.

[206] Davidson uses just this metaphor in "Three Varieties of Knowledge" (2001*b* (1988): 214): "Given the richness of the structure represented by the set of one's own sentences, and the nature of the connections between the members of this set and the world, we should not be surprised if there are many ways of assigning our own sentences to the sentences and thoughts of someone else that capture everything of relevant interest."

meanings to sentences in the object language, to keep track of the phenomenon that his theory of interpretation deals with. On this basis, while recognizing (1) and (2) are not in fact equivalent, he may, in giving a theory of his subject matter, relativize assignments of interpretations to the 'scales' he arrives at by different routes in interpretation. These scales would be identified by the whole system of interpretation. He would then be using the meanings of his sentences to keep track of a phenomenon which had a structure less complicated than the structure of the relations among the meanings of his sentences. That would account for why different assignments of meanings to object language sentences work equally well. Thus, by adopting the hypothesis that the relations among the sentences in the object language were essentially less rich (admit of fewer distinctions) than those among the sentences in the metalanguage, one could maintain the thesis of indeterminacy despite the fact that, in general, meaning is not relativized to anything other than language, and the fact that different verifiable theories assign incompatible meanings to object language sentences. (In this way, we might explain why we can keep track of the behavior of pets equally well by assigning them any number of beliefs we would regard as different in ourselves: 'Wang-Tzu expects Professor Ludwig to be home soon' will do as well as 'Wang-Tzu expects his master to open the door in the near future' as far as keeping track of overt behavior goes.)

As far as we can tell, this is the *only* way the analogy could be used to try to save the indeterminacy thesis. However, the very asymmetry postulated between the metalanguage and object language on this way of drawing the analogy, which is what allows it to serve as a way of making sense of the claim of indeterminacy despite the strict incompatibility of the theories confirmable from the radical interpreter's standpoint, is also why it cannot protect radical interpretation from the objection we have leveled. The claim on behalf of the procedures of the radical interpreter is that:

> (The Claim) For any speaker, an interpretation theory
> confirmed by the procedures of the radical interpreter will
> be a correct theory for that speaker's language.

However, we have shown that for a radical interpreter to be in a position to claim that his procedures have yielded a correct theory, he must be able to justifiably hold also:

> (The Assumption) The relations among the object lan-
> guage sentences are not as structurally rich as those among
> the sentences of the interpreter's language.

246

The radical interpreter is himself a speaker, however, and so subsumed by the generalization expressed in the Claim. Manifestly, then, the interpreter will not be in a position to confirm a correct theory about a speaker of his own language, because in that case the Assumption *is false by hypothesis.*[207] Thus, if the foregoing reasoning is correct, radical interpretation is *not* in principle possible.

It should be noted that it was crucial to this line of argument that we took the goal of the interpreter to be to arrive at interpretive *TF*-sentences. If his goal were only to arrive at true *TF*-sentences, the present objection would collapse. Restating as we did the answer to question (Q1) in Chapter 11, 'What can we know that would enable us to interpret any potential utterance of a speaker?', helped to highlight this requirement, and so to elicit more clearly what the difficulties are that stand in the way of success at radical interpretation. We suspect part of the reason this difficulty has not been so readily apparent is due to unclarity about what the interpreter has to know to interpret another's speech that has arisen from the way Davidson has answered question (Q1).

Where does this leave us with the claim that the concepts deployed in the interpreter's theory are purely theoretical concepts which ensure that empirically equivalent theories that account for all the evidence state the same facts? The answer is that we must give up either the claim that the concepts are in the relevant sense purely theoretical, or that all the relevant evidence is available to the radical interpreter, or that the radical interpreter has brought to bear all of the a priori theory available. We see little hope for eking out enough additional constraints by appeal to what can be established a priori to help much. If this is right, the upshot is that we must reject either the idea that the radical interpreter has available all the evidence relevant to the deployment of these concepts, or the assumption that they are purely theoretical concepts of the relevant sort in the first place, or both. We trace out the ramifications of this for other theses Davidson has argued for on the basis of reflection on radical interpretation primarily in Part III.

---

[207] This matter will also come up in our discussion in Ch. 21.

16

Development of a Unified Theory of Meaning and Action

> The immediate psychological environment of linguistic aptitudes and accomplishments is to be found in the propositional attitudes, states or events that are described in intensional idiom; intentional action, desires, beliefs, and their close relatives like hopes, fears, wishes and attempts. Not only do the various propositional attitudes and their conceptual attendants form the setting in which speech occurs, but there is no chance of arriving at a deep understanding of linguistic facts except as that understanding is accompanied by an interlocking account of the central cognitive and conative attitudes.
>
> (Davidson 2004 (1980): 151–2)

In this chapter, we explain a development in Davidson's account of the procedures of the radical interpreter. The development involves bringing to bear more explicitly the constraints imposed by the framework of decision theory on an interpretation of another. Application of decision theory to explanation of behavior requires assigning subjective probabilities— or degrees of belief—and desirabilities—or degrees of value—in explaining action. These assignments are of particular importance in interpreting "non-observation" terms. We explain the motivation for the development in §1. In §2, we discuss the problem of determining degrees of belief and desirabilities, and Davidson's solution in §3. In §4, we summarize the new procedure of interpretation, and discuss its implications for the conclusions reached so far.

1. Interpretation and Attitudes

We have already indicated that interpreting another's speech is to be conceived of in the context of a general account of the contents of his attitudes and the explanation of his actions. This connection is apparent immediately in the standard explanation for a speaker's hold true attitudes, which is to yield simultaneously an interpretation of his sentences and the assignment of content to his beliefs. But the connections between a general theory of a speaker's actions and attitudes and an interpretation of his speech are tighter and more complex than this suggests. Of course, assuming we have identified a speaker's attitudes towards sentences, not just his hold true attitudes, but also his attitudes of fearing a sentence true, hoping it true, desiring it true, preferring the truth of one sentence to another, and so on, the interpretations assigned to the speaker's sentences will yield assignments of contents to his fears, hopes, desires, and so on. These assignments will yield predictions about how the agent will act in various circumstances, which can be checked, and used to correct one's assignments of contents, and so in turn interpretations of the speaker's sentences. (This assumes that for each, or at least most, of a speaker's attitudes, he has a corresponding attitude toward the truth of a sentence of his that would express the content of the attitude, and that this attitude is a result of his knowing the meanings of his sentences and finding appropriate the relevant attitude toward the sentence on the basis of the attitude whose content the sentence expresses. Thus, we are here assuming that in general if, for example, an agent desires that *p*, and believes (or knows) that *s* means that *p*, he will desire that *s* be true. It is not altogether clear this assumption is correct. One need not desire what is necessarily equivalent to what one desires, even if one sees it is necessary and sufficient for the satisfaction of one's desire.) This suggests we could regard an interpretation theory as a combined theory of meaning and action, that is, a theory which aims both to assign interpretations to a speaker's sentences and contents to his actions. The primary evidence for the former is sentences held true, and for the latter is the speaker's preferences as exhibited in his actions.

So far we have been assuming that identifying a speaker's hold true attitudes would suffice to yield an interpretation of every sentence in his language. Hold true attitudes offer insight initially into how to interpret occasion sentences. Since any term can appear in an occasion sentence, it is plausible to suppose the interpretations assigned to occasion sentences will provide evidence for the interpretations of all terms in the language. However, with terms "more or less remote from what is immediately observed" (Davidson 2004

(1980): 157), interpreting them correctly, even in occasion sentences, will depend upon seeing how they are used in non-occasion sentences, and, in particular, will depend on how the speaker treats occasion sentences as supporting sentences containing them, and what occasion sentences he treats as consequences of sentences which contain them. That is, the interpretation of terms whose application conditions are guided by a complex theory in which they are embedded will depend upon tracing out the connections of support between sentences about the immediately observable and the sentences more remote from it (theoretical sentences, say). Since support relations will typically be weaker than entailment, what is wanted is a measure of the degree to which a speaker takes a given occasion sentence (against the background of the rest of his theory) to support a theoretical sentence. This will often be reflected in how his confidence in the truth of a theoretical sentence increases or decreases with corresponding increases or decreases in his confidence in the truth of occasion sentences.[208] Once we recognize the importance of degree of belief in this context, we can also see it will be of central importance even in the case of interpreting occasion sentences, since often we will hold true sentences about events in our environment with less than perfect confidence. ("It looked like a rabbit, but I only caught a glimpse of it, so I'm not completely sure it was.") Information of this sort would obviously be of great help in interpreting observation sentences.

This means that we ultimately want to look not just at hold true attitudes, but also at the degrees of confidence a speaker has in the truth of his sentences, and, likewise, for optative attitudes toward sentences, the degree to which the speaker desires the sentence to be true, the degree being determined by the ranking of sentences in one's preferences. We may expect, then, that a fully worked-out interpretation theory would need to utilize both degrees of confidence in the truth of sentences (subjective probabilities) and relative desirabilities assigned to the truth of sentences.

2. The Problem of Assigning Desirabilities and Degrees of Belief

This introduces a thus far overlooked problem, however. If correctly assigning interpretations to sentences requires identifying subjective probabilities and desirabilities, how can this be done without assuming what our interpretation

---

[208] See Davidson 2004 (1980): 157.

theory is supposed to yield? The method introduced by Ramsey (see Chapter 12) to extract probabilities and desirabilities from evidence in the form of choices among gambles *presupposes* we can interpret the subject's speech, that is, that we are able to identify already the speaker's attitude contents, that is, his attitudes toward gambles, which would typically be determined experimentally by presenting him with the gambles and asking which he preferred. This is not information to which the radical interpreter can help himself.

Davidson's unified theory of meaning and action, a refinement of the account of radical interpretation offered in his earlier papers, aims to provide a solution to this problem.[209] To solve the problem of breaking into the circle of meaning and belief, we chose an attitude which is a vector of both, namely, the attitude of holding a sentence true. The more general problem can be treated in a parallel fashion. We need to identify an attitude which can be used as evidence simultaneously for a speaker's subjective probabilities, desirabilities, and meanings.

The solution lies in the attitude of preferring one sentence true to another. This is the analog of holding true for radical decision theory. For an agent's preferences among alternatives are expressed in his actions. In Jeffrey's version of decision theory,[210] which is the decision-theoretic framework that Davidson adopts, the agent is represented as having attitudes toward propositions. We cannot help ourselves to propositions. To do so is equivalent to helping ourselves to the contents of the agent's preferences. However, on the assumption that if the agent prefers p to q, and knows that s means that p and s' means that q, then he will prefer the truth of s to the truth of s', we can be assured of a source of data which preserves patterns among preferences without presupposing we know in detail their contents. We prefer one sentence true to another because we place more value on the state of affairs expressed by the one than by the other. This can be because of the intrinsic value we place on each state of affairs, or because of the values we place on their possible consequences and our estimate of the likelihood of their coming about in the event that the sentences that express them are true. The latter case is of special interest in the present context, for, typically, we do not act for the sake of acting, but for some further end, and our deliberations about what to do even in the most mundane matters involve complicated means–end reasoning (the reasoning need not be explicit). In these cases, the preference for q over t can be represented as a result of the computation represented in (1), where n

[209] See Davidson 2004 1980, 1985*a*, 1990*b*: appendix.   [210] Jeffrey 1983.

and m are the number of possible outcomes, and 'p', 'q', 'r', and 't', together with subscripts, represent the contents of attitudes, and 'des(x)' and 'prob(x)' are functions from contents of desires and beliefs to numbers representing the degree of value and belief assigned to the contents, respectively. 'prob(x/y)' expresses the probability of x given y, which may be understood as the degree of confidence the agent would assign to x, *ceteris paribus*, if he accepted y.

$$(1) \quad \sum_{i=0}^{n} \text{des}(p_i) \times \text{prob}(p_i/q) > \sum_{i=0}^{m} \text{des}(r_i) \times \text{prob}(r_i/t)$$

This computation will be mirrored by one involving sentences represented in (2), where the agent believes (knows) that s expresses the state of affairs that q and so on.

$$(2) \quad \sum_{i=0}^{n} \text{des}(s_i) \times \text{prob}(s_i/s) > \sum_{i=0}^{m} \text{des}(s_i') \times \text{prob}(s_i'/s')$$

Thus, starting with preferences among sentences, knowledge of which does not presuppose detailed knowledge of the contents of attitudes, we may hope, applying suitable constraints, to derive subjective desirabilities, subjective probabilities, and meanings.

3. The Solution

The procedure Davidson outlines does not replace his earlier description of radical interpretation, but subsumes it. First, we will lay out the procedure. Then we will comment on it.

The primary task to be solved is identifying either the probabilities or desirabilities attached to sentences. If we had either, we could solve for the other. Once we had subjective probabilities, we could use these in conjunction with our earlier procedure to produce a finer-grained portrait of the conditions under which speakers hold sentences true, and arrive at correlations between hold true attitudes and environmental conditions we take to be interpretive of the sentences held true.

We take Jeffrey's formulation of decision theory as our framework,[211] modified to apply to (meaningful) sentences, which consists of the following axioms (where 'prob(x)'='the probability that s is true', and 'des(s)'='the

---

[211] Jeffrey wrote the first edition of *The Logic of Decision* at Stanford from 1961 to 1964, and so would have been in contact with Davidson at the time (and acknowledges his help in the preface: "the inception of this book owes much to the stimulation of Donald Davidson and Patrick Suppes [at Stanford]"); hence, Davidson's deep and early familiarity with Jeffrey's version of decision theory.

desirability of *s*'s truth'):[212]

I. Probability axioms

(a) $\text{prob}(s) \geq 0$;

(b) $\text{prob}(T) = 1$;

(c) if $\ulcorner s$ and $r \urcorner$ is necessarily false, then $\text{prob}(\ulcorner s$ or $r \urcorner) = \text{prob}(s) + \text{prob}(r)$ (where 'T' represents a tautology).

II. Desirability axiom

If $\text{prob}(\ulcorner s$ and $r \urcorner) = 0$ and $\text{prob}(\ulcorner s$ or $\urcorner r) \neq 0$, then

$$\text{des}(\ulcorner s \text{ or } r \urcorner) = \frac{\text{prob}(s)\text{des}(s) + \text{prob}(r)\text{des}(r)}{\text{prob}(s) + \text{prob}(r)}$$

The procedure has two main steps. In the first, we identify the logical constants in the object language. In the second, we use these to assign a probability ranking to sentences in the object language for the subject, and then use these in turn to determine his desirabilities. The procedure employed in the second stage has been worked out by Jeffrey. Davidson's contribution is to show how to identify the logical constants in the language by relying solely on preferences among sentences. First we present Davidson's proposal. Then we outline its role in the fully revised characterization of radical interpretation.

Our aim is to identify a pattern among preferences of sentences that will enable us to identify certain particles as logical constants. Thus, we must presuppose we can identify truth-functional connectives in the language.[213] The key to the appropriate pattern must be found in the application of the

[212] See Jeffrey 1983: ch. 5. Jeffrey's account is more general than the sketch of the relation between preference, probability, and desirability just given, since it sees the desirability of propositions as a matter of the sum of their desirability in various possible situations weighted by the probability of the situation obtaining, independently of thinking of the proposition as having consequences for one's acting, though each of these can be accounted for in Jeffrey's system.

[213] This is not an entirely innocent assumption. For we need not just to identify sentential connectives, but those that are truth-functional connectives. To do this, it looks as if we need to show that the truth or falsity of the containing sentence depends only on the truth or falsity of the contained sentences. It is hard to see how to do this without determining at the same time which truth function the connective represents. In the end, it may be better to think of all of the constraints being applied to the evidence at once to determine the best overall fit.

above axioms, and of II in particular. To see how, let '*r*' be 'not-*s*'. Then we have from II:

$$(3) \quad \text{des}(s \text{ or not-}s) = \frac{\text{prob}(s)\text{des}(s) + \text{prob}(\text{not-}s)\text{des}(\text{not-}s)}{\text{prob}(s) + \text{prob}(\text{not-}s)}$$

We assume an agent is indifferent to tautologies, and assign 0 as the value of any sentence to which he is indifferent. Utilizing the fact that $\text{prob}(\text{not-}s) = 1 - \text{prob}(s)$, we can solve for $\text{prob}(s)$, to derive:

$$(4) \quad \text{prob}(s) = \frac{-\text{des}(\text{not-}s)}{\text{des}(s) - \text{des}(\text{not-}s)}$$

Note that here we must assume that $\text{des}(s) \neq \text{des}(\text{not-}s)$. This is equivalent to:

$$(5) \quad \text{prob}(s) = \frac{1}{1 - \frac{\text{des}(s)}{\text{des}(\text{not-}s)}}$$

(provided $\text{des}(\text{not-}s)$ is not zero, of course). The interest of this formula is that it shows that, since probabilities must be between 0 and 1, inclusive, if we assign 0 to a tautology, for *every* non-tautological sentence, it cannot be that it and its negation are both less desirable than a tautology or more. For in that case, $\text{prob}(s)$, by the above formula, would be greater than 1. This can also be seen from (4), since if $\text{des}(s)$ and $\text{des}(\text{not-}s)$ were both less than zero, if $\text{des}(s)$ were less than $\text{des}(\text{not-}s)$, the ratio would be less than zero, and if $\text{des}(s)$ were greater than $\text{des}(\text{not-}s)$, the ratio would be greater than 1. Similarly, if both were greater than zero, if $\text{des}(s)$ were greater than $\text{des}(\text{not-}s)$, the ratio would be less than zero, and if it were less than $\text{des}(\text{not-}s)$, the ratio would be greater than 1. This informs us about what pattern of preferences we will find between a sentence, its negation, and any logical truth, T, namely,

(6)   If $\text{des}(s) > \text{dess}(T)$, then $\text{des}(\text{not-}s) \leq \text{des}(T)$;
       If $\text{des}(\text{not-}s) > \text{des}(T)$, then $\text{des}(s) \leq \text{des}(T)$.

Suppose we had identified a logical truth in the object language (let it be T). And suppose also we had identified a one-place truth-functional connective, '@'. If we found that for our subject,

(7)   For all object language sentences ϕ, if $\text{des}(\phi) > \text{des}(T)$, then $\text{des}(\ulcorner @ \phi \urcorner) \leq \text{des}(T)$ *and* if $\text{des}(\ulcorner @ \phi \urcorner) > \text{des}(T)$, then $\text{des}(\phi) \leq \text{des}(T)$,

we would have found a pattern that identifies '@' as negation.

The trouble with this suggestion is that we cannot be sure of identifying a logical truth (as opposed to an obvious truth) without already having an interpretation of some logical constants. We need to look, then, for a structure in T that guarantees it is a logical truth in the context of (7). That is, we need to find a pattern of truth-functional connectives in T as well as in the sentence we are testing, which will guarantee that if (7) holds for all sentences in the pattern, a unique interpretation is forced on the logical constants employed. This will obviously be easier if we look to use the same constant in T as we use to form the negation of the sentence whose desirability we compare with that of T. We have this in the Sheffer stroke '|'. (This is usually given one of two interpretations, either *not both p and q* or *not either p or q*—Davidson gives the first.) The negation of a sentence ϕ can be represented as $\ulcorner \phi|\phi \urcorner$. For the logical truth, let us choose the following: $\ulcorner (\psi|\theta)|((\psi|\theta)|(\psi|\theta)) \urcorner$.[214] This is equivalent to $\ulcorner$ not-$((\psi|\theta)$ and not-$(\psi|\theta)) \urcorner$, which is a logical truth, $\ulcorner$ not-$(\psi|\theta)$ or $(\psi|\theta) \urcorner$ (on the *other* standard interpretation of the Sheffer stroke, it is equivalent to a necessary falsehood, $\ulcorner$ not-$((\psi|\theta)$ or not-$(\psi|\theta)) \urcorner$). Substituting in (7), converting and quantifying over the new variables, we get:

(8) For all object language sentences ϕ, ψ, θ if des$(\phi) > $ des$\ulcorner (\psi|\theta) |((\psi|\theta)|(\psi|\theta)) \urcorner)$, then des$\ulcorner \phi|\phi \urcorner) \leq$ des$\ulcorner (\psi|\theta)|((\psi|\theta)|(\psi|\theta)) \urcorner)$ *and if* des$\ulcorner \phi|\phi \urcorner) > $ des$\ulcorner (\psi|\theta)|((\psi|\theta)|(\psi|\theta)) \urcorner)$, then des$(\phi) \leq$ des$\ulcorner (\psi|\theta)|((\psi|\theta)|(\psi|\theta)) \urcorner)$.

Now, suppose '|' is a logical constant in the object language which we are seeking to interpret, so far unidentified, but we discover (8) to be true of it for our subject. If we know a sentence of the form $\ulcorner \phi|\phi \urcorner$ is not a logical truth (or falsehood), we can be sure '|' is the Sheffer stroke. (If a sentence of the form $\ulcorner \phi|\phi \urcorner$ were a logical truth (or falsehood), its desirability (and that of its negation) would be zero, and the antecedents of both conditionals would be false, for all sentences.) It is sufficient for this that there be sentences ϕ, ψ, such that des$\ulcorner \phi|\phi \urcorner) \neq$ des$\ulcorner \psi|\psi \urcorner)$, if we assume, as we have been, that agents are indifferent to logical truths.[215]

It is clear that if '|' were the Sheffer stroke, (8) would be true for all sentences in the subject's language. (This is, of course, an idealization—in practice, we would look for the pattern to hold for a wide enough range of cases, and to be able to explain lapses.) Why is it necessary? The reason is we know that '|' is a truth-functional connective, and that $\ulcorner \phi|\phi \urcorner$ is not a tautology or a necessary

---

[214] It is not clear why Davidson chooses such a complicated logical truth. A simpler logical truth would do as well, e.g. something of the form $\ulcorner (\psi|(\psi|\psi)) \urcorner$. All the considerations which will be brought to bear below will apply as well to the simpler form.

[215] The assumption is justified by the claim that one can desire something only if one does not believe it to be true, and the (idealized) assumption that one believes all logical truths.

falsehood: in this case a pattern among preferences of the sort exhibited in (8) will obtain only if it is a pattern of the sort exhibited in (7). While there are other truth table assignments to '|', such as (TFTT),[216] that will make $\ulcorner (\psi|\theta)|((\psi|\theta)|(\psi|\theta)) \urcorner$ a logical truth, the pattern in (7) will be exhibited only if at the same time the connective makes $\ulcorner \phi|\phi \urcorner$ the negation of ϕ (given that $\ulcorner \phi|\phi \urcorner$ is not a logical truth or logical falsehood). Only interpreting '|' as (FFFT) or (FTTT) will secure this, which are the two traditional interpretations of the Sheffer stroke.[217] (In the appendix we offer an alternative way of identifying the Sheffer stroke using the same resources which is simpler.)

Once we have identified the Sheffer stroke, we can identify other logical constants; as we know, $\ulcorner \phi|\phi \urcorner$ is equivalent to the negation of ϕ, and we can distinguish, indeed, between the two interpretations of the Sheffer stroke simply by discovering whether the agent holds true or holds false (sentences of the form) $\ulcorner (\phi|(\phi|\phi)) \urcorner$. Of course, we do not need to assume that the object language contains a binary logical connective that is equivalent to the Sheffer stroke. The technique outlined above would work as well for a complex of connectives that was equivalent to the Sheffer stroke, $\ulcorner -(\phi\&\psi) \urcorner$, for example. Once we have identified the logical constants, we can employ Jeffrey's axioms to assign probabilities to sentences, given preferences among sentences.

The key to determining probabilities, once we have identified logical constants, is to identify a logical truth, which we can assign the value 0.

---

[216] This is the series of truth values assigned to the sentence when assignments to the components are TT, TF, FT, FF, respectively.

[217] Davidson's discussion is compressed. He fails to note that there are two interpretations of the Sheffer stroke that will make $\ulcorner \phi|\phi \urcorner$ the negation of $\ulcorner \phi \urcorner$. Jeffrey claims it does not make sense to assign a desirability to logical falsehoods. He bases his claim on the assumption that the rule for computing the desirability of a proposition (or sentence) is the following: "the desirability of a proposition is a weighted average of the desirabilities of the cases in which it is true, where the weights are proportional to the probabilities of the cases" (Jeffrey 1983: 78). Since a necessary falsehood is never true (there is no way for the world to be that would make a necessary falsehood true), the description is non-denoting for a necessarily false proposition. Desirabilities in decision theory are supposed to track attitudes of an ideal agent. Underlying this rule is presumably the assumption that an agent desires complete states of the world, so that desires for individual propositions can be reduced to desirabilities of the states of the world they would play a role in describing. It is assumed the agent places values only on ways (he believes) the world could be, and has no mistaken beliefs about the way the world could be. However, even if we were to abandon this assumption, which is not demanded by Jeffrey's axioms, the utility of the procedure is not undermined. If we assume a desirability can be assigned to a logical falsehood, from the desirability axiom, we can deduce that it must be assigned the same value as a tautology. But given this, if the pattern in (8) holds, we will know we have identified the Sheffer stroke on one of its interpretations, and then we can identify other logical constants, since, as we have seen, negation is definable in terms of the Sheffer stroke regardless of which interpretation is chosen. Even apart from this, as we note below, we can test to see whether $\ulcorner (\psi|\theta)|((\psi|\theta)|(\psi|\theta)) \urcorner$ is held to be true or false by the agent, and so determine which interpretation is appropriate.

Then, to find the preference ranking among sentences for the agent, we order them on a scale above and below the ranking of T. We assign numbers to the sentences in the preference ranking so as to preserve their ordering, and then use equation (5) to assign probabilities to sentences. If we had assigned the following rankings to a sentence ϕ and its negation $\ulcorner$not-$\phi\urcorner$,

$$
\begin{array}{cc}
2 & \phi \\
0 & T \\
-1 & \text{not-}\phi
\end{array}
$$

the probability of ϕ would be 1/3. Likewise, if for some sentence ϕ, des(ϕ) = des($\ulcorner$not $-\phi\urcorner$), then prob(ϕ) = 1/2. Thus, from a full ranking of sentences, recoverable from an exhaustive pairwise ranking, one can recover all the information relevant to subjective probabilities, given the assumptions about how to determine the desirability of a sentence.[218]

4. Summary of the Revised Procedure and Discussion

As mentioned above, the unified theory of meaning and action refines the procedure of the radical interpreter described above, rather than replacing it. The new procedure can be outlined as follows:

Stage 1

Use patterns among preferences to identity truth-functional connectives as above, and, thence, logical truths.

Stage 2

Use Jeffery's technique to assign subjective probabilities and desirabilities to sentences.

Stage 3

Identify hold true attitudes (and their associated degree of belief) toward occasion sentences in particular, and use information about the conditions

---

[218] There will be many different ways of assigning numbers to desirabilities and probabilities that will preserve the preference ranking in conformity with Jeffrey's axioms for decision theory. See Jeffrey 1983: ch. 8 for details. A study of this also helps us gain greater insight into Davidson's claim that, in assigning one's own sentences to another's in the context of an interpretation theory, the possibility of arriving at different interpretation theories is not a matter of underdetermination, but indeterminacy. For reasons we have given in Ch. 15, we believe the parallel does not hold.

under which they are held true, and to what *degree*, to formulate L_R-sentences:

> (L_R)   For times t, speakers S, *ceteris paribus*, S holds true (to degree R)s at t iff p.

Stage 4

The modification of the form in which the data for the truth theory is cast will require a modification to how the principle of charity (interpreted as Grace) is formulated and employed. Previously, we required a speaker's belief be prompted by a condition which is expressed using a sentence which gives the content of the belief (which guarantees it is true). What should replace this? Consider an L_R sentence. When R is close to 1, we will want to use pretty much the same assumptions outlined in Chapter 12, that is, we will assume that the belief prompted by the conditions expressed in the L_R sentence has its content given by the sentence that expresses those conditions. As R falls off from 1, but is still above $1/2$, we will expect to find that the conditions that the hold true attitude (with associated degree of belief) is associated with provide evidence that supports the belief to that degree. Correspondingly, we should expect associated hold true attitudes directed toward sentences which express that the evidence conditions obtain whose degrees are close to 1. We will look for assignments of contents which make sense of these interrelated attitudes. If a speaker holds true s to degree n (not close to 1 but above $1/2$), and holds true s' with degree of belief close to 1, in the same circumstances, after our tentative assignment of a T-sentence on the basis of the L_R-sentence for s', if its truth conditions provide evidence to degree n for the truth of another sentence s^* of the metalanguage, we may take this as prima facie evidence that s^* gives interpretive truth conditions for s. Similarly, when degrees of belief in the truth of sentences are below $1/2$, we will look for sentences held true with degree of belief close to 1 whose assigned truth conditions provide evidence against those sentences being true to the appropriate degree. Of course, there is ample room for slippage in these assignments, and the correct assignments must emerge from the best overall fit of evidence to data.

Stage 5

Use the T-sentences arrived at in stage 4 to formulate an initial truth theory which entails them.

Stage 6

Employ information about subjective probabilities to formulate hypotheses about axioms for theoretical terms and sentences in the language.

Stage 7

Make predictions about the agent's actions and the circumstances in which he will hold true (to various degrees) various so far untested sentences, and test the predictions, modifying hypotheses until theory and observation converge.

Obviously, this omits many details and subtleties, but it indicates the place of the new techniques in Davidson's previous account of radical interpretation.

The main object of Stage 1 is to identify the logical constants in the object language to enable us to assign subjective probabilities and desirabilities. That the a priori constraints on the relations among desirabilities, subjective probabilities, and preferences give rise to patterns that restrict the interpretation of particular logical constants or configurations of logical constants is a potent illustration of how these sorts of holistic constraints provide important clues to interpretation. We should note, however, that this is not the only sort of clue to the meanings of logical constants we can exploit. It is important that to employ the technique described above at all, we must first have a syntactical description of the object language and have identified the category of truth-functional sentential connectives. This indicates the extent to which the above procedure is partially artificial, since an identification of the logical constants *as* logical constants would probably not proceed completely independently from trying out various hypotheses to see how well they helped to predict both behavior and what we take to be hold true attitudes and relations among hold true attitudes. The latter provides a important independent source of clues to the identification of logical constants. Suppose we have identified a binary sentential connective '@', but do not yet know whether or not it is a truth-functional connective. Representing degree of belief by a subscript on 'holds', suppose we find that (9) and (10) are true.

(9) For all ϕ, ψ, S holds$_R$ true $\ulcorner \phi @ \psi \urcorner$ at t iff S holds$_R$ true ϕ at t or S holds$_R$ true ψ at t iff S holds$_R$ true $\ulcorner \psi @ \phi \urcorner$

(10) For all $\phi, \psi, \theta, \delta$ such that S holds$_R \phi$ and θ alike in truth value and ψ and δ alike in truth value, S holds$_R$ true $\ulcorner \phi @ \psi \urcorner$ at t iff S holds$_R$ true $\ulcorner \theta @ \delta \urcorner$ at t.

259

(We are not assuming we know which degree of belief to assign, only sameness of degree of belief.) In practice, of course, we seek such patterns to hold for the most part, and expect explanations when they do not, such as that the sentences are too long. If we found (9) and (10) to be (approximately) true for a speaker and a sentential connective '@', we would identify '@' as disjunction; no other interpretation is possible. The relation is symmetric, extensional, and sentences in which it is the main connective are held true to a certain degree iff one or the other of its two main component sentences is. Similar observations apply to the other sentential connectives we could identify in the object language. Thus, Stage 1 in the above procedure is not necessary in order to identify logical constants and proceed with the rest of the task of interpreting a speaker; what it does is provide an additional test, and illustrates, as we said, the way in which these constraints on the interaction between preference, belief, and desire constrain interpretations of the subject's speech.

The procedure for the unified theory of meaning and action modifies that outlined in Chapter 12. Do such revisions undermine the results reached in Chapter 15? No. The radical interpreter must still make use of L_R-sentences for sentences for which the degree of belief is high in order to arrive at interpretive *TF*-sentences. Unless attention to degree of belief and desirabilities assigned to sentences forces a unique selection of L_R-sentences (unique up to the interpretiveness of the corresponding *TF*-sentences, from the point of view of the interpreter's language), which seems implausible (again, recall the thought experiment of Chapter 15, §5), the interpreter cannot regard the different interpretation theories he confirms as all saying the same thing, and so cannot regard them all as correct; and, as we observed, there is no refuge in the thought that the object language may simply be conceptually poorer than the metalanguage, because this cannot be so in general, on pain of making each interpreter of another speak a language no other could! If there is still underdetermination after taking into account the full power of the constraints imposed by decision theory, it shows not that there is indeterminacy, but that radical interpretation starts from too impoverished a set of data (or too few constraints) to justify a correct interpretation theory.

Appendix: An Alternative Method of Identifying Logical Connectives

In this appendix we describe a different method for identifying the equivalent of the Sheffer stroke by attention to patterns among prefer true attitudes directed toward sentences than the one presented in the body of the chapter, which was suggested to us by Piers Rawling (see Rawling 2002).

Suppose we know '|' is a binary truth-functional connective, and we wish to test for whether it is the Sheffer stroke. It is if, and only if, its truth table is either FTTT or FFFT. Suppose we know for a given agent S, restricting our quantifiers to sentences in S's language,

(A) For all sentences ϕ, des(ϕ) $\neq$ des($\ulcorner \phi|\phi \urcorner$);
(B) There are sentences θ, ψ, such that des($\ulcorner \theta|\theta \urcorner$) $\neq$ des($\ulcorner \psi|\psi \urcorner$).

We assume the desirabilities of truth-functionally equivalent sentences are the same (see n. 217). (B) suffices to show that $\ulcorner \theta|\theta \urcorner$ is not a logical truth or falsehood and that the domain of quantification is not empty. Since by hypothesis '|' is a truth-functional connective, it follows that $\ulcorner \theta|\theta \urcorner$ is equivalent to the negation of θ, that is, that whether a sentence is true or false, the application of '|' to it yields a sentence logically equivalent to its negation. Thus, the truth table for '|' is represented by one of the columns under '$\theta|\psi$' in Figure 2.

To show '|' is the Sheffer stroke, we would need reason to rule out the middle two columns. Suppose we know also about S that:

(C) For all sentences θ, des(θ) $\neq$ des($\ulcorner \theta|(\theta|\theta) \urcorner$);
(D) For all sentences ψ, des($\ulcorner \psi|\psi \urcorner$) $\neq$ des($\ulcorner \psi|(\psi|\psi) \urcorner$).

ψ	θ	$\theta\|\psi$			
T	T	F	F	F	F
T	F	T	T	F	F
F	T	T	F	T	F
F	F	T	T	T	T

Figure 2

θ	$\theta\|\theta$	$\theta\|(\theta\|\theta)$			
T	F	T	T	F	F
F	T	T	F	T	F
Options:		1	2	3	4

Figure 3

Consider Figure 3, which displays the values of θ, $\ulcorner \theta|\theta \urcorner$, and $\ulcorner \theta|(\theta|\theta) \urcorner$ which are compatible with the assignments in Figure 2. (C) is incompatible with option 2. (D) is incompatible with option 3. Thus, if we know (A)–(D), we can identify '|' as the Sheffer stroke (of course, as above, in practice, we will look to find that for the most part these hold, and seek to explain why they do not when they should, if we arrive at the hypothesis that '|' is the Sheffer stroke). In effect, as Rawling points out, this method relies just on the fact that we have a relation which holds between two sentences just in case they are not truth-functionally equivalent. The same argument can be repeated for any such relation.

17

The Reality of Language

> I conclude that there is no such thing as a language, not if a language
> is anything like what many philosophers and linguists have supposed.
> There is therefore no such thing to be learned, mastered or born with.
>
> (Davidson 1986: 446)

In "A Nice Derangement of Epitaphs," Davidson declares there is "no
such thing as a language" (1986: 446), at least not in a sense which many
philosophers of language and linguists have wanted to maintain. He claims
to have himself held a view of the sort he seeks to discredit. In this chapter,
we will examine his argument against languages (in the relevant sense). It will
be crucial, of course, to clarify the conditions that he is placing on something
being called "a language," in whatever sense it is in which the conclusion
denies there are any.

Critics have thought Davidson's own program in the philosophy of language
is undercut if his argument succeeds. Ian Hacking, for example, has observed,
"'True-in-L' is at the heart of Davidson's philosophy. What is left, if
there is no such thing as an L?" (1986: 447). A similar line is taken by
Dorit Bar-On and Mark Risjord: "Unless Davidson's radical claim is a
departure from his developed views, the Davidsonian program appears to
have undermined itself" (1992: 163). Indeed, they go on to say that the
thesis "in an important sense... robs the [Davidsonian] program of subject-
matter and empirical content" (p. 164), and they point out (p. 187) that
Davidson does not in fact abandon the use of the notion of a language
after "A Nice Derangement of Epitaphs." Michael Dummett has remarked,
"The occurrence of the phenomena that interests Davidson is incontrovertible: but how can an investigation of them lead to the conclusion that
there is no such thing as a language?" (1986: 465). Davidson's admission

that he held a view of the sort he rejects has added fuel to the charge. Other commentators, however, have come to his defense (Ramberg 1989; Pietroski 1994).

It is obviously crucial for assessing Davidson's project in the theory of meaning to determine whether his position in "A Nice Derangement of Epitaphs" represents a radical departure from his prior program, and, in particular, one which threatens to undermine his earlier work or its continuation. We will argue that, once it is understood exactly which thesis he is attacking, it is hard to see how it undermines anything he has previously maintained, and that it is, in a certain sense, just a further articulation of consequences of his basic methodological stance. We will also argue that there is no reason for him to suspend his use of the notion of a language in a perfectly respectable sense (distinct from the one he attacks) that comports with his theoretical aims. It may also be doubtful that the argument undermines any beliefs any reasonably sophisticated philosopher or linguistic has held, including Davidson.

So, we will begin in §1 by carefully examining Davidson's target. In §2, we will consider his argument for undermining his target position. Our aim will be to clarify as best we can what we take to be the line Davidson pursues. We will not follow precisely its development in his hands, partly to try to elicit more clearly what is going on in his argument, and partly to make the discussion more tractable, and also to position ourselves to register, we hope, illuminating comments about it. In §3, we will consider some principal responses to Davidson's argument, in the light of our exposition. And, finally, §4 offers a brief conclusion.

Three of Davidson's papers are particularly relevant to this discussion. In order of appearance, they are "Communication and Convention" (2001*b* (1983)), "A Nice Derangement of Epitaphs" (1986), and a follow-up paper addressed to Dummett's concerns, "The Social Aspect of Language" (1994*b*). "Convention and Communication," though its primary focus is not the same as that of "A Nice Derangement of Epitaphs," already, if more briefly and with milder rhetoric, announces the latter's main theme, and advances essentially the same reasons for it.

1. The Target

The crucial question for understanding Davidson's argument is what he means by 'language'. He is concerned in the first instance with two interrelated questions:

(1) What is the role of convention in communication, and
(2) What role does the knowledge an interpreter brings to a communicative interaction play in communication?

(1) and (2) are obviously connected. It is typically thought that prior knowledge of conventions about the use of words in a speaker's language plays a significant role in communication. In a sense, Davidson does not deny this. For he does not deny we know facts about the conventions according to which words are used, nor does he deny that this knowledge, possessed prior to interpreting others in our linguistic community, can play a useful and important role in interpreting them. Rather, what he denies is that such knowledge is *essential* to interpretive success, that is, he wants to deny that prior knowledge of conventions about the use of words in a speaker's language is either necessary or sufficient for communication (Davidson 1994*b*: 3).

His negative conclusion is prompted by uses of words that are at odds with their dictionary (or customary) meaning in the speaker's linguistic community, but which nonetheless fail to impede communication significantly. The title of "A Nice Derangement of Epitaphs" is taken from a line from Sheridan's play *The Rivals*, spoken by a certain Mrs Malaprop, from whose name the expression 'malapropism' is derived. A malapropism is a ludicrous misuse of a word, especially when that misuse results from a speaker mistaking a word for one similar in sound which does express the meaning he intends. For this reason, it is usually easy to determine what a speaker intends to convey when guilty of a malapropism, as with Mrs Malaprop's attempt to convey that something was a nice arrangement of epithets. Malapropisms are common. The sports pages of most papers yield a rich harvest. Here is a sample from a highly respected NFL head coach, "We know that if we've got our head between our tails, we can get embarrassed very quickly."[219] It's funny, but we have no trouble understanding what he meant to convey.

Mistakes are not the only occasions on which we take another to have intended, in some sense, something other than what the words he used literally mean in his community's language. Words may be used with a non-standard meaning, if a speaker knows it will be clear to an interpreter exactly how he intends them to be understood. Hearing Mrs Malaprop, we may reuse some of

---

[219] Mike Shanahan, quoted in *Jacksonville Times-Union* (12 Dec. 1999). In this case, it may be more plausible to suppose the lapse was an error in performance rather than in competence.

her misused words in fun, saying, "And that's a nice derangement of words," intending them to be understood as meaning what they were *misunderstood* to mean (and then meaning them ironically), without misunderstanding them ourselves.

This phenomenon prompts Davidson to distinguish between literal meaning, or what he calls 'first meaning', and conventional (or dictionary) meaning. Our utterance in the imagined context will be understood to mean "And that's a nice arrangement of words," but only ironically, that is, we will be taken to have meant, by so meaning with these words, that it was *not* a nice arrangement of words. Here we find the familiar separation of literal and speaker meaning, even though the words were not used with conventional meanings. This distinction between first and conventional meaning can in turn be seen as a key to what underlies Davidson's rejection of one conception of the role of convention in communication, and one conception of a language, according to which language consists of conventional meaning bearers (and how that is understood is important), knowledge of which is necessary and sufficient for communication.

First meaning is what a speaker intends his words to be understood to have so as to form the basis for subsequent effects achieved by his using the words he does; as Davidson puts it, it is the meaning he intends to be "first in order of interpretation" (Davidson 1986: 435). Various forms of non-literal meaning always play off of the literal meaning of an utterance. Grasping a metaphor or literary figure involves first understanding what the words literally mean. Consider these lines from Shakespeare's Sonnet 73.

> That time of year thou mayst in me behold
> When yellow leaves, or none, or few, do hang
> Upon these boughs which shake against the cold,
> Bare ruined choirs, where late the sweet birds sang.

The image would be lost on us if we did not understand what these words literally meant, if we did not understand that, for example, 'choir' means that part of the church appropriated to the singers, and specifically the chancel eastward of the nave that is screened off with open lattice work from the rest of the church and the audience, and in which the services are performed. Understanding the intent involves understanding first what the words literally mean, which together with their use in application to a person, prompts us to see certain analogies, and to make certain associations, as we are intended to.

266

Or, consider the following passage from Tennyson's *Ulysses*:

> How dull it is to pause, to make an end
> To rust unburnished, not to shine in use,
> As though to breath were life!

To understand Tennyson's intent, the analogies he wants us to see between a thing polished or rubbed smooth and bright by use and a person, the associations he wants us to make, requires we first understand the literal meaning of his words, their first meanings. He intends that we see the analogies by first understanding his words to mean just what they do in more prosaic uses, then to realize that the intent of his utterance, since his literal meaning involves a category mistake, is to be found in certain analogies and associations suggested by the words with their literal sense.

Usually, we take it for granted that what words literally mean is determined by public norms governing their usage in a speaker's linguistic community. But the distinction between literal and speaker meaning survives non-standard uses of words, and so the distinction itself must be relativized to a speaker. When a speaker uses his words in accordance with public norms, his literal, that is, first meanings, will correspond with dictionary meaning. But the two can come apart. They coincide when the competent speaker intends that any further meaning which attaches to his words be arrived at by first interpreting the words in accordance with public norms. They diverge when he intends that the words he utters be interpreted in the first instance in a way that does not correspond with dictionary meaning, whether intentionally or inadvertently. (One could insist that 'literal meaning' be reserved for dictionary meaning or conventional meaning; however, this would be to a verbal quibble, for we would still need something like the distinction between first and speaker meaning, where first and dictionary meaning need not coincide.)

The reason it is important to distinguish first meaning from conventional meaning is that the former is essential to all communication, and, indeed, to all linguistic uses of language. If we misidentify the two, then we will be led to suppose that conventional meaning is also essential to all linguistic communication. Davidson does not explicitly draw this connection, but seeing it is there helps to throw into better definition the thought underlying his argument.

We are now in a position to state more precisely what Davidson's target is, and also to see what might motivate the picture he wants to oppose.

This position is articulated with the three following "plausible principles concerning first meaning in language."

(1) *First meaning is systematic.* A competent speaker or interpreter is able to interpret utterances, his own or those of others, on the basis of the semantic properties of the parts, or words, in the utterance, and the structure of the utterance. For this to be possible, there must be systematic relations between the meanings of utterances.

(2) *First meanings are shared.* For speaker and interpreter to communicate successfully and regularly, they must share a method of interpretation of the sort described in (1).

(3) *First meanings are governed by learned conventions or regularities.* The systematic knowledge or competence of the speaker or interpreter is learned in advance of occasions of interpretation and is conventional in character. (Davidson 1986: 436)

Davidson's target is (3) in particular, when interpreted as saying that first meanings are governed essentially by learned conventions or regularities. (3) is equivalent to identifying first meaning, conceived of in its role as what words are intended in the first instance to be interpreted as meaning, with conventional meaning of the sort expressed by dictionary definitions.

How is the rejection of (3) connected with there being no such thing as a language? The connection is made as follows. First, we plausibly hold that to be able to interpret a speaker , we must know which language he is using on the occasion of interpretation. Second, we identify the language that he speaks as determined by what he intends the first meanings of his words to be at that time. Third, we identify first meanings, as in (3), with conventional meanings of the words in his linguistic community. Thus, we arrive at a conception of language as something essential to interpretation, because knowledge of a speaker's first meanings is essential to interpretation, and such knowledge consists (by the identification of first meanings with conventional meanings) in mastery of conventions determined by community practices, mastery of which must necessarily be acquired prior to interpretation. On this conception, a language is (*a*) a vocabulary and set of rules determined by conventions in a linguistic community which (*b*) is mastered by members of the community, and mastery of which is both (*c*) necessary and (*d*) sufficient for interpreting its speakers.

It is evident that arguing against the existence of anything called a 'language' in this sense does not commit one to there not being languages in any respectable sense. For convenience, when we speak of a language as characterized by (*a*)–(*d*), we will write '*language*'. Henceforth, we will restrict 'language' for use to characterize a meaningful vocabulary and set of rules which determine the meanings of sentences formed using it. Every *l a n g u a g e* is a language the meanings of whose words are determined by linguistic conventions in a community which are mastered by its members, and mastery of which is necessary and sufficient for interpreting its speakers. Though Davidson does not draw this distinction, as we will see, it is nonetheless implicit in his discussion, and will aid us in discussing the implications of his argument.

2. The Argument

Part of the argument against there being *l a n g u a g e s* has already, in a sense, been adumbrated, but we will fill in the details in this section.

Two things need to be established. (1) The first is that knowledge of the conventional meanings in a linguistic community of the words that a speaker uses (henceforth, 'knowledge of conventional meanings') is insufficient for interpreting him. This can be understood in a stronger and a weaker sense. (*a*) In a weaker sense, the claim is that knowledge of conventional meanings does not guarantee correct interpretation, so that on occasion, perhaps quite often, additional facts must be adduced to arrive at a correct interpretation of a speaker. (*b*) In a stronger sense, the claim is that we must always bring to bear other knowledge in addition to knowledge of conventional meaning to correctly interpret a speaker. We will consider how the evidence bears on both (*a*) and (*b*). (2) The second thing that needs to be established is that knowledge of conventional meanings is unnecessary for interpreting another speaker. This too can be taken in a stronger and a weaker sense. (*c*) The weaker interpretation is that in principle (if not in fact, given our limited epistemic capacities) knowledge of conventional meanings can be discarded. (*d*) The stronger claim is that as a matter of fact, speakers being as they are, no knowledge of conventional meanings is required for them to succeed in interpretation.

(1) The argument against sufficiency appeals to facts we previously surveyed which motivated distinguishing conventional meanings from literal or first meanings, where the latter are understood as necessary for all communication. What the data show in the first instance is that people do speak misusing words relative to the public norms of their linguistic community, but not so as to prevent their audience from figuring out, as we can put it, what they would have said, had they used their words in conformance with public norms. What this comes to is that their audience correctly interprets their words to mean what they intended them to think they mean. We will take up some worries about this below, but for now our interest is in the consequences of accepting it.

If this is the right way to interpret the data, it follows immediately that knowledge of conventional meanings is not sufficient in sense (*a*) for interpretation. It is true that in these cases our knowledge of conventional meanings plays a role in our coming to correctly interpret the speaker's words, since it is in part by recognizing their inappropriateness in the context that we come to assign a different meaning to them. But we also rely on the knowledge that it is unlikely that the speaker in the circumstances would have wanted to say what the words literally say, and knowledge of certain kinds of errors we know people are liable to make in speaking and in learning public norms for the use of words. This seems obvious and incontrovertible. It is very likely that every speaker has at least once misused a word relative to his community's norms, and has still been understood. This happens whenever we are corrected, the right word being supplied, since such correction requires knowing what we intended to say. Misuse of words relative to public norms is the occupational hazard of speaking. Understanding people despite their linguistic foibles is a routine exercise of charity.

It is not as obvious that (*b*) is correct, nor is it clear Davidson meant to argue for (*b*) rather than just (*a*). At least one sympathetic commentator has suggested Davidson's target is (in effect) (*b*), which of course entails (*a*), though not vice versa (Pietroski 1994: 105). The case against (*b*) is as follows. Surely, it might be said, while people do make mistakes from time to time, or use words deliberately with a non-standard meaning, often they do not. And even if no one is an ideal speaker, for example, of English, in the sense of grasping completely the entire English vocabulary with all its variants and specialized suburbs, surely there are very competent and responsible speakers of English who are paragons of erudition, and who do not misuse what words they deploy in speech intentionally or unintentionally (they are known as pedants). And it is at least plausible that on many occasions there is no call for reinterpreting what another says by assigning non-standard meanings to his words. In these cases, it is just plain false that any knowledge must be brought to bear in addition to knowledge of the conventional meanings of the words uttered. Thus, while knowledge of conventional meanings does not guarantee interpretive success, sometimes it is all that is needed.

A counter-argument rests on the observation that the possibility a speaker has not used his words in conformity with public norms is ever-present. Thus, in interpreting a speaker as meaning with his words exactly what we understand those words to mean according to public norms, we believe that he is using them in accordance with public norms, that is, that he is not mistaken and does not intend us to recognize that he intends us to interpret his words in a non-standard way. In order for our so interpreting him to be justified, this belief must also be justified. But since its justification will invoke more than knowledge of conventions for the use of words, and even that the speaker is a member of the appropriate linguistic community, it follows that knowledge of conventional meaning is never sufficient for interpretive success.

There is truth in both the objection and its response. It does seem obvious, once we turn our attention to the matter, that deploying our knowledge of conventional meaning to interpret a speaker does require our supposing, and believing justifiably (assuming our interpretation is to be justified) that he is speaking in conformity with public norms.[220] And this is something that requires knowledge of more than just conventional meanings. At the same time, it also seems clear that we routinely and successfully interpret others on the basis of taking them to mean what their words mean according to public norms. We do so because we often have good reason to think others, particularly our intimates, in most circumstances, are using words in conformance with public norms, and we are adept at noticing signs when they are not. Acknowledging these facts, the question whether (*b*) is justified boils down to what we intended by saying that knowledge of conventional meanings is sufficient for interpretive success. If we meant simply that sometimes, even often, we are not called upon to revise our view that the speaker speaks with the majority, then (*b*) should be rejected. If we meant simply that knowledge of conventional meanings all by itself sometimes suffices for interpreting another as speaking in accord with public norms, then, since this is not so, we should accept not just (*a*), but (*b*) as well. Indeed, in this case, (*b*) follows simply from the observation that human beings are in general fallible.

Our discussion can be recast in terms of a distinction Davidson introduces between a speaker's and an interpreter's prior and passing theories, and it will be useful to do so in anticipation of later argumentation (Davidson 1986: 441–2). We begin with the more central distinction between an interpreter's prior and passing theories. The theories in question are not ones the interpreter is actually supposed to hold, but rather ones a theorist uses in characterizing the interpreter's dispositions to understand a particular speaker.

---

[220] This might be challenged on the grounds of a general rejection in epistemology of the need to justify what might be called default assumptions. That is, it might be maintained that our beliefs about what others in our community mean by their words and actions are justified by default: unless circumstances depart from the norm, in some way that we should notice, the beliefs we have automatically are justified without appeal to anything. They must be actively justified only when circumstances depart in certain specific ways from the norm. Perhaps this would motivate a rejection of (*b*). But to pursue this issue in epistemology would take us too far afield, and is not likely to shed much additional light on the issues of direct concern to us here.

In a communicative exchange, an interpreter always stands ready to modify how he is disposed to understand a speaker in the light of information provided by the context and what the speaker has already said. The prior theory for the interpreter is the one that characterizes his disposition to interpret the speaker prior to the onset of a communicative exchange. The passing theory for the interpreter is one that characterizes his dispositions to interpret the speaker's utterances in the midst of the communicative exchange. (In the limit, the passing theory is the theory applied to each distinct utterance in the conversation by the speaker.) Prior and passing theories for interpreters are always relativized to particular speakers and times or time intervals.

As with the interpreter, the prior and passing theories for the speaker are to be thought of as relativized to interpreters and times. The prior theory of the speaker is, Davidson says, "what [the speaker] *believes* the interpreter's prior theory to be, while his passing theory is the theory he *intends* the interpreter to use" (1986: 442). The passing theory is the one, then, which expresses what words in his mouth mean while he is talking to the interpreter. Davidson says it is the theory he *intends* the interpreter to use, but in light of his own admonishments that we are not to take seriously the idea that communicators hold full-blown meaning theories (1986: 438, 441), it seems appropriate to interpret him to mean that the passing theory for the speaker is what characterizes his dispositions to speak during a communicative exchange, and expresses how he intends to be interpreted. As Dummett has pointed out, it looks as if there is an asymmetry in the distinction between prior and passing theories for interpreter and speaker (1986: 460). For the interpreter, the prior and passing theories are representations by the theorist of how the interpreter is disposed to interpret the speaker prior to, and during, a communicative exchange. For the speaker, the prior theory is *what* the speaker *believes* the interpreter's prior theory is. This is not exactly the same as how the speaker is disposed to interpret the interpreter prior to the interpretive exchange, which would be parallel to the interpreter's prior theory.

Dummett is right about the asymmetry, but mistaken about the content of the speaker's prior theory. He says it is a second order theory, a theory about a theory, presumably because Davidson describes the speaker's prior theory in terms of the speaker's beliefs about what the interpreter's prior theory is. However, it is a mistake to suppose Davidson assumes that the speaker has formulated a meaning theory he explicitly believes to be held by the interpreter. This would, if Davidson is right, make both the theorist and the speaker wrong. So, his remark about what the speaker believes must be a shorthand and misleading way of saying something which could be captured from the theorist's perspective without attributing detailed beliefs about semantic theories to the speaker. What is it, though? The prior theory for the speaker is *a first order theory* that characterizes the speaker's dispositions to use words *conditional on* his wanting to use those words in accordance with how he would suppose the interpreter to interpret them by default. So, it is not, as Dummett says, a second order theory. In part, Dummett's mistake arises from misreading the passage. In Davidson's locution 'what the speaker believes the interpreter's prior theory to be', the theory being denoted is the theory x such that x is believed by the speaker to be the interpreter's prior theory. This is a first order theory. Its content is not given by the content of the speaker's beliefs about the interpreter.

In short, what are these theories theories of? They are theories of languages which aim to model dispositions of interpreter and speaker. For the interpreter, the prior and passing theories model his dispositions to interpret the speaker prior to, and during, the communicative exchange. For the speaker, the prior and passing theories model, respectively, his dispositions to speak as his interpreter would by default understand him, conditional on his wanting to be so understood *prior to* the communicative exchange, and his dispositions to speak *during* the communicative exchange. At any given time, determinate facts about the speaker's dispositions to use words fix what they mean. Thus, the speaker's dispositions determine at a time in question how to understand each of the infinity of sentences which can be grammatically formed from words to which he then has dispositions attached. In the sense of 'language' at the end of §1, according to which a language is characterized by a meaningful vocabulary and set of rules which determine the meanings of sentences formed using it, they are theories of languages the speaker can speak at a time. Prior and passing theories for both interpreter and speaker are theories about the speaker's language (specifically about the language he intends to use in speaking to the interpreter). The difference is that, for the interpreter, they characterize his dispositions to interpret the speaker (these theories may not work for his own dispositions to speak to the speaker), while, for the speaker, they characterize his dispositions to speak, conditionally for the prior, and actually for the passing, theory.

Davidson, of course, suggests that we think of these theories as cast in the form of truth theories for the speaker. However, nothing hinges on his way of thinking of them.

Let us now recast the issue about whether there is any such thing as a *language* in terms of the distinction between prior and passing theories. The thesis Davidson wants to argue against is that successful communication requires both an interpreter's and a speaker's prior theories (at least the portions relevant to the communicative exchange) to correctly capture the conventional meanings of the speaker's words, and to coincide with their passing theories. This position identifies first meaning with conventional meaning. His objection against it, then, is that successful interpretation depends solely upon an interpreter's and speaker's passing theories coinciding. The prior and passing theories of the interpreter can differ from one another, as can those of the speaker; and the prior theories of interpreter and speaker need not be the same, even though they succeed in communication, because they converge on a passing theory. Prior and passing theory may both diverge from a correct meaning theory of a speaker's words according to public norms. Passing theories are often modifications of prior theories in light of inferences about what the speaker really means in the context (or, for the speaker, about how the interpreter is understanding and will understand him), and prior theories for particular speakers may themselves diverge from public norms, that is, they may not treat the speaker as speaking in perfect conformity with those norms.

How is knowledge of conventional meaning in fact related to prior and passing theories? We typically suppose members of our linguistic community will speak for the most part in accordance with public norms, as we do, though we recognize there will be deviations from public norms (of course, we may also deviate unknowingly from public norms, as most of us recognize, but are not in a position to do anything about it). We might be said to have dispositions characterizable using a generalized prior theory, one which can be thought of as generalizing over members of the linguistic community. The dispositions this theory characterizes, or models, are conditioned by what we believe words in our linguistic community to mean according to public norms. This theory would aim to capture what would usually be deemed as our competence in the public language, the language of our community.

This answers a question Davidson asks in "A Nice Derangement of Epitaphs" (p. 444), when he despairs of identifying prior and passing theories for particular speakers with linguistic competence: "Is there any theory that would do better?" Yes, the theory that characterizes our dispositions to interpret someone as, so far as we can tell, an ideal speaker of the public language. This theory characterizes our competence in the public language. To the extent that it corresponds to the public norms, we can be said to be competent in the public language. This is obviously not what Davidson calls a framework theory, "a basic framework of categories and rules, a sense of the way English (or any) grammars may be constructed, plus a skeleton list of interpreted words for fitting into the basic framework" (Davidson 1986: 444). What Davidson has in mind by a framework theory does not provide an interpretation of all of the vocabulary, and it is apparently not guaranteed even to provide all the details of the grammar of English.

When we encounter a speaker (or interpreter) for whom we have no clues to idiosyncratic usage, we are apt to treat him by default as in perfect accord with public norms. The prior theory for us will then be the instantiation of the generalized theory to the individual. As we learn more about the speaker's or interpreter's idiosyncrasies (or flights of fancy), our dispositions to interpret or speak will be modified. This shows up in the prior and passing theories as their characterizing the speaker's language as distinct from the language determined by public norms.

How are these facts, then, related to the denial that there are any such things as *languages*? Clearly, nothing in any of these considerations would lead us to deny a speaker is speaking a language when interpreted. In fact, the account presupposes it, for otherwise prior and passing theories would lack a subject-matter. One can speak a language, though, without speaking a *language*. A *language* is a language that meets certain additional conditions. The chief of these is that it play a certain role in communication. It is learned prior to communicative exchanges. It is all that one need know for successful interpretation. It is such that knowing it is necessary for successful communication. And it is identical with what one learns in learning which public norms attach to words (in the relevant linguistic community), that is, it is the public language. Given this, to deny that knowledge of public norms for the use of words is sufficient for successful communication is to deny that there are *languages*.

It is a bit odd, however, to cast the thesis in this form, and that may be why commentators have been misled about its import. We doubt anyone thought all these conditions were necessary for something's being a language. The position that the public language *plays* the relevant roles is one we can *imagine* someone holding. But then the more natural way to put Davidson's negative thesis would be to say that knowledge of the public language is neither sufficient nor necessary for successful communication. This way of framing the thesis puts it in a more plausible light, but makes it appear less exciting.

We have characterized the thesis under attack as that speakers communicate successfully with one another by bringing to bear their identical competence in speaking and in interpreting public languages. Davidson often puts the thesis in a more general form, as the claim that speakers and interpreters bring to a communicative exchange an identical competence both necessary and sufficient for communicative success. ("The problem we have been grappling

275

with depends on the assumption that communication by speech requires that speaker and interpreter have learned or somehow acquired a common method or theory of interpretation—as being able to operate on the basis of shared conventions, rules or regularities" (1986: 446).) This would be so only if shared prior theories, however derived, were necessary and sufficient for communication. If the argument surveyed above is correct, then this position is mistaken, and the denial of the more general thesis, which would have been seen as founded, in any case, on the more specific, is established as well.

Does any of this undermine the idea that many actual speakers share a language in a fairly robust sense that accounts for the ease with which they communicate with one another? Presumably not. The thesis Davidson is attacking requires prior and passing theories be both shared and exactly alike. It is doubtful anyone would have wanted to claim anything that strong. So, its denial leaves plenty of room for thinking that the prior and passing theories, for most interpreters and speakers in a linguistic community, share a lot in common, certainly enough to make sense of the idea that they share a language. We can think of this simply as that shared subset of the axioms that characterize their prior or passing theories: given any overlap, they share a language. Of course, this will never be the whole of what is thought of as the public language: but none of us is master of that, and no one could ever seriously have thought otherwise.[221]

Before tackling the second half of Davidson's argument, we want to consider briefly an objection to his account about what transpires in understanding what someone has said who, through confusion about the public meanings of words, is guilty of a malapropism. This case differs from the deliberate use of a word to mean something non-standard. A speaker who unknowingly misuses a word intends to be using it in accordance with public norms. A speaker utters 'Lead the way and we'll precede', and intends that we understand 'precede' to mean *proceed*, and intends to mean by 'precede' what it means according to public norms, that is, *precede*. Davidson appears committed to saying that the word as used by the speaker means what he thought it meant, despite his intending it to be interpreted according to public norms. An objection here might take either of two forms. First, it might be urged that the speaker's intention for it to be interpreted according to public norms takes priority over his intention to use it to mean *proceed*. This might be urged on

---

[221] It is doubtful Davidson would want to quarrel with any of this. In Davidson 1994*b*: 3, he says, "I am happy to say speakers share a language if and only if they tend to use the same words to mean the same thing, and once this idea is properly tidied up it is only a short uninteresting step to defining the predicate 'is a language' in a way that corresponds, as nearly as may be, with ordinary usage."

grounds that if it were disclosed to the speaker that 'precede' means *precede*, and not *proceed*, he would acknowledge having said something absurd or silly. Thus, he takes himself to have said something appropriately understood relative to his community's norms, and not relative to what he thought it meant. If this is right, then, in these cases, at least, the passing theory should not diverge from the theory of the public language, despite the speaker's dispositions to use words failing to comport with public norms. Second, it might be urged that when the speaker's intentions are confused in this way, it is improper to assign a meaning to his word. We cannot say it meant either *precede* or *proceed*.[222]

Even granting these objections, however, does not seriously undermine Davidson's position. For there are other cases in which the passing theory, and, indeed, the prior theory, may diverge from public norms where the speaker is *not* confused about the public norms, but still uses his words deliberately in a non-standard sense. In these cases, he cannot be accused of intending them to be interpreted according to public norms, and so the opportunity for the above objection does not arise. This would not suffice to show that knowledge of conventional meanings *alone* is no guarantee of success in communication. At most, the objection would show it is a mistake to try to make the point by appeal to unknowing misuses of words relative to public norms.

Even so, it might be urged that what we should say about the case of unknowing misuses of a word is neither that the speaker means what the word means according to public norms, nor that he means nothing, nor that he means straightforwardly only what he thought it meant, but, rather, something more nuanced. Namely, it might be said, he intended it to be interpreted according to public norms—and, so interpreted, it does not mean what he wanted to say—but that he wanted to say something whose content can be given by what he thought his words meant. A theory that captures all of this is the theory we should use when we want to ignore his mistake about how words are used in the community. Communication could proceed for all practical purposes without bothering to correct him, and we need not decide his words must mean just the one thing or the other in light of his conflicting intentions.

(2) We now turn to the second thesis Davidson aims to defend, namely, that prior knowledge of conventional meaning is not necessary for successful communication. Since the thesis Davidson attacks claims prior knowledge of

---

[222] For slips of the tongue and other performance errors untraceable to mistakes about what words mean in the public language there is an even stronger pull to say their words mean literally what they do in the language, since speakers will readily acknowledge they did not say what they meant to, even by their own lights.

conventional meaning is both sufficient and necessary, his attack on sufficiency is enough to refute it. However, it is clear he also thinks knowledge of conventional meaning is unnecessary for successful communication. We distinguished a stronger and weaker version of his claim. The stronger version is that as a matter of fact, given our cognitive abilities, we could interpret someone without prior knowledge of any conventional meanings attached to his words. The weaker version is that it is in principle possible for interpretation to proceed independently of any prior knowledge of conventional meaning.

The thesis that knowledge of conventional meaning is unnecessary for communication comes out clearly in "Communication and Convention,"

Knowledge of the conventions of language is ... a practical crutch to interpretation, a crutch we cannot in practice afford to do without—but a crutch which, under optimum conditions for communication, we can in the end throw away, and could in theory have done without from the start.   (Davidson 2001*b* (1983): 279)

It is not entirely clear whether Davidson thinks that, without expanding our cognitive powers, we could in fact interpret others without relying upon shared knowledge of prior conventions or established regularities, interpreting deviancies in the light of the standard practice. What we could do in theory may require suspending certain of our current limitations. We take first, then, the question whether shared knowledge of prior conventions is in principle necessary for interpretive success.

In asking this question, it is important not to suppose speaker and interpreter are required to employ the same conventional meaning bearers in speech. All that is required for the thesis to be true is that they share prior knowledge of the conventional meanings of the words they use, whether they are the same words or not, with the same conventional meanings or not, in speaking. One party to a conversation could speak Mandarin, another French and each understand the other perfectly.[223]

The question whether it is in principle possible to interpret another without appeal to prior knowledge of conventions can be put usefully this way: is there knowledge an interpreter could in principle have, leaving aside natural limitations of knowledge and perspicacity, which would enable him to correctly interpret a speaker of whom he had no prior knowledge at some given time? Setting aside natural limitations of knowledge and cognitive abilities,

---

[223] Within some linguistic communities, there are systematic differences in the vocabulary used by subgroups. In Japanese, men and women are supposed to use systematically different forms for certain grammatical particles and pronouns. It is easy to imagine extending this social arrangement so that two groups in the same linguistic community used entirely non-overlapping vocabularies.

this is equivalent to asking whether there are facts independent of linguistic conventions that determine (or could determine) what a speaker means by his words. The fact is that if Davidson's basic methodological stance on matters of meaning is correct, then the answer to this question is clearly affirmative.

A speaker's dispositions to use words, as he is disposed to in his environment, fix their meanings. More cautiously, if the speaker does not intend his words' meanings to be determined by conventions in his linguistic community, then what his words mean is determined by his dispositions to use them. If we grant an interpreter knowledge of a speaker's dispositions to use words in his environment, then the interpreter knows everything he must in order to correctly interpret the speaker's words. Indeed, if knowledge of a speaker's dispositions plus knowledge that he is of the same psychological type as oneself is sufficient for correctly determining what his words mean, it will be in principle possible to interpret another speaker without relying on any prior knowledge of any conventions or regularities for the use of his words. Two gods could speak to each other, each relying on knowledge that the other knew all of his dispositions, without any need to appeal to knowledge of how either had used or understood words in the past.

It is much more difficult to decide whether *we* could get by without the crutch of conventions and established regularities. We clearly cannot know what someone's dispositions to use words are without either having observed him over a period of time, or located him within a linguistic community whose regularities in word use we have antecedently learned. Even with his complete physical description and a correct theory of physics, the computational problem would be intractable. We simply are not gods. There is no prospect for knowing what someone means by his words at a time with no grounds whatsoever to think that, prior to the communicative interchange, he uses them one way rather than another. The role that participation in a speech community plays in actual communicative practice is to provide us with grounds for thinking a speaker is disposed to use words in a certain way. It is, perhaps, imaginable that two speakers could interact and by mutual consent converge on a changing passing theory which deviates further and further from public norms, and perhaps in some systematic way that does not leave any words with stable meanings. But even this, clearly something not within our powers, would rest on prior knowledge of public conventions.

It might be objected that, in fact, field linguists can break into alien languages. Of course, this is correct. But they do so by figuring out the regularities in the uses of words by their subjects, which is a matter of learning which conventions govern their words in their linguistic community. Knowledge of conventions for word use seems, for us at least, to be essential for communicative success, even if it is not a matter of necessity that we always interpret words in accordance with public conventions.[224]

So far, we have been concerned with whether knowledge of public conventions for word use, or prior knowledge of conventions, even if adhered to only by individuals involved in a particular communicative exchange, is necessary or sufficient for communicative success. In practice, it is insufficient; in principle, it is unnecessary. But, it might be maintained that, nonetheless, conventions in a sense are necessary for communication. This, of course, depends on how we are to understand what it is to participate in a convention, or to understand words in accordance with one. In "Communication and Convention," Davidson argues conventions are unnecessary for communication. His conclusion rests on both of the kinds of considerations so far reviewed, but also on a certain conception of what a convention is that derives from the work by David Lewis.[225]

For Lewis, the most relevant component in a characterization of convention is the notion of a regularity. In particular, he says:

a regularity R in the behavior of members of a population P, when they are agents in a recurrent situation S is a *convention* if and only if it is true that, and it is common knowledge in P that, in almost any instance of S among members of P,

(1) almost everyone conforms to R;
(2) almost everyone expects almost everyone else to conform to R;
(3) almost everyone has approximately the same preferences regarding all possible combinations of actions;
(4) almost everyone prefers that any one more conform to R, on condition that almost everyone conform to R;

---

[224] Suppose you encounter someone in a context where there is no reason to think he is a member of your speech community, and he utters words that sound like English. Suppose you interpret them as English with success. Is this an instance of interpreting someone correctly without prior knowledge of shared conventions? The question is whether you know that you have interpreted him correctly without acquiring knowledge of what conventions he intends his words to be governed by. Guessing correctly is not knowledge, though you may quickly become assured you have guessed correctly by his reaction to what you say and do in response to his utterances. In this case, it looks as if speaker and hearer do adhere to like conventions, and a trial at communicating on this assumption quickly confirms it. But knowledge of correct interpretation succeeds the trial rather than precedes it.

[225] Davidson does not quote Lewis's final version, but a preliminary one of his analysis of convention, although in a relevant respect they are identical, i.e. in treating a convention as a regularity.

(5)   almost everyone would prefer that any one more conform to R', on condition that almost everyone conform to R',

where R' is some possible regularity in the behavior of members of P in S, such that almost no one in almost any instance of S among members of P could conform both to R' and to R.   (Lewis 1969: 78)

If Lewis means here, as it is natural to interpret him, an *actual* regularity in behavior, then his account requires that there be instances, presumably many, of the kind of behavior constitutive of the conventional behavior for there to be a convention of the kind in question. If this is a necessary feature of convention, then conventions are neither sufficient nor in principle necessary for communicative success, however important a role they play in actual communicative success.

However, is an actual regularity a necessary feature of a convention? Why can we not establish conventions that have not yet been followed, for example, as when we explicitly establish conventions for governing forms of behavior we already engage in? When a group of nations agrees upon conventions to govern the treatment of prisoners of war, or non-combatants in war zones, these conventions are in effect from the time of the agreement, whether or not there is an immediate scope for their application. If we agree to the conventions, and dispose ourselves to follow them, then they in effect exist, even before anyone's behavior is governed by them. Indeed, we could even have conventions for governing behavior in situations which *never* arise, for example, governing contact with an extraterrestrial intelligence.[226]

What, then, is necessary for conventions? For present purposes, we would like to suggest a slight modification of Lewis's characterization to apply to conventions that hold in a community, though particular behavior has not yet been governed by them. The characterization does not require explicit agreement. Let us say that during a time interval t, a convention obtains in a population P to behave in accordance with a rule R in a situation type S just in case it is true that, and it is common knowledge in P that, in almost any instance of S among members of P,

(1)   almost everyone conforms to R;[227]

---

[226] Although Lewis's characterization is strictly about the conditions under which *a regularity* in behavior in a community is a convention, and not of what *a convention* is, it is clear that he thinks only regularities are conventions. He says as much flatly at one point—"A convention is a regularity in behavior" (Lewis 1969: 51)—and it is presupposed in much of his discussion.

[227] This does not require that everyone actually engage in behavior in accordance with R in situations of type S, but only that they are disposed to do so, since S may not occur. For our purposes, all that is important in calling R a rule is that it is a statement of a pattern of behavior

(2)   almost everyone expects almost everyone else to conform to R;

(3)   almost everyone has approximately the same preferences regarding all possible combinations of actions;

(4)   almost everyone prefers that any one more conform to R, on condition that almost everyone conform to R;

(5)   almost everyone would prefer that any one more conform to R', on condition that almost everyone conform to R'

where R' is some possible rule governing the behavior of members of P in S, such that almost no one, in almost any instance of S among members of P, would conform both to R' and to R.

This modified characterization differs from Lewis's by being about the conditions under which a convention obtains to behave in accordance with a rule, rather than being about a condition on when a regularity is a convention. We might say the relation between them is that a regularity in behavior in a community is a convention when it arises because of a convention to behave in accordance with a rule. This provides a plausible characterization of when a convention obtains in a community which does not require past regularity of behavior.[228] Indeed, it does not even require future regularity of behavior, since the situation the rule governs may never occur, and also because it does not require members of the community to adhere to the convention in the future, for it to qualify as a convention now.

If 'convention' is understood in this sense, then it is crucial to couch Davidson's point in terms of prior knowledge of conventions. For the speaker and the hearer in a communicative exchange do understand the speaker to be intending to use words in accordance with certain rules. These rules will meet the conditions for there being conventions to behave in accordance with them. Only the speaker and interpreter are required. The conventions which govern their communication need not be stable. But since the speaker and interpreter need to converge on a passing theory for successful communication, they must converge on a common set of rules governing the speaker's use of words, that is, on shared conventions. In this sense, conventions are necessary for communicative success, at least in so far as it is *linguistic* communication.[229]

---

in situation type S; one conforms to the rule if one's behavior in the situation type exemplifies the pattern.

[228] We are not concerned with whether this is exactly right. What is important for our point is just that it is close enough that any refinement will yield the same results for our interests, namely, that convergence on a passing theory amounts to mutual agreement on conventions.

[229] It might be thought that the requirement that everyone conform to the rules will require speaker and hearer to speak in the same way. But the formulation is not so restrictive, since the rule

Does this undermine any of Davidson's conclusions? So far as we can see, no serious damage is done. Some re-expression of his conclusion is required if what we say about convention is correct. But to say conventions are required for communication, given what we mean by that, is not to say anything which conflicts with anything Davidson is maintaining. And in fact in our discussion, looking ahead, we have worded things in a way that avoids any difficulty. Our characterization of conventions, which allows them to exist in the absence of antecedent regularities in a community, or on a speaker's and interpreter's part, helps render more palatable a claim Davidson makes at the end of "Communication and Convention" (2001*b* (1983): 280), namely, that: "philosophers who make convention a necessary element in language have the matter backwards. The truth is rather that language is a condition for having conventions." If we are right, then there is a sense in which we can have our cake and eat it too. Convention is essential to language. But prior shared conventions are not. We cannot, however, quite stretch this to sanction the claim that language is a condition for having conventions, though it is clear why Davidson should think this is so, since he is committed to language being necessary for thought, and clearly thought is necessary for conventions (Davidson 2001*b* (1977)). We postpone until Chapter 22 discussion of the relation between language and thought.

Suppose we are mistaken about what is expressed by 'convention' in English, and that, as Lewis thinks, nothing is a convention unless it is a regularity. Would this be significant? We do not think so. This would mean that there is a historical component to the common notion of convention. It would not show that a central part of this historical notion is neither necessary nor sufficient for linguistic communication. Though people who think language is necessarily conventional have probably not carefully distinguished between the historical and ahistorical conceptions of convention, it seems most likely that they have thought that language must be conventional, roughly, because (in the relevant community) its vocabulary is governed by (in a certain sense) arbitrary rules which everyone expects, and wants, everyone else to obey.[230] Clearly, we miss something important if we flatly deny communication must rely on

can be that everyone interpret the speaker in accordance with a certain set of rules, including the speaker.

[230] Consider a remark by Alston, which probably represents the attitude of many philosophers: "what really demarcates symbols is the fact that they have what meaning they have by virtue of the fact that for each there are rules in force, in some community, that govern their use ... Henceforth, we shall feel free to use the term 'conventional' purged of misleading associations, as shorthand for 'on the basis of rules.' " (Alston 1964: 57–8).

conventions, because we believe convention has a historical component, that the rules must have been followed in the past. Here what is needed is a further distinction marking the difference between the historical and ahistorical conceptions. The observation that language is not necessarily conventional, because the historical requirement may not be met in possible communicative situations, appears, then, to be less damaging to traditional views about the relation of convention to linguistic communication.

3. Reactions

We turn now to reactions to Davidson's thesis that "there is no such thing as a language, not if a language is anything like what many philosophers and linguists have supposed." If our account of his argument and its import is correct, at least some of these critical reactions have been based on mistakes about what Davidson was arguing for.

(*a*) In "The Parody of Conversation," Ian Hacking says, "True-in-*L* is at the heart of Davidson's philosophy. What is left, if there is no such thing as an *L*?" (Hacking 1986: 447). Hacking does not, however, think Davidson is committing "philosophical suicide" (p. 448). He recognizes Davidson has something quite specific in mind about what a language is in his claim that "there is no such thing as language." However, he thinks Davidson's views require more revision than he sees Davidson as willing to admit. We first consider what Hacking thinks Davidson has to abandon, and then whether he must do so.

Hacking treats the '*L*' in 'true-in-*L*' as in effect a variable. It would be better therefore to write 'true in *L*'. He recognizes that denying there are languages in the sense of Davidson's claim, that is, denying that there are *languages*, does not show there are no values for '*L*'. If we divorce these from our usual notion of language, however, he says they just become formal systems required because they allow us to recursively generate assignments of truth conditions to speakers' utterances of sentences of *L*. His objection is to the utility of even *such* languages in interpretation, if we take to heart Davidson's observations about the way in which our interpretations of what speakers say is determined so much by what we infer about their intentions in the context in which we hear them speak. We do not, Hacking says, utilize "one whole recursive system that goes on forever spinning unintelligible deductions," but "rather . . . a whole bunch of tricks for seeing what connects with what" (p. 456). Thus, an account of how interpretation succeeds does not require us to treat the knowledge that interpreters (and speakers) have that enables them to communicate as represented by a full-blown Tarski-style truth theory for a formally specified language L.

> The more one thinks of conversation as evolving passing theories, the more open one may be to a lot of different passing theories about different aspects of a person's life. These 'theories' are clumps of expectations about the beliefs, desires and ways of talking of the other . . . I am calling in question only . . . [the] idea that we construct a "total" theory of the other. To suppose that in interacting with another person, we construct such a total theory as we construct a passing systematic theory of truth for him is to force upon ourselves a parody of conversation.   (p. 457)

Thus, the heart of his objection is that Davidson's observations about how passing theories diverge from public norms shows we do not, contrary to what Hacking thinks Davidson maintains, bring to bear anything like a total theory of interpretation for a speaker in conversation. The right question about his conclusion is whether it contradicts anything important in Davidson's view. We think not.

First, Davidson, of course, does not think the theories we as theorists construct to describe an interpreter's dispositions to interpret another (*mutatis mutandis* for a speaker) are theories interpreters *bring to bear* in their interpretations. In Hacking's discussion, he often talks as if the theories in question were explicitly held theories, theories that include, for example, propositions about whether someone intends to be speaking with the English-speaking community, or a different language. These theories, however, are ways of modeling how an interpreter is disposed to interpret, and a speaker to speak, not theories they are presumed to actually hold.

Hacking's claim can be recast, though. The claim that the interpreter does not bring a total theory to interpretation of a speaker becomes the claim that a model of the interpreter's dispositions to interpret the speaker will not provide a complete interpretation theory for him. For a speaker, it is not clear that there is a parallel claim, since our theory of his dispositions to speak to the interpreter will presumably cover all the vocabulary the speaker is willing to use in speaking to that interpreter at that time. Henceforth, we restrict attention to interpreters. The claim that interpreters apply many partial theories is recast as the claim that a model of the interpreter's dispositions should include many distinct models.

Two remarks are in order. First, the claim that we should model the dispositions of interpreters and speakers using many partial theories looks insignificant. Presumably these theories will be for distinct ranges of vocabulary, or at least ranges with considerable non-overlap. But then they could all be combined into a single theory for the entire vocabulary without loss. This is just a matter of bookkeeping. Second, with regard to the claim that a model of the interpreter's dispositions to interpret a speaker will not provide a full theory of interpretation for the speaker's dispositions to speak to the interpreter, this certainly seems likely to be often true for actual interpreters. But it is hard to see why this should lead us to the conclusion that there is something wrong with giving a characterization of the interpreter's dispositions in terms of a truth theory for L. What it shows is only that the vocabulary of L we choose will often be a subset of the vocabulary the speaker is willing to use in speaking to the interpreter. The convergence on passing theories for the vocabulary the speaker actually employs is what is required for communicative success. Thus, these observations go no way toward showing "we do not want L at all, for its chief force was to be part of a recursive system" (p. 456).

(*b*) Dorit Bar-On and Mark Risjord have argued that "giving up the concept of a language does threaten to undermine Davidson's original program ... in an important sense it robs the program of subject-matter and empirical content" (1992: 164). This is a serious charge. But we can already see it likely rests on a mistake about what Davidson is arguing. Bar-On and Risjord also argue that two arguments for the claim that there is no such thing as a language, which they find in a book by Bjorn Ramberg on Davidson's philosophy of language, are bad arguments (Ramberg 1989). They are bad arguments, but since they are not arguments that Davidson himself gives, we will not discuss them here (see Pietroski 1994 for discussion). We instead will concentrate on the reasons Bar-On and Risjord advance to show Davidson's conclusion undermines his entire semantic program. This will establish which conception of language they are working with, and it will usefully elicit a mistake about their conception of what a passing theory is answerable to.

Their charge against Davidson rests on a claim he makes in "The Structure and Content of Truth," which Bar-On and Risjord quote:

the question whether a theory of truth is true of a given language (that is, of a speaker or a group of speakers) makes sense only if the sentences of that language have a meaning that is independent of the theory (otherwise the theory is not a theory in the ordinary sense, but a description of a possible language) ... If the question can be raised ... the language must have a life independent of the definition ... (Davidson 1990*b*: 301)

Their charge is that if there is no such thing as a language, the independence required is "bound to go unfulfilled," and the original Davidsonian program "would be robbed of its intended subject matter and its promised empirical content" (Bar-On and Risjord 1992: 187).

The first remark to make is that Davidson, of course, is not arguing against languages, but only *languages*, that is, a language learned antecedent to communicative exchanges, shared by communicators, and necessary and sufficient for communication. But this does not mean that no language is shared in communication by the interpreter and speaker. It does not even mean they do not share a language for some time, so that the passing theory from each moment to the next does not change during that interval.

It would be a mistake, however, to reject Bar-On and Risjord's objection solely on this ground. For the reason Bar-On and Risjord advance for their charge survives this correction about Davidson's target. They claim that an interpreter's passing theory does not meet the conditions for being about a language that has a meaning independent of the theory in the sense required in the passage quoted from Davidson above. Here is their argument (Bar-On and Risjord 1992: 187–8).

[i] On the picture that emerges from the later Davidson . . . the axioms and structural pattern laid out by an interpreter's truth theory must not be regarded as representing a set of rules or conventions antecedently mastered by speakers and discovered by an interpreter. [ii] They must not themselves be regarded as capturing something having independent existence . . . But then the only thing that could be said to have 'a life independent of the [truth] definition' would be individual utterances uttered by speakers, considered in isolation . . . In a languageless Davidsonian semantics, then, an interpretation theory becomes what Davidson has called a "passing theory," where "knowing a passing theory is only knowing how to interpret a particular utterance on a particular occasion." (Numbering added; the quotation is from Davidson 1986: 443.)

Bar-On and Risjord argue that for the subject-matter of the theory to have a life independent of the theory, there must be constraints on the choice of a correct theory that are unavailable if we regard the passing theory as aiming merely to provide a correct interpretation of an utterance of the speaker at a time. This is represented in the move from [i] to [ii] above. They also complain that such theories are clearly not about what linguists, and apparently Davidson, have been interested in, namely, natural languages like English, German, French, Swahili, and so on. What is missing for the passing theory, they say, is a holistic constraint, namely that "the totality of *T*-sentences [entailed by the theory] . . . optimally fit evidence about sentences held true by native speakers" (Davidson 2001c (1973): 139). They argue that "the holistic requirement underpins the independence requirement by giving us reason to believe that a truth theory is capturing something independent" (Bar-On and Risjord 1992: 189).

If Bar-On and Risjord were right that the subject-matter of the passing theory by itself precluded the possibility of conceiving of its subject-matter as independent of the theory, there would be a problem for Davidson, even if we granted that there was still some conception of language at work in the passing theory. For Davidson clearly does want the passing theory to be an empirical theory responsible to something independent of it.

The charge, however, does not stick. The move to [ii] from [i] is a *non sequitur*. Before we say why, though, it is important to note that, as we argued in §2, we can easily admit that there is no such thing as a $language$, while at the same time preserving the view that there are natural languages, and that we can speak intelligibly of mastery of such languages, though passing theories of members of one's community are apt usually to diverge from the theory for the portion of the natural language the speaker speaks. Recall, the theory for the natural language is an abstraction from the usages of members of the linguistic community as a whole. Any individual member of the community is likely to have idiosyncrasies in his speech. That is, most members of any speech community will make mistakes about community usage for at least some portion of the vocabulary they use, even if limited and minor. So, our passing theories for them will not be exactly the same as the theory we formulate by abstraction from the usage of the community as a whole. Therefore, nothing in "A Nice Derangement of Epitaphs" undercuts the application of Davidson's methods to the investigation of natural languages. All that they require is that we not conceive of knowledge of the natural language as being either sufficient or necessary (in principle) for communication.

Now let us turn to the question whether the fleeting utility of the passing theory undercuts the thought that it has a subject-matter independent of theory. It will help first to put this issue in perspective. Davidson distinguishes between prior and passing theories in the interest of giving a more detailed account of what goes on in communication and, in particular, of what is essential and what role prior knowledge, particularly of convention, plays in communication. Prior and passing theories are relativized to times, and are formulated for both interpreters and speakers, conceived of as directed at particular speakers and interpreters, respectively. They characterize dispositions to use words by interpreter and speaker in light of to whom each believes himself to be talking. In Davidson's earlier work, these distinctions were simply not marked. It is clear that there he was largely concerned with modeling the dispositions of a speaker to use words at a time. He assumed that we could without danger suppose that the speaker's dispositions were stable over time, and stable with respect to members of his linguistic community, whose dispositions could be taken to be largely the same.[231] The distinction between prior and passing theories, with their relativization to speaker or interpreter and times, gives us tools to provide a more detailed account of how actual communication proceeds. But it is not a radical break with his previous approach. In particular, the justification of a passing theory for interpreter or speaker is still responsible to what sentences each holds true, prefers true, etc., and would hold true, prefer true, etc., in what circumstances in their environments, in the relevant language (for the interpreter, the language he expects the speaker to speak, for the speaker, the language he intends to speak). These facts are independent of the theory and give it its empirical content; they are ultimately about the interpreter's and speaker's dispositions to respond to events and objects in their environments. We still want "the totality of T-sentences [entailed by the theory] ... [to] optimally fit evidence about sentences held true by native speakers."

Let us concentrate for the moment on the passing theory for the interpreter, as Bar-On and Risjord do. The passing theory that describes an interpreter's dispositions to interpret a speaker aims to capture not just how the interpreter would interpret what the speaker actually says at that time, but anything that the speaker might then say. Of course, an interpreter may not be prepared to interpret everything a speaker might say to him, and his interpretive repertoire may be augmented as a conversation proceeds. But the passing theory for the interpreter is responsible to the entire vocabulary he is prepared to interpret if used by the speaker, and so to his attitudes toward the truth of sentences formed using that vocabulary, actual and potential.

In the case of the speaker, it is even more obvious that the passing theory is responsible for the entire vocabulary that he is prepared to use with the interpreter. That means it is responsible to his dispositions to use that entire vocabulary in response to events and objects in his environment, not just to what is actually uttered at a time, but anything the speaker might utter at that time, that is, for the whole of the language the speaker brings to the communicative exchange. In this respect, there is no difference between the views Davidson expressed in his earlier papers and his views expressed in "A Nice Derangement of Epitaphs."

---

[231] Could Davidson have failed to see these assumptions as idealizations? Presumably not. Then in what sense could he have held the conception of language which he criticizes?

Bar-On and Risjord may have been misled by Davidson's habit of saying of the interpreter's and speaker's passing theories that they were theories formulated by the interpreter and speaker for the purposes of interpreting and speaking, respectively. They might have supposed that the point of the passing theory for the interpreter is simply to get right what a speaker is actually saying at any given time, and the point of the passing theory of the speaker is to get right only how his interpreter will interpret what he actually says at that time. In this case, it may have seemed to them that all the usual constraints relevant to pinning down the rest of the language are irrelevant, since those portions of the language are not used on the occasion in question. Indeed, in a passage Bar-On and Risjord quote, Davidson says something that sounds very much as if he had this in mind: "knowing a passing theory is only knowing how to interpret a particular utterance on a particular occasion" (Davidson 1986: 443). This is certainly not a very apt way to put his point, which can only be that, for each distinct utterance, there is a sense in which a distinct passing theory is relevant, that is, the one which is about the interpreter or speaker at that time.[232] In fact, the passing theories for interpreter and speaker are not theories they bring to bear on communication, but theories we, as theorists, formulate to describe their dispositions. It is clear what they are responsible to, which gives them their empirical content, namely, the dispositions of the interpreter and speaker at the time that the passing theories are about.

The mistake in moving from [i] to [ii] above is to think that the only thing a truth theory could be held responsible to is "a set of rules or conventions antecedently mastered by speakers and discovered by an interpreter." This has never been Davidson's view. The primary subject of interpretation has always been the individual speaker. Public languages with their conventions for use of words are abstractions from the dispositions of communities of speakers. What gives life to any empirical truth theory or meaning theory, and to views about public conventions for the use of words, is ultimately the dispositions of individual speakers to use words.

In sum, then, the charge Bar-On and Risjord register is independent of mistaking Davidson's target, but is still founded on a failure to take to heart his admonition that talk of prior and passing theories is talk about theories for the interpreter's and speaker's dispositions. With this clearly in view, there will not be a tendency to withhold empirical content to the theories, or to affirm

---

[232] This is an artifact of taking the theory to be about a particular small time. There is no reason not to formulate a theory which aims to capture an interpreter's or speaker's dispositions over a extended period of time, if their dispositions to interpret and speak remain stable. This would amount to their passing theories not changing over the interval.

that the constraints they must meet diverge from those Davidson has specified in earlier writings.

(*c*) Davidson and Dummett have been engaged in a debate in and out of print for nearly two decades about issues raised by "A Nice Derangement of Epitaphs." It is a debate remarkable for its elusiveness, for they often seem at cross-purposes, and it is unclear in the end whether serious disagreement separates them. We will discuss two rounds of exchange, the first constituted by "A Nice Derangement of Epitaphs" (Davidson 1986) and "A Nice Derangement of Epitaphs: Some Comments on Davidson and Hacking" (Dummett 1986), and the second by "The Social Aspect of Language" (Davidson 1994*b*) and Dummett's reply (Dummett 1994). We will concentrate on the more recent exchange, since it gets past obvious misunderstandings in the first (for example, whether Davidson intended to be attributing to interpreters and speakers knowledge of the content of prior and passing theories, and, to some extent, about whether he meant to deny we learn and use public languages in communication—he did not).

In "The Social Aspect of Language," Davidson characterizes the issue between himself and Dummett as about whether the idiolect or language (in the sense of public language) is conceptually primary. In more detail, he locates the disagreement between them as this:

What bothers Michael is . . . my failure to appreciate that the concept of a speaker meaning something by what he says depends on the notion of a shared language and not the other way around. My mistake, in his eyes, is that I take defining a language as the philosophically unimportant task of grouping idiolects, whereas he thinks I have no non-circular way of characterising idiolects.   (Davidson 1994*b*: 3)

To adopt the view that the idiolect is primary is not to deny that language is social. But it is to raise a question about what constitutes its essential social element.

The connection between Davidson's thesis that prior shared knowledge of public conventions for the use of words is neither necessary nor sufficient for communication and the thesis that the idiolect, not the public language, is conceptually primary, is that if prior knowledge of the (or a) public language is not necessary or sufficient for communication, then our core understanding of linguistic communication is independent of our conception of a prior shared public language. We understand what linguistic communication is even in the absence of an enduring public language; so, our conception of it derives from our conception of something prior to it, namely, overlap of idiolect: stable overlap of idiolect, then, gives rise to the idea of an enduring public language.

Davidson imagines three critical responses. The first is that taking the idiolect as basic fails to account for our holding ourselves to a public norm in speaking. The second is that in practice we cannot get along without prior knowledge of a public language. The third is that, without one, we have no answer to Wittgenstein's question about what makes the way we go on the right way.

To the first, Davidson protests that there is no obligation to speak as others do, and that the reason we hold ourselves to a public norm is adequately explained by its utility. (There could arise a responsibility to speak to others in conformity to public norms, where an antecedent responsibility to cooperate in certain enterprises is in place, and where speaking the same as others is important for success: but this is a derived, and not an original, obligation, and it is not to public norms but to those to whom one is speaking. Davidson takes his criticism here to have Dummett as its target. Dummett declines the role, and rather adopts something close to the view we have just sketched (Dummett 1994: 266), claiming Davidson has misinterpreted him.) To the second response, Davidson says rightly that it is irrelevant to the theoretical issue. Davidson's response to the third is not as clear. Consider this passage.

My proposal takes off from this observation: what matters, the point of language or speech or whatever you want to call it, is communication, getting across to someone else what you have in mind by means of words that they interpret (understand) as you want them to . . . The intention to be taken to mean what one wants to be taken to mean is, it seems to me, so clearly the only aim that is common to all verbal behavior that it is hard for me to see how anyone can deny it . . . if it is true, it is important, for it provides a purpose which any speaker must have in speaking, and thus constitutes a norm against which speakers and others can measure success of verbal behavior. (Davidson 1994*b*: 11)

His suggestion appears to be that the norm that determines correct or incorrect interpretation is provided by a speaker's intentions in using words, though he adds that this does not imply a speaker's words mean whatever he wants or intends them to mean. It does not, because for his words to mean what he intends, it must be possible to succeed in communicating with a reasonable interpreter, when he uses them in accordance with those intentions. In this sense, communication is the source of meaning, though intending is essential to meaning, and provides its normative element.

There is one more point Davidson advances, which may be connected with the last, though it is unclear, which takes the form of an answer to Wittgenstein's question about what makes it the case that we go on in the same way we have before. Wittgenstein intended this to be equivalent to the question what makes it the case that we follow one rule rather than another. This makes it look as if Wittgenstein's question is the one we have just addressed, since to mean something by one's words is to have used them in accordance with a rule. Intending to mean the same thing by the same word, then, should supply the answer to the question. But Davidson goes on to give a different answer.

So far as we can tell, his answer is that one goes on in the same way provided one is a member of a social group minimally consisting of two people who have correlated each other's reactions to some common stimuli with the stimuli. One goes on in the same way if one does not frustrate the other's natural inductions about one's behavior. This is supposed to be the minimal social element in answering the question what it is to go on as before.

It is unclear to us how this answer is connected with identifying intentions as providing the guide to whether one has interpreted another correctly. The proposal does not in fact seem sufficient to account for someone's going on the same as before, at least if this means responding in the same way to the same stimuli. If two people make the same mistake about a stimulus, for example, and have the same reaction, which they have come to expect in the light of what they mistook the stimulus for, on Davidson's proposal they would have gone on in the same way. But in a clear sense they did not: they reacted differently from usual, assuming they usually get it right. But neither detected the error.

In any case, this would not be sufficient for following a rule. Suppose something consistently amuses both A and B, and they notice this about each other, and enter into the relevant natural deductions. This has so far nothing to do with rule following or speaking a language. So, whatever question Davidson's answer addresses does not seem to be the question Wittgenstein was posing.

We suspect there is no informative answer to the question what is it to go on as before in the sense of following the same rule. To suppose there is is to suppose rule following can be reduced to something else. But there is no reason to think this is so. Thus, Davidson's first answer, that it is in virtue of our intending to go on as before, is likely to be as informative an answer as is possible.

Dummett, in his reply to Davidson, concedes, straight off, that "Davidson is quite right that sharing [a language in the sense he has characterized] is neither necessary nor sufficient for communication, and he is right for the right reasons" (Dummett 1994: 257). He disclaims ever having held the view criticized. However, he denies this is central in the debate about whether the common public language or idiolect is conceptually primary. That knowing a common language, in the usual sense, is neither necessary nor sufficient for communication, Dummett says, does not show it is unimportant for our philosophical understanding of linguistic communication.

However, Dummett does not clarify what he takes the question about the primacy of the common language over the idiolect to be. He clearly does not think the primacy of the common language requires that knowledge of it be necessary and sufficient for communication. It is not sufficient, because knowing the public language speakers may deliberately deviate from it, or use it non-standardly; then they cannot be understood solely on the basis of knowledge of the public language. It is not necessary because a speaker mistaken about the common language may still be successfully understood. In what sense, then, could one maintain that a common language is central to an investigation of linguistic communication?

One suggestion might be that although shared knowledge of a common language is not necessary or sufficient, without some prior shared know-ledge of conventions for the use of words, linguistic communication would be impossible. If our discussion in §2 is correct, however, not even this is required in principle.

Dummett, however, takes the issue apparently to hinge on whether two speakers could communicate using different vocabularies (Dummett 1994: 263). He says, granting its possibility, it would still be the case that the two speakers share a language, for though each speaks using different words, each presumably could use the other's words, given that he can interpret the other.[233] But true or not, this is not the issue. The real issue is whether the speaker and interpreter must have prior knowledge of shared conventions. For this, it would suffice, as we noted, that they learn a prior language one speaks and the other interprets, though neither speaks the other's language.

Because of this misunderstanding, it is unclear whether Dummett disagrees with Davidson over the central issue. The reason is that Dummett does not raise the question whether *prior* shared knowledge of rules governing meaning bearers is essential to communication, rather than simple shared knowledge at the time of communication of rules governing meaning bearers. Furthermore, the question is not whether such prior knowledge is in fact required, but, as Davidson has made clear, whether it is in principle required.

---

[233] Is this clearly true? It is easy to imagine someone who has the capacity to understand a language spoken to him, but who cannot speak it; otherwise, those who are dumb but not deaf could not master a language to the extent of understanding others when they were spoken to, a manifest falsehood. Certainly, to survive these sorts of cases, the claim would have to be carefully qualified.

It may well be that Dummett's insistence on the importance of a public language is really an insistence on the importance of there being shared mastery of a common set of rules governing meaning bearers for linguistic communication to take place. If this is so, it does not conflict with any doctrine Davidson has advanced. For this would be merely to hold that, on the ahistorical conception of convention, shared mastery of conventions is necessary for communication. Moreover, even if Dummett wants to insist that for actual speakers, prior knowledge of a public language (not necessarily complete overlapping) by participants is necessary for communicative success, this would not yet constitute a conflict, since it is doubtful Davidson would deny this.

Thus, in the end, it remains, as Dummett says, "obscure . . . how far apart Davidson and I really are on the strictly philosophical issues" (Dummett 1994: 265).

4. Conclusion

The main purpose of this chapter has been to determine whether Davidson's—on the face of it—astonishing claim that "there is no such thing as a language, not if a language is anything like what many philosophers and linguists have supposed" departs from, and undermines or conflicts with, his earlier work, as commentators have supposed. Our answer is resoundingly 'no'. Indeed, in a clear sense, the views expressed in "Communication and Convention," "A Nice Derangement of Epitaphs," and "The Social Aspect of Language" are a natural development of his work on radical interpretation. If one takes the standpoint of the radical interpreter as basic in investigating matters of meaning and thought, it will be natural, since radical interpretation can focus on a single individual, to take the individual's dispositions to be fundamental to the possibility of linguistic communication. Communication is possible iff a radical interpreter could determine from the speaker's dispositions what he means by his words at the time. No one doubts a speaker's dispositions to use words can change over time. In the limit, they could change from instant to instant. The view that the speaker's dispositions fix the meanings of his words, a view implicit in taking the stance of the radical interpreter toward the speaker to be fundamental, means, then, that in principle no facts about his actual prior or subsequent behavior are relevant, and, hence, no facts about his participation in conventional practices in the use of words. The phenomenon of a public shared language, while undoubtedly important to understanding how actual linguistic communication proceeds, will then appear to be nonetheless not a fundamental feature of linguistic communication as such.

Davidson's conclusion does not entail that speaker and interpreter do not share, for the space of a successful communicative encounter, a language in a perfectly robust sense, even one which supports their sharing conventions for word use. In fact, his view requires it, because it requires "sharing" passing theories. Therefore, his conclusion does not rob interpretation theory of its subject-matter. Nor does it not imply there are no such things as what we think of as public or natural languages: English, Danish, Thai, Turkish, Greek, Polish, Pashto, and so on. Nor does it imply we do not learn such languages, nor that such learning plays no important role in our ability to understand others around us.

We have seen that when commentators object that "A Nice Derangement of Epitaphs" undermines the body of Davidson's work on interpretation theory, this is because they do not attend carefully enough to exactly what conception of language he is attacking. Davidson is guilty of inviting misunderstanding. It is much more natural to put his thesis as saying knowledge of public languages is neither necessary nor sufficient for communicative success, using 'language' in its ordinary sense, or a mild variant of it. But, instead, he chose to characterize a language as something that must (i) be learned and shared by speaker and interpreter prior to a communicative exchange, (ii) *and which* is in addition necessary and sufficient for any communicative success, and so packaged his thesis as denying that there are languages, albeit with a qualification that points toward the rather strange construal of 'language' at issue in the claim. Nonetheless, the objection rests on a misunderstanding, and Davidson's thesis is much less surprising and much more plausible than at first appears. In the end, it is not clear that Davidson and his critics differ substantially on relevant philosophical issues, though sometimes persistent misunderstandings occlude the precise areas of agreement and disagreement.

To conclude, we urge that, even if Davidson's thesis is granted, there is a point to paying attention to the role of a public language in human linguistic communication, and according public language a central role in our philosophical understanding of human linguistic communication. Its role will not be one it has in virtue of our being linguistic beings, but in virtue of our being the epistemically and cognitively limited linguistic beings we are. While gods may dispense with prior knowledge of shared conventions, it is doubtful we ever could. A philosophical understanding of our communicative practices and communicative successes may well have to locate a central place for mastery of a public language, on pain of distorting our understanding of what makes communication possible *for us*. And so, *pace* Davidson, we should *not*, in fact, "give up the attempt to illuminate how we communicate by appeal to conventions" (Davidson 1986: 446). An analogy may be appropriate. Philosophical understanding of the epistemic position of an omniscient being, a being with direct knowledge of everything (assuming it is possible), has no need for an account of how such a being could come to know things about its environment on the basis of, for example, sensory experience. So, one might say, an account of how sensory experience plays a role in *our* knowledge of our surroundings should not be thought of as pertaining to the *essence* of knowledge. It is for us merely a crutch, in principle dispensable. Suppose all of that is true. Nonetheless, we would not have an adequate philosophical understanding of *our* epistemic position if we did not pay attention to the central role sensory experience plays *for us* in gaining knowledge of the world. Similarly, we would not have an adequate philosophical understanding of *our* communicative abilities if we did not pay attention to the central role that mastery of public languages plays *for us* in enabling us to communicate with one another successfully. Thus, there is a way of accepting Davidson's conclusion, while also maintaining there is nothing misguided about the attention many philosophers have given to the role of public languages in our communicative practices. On that happy note, we conclude this chapter.

Summary of Part II

In Part II, we have examined the role of radical interpretation in Davidson's overall project in the theory of meaning. The point of so doing is to consider in detail how to confirm an interpretation theory for another speaker. As we have seen, an interpretation theory, in its broadest sense, is a theory both of the meanings of a speaker's words and of the contents of his attitudes. It can be seen as having an a priori structure given by the central concepts it deploys, that of meaning, truth, reference, and satisfaction, on the side of the meaning theory, and of belief, desire, intention, preference, action, and the like, on the side of agency. The primary form in which Davidson casts a meaning theory is a Tarski-style truth theory. The core of the theory of agency is decision theory. Together, these impose powerful constraints on the empirical application of an interpretation theory. The theory has an infinite number of consequences. The hope is that the structure imposed by the a priori constraints, together with meager evidence applied at a potential infinity of points, suffices to justify an interpretive truth theory. One payoff of the theory of radical interpretation is the light it sheds on the interconnections, though not strong enough to support a claim of reducibility, between the family of concepts employed in the theory and the concepts employed in the description of its evidence. If it could be shown, either in a detailed account of the procedure, or a priori, that radical interpretation must be possible for any speaker of a language, we would have limned the fundamental structure of language and agency in an examination of the procedures of radical interpretation. In addition, we would be entitled to take as truths about the nature of language, meaning, and the attitudes, anything indispensable for radical interpretation.

The project so construed is not undermined, as critics suppose, by Davidson's denial in later work (surveyed in Chapter 17) that prior knowledge of public conventions must play an essential role in understanding communication. Indeed, this claim naturally issues from his fundamental methodological stance, which places the project of eliciting an account of the meaning of a speaker's words and the contents of his attitudes from an account of how he is disposed to react to events and conditions in his environment at the center of an account of what it is to be a linguistic being.

For that project, however, we have argued that the causal structure of the world in which a speaker is embedded is insufficient to extract from the constraints examined a theory of the speaker's words and actions that we can know to be correct. Additional constraints are required. In outline, the argument is that we know there are more correlations between hold true attitudes and conditions in a speaker's environment than can be employed as evidence for a single consistent theory of interpretation. Thus, an interpreter must choose between sets of correlations which will lead to incompatible interpretation theories. The constraints imposed by the a priori theory of rationality are not enough to determine a unique one. We cannot explain away underdetermination of theory by evidence in radical interpretation as indeterminacy no more harmful than the difference between reporting temperatures using the Centigrade or Fahrenheit scales, for that requires, absurdly, that the interpreter's language must itself have less structure than it has.

However, even if all of this is correct, it does not undermine the importance of reflection on the project of radical interpretation in the philosophy of language. Understanding how interpretation of the speech of another is possible, and under what conditions it is possible, is central to understanding the nature of language, which we do not understand apart from linguistic communication. Discovering what additional constraints are required will shed important light on the nature of linguistic communication and the central concepts of a theory of meaning and action.

Nonetheless, the claim that radical interpretation is possible under the constraints Davidson gives is important for many of the theses he has aimed to found on reflection on radical interpretation. The constraints he focuses on we can know to apply a priori. In this case, if we know radical interpretation can succeed within those constraints, whatever must be true about a speaker for that to be so is constitutive of speakers as such, and so, of us. If we must add additional constraints, and some involve assumptions about subjects of interpretation which are not conditioned simply by their being speakers, but are contingent assumptions about, for example, their psychology, then a number of important theses Davidson has maintained on the basis of reflection on radical interpretation will (apparently) be undermined, or, at least, their status as a priori truths about speakers and thinking beings will be undermined; and, consequently, their relevance to traditional philosophical debates about our metaphysical and epistemic relations to the world will be undercut.

Part III will be largely concerned with these matters. We will consider a variety of important theses in the philosophy of language (e.g. the inscrutability of reference), metaphysics (conceptual relativism and the nature of truth), epistemology (the impossibility of massive error), and the philosophy of mind (the relational individuation of thought content, the nature of first person authority), which Davidson has grounded in his reflections on and description of the radical interpreter's procedure. In the course of this, we will return to major themes of this part, and consider in particular various suggestions for how to deal with problems raised here.

Part III

Metaphysics and Epistemology

Ironically perhaps, my starting point is the same as Descartes': what I
know for certain is that thought exists, and I then ask what follows. Here,
however, the similarity with Descartes ends.

(Davidson 2004b (1995): 5)

1. Introduction

In Part III, we take up a number of important developments in Davidson's
work based upon reflections on the project of radical interpretation and the
central role in it that Davidson gives to a truth theory. A number of these
themes turn out to be central to a defense of the possibility of radical interpretation and, in the course of exposition and criticism, we will also aim to make
these clear connections.

We begin, in Chapter 18, with Davidson's celebrated argument against
the possibility of conceptual schemes radically different from our own. Concepts are the common currency of different thoughts. To claim that there
cannot be conceptual schemes radically different from our own is to claim
that, though there can be some failure of overlap between the concepts that
different thinkers employ, there must be enough overlap to ensure the possibility of communication between them. Davidson casts this as an argument
against conceptual relativism. There are, though, two theses that have sometimes gone under the label 'conceptual relativism', and it is important to be
clear about which one is Davidson's principal target. One is the view that
truth is relative to a conceptual scheme. The other is that there can be different non-overlapping, (or minimally overlapping) conceptual schemes (sets of

concepts). These theses are not unconnected, but they are not the same. The latter might best be called conceptual pluralism, and is Davidson's main target. The former is a secondary target and Davidson aims to undermine it by undermining conceptual pluralism. The connection is that if everyone must share a conceptual scheme, there is not more than one conceptual scheme for truth to be relative to, and, hence, the claim that truth is relative to a conceptual scheme has no work to do. However, these theses are distinct, since one can certainly deny truth is relative to a conceptual scheme (in any interesting sense), while admitting the possibility of radically non-overlapping conceptual schemes.

In Chapter 19, we take up Davidson's important arguments for the impossibility of massive error, particularly in our empirical beliefs, and his arguments for externalism about thought content—the view that the contents of our thoughts are determined by our relations to things in our environments (past and present). These arguments rest directly on assigning radical interpretation a fundamental role in understanding language and thought.

In Chapter 20, we consider Davidson's account of first person authority, that is, the special warrant that a person's own statements about his thoughts are accorded. As we remarked in Chapter 15, one source of a challenge to Davidson's basic methodological position on meaning and thought, namely, that we should take the radical interpreter's stance as conceptually basic, is the fact that we do not in our own case go on behavioral evidence in saying what we think. This suggests, at least, that behavioral evidence may fail to provide sufficient grounds for thought attribution, absent independent reasons to think that it is associated with a first person point of view. Thus, it becomes important, indeed crucial, to a defense of Davidson's methodological stance to exhibit first person authority as arising from reflection on what it is necessary to assume in interpretation.

In Chapter 21, we take up Davidson's arguments for the inscrutability of reference. This is the view that what our singular terms refer to, and what falls in the extensions of our predicates, is inscrutable in the sense that there are many equally good assignments which capture all there is to be captured about sentential meaning. This is obviously connected with the thesis of the indeterminacy of interpretation, but has some distinctive features, and rests in part on the claim that the concept of reference is a theoretical concept whose content is exhausted by the role it plays in accounting for the truth of sentences. This argument too rests in part on taking the stance of the radical interpreter, and the fact that his first access to another's language goes through identifying hold true attitudes, to be methodologically basic.

In Chapter 22, we consider arguments Davidson has developed more recently which aim to ground what is perhaps his most fundamental assumption, namely, that psychological and linguistic concepts are *theoretical* (particularly in the way required to give rise to indeterminacy by what appears to be empirical underdetermination), or, alternatively, that the third person stance, essentially the stance of the radical interpreter, is conceptually basic in understanding meaning and the psychological attitudes. These arguments aim to show that there is a fundamental connection between the possibility of having beliefs, and so any propositional attitudes, and having the concept of truth (or, as Davidson says equivalently, of objectivity), and a fundamental connection, in turn, between having the concept of truth and having and using a language. The argument rests on the requirement that any concept which we possess have some scope for application in our experience. The concept of objectivity or truth, Davidson argues, could be deployed by us, that is, we could make sense of our possession of it, only if we conceive of ourselves as specifically *linguistic* agents.

The theses we examine in this part are clearly not independent of one another. The most fundamental is the assumption that the concepts we deploy in thinking about language and thought are theoretical concepts whose character determines that empirically equivalent theories, after all the evidence is in, state the same thing. The other theses all rest to some degree on this one. Yet, the other arguments provide indirect support by aiming to show that this fundamental methodological stance issues in a coherent and persuasive picture of the nature of language and thought and their place in the natural world. Thus, for example, as we have noted above, the account of first person authority from the third person standpoint aims to meet a direct challenge to the coherence of the basic methodological stance. The argument for the impossibility of alternative conceptual schemes, as we will show, plays an important role in the argument for the impossibility of massive error. The thesis that only linguistic agents are believers is presupposed by the arguments for the impossibility of radically different conceptual schemes, for the impossibility of massive error and for externalism about thought content, and the account of first person authority, since all of these arguments depend on reading off from what is necessary for interpretation facts constitutive of belief, which presupposes that believers are by their very nature interpretable. The argument for the necessity of language for belief is at the same time an argument for a very strong publicity requirement on language. Thus, most of the arguments we examine in what follows provide at least indirect support for the others by combining with them to present a comprehensive and coherent account of the nature of language and thought from a resolutely third person point of view.

The account that emerges is impressive. Yet, in the end, its persuasiveness must rest on more than just the seamless interlocking of its separate theses. The detailed arguments for the theses must themselves withstand critical scrutiny. Our position, signaled in Part II, is that in the end they do not. In arguing for this, particularly in arguing against the availability of a transcendental guarantee of success in radical interpretation founded on reflection on what is required simply to have beliefs, we complete the argument of Part II for the impossibility of radical interpretation, at least when it is characterized in a way that will support the theses we examine in Chapters 18–22.

18

The Impossibility of Alternative Conceptual Schemes

> The dominant metaphor of conceptual relativism, that of differing points
> of view, seems to betray an underlying paradox. Different points of view
> make sense, but only if there is a common co-ordinate system on which
> to plot them; yet the existence of a common system belies the claim of
> dramatic incomparability.
>
> (Davidson 2001c (1974): 184)

Davidson's main concern in "On the Very Idea of a Conceptual Scheme" is
with the intelligibility of the concept of a conceptual scheme, at least when
it is to be understood in a way that allows it to do interesting work. There
are two different doctrines the concept of a conceptual scheme is used to
state, both of which are targets in Davidson's discussion, though they are
not always distinguished. The first is the relativity of truth to a conceptual
scheme (or reality). The second is the possibility of a plurality of fundamentally
different conceptual schemes. The first is the doctrine that what is true (or so)
according to, or relative to, one scheme may not be true (or so) according
to another; the second is that there can be conceptual schemes which share
nothing in common and, in particular, no concepts. While the former makes its
appearance in Davidson's discussion, the latter is his main target. There is this
connection between them: if there cannot be a plurality of different conceptual
schemes, then talk of truth being relative to a conceptual scheme is idle. There
seems, however, no incompatibility between holding that there is a plurality
of conceptual schemes, although truth is not relative, in any interesting sense,
to scheme (we will return to this below).

1. Conceptual Schemes

In this section, we take up the questions what a conceptual scheme is, and what is required to make sense of someone's having one.

First, then, what is a conceptual scheme? It is natural to say that it is a set of concepts the totality of which is minimally sufficient for it to be the set of concepts of some possible thinker. So understood, not every set of concepts will count as a conceptual scheme, since some sets of concepts may be too small, or inappropriately constituted, to be a minimal set of concepts that a thinker could operate with.

Davidson, however, identifies conceptual schemes with sets of inter-translatable languages (Davidson 2001*c* (1974): 185). This requires at least two assumptions. The first is that only speakers have concepts. This is equivalent to saying that only speakers have thoughts. We will accept this assumption for the time being; it is argued for in "Thought and Talk" (Davidson 2001 (1975)) and "Rational Animals" (Davidson 2001*b* (1982)), and we will consider it in Chapter 22. The second is that any concept a speaker possesses, and any thought he could think, is expressible in his language. (We think of a language here as something usable for communication; hence, something that could be learned by a concept possessor.) Together these assumptions entail that there can be a difference in conceptual scheme between two people only if some portion of the language one speaks is not translatable into any portion of the other's. Where one language is partially translatable into another, there is partial overlap between conceptual schemes. When no portion of one language is translatable into another, there are two radically or completely different conceptual schemes.

Given the identification of conceptual schemes with sets of inter-translatable languages, whether we can make sense of radically different conceptual schemes reduces to whether we can make sense of two languages not being at all inter-translatable (or such that "no significant range of sentences in one language could be translated into the other": Davidson 2001*c* (1974): 185). The idea that there can be non-inter-translatable languages stands in need of defense. If we cannot show in detail that it makes sense to talk of radically or completely different conceptual schemes, then it does not.

Davidson argues that making sense of talk of non-inter-translatable languages requires a criterion for when a form of behavior counts both as speech behavior, and as speech that cannot be translated into our own. There are two ways to interpret his request for a criterion. According to the first,

306

what we want is a condition at least sufficient for the required state of affairs to obtain, and which makes sense in detail of its obtaining (the condition that it is speech behavior and not translatable into our own language is supposed to fail to satisfy the second conjunct of the requirement). Call this an 'individuation criterion'. According to the second, what we want is a way of *telling* that certain behavior is speech behavior and not translatable into our own language. Call this an 'identification criterion'. It is unclear whether Davidson intends the first or the second criterion, or whether he regards the second as required to satisfy the first. We will consider the success of his argument on both readings.

The following passage suggests that Davidson intends the second reading, that is, that he requires that in order to make sense of there being alternative conceptual schemes, in the sense of non-inter-translatable languages, we be able to *tell* that someone is speaking a language we cannot translate into our own:

It is tempting to take a very short line indeed: nothing, it may be said, could count as evidence that some form of activity could not be interpreted in our language that was not at the same time evidence that that form of activity was not speech behavior. If this were right, we probably ought to hold that a form of activity that cannot be interpreted as language in our language is not speech behavior. Putting matters this way is unsatisfactory, however, for it comes to little more than making translatability into a familiar tongue a criterion of languagehood. As fiat, the thesis lacks the appeal of self-evidence; if it is a truth, as I think it is, it should emerge as the conclusion of an argument.   (Davidson 2001c (1974): 185–6)

The suggestion implicit in this passage is that to make sense of there being languages not translatable into our own would be to be able to describe evidence that someone had a language not translatable into our own, and so to have an identification criterion for there being non-inter-translatable languages. That this is what Davidson has in mind is reinforced by his observation that to identify someone as having a language requires identifying him as having attitudes, but identifying someone as having attitudes requires interpreting his language: "it seems unlikely that we can intelligibly attribute attitudes as complex as these to a speaker unless we can translate his words into ours" (Davidson 2001c (1974): 186).

2. Scheme and Content

In this section, we consider what the contrast between a scheme and its content comes to, and the two central metaphors for making sense of radically differing

307

conceptual schemes that Davidson considers. We begin with considerations about the relation between the scheme–content distinction, and the connected distinction between analytic and synthetic sentences.

The idea of a *multiplicity of (possible) worlds*, as Davidson remarks, is not the same as the idea of a *multiplicity of points of view* on a *common world*. The central metaphor of conceptual relativism is the latter rather than the former. They may be thought to be connected, however, in the following way. The former arguably presupposes the analytic/synthetic distinction. This is because it presupposes the distinction between the necessary and the possible, which has been traditionally explicated by appeal to the analytic/synthetic distinction. This supplies a suggested connection. For rejecting the idea of a multiplicity of worlds requires, if we accept the traditional view, rejecting the analytic/synthetic distinction, and this, while not required for it, may still encourage conceptual relativism, by encouraging the thought that meaning is dependent on theory.[234] (The cluster view of meaning was instrumental in the early arguments of Feyerabend and Kuhn that before and after scientific revolutions scientists speak different languages.) For, if meaning is dependent on theory, then a change in theory leads to a change in meaning. Radical change in theory may lead then to a radical change in meaning, and, thus, to a radically different conceptual scheme, that is, a language not translatable into that of any radically different theory. In this way, one might argue that it must be possible that there be radically different conceptual schemes, because there clearly can be radically different theories. (Perhaps no one, anymore, would wish to say that every change in theory results in a complete change in the language one speaks, if, indeed, anyone ever intended to endorse this implausible view.)

Davidson's objection to this line of argument is that it does not meet the requirement laid down above, namely, that it provide a criterion for someone speaking a radically different language. To do this, one needs to

---

[234] One of us (Ludwig) would not endorse this connection, on the basis of the argument sketched in n. 236, which, if correct, shows that rejecting the analytic/synthetic distinction is equivalent to rejecting the concept of meaning. If this is correct, then one would not be inclined to think that if the analytic/synthetic distinction is rejected, all meaning must be dependent on theory, for the rejection of the distinction would be a rejection of the concept of meaning as well. The path Davidson indicates to the conclusion (without committing himself to it) is the following (Davidson 2001c (1974): 187–8): "The distinction between theory and language depends upon the distinction between analytic and synthetic sentences. Why is that? The idea is that the language is fixed by its analytic sentences: these provide the framework for empirical variation of theory in a fixed language. If we abandon the idea that there are analytic sentences, then (the argument goes) all sentences are synthetic, and we cannot make sense of the idea of theory variation within a fixed language. Thus, language varies as the theory does."

show that before and after some change in theory, or between holders of different theories, there really is complete non-inter-translatability of theory, while still showing that the other *has* a theory, and so a language. For this reason, Davidson says that "giving up the analytic–synthetic distinction has not proven a help in making sense of conceptual relativism" (Davidson 2001c (1974): 189).[235]

This leaves us with the thought that, even giving up the analytic/synthetic distinction, and so the idea of a sentence true in virtue of meaning, as opposed to true in virtue of meaning plus the way the world is, one can retain the distinction between sentences and their contents.[236] The latter are explained by their relation, in the context of a theory, to evidence for the former, which, in the empiricist tradition, is identified with sensory experience. This, a dualism of "conceptual scheme and empirical content," the "third dogma of empiricism," as Davidson calls it (2001c (1974): 189), is essentially Quine's position in "Two Dogmas of Empiricism" (Quine 1953) and *Word and Object* (Quine 1960), which Davidson has in mind here.

The central suggestion is that we can make sense of different conceptual *schemes* by making sense of sets of sentences, overall theories, standing in different *relations* to what gives any such theory its *content*, namely, the evidence for the theory, sensory experience. The differing relations are to give rise to differing contents. Davidson identifies two main families of metaphors for the relation: theories organize (systematize, divide up) experience, or they fit (predict, account for, face) experience. The strategy of Davidson's argument

---

[235] There is another objection that can be raised. Proponents of the view that changes in theory lead to changes in meaning typically suppose that there is something in common between different theories to which they are responsible, the evidence or observations which count against the one and for the other. For there to be this common ground, however, the proponents of different theories must share the concepts required to describe the common evidence. Theory comparison undercuts the possibility of radical non-overlap of conceptual scheme. In fact, neither Feyerabend nor Kuhn supposed that scientists working with different theories failed to agree on what number a needle on a dial is pointing to, or whether the lights are on in the lab, even if they disagreed about other descriptions of these things. So, it is unclear that any of the proponents of the cluster theory of meaning really had anything quite as radical in mind as Davidson's target. This remark is obviously connected with the next line taken up by Davidson.

[236] One of us (Ludwig) thinks this is incoherent, but in any case, in the main discussion, we will assume it is true for the sake of argument. If it is not, then it offers no refuge for conceptual relativism. The objection to it is that by maintaining a distinction between sentences and content, one is *ipso facto* maintaining a distinction between sentences and meaning. Given that syntax is independent of semantics, it seems possible to formulate analytic sentences with some elementary logic. Thus, the argument goes, giving up the analytic/synthetic distinction is equivalent to giving up on meaning and content altogether, or on elementary logic, and so, the argument goes, there is no intelligible option to accepting an analytic/synthetic distinction. This argument is, however, controversial, and one of us in particular (Lepore) is skeptical about it.

is to show that neither metaphor can be cashed out without presupposing that there is no complete breakdown in translation between the different theories.

3. Attacking the Metaphors of Conceptual Relativism

In this section, we consider Davidson's attack on the two metaphors of conceptual pluralism. The first, the idea that schemes organize differently a common world, is dispensed with relatively quickly. Davidson's argument for the impossibility of radically different conceptual schemes is completed by arguing that, when we turn to the second metaphor and trace out its consequences, we will see that it is equivalent to taking a theory to be true, and that reviewing what the concept of truth requires shows us that to make sense of a theory merely being true requires seeing the theory as translatable into a language we understand.

(a) Different Schemes *Organize* Differently the Same World

The difficulty with the metaphor of organizing is straightforward. Organizing something (the world) requires thinking of it as composed of a number of distinct particulars or features which can be classified in some more or less simple ways. To suppose that different theories aim to organize a common subject-matter, whether or not it is experience, is to presuppose that they in fact have a common subject-matter, that is, that they have predicates in common which classify particulars in the same ways, or are about the same features, which belies complete failure of translatability. Thus, appeal to different ways of organizing a common subject-matter fails to provide a ground for making sense of completely different conceptual schemes. This brings out a basic tension in the metaphor of conceptual schemes as different points of view on one world. Thus, while pursuit of this metaphor might lead to making detailed sense of *differing* conceptual schemes, it requires presupposing that failure of translation between the languages that express them is at most partial. The argument is more general than is suggested by its application to the empiricist conception of what determines content. What gives rise to a problem is the requirement that there be a common subject-matter being organized, and not the nature of that common subject-matter.

(b) Different Schemes Account Differently for the Same Evidence

This leaves the idea that what makes something, a set of sentences, into a conceptual scheme, is a relation of fitting or predicting or accounting for evidence. Davidson reduces this in two stages to the view that a conceptual scheme is a largely true theory. We will consider the reduction, then Davidson's argument against the possibility of radically different conceptual schemes so considered, and then return to the shift here from thinking of a conceptual scheme as *a language or set of concepts* to thinking of it as *a theory*.

Two assumptions are required to reduce the idea that a conceptual scheme fits the (sensory) evidence to the idea that it is a true theory.

(1) Sensory evidence is to be understood as "the totality of possible sensory evidence past, present, and future." (Davidson 2001*c* (1974): 193)

(2) "for a theory to fit or face up to the totality of possible sensory evidence is for that theory to be true." (Davidson 2001*c* (1974): 193)

Underlying (1) and (2) is the thought that terms of a theory are introduced explicitly in the context of giving an account of the evidence the theory is meant to accommodate, and that they do not have a role in the language independently of that given to them in the context of the theory. Therefore, the thought continues, the content of these theoretical terms is exhausted by their role in accounting for evidence. In particular, on this view, if a theory accommodates all the possible evidence, there is no additional question about whether the world is the way the theory says it is. This would presuppose that there were some fact of the matter about what the theoretical terms in the theory meant which went beyond their contribution to accounting for possible evidence for the theory. This view, applied to interpretation theory, underlies Davidson's thesis of indeterminacy of interpretation (Chapter 15), and his view that reference is inscrutable, as we will see (Chapter 21)—of behavioral evidence, Davidson says that "such evidence is all that matters to questions of meaning and communication" (2001*a* (1979): 227).

Given (1) and (2), the question whether there can be different conceptual schemes reduces to the question whether we can provide a criterion for whether a theory is true but untranslatable into our own language. "The question whether this is a useful criterion is just the question how well we understand the notion of truth, as applied to language, independent of the notion of translation" (Davidson 2001c (1974): 194).

Our clearest insight into truth is provided by Tarski's Convention T (and its variants), Davidson says. A definition of a truth predicate for a language (in another) must entail (setting aside context sensitivity) all sentences of the form,

(3) s is T iff p

where 'p' is replaced by a sentence that translates s. For another's theory to be true, it must be the case, then, that there is a truth theory for his language, and the sentences which are part of his theory are true, which means that, in the corresponding T-sentences in the truth theory for his language, the right hand sides obtain. So, to *tell* whether a sentence in another's language (or theory) is true or not, we need a T-sentence for it. Then by ascertaining whether the right hand side holds, we can tell whether it is true. But to be in possession of a T-sentence (in the sense intended), we must know it and know that it is a T-sentence, and that requires knowing that the sentence that replaces 'p' is a translation of s; since the T-sentence, if it expresses knowledge we have, must be stated in a language we understand, s must be translatable into a familiar language, and so, it is not a sentence in a non-translatable language. If this is right, there is no hope of telling that a theory stated in another language is (largely) true (and so represents a conceptual scheme or theory at all, on the present line of thought) unless it is (largely) translatable into one's own language.

4. Evaluating the Argument for the Impossibility of Radically Different Conceptual Schemes

Are these arguments successful? It should be noted first that both of them are most plausible if we interpret Davidson as requiring an identification criterion for making sense of alternative conceptual schemes, rather than just an individuation criterion. This is seen most clearly in the case of the argument against the fitting metaphor. For there it is explicit that it is the requirement that we *tell* that a theory is true that generates the requirement that we translate the other's sentences into our own language. For it is the requirement that we can tell the other's sentences are true that generates the requirement that we can state the T-sentences for their language in our own language, and that requires in turn translatability of the other's sentences into our language. If we ask merely for a condition for the sentences of his theory to be true, then we can state that condition in terms of truth without presupposing that any of his sentences is translatable into one of ours. The condition is that (*a*) there be an interpretive truth theory for his language, and that, (*b*) for the sentences in his theory, the right hand sides of their *T*-sentences be true.

The requirement that we have an identification criterion is also implicit in the argument against the metaphor of organizing. For it is only if we are required to tell that a putatively alternative scheme is organizing something that it seems necessary to suppose that we can identify what it is organizing in ways different from our own. That is what leads to the conclusion that the supposed alternative conceptual scheme is not expressed in a language that is completely non-translatable. If we ask merely for a individuation criterion, we might appeal to organization, not of some common subject-matter, but of different subject-matters. Different schemes, on this view, would count as schemes, because their function was to organize (classify) something given to their users, but could be radically different only in so far as they organized different things, and, in particular, things that could not be talked about in other schemes. (Whether even this much could be granted without already presupposing some features of the language in common, such as the basic logical apparatus, we will not pursue here; independently of pursuing this worry, we hope to demonstrate that there cannot be radically different conceptual schemes for linguistic beings.)[237]

For this reason, we think it is most plausible to suppose that Davidson does intend to be requiring an identification criterion for alternative conceptual schemes in order to make sense of the idea. What would justify requiring

---

[237] One might aim to keep the idea that there is something common to all conceptual schemes which is organized, compatibly with denying that there is any conceptual overlap, by conceiving of conceptual schemes in a broadly Kantian way as operating on the same "raw given" in experience, in such a way that what is brought under a concept is the result of the organization of the raw given by the conceptual scheme (the a priori categories of the understanding). On this view, different schemes bring different kinds of objects under concepts by their very nature, though there is something they all organize which is for each scheme below the level of conceptualization. The given in experience would not be something describable in any scheme, for bringing something under a concept would presuppose it was thereby organized as an object of a certain kind conforming to the requirements at least of certain general concepts. This would (formally) avoid the objection that to speak of different schemes organizing the same thing presupposes shared concepts. However, this is purchased at the cost of introducing a notion of organization, and a notion of something organized which are unclear in detail, and of making mysterious what our position as theorists whose cognitive capacities are being described is with respect to the theory we describe ourselves with. In any case, if Davidson is appealing to an identification criterion, then he would object that this view leaves us with no way to identify anyone as having a conceptual scheme who does not organize experience as we do. (We are indebted to Peter Klein for discussion which prompted this note.)

313

an identification criterion, rather than an individuation criterion? One might argue that a non-trivial individuation criterion requires an identification criterion; that is, to explain in detail what would constitute someone speaking a language not translatable into one's own would require more than just employing a small set of interrelated concepts, such as truth, meaning, classification, etc., to describe an activity, and adding that the activity so described is not speech behavior that is interpretable in one's own language. To give the idea plausibility, to show how it could be so, one might argue, requires giving substance to the idea that the concepts could be applied in the absence of translatability in a language one speaks. But, further, to give substance to the idea that the concepts can be applied in the absence of translatability into a language one speaks seems to require thinking of what evidence there could be that these concepts did apply in particular cases, which leads to the requirement of an identification criterion.

The requirement that we have an identification criterion for alternative conceptual schemes to make sense of them can also be seen as following from the view we attributed to Davidson in Chapter 15 about the special character of the central concepts involved in thinking about languages, namely, the concepts of meaning, truth, reference, and satisfaction. On that view, they are theoretical concepts. Their application is justified by appeal to behavioral evidence. And their content is exhausted by their roles in accounting for the evidence for their application in a way that ensures that theories empirically equivalent after all the evidence is in state the same facts. In light of this, the claim that the concept of language, for example, applies or could apply to an activity in the absence of its being translatable into our language requires that we explain how we could *apply* the concept *on the basis of behavioral evidence* in a way that does not require simultaneously that we find the language to be translatable into our own. This marks an important connection between Davidson's arguments against the possibility of radically different conceptual schemes and his basic methodological stance in radical interpretation.

We want to return now to a puzzle we passed over in explaining Davidson's argument against the possibility of radically different conceptual schemes conceived of as true theories. That is the shift in the conception of the individuation of conceptual schemes as sets of inter-translatable languages to their individuation as true but different theories. It is this shift that allows Davidson to argue that an identification criterion for a true theory would require that it be translatable into one's own language. The idea that a conceptual scheme is a theory, however, is at odds not only with the way we originally introduced the notion, namely as a set of concepts, but also with the way we then explicated it in terms of a set of inter-translatable languages. For many different theories can be stated in a given language or using a given set of concepts. Thus, the shift of target looks like a change of subject.

(Note that if we were to adopt this identification of conceptual scheme with true theory, we would be forced to deny that anyone possessing a (largely) false theory had a conceptual scheme. That is, to possess a conceptual scheme at all would be to possess a largely true theory or view of the world. This is, of course, a position Davidson has argued for independently, and which we take up in the next section.)

The explanation of why this shift takes place may lie in part in the route that Davidson takes to this suggestion. For the metaphors of organizing or fitting reality were introduced against the background of an argument for radically different conceptual schemes based on the rejection of the analytic/synthetic distinction and the consequent suggestion that we should have to treat any theory change as change of language. In this case, different theories *ipso facto* represent different languages, and so, the identification is innocent.

However, there is no reason why someone who wishes to employ these metaphors is required also to think that we must reject the analytic/synthetic distinction. So, the rejection of them as providing a means of making sense of radically different conceptual schemes should not rest on interpreting them against the backdrop of the rejection of the analytic/synthetic distinction. In any case, the view that language changes with theory change is on its face absurd. If conceptual relativism rested on this doctrine, that would in itself be sufficient to refute it.

It might be said, though, that the fault really just lies with the metaphor of fitting itself. In this case, there can be no objection to the shift, for the change of subject is dictated by the change of metaphor. However, there does seem to be a way of interpreting the suggestion that a conceptual scheme is a tool for predicting experience, or for enabling us to fit theory to evidence, that does not require us to identify the conceptual scheme with the theory. This is to think of different conceptual schemes as different sets of concepts, or differ- ent non-inter-translatable languages, which enable us to state different classes of theories. If we suppose that different classes of theories so characterized may be, as classes, more or less well suited for fitting a particular stream of experience or particular set of data, then we can make sense of the role of dif- ferent conceptual schemes as enabling our theories to fit their evidence without identifying conceptual schemes with the theories.

If we understand the role of the fitting metaphor in this way, we would not identify conceptual schemes with true theories, but with classes of theories.

315

The test for whether another possessed a conceptual scheme would then not be whether he had a true theory (so that what is required for identifying another as having a true theory would not be relevant), but whether he possessed something which could be used to form a theory that could fit some possible stream of experience or set of evidence.

It is not clear that this is much help for the proponent of radically different conceptual schemes, because this is equivalent to saying that another has a theory or is in a position to have a theory (whether true or not). And this seems to be equivalent to saying that one has a language. So, we are back to the question of how we would identify someone as having a language without finding that it was translatable into our own.

The shift to conceiving of having a conceptual scheme as having a theory, or being able to have a theory, capable of being true or false, suggests that if we could show that another made utterances that had truth values, that is, were either true or false, we would be in a position to identify him as having a language. It might be said, however, in line with Davidson's own argument, that since identifying someone's utterances as true or false requires identifying them as meaningful, and identifying them as meaningful requires identifying their meanings, even identifying someone as making utterances that are truth-valued requires translating their language.

There is a natural objection to make at this point, which would apply both to the last suggestion and to Davidson's original argument. That is that Davidson himself assumes that we can identify others' hold true attitudes toward sentences independently of finding out what they mean. This is assumed in his description of the radical interpreter's procedure. But if we can identify others' hold true attitudes toward sentences, then we have identified them as thinkers without having translated their language. Thus, it might be objected, Davidson bears witness against himself. If he is right that we can identify a speaker's hold true attitudes without knowing what his sentences mean, then we can identify another as having a language without translating it into our own. On the other hand, if he is right that we cannot identify another as a speaker or thinker at all without translating his words into our own, then Davidson's description of the procedure of the radical interpreter is undermined.

To respond to this Davidson must maintain that evidence that someone has a range of hold true or other attitudes toward sentences must ultimately be backed up by showing that, on that assumption, we can go on to assign meanings to the sentences and contents to the attitudes in a way that makes sense of his behavior. Thus, we must represent the initial identification of a speaker's hold true attitudes as a hypothesis, which must ultimately be surrendered if it does not lead to a workable interpretation theory for the supposed speaker. This brings Davidson's position in "On the Very Idea of a Conceptual Scheme" into line with his account of the procedure of the radical interpreter.

We can mention one further difficulty for the view that we make sense of a conceptual scheme by thinking of it as a theory or set of possible theories, namely, that to the extent to which we think of the theories as responsible to the same kind of evidence (e.g. sensory experience), we must, as in the case of the metaphor of organization, think of them as having a common vocabulary. For what supports a theory must be sentential or propositional in form, that is, statements about sensory experience. If different classes of theories are responsible for the same evidence in this sense, then the languages in which they are stated cannot be completely non-inter-translatable. To suppose they were would require thinking of them as addressing different kinds of evidence.

We have identified the assumption that we can make sense of an alternative conceptual scheme only if we have an identification criterion for them as crucial to the success of Davidson's arguments. This in turn seems to rest on the view that the concepts of the theory of interpretation are theoretical concepts of the sort that give rise to indeterminacy. Whether the concepts of the theory have this character is not an issue we will raise here, but rather in Chapter 22, for the assumption underlies Davidson's discussion of each of the topics we will discuss in this part. However, it will be useful to consider our position with respect to conceptual relativism, if this assumption cannot be sustained. First, we wish to know whether we have reason to reject the relativity of truth to a scheme even if we do not succeed in rejecting the possibility of a plurality of conceptual schemes. Secondly, we wish to know whether arguments in addition to those that Davidson has adduced can be brought forward to reject the possibility of a plurality of radically different conceptual schemes, without appeal to the assumption that the central concepts of interpretation are theoretical concepts (in the sense discussed).

The doctrine of the relativity of truth to a conceptual scheme is indefensible independently of any commitments to the theoretical character of the concepts of truth, meaning, or reference. The reason is to be found in the connection between meaning and truth exemplified in Tarski's Convention T, when we make explicit the relativization of truth to a language, as in (4), where, as usual, 'p' is replaced by a sentence that translates s.

(4) s is true in L iff p.

317

The connection between meaning and truth that underlies the adequacy of Tarski's Convention T as a test of the extensional adequacy of a truth theory is, as we have mentioned before, expressed by the schema (5).

(5)   If s means that p in L, then s is true in L iff p.

If this is correct, then the truth conditions in that language of a sentence in a language are fixed by its meaning. Languages are individuated by their syntax and semantics, so saying what language a sentence is to be evaluated relative to fixes its meaning and, hence, in that language, its truth conditions. This, together with the way the world is, fixes its truth value. This shows that there can be none but a harmless and uninteresting relativism of truth to a conceptual scheme, namely, the familiar relativism of truth to a language.

The excitement of the doctrine of conceptual relativism lies in the thought that, by shifting from the point of view of one conceptual scheme to another, a true sentence may become a false one, while retaining its meaning. For if the meaning of the sentence is not the same in one scheme as it is in another, there is nothing surprising in the thought that its truth value is not the same in both. But to suppose that its truth value is different relative only to different schemes, while its meaning is invariant is incoherent. If the meaning of a sentence is the same relative to two schemes, that is, if relative to scheme 1, a sentence s means that p, and relative to scheme 2, it means that p, then that is in effect the same as saying that s means in the language L_1 of the first scheme the same as it does in the language L_2 of the second scheme. This can be put by saying:

(6) s means that p in L_1 iff s means that p in L_2.

From (5) and (6) we can deduce (7).

(7) s is true in L_1 iff s is true in L_2.

That is, given the way the world is, s is true relative to both schemes, or false relative to both. Thus, on the one hand, to suppose that a sentence could be true relative to one conceptual scheme and false relative to another in which it means the same thing is to suppose a contradiction. And, on the other, to suppose a sentence is true relative to one conceptual scheme and false relative to another in which it means something different is to suppose something that is of no consequence. There is, then, no interesting sense in which truth can be relative to a conceptual scheme. This holds even if there is a plurality of different conceptual schemes. What it shows is that if there can be radically different conceptual schemes, they must be conceived of as being about different aspects of the world, that is, as employing concepts which are about different things or features of things.

Can we make headway against the possibility of a plurality of conceptual schemes without the assumption Davidson draws on? Yes, we can, by exploiting another point Davidson makes, but which he does not apply in this connection. If we adopt the point of view that having a conceptual scheme is a matter of speaking a language, then we can be certain than anyone who has a conceptual scheme shares with anyone else who has a conceptual scheme a certain family of concepts. Speaking is an intentional activity. It involves thinking of sentences as meaning one thing or another, and having the ability to form intentions directed toward one's potential interlocutors, as well as to form beliefs about one's potential interlocutor's utterances, and engage in certain patterns of inference involving these utterances and concerning the interlocutor's intentions, beliefs, desires, and so on. Thus, to be a language speaker is to possess a large connected family of concepts, including those of sentence, term, meaning, truth, number, reference, intention, belief, desire, action, agency, communication, event, particular, causation, and so on. Given the principle that any thought a person can think is expressible (potentially) in his language (a condition on our identifying sets of inter-translatable languages with conceptual schemes), we can conclude that there cannot be radically different conceptual schemes in the sense of completely non-inter-translatable languages.

This leaves open how much else might need to be shared between speakers of different languages, and there may well be quite a bit more that would be needed to make sense of someone's speaking a language. So far as the argument goes, however, it allows that all of a speaker's other general terms may express concepts which find no echo in one's own thought. This may be far less than what Davidson hopes to have established, but it does suffice to show the absurdity of the idea of completely non-overlapping conceptual schemes, and the importance of trying to make sense in detail of the possibility.[238]

---

[238] The argument Davidson gives against the possibility of non-linguistic creatures with beliefs would secure this result also (see Ch. 22), since it requires that any creature with beliefs have the concept of belief, and presumably that would require their having a host of related concepts, desire, action, intention, etc. The current argument is in any case hostage to the argument that all believers speak a language, for otherwise the conclusion would at most show that all linguistic beings must share some concepts. It may be that the argument can be extended to non-linguistic beings, if being an agent as such requires possession of psychological attitude concepts. This would be so if acting requires rationalization of the act performed by an instrumental belief–desire pair. For the belief would involve conceiving of something as an action and, hence, as having appropriate attitudes in its etiology.

Davidson also considers the possibility of partial non-overlap of conceptual schemes, and argues that partial failure of translation presupposes a vast background of agreement. If this is right, then the observation above that there must be partial translatability secures that the overlap between any two possible conceptual schemes must be quite large. However, the argument for this is closely connected also with the argument against the possibility of massive error, and so will be dealt with in the next chapter on that topic.

5. Conclusion

We have reached the conclusion that Davidson's arguments against radically different conceptual schemes are successful only if his demand that we have an identification criterion for other conceptual schemes is legitimate. This requirement is not obviously legitimate. Often it seems enough that we know what would have to be the case for something to obtain in order to make sense of it, not that we be able to tell whether what would have to obtain does. But we have not issued a final verdict on this, because the question whether the concepts deployed in interpretation theory are relevantly theoretical is central to deciding the issue. If they are, their content is exhausted by how they help us keep track of the data they are introduced to manage. In this case, the idea that the data do not support their application in detail, though they apply, will look to be, at the least, very puzzling, and perhaps incoherent. If they are not, then the requirement of an identification criterion remains unsupported, and is not self-evident, so the argument must then be judged unsuccessful. This issue we take up again from different standpoints in Chapters 20 and 22. In Chapter 20 we evaluate Davidson's account of first person authority. In Chapter 22 we consider his arguments for the primacy of the third person point of view on meaning and psychology. We argue that Davidson's account of first person authority is inadequate, and that he fails to provide a transcendental argument for the primacy of the third person point of view. In consequence, we judge that his argument against radically different conceptual schemes fails. We have argued independently, however, that we cannot make good sense of complete non-overlap of conceptual schemes for linguistic beings. The argument rests on our concept of a linguistic being, and not on the requirement that we be able to identify someone as having a conceptual scheme for us to make sense of it.

We have also argued that, whatever the judgment reached about the possibility of radically different conceptual schemes, the thesis that truth is relative to a conceptual scheme is specious. Conceptual schemes are individuated by their concepts. These fix the meanings of terms in the language they are associated with. This fixes their truth conditions. Truth is relative to nothing except what fixes meaning and the world. Meaning and world being fixed, truth is invariant. Where truth varies while the world does not, meaning must vary as well. At most, different conceptual schemes in which different truths are advanced are not of different realities, but of different portions of one reality. The excitement of conceptual relativism conceived of as the relativity of truth (and so the thought goes, reality) to scheme vanishes as soon as the unclarity in our thinking is removed.

19

Externalism and the Impossibility of Massive Error[239]

> What stands in the way of global skepticism of the senses is, in my view, the fact that we must, in the plainest and methodologically most basic cases, take the objects of a belief to be the causes of that belief.
>
> (Davidson 2001a (1983): 151)

Davidson argues for the impossibility of massive error, and for a form of externalism about thought content—the view that our thoughts' contents are individuated at least in part by our relations to our environment—in a number of articles, beginning with "The Method of Truth in Metaphysics" (2001a (1977)), and including "Empirical Content" (2001a (1982)) and "A Coherence Theory of Truth and Knowledge" (2001a (1983)).[240] There are two main versions of Davidson's argument for the impossibility of massive error that have been discussed, though it is not clear Davidson intended to give two different arguments.[241] The first is the omniscient interpreter argument; the second we will call the argument from the principle of charity. We take these in turn.

---

[239] Some of the material in this chapter is derived from Ludwig 1992b.

[240] See also "The Myth of the Subjective" (Davidson 2001a (1988)), "The Conditions of Thought" (1989), "The Structure and Content of Truth" (1990b), "Representation and Interpretation" (2004 (1990)), "Three Varieties of Knowledge" (2001b (1988)), "Epistemology Externalized" (2001 (1991)), and "What is Present to the Mind" (2001 (1989)). For some reflections on calling his position a coherence theory of truth and knowledge see Davidson 2001a (1987), in which he rejects both the coherence and correspondence theories, and identifies the central theme as showing that belief and truth are interconnected.

[241] Davidson has said in conversation that he wished he had never mentioned the omniscient interpreter.

1. The Omniscient Interpreter Argument

The omniscient interpreter argument appears primarily in "The Method of Truth in Metaphysics," though there is a passing, but inessential, reference to an omniscient interpreter in "A Coherence Theory of Truth and Knowledge" (Davidson 2001*a* (1983): 150–1). The argument can be laid out as follows.

(1) Necessarily, to interpret another correctly requires finding him largely in agreement with oneself.

(2) It is possible that one be interpreted correctly (other things being equal) by an omniscient interpreter.[242]

(3) Therefore, one must have largely true beliefs, i.e. one cannot be in massive error about the world.

By an omniscient interpreter, Davidson means an interpreter with complete knowledge of the world *except* for knowledge of the attitudes of speakers and the meanings of their sentences. This ensures that an omniscient interpreter would have to learn about our attitudes and the meanings of our sentences by the methods of the radical interpreter. The 'other things being equal' clause is required because what is intended is that we would be interpretable by an omniscient interpreter given our current beliefs and language, in our current environment, not in counterfactual circumstances in which we speak a different language or have different (and mostly true rather than mostly false) beliefs.[243]

If it is possible that one be interpreted (as currently situated) by an omniscient interpreter (one who has only true beliefs about his environment and the world in general), and if to be interpreted by another one must be found to be largely in agreement with him, then (as currently situated) one's beliefs must be largely true. For suppose that one's beliefs were not largely true. Then someone with largely true beliefs about the same matters, in order to interpret one correctly, would have to find one largely in agreement with him. But he

---

[242] We will be assuming throughout the rest of the discussion that for one person to be able to interpret another is for him to be able *correctly* to interpret any sentence he may utter. We will henceforth drop the modifier 'correctly' from 'interpret' and its variants.

[243] Through failure to appreciate this, some authors have been led to think that Davidson must suppose that in every possible world there is an omniscient being in order for the argument to be sound, on the grounds that our possibly being interpreted by an omniscient interpreter entails nothing about whether our *actual* beliefs are largely true or not. See Foley and Fumerton 1985.

could not find one largely in agreement with him. Therefore, he could not interpret one correctly. An omniscient interpreter would by hypothesis have largely true beliefs about every subject matter (excepting at the start facts about meaning and thought). Therefore, if one did not have largely true beliefs, it would not be possible for one (as one is currently situated) to be interpreted by an omniscient interpreter, contrary to (2).

An initial question that arises is whether we can make good sense of the conclusion, given that we have indefinitely many beliefs. What does it mean to say that we have largely true beliefs, or that most of our beliefs are true, if we have an infinite number of beliefs? First, it is not clear that it is correct to say we have an infinite number of beliefs. If so, then no problem presents itself here. However, Davidson often talks as if we have an indefinitely large number of beliefs, so it would be well to be able to explicate the idea of most of our beliefs being true in a way that does not require the number of them to be finite. One suggestion is to require that a belief selected randomly from among one's beliefs be highly likely to be true. But a better approach is to explicate the content of the conclusion in terms of how an interpreter proceeds in constructing an interpretation for a speaker, for he starts with the assumption that all of a speaker's beliefs are true, and makes adjustments when it is required to make the speaker out to be more rational than otherwise. The initial assignments of contents to attitudes are made on the basis of a picture of the speaker's beliefs as largely true from the interpreter's point of view. In following this procedure, then, from the point of view of the interpreter, the area of disagreement will always be small relative to that of agreement, no matter how far the process is carried.

Suppose premises (1) and (2) are true. How much does the conclusion that we have largely true beliefs show? A question arises here because, if we have an indefinitely large number of beliefs, then it is possible that most of our beliefs are true, even though most beliefs about various categories of facts we are specially interested in are false, for example, beliefs about other minds, about the external world, about the future, about our own minds, and about contingent general truths. In "The Method of Truth in Metaphysics," the argument Davidson offers for the claim that an interpreter must find the speaker he interprets largely in agreement with him depends on the claim that "Beliefs are identified and described only within a dense pattern of beliefs" (2001*a* (1977): 200). This rests on the view that concept possession depends upon having a large set of general beliefs which are constitutive of having the concept, and are true in virtue of their conceptual contents (see Chapter 14, §2). This, however, would secure only that most of our a priori general beliefs are true.

And this falls far short of addressing any traditional skeptical arguments about our empirical beliefs.[244]

The argument shows more, however, than just that most of our a priori general beliefs are true, because success at interpreting another through the procedures of the radical interpreter depends on more than just finding agreement on a priori patterns of general beliefs. Crucially, it depends on the principle of charity (or a stronger principle) in application to *L*-sentences, as we saw in Chapter 12. Since assigning meanings to sentences in this way depends upon the interpreter's assuming that the speaker is mostly right about his particular beliefs about his environment (so far as the interpreter can tell, of course), the assumption that one is interpretable via the methods of the radical interpreter also will require the interpreter to find the speaker largely in agreement with him on the nature of the speaker's environment. Thus, if the interpreter is right about the nature of the speaker's environment, as an omniscient interpreter is by hypothesis, the speaker, if intepretable by him, is likewise mostly right about his environment. Thus, if the argument is sound, the conclusion would show not just that a speaker is mostly right in his general a priori beliefs, but also in his beliefs about his environment. So, if the premises are in addition knowable a priori, this provides a refutation of one of the assumptions of traditional skepticism about the external world, namely, that it is conceptually possible that most of our beliefs about our environment be false. Furthermore, if we know that most of our beliefs are true, then there is a presumption for any given belief that it is true. Every belief, then, will start out with a kind of

---

[244] Davidson later addressed this objection in "Epistemology Externalized" (2001 (1991): 195). "It is possible to try to avoid this conclusion [that most of our empirical beliefs are true] by arguing that a belief such as that a mouse is a small, four-footed animal is true by virtue of the concepts alone—it is an analytic truth—and so is not really about the world. One could then still say all our beliefs about the world might be false. This line is not available to someone who, like me, does not think a clear line between analytic and synthetic truths is there to be drawn. But even if there are indubitably analytic truths, it is not plausible that these serve to eliminate the host of cases in which concepts are individuated by multiple empirical criteria." But this does not wholly meet the objection. The sorts of beliefs one must attribute to someone to sustain the attribution of a certain concept to him will be general beliefs. The sorts of beliefs we want to know are true in order to respond to philosophical skepticism are beliefs about particulars. Davidson in fact acknowledges this: "What [the argument from the holistic character of empirical belief] shows is that we cannot harbor particular false (or true) beliefs about individual objects unless we have many true beliefs about the nature of such objects. This leaves open the possibility that we may be wrong in all our particular beliefs about what exists in the world, and this would be a pretty extreme skepticism, though not quite total" (ibid. 195). Davidson goes on in this article to argue that we cannot make intelligible from the interpreter's standpoint mostly false beliefs about particulars. This involves a shift from considerations about what general beliefs one must attribute to another to sustain attribution of a concept to him to considerations about what an interpreter must assume to succeed in interpretation.

default warrant on this view. If the warrant is not defeated by conflict with other beliefs in the light of principles of good evidence, it will be justified. Thus, the transcendental guarantee that we have mostly true empirical beliefs will provide a framework for a positive program in epistemology.

How much can we show on the basis of this general transcendental guarantee that most of our beliefs are true? The argument does not show directly that we cannot have mostly false beliefs about the minds of others, for it is not clear that mostly true beliefs about other minds are required for success in interpretation. However, we will see that the most plausible argument Davidson can offer for the second premise will show, if correct, that there can be no difficulty, in principle, about learning about the minds of others, as far as their propositional attitudes go. Can the argument be made to solve the problem of induction by offering a general guarantee that our general beliefs that cover the future and the unobserved are true? It does not seem that it has any direct bearing on the problem of induction. Speakers' beliefs about generalizations whose domains are infinite need not be true in order for one to succeed in interpreting them; those beliefs do not, therefore, receive the blessing of interpretation.

2. Evaluating the Omniscient Interpreter Argument

We turn now to the question what reasons we can adduce for accepting premises (1) and (2) of the omniscient interpreter argument. (1) is supposed to be supported by reflections that we have already reviewed in Chapter 12, namely, the need to apply the principle of charity in interpretation, and the requirement that one attribute to a speaker many true general beliefs involving the concepts at play in any attitude one attributes to him. We leave aside for now any further examination of this premise and its grounds. (2) must be supported by two thoughts. The first is that, as Davidson puts it,

(4)   "there is nothing absurd in the idea of an omniscient interpreter" (2001*a* (1977): 201).

That is, it is possible (other things being equal) for there to be an omniscient interpreter. The second is (5).

(5)   We are potentially interpretable (other things being equal) by any possible interpreter.[245]

[245] Here is a clear expression of this idea from "The Myth of the Subjective" (Davidson 2001*a* (1988): 46–7, emphasis added): "to recognize [skepticism about other minds is ruled out] is not to answer the question what conceptual conditions do we place on the pattern of thought that make

(5) is required in addition to (4), because even if we grant the possibility of an omniscient interpreter, this would not guarantee that we were mostly right about the world unless we were interpretable by an omniscient interpreter (as we are presently situated). If we had mostly false beliefs, and another speaker mostly true beliefs, the requirement that, for one speaker to interpret another correctly, they must be largely in agreement with one another would simply show that we could not be interpreted by him.

We can see an important connection between the argument for the impossibility of radically different conceptual schemes and the assumption that we are interpretable with our current beliefs and in our current environment by any possible interpreter. If making sense of someone speaking a language at all requires an identification criterion, and this requires that we find another's language translatable into our own, then every language speaker must be potentially interpretable by every other. Seen in this light, the argument against the possibility of radically different conceptual schemes provides at the same time a crucial assumption of Davidson's argument against the possibility of massive error. If correct, this also provides a kind of transcendental argument against skepticism about other minds; this is of a piece with Davidson's view that the central concepts of interpretation theory should be treated as theoretical concepts whose content is exhausted by their role in accounting for the evidence, in this case, behavior, as previously discussed.

There is also a connection in the other direction: for if one could establish independently of the argument against radically different conceptual schemes that every language speaker had mostly true beliefs, one could support the claim that to have a conceptual scheme is to have a true theory, and thereby argue, as sketched in the previous chapter, that if we need an identification criterion for another having a conceptual scheme, it would require translation into our language, since that is the only way to identify another's theory (beliefs) as largely true.

What about (4), the assumption that it is possible that there be an omniscient interpreter? This may seem to be an innocent enough assumption.[246] Indeed,

---

it possible for an interpreter to progress from observed behavior to knowledge of the intentional attitudes of another. That this question has an answer, however, is guaranteed by the fact that *the nature of language and thought is such as to make them interpretable*."

[246] One minor and reparable difficulty with Davidson's appeal to the possibility of an omniscient interpreter is that it presupposes that the interpreter has all true beliefs, although for us, who are fallible speakers, this is a fact that could not emerge in the context of interpretation. According to Davidson, however, that context exhausts the relevant facts: what cannot emerge in the context of interpretation cannot be a matter of meaning or belief. Thus, we should not be able to make clear

we can get a sense of the cleverness of the supposition by noting that some traditional skeptical hypotheses which are constructed so as to be incompatible with what we believe, such as Descartes's evil genius hypothesis, contain an omniscient (though malevolent) interpreter. If all thinkers are speakers, and all speakers are potentially in communication with one another, but only by way of the procedures of the radical interpreter, then these hypotheses are incoherent, since they require a speaker to be mostly wrong about his environment, but to be interpretable by an omniscient interpreter, who by hypothesis exists. Nonetheless, the assumption, when we spell it out, in the context of radical skepticism about the external world, is not as innocent as it seems.

We should note first that the assumption is not just that there could be an omniscient interpreter, but that there could be one in a world in which we are situated as we are, and in which if there were, he would know something which would serve him as evidence for interpreting us. To see why this is an issue, consider a nonspatial world in which we are immaterial beings whose experiences are unconnected with events in any space, Leibnizian monads, as it were, whose experiences unfold by way of an internal principle of change. In such a world, even if there were an omniscient interpreter (of the sort we are considering, that is, one who does not start out with beliefs about others' attitudes and so on), he could not interpret us, because nothing in that world would serve him as evidence for interpretation, even though he has only true beliefs about the world. If this is possible, then to know not just that there could be an omniscient interpreter who interprets us in some possible world, but one who interprets us correctly in a world of the same type as the actual world with respect to our situation and dispositions, we would have to know that the world is at least spatial. For its being spatial is a necessary condition on there being public evidence of the sort that the interpreter would rely on. If we cannot rule out a priori that the world is nonspatial, then premise (2) would have to be supported at least in part a posteriori. However, this would presuppose what is in question in the context of skepticism about the external world, namely, that we can have knowledge of the external world.

Another way to see that accepting the assumption that there can be an omniscient interpreter who could interpret us is suspicious against the current background of assumptions is to consider a possibility which seems at least

sense of a speaker all of whose beliefs are true. However, the repair is simple: we want, not an omniscient interpreter, but an interpreter who is mostly right about the world, and in particular, mostly right about our environments. Henceforth, we understand the phrase 'omniscient interpreter' in this way. It is an interesting sidelight that this argument, if sound, shows that there could not be an omniscient being, and, hence, that there could not be a God as traditionally conceived.

prima facie plausible, namely, that there be an interpreter who, in contrast to the omniscient interpreter, is not largely right, but largely wrong about our environment.[247] Unless we already have a reason to suppose that a speaker or interpreter must be largely right about his environment, we have no reason to oppose this possibility. But if there can be an interpreter who is mostly wrong about our environment, then if he is required to find us mostly in agreement with him in order to interpret us, then together with the assumption that we are (situated as we in fact are) interpretable by him, we can conclude, not that we have mostly true beliefs about our environment, but mostly false beliefs. What is wanted is some reason to suppose that the hypothesis of the "omni-ignorant interpreter" (understood not as an interpreter all whose beliefs are false, but one most of whose beliefs about our environment are false) who could interpret us, as we are, is less plausible than that of the omniscient interpreter who could do so. If we had an argument to show, however, that there could not be an omni-ignorant interpreter who could, as we are, interpret us, then we would already have an argument against skepticism about the external world. It seems, then, that the omniscient interpreter argument is unsuccessful, because we will be in a position to accept one of its assumptions only if we can independently show skepticism about the external world to be false.

3. The Argument from Interpretation

The omniscient interpreter argument is not Davidson's considered argument for the impossibility of massive error in our empirical beliefs. There is a more straightforward argument available, grounded in considerations about the procedure of the radical interpreter, which Davidson gives in "Empirical Content" (2001a (1982)), "A Coherence Theory of Truth and Knowledge" (2001a (1983)), and other papers.[248] The argument can be laid out as follows.

(1) To be a speaker is to be interpretable by other speakers.[249]
(2) To be interpretable by other speakers, one must be largely right, not only in one's general beliefs, but in one's beliefs about one's environment.

---

[247] We say mostly wrong about the environment because to attribute attitudes at all to an interpreter, we must, of course, attribute to him a supporting cast of beliefs which are conceptually true.

[248] Davidson 2001a (1988), 1990b, 2004 (1990), 2001b (1988), 2001 (1990), 2001 (1989).

[249] In later work, Davidson has endorsed an additional requirement: that to be a speaker, one must be interpreted by other speakers. Considerations that count against the weaker thesis will count against the stronger. We examine the stronger thesis in Ch. 22.

(3)   Therefore, to be a speaker is to be largely right, not only in one's general beliefs, but in one's beliefs about one's environment.

We appealed to (1) here in the omniscient interpreter argument in support of its second premise. The important difference between the two arguments lies in the difference between the first premise of the omniscient interpreter argument and (2) here. The earlier premises required that for anyone to interpret another speaker, the first person must find the speaker to be largely in agreement with him. This leaves open whether they agree on truths or falsehoods. If we consider, however, the description of the procedure of the radical interpreter in Chapter 12, the principle of charity does not say that the interpreter must find the speaker to be in agreement with him: the required assumption is that the speaker's beliefs about his environment be mostly true. (This, of course, is secured also by the stronger principle that we argued Davidson needs, namely, Grace.) If an interpreter is to succeed in interpreting a speaker, he too must have largely true beliefs about the speaker's environment, and this will result in the speaker and interpreter agreeing about the nature of the speaker's environment. However, the assumption made in order to connect an interpreter's evidence with an interpretive truth theory is not that the interpreter and speaker are in agreement, but that the speaker is mostly right about his environment. So, on the assumption that radical interpretation is possible, the proper way to state the requirement on a speaker is that his beliefs about his environment be mostly true. We can thus bypass the appeal to an omniscient interpreter and appeal directly to its being necessary that a speaker be interpretable, and a necessary condition on that, namely, that the speaker's beliefs about his environment be mostly true.

Both of the premises required by the argument are to be considered a priori truths. If we take the procedure of the radical interpreter, as Davidson does (and must, for this argument to be effective), to be a rational reconstruction of how one could be justified in interpreting any speaker, and further assume that, of necessity, every speaker is interpretable, then what we must assume in order to interpret any speaker can be seen as constitutive of the nature of speakers. It is then constitutive of speakers, if this is right, that they have mostly true beliefs about their environment. If we did not take the premises of the argument to be a priori truths, then we would not be in a position to respond to traditional skepticism about the external world. For then we would have to know the premises a posteriori, and this would involve having knowledge of the external world. The skeptic purports to have an a priori argument against the possibility of knowledge of the external world.

To appeal to such knowledge in the face of his argument is question begging. This is one point at which we see the importance of taking Davidson to be supposing that he has an a priori argument for the possibility of success in radical interpretation. Without it, the argument against skepticism collapses. We might as well blandly appeal to knowledge that this is one hand and this another.[250]

We are in a position to infer more than just that a speaker's beliefs about his environment are mostly true. For, as we saw in Chapter 12, the procedure of the radical interpreter necessarily involves taking, by and large, the speaker's beliefs which are directed toward his environment (these are the beliefs which underlie hold true attitudes toward occasion sentences) to be about what typically causes them, or, more specifically, it involves supposing that the contents of his hold true attitudes directed toward his environment are given by the conditions with which the interpreter identifies them as nomically correlated.[251] (For the moment we ignore the difficulty presented by the possibility of multiple starting points for interpretation.) Thus, we can also conclude that it is constitutive of a speaker's environmentally directed beliefs that, by and large, they are about their typical causes. In this sense, we can say that beliefs about

[250] It is worth considering here the relevance of Davidson's occasional denials that he thinks that there is a sharp line between analytic and synthetic truths. It is not entirely clear whether in saying this he is denying there is any distinction at all, or only maintaining that these are vague predicates. The question in the current context is whether this rejection is also a rejection of the distinction between a priori and a posteriori knowledge. If it is, this undercuts another assumption of traditional skeptical arguments, namely, that we can have a priori knowledge of the premises of skeptical arguments, a requirement on such arguments not being self-defeating. It is not easy to determine what Davidson's attitude toward this issue is. On the one hand, he says he does not think a sharp line can be drawn between the analytic and synthetic. On the other, he does not purge his vocabulary of modal terms, or hesitate to characterize some of his conclusions as showing something about what is constitutive of a certain kind of thing (meaning or belief, for example). And many of his arguments appear to aim at conceptual analyses, or at least conceptual articulation, and to reach conclusions that are not merely empirical observations. Furthermore, Davidson's responses to skeptical arguments seem to aim to meet the skeptic on his own ground, rather than simply deny a presupposition of his position. One way to reconcile these features of his views is to suppose that he does not think that the positivist explanations of modal notions and the a priori/a posteriori distinction in terms of the analytic/synthetic distinction are correct.

[251] Strictly speaking, since Davidson holds that causal relations hold among events, we must say that beliefs are, by and large, about those events which typically cause their subject to acquire them. But this in turn is not quite right either. For, as was made clear in the discussion of the procedure of the radical interpreter, belief contents will be read off from the *L*-sentences which are used to derive *T*-sentences for the purposes of projecting an interpretive truth theory for the speaker's language. (This does not mean that every *L*-sentence is used to read off a speaker's belief contents, since some will be rejected for the purposes of deriving interpretive *T*-sentences by holistic constraints on attitude attribution.) We will follow Davidson in this discussion, talking loosely of beliefs being about the events that cause them, but underlying this is the more refined picture of Ch. 12.

a speaker's immediate environment, and beliefs more generally, since their contents in general will depend on the contents of such beliefs, are partly individuated by their typical causes. Had they had different causes, then their contents would have been different, regardless of whether the speaker differed otherwise. If this is correct, it shows that propositional attitude contents are relationally individuated; that is, to put this another way, the property of having an attitude with a certain content, one which involves concepts used in application to the speaker's environment, is a relational property, in the sense that having it requires the existence of something besides the speaker.[252]

In "A Coherence Theory of Truth and Knowledge," Davidson calls his position a kind of coherence theory of truth. This is misleading, though he is clear about what he intends. If the above argument is correct, any speaker must have a coherent set of beliefs which are largely true as a condition on being a speaker or having any beliefs at all. In this sense, we could say that any coherent set of beliefs is a largely true set of beliefs. However, this is not to say that what makes the beliefs true is the fact that they form a coherent set of beliefs. One explanation of their truth is that they represent the world as being thus and so, and (on the whole) the world is thus and so. Another is that it is the nature of belief, as Davidson puts it, to be true, or, perhaps more accurately, it is of the nature of believers to have mostly true beliefs. This does not constitute, of course, an analysis of truth in terms of coherence, which was the object of the traditional coherence theory of truth. If anything, the explanation goes in the other direction. To have beliefs, most of one's beliefs must be true. For most of one's beliefs to be true, they must be, by and large, coherent.

As in the case of the similar conclusion of the omniscient interpreter argument, once we have a transcendental guarantee that most of our empirical beliefs are true, we are in a position to state under what conditions a belief is warranted. Every belief starts out with a presumption of truth. If it survives the test by our other beliefs in the light of principles of good evidence, it counts as justified. Thus, we at once undermine the traditional assumption of the skeptical arguments about the external world that propositions about the mind are logically independent of those about the external world, and provide a program for identifying justified beliefs about the external world.

---

[252] More carefully, we will say that a property P is a relational property iff: necessarily, for any x, x has P only if there is a y such that y is not identical with x or any part of x, and y is not a necessary existent.

4. Evaluating the Argument from Interpretation

Is the argument successful? Whether premise (2) is true depends on how exactly it is to be understood. If we are thinking of our interpreters as restricted to the evidence and methods of the radical interpreter, then we can agree that the second premise is correct. For then it is simply the claim that if one is interpretable from the radical interpreter's standpoint, then one must be largely right about one's environment. On the other hand, if we do not so restrict how we think of potential interpreters, and require only systematically correct assignments of interpretations for interpretation, then it is not inconceivable that two brains in a vat could be interpreters of one another fortuitously, although most of their shared beliefs about particular events and objects in their environment were false. We will suppose, however, that Davidson has the first reading in mind throughout.

Premise (1) is ambiguous as stated. It admits of (at least) two readings, one weaker, and one stronger. We have implicitly been appealing to the stronger, but the appeal of premise (1), we will argue, rests on the weaker reading. For the premise to do the work it must in the argument, it must take the following form:

(1*a*)   For *any* speaker *s*, and *any* speaker *s'*, and *any* environment *e*, *s* is interpretable by *s'* in *e*.

A weaker reading is the following:

(1*b*)   For any speaker *s*, it is *possible* that there be *a* speaker *s'*, and *an* environment *e*, such that *s* is interpretable by *s'* in *e*.[253]

Clearly, (1*b*) is not strong enough for the argument to go through. For (1*b*) can be true provided that it is possible for one to have true beliefs about one's environment in some environment, but it does not require that in every circumstance one has mostly true beliefs about one's environment (for example, when one is a brain in a vat).

---

[253] There are other interpretations as well which fall between these two. We could interpret (1) as:

(1*c*)   For any speaker *s*, there is a speaker *s'* such that in any environment *e*, *s'* can interpret *s* in *e*.

This would allow for the possibility of radically different conceptual schemes, but not for one to be in massive error about one's environment. Davidson is committed to the strongest of these interpretations, while only the weakest is justifiable on the basis of considerations of the necessary publicness of language.

The appeal of premise (1) lies in the thought that language is essentially a medium for communication between different speakers, so that it is incompatible with someone being a speaker of a language to suppose that he could not interpret and be interpreted by others. Thus, we can say that because of the nature of language, in particular, its essential publicness, every speaker is necessarily interpretable. However, the reflection on the role of language as a medium for communication supports only the observation that no one can be a speaker unless he *can* communicate with others, in *appropriate* conditions. If we think of language as a tool for communicating with others, what is required for it to be such a tool is only that there are circumstances in which it can be used to achieve its end. It is not required that having a language give one magical powers to communicate with and be understood by others in any circumstances whatsoever. But that is what (1*a*) requires: that one be interpretable in any possible world, in any possible environment, as a brain in a vat, as a disembodied spirit, in a lifelong dream. The necessary publicness of language does not require this.

If premise (1*a*) were true, the argument advanced earlier to cast doubt on our being able to know a priori that it is possible for an omniscient interpreter to interpret us in a world in which we are situated as we actually are would be undermined. According to that argument, we would have to know at least that the world is spatial in order to know that we could be interpreted by an omniscient interpreter. For a nonspatial world would provide no evidence for interpretation. But if (1*a*) were true, in a possible world in which no evidence is available for interpretation, there would be no speakers.

The question whether (1*a*) is true is connected with the question whether the central concepts of interpretation theory are theoretical concepts whose contents are exhausted by their role in accounting for behavior. If the proper evidence for an interpretation theory is behavior, non-intentionally and non-semantically described, it would not be appropriate to describe anything not displaying behavior of a sort that could be interpreted on the basis of public clues as a speaker. This shows that the assumption that the concepts of belief, meaning, and so on, are theoretical in this sense is stronger than what is required to accommodate the observation that language is essentially a medium for communication, and as such must allow for speakers to be interpreted on the basis of public evidence. Thus, it derives no support from the observation that language is necessarily public, unless one can show that a speaker could be interpreted in some environment by some speaker on the basis of public evidence only if the content of the concepts deployed in interpretation were exhausted by their role in accounting for behavior. This assumption, then, emerges as perhaps the most basic one in Davidson's project in radical interpretation. If it is granted, he should be in a position to establish most of his main conclusions.

Evaluation of this assumption will be spread out over the rest of the chapters of Part III, in each of which we approach it from a different direction.

5. Comparison with Other Sorts of Externalism about Thought Content

Before closing this chapter, it will be useful to compare the form of externalism to which the arguments of Davidson's examined here give rise to other forms in the contemporary literature.[254] All externalist theories of thought content hold that some of our thoughts at least depend on our relations to our environments for their contents. Not all such theories hold that the contents of all of our thoughts so depend, or that we could not have any of the thoughts we currently have, if we were in a different environment. It should be readily granted by those who accept the direct reference theory of proper names that no one (other than Muhammad Ali) can believe that Muhammad Ali was the greatest heavyweight boxer of the twentieth century without something besides himself existing, namely, Muhammad Ali. This is a mild form of externalism, and can readily be granted even by Cartesian skeptics, for they will maintain that such thoughts are not the sort to which we have non-inferential access, but are rather thoughts we can know we have only in so far as we know there is someone who is Muhammad Ali.[255] Philosophically interesting accounts are those which hold that thoughts we express using general terms, and of which we have non-inferential knowledge, have their contents determined relationally in a way that guarantees that they are apt for truth. We henceforth restrict our attention to such theories.

Some externalist theories of thought content appeal in part to facts about the evolutionary history of our species in accounting for our thought contents.[256] These theories make a fundamental methodological mistake if they aim to be contributing to the conceptual analysis of thought content. The theory of evolution is itself an empirical theory. Its truth is contingent. But

---

[254] Some material in this section is adapted from Ludwig 1996*a*.

[255] See Ludwig 1996*c* for a defense of a Cartesian theory of singular thought that incorporates this feature.   [256] See e.g. Millikan 1984 and Papineau 1987.

our knowledge of whether we have thoughts is not contingent on its truth. There is no incoherence in supposing that we should find one day that, in fact, evolutionary theory is false. No theory about why our thoughts have their contents that appealed essentially to the truth of evolutionary theory, then, could provide a conceptual analysis of thought content. If it did, it would be incoherent to suppose we could discover that evolutionary theory was false, and, indeed, we would have an a priori route to its confirmation from our knowledge of our thoughts. But this is not so. However, only a conceptual analysis—broadly construed to include conceptual articulation—will provide us with the kind of theory which we seek in traditional philosophical inquiries into the mind–world relation of the sort prompted by, for example, Cartesian skepticism about the external world.

All other contemporary externalist theories are broadly causal theories in the sense that they hold that facts about our causal or nomic relations to our environments, past or present, determine our thought contents. There are a number of different cross-cutting criteria we can employ to classify such theories. First, there is the distinction between diachronic and synchronic externalism. Diachronic externalism holds that facts about our history of past causal interactions with our environments are of central importance to what thought contents we have. Some hold that some past period is of special import- ance, a learning period.[257] Some hold that our thought contents are more or less continuously sensitive to causal interactions with our environment for some period stretching from the present into our pasts. Synchronic external- ism holds that our thought contents depend only on our current environment and our dispositions to respond to it, so that our thought contents are not historical facts about us, but rather facts about our potentialities in relation to our current environments.

We can also distinguish between social externalism and physical external- ism. Social externalism holds that our thought contents are determined in part by our social environments, specifically, by how others in our linguistic com- munities use words.[258] Physical externalism holds that our thought contents are determined in part by our relations to our physical, nonsocial environ- ments. While these are independent, they are not incompatible, and one could hold one or the other only, or both, consistently.

Davidson's externalism is a form of physical externalism. As we dis- cussed in Chapter 17, his basic methodological stance is opposed to treating

---

[257] See e.g. Dretske 1988.   [258] See Burge 1979, and also Putnam 1975.

336

what one thinks and means by one's words as fundamentally dependent on how others use words or have used words. Thus, Davidson's route to his externalist position would, if correct, also undermine social externalism. The next question to raise is whether he is a synchronic or diachronic externalist. So far as we can see, the arguments we have considered in this chapter do not require us to think that there is any historical element at all in what fixes thought content. From the standpoint of the radical interpreter, what is important is what the speaker's environment is like, and what his dispositions are to respond to changes in his environment. These are the facts that determine the correct interpretation theory. Since we do not have magical access to nomic facts, in practice, to discover a speaker's dispositions, we must observe his interactions with his environment. But this no more means that what we thereby discover is a historical fact about him than does the use of induction in science generally show that the dispositional properties of things we thereby discover are really historical properties of them. Thus, reflection on taking the radical interpreter's standpoint as methodologically basic appears to recommend a form of synchronic externalism. On this view, once we have fixed a speaker's dispositions, we have fixed what determines, relative to any environment, what his thoughts in that environment will be (if any, perhaps), that is, the speaker's dispositions determine a function from environment to classes of empirically adequate interpretation theories.

However, this is not in fact the position Davidson adopts. He holds rather that there is a historical element to thought content. His argument consists of a thought experiment, given in the following passage.

Suppose lightning strikes a dead tree in a swamp; I am standing nearby. My body is reduced to its elements, while entirely by coincidence (and out of different molecules) the tree is turned into my physical replica. My replica, Swampman, moves exactly as I did; according to its nature it departs the swamp, encounters and seems to recognize my friends, and appears to return their greetings in English. It moves into my house and seems to write articles on radical interpretation. No one can tell the difference.

But there *is* a difference. My replica can't recognize my friends; it can't *recognize* anything, since it never cognized anything in the first place. It can't know my friends' names (though of course it seems to); it can't remember my house. [*] It can't mean what I do by the word 'house', for example, since the sound 'house' Swampman makes was not learned in a context that would give it the right meaning—or any meaning at all. Indeed, I don't see how my replica can be said to mean anything by the sounds it makes, nor to have any thoughts.   (Davidson 2001*b* (1987): 19)

337

The argument here is a straightforward appeal to intuitions.[259] It does not find its ground in reflection on what is required for radical interpretation, since clearly a radical interpreter could by the usual methods assign thoughts to Swampman and meanings to his utterances. Indeed, there seems to be a tension between the intuitions that Davidson has about this thought experiment and his view that the procedures of the radical interpreter are the fundamental standpoint from which to consider questions of thought and meaning. The Swampman certainly has all it takes to be radically interpreted (if any of us does). Why should it matter how long he has been around?

We can of course grant many of the things Davidson says in the quotation above. The Swampman has not learned a public language; arguably he does not speak English if that requires having been inculcated into the English speaking community. He does not remember anything prior to his creation. He does not recognize anyone he meets for the first time. In fact, we can readily grant everything up to [*] in the passage, for none of that requires that the Swampman's history play any role in what thoughts he has now. The work is all done in the last two sentences.

It would not be inconsistent to add to the a priori requirements on agency a requirement that an agent have been in causal interaction in the past with enough things to ground his thoughts about things in general. In this case, the interpreter would just impose this historical requirement on the grounding of an interpretation theory on top of everything else. So, the problem is not that the resulting position would be inconsistent. Rather, the problem is that this historical component looks to require a grounding different from, say, the appeal to decision theory as providing a basic framework for attitude attribution, since it is not tied up with our conception of the patterns of attitudes which are required for agency. It looks as if this additional requirement, on Davidson's view, should emerge from reflection on what must be so for success in radical interpretation. But it does not. And thus it appears to be a view that to some extent undercuts the view that the radical interpreter's standpoint is basic.

Let us leave aside now this worry about whether the historical component Davidson adds to his externalism is in tension with his basic methodological stance to ask how convincing the thought experiment itself is. It is certainly true that many contemporary philosophers would endorse the conclusion. But it is much less clear why. The passage in which Davidson recounts the thought

---

[259] Davidson apparently intends it to be making the same point that is made by Putnam's Twin Earth thought experiment, though the way the latter proceeds is rather different.

experiment seems in fact designed to deliver the verdict by a sleight of hand. Most of the relevant passage before [*] is about Swampman's lacking certain epistemic states that would require him to experience things before he existed. The transition to the claims about what he could mean or think is made without remark, as if the same sorts of considerations were simply being extended, though this is patently not so. It is doubtful that the thought experiment carries much persuasive force. We do not share Davidson's intuitions, and it seems clear enough that many people will not. In fact, most people without a philosophical theory to defend will readily suppose that Swampman does have thoughts, and that he means by his words, on the whole, what we mean by them.[260] (There will be problematic cases, since knowing the referents of some of the proper names he uses would require him to have knowledge of things that happened before he came into existence.)

The final question to ask is whether Davidson's externalism is reductive or non-reductive. The answer is the latter. Davidson does not give a prescription for reading off sufficient non-psychological conditions for someone to have the thoughts he does. Rather, the conditions that Davidson specifies, in so far as he does, themselves use psychological terms. In effect, he gives the following condition for x having a certain thought with the content that p and the mode M, represented by $M(x, p)$.

> For any x, $M(x, p)$ iff there is an interpretation theory $\mathcal{I}$
> such that $\mathcal{I}$ is confirmable from the standpoint of a radical
> interpreter for x, and $\mathcal{I}$ entails that $M(x, p)$.

This provides no guarantee that there will be any way of specifying non-mental conceptually sufficient conditions for the attribution of an attitude to an agent.

It is worth remarking finally on two other features of Davidson's argument for externalism which distinguish it from most others. First, as the previous paragraph indicates, his account of how attitude content is fixed is holistic in the sense that there is no saying what attitudes an agent has without formulating an adequate overall theory of his psychology, that is, there is no way to specify conditions for someone's having an attitude independently of specifying conditions for his having a host of attitudes. The conditions that determine

---

[260] Perhaps Davidson himself should not take his thought experiment too seriously. In "Epistemology Externalized" (2001 (1991): 199), he says, "I have a general distrust of thought experiments that pretend to reveal what we would say under conditions that in fact never arise." (This is a slight, but important, mischaracterization of thought experiments, which in general are not about what we would *say* in counterfactual circumstances, but what would be *so*.)

that someone has an attitude, and what its content is, do not attach primarily to the attitude itself, but rather to the agent who has it.[261] Second, unlike many arguments for externalism, Davidson's argument does not rely on first establishing that the meanings of our terms are fixed by what they are used in application to in our environment, and then arguing that, since we use them in attitude attributions, all our thought contents must likewise be determined by our relations to our environment (this is the way one would argue for externalism by appeal to the sort of Twin Earth thought experiment introduced by Putnam 1975). This sort of argument relies on assumption [A].

> [A]   If it can be demonstrated that some attitudes attributed using sentences of natural languages are relationally individuated, then there are no thoughts which are not individuated relationally, that is, it is of the nature of representational content that it be relational in character, if the semantics of terms used to attribute attitudes is determined in such as way as to make the attitudes attributed relational in character.[262]

[A] is not typically argued for, and this represents a gap in typical semantic arguments for externalism about thought content. Davidson's argument, however, if successful, would bypass this assumption, since his argument for our thought contents being fixed by our causal interactions with our environment falls out of the need to suppose this is so in order to guarantee success in radical interpretation, which is seen as a condition on being a speaker or thinker at all.

6. Conclusion

To conclude, we have examined two arguments of Davidson's, or what appear to be two arguments, for the claim that belief, and empirical belief in particular, is by its nature veridical: the omniscient interpreter argument and the argument from interpretation. It is not clear, in the end, whether Davidson intends to be offering distinct arguments here, or whether his appeal to an omniscient interpreter was intended merely to be a way of highlighting the fact that successful interpretation requires seeing a speaker as mostly right about his environment. The omniscient interpreter argument, taken at face value, seems to require us to know something about ourselves which qualifies as knowledge of the external world, namely, that we are so situated that an

---

[261] Contrast this with Fodor's asymmetric dependence condition in Fodor 1987, 1990*a*.

[262] See Ludwig 1996*a* for further discussion of the role of this assumption.

omniscient interpreter could correctly interpret us. Thus, to be in a position to accept the premises of the argument, we would have to have established already that we could have knowledge of the external world. Of course, this objection could be overcome by insisting on a stronger premise, namely, that we are, as we are situated, correctly interpretable by any possible interpreter, on the basis of behavioral evidence.[263] This, however, leads directly to the argument from interpretation. If we have this stronger premise in place, we can dispense with the appeal to the possibility of an omniscient interpreter, and argue more directly for the conclusion. For, granting Davidson that to correctly interpret another, we must find him to be largely right about his environment, if any speaker is *ipso facto* correctly interpretable on the basis of behavioral evidence[264] in *any* environment, then *any* speaker must be largely right about his environment. The question that arises about this argument is whether we have reason to believe the crucial assumption that any speaker is interpretable in any environment by any other. We have argued that the primary source for the justification of this assumption, namely, the undeniable fact that we cannot think of someone possessing a language who could not in principle communicate with others using it, supports only the weaker principle that any speaker is interpretable in *some* environment by *some* speaker. Davidson's argument requires the middle quantifier to be a universal quantifier. (The last must be a universal quantifier to secure the thesis of the impossibility of radically different conceptual schemes.) Some other ground than reflection on the fact that language is a medium or tool for communication must be found if the argument is to be supported. We noted that, if Davidson could establish that the concepts we deploy in thinking about meaning and psychological attitudes are theoretical concepts whose content is exhausted by purely behavioral evidence for their application, then he could support the stronger assumption needed. We reached a similar conclusion about the success of

---

[263] This in itself may be thought to be question begging, for this presupposes that someone just like us could know our surroundings. But, though true, this is not really question begging, for the requirement is supposed to drop out of reflection on what it is to be able to speak a language, and the connection between speaking a language and being interpretable is supposed to be established a priori. One might also object that it is all very fine to establish such a connection, but that all that does is raise the question whether we do speak a language in the relevant sense. However, Davidson maintains that we do not think at all unless we speak a language in the relevant sense, and if the argument for that is successful, since we know without empirical investigation that we think, we can infer we can speak a language in the relevant sense.

[264] The proviso is important, since we might imagine interpreting another as mostly false if we did it indirectly, by considering how to interpret him in what we take to be a favored environment rather than the one he is in e.g. we might consider assigning thoughts to a brain in a vat by considering how we would interpret him if he were in a body in a normal environment.

Davidson's argument for the impossibility of radically different conceptual schemes.

This should be no surprise. In the end, these questions depend upon the fundamental character of the concepts we deploy in posing them. There is no more fundamental question about them than the one raised by Davidson's fundamental stance on their third person, theoretical character. Again, we return to his arguments for this in Chapter 22.

We have also surveyed briefly the field of externalist theories in the contemporary literature with an eye to saying where Davidson's views fit in. His basic methodological stance recommends a form of physical, synchronic, non-reductive externalism. He adds to this a historical component not directly motivated by his basic methodological stance. We have suggested that the actual thought experiment he brings to bear in support of this is not persuasive, and that there is a tension between this additional component and his basic methodological stance, even if there is no outright inconsistency in the resulting position.

20

First Person Authority[265]

> It is long out of fashion to explain self-knowledge on the basis of intro-
> spection. And it is easy to see why, since this explanation only leads to the
> question why we should see any better when we inspect our own minds
> than when we inspect the minds of others.
>
> (Davidson 2001a (1984): 5)

In Chapter 15, we raised, but put aside for later consideration, an objection regarding the central concepts of the theory of interpretation as theoretical concepts. The objection was that in their application to ourselves, we evidently do not apply them on the basis of behavioral evidence, and we apparently have a special, though defeasible, authority over our own mental states. The asymmetry between how we tell or know in our own cases what our mental states are and how others tell, and between the authority with which we can say what our mental states are and that with which others can say, seems incompatible with seeing the content of the concepts of belief, meaning, and so on being exhausted by their role in explaining behavior. In addition, by now a standard criticism of accounts of thought content that hold that an individual's thought contents are partially or wholly determined by the individual's relations to his physical environment is that such an account is incompatible not just with our special authority to say what our own mental states are, but with our being in any position to know what they are at all.[266] Our special warrant for saying what our beliefs are seems to be threatened by relational theories of thought content, because the contents of our thoughts, according to these views, are determined by our relations to objects and events in our environment about which we are

---

[265] Material in this chapter is adapted from Ludwig 1994.

[266] See e.g. Brueckner 1986; Boghossian 1989; Ludlow and Martin 1998. The literature on this issue, pro and con, is now quite large.

not authoritative. Surely, the complaint goes, we can be no more authoritative about the contents of our beliefs than we are about what determines those contents. Moreover, our having any knowledge of the contents of our thoughts seems threatened, for our knowledge of facts about our environments seems to rest on prior knowledge of the contents of our thoughts. But if our thought contents are determined by their relations to objects and events in our environments, it seems we must know first about our environment before we can know about our thoughts. Thus, it seems that if the relational account is correct, we could know either of these things only if we *first* knew the other, which must give rise to a thorough skepticism about the contents of our thoughts.[267] the challenge which first person knowledge and authority presents to Davidson's assumptions of the theoretical character of the concepts of interpretation theory, and of relational individuation of thought contents, is taken up primarily in "First Person Authority," in which Davidson offers an explanation for the presumption that "[w]hen a speaker avers that he has a belief, hope, desire or intention, . . . he is not mistaken" (Davidson 2001*a*: (1984), 3) by grounding it in the assumptions which an interpreter must make in order to succeed at interpretation. Davidson has offered some apparently different considerations, though much more briefly (see Davidson 2001 (1991): 197–8). In this chapter, we examine the adequacy of Davidson's primary response to the challenge, and consider briefly other suggestions he has made.[268]

1. The Explanandum

To begin, it is important to get a clear view of what phenomena need to be accounted for. We begin with some terminological distinctions that will aid in identifying our explananda.

We press into technical service the term 'ascription' to mean any *thought* or *belief* whose content would be expressed by a sentence of subject–predicate

---

[267] We do not endorse these criticisms. We do not believe that externalism about thought content by itself does entail that we do not have first person knowledge. It does so, however, together with two independently plausible assumptions: (1) knowledge of our own thoughts supervenes on the subjective character of our conscious mental states; (2) the subjective character of our conscious mental states is not determined relationally. From this it follows that if we have knowledge of our own thoughts, they are determined non-relationally. For a fuller discussion, see Ludwig 1992*a*, 1990: ch. 6.

[268] In "The Myth of the Subjective" (Davidson 2001*a* (1988)), Davidson says it is first person authority which gives rise to the idea that there is an epistemic priority of thought to the world, and so leads to skepticism. Thus, explaining first person authority without the assumption of epistemic priority becomes central also to responding to skepticism.

form, such as 'Caesar was ambitious'. Thus, Cassius' *belief* or *thought* that Caesar was ambitious is an ascription on this usage. A *self*-ascription, we will say, is an ascription whose subject is the thinker. Thus, a thought that one is flying is a self-ascription. A *reflexive* ascription is a self-ascription which one would attribute to oneself using a sentence of the form [1], or would be attributed to one by another using a sentence of the form [2], examples of which are given in [3] and [4].

[1]   I believe that I ϕ.
[2] α believes that he (or she or it) ϕ.
[3]   I believe that I was born in Tulsa.
[4]   Ludwig believes that he was born in Tulsa.

Thus, someone's thought that he is hungry or that he is tall is a reflexive self-ascription. A self-ascription need not be a reflexive ascription, as one can express a self-ascription using a sentence in which one picks oneself out with a description or a proper name. The difference is important. First person knowledge and authority extends generally only to reflexive ascriptions of mental states. We will call these first person ascriptions. Reports of a speaker's first person ascriptions we will call first person reports. (We call our knowledge and warrant here first person knowledge and authority because the canonical form for its expression by the subject is a sentence of the form [1].) One is not specially authoritative, and possesses no special kind of knowledge about, for example, one's location or height; and even in the case of ascriptions of mental states, if the thought one has is expressed using a proper name or description, there is no presumption (independently of other assumptions) that one is specially placed with respect to its truth. No doubt, with respect to many of one's properties, such as height, profession, location, year of birth, number of children, and the like, proximity to and familiarity with oneself places one in an advantageous position. But in principle, at least, someone else could be as well placed, and perhaps better placed, than oneself with respect to these sorts of properties. In contrast, it seems scarcely intelligible that someone else could be as well placed or better placed than one is oneself with respect to whether one believes that one is hungry, or in pain, or a closet Republican.

To the extent to which we can make sense of ourselves as being in a better position to say what someone else's mental states are, this is limited to his dispositional mental states, and we cannot, in any case, be in a better position generally than another with respect to his dispositional mental states, but only in rather exceptional cases; and, moreover, when we can make sense of this, it requires an elaborate backing story, which in the end depends for

345

confirmation on the subject's being able to be brought by some appropriate method to acknowledge it.[269] In the case of conscious or occurrent mental states, even these stories fail us.

Despite the possibility of conceiving of circumstances in which someone else is better placed than oneself with respect to some of one's dispositional mental states, our first person authority generally extends to them. We are presumed, in most cases, to be better placed with respect to our dispositional mental states than are others because they are in part dispositions to have particular conscious or occurrent mental states whose contents and modes give the contents and modes of the dispositional states of which they are manifestations. For example, the dispositional belief that Antigua lies in the Caribbean is in part manifested on appropriate occasions in an occurrent belief that Antigua lies in the Caribbean. A gap remains because our dispositional states are not always manifested in consciousness, and it is the possibility that such dispositional states may be blocked from being manifested in consciousness that gives rise to the possibility of psychoanalytic explanations of behavior, or, more generally, the possibility of someone else's being in a better position than we are to say what our dispositional mental states are.

Central to our special knowledge and warrant about our mental states is our special knowledge and warrant about our conscious mental states. That we have first person knowledge of our own conscious mental states explains both our special warrant about them, and our knowledge and special warrant about our dispositional mental states.

For future reference, we summarize the results of this discussion in the following theses, [*E1*]–[*E4*].

> [*E1*] Necessarily, no one is in as a good an epistemic position to ascribe conscious or occurrent mental states to a thinker as the thinker is himself.

---

[269] We are thinking, of course, of a broadly Freudian conception of the unconscious, claims about which, to be confirmed, must ultimately be capable of being acknowledged by the subject as the result of therapy. There is, of course, a tradition in psychology, which has been taken up by many, though not all, workers in recent cognitive science, that holds that many of the mechanisms which underlie our cognitive abilities can be explained by appeal to in principle unconscious mental processing. It is clear that first person authority and knowledge would not extend to such mental states, which are postulated as the best explanation of our having certain cognitive abilities, but not supposed to be accessible to the subject, since subjects do not in fact report having them, or show in any way that they are integrated with the thoughts we would ordinarily attribute to them. Whatever the status of such attributions, they are not our current subject, and no consideration relevant to such attributions will undermine our current discussion. See Ludwig 1996*b* for an extended discussion of these issues in the context of inferential theories of perceptual achievement.

[E2] Necessarily, no one is in general in as good a position to ascribe
dispositional mental states to a thinker as the thinker is himself.

[E3] Necessarily, no one is in general in as good a position to ascribe
mental states to a thinker as the thinker is himself.

[E4] Necessarily, a speaker's sincere first person reports have more evidential weight than reports about the speaker's mental states by
others.

[*E1*] together with the fact that dispositional mental states are in part dispositions to have occurrent mental states which give them their content explains
[*E2*]. [*E1*] and [*E2*] entail [*E3*], and [*E3*], with some readily evident epistemic principles, entails [*E4*]. Clearly, [*E1*] is the central phenomenon to
be explained.

The asymmetry in epistemic position is connected of course with a difference between the way one knows one's own mental states and how others
know them. When attributing thoughts to others, one relies essentially on their
behavior (or records of their behavior); in the case of attributing first person
ascriptions to oneself, one does not rely on evidence at all and does not have
to consult one's behavior. If one had to rely on one's own behavior as others
do, one would not necessarily be better placed to say what one's mental states
were. Although knowing something in a different way, or not on the basis of
evidence, does not in itself guarantee that what is known is known better, we
may expect that this difference in how one knows one's mental states (first
person knowledge) and how others know them underlies one's first person
authority.

Davidson aims to explain the asymmetry between our knowledge of our
mental states and our knowledge of the mental states of others (or, alternatively, the asymmetry between our own knowledge of our mental states and
the knowledge others have of them) by explaining a closely related asymmetry: why "[w]hen a speaker avers that he has a belief, hope, desire or
intention, there is a presumption that he is not mistaken, a presumption that
does not attach to his ascriptions of similar mental states to others" (Davidson
2001*a* (1984): 3).[270] This is a variant of [*E4*] above. Our main question will
be how far Davidson has succeeded in explaining this asymmetry in authority, and to what degree it explains the related asymmetry in our knowledge
of our own and others' mental lives, represented by [*E3*]. We will argue that

---

[270] Here Davidson uses 'ascription' in the sense of speech act, of course, not in the technical sense
introduced at the beginning of this chapter.

Davidson's explanation is unsuccessful on both fronts, and, further, that the hope for an illuminating explanation of the special epistemic status of first person ascriptions is a philosophical *ignis fatuus*.

A successful philosophical explanation of the asymmetry between our warrant for first person ascriptions of mental states and other ascriptions[271] of mental states should meet the following criteria of adequacy, [*C1*]–[*C3*].

[*C1*] The explanans must entail the explanandum.

[*C2*] The explanans must not contain explicitly a statement of the asymmetry to be explained, or any asymmetry which stands in need of an explanation at least as much as the original asymmetry.

[*C3*] The explanans must be conceptually prior to the explanandum.

[*C1*] is a minimal condition on the relevance of the explanans to the explanandum. [*C2*] is a minimal condition on the informativeness of the explanation. It requires that the explanans not be a mere redescription of the explanandum, or rely on an unexplained asymmetry at least as mysterious as the original one. [*C3*] requires that the explanans be illuminating.

The asymmetry that Davidson investigates is in three ways narrower than [*E3*]. First, Davidson restricts his attention to propositional attitudes. Second, among the propositional attitudes, he restricts his attention to belief. Third, he restricts his attention to linguistic beings (as we have seen, this restriction is in play crucially in Davidson's arguments from the nature of radical interpretation to the nature of the propositional attitudes—we take up the argument for it in Chapter 22).

Given the third restriction, Davidson argues that we can legitimately reformulate the question why we have a special warrant for first person ascriptions of mental states as the question why we speak with special authority in reporting our own mental states: "if one can speak with special authority, the status of one's knowledge must somehow accord; while if one's knowledge shows some systematic difference, claims to know must reflect the difference" (2001*a* (1984): 3). The latter question can in turn be reformulated as the question why an interpreter of a speaker should give the speaker's first person reports special evidential weight in attributions of attitudes to him, [*E4*]. This question can without loss, Davidson says, be treated as the question, "what explains the

---

[271] The asymmetry can be stated in either of two equivalent ways: first, as the asymmetry between one's warrant for ascribing mental states to oneself and to others; second, as the asymmetry between one's warrant for ascribing mental states to oneself and others' warrant for doing so. These are equivalent for our purposes, because the explanation of either will provide an explanation of the other.

difference in the sort of assurance you have that I am right when I say 'I believe Wagner died happy' and the sort of assurance I have?" (2001*a* (1984): 11). Thus, Davidson is committed to the following conditionals [5]–[7].

[5] If we explain the difference in the warrant we each have that one of us is right when that one states what he believes, then we will have explained the difference in warrant between first person ascriptions of beliefs and other ascriptions of beliefs.

[6] If we have explained the difference in warrant between first person ascriptions of beliefs and other ascriptions of beliefs, we will be in a position to explain the difference in warrant between first person ascriptions of propositional attitudes and other ascriptions of propositional attitudes.

[7] If we are in a position to explain the difference in warrant between first person and other ascriptions of propositional attitudes, we will be in a position to explain the difference in warrant between first person and other ascriptions of sensations and other non-propositional mental states.

The success of Davidson's overall strategy in explaining first person authority depends upon the truth of these conditionals, and upon the claim that if we explain the asymmetry for linguistic beings, there will be no separate task required for non-speakers, or at least that if there is, it will not reflect adversely on the adequacy of the explanation for linguistic beings. We will for now restrict our attention to assumption [5].

2. Two Explanations

There are suggestions of at least two explanations of the special weight accorded to first person reports in Davidson's discussion. We first lay out the general form of the argument, and then what seem to be the two principal explanations for the crucial premise in the argument, which are suggested in the discussion.

The asymmetry Davidson aims to explain in the first instance, and upon which the original asymmetry is said to rest, is that between one's own warrant for thinking that one has said something true in making a first person report and someone else's warrant for thinking that one has said something true. As a preliminary stage in the explanation, we can observe that if anyone knows that one holds true a sentence *s* on a particular occasion of utterance, and what one means by that sentence, he is in a position to know what belief one expresses with that utterance. Let us suppose that both *A* and *B* know that *B* holds a sentence *s* true, and that both know *that B* knows what *s* means. We have in this, Davidson notes, assumed no asymmetry between the knowledge that *A* and *B* have. Now, however, "there is this difference between [*A* and *B*], which is what was to be explained: on these assumptions, [*B*] know[s] what [he] believe[s], while [*A*] may not" (Davidson 2001 (1984): 12).

This assumes that *B* infers from his knowledge of the meaning of *s* and his belief that *s* is true that he believes what *s* expresses, that is, if *s* means, for example, that Wagner died happy, that he believes that Wagner died happy. Thus, for this observation to serve as a general account, as Davidson intends, of a presumption that one knows what one believes, we must assume that, by and large, (i) if someone holds a sentence *s* true, and knows the meaning of *s*, then he believes what *s* expresses; (ii) if someone believes that *p*, then there is a sentence *r* which expresses what he believes, and which he holds true; (iii) speakers know (i) is true; and (iv) speakers will generally infer from (i), knowledge of what sentences they hold true and knowledge of what they mean, what they believe.

Let us grant all of this for now. As we noted in Part II, assumptions (i)–(iii) appear also in Davidson's account of the procedure of the radical interpreter ((iv), as we will have occasion to note, looks problematic from that standpoint, however). Even so, we do not have an explanation of our asymmetry. Even if it follows from the fact that both *A* and *B* know that *C* holds true *s*, and that *B* knows what *C* means by *s*, that *B* knows (or at least is in a position to know) what *C* believes, while *A* may not know (or be in a position to know) what *C* believes, this does not show that *B*'s pronouncements about *C*'s beliefs should in general be given special evidential weight in attributing beliefs to *C*. So far as anything we have said yet goes, *B*'s knowing what *C* means by *s* while *A* does not may be entirely fortuitous. Davidson recognizes this. "It remains to show why there must be a presumption that speakers, but not their interpreters, are not wrong about what their words mean" (Davidson 2001 (1984): 12). What we must show, then, is why there should be a presumption that *B* knows what *C* means by *s* when *B* is identical with *C*, while there is no such presumption when *B* is not identical with *C*.

Once we have shown this, on the assumption that both *A* and *B* know that *B* holds true the sentence *s*, we can show that there is a presumption that *B* knows (or can know) what *B* believes, while there is no such presumption in the case of *A*. The argument, which we call the 'master argument', can be laid out as follows, first for the case of a single sentence, then more generally:

(1) *A* knows that *B* holds true *s*.

(2) *B* knows that he holds true *s*.

(3) There is a presumption that *B* knows what he means by *s*, while there is no presumption that *A* knows what *B* means by *s*.

(4) For all *x*, if *x* holds true *s*, and *x* knows the meaning of *s*, then *x* believes what *s* expresses.

(5) For all *x*, for all *y*, if *x* knows that *y* holds true *s*, and knows what *y* means by *s*, and *x* knows (4), then *x* knows or is in a position to know what *y* believes in holding true *s*, i.e. to know that *y* believes that *p*, where '*p*' is replaced by *s*.

(6) *A* and *B* both know (4).

(7) Therefore, by (1)–(6), there is a presumption that *B* knows or is in a position to know what he believes in holding true *s*, while there is no presumption that *A* does.

To extend this result to all of *B*'s beliefs, we must assume (8) and (9), and then modify (3) to cover all sentences B holds true, as in (10).

(8) For all *x*, if *x* believes that *p*, then there is a sentence *r* which expresses what *x* believes, and which *x* holds true.

(9) For all sentences *s*, if *B* holds true *s*, then *B* knows that he holds true *s*.

(10) For all sentences *s*, if *B* holds true *s*, then there is a presumption that *B* knows what *s* means, while there is no presumption that *A* knows what *B* means by *s*.

Then, even assuming *A* and *B* both know with equal warrant what sentences *B* holds true, we have (11).

(11) For all sentences *s*, if *B* holds true *s*, then there is a presumption that *B* knows what he believes in holding true *s*, while there is no presumption that *A* does (by (4)–(6), (9), (10)).

(12) Therefore, for any belief of *B*'s, there is a presumption that *B* knows what he believes, while there is no presumption that *A* knows what *B* believes (by (8) and (11)).

351

(13)   Therefore, *B*'s sincere reports of his self-ascriptions of beliefs should be accorded special evidential weight in attributions of beliefs to him (by (12)).[272]

Although a number of these premises are questionable, (10) (or, in the more restricted argument, (3)) is the crucial premise, in the sense that it is the source of the asymmetry derived in the conclusion. What is the argument for it? The answer is supposed to lie in reflections on the different roles of the interpreter and speaker in communication. At first, Davidson seems to suggest that the asymmetry is to be explained by appeal to an asymmetry in the evidence that the speaker and interpreter go on:

> A hearer interprets (normally without thought or pause) on the basis of many clues: the actions and other words of the speaker, what he assumes about the education, birthplace, wit, and profession of the speaker, the relation of the speaker to objects near and far, and so forth. The speaker, though he must bear many of these things in mind when he speaks, since it is up to him to try to be understood, cannot wonder whether he generally means what he says.
> ... [Thus, t]he asymmetry rests on the fact that the interpreter must, while the speaker doesn't, rely on what, if it were made explicit, would be a difficult inference in interpreting the speaker.   (Davidson 2001*a* (1984): 12–13)

To stop here, however, is not to explain the asymmetry, for all we have done is to invoke another asymmetry whose relation to the asymmetry in warrant remains mysterious. That the interpreter must go on behavioral evidence, while the speaker does not go on evidence at all, is properly part of the description of the puzzle, not its solution. As Davidson himself remarks in an earlier passage, "claims that are not based on evidence do not in general carry more authority than claims that are based on evidence, nor are they more apt to be correct" (Davidson 2001*a* (1984): 5). What we need minimally, in addition to this asymmetry in evidence, is some reason to think that in this case the speaker's reports about his mental states, in addition to not being based on evidence, are "apt to be correct." Showing this is the main burden of the following passages, (I) and (II), in which different arguments are suggested.

---

[272] One difficulty we will not dwell on here is that this style of argument cannot explain why reflexive self-ascriptions appear to have a special status. It seems that someone could fail to be authoritative about a thought announced using a proper name that refers to himself, while this does not appear to make sense for reflexive self-ascription. See Ludwig 1996*c* for an explanation of this phenomenon.

(I) The speaker, after bending whatever knowledge and craft he can to the task of saying what his words mean, cannot improve on the following sort of statement: 'My utterance of "Wagner died happy" is true if and only if Wagner died happy'. An interpreter has no reason to assume this will be *his* best way of stating the truth conditions of the speaker's utterance. (Davidson 2001 (1984): 13)

(II) [Imagine] a situation in which two people who speak unrelated languages, and are ignorant of each other's languages, are left alone to learn to communicate... Let one of the imagined pair speak and the other try to understand.... The best the speaker can do is to be *interpretable,* that is, to use a finite supply of distinguishable sounds applied consistently to objects and situations he believes are apparent to his hearer... [I]t is... obvious that the interpreter has nothing to go on but the pattern of sounds the speaker exhibits in conjunction with further events (including, of course, further actions on the part of both speaker and interpreter). It makes no sense in this situation to wonder whether the speaker is generally getting things wrong. His behavior may simply not be interpretable. But if it is, then what his words mean is (generally) what he intends them to mean... There is a presumption—an unavoidable presumption built into the nature of interpretation—that the speaker usually knows what he means. So there is a presumption that if he knows that he holds a sentence true, he knows what he believes. (Davidson 2001 (1984): 13–14)

It is not clear that Davidson intends to be giving two separate arguments in these passages. Yet, the first passage suggests a ground for the asymmetry which seems quite different from that suggested in the second, and which is of sufficient interest to justify examination, whether or not Davidson intends to be presenting a separate argument there.[273] Therefore, we treat each passage as offering a different argument.

In the first passage, our attention is drawn to the following asymmetry. If a speaker desires to state the conditions under which a sentence of his is true in virtue of what the sentence means, he can do no better than to employ disquotation. (Whether *this* is so, we will question—but for now our goal is exposition.) In the case of an interpreter, whose language must at least initially be assumed to be different from that of the speaker, even if the interpreter uses

---

[273] That Davidson does intend the first passage to play an important role in the argument is suggested by the following (2001 (1989): 66), "it does not make sense to suppose I am *generally* mistaken about what my words mean; the presumption that I am not generally mistaken about what I mean is essential to my having a language—to my being interpretable at all. To appeal to a familiar, though often misunderstood, point: I can do no better, in stating the truth conditions for my utterance of the sentence 'The Koh-i-noor diamond is a crown jewel' than to say it is true if and only if the Koh-i-noor diamond is a crown jewel." In a footnote, Davidson refers the reader to "First Person Authority" for a more detailed discussion.

a sentence syntactically identical with a sentence the speaker utters, there is no guarantee that disquotation in the interpreter's language will yield the correct truth conditions of the speaker's utterance. If in our language 'dog' means what 'cat' does in yours, and vice versa, then applying disquotation to your sentence, 'dogs chase cats', will yield the wrong interpretation in our language. No such possibility is open when the speaker uses disquotation for his own language, since the sentence he uses on the right hand side of the biconditional and the sentence he names on the left hand side are in the same language. Thus, we may say that a speaker who employs disquotation will not be able to make a mistake in stating the truth conditions of his sentences; he will state the truth conditions of his sentences in a way that ensures that the sentences he uses in stating the truth conditions provide interpretations of them. On the first line of argument, we conclude from this that the speaker is in general in a better position to state the truth conditions of his sentences in a way which exhibits their meaning than the interpreter, and therefore can be presumed to know what his words mean, while no such presumption attaches to the interpreter's assignments of truth conditions to the speaker's utterances in the interpreter's language. Let us call this 'argument I', which we can represent as consisting of the following steps, (1)–(4).

(1) A speaker can always correctly state the truth conditions of his sentences by using on the right hand side of the biconditional which he uses to state its truth conditions the sentence which he names on its left hand side.

(2) An interpreter of the speaker cannot be sure that disquotation in the interpreter's language will yield a correct statement of the truth conditions of the speaker's utterance.

(3) Therefore, a speaker is always in a position to correctly state the truth conditions of his sentences, while the interpreter is not.

(4) Therefore, there is a presumption that a speaker knows the meanings of his words, while there is no such presumption that his interpreter does.

In the second passage, we are asked to imagine two individuals who wish to communicate with one another, but who share no common language. We consider the situation from the point of view of the interpreter. The aim is to show that an interpreter must, as a part of his project, assume that a speaker knows the meanings of his words.

We can note first that an interpreter must assume that a speaker is trying to communicate with him; otherwise, the interpreter will not have any reason to treat any of the speaker's actions as speech acts. Thus, the interpreter will assume that the speaker intends to be supplying clues to the meanings of his utterances. The speaker can do no better than to talk about features of his environment he believes to be salient to his interpreter. Since the interpreter has only the speaker's utterances in the presence of conditions and events in their shared environment to go on, the interpreter must assume that the speaker is largely rational and has true beliefs about his environment, and in particular about features of the environment salient to the interpreter. "It makes no sense," Davidson says, "in this situation to wonder whether the speaker is generally getting things wrong" (2001 (1984): 14). This is just the principle of charity,[274] which is required because the only strategy available to the interpreter in assigning interpretations to a speaker's utterances is to assume that the salient conditions in his environment that cause the speaker's hold true attitudes provide their truth conditions. In practice, of course, the interpreter's first access to hold true attitudes is through the speaker's assertions about events and conditions in his environment. It is at this point that an assumption enters about the speaker's knowledge of the meanings of his words. For if one is to take the speaker's assertions to be a guide to his hold true attitudes, which in turn are to be a guide to his beliefs about his environment, one must assume that the speaker knows what his words mean, for we suppose his hold true attitudes in general are the result of his beliefs about his environment and the meanings of his words. (Note this assumption for later reference.) To attach the conditions that make the speaker's beliefs true to the sentences he holds true, we must suppose his beliefs about what his sentences mean are reliably true; this is expressed in his applying them systematically and correctly to objects and events in his environment on the basis of his beliefs. In this sense, the speaker knows what his words mean. The interpreter has no choice but to assume that the speaker is mostly right about what his words mean, on pain of losing the subject of his interpretation. Thus, the assumption is forced on the interpreter in virtue of his commitment to carrying out his project, to treating his subject as a speaker; while, of course, no such assumption must be made about anyone else's having knowledge of the meanings of the speaker's terms. Let us call this 'argument II'. Its crucial steps are these.

(1) A speaker is interpretable only if he can apply words consistently to objects and events in his environment with the intention of stating what he believes about them.

---

[274] In its strengthened form, i.e. Grace. See Ch. 12.

(2) If a speaker can apply words consistently to objects and events in his environment with the intention of stating what he believes about them, then he knows the meanings of his words.

(3) Therefore, if a speaker is interpretable, the speaker knows the meanings of his words.

(4) It is an assumption of the project of interpretation, then, that the subject of interpretation knows the meanings of his words; no such assumption must be made about anyone else's knowledge of the speaker's words.

Each of arguments I and II independently supports premise (10) of the master argument (with the additional plausible assumption that most of the sentences a speaker holds true will be sentences in his language). Thus, if either argument is successful, provided that the master argument is successful, we have a ground for an asymmetry between the weight attached to B's sincere reports of his beliefs and that attached to A's reports of B's beliefs, and between the knowledge that B has of his beliefs and the knowledge that A has of B's beliefs.

If these arguments are sound, and provide an adequate explanation for first person authority, then they promise an elegant solution to the problems posed at the beginning of this chapter. The strategy of the argument is to show that the problematic features of our knowledge of our own mental states, the fact that we do not go on behavioral evidence in our own case, and that there is a presumption that we are right in what we sincerely say about our own mental states, are themselves a result of adopting the priority of the third person point of view over the first person point of view in the application of psychological and linguistic concepts. The relational theory of thought content, the possibility of knowledge of other minds, and the asymmetry between first person knowledge and authority and third person knowledge and authority about mental states all spring from adopting the standpoint of the radical interpreter as conceptually fundamental for investigating meaning and related concepts. The result is a unified philosophical account of our knowledge of our own and other minds and the world around us of great elegance and beauty.

3. Evaluating the Account of First Person Authority

We turn now to an evaluation of Davidson's argument, in two stages. First we raise the question whether the master argument explains what it is supposed to.

Second, we examine the two arguments advanced in support of the crucial premise, (10), of the master argument.

(a) The master argument

A preliminary observation we should make is that Davidson's official explanandum, [8], is not sufficient to establish any special authority for first person ascriptions we may have, nor entailed by the asymmetry that Davidson explains.

> [8]   There is a "difference in the sort of assurance you have that I am right when I say 'I believe Wagner died happy' and the sort of assurance I have".

It is not sufficient to establish any special authority for our first person ascriptions because it is compatible with one's knowing that one is right when one says 'I believe Wagner died happy' that one is ignorant of the meanings of one's words. If one is, then despite knowing that one is right, one will not know what one believes in virtue of knowing that one is right. By the same token, since the asymmetry Davidson explains is an asymmetry in knowledge of the meanings of our words, it could not by itself explain an asymmetry in our warrant for thinking one had said something true when saying, 'I believe Wagner died happy'.

In itself, this shows only that Davidson initially misstated the explanandum for the explanation he goes on to give. But it points to an important flaw in the master argument. Unless sentences such as [8] are true and Davidson has an explanation of their truth, he will not be in a position to explain the asymmetry we began with between our warrant for first and other person ascriptions, or that between first and other person reports. The reason is as follows.

Davidson's explanation of first person authority rests on an explanation of an asymmetry between the knowledge that a speaker and interpreter have of meanings of the speaker's words. This asymmetry between the knowledge one has of one's own words and an interpreter's knowledge of the meanings of one's words is most striking in the case of an interpreter who is not a member of one's speech community. To test whether this asymmetry is the real or only source of first person authority, we can consider the best possible case of another person knowing the meanings of one's words, in order to see to what degree this reduces the asymmetry between first and other person ascriptions of mental states.

357

Let us consider, then, not just people who are members of the same speech community, but people who are raised together, and are regular interlocutors. Let us consider, for example, twin brothers, *A* and *B*, who have been raised together, who went to the same schools, who have most of the same interests, and who spend most of their time together.[275] In this situation, their knowledge of each other's idiolect may be presumed to be almost perfect. While there is perhaps still some sense in which *A* may know better what *A* means by his words than his brother does, still *B* is in an excellent position to interpret *A*'s words. If the asymmetry between self-ascriptions and other ascriptions depends solely on an asymmetry between one's knowledge of the meanings of one's own words and others' knowledge of their meanings, in this situation, we should expect the asymmetry in knowledge or warrant to be almost completely eliminated. For all practical purposes, *A* and *B* should each know the other's thoughts as well as they know their own. But—of course—the asymmetry is not eliminated, nor even very much reduced. *A* knows, for example, for each of his conscious thoughts, that he is thinking it, and what he is thinking; *A*'s twin *B*, of course, although his position with respect to his own conscious thoughts is equally good, for the most part does not know or even have very many detailed beliefs about *A*'s conscious mental states. Most of what *A* thinks may never be indicated in any way in his behavior. This does not prevent his knowing what he is thinking, but without behavioral evidence of some kind, his twin would not be able to know any of his thoughts. This same point, of course, extends to their dispositional states, which *A* can know about without consulting his behavior, while his twin cannot. Thus, their nearly equal knowledge of the meanings of the words in *A*'s idiolect goes only a very little way toward eliminating the asymmetry in their knowledge of his thoughts. Even when we turn to consider those of *A*'s thoughts to which he gives verbal expression, we find that equal knowledge of the meanings of *A*'s words is not by itself enough to eliminate an important asymmetry between his knowledge and *B*'s knowledge of his thoughts. For, even in this case, there is an inference which *B* would need to make, which *A* would not. For *B* would need to have reason, grounded in past experience, present circumstances, and behavioral evidence, to believe that *A*'s assertion is sincere, while *A* would need no such evidence. This asymmetry in their positions is not explained by an asymmetry in their knowledge of the meanings of the words in the sentences *A* utters.

---

[275] One could imagine two molecular twins from twin earths, brought together in full knowledge of their having identical verbal dispositions.

Once we remind ourselves of these features of our authority and knowledge about our own thoughts, we can hardly expect an asymmetry in the knowledge we and others have of the meanings of words in our idiolects to be an adequate explanation of the asymmetry between the warrant we have for first and other person reports, or first and other person ascriptions of mental states. An asymmetry in knowledge of meanings would seem adequate only if we restricted our attention to knowledge of thoughts which are expressed verbally, and which we are allowed to assume are sincerely expressed. Much of the asymmetry between our knowledge of our own and our knowledge of others' thoughts comes from our knowledge of thoughts to which we and they do not give verbal expression. This difference is what underwrites [8].

This problem is clearly reflected in Davidson's argument. For an asymmetry in the knowledge of the meanings of our words to be sufficient to account for the asymmetry in warrant between self-ascriptions and other ascriptions, there would have to be no need for an asymmetry in the knowledge expressed in (1) and (2) in the master argument.[276] However, if there were no asymmetry in the knowledge expressed in (1) and (2), it would not necessarily always be the case that a speaker knew with greater warrant what he thought than his interpreter, because although he might know with better warrant what his words meant, he might not know with as great a warrant as his interlocutor what sentences he held true. Thus, without an asymmetry between one's own knowledge of which sentences one holds true and that of an interpreter, we are not guaranteed an asymmetry between one's knowledge of one's own and of others' attitudes, and consequently we are not guaranteed that a speaker's own reports of his mental states should be accorded more weight than those of others.

Our first objection to Davidson's explanation, then, is that, even if we grant the correctness of the explanation of the asymmetry between our knowledge of the meanings of our own words and of the meanings of others' words, we have not explained the asymmetry in warrant between first and other person reports. We want to explain why, necessarily, one is always in a better position to know and say what one believes, etc., than anyone else. The explanans does

---

[276] This point was first made to one of us by Bruce Vermazen in 1987. We think Davidson was aware of this deficiency in the argument at the time he wrote "First Person Authority," for his conclusion is that, for any speaker, "there is a presumption that if he knows that he holds a sentence true, he knows what he believes" (Davidson 2001 (1984): 14). Clearly, the conditional conclusion cannot support our original explanandum, which is not a conditional. Davidson cannot have been unaware of this fact. We suggest, therefore, that he regarded his argument as only a partial explanation of first person authority.

not entail this explanandum. This violates our first criterion of adequacy. For the explanans to entail the explanandum, we must add to the explanans that the speaker is presumed to know what sentence he holds true, while there is no such presumption on the part of the interpreter. This, however, would violate our second criterion of adequacy, that we not rely in our explanation on any asymmetry which stands just as much in need of explanation as the original.[277]

A second objection against the master argument is that it misrepresents what our knowledge of our own propositional attitudes comes to. For the argument to succeed, we must represent our knowledge of the content of our propositional attitudes as composed of two separate bits of knowledge: first, knowledge of which sentences we hold true; second, knowledge of the meanings of our sentences. From these two items of knowledge, we can infer the contents of our beliefs. However, it seems clear that our knowledge of the contents of our beliefs does not in this way consist of knowledge of sentences we hold true and knowledge of their meanings.[278] First, it should be clear that no such inference takes place when we report our mental states. Second, if our knowledge of the contents of our attitudes depended on first knowing both of these things separately and prior to our knowledge of any attitude content, we could not know the contents of our beliefs. For to know that one believes that *s* is true is to know the content of one of one's beliefs. Thus, if one needed to know these two things prior to knowing what one believed, one could never know what one believed. Our knowledge of the contents of our beliefs, then, is not correctly represented as (generally) based on an inference from knowledge of what sentences we hold true and what those sentences mean. Someone else could be in that position with respect to us and, so, come to know what we believe on the basis only of such knowledge, but we could not be in that position in general with respect to ourselves. It is a mistake, then, to attempt to explain an asymmetry in knowledge or warrant for first person ascriptions by appeal to an asymmetry in knowledge of meanings of one's idiolect.

There is a further oddity about Davidson's appeal to this direction of explanation in explaining first person knowledge and authority. In our discussion of the procedure of the radical interpreter in Chapter 12, we observed that the reason we can treat hold true attitudes as part of the evidence for an interpretive

[277] It is also worth remarking that appeal to knowledge of meanings could at most help with knowledge of the contents of propositional attitudes, not with the distinctions among different propositional attitudes, knowing that one believed that *p* rather than desired that *p*, for example.

[278] We are indebted here to Charles Siewert.

truth theory for a speaker is that we can suppose that, by and large, a speaker's hold true attitudes were a result of, that is, inferred from, his beliefs and his knowledge of the meanings of his sentences. This, however, presupposes (as, indeed, it ought) that the speaker's knowledge of the meanings of his sentences is not prior to his knowledge of the contents of his beliefs, and that both are prior to his knowledge of what sentences he holds true. Indeed, in the previous section of this chapter, when explaining argument II, we relied on the assumption that a speaker knows what he believes independently of knowing what he means by his words.

Now we turn to some objections to Davidson's explanation of the assumption that a speaker knows better than his interpreter what the meanings of his words are, and his use of this argument in his explanation of why a speaker's first person reports ought to be accorded special evidential weight.

(b) Supporting argument 1

We identified two different arguments. The first is in passage (I). This argument for an asymmetry relies on the fact that when a speaker gives truth conditions of utterances in his language, he uses the language for which he gives truth conditions, while the interpreter may use another language. Leaving aside any other concerns about this, it would explain the asymmetry in knowledge of the meanings of the expressions in the speaker's language only if (i) it were not possible for the interpreter also to use the speaker's language to state the truth conditions of the speaker's sentences, and (ii) the speaker's stating the truth conditions of sentences in his language were sufficient for him to know the meanings of them in his language. Neither of these conditions is met. This means that in argument I premise (3) does not follow from premises (1) and (2), and that premise (4) does not follow from premise (3).

Suppose that *A* speaks language *L* and *B* speaks language *L'*, and that *L* and *L'* are different languages. Let us consider how *A* and *B* would typically state the truth conditions of a sentence *s* in *A*'s language *L*.

[9]   *A* (in *L*): *s* is true in my idiolect [i.e. *L*] iff *p*
[10] *B* (in *L'*): *s* is true in *A*'s idiolect [i.e. *L*] iff *p*

We indicate in brackets in what language the sentences uttered by *A* and by *B* are spoken. Given that *A*'s idiolect is *L*, *A* is guaranteed to get the truth conditions of *s* right in [9] if he uses *s* in place of '*p*'. By the same token, however, if *A*'s idiolect is *L*, *B* is not guaranteed to get the truth conditions of *s* right in [10] if he uses *s* in the place of '*p*', given that *L* and *L'* are different languages, and *B*'s statement is in *L'*.

While this is true, it is not sufficient to explain an asymmetry in *A*'s and *B*'s knowledge of what *A* means by his words. It would be sufficient only if it were not possible for *B* to state the truth conditions of a sentence *s* in *A*'s language, which we can represent as follows:

[11]   *B* (in *L*): *s* is true in *A*'s idiolect iff *p*.

But there is clearly in principle no reason why *B* cannot do this provided that *L* is a language which can be spoken by more than one person, which is a necessary condition on *L*'s being a language. If *B* states the truth conditions of *s* as in [11] using *s* in place of '*p*', then *B* is guaranteed to get the truth conditions of *A*'s sentence right for the same reason that *A* is in [9]. Thus, there does not seem to be any necessary asymmetry between the ability of *A* and *B* to state the truth conditions of *A*'s sentences in *A*'s language. It does not follow, then, from the fact that *A* can always state the truth conditions of his sentences in his language correctly by disquotation, while *B* cannot necessarily state the truth conditions of *A*'s sentences by disquotation in *B*'s language, that a speaker is always in a position correctly to state the truth conditions of his sentences, while an interpreter is not.

Furthermore, since it is clear that *B* could state the truth conditions of *A*'s sentences in *A*'s language without understanding it (mimicking *A* would do), *A*'s being able to use *A*'s language to state the truth conditions of his sentences is not sufficient for *A* to understand his own sentences. Thus, *A*'s always being able to state the truth conditions of sentences in his language could not be sufficient to explain an asymmetry between his and *B*'s knowledge of the meanings of the words in *A*'s language, because it would not be sufficient for *A* to know what his words meant.

This difficulty might be circumvented by stipulating that one cannot state the truth conditions of a sentence in a language unless one understands that language. But this is simply to acknowledge that being able to state the truth conditions of a sentence in a language is no explanation of one's knowledge of the meaning of the sentence, since it presupposes that knowledge; thus, any appeal to an asymmetry between the warrant for a speaker and interpreter in stating the truth conditions of the speaker's sentences simply presupposes an asymmetry in their knowledge of the meanings of the speaker's sentences.

Have we overlooked the asymmetry that is really doing the work here? It might be said that, although *A* and *B* can both state the truth conditions of *A*'s sentences in *A*'s language, only *A* is guaranteed to be in a position to know that he is stating the truth conditions of his sentences in *his* language. Even granting the premise for the sake of argument, this is not enough to ground an asymmetry between A's and B's knowledge of the meanings of sentences in A's language.[279] There is, perhaps, a trivial sense in which A knows that he is stating the truth conditions of his sentences in his language: he knows he is stating them in a language he speaks, and thus needs no independent check on whether the meanings of the sentences he uses are appropriate for giving the truth conditions of his sentences. However, this does not entail that he has any special authority about the meanings of the sentences in his language, for he could know he is stating the truth conditions of his sentences in his language, for the reason given, even if he did not know their meanings.

There is one final point to be made about this appeal to the possibility of stating the truth conditions in one's own language by disquotation, a technical point which we have put aside to see how far we could get with the argument on its own terms, but one which shows in a connected way why the explanatory strategy we have just considered is doomed. That is that one cannot generally state truth conditions for one's language by disquotation. The reason is, of course, that most of one's sentences are context sensitive. Thus, the form of sentence for stating their truth conditions must employ a truth predicate relativized to speaker and time, and in general we will find bound variables on the right of the embedded biconditional. So knowing how to state the truth conditions of one's sentence cannot amount merely to knowing how to disquote. One has to know what one's sentences mean, so as to know how what they express is to be relativized to context. Nor would it be appropriate to say that one could use disquotation on any given occasion to explain what one's sentences mean. First, for context sensitive sentences, part of what they mean is brought out by stating relativized truth conditions, namely, their context sensitivity. Thus, one cannot give the truth conditions for 'I am tired' by way of the biconditional [12], since just being able to do this will not show that one knows that 'I' is a context sensitive term, rather than a proper name, as in [13], which looks the same.

[12] 'I am tired' as spoken by me now is true iff I am tired
[13] 'N is tired' as spoken by me now is true iff N is tired.

---

[279] But why, after all, should there be any difficulty about B knowing that he is stating the truth conditions in A's language? He listens to A, and repeats his sentence, intending it to be understood relative to his language.

Furthermore, disquoting some sentences will in fact yield mistaken truth conditions because they interact with the syntax of the containing sentences, as in [14].

> [14]   'Anyone can do it' as spoken by me now is true if, and only if, anyone can do it.[280]

The difficulty here is that 'Anyone can do it' when it is used by itself is interpreted as equivalent to 'Everyone can do it', but when it is embedded in a biconditional as in [14], it is interpreted as equivalent to 'Even one can do it'.

(c) Supporting argument II

The second line of argument we identified holds that a speaker is interpretable only if he can consistently apply words to objects and events in his environment with the intention of stating his beliefs. Since, in the absence of an external check by his linguistic community on the appropriateness of his use of his words, getting it right can come to no more than using his words consistently,[281] it follows that if the speaker can be interpreted, he knows what he means by his words. From this it follows that an interpreter must assume that a speaker knows the meanings of his words, since it is a presupposition of his project that his subject is interpretable.

As it stands, this argument is incomplete, for all it shows is that *if* a speaker is interpretable, he knows the meanings of his words. While this may be enough to ensure that if an interpreter intends to interpret a subject, he is committed to assuming that the subject knows the meanings of his words, this does not show that every speaker knows the meanings of his words, or is a special authority on what his words mean. However, that every speaker is interpretable is, of course, something that Davidson holds on independent grounds, so he will feel free to appeal to it here, especially in the light of showing that his position has the resources to explain first person authority. Even apart from this, a weaker assumption will do, namely, that the speaker is interpretable in some environment, and that a speaker's knowledge of the meanings of his words is exhibited in his correctly applying them in an environment in which he is

---

[280] This is adapted from a criticism of Hintikka's (1975) of applying Tarski-style truth theories to natural languages. The criticism of using truth theories in Tarski's style in application to natural languages fails once we move away from the disquotational paradigm, which is required in any case to accommodate context sensitive sentences.

[281] In the light of the discussion of Ch. 17, we should take this to come to being disposed to use his words in a definite way at the time of interpretation.

mostly right and interpretable. This minimal requirement on the publicity of language will be sufficient to ensure that any speaker knows the meanings of his words, if knowing the meanings of his words is necessary for interpretation.

But even so, we *do not* have an *explanation* of first person authority. The form of our argument is the following: one speaks a language only if one is interpretable; one is interpretable only if one is mostly right about the meanings of one's words; therefore, one speaks a language only if one is mostly right about the meanings of one's words. We have here two options for explaining why a speaker knows the meanings of his words. First, he knows the meanings of his words because he is interpretable. This is unsuccessful because it gets the order of the explanation backwards. It meets our first two criteria of adequacy, but not the third. A speaker knows the meanings of his words not because he is interpretable, but is interpretable because he knows the meanings of his words. Second, one might say that he knows the meanings of his words because he speaks a language. This looks initially more promising. But the difficulty here is again that this explanation provides no philosophical illumination of the explanandum. For our conception of what it is to be a being who speaks a language is that it is to be a being who uses his words consistently in his application of them to objects and events in his environment in communicating with other members of his linguistic community. To say this is to say that a speaker is someone who, *inter alia*, knows the meanings of his words. Suppose we say that an X is anything that is A, B, and C. We cannot then explain why s is A by saying that it is X, for this cites no fact deeper than that for which we sought an explanation. And so, in citing the fact that someone speaks a language, we cite a fact which is no deeper than that which we wanted explained.

Another independent difficulty arises in using argument II as part of an explanation of the special authority that attaches to first person reports, and of the special warrant of first person ascriptions. The difficulty is that the argument presupposes and depends upon the asymmetry between the speaker's knowledge of his attitudes and the interpreter's. (This is related to a problem raised for the master argument, namely, that it fails to account for the kind of asymmetry there is between one's knowledge of one's thoughts and others' knowledge of them except relative to the assumption that one knows better what sentences one holds true.) To see this, notice that, in our description of the interpreter's assumptions in the interpretive project, we treat the speaker as a rational agent who is trying to communicate with the interpreter. This provides us with an explanation of his consistent use of words to express his beliefs, which is a necessary condition of his being interpretable. The speaker typically uses, for example, the same vocable, 'vade mecum', whenever he wants to say what he believes about a salient useful guidebook in his environment. This presupposes that the speaker knows what he believes about his environment, that he knows how he has used his words in the past, which requires him to know what he believed in the past, and that he knows what he intends. Otherwise, there would be no guarantee that he would be using his words correctly in saying what he believes about his environment. If the speaker were not a better authority on what he believed than his interpreter, then the speaker would not be in a better position to know what he means by his words. Thus, in order to explain the asymmetry between the speaker's knowledge of the meanings of his words and the interpreter's, we must presuppose an asymmetry between the speaker's knowledge of his attitudes and the interpreter's knowledge of them. To attempt to turn from this to explaining the asymmetry between the speaker's and interpreter's knowledge of the speaker's attitudes by appeal to an asymmetry between the speaker and interpreter's knowledge of the meanings of the speaker's words is to presuppose in one's explanans the explanandum. We cannot then expect to use this asymmetry between the knowledge that a speaker and interpreter have of the speaker's words to explain the asymmetry between their knowledge of the speaker's attitudes.

A final concern we have about the explanation that Davidson offers, which does not focus on the details of the argument, is that it does not give any role to consciousness in explaining the special warrant we have for our first person reports, and in explaining the special warrant of first person ascriptions. An understanding of consciousness must play a central role in our understanding of our special epistemic position with respect to our own mental states. No argument or explanation which omits to mention consciousness can be correct, because being conscious is a necessary condition on knowing what our own mental states are. Yet, if Davidson's explanation were correct, it would seem that a being with propositional attitudes who was not a being capable of consciousness (if this is possible) would know just as well as one who was conscious what the contents of its propositional attitudes were. However, if such a being could be said to know anything about its own mental states, it would not be in the same sense in which we know what our mental states are. Thus, a successful explanation of the asymmetry between first and other person ascriptions must entail that the knower is conscious. Davidson's explanation does not meet this requirement.

Another way to see why consciousness must play a central role in our understanding of our knowledge of our own mental states is to consider the difference between our knowledge of our mental lives when we are awake, and when we are asleep and not dreaming. Clearly, there is a vast difference here in our knowledge of our mental states. This difference cannot be explained without reference to consciousness. But Davidson's argument does not have the resources to make any distinctions between periods of consciousness and unconsciousness. The knowledge that Davidson's master argument appeals to, knowledge that one holds certain sentences true, and knowledge of the meanings of one's terms, can be understood dispositionally. So understood, it does not distinguish between one's knowledge of one's mental life when one is conscious, and when one is unconscious.

This complaint with Davidson's argument is connected with our identifying, in §1, [*E1*] as the primary source of first person authority. Davidson's argument cannot explain [*E1*] because it cannot single out consciousness for a special or primary role in our knowledge of our own mental lives.

There is one final point that should be made in this regard. We have not so far marked out sensations as a distinct class of conscious mental states. Davidson sets them aside explicitly. It is clear that his arguments could at most explain why we have special warrant for our ascriptions of propositional attitudes such as beliefs and desires to ourselves, since it depends upon an asymmetry in knowledge of meanings, which is irrelevant to mental states that do not have propositional contents. Pains, itches, anger, hunger, and the like would not be covered by this explanation. Thus, [7], which we noted was required for the success of his argument, is left unsecured. Moreover, this should call into question by itself the adequacy of the explanation of our knowledge and authority about our propositional attitudes, since there is good reason to think that there should be a unified explanation of our knowledge of all our conscious mental states.

The real source of first person authority is first person knowledge. We know about our own mental lives in a way that is different in kind from that of anyone else. This knowledge of our own mental lives is not based on observations or knowledge of our behavior, and is non-inferential. Since facts about our behavior do not entail that we have mental states or, if we do, what they are, someone who is in the position of having to infer what our beliefs are from our behavior is always at risk of getting it wrong. These facts are in themselves enough to explain why we are generally better placed to say what we believe, desire, intend, etc., than others are. Whereas they must make an inference which puts them at epistemic risk, we need make no such inference in order to know. This is not, of course, a satisfying explanation. It rests the asymmetry in warrant for first and other person reports and ascriptions on an asymmetry in the way we know our own and others' mental states. To explain the former adequately we cannot just cite the latter, without having an explanation of it in turn.

For first person knowledge, however, there is little hope of a philosophically illuminating explanation. We do not dispute the claim that for one speaker to interpret another, he must assume, and it must be true, that the subject of interpretation knows the meanings of his words *and* the contents of his propositional attitudes. We do not see, however, that these facts about interpretation explain the subject's knowledge in any way that helps to blunt the challenge non-inferential knowledge of thought contents presents to Davidson's basic methodological stance. The reason that we must assume that a speaker knows what he thinks, desires, means, etc. is not because this is necessary for us to interpret him, though this is correct, but because it is a part of our conception of what it is for anything to be a rational agent. A rational agent is one who acts on the basis of his beliefs and desires in a way exemplified by rationalizing explanations of actions. This presupposes patterns of interaction among beliefs and desires that display an awareness of their contents. The only way to make sense of a failure of self-knowledge is to try to imagine that someone's actions fall into incoherence. Too much incoherence in someone's behavior, however, convinces us not that they fail to know the contents of their attitudes, but that they are not, after all, agents. This is an insight we owe to Davidson. However, to notice this connection between rational action and self-knowledge is not to provide an explanation of the latter. We invoke it in our explanation of what it is to be a rational agent. And so saying that we are rational agents does not constitute an illuminating explanation of that fact about us. We cannot do better in striving for philosophical illumination than to recognize the role that non-inferential knowledge of our own mental states plays in our conception of the kind of beings that we are. This is not to explain first person knowledge, but to recognize it as something we can appeal to in explaining other things, as an end point of explanation.

This goes no distance toward showing that the third person perspective on psychological states and meanings is primary, and that the content of linguistic and psychological concepts is exhausted by their roles in keeping track of behavior. On the contrary, it seems to show that our a priori conception of a rational agent is one of a being who has non-inferential knowledge of its own psychological states, and, if it is a speaker, the meanings of its sentences, and who therefore must regard its attempts to interpret others as attempts to discover facts which are not exhausted by what is recoverable from observations of behavior; if there are two possible assignments of meanings and attitude contents to a speaker's sentences and attitudes, from the interpreter's standpoint, the possibility that one is right and the other is wrong remains open, because the interpreter must recognize the possibility of a perspective on those thoughts and meanings which is not dependent on recovering them from behavioral evidence.

4. Does Externalism Make Thoughts Self-Verifying?

We turn finally to a different explanation Davidson has offered of the asymmetry in our knowledge of our thoughts and others' knowledge of them. In "Epistemology Externalized," he argues against the view that externalism entails we do not know the contents of our own thoughts. In the course of this, he offers what appears to be a new explanation for why, if externalism is true, it cannot be that we are wrong about what we think.[282] The explanation goes as follows.

An interpreter must discover, or correctly assume on the basis of indirect evidence, what the external factors are that determine the content of another's thought; but since these factors determine both the contents of one's thought and the contents of the thought one believes one has (these being one and the same thought), there is no room for error about the contents of one's own thoughts of the sort that can arise with respect to the thoughts of others.   (Davidson 2001 (1991): 197–8)

---

[282] Davidson represents the argument as showing that externalism does not entail that we do not know the contents of our own thoughts, and cites "Knowing One's Own Mind" (2001*b* (1987)) as a place he has "argued this at length" (2001 (1991): 197). However, the argument he goes on to give appears to aim to show that externalism requires self-knowledge, and does not appear in "Knowing One's Own Mind." He argues there that the reason many have thought that it does is that they have harbored a view of thoughts as objects of the mind. When it is suggested that the objects of the mind are individuated by their relational properties, so the explanation goes, we think we cannot know what our thoughts are, because to know them conceived of as objects would require knowing everything about them, and we cannot know everything about any object. "The basic difficulty is simple: if to have a thought is to have an object before the mind, and the identity of the object determines what the thought is, then it must always be possible to be mistaken about what one is thinking. For unless one knows *everything* about the object, there will always be senses in which one does not know what object it is" (Davidson 2001*b* (1987): 37). We doubt this is what has motivated the view that if externalism is true, then we cannot know what we think. This argument, if sound, would undermine knowledge of thoughts, whether or not they were individuated relationally, as long as they were treated as objects of some kind. The only argument to show that we do in fact have knowledge of our own thoughts in "Knowing One's Own Mind" occurs in the last paragraph (ibid. 38), and appeals to the necessity of a person's knowing what his words mean: "unless there is a presumption that the speaker knows what she means, i.e., is getting her own language right, there would be nothing for an interpreter to interpret." This simply points to the argument given in "First Person Authority" (Davidson 2001 (1984)).

It is not entirely clear from this passage how the argument is supposed to go. But the idea seems to be the following. When another attributes a certain content to one of one's thoughts, he assigns it its content on the basis of external factors, which constitute his evidence. Evidently, he can think of a thought of yours as having a certain content and get it wrong, from being too hasty, or not assessing the evidence correctly. Can a similar mistake arise in one's own case, that is, can one think of one of one's own thoughts, and mistake its content, in the way that another may do so? The answer is supposed to be 'no'. For suppose one believes that p, and that one forms a belief about that belief to the effect that one believes it. To form a belief about one's belief that p is to believe that one believes that p. What individuates the latter, the belief that one believes that p, is what individuates one's belief that p itself, since for both their identity is determined once we say what goes in for 'p'. But the same factors fix that in both cases. Thus, once one has the belief about one's belief, it cannot be mistaken, whereas this is not so when someone else has a belief about one of one's beliefs.

We must admit some uncertainty about whether this is what Davidson intended. But this is all that the passage suggests to us. If this is the explanation, then there are a number of reasons to find it unsatisfying.

First, we should ask what the explanation must show, if it is to do the job Davidson's needs it to do. What we want is an explanation of first person knowledge and authority from the standpoint according to which psychological concepts are theoretical concepts whose contents are exhausted by behavioral evidence for their application. The explanation must explain why we know differently, and better, what our conscious thoughts are than anyone else.

Does the explanation just canvassed do this? No. First, the basic fact it appeals to has nothing whatsoever to do with externalism or the view that psychological concepts are theoretical in character. The basic idea is just that if one forms a belief about one's belief that p, that belief is guaranteed to be right: this is not true for someone else who forms a belief about that belief, because it is not *his* belief. Thus, even if this explanation explains something, it does not do so by relying on anything distinctive about Davidson's views. It cannot therefore play the kind of role required in a defense of the view that psychological concepts are theoretical concepts.

Second, note that the explanation aims to explain why, if we have a belief about a belief of ours, we cannot be wrong about its content. It does not explain why we know what beliefs (desires, and so on) we have in the first place. That is to say, the explanation starts out with the assumption that one has identified correctly a certain belief one has, and asks whether one could go wrong about its content, given that one had a belief about it. But if we think about our knowledge of our thoughts as divided into these two stages, first we pick out a belief we have, then we say what its content is, then we need also an explanation of how in our own case we manage to correctly identify our beliefs.[283]

Third, waiving this consideration, the argument relies on the following assumption. To form a belief about a belief that *p* one has is to believe that one believes that *p*. But this is not so. One may believe that one believes that *p* but not believe that *p*, and one may believe of a belief that one has that it is a belief that *p*, when it is not. We do not say this could be generally so, only that there is nothing incoherent about it. The mere fact that a belief is one that one has oneself does not guarantee that one will have correct beliefs about its content, if one has any beliefs about its content at all, as if we could not make sense of what it would be to believe falsely that a belief of one's was a belief that *p*. We cannot make good sense of *massive* error about one's own beliefs. By and large, if we believe that *p*, then we are in a position to warrantedly believe that we do. But that fact still stands in need of explanation. If what we have said in the previous section is correct, there will be no illuminating explanation of this, for the concept of an agent is fundamentally an epistemic concept.[284]

5. Conclusion

If the arguments presented in this chapter are correct, then the challenge that first person knowledge and authority presents to the conception of psychological and linguistic concepts as theoretical concepts has not been met. The challenge can be expressed in the following argument.

(1) The justification for believing that something falls under a theoretical concept must be inferential.

(2) We have non-inferential knowledge of the contents of our psychological states and of the meanings of sentences in our language.

---

[283] In fact, this way of thinking about the task seems to us to be infelicitous. What we are interested in knowing is why one's own beliefs which one would express by a sentence of the form 'I believe that I believe that *p*' are generally warranted, while if someone else believes that one believes that *p*, we have not the same assurance that he is right. But if we resist talking about beliefs as objects, it becomes impossible to say what argument Davidson could have in mind in the passage we have quoted.

[284] We can note in passing also that the form of explanation would not make sense of the special role that consciousness plays in first person knowledge, nor is it obvious how it could be extended to knowledge of mental states other than propositional attitudes.

(3) Therefore, (these) psychological and linguistic concepts are not theoretical concepts.

Davidson's strategy is to show that (1) is mistaken by arguing that non-inferential knowledge at least of meanings is a consequence of a view according to which psychological concepts are theoretical concepts deployed in the first instance from the third person perspective on the basis of behavior. Davidson's main argument appeals to the claim that we must assume in interpretation that another knows the meanings of his words, while no such assumption is required of the interpreter. This is to provide a basis for the special epistemic position we are in with respect to our own thoughts by giving it a basis which does not require investigation of the world around us. As we have shown in this chapter, the attempt fails, for at least two reasons. First, the fact that we must assume a speaker knows what he means to interpret him does not itself constitute an explanation of his knowledge. Second, the appeal presupposes, but does not explain, an asymmetry in first person knowledge. For unless we also assume an independent asymmetry in knowledge of what one thinks, the master argument fails to establish an asymmetry in first person authority, even granting one in knowledge of meanings. In addition, what we think of as the main argument for the asymmetry in knowledge of meaning, argument II, presupposes that the agent independently knows what he thinks. The first point though, is the most important one. For there is clearly a more direct argument available to Davidson, which shows that someone who does not know what he thinks is not interpretable. This just rests on the observation that we count nothing as an agent unless it is by and large rational, and that presupposes that the coherence of its behavior in light of the attitudes we attribute to him expresses his knowledge of what he thinks. Evidence that he did not know what he thinks would at the same time be evidence that showed his behavior not to be fully rational, in the light of the attitudes attributed to him: too much of this, and we lose our grip on the idea that he is an agent at all. The trouble with this is that it provides no explanation of first person knowledge, any more than the need to assume a speaker is by and large rational in order to interpret him explains why he is rational. That someone knows what he thinks falls out of our conception of an agent, and is not something that is explained by the need to assume it in interpretation.

21

Inscrutability of Reference[285]

What no one can, in the nature of the case, figure out from the totality of
the relevant evidence cannot be part of meaning.

(Davidson 2001a: 235)

The *indeterminacy of interpretation* is the thesis that there are many correct
interpretation theories for any speaker which nonetheless assign different interpretations to the speaker's sentences. The *inscrutability of reference* entails, but
is not entailed by, the indeterminacy of interpretation: it is the thesis that reference schemes for any speaker's language which assign different referents to
his singular terms and extensions to his predicates are equally correct, *provided*
they result in the same assignments of truth values to object language sentences

---

[285] This chapter presupposes some familiarity with the satisfaction relation used in definitions of truth for a language with quantifiers. This topic is discussed in *Truth-Theoretic Semantics*,
chapters 2–3. The satisfaction relation is invoked to handle quantification. The satisfaction relation holds between an open sentence and an object or sequence of objects when the result of
interpreting the free variables referring to those objects is true, where variables in their sequence
are matched to the objects in theirs. We may say the predicate is true of the object or of the
sequence of objects, or reversing the order of the relata, that the object or sequence of objects satisfies the predicate. We may also talk of a function which assigns objects to variables as satisfying
a predicate; it satisfies it when the result of interpreting the free variables in it as referring to the
objects assigned to them by the function is true. We say a universally quantified open sentence
with respect to a variable v is true just in case no matter what a function assigns to v the result is
true. To handle multiple quantification, where we must keep track of which variables are bound
by which quantifiers (e.g. in 'for any x, there is some y, such that $x > y$'), we say a universally
quantified sentence with respect to v is satisfied by a function just in case every function that
differs from it at most in what it assigns to v satisfies the sentence; for existential quantification
we require that at least one function that differs from it at most in what it assigns to v satisfy the
sentence. The effect of this is to keep track as we evaluate quantifiers in sequence of which deal
with which variable in the right order. So for our example above we have it that: f satisfies 'for
any x, there is some y, such that $x > y$' iff for every f' that differs from f at most in what it assigns
to 'x', f' satisfies 'there is some y, such that $x > y$' iff for every f' that differs from f at most in
what it assigns to 'x', for some f'' that differs from f' at most in what it assigns to 'y', f'' satisfies
'$x > y$'. Then we say that a sentence is true iff it is satisfied by all functions; it is clear that it doesn't
matter what function we start with for quantified sentences which contain no free variables, so if
any of the functions satisfy a quantified sentence, all of them will.

(relativized to context).[286] A reference scheme can be thought of as given by the non-recursive semantic axioms (i.e. those that assign satisfaction and reference conditions to object language expressions) for a truth theory for a language. These axioms assign referents to proper names, satisfaction conditions, and so extensions, to predicates (perhaps relative to times for tensed predicates), and referents relative to context (speakers and times) for indexicals and demonstratives. The inscrutability of reference entails the indeterminacy of interpretation, since it is sufficient for the truth conditions assigned to a sentence by two theories to give different interpretations (in the context of our whole theory) that predicates and singular terms used to state them have different extensions and referents, respectively.[287] We treat the inscrutability of reference apart from the indeterminacy of interpretation because Davidson employs additional arguments to show reference is inscrutable, which it will be useful to examine separately, and also because additional difficulties arise for inscrutability of reference, due to the particularly dramatic forms of indeterminacy it sanctions. Davidson's papers especially relevant to this issue are "Reality without Reference" (2001*b* (1977)) and "The Inscrutability of Reference" (2001*a* (1979)). Our discussion will focus mainly on the latter.[288]

1. The Argument for the Inscrutability of Reference

The argument for inscrutability is straightforward. We introduce some terminology to help state the argument clearly. A truth theory $\mathcal{T}$ employs

---

[286] As Davidson puts it, "there is no way to tell what the singular terms of a language refer to, or what its predicates are true of, at least no way to tell from the totality of behavioural evidence, actual and potential, and such evidence is all that matters to questions of meaning and communication" (2001*a* (1979): 227). And since such evidence is all that matters to questions of meaning, there is no fact of the matter beyond what empirical patterns are captured by all empirically equivalent theories for a given speaker. Again, Davidson says, "Everyday linguistic and semantic concepts are part of an intuitive theory for organizing more primitive data, so only confusion can result from treating these concepts and their supposed objects as if they had a life of their own" (2001*a* (1974): 143). Wallace puts the same idea, more generally, in the following way (1977: 159): "There are some concepts whose role is exhausted in inducing a certain organization on some other concepts. The role of these special concepts is to bring to the surface of language a potential for structure already present in those other concepts. To give an implicit definition of such a concept is to state axioms which tie it together with the concepts it organizes, and which make explicit all such ties. With axioms in hand we can say: any concept of X conforms to all of these requirements; and any concept which conforms to all these requirements is a concept of X."

[287] The indeterminacy that is supposed to be established by the argument for the inscrutability of reference does not establish forms which allow variation in the truth values of sentence across different interpretation theories.

[288] Davidson cites Wallace 1977 and Field 1974, 1975 as important influences. We are, however, mainly concerned with Davidson's development of the thesis.

a reference scheme $\mathcal{R}$ iff $\mathcal{R}$ gives the non-recursive semantic axioms of $\mathcal{T}$; we abbreviate this as '$\mathcal{T}$ employs $\mathcal{R}$'. Let '$s_{\mathcal{T}}$' represent the canonical theorem for $\mathcal{T}$ for a sentence s. Let '$\mathcal{T}$' and '$\mathcal{T}'$' range over Tarski-style truth theories, and '$\mathcal{R}$' and '$\mathcal{R}'$' range over reference schemes. We use 'true$_{\mathcal{T}}$' and 'true$_{\mathcal{T}'}$' to translate the truth predicates characterized by $\mathcal{T}$ and $\mathcal{T}'$, respectively. First we define the notions of *equivalent reference schemes* for a language and *non-identical reference schemes* for a language.

(Def.)   For any $\mathcal{R}$, $\mathcal{R}'$, and any $\mathcal{T}$, $\mathcal{T}'$, such that $\mathcal{T}$ employs $\mathcal{R}$, and $\mathcal{T}'$ is obtained from $\mathcal{T}$ by replacing $\mathcal{R}$ by $\mathcal{R}'$, for any $s_{\mathcal{T}}$, $s_{\mathcal{T}'}$, $\mathcal{R}$ and $\mathcal{R}'$ are equivalent iff$_{\text{df}}$ $s_{\mathcal{T}}$ is true$_{\mathcal{T}}$ iff $s_{\mathcal{T}'}$ is true$_{\mathcal{T}'}$.

(Def.)   For any $\mathcal{R}$, $\mathcal{R}'$, $\mathcal{R}$ is non-identical to $\mathcal{R}'$ iff$_{\text{df}}$ $\mathcal{R}$ and $\mathcal{R}'$ do not assign the same referents to singular terms or do not assign the same extensions to predicates.

The argument for inscrutability can now be given in terms of these notions.

(1)   For any $\mathcal{T}$, $\mathcal{R}$, and speaker S, if $\mathcal{T}$ is an interpretive truth theory for S which employs $\mathcal{R}$, then there is a truth theory $\mathcal{T}'$ for S which is like $\mathcal{T}$ except for employing a reference scheme $\mathcal{R}'$ equivalent to but non-identical with $\mathcal{R}$.[289]

(2)   For any $\mathcal{R}$, $\mathcal{R}'$ such that $\mathcal{R}$ is equivalent to $\mathcal{R}'$, for any $\mathcal{T}$, $\mathcal{T}'$, such that $\mathcal{T}$ employs $\mathcal{R}$ and $\mathcal{T}'$ is like $\mathcal{T}$ except for employing $\mathcal{R}'$, if either $\mathcal{T}$ or $\mathcal{T}'$ is interpretive, both are.[290]

(3)   For any speaker, there is at least one interpretive truth theory.

(4)   Every interpretive truth theory employs a reference scheme.

(5)   Therefore, for any speaker S, there are at least two correct reference schemes for S's language which assign different referents to his singular terms and different extensions to his predicates, that is, reference is inscrutable.

(3) and (4) are uncontroversial. So the argument has only two significant premises. We begin with (1), and then turn to the more fundamental assumption (2).

---

[289] We talk of truth theories for speakers rather than languages because, as we will see, Davidson's account of the relativity of reference involves relativizing truth theories to languages, while claiming that theories relativized to different languages can be equally good theories for interpreting speakers.

[290] Davidson says "Another assumption that is clearly needed if we are to conclude to the inscrutability of reference is that if some theory of truth . . . is satisfactory in the light of all relevant evidence (actual or potential) then any theory that is generated from the first theory by a permutation will also be satisfactory in the light of all relevant evidence" (2001a (1979): 230), where, of course, being satisfactory in the light of all relevant evidence in this sense is being correct.

2. The First Premise of the Argument for the Inscrutability of Reference

We examine in detail here one argument Davidson advances for (1), which involves introducing a permutation function. It should be noted that the procedure described in Chapter 15 is likely to allow for different reference schemes also, so that the argument here is not the only way to establish the possibility of the inscrutability of reference. The argument goes as follows. First, we consider a one-to-one non-identity mapping from objects in the universe onto themselves, that is, a mapping in which each object is mapped onto just one other object, and none is mapped onto more than one, and which does not map every object onto itself. Let ψ be such a mapping. We can generate from a reference scheme $\mathcal{R}$ an equivalent (in the sense above) but non-identical one $\mathcal{R}'$ using the permutation function ψ. We let 'Ref$_{\mathcal{R}}(x)$' and 'Ref$_{\mathcal{R}'}(x)$' be the reference functions for singular terms, and 'sat$_{\mathcal{R}}(x,y)$' and 'sat$_{\mathcal{R}'}(x,y)$' be the satisfaction functions for schemes $\mathcal{R}$ and $\mathcal{R}'$, respectively. Initially, we will show how to construct an equivalent but non-identical reference scheme $\mathcal{R}'$ from a scheme $\mathcal{R}$ for a language without context sensitive expressions. This is the procedure Davidson follows. We will return to the question how to do it for a language with context sensitive expressions later, to see what additional complications may arise. We construct Ref$_{\mathcal{R}'}(x)$ from Ref$_{\mathcal{R}}(x)$ as in [1],

[1]   For all α, x, if Ref$_{\mathcal{R}}(\alpha) = x$, then Ref$_{\mathcal{R}'}(\alpha) = \psi(x)$.

where 'α' ranges over singular referring terms and 'x' over objects. Now, let '$\mathbf{r}_n$' represent a vector of n variables (an ordered n-tuple of variables). Quantification over these variables will be represented as 'For all $\mathbf{r}_n$, ϕ' (i.e. if $\mathbf{r}_n = <x_1, x_2, \ldots, x_n>$, then 'For all $\mathbf{r}_n$, ϕ'='For all $x_1, x_2, x_3, \ldots, x_n, \phi$'). A predicate '$F$' with $\mathbf{r}_n$ free variables will be represented as '$F(\mathbf{r}_n)$'. '$f(\mathbf{r}_n)$' represents an assignment by a function f of objects to the variables $\mathbf{r}_n$, and '$F(f(\mathbf{r}_n))$' represents the result of replacing each free variable x_i in 'F' with $\ulcorner f(x_i) \urcorner$. We construct 'sat$_{\mathcal{R}'}(x,y)$' from 'sat$_{\mathcal{R}}(x,y)$' as in [2], where '$F'$' meets the condition specified in [3].[291]

---

[291] There is a mistake in Davidson's exposition of the construction of a new reference scheme from an old one in "The Inscrutability of Reference." "If we have a satisfactory scheme of reference for a language that speaks of this universe, we can produce another scheme of reference by using the permutation: whenever, on the first scheme, a name refers to an object x, on the second scheme it refers to $\phi(x)$; whenever, on the first scheme, a predicate refers to (is true of) each thing x such that Fx, on the second scheme it refers to each thing x such that $F\phi(x)$" (Davidson 2001a (1979): 229). The last clause should read 'whenever, on the first scheme, a predicate refers to (is true of) each

[2]　For all ϕ, f, $\mathbf{r_n}$, if $\mathrm{sat}_{\mathcal{R}}(\phi, f)$ iff $F(f(\mathbf{r_n}))$, then $(\mathrm{sat}_{\mathcal{R'}}(\phi, f)$ iff $F'(f(\mathbf{r_n}))$.

[3]　For all $\mathbf{r_n}$, $F(\mathbf{r_n})$ iff $F'(\psi(\mathbf{r_n}))$.

[3] ensures that the extension of 'F''' is the set of things onto which ψ maps the members of the extension of 'F''. We show now that any reference scheme $\mathcal{R'}$ constructed in this way from a scheme $\mathcal{R}$ is equivalent to $\mathcal{R}$. This requires showing that for a T-theorem canonically provable in $\mathcal{T}$ employing $\mathcal{R}$ of the form [4], the truth conditions are extensionally equivalent to those in the corresponding T-theorem for $\mathcal{T'}$ which is like $\mathcal{T}$ except for employing $\mathcal{R'}$ instead of $\mathcal{R}$, as in [5].

[4]　s is true$_{\mathcal{T}}$ iff p

[5]　s is true$_{\mathcal{T'}}$ iff q

This is equivalent to showing that p iff q. Since the satisfaction axioms for $\mathcal{T}$ and $\mathcal{T'}$ for primitive non-recursive terms are materially equivalent, and no changes are made to recursive terms, for sentences without proper names it is easy to see they will be true in exactly the same circumstances. What about those with proper names? It is easy to see that the result obtains here as well. Suppose a proper name on the original reference scheme refers to an object x that falls in the extension of a predicate ϕ. In the new reference scheme, the proper name refers to $\psi(x)$. But the extension of ϕ in the new scheme is the set of objects onto which ψ maps the extension on the original scheme, that is, if $x \in \mathrm{ext}(\phi)$ on $\mathcal{R}$, then $\psi(x) \in \mathrm{ext}(\phi)$ on $\mathcal{R'}$. Thus, if $\mathrm{Ref}_{\mathcal{R}}(\alpha)$, that is, x, falls in the extension of ϕ on the original scheme, $\mathrm{Ref}_{\mathcal{R'}}(\alpha)$, that is, $\psi(x)$, falls in the extension of ϕ on the new scheme. This establishes (1) for languages not containing context sensitive elements.

It will be useful to see how this would be extended to context sensitive terms, which would be required to show the result holds for natural languages. We take as samples the demonstrative 'that', the first person pronoun 'I', and tense. We need to consider tense first, since this requires rethinking how to construct new predicates to assign extensionally equivalent satisfaction conditions to our original predicates. The simplest thing to do is to consider a one-to-one permutation function which maps objects at times onto objects which exist at that time, $\psi(x, t)$, which is not the identity mapping of objects at a time. Then our aim is to construct from a tensed predicate, say 'is snow' a new predicate 'is snow'' so that [6] obtains.

---

thing x such that Fx, on the second scheme, it refers to (is true of) $\phi(x)$'. The extension on the new scheme should be the image of the old under the permutation.

[6]   For all x, t, x is snow at t iff $\psi(x, t)$ is snow′ at t.

Consider now the demonstrative 'that'. Evidently, to get correct truth conditions, if we provide a reference axiom for 'that', we must ensure that what 'that' refers to on an occasion of use is appropriately related to what would be referred to in our original scheme of reference. The natural suggestion is [7], where 'Ref$_\mathcal{R}(S, t)(x)$' is read as 'the referent of x in $\mathcal{R}$ understood as if spoken by S at t'.

[7] $\text{Ref}_{\mathcal{R}'}(S, t)(\text{'that'}) = \psi$(the object potentially demonstrated by S at t, t).

Putting [7] together with the satisfaction axiom for 'is snow' which uses 'is snow′' and substituting, we arrive at [8].

[8]   For all functions f, speakers S, times t, $f\,\text{sat}_{\mathcal{R}'}(S, t)$ 'That is snow' iff ψ(the object potentially demonstrated by S at t, t) is snow′ at t.

For the indexical 'I', we will have [9], which combined with a predicate such as 'am tired' and an appropriately constructed alternative predicate 'am tired′', will yield [10].

[9] $\text{Ref}_{\mathcal{R}'}(S, t)(\text{'I'}) = \psi(S, t)$

[10]   For all functions f, all speakers S, all times t, $f\,\text{sat}_{\mathcal{R}'}(S, t)$ 'I am tired' iff $\psi(S, t)$ is tired′ at t.

Clearly, given how we have constructed the new predicates and determined the referents of the context sensitive terms, we have [11] and [12].

[11]   For all t, S, the object potentially demonstrated by S at t is snow at t iff ψ(the object potentially demonstrated by S at t, t) is snow′ at t.

[12]   For all t, S, S is tired at t iff $\psi(S, t)$ is tired′ at t.

The extension to context sensitive terms, while straightforward, does, as we will see, introduce important new elements into the discussion.

3. The Second Premise of the Argument for the Inscrutability of Reference

We turn our attention to premise (2), which is obviously the contentious one. Is (2) correct? The answer, in the light of previous discussion, is that it is *not*, even by Davidson's own lights.

378

The inscrutability of reference is a form of indeterminacy of interpretation. So, the arguments we advanced against indeterminacy in Chapter 15 apply here as well. We will cover the objections that overlap briefly. But there are also objections that can be raised against the inscrutability of reference inapplicable to milder forms of indeterminacy. We will examine these first. In the next section, we will consider some responses to objections we introduce here.

The first point we wish to highlight is that when we apply the permutation argument to a natural language in which we have to accommodate indexicals and demonstratives, we get strange and even paradoxical results.

First, notice that in [7], we specify the original referent in terms of which we formulate our modified axiom by talking about what the speaker demonstrates. Thus, our original theory is committed apparently to the speaker's having referred to a particular object, which cannot be guaranteed to be the same object as the object to which the permutation would take us. This presents us with two problems immediately. First, Davidson is committed to saying that, *although a speaker may demonstrate one object, the demonstrative he uses could just as well be taken to be referring to a different object.* This is a result to be avoided if possible, since the function of a demonstrative is to refer to the object the speaker demonstrates in using it.

Second, nothing restricts what object a permutation can take the originally demonstrated object to. The object may be one with which the speaker has no causal or perceptual contact, and no way of knowing about, from the point of view of the interpreter. It is hard to see how assigning such an object to a use of a demonstrative could be compatible with the principle of charity, or any common-sense principles of interpretation.

It might be suggested that the objection based on [7] can be avoided by holding, not that referents are assigned to 'that' on the second scheme by applying the permutation function to what the speaker demonstrates, but rather that *on the second scheme* the speaker demonstrates the object to which the permutation takes what the speaker demonstrates *according to the first scheme.*[292] But this is confused. A reference scheme is about what referring terms in a language refer to, and what the extensions of predicates in the language are; it is not about what speakers demonstrate. So, a reference scheme does not speak directly to what a speaker demonstrates at all. The notion of demonstration invoked in axioms for demonstratives is a term of the metalanguage, not the object language. Moreover, it would hardly make sense to say that the speaker always demonstrates at least two objects, even if we could make sense of relativizing

---

[292] Wallace 1977: 148–9 makes a suggestion like this.

the demonstrations to a reference scheme. Of course, sometimes a speaker may demonstrate more than one object on a given occasion, but he may also not do so. And the problem is really worse than this suggests. For given any object at a time there is a permutation that will take it to any other object at that time. So any time a speaker demonstrates an object, on the present suggestion, for any other object at that time, there is a scheme according to which he demonstrates it. So if a speaker demonstrates any object at a time, he demonstrates every object at that time.

Perhaps it will be objected that this is to take the suggestion in the wrong way, and that the suggestion is really just that we should rewrite the axiom as in [7'].

[7']   Ref$_{\mathscr{R}'}$ (S, t)('that') = the object demonstrated' by S at t

We explain 'x is demonstrated' by S at t' as in [13].

[13]   For any x, x is demonstrated' by S at t iff$_{df}x = \psi$(the object demonstrated by S at t, t)

But, as a response to the original objection, this is fatuous, since the definition of 'x is demonstrated' by S at t' makes use of the relation between speaker and object we were trying to avoid. [7'] simply draws a veil over the absurdity. It does not remove it.

We get strange results also when we consider the account of the referent of a use of the first person pronoun. For if Davidson were right that an alternative reference scheme which used [9] were as good as the one we started with, then there is *no fact of the matter* whether when one says 'I am in pain' one is talking about oneself or a distant quasar. This of course plays havoc with the suggestion that one announces with that sentence something which one knows non-inferentially; no one thinks one can know something non-inferentially about distant stellar objects.

A related problem is that, in the new reference scheme, none of the interpretations assigned to one's predicates is guaranteed to make them psychological predicates, that is, it could turn out that in one's language one lacks the resources to talk about mental states. How we could make sense of someone as a rational agent in that case is mysterious. Yet the theory of agency which the interpreter brings to bear is constitutive of his subject-matter. If his interpretation leads him to a position in which he cannot make sense of his subject as a rational agent, then by his own lights it must be mistaken.

In short, for a coherent theory of interpretation of a speaker of a natural language, it does not look as if we are free to use any theory constructed by use of a permutation function as above from one we have confirmed. The additional axioms needed for demonstratives and indexicals, and the requirement that we see the speaker as a rational agent with attitudes that rationalize his actions and make sense of his speech behavior, place important constraints on what reference function we use in our truth theory for his language.

The second point to notice is that what we required for an equivalent reference scheme is merely extensional equivalence between two truth theories. We can achieve that by a systematic remapping of singular referring terms onto objects, and by providing, for each predicate '*F*' (in the metalanguage) used to give satisfaction conditions for a predicate in the object language, a new predicate '*F''* which meets condition [3], repeated here.

[3]   For all r_n, $F(r_n)$ iff $F'(\psi(r_n))$

But note that all that is required is that [3] be as a matter of fact true. However, Davidson requires that the theorems of an interpretive truth theory be laws (this is a consequence of its being treated as an empirical theory). Constructing a new theory from an empirically confirmed theory by the method that employs [3] will not guarantee that the new theory's theorems are natural laws, that is, are projectible and support counterfactuals. By Davidson's own lights, then, not every equivalent reference scheme should be seen as equally adequate.

This problem, of course, could be remedied by requiring that the predicate '*F''* we choose renders [3] a law, and thus counterfactual supporting. It should be noted, however, that the extra constraint here makes more difficult the task of showing that we will be able to find predicates that pick out exactly the right objects, for the construction to work.

But apart from this, we can see that the issue here is the same one we addressed in Part II in considering what constraints must be added to a truth theory to ensure that its theorems are interpretive. There we concluded that being true laws, and even being conceptually or logically necessary, was not sufficient to ensure that the truth conditions given were interpretive. So even if we required that [3] be a necessary truth, we would not thereby ensure that the new theory is interpretive, even if we grant that the theory from which it is derived is interpretive.

We saw earlier (Chapter 11) that one way of conceiving of how to place extra constraints on the theory was to require it to be empirically confirmable from the standpoint of a radical interpreter. This does not, we think, add anything new. But if we suppose for the sake of argument it does, and is sufficient for a theory to be interpretive, the question whether two truth theories constructed from equivalent reference schemes were both interpretive, if either was, would boil down to whether both were confirmable from the standpoint of a radical interpreter, if either was. This will depend on how narrowly we interpret confirmable from the standpoint of a radical interpreter. For the truth of the derived theory is guaranteed by that of the original, so if we have confirmed the original, we will be in a position to infer the derived theory, and to have as good a justification for thinking it true as the original, if we can actually confirm appropriate equivalences of the form [3]. But if we are to have any hope that empirical confirmability will suffice for interpretability, we should restrict the term 'empirically confirmed' to theories which are originally confirmed by direct application of the methods of the radical interpreter. If we so understand the restriction, however, we must also give up the permutation argument as a way of showing that reference is inscrutable, because theories constructed by this method will not be guaranteed to be empirically confirmable in the relevant sense.

The reasons advanced against indeterminacy of interpretation in Chapter 15 also apply here. It seems clear, for example, that an interpreter cannot regard truth conditions for an object language sentence as providing the same interpretation of the sentence, when the referents of the singular terms and extensions of the predicates are different. Thus, the interpreter must regard theories $\mathcal{T}$ and $\mathcal{T}'$, obtained from a reference scheme equivalent but non-identical with the one used for $\mathcal{T}$, as interpreting object language sentences differently, and cannot suppose both are right, except on the assumption that the content of the object language sentences is less 'fine-grained' than that of the metalanguage's sentences. As we have observed, this shows that the procedure of the radical interpreter cannot always recover all the semantic distinctions to be drawn in an object language because it would be unable to do so for the interpreter's language. That is, since it is possible for two people to speak the interpreter's language, but the interpreter could not recover from evidence distinctions in another's language that were as fine-grained as those in his own, it follows that the procedure of the radical interpreter cannot always recover the semantic distinctions in an object language.[293]

---

[293] It is important to note that our objection is not the most common one to the inscrutability of reference, namely, the appeal to a special relation which words by themselves are supposed to bear to objects in the world, which secures for them a determinate reference. We agree with Davidson that if you make the adequacy requirement on a correct theory weak enough, then no appeal to any such relation would be effective. For whatever the relation was, whether causal, or anything else, one could construct different theories which appeal to different relations between words and what they would be said to refer to, which would hold whenever the appropriate causal relation held between the object language word and some object or objects (at least, waiving the worry about whether we can find some appropriate relational term). For any relation we can state between a word and some

The appropriate conclusion to draw is that (2) is unsupportable, and, indeed, false.

4. Responses

We turn now to responses suggested by what Davidson has written, and to distinguish our criticism from others Davidson has considered.

One response is suggested in the following passage:

> The semantic features of language are public features. What no one can, in the nature of the case, figure out from the totality of the relevant evidence cannot be part of meaning. And since every speaker must, in some dim sense at least, know this, he cannot even intend to use his words with a unique reference, for he knows that there is no way for his words to convey this reference to another.   (Davidson 2001*a* (1979): 235)

The last sentence here is not central, and even seems to be in tension with the first, since it suggests a speaker at least understands what it would be to use a word with a unique reference—something Davidson cannot countenance. The central claim is the first: since meaning is necessarily public, if from public clues an interpreter cannot recover a supposed semantic feature of a speaker's words, there cannot be any such feature. Thus, if there is supposed to be a feature of a proper name, such as 'Gottlob Frege', as used by a speaker, which determines that it refers to Gottlob Frege, rather than Bertrand Russell or G. E. Moore, this can at best be a kind of illusion.

Put this way, the conclusion throws more doubt on the theory that leads to it than it does on our ability to refer to Frege, rather than Russell or Moore. We have discussed in part the suggestion that the public character of language may lead to startling conclusions about the nature of language and thought. We are willing to grant that if anyone speaks a language, then he is interpretable by some speaker in some environment. If there is no environment in which any speaker could be interpreted by any speaker so as to be referring uniquely, then we would have to give up the idea that unique reference is possible. But how this could be so is something we think no one has any clear grasp on.

Is it true that we have reason to think that no one could recover from public clues facts about what other speakers are referring to in a way that would rule out the inscrutability of reference? At most, what Davidson has shown

object, $R(\alpha, x)$, we look for a binary relation whose extension meets the following condition: for any x, $R(\alpha, x)$ iff $R'(\alpha, \psi(x))$.

is that this could not be done from the standpoint of the radical interpreter. The case for its being possible rests on the claim that none of us could be in a better position than the radical interpreter to interpret another. This, in turn, we have argued, rests on the assumption that linguistic and psychological concepts are theoretical. We have seen reason to doubt this assumption in a previous chapter. There remains the task of showing that we could have knowledge sufficient to interpret others in an appropriate environment. We postpone this task until the next chapter, and so leave the further defense of our argument here against the current line of objection until then.

A second response is to argue that the assignment of referents to a speaker's words on two interpretation theories with equivalent but non-identical reference schemes are not in conflict with one another because we have overlooked a crucial relativization. (2) may be maintained after all, once we take into account the relativization. (This should sound familiar: we considered a like response to our argument in Chapter 15 against the indeterminacy of interpretation.) In Davidson's hands, this claim of relativity is not that *ontology* is relative to a scheme of reference. As he says, if you can fix ontology, even if relative to a scheme of reference, for a language, there can be determinate facts about reference, once an arbitrary choice of relativization has been made. And this is something that Davidson denies can be done. What relativization Davidson thinks is allowable and needed is indicated in the following passages.

All that we can say gets fixed by the relativization is the way we answer questions about reference, not reference itself. So it seems to me the natural way to explain the sometimes needed explicit relativization is a familiar one: we take the speaker to be speaking one language or another. If we take his word 'rabbit' to refer to rabbits, we take him to be speaking one language. If we take his word 'rabbit' to refer to things that are ϕ of rabbits, we take him to be speaking another language. If we decide to change the reference scheme, we decide that he is speaking a different language. In some cases the decision is ours; some languages are identical in that their speakers' dispositions to utter sentences under specified conditions are identical. There is no way to tell which of these languages a person is speaking.   (Davidson 2001*a* (1979): 239)

There is, then, a reasonable way to relativize truth and reference: sentences are true, and words refer, relative to a language. This may appear to be a familiar and obvious point, and in a way it certainly is. But there are some subtleties in how we understand it. It is not, for example, an empirical claim that 'Wilt' refers to Wilt in *L*. For if this were empirical, *L* would have to be characterized as *the* language spoken by some person or persons at a given time. Such a characterization would not serve our purpose, since we admit that it is not entirely an empirical question what language a person speaks; the evidence allows us some choice in languages, even to the point of allowing us to assign conflicting truth conditions to the same sentence. But even if we consider truth invariant, we can suit the evidence by various ways of matching words and objects. The best way of announcing the way we have chosen is by naming the language; but then we must characterize the language as one for which reference, satisfaction, and truth have been assigned specific roles. An empirical question remains, to be sure: is this language one that the evidence allows us to attribute to this speaker? (ibid. 240)

We must think of the interpreter's claims about the meanings of a speaker's words as relativized to a language. Then it will be true, on one theory, that the speaker's word 'Gottlob Frege', for example, does not refer to Bertrand Russell, but to Gottlob Frege. And it will be true, on a different theory, that his word 'Gottlob Frege' refers to Bertrand Russell. But the theories will not be inconsistent, because they will be relativized to different languages. The claim then is that it is indeterminate which of these languages the speaker speaks.

This provides no refuge from the problem we have just presented, which is that, from the interpreter's point of view, different, conflicting claims are being made about the speaker's words. For the theories are being used to give interpretations of the speaker's words, and they give different interpretations. The interpreter can make sense of each being equally good only by thinking of the speaker's language as not being as rich as his own. For the interpreter can clearly distinguish between these different languages. He knows that the referents in one are not the same as the referents in the other. His language therefore is rich enough to distinguish between them. He cannot therefore regard his own language as subject to the same indeterminacy that he is supposed to think of his subject's language as being subject to. But then it cannot be a fact about languages possessed by people as such that reference is inscrutable.

Consider also our position as theorizers. We are supposed to understand talk of these languages to which reference is being relativized. We are supposed to understand that they have words with semantic properties which determine uniquely the referents of words and extensions of predicates. But languages have no lives independently of communities of people who use them, and we can surely make no sense of semantic properties which we cannot understand to arise out of the use of a language by a linguistic community. So if we so much as understand the relativization that Davidson talks about here, which we surely do, then we do understand what it is for a word someone uses to refer uniquely, and we know that if Davidson's argument is valid, it cannot be sound. The difficulty that Davidson's relativization runs into is similar to the difficulty Davidson raises for Quine's thesis of ontological relativity. Davidson objected to Quine that if we can fix the referents of terms relative to anything, then there can be a fact of the matter about what expressions refer to. This is still so if what we relativize to are languages.

A final topic we want to consider is the question whether some defense of the inscrutability of reference can be found in the thought that the concepts of reference and satisfaction are understood only relative to their contributions in the context of a truth theory to the truth conditions of sentences. Let us grant that we do not understand reference and satisfaction apart from their contribution to truth conditions. Nothing follows from this about the inscrutability of reference. For the relevant notion of truth conditions here is interpretive truth conditions. Thus, the relevant notion of reference and satisfaction is interpretive reference and satisfaction. An argument to the inscrutability of reference would have to first show that different assignments of reference and satisfaction conditions to primitive non-recursive terms did not lead to differences in the interpretiveness of truth conditions thereby generated. Such claims would have to be argued for independently of any claims about the interconnection of the concepts of truth, meaning, reference, and satisfaction.

5. Conclusion

We conclude, pending only the next chapter in this part, that the permutation argument for inscrutability fails, both because it should be regarded by Davidson as not meeting constraints on a truth theory's being interpretive he has himself laid down, and because it fails to introduce any new considerations to blunt our earlier arguments against indeterminacy.

22

Language, Thought, and World

...the acquisition of knowledge is not based on a progression from the subjective to the objective; it emerges holistically, and is interpersonal from the start.

(Davidson 1991: abstract, p. 191)

The solipsist's world can be any size; which is to say, from the solipsist's point of view it has no size, it is not a world.

(Davidson 2001 (1992): 119)

In this last chapter of Part III, we are concerned principally with the question what support can be found in Davidson's work for what we have called his most fundamental assumption, namely, that we can properly treat psychological and linguistic concepts as theoretical concepts whose purpose is to enable us to systematize and keep track of behavior neutrally described— or, to put it another way, the assumption that the third person stance, as embodied by the stance of the radical interpreter, is conceptually basic in understanding meaning and psychological attitudes.[294] If it can be shown that the third person stance is conceptually basic in understanding meaning and psychological attitudes, we would have good reason to suppose that the

---

[294] By 'the third person stance', or 'the third person point of view', we mean our conception of a shared perspective on a common public world. Following many, we call it the 'third person' point of view to emphasize the fundamental role of others in our understanding of it. To say that such a point of view is fundamental or basic is to say that our conception of ourselves as occupying other perspectives on the world—and here the primary contrast is the first person perspective—depends on our thinking of ourselves as already occupying the third person perspective. In other words, if the third person perspective is primary, we cannot have (or think of ourselves as having) a first person perspective on our own thoughts, except in so far as we already have (or think of ourselves as having) a perspective on a public world shared with others.

apparently intractable problems we have found for radical interpretation can be circumvented, even if we do not yet see in detail how to do it. This would also force on the philosophical tradition a fundamental reorientation. Thus, the arguments we examine in this section are of crucial importance for the overall evaluation of Davidson's position, as well as our understanding of methodology in philosophy in general. On matters as large and fundamental as these, we do not expect to have a final say. Our object is to evaluate the state of the game as best we can up to this point.

We noted in Chapter 18 that the observation that language is a medium or tool for communication is not enough to secure without further argument a sufficiently strong form of the publicness of language to support Davidson's program. The difficulty is to show two things. The first is that speaking requires being interpretable by any possible speaker in any possible environment. The second is that the basic concepts of interpretation theory have their content exhausted by their role in tracking behavior. It looks as if these theses will stand or fall together.

The reason that the requirement that language be conceived of as enabling speakers to communicate with one another is too weak is that this conception of language is compatible with the enabling conditions being met only in some circumstances, with respect to some kinds of speakers. This leaves open the possibility of radical error about one's environment, and for significantly differing (though not completely, if our earlier arguments are correct) conceptual schemes. It also leaves open the possibility of taking the first person standpoint as epistemically basic in thinking about our knowledge of our own minds, the external world, and the minds of others. To put it another way, even the protagonist of Descartes's "First Meditation" could accept that language is public in the sense that, in an appropriate environment, faced with another member of his linguistic community (or someone enough alike him as to be apt to think about and desire, at bottom, similar sorts of things), he could be interpreted by him (and justifiably so, contingent on a general solution to the problem of knowledge of the external world).

This issue of the public nature of facts about meaning and propositional attitudes is connected with another of considerable importance, namely, the question whether language is required for thought.

We have already seen the assumption that language is necessary for thought at work in a number of Davidson's arguments. For example, in the argument against the possibility of a plurality of radically different conceptual schemes, we assumed that a conceptual scheme could be identified with a set of inter-translatable languages, which assumes that only linguistic beings have conceptual schemes. In the argument for the impossibility of massive error, the conclusion that belief is by its nature largely true clearly rests on the assumption that belief is by its nature linguistic. The explanation of first person authority rested on appeal to an asymmetry in knowledge of meanings: this cannot be the right explanation for why thinkers have a special knowledge of their own thoughts, except in so far as all thinkers are speakers of a language.

Indeed, the assumption that only speakers of a language are thinkers *must* be in the background in any argument that aims to proceed from assumptions a radical interpreter must make to conclusions about the nature of the propositional attitudes. For if there can be non-linguistic beings who have propositional attitudes, then conclusions reached on the basis of what must be assumed about linguistic beings in order to interpret them would not extend to non-linguistic beings, and, hence, could not be characterized as revealing anything about the nature of beliefs, etc., as such. Furthermore, if the conclusions reached can at best be seen as restricted to linguistic beings, those conclusions themselves will be in danger of being undermined. For the question would arise why, if our conception of belief and other attitudes is independent of what it is to speak a language, and so independent of interpretation, we should conceive of the standpoint of interpretation as the sole standpoint from which to understand our beliefs, and other attitudes, even as linguistic beings. Why insist so strongly, for example, on the possibility of being interpreted from the standpoint of the radical interpreter, which underlies the strong results about the nature of our beliefs that Davidson reaches? The question of the relation between language and thought is of central importance, however, for another reason also, for one of Davidson's arguments for language being essential to thought, which relates the possibility of thought to actual communication, *if successful*, would at the same time support a very strong version of language being necessarily public, and would support the main premise of the argument for the primacy of the third person point of view.

We will trace the following route through these issues (the relations between the arguments we discuss are illustrated in Figure 4). We begin first with the main arguments for the necessity of language for thought, the *argument from holism* (A) and the *argument from the concept of belief* (B), respectively. The first argues that only the complex pattern of behavior found in linguistic communication suffices to ground attributions of complexes of propositional attitudes to beings. The second argues that a condition on having belief is that one have the concept of belief, and a condition on this in turn is that one possess a language. (A) is inconclusive. We turn to supporting arguments for the each of the main premises of (B).

389

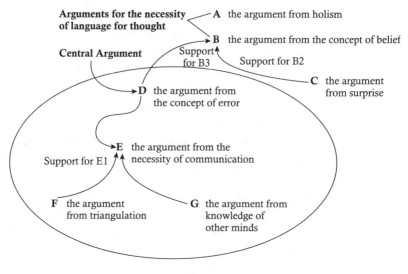

Figure 4

The first argument for the main premises of the argument from the concept of belief, the *argument from surprise* (C), seeks to support the connection between having beliefs and having the concept of belief by appeal to the requirement that one have the capacity for surprise for belief, and the concept of belief for the capacity for surprise. While we fault the argument, we grant the conclusion on other grounds.

The second argument for the main premises of the argument from the concept of belief, the *argument from the concept of error* (D), is of central importance. It seeks to support the claim that one can have the concept of a belief only if one possesses a language. It argues that in, but only in, the context of communication is there scope for the application of the concept of error, without which one cannot have the concept, but also that the concept of error is a condition on having beliefs. The form of argument, if successful, secures the necessity of language for thought, but also something stronger, namely that actual communication (present or past) is a precondition on having the concept of belief. This leads to the conclusion that the third person stance is methodologically and conceptually fundamental (*the argument from the necessity of communication* (E)). The argument from the concept of error may be fairly called a transcendental argument for the necessity of communication for thought because it seeks to establish that communication is a precondition for thought, that is, that in the absence of conditions which enable actual communication, it is not possible for there to be thought. If successful, it also

390

constitutes part of a transcendental argument for the primacy of the third person point of view: we must treat the third person point of view as fundamental, as a condition on making sense of the possibility of any thought at all. We argue, however, that the argument from error is not successful. It suffers from a traditional weakness of transcendental arguments, namely, that it is difficult to see why the conditions required for the possession of a relevant mode of representation—here the concept of error—cannot be satisfied subjectively, rather than objectively. That is to say, arguments which aim to show that deploying certain concepts correctly is a necessary condition of thought or consciousness must show that their deployment in thought involves actually bringing their objects under them rather than its just seeming so to their possessors. In addition, it is doubtful whether the specific conditions Davidson suggests are necessary for having the concept of belief, such as the capacity to be surprised, are, in fact, required.

We turn, then, to consider a different kind of argument that has appeared in recent work of Davidson's, which we call *the argument from triangulation* (F). The notion of triangulation between speakers and a common object of thought is employed as an analogy by Davidson, illustrating his transcendental argument, as early as "Rational Animals" (2001*b* (1982)). However, what we are calling 'the argument from triangulation' makes a different use of the idea; it attempts to establish that communication is a necessary condition on solving the problem of making sense of what a thought could be about. If successful, it also promises to provide a response to the objections advanced in Chapter 15 that too much indeterminacy is permitted by the constraints upon the radical interpreter's project. This argument, however, presupposes the primacy of the third person point of view, rather than providing independent support for it. In addition, we argue that, even granting that assumption, it fails to solve the problem it sets itself.

Finally, we turn to another form of argument that we think can be detected in Davidson's work, which presents acceptance of the primacy of the third person point of view as the only possible solution to the problem of our knowledge of other minds (G). We argue that this has not been adequately supported.

In concluding, we step back from the details of the arguments to consider the position Davidson reaches, which emphasizes the interconnection between our knowledge of our own minds, the minds of others, and the external world; the interest and importance of his position is not necessarily undermined, if his arguments are not conclusive. Its profoundly anti-Cartesian stance illuminates possibilities for understanding our epistemic position in the world which are themselves of great importance. It may be that on issues as fundamental as these, no wholly persuasive and non-question-begging arguments will be available, and that the choice between different stances must be made on the basis of holistic criteria, that is, considerations about how well (though imperfectly) each position accommodates the weighted totality of our pre-analytic beliefs.

1. The Main Arguments for the Necessity of Language for Thought

Davidson has at least two arguments for thinking that non-linguistic beings are incapable of thought. The first, while in a way a warm-up for the second, is interesting in its own right, and is connected with important themes in our discussion of radical interpretation. The argument focuses on the contrast between the holistic nature of attitude attribution, and the kind of evidence available for the attribution of attitudes in the absence of verbal behavior.

A. The argument from holism

(A1)   Beliefs and other propositional attitudes are ascribable only in dense networks of such attitudes.

(A2)   Attributing a dense network of propositional attitudes to another requires for support a rich pattern of behavior that gives substance to the attributions.[295]

(A3)   The pattern of behavior required cannot be exhibited in the absence of verbal behavior interpretable as speech acts.

(A4)   Therefore, only linguistic animals can have propositional attitudes.

---

[295] Assumptions (A1) and (A2) are central to Davidson's view of the nature of the attitudes. This comes out, e.g., in "Rational Animals" (2001*b* (1982)) and in "The Method of Truth in Metaphysics" (2001*a* (1977)). Support for attributing the third assumption to Davidson can be found in "Rational Animals" (2001*b* (1982): 98): "If we really can intelligibly ascribe single beliefs to a dog, we must be able to imagine how we would decide whether the dog has many other beliefs of the kind necessary for making sense of the first. It seems to me that no matter where we start, we very soon come to beliefs such that we have no idea at all how to tell whether a dog has them, and yet such that, without them, our confident first attribution looks shaky." And: "a very complex pattern of behavior must be observed to justify the attribution of a single thought. . . . I think there is such a pattern only if the agent has language" (ibid. 100). See also (Davidson 2004 (2001)), e.g., "a creature with propositional attitudes is equipped to fit a new concept into a complex scheme in which concepts have logical and other relations to one another. Speechless creatures lack the conceptual framework which supports propositional attitudes" (p. 137); these considerations are also tied in with what it is to have the concept of error (e.g., p. 141).

The argument is, in the nature of the case, rather inconclusive, as Davidson recognizes. If the premises are true, so is the conclusion. The problem lies in sustaining premise (A3). One can easily feel sympathy for the thought that there is something arbitrary about saying that Rover thinks the cat went up that tree, rather than saying that Rover thinks the furred quadruped scurried up an oak. What further behavior Rover could display that would distinguish between the two attributions, or any number of others, is mysterious. Yet, there *is* a pattern of activity that seems to be captured *equally well* by any of these, but not by, say, attributing to Rover the belief that the cat disappeared into thin air. Indeed, *here* is a likely place to apply Davidson's favored analogy for explaining the indeterminacy of interpretation: like the different scales we could use in measuring temperature, the different belief sentences we use to keep track of Rover's behavior (each requiring a supporting pattern of related ascriptions) all equally well capture the phenomenon that interests us, which is different from saying that no phenomenon of the kind is of interest at all. What the indeterminacy suggests is that the particular concepts we employ in attributing beliefs to one another are richer in content and structure than any which we could legitimately attribute to a dog or any other non-linguistic animal. Since we do not have ready-made words which express concepts of the requisite grain, we perforce use our own, which necessarily overdescribe the contents of Rover's attitudes. There is no reason in *this* to suppose that he has no attitudes at all, but only that our sentences are not tailored to capture exactly their truth conditions. (This is essentially the line of thought taken up in Jeffrey 1985.)

In any case, Davidson does not rest the burden of his position on (A), perhaps for reasons similar to those given. His primary argument for language being essential to thought proceeds rather through reflection on what is required to have beliefs, namely, the concept of belief, and, in turn, the concepts of truth, error and objectivity, and on what is required to have these concepts.[296]

B. The argument from the concept of belief

(B1)   One can have propositional attitudes (thoughts) only if one has beliefs.

(B2)   One can have beliefs only if one has the concept of belief [C].

(B3)   One can have the concept of belief only if one has a language [D].

---

[296] See Davidson 2001*b* (1982): 102–6 and 2001 (1975): 170.

> (B4)   Therefore, one can have propositional attitudes (thoughts) only if one has a language.

The argument for the first of these premises is that propositional attitudes, such as beliefs, desires and intentions, are understood as attitudes of a being capable of expressing agency. This requires that the attitudes it has be interrelated in kind and content. Agency is expressed in action, and actions are, in the standard case, the results of intentions, which are rationalized by the agent's desires and his beliefs about how to satisfy his desires in action. Belief and desire are basic in the sense that other propositional attitudes are understood at least in part in relation to these. For example, hope involves (at least) a desire for what is hoped for and a belief that it is not actual; fear involves a desire that what is feared not obtain and (typically) a belief that it does or might, and so on. Since belief and desire underlie other attitudes, and belief is necessary along with desire in any agent, someone can have any propositional attitude only if he has beliefs. The issue lies with the second and third premises, (B2) and (B3).[297]

2. The Argument for the Claim that Having Beliefs Requires Having the Concept of Belief

Davidson offers an argument for (B2) in "Rational Animals."[298]

C. The argument from surprise

> (C1)   One can have a general stock of beliefs only if one can be surprised.

---

[297] However, for a more skeptical view of the question whether (B1) is in good standing, see Fodor and Lepore 1992.

[298] The relevant passage is 2001*b* (1982): 104: "Surprise requires that I be aware of a contrast between what I did believe and what I come to believe. Such awareness, however, is a belief about a belief: if I am surprised, then among other things I come to believe that my original belief was false. I do not need to insist that every case of surprise involves a belief that a prior belief was false . . . What I do want to claim is that one cannot have a general stock of beliefs of the sort necessary for having any beliefs at all without being subject to surprises that involve beliefs about the correctness of one's own beliefs. Surprise about some things is a necessary and sufficient condition of thought in general. This concludes the first part of my 'argument'." Davidson appears to offer a reason distinct from, if closely related to, this in "Thought and Talk": "Someone cannot have a belief unless he understands the possibility of being mistaken, and this requires grasping the contrast between truth and error— true belief and false belief" (2001 (1975): 170). This is slightly less committed than premise (C1), but, like (C1), it seems scarcely less at issue than the conclusion which it transparently embeds.

(C2) One can be surprised (that is, come to realize that one or more of one's beliefs (expectations) was not correct) only if one has the concept of belief.

(C3) Therefore, one can have beliefs only if one has the concept of belief [B2].

The questionable premise is (C1). For it can be granted that to be surprised about the correctness of one's own beliefs is in part to think that one's beliefs were false, and so requires that one have the concept of belief. But why do we have any more reason to think that one can have a general stock of beliefs only if one can be surprised than we do to think that one can have any thoughts or beliefs at all only if one has the concept of belief? It is sometimes said, for example, by child psychologists, that children (who have already acquired some language) pass through a developmental stage in which they are unable to recognize that they have had false beliefs (Gopnik and Astington 1988; Perner *et al.* 1987). If so, they are equally incapable of being surprised (at least in the relevant sense). We seem then straightforwardly to have evidence that they do not have beliefs, *if* that requires being capable of being surprised. And, then, if Davidson were right, they would have no propositional attitudes at all. Yet, this is vastly implausible in these cases, for the children have in fact already acquired some language mastery, and it is by asking them questions that psychologists have arrived at the view that they do not recognize that they have had false beliefs.

The second premise of (B) stands in need of support because it is not obvious that attributing beliefs to someone requires thinking of him as having the concept of belief. It is hard to see how the support offered by (C) advances the case, for it is no more obvious that attributing beliefs to someone requires thinking of him as being capable of being surprised. Imagine, for a moment, an omniscient being. By hypothesis he has beliefs, but he is obviously incapable of being surprised. If anything, the supporting argument seems to take us further from our goal.

The goal is attainable, however, if we reflect on what is required simply by identifying something as an agent, that is, as capable of acting intentionally. This we have already admitted is necessary, if one is to have any attitudes at all, and belief in particular. If we can show that nothing is an agent that lacks the concept of belief, we will have shown that nothing can have a belief without the concept of belief. The argument for this goes as follows.

To have belief is to be an agent. To be an agent is to be capable of acting. To be capable of acting, one must be able to have intentions, and one's beliefs and desires must be coordinated in the right way to provide rationalizations of one's potential actions. In particular, since rationalizations require thinking of the relation between potential actions and their consequences, they require agents to be capable of forming beliefs with contents of the form,

If I do A, then p.

However, the antecedent clearly expresses the concept of action. So, to engage in the means–end reasoning which is the characteristic pattern of rationalization, an agent must have the concept of an action. The concept of an action, however, is closely bound up with that of intention, belief, and desire; no one without these concepts could have the concept of an action. Thus, anyone capable of acting intentionally, that is, any agent, must have, *inter alia*, the concept of belief.

We find an alternative route to the same conclusion through reflection on the nature of intention, for intention contains a self-referential element. If one intends to serve a rarebit, it is not enough for one to have carried out one's intention that one do something which results in one's serving a rarebit. Rather, one must serve a rarebit as an intentional result of intending to do so. The satisfaction conditions of attitudes must be represented in their contents, however, so the content of the intention must be represented by the agent (minimally) as follows:

I intend that I serve a rarebit as a result of this intention to do so.

But this requires that the subject have the concept of intention, and one can have the concept of intention only if one has the concepts of belief, desire, and action. Thus, we are led by another argument to the same conclusion: one cannot be an agent without having the concepts of belief and other related propositional attitudes.

If this is right, it requires us to make sense of attributing to non-linguistic animals like dogs the concepts of action, belief, desire, intention, and the like. It may seem doubtful to many that it is legitimate to do so. It is not, however, obvious that it is incoherent. Given how we have argued for the necessity of having the concept of belief, action, desire, intention, and the like, it is clear that whatever evidence one has that non-linguistic animals are acting intentionally is equally evidence that they possess the relevant concepts, at least in some rudimentary form—whatever is required for conceiving of them as instantiating the right patterns of explanatory attitudes toward their own actions.

3. The Argument for the Claim that to Have the Concept of Belief One Must Have a Language

The burden of argument (B) comes down, then, to the third premise (B3). We reconstruct the argument as follows.[299]

D. The argument from the concept of error

(D1)   To have the concept of a belief, one must have the concept of error, or, what is the same thing, of objective truth (that is, a way things are independent of how one believes them to be).

This is to say that having the concept of belief is having the concept of a state which is capable of being true or false; to understand this is to understand the contrast between the merely subjective, what one merely believes, and how things really are, the objective world; when the former "matches" the latter, one's beliefs are true, otherwise false.

---

[299] We draw here on a number of sources, but principally "Thought and Talk" (Davidson 2001 (1975)), "Rational Animals" (2001*b* (1982)), "Three Varieties of Knowledge" (2001*b* (1988)), and "The Myth of the Subjective" (2001*a* (1988)). Here, e.g., are the relevant passages from "Rational Animals": "Much of the point of the concept of belief is that it is the concept of a state of an organism which can be true or false, correct or incorrect. To have the concept of belief is therefore to have the concept of objective truth" (p. 104). Now, we demand that we find in behavior some reason to suppose that a creature has the concept of belief, or, more particularly, is capable of being surprised. "What *would* show command of this contrast [i.e., of the possibility of false belief, belief which represents the world one way, when it is another]? Clearly linguistic communication suffices. To understand the speech of another, I must be able to think of the same things she does; I must share her world. I don't have to agree with her in all matters, but in order to disagree we must entertain the same propositions, with the same subject matter, and the same concept of truth. Communication depends on each communicant having, and correctly thinking that the other has, the concept of a shared world, an intersubjective world. But the concept of an intersubjective world is the concept of an objective world, a world about which each communicant can have beliefs. I suggest, then, that the concept of intersubjective truth suffices as a basis for belief and hence for thoughts generally. And perhaps it is plausible enough that having the concept of intersubjective truth depends on communication in the full linguistic sense. To complete the 'argument', however, I need to show that the *only* way one could come to have the belief-truth contrast is through having the concept of intersubjective truth. I confess I do not know how to show this. But neither do I have any idea how else one could arrive at the concept of an objective truth" (p. 105). For this argument sketch to succeed, we must require that something show in a being's behavior command of the concept, to make sense of its possessing it (premise (D2) in the text). In the passage quoted here, Davidson says that communication suffices (premise (D3)), but, though he says it is the only way he can see for command of the concept of belief to be exhibited, he does not commit himself to its being necessary. In a later paper, however, Davidson makes the claim of necessity (premise (D4)): "Only communication can provide the concept, for to have the concept of objectivity . . . requires that we are aware of the fact that we share thoughts and a world with others" (2001 (1991): 202).

> (D2)   The claim that a creature possesses the concept of error, or object-
> ive truth, stands in need of grounding, that is, we need some
> account of how a creature is able to have such a concept, what
> conditions must be in place in order for the creature to have it: this
> must take the form of explaining how there could be scope in the
> creature's behavior or experience for application of the concept.

Although this premise is never made explicit by Davidson, the demand it
expresses is presupposed by the argument sketch he gives. We will say more
about this in the comment on the next two premises, (D3) and (D4).

> (D3)   We can understand how a creature who was in communication
> with other creatures could have the concept of error, as a tool
> used in interpretation to achieve a better rational fit of a speaker's
> behavior to the evidence we have for his beliefs and meanings; that
> is, the concept would have some work to do (it would have some
> scope for application) for interpreters of others' speech.
>
> (D4)   There is scope for the application of the concept of objective truth
> in a creature's behavior or experience only if it is (or has been) in
> communication with others.

These two premises are the core of the argument. Premise (D3) tells us that
there is scope for the application of the concepts of truth and error for creatures
who are in communication with one another. We wish to see our interlocutors
as rational as possible; too much deviance from norms of rationality undercuts our ability to see others as agents at all. Often, we can make out others
to be rational only by supposing that they have false, though, from their perspective, well-justified beliefs. Much of what we do would not make sense on
the assumption that we had full information about our environments and the
consequences of our actions. Then premise (D4) tells us that there is scope
for the application of the concepts of truth and error *only* in the context of
communication. Thus, (D3) tells us there is one way, (D4) that there is no
other. (Strictly speaking, (D3) is not needed for the argument; but it evidently
serves as part of the motivation for (D4).) We can see here the importance
of (D2): for given that we need to give a ground for the possession of the
concept, which is to be looked for in its having a role to play in the activities of
the creature who possesses it, if the only kind of activity which could support
a role for it were communication, no creature who was not a communicant
would possess the concept.

(D5) Therefore, from (D2)–(D4), to have the concept of error or objective truth one must be (or have been) in communication with others.

To require that one actually be in communication with others to have the concept of truth or error is obviously too strong. Although Davidson sometimes seems to state the conclusion this strongly, it is clear that he intends the weaker conclusion (and, in any case, nothing he wishes to rest on the conclusion requires anything stronger). This conclusion still might be thought to be stronger than warranted, even granting that communication is conceptually central to the concept of objectivity, or true and false belief. We will return to this question below.

(D6) Therefore, from (D1) and (D5), to have the concept of belief, one must have a language, and be (or have been) in communication with others [i.e. B3].

This, together with the assumption that to have belief, one must have the concept of belief, gets us to the conclusion that to have belief, one must be or have been in communication with another; and since all thought requires belief, every thinker must be a communicant.

4. The Argument to the Primacy of the Third Person Point of View

If this is right, then it promises an answer to the question how we can provide a priori support for the presupposition of radical interpretation, namely, that one can arrive at a justified interpretation from the epistemic standpoint of the radical interpreter, and the assumption implicit in the presupposition, namely, that psychological and linguistic concepts are theoretical concepts whose contents are exhausted by their roles in accounting for behavior. The argument would proceed as follows.

E. The argument from the necessity of communication

(E1) Necessarily, every thinker is in communication, or has been in communication and potentially is in communication, with others.

(E2) Therefore, necessarily, every thinker is interpretable in any environment in which he is located, by any other speaker.

(E3) Therefore, radical interpretation is possible, and the only content that can be given to psychological and linguistic concepts is provided by their role in accounting for behavior, in the context of a theory of interpretation formulated from the third person standpoint.

This is not an argument that Davidson has given explicitly. But it represents a plausible way of connecting the considerations put forward in argument (D), and in other arguments, (F) and (G) below, with his basic methodological assumption. Our main concern will be with whether adequate justification is provided for (E1) by argument (D). Before we turn to that, however, it is worth noting that we have put (E2) in a particularly strong form. This is needed to guarantee success at radical interpretation. However, it is more than can be supported by (E1), which does not require that one be interpretable by any other speaker (only some), and does not require that one be interpretable in any environment (only that one be or have been correctly interpreted in some). So, there is a sense in which the result still falls short of what Davidson needs, even granting the soundness of argument (D). Still, it would guarantee a form of the primacy of the third person standpoint, since it would require us to think of it being a condition on our being thinking beings that we be or have been in communication with others about a shared world.

5. Evaluating Argument (D)

We turn now to evaluation of argument (D). Premise (D2), repeated here, is central.

(D2) The claim that a creature possesses the concept of error, or objective truth, stands in need of grounding, that is, we need some account of how a creature is able to have such a concept, what conditions must be in place in order for the creature to have it: this must take the form of explaining how there could be scope in the creature's behavior or experience for application of the concept.

Its justification is as follows. To think of any creature as having a certain concept is to think of it as deploying the concept in thought. But to think of the creature as deploying the concept in thought is to think of the creature's range of activities as requiring or providing proper scope for the deployment of the concept. Thus, any attribution of a concept to a creature requires a grounding in the following sense: it must be possible to conceive of the creature as engaging in a range of activities which gives play to the concept in question.

There is a strong and weak interpretation of this open to us. The strong interpretation holds that thinking of the creature as deploying a concept requires thinking of it as *correctly* deploying it in some of its activities, in the sense of applying it correctly to objects. On the strong interpretation, to deploy correctly the concept of a spatial object, for example, would require there to be spatial objects of which one thinks correctly that they are spatial objects. This is the objective application of the concept. The weak interpretation holds that thinking of the creature as deploying a concept requires thinking of it as engaging in patterns of thought, some of whose contents involve the concept, which give point to the deployment of the concept *from the thinker's point of view*. On the weak interpretation, it must only seem to the thinker that he deploys the concept correctly in application to objects, not that he actually apply it correctly to any object. This is the subjective application of the concept. The difference is important, as we will see. It corresponds to the distinction between the third and first person point of view.

We turn to premises (D3) and (D4). It is easy to grant premise (D3). It seems clear that communication involves not merely the concept of belief, but of meaning, intention, action, desire, language, communication, and a rich pattern of other psychological and linguistic concepts. The particular application Davidson emphasizes arises from the usefulness of the contrast between belief and truth, which allows the interpreter to sometimes count a speaker wrong, in order to provide overall a smoother interpretation of his words, and to make better sense of him as a rational being. The most problematic premise is (D4).

There are two difficulties we wish to highlight. The first is why we should suppose that scope for the application of the contrast between true and false belief should be provided only in the context of communication. It seems sufficient for the range of a creature's activities to give rise to the application of the contrast that its activities give rise to the possibility of error. What is required is simply that we describe some activity an agent could engage in which would involve making mistakes, but not involve essentially communication. It is clear that, in asking what grounds the attribution of the concept to a creature, we are not asking for a story about how the creature could acquire the concept. It would be beside the point to ask for a brute causal story. And it could not be a request for a story about how a creature with beliefs could acquire the concept of error by engaging in certain sorts of activities. For the aim of the argument is to show that without the concept of error, and so the concept of belief, one cannot have beliefs at all. What we want is a description of an activity which gives point to the application of the concept of error. But once put like this, it seems easy to specify contexts in which there would be a point to deploying the concept of error which do not involve communication.

First, to put it in the vein Davidson does, the usefulness of the contrast between true and false belief can be seen to lie in part in our ability to provide an overall smoother account of the nature of the world around us by sometimes attributing false beliefs *to our past selves*. Accustomed to the persistence of solid objects, one glances at a table and comes to believe there is a book lying there. Looking up moments later, one sees nothing there where one had thought there was a book. One may achieve a smaller overall adjustment of one's theory of the world by supposing that one was mistaken the first time around, rather than supposing solid objects go out of existence without explanation.

Second, looking to others, we can see a similar utility in the context of explaining action, without having to imagine the possibility of communication. Provided that we can recognize that others have attitudes without supposing them to be speakers (the point at issue), we will sometimes be better able to make sense of them as rational agents by supposing their beliefs mistaken. Take the case of the dog barking up the wrong tree. Without the contrast between true and false beliefs, we are at a loss to make sense of the dog's behavior, given that we believe that the cat is up the elm and not the oak tree. Taking the dog to have false beliefs restores his sanity and our sense of order. If we understand how communication is supposed to give scope to the application of objective truth, it is hard to see why theory construction and action explanation do not provide just as much scope and point for its application.

Third, the contrast between true and false belief can also have a role to play in purely theoretical reflection. In thinking over a proposed solution to a problem in geometry or a proof in number theory, one may come to believe that one made a mistaken inference, or employed a false principle, because, for example, one sees that it is incompatible with something else one regards as more certain. Thus, it seems dubious that communication is the only context in which there is scope for the application of the concept of error.

Putting this point aside, another, more general, difficulty faces any strategy like Davidson's that attempts to move from observations about the conditions under which we can have certain concepts to objective features of the world. Both the strategy and the difficulty are familiar. The novelty lies in Davidson's application. To see the difficulty, we can remind ourselves of the strategy's application in a different context, Strawson's transcendental argument in *Individuals* for knowledge of an external reality (Strawson 1959). The broadly Kantian argument proceeds (in outline) by trying to show that a condition for the possibility of experience is that we deploy concepts of objects in experience. Even granting the soundness of the argument, however, its conclusion falls short of establishing that we ever bring actual objects under our concepts: what is established is, rather, that we must think of ourselves as deploying the concept of an object, and must deploy it to have any experience at all. The point at which this issue arises in the above argument is in the interpretation of premise (D2). It is the strong interpretation Davidson needs. However, it is hard to see that any intuitive consideration justifies more than the weak one. On the weak interpretation, however, at most, Davidson could get the conclusion that we must think of ourselves in communication with others in order to have the concept of belief, truth, and objectivity. Even if there were scope for the correct application of the concept only in the context of actual communication, if possession of the concept requires only thinking of oneself as being in a situation in which the application of the concept has a point, we could not conclude that we have ever actually been in communication with others from knowledge that we possess the concepts of belief, truth, and objectivity. A gap remains between thinking of ourselves as being in communication with others and actually being so.

We conclude that the case has not been made for the necessity of communication for thought; therefore, even were the argument (E) for the possibility of radical interpretation valid, the case would not have been made for its premises.

At the end of "Rational Animals," Davidson offers the following analogy:

> If I were bolted to the earth, I would have no way of determining the distance from me of many objects. I would only know they were on some line drawn from me toward them. I might interact successfully with objects, but I could have no way of giving content to the question where they were. Not being bolted down, I am free to triangulate. Our sense of objectivity is the consequence of another sort of triangulation, one that requires two creatures. Each interacts with an object, but what gives each the concept of the way things are objectively is the base line formed between the creatures by language. The fact that they share a concept of truth alone makes sense of the claim that they have beliefs, that they are able to assign objects a place in the public world. (2001*b* (1982): 105)

The analogy is between two things: (i) how the possibility of observing an object from two positions a known distance apart gives content to the idea of its distance from one and (ii) how the possibility of observing another who is observing the same object we observe gives content to the idea of objective truth. Essential to Davidson's argument is that only this could give rise to the idea of objective truth. It is this to which we have mainly objected. To recur to the analogy, the richness of the conceptual system in which the concept of distance plays a role gives rise to the possibility of the application of the concept even from the point of view of a stationary observer. For if objects move relative to oneself, one can give substance to the idea of distance as well as if one moves oneself. Similarly, the conceptual system in which the concept of truth plays a role can occasion the possibility of the application of the concept even in the absence of supposing oneself in communication with another, in adjusting theory to new information, adjusting for consistency, and in accounting for the behavior of others even in the absence of their speaking.

6. The Argument from Triangulation

The idea of triangulation has appeared in another context in Davidson's work, which it will be appropriate to turn to now. In the argument for the necessity of language for thought, the idea of triangulation is essentially that of the context of communication: each of two individuals (at least) find themselves responding to the same object and to each other, thereby forming a triangle, where, as Davidson says, the base line is the communication between them. Whether or not it is only in this context that the idea of objective truth, or error or belief, can arise, this triangulation is essential to communication, and Davidson has employed the observation to argue from a different point of view for the conclusion that every speaker is, or has been, in communication with other speakers. While Davidson does not always cleanly separate the two arguments, it is clear that they must be taken separately.

Here is how Davidson puts the thought at one point:

Without this sharing of reactions to common stimuli, thought and speech would have no particular content—that is, no content at all. It takes two points of view to give a location to the cause of a thought, and thus to define its content. We may think of it as a form of triangulation: each of two people is reacting differentially to sensory stimuli streaming in from a certain direction. Projecting the incoming lines outward, the common cause is at their intersection. If the two people now note each others' reactions (in the case of language, verbal reactions), each can correlate these observed reactions with his or her stimuli from the world. A common cause has been determined. The triangle which gives content to thought and speech is complete. But it takes two to triangulate. (2001*b*: 212–13)

Again:

Adding a second person . . . narrows down the relevant cause to the nearest cause common to two agents who are triangulating the cause by jointly observing an object and each other's reactions. The two observers don't share neural firings or incoming photons; the nearest thing they share is the object prompting both to react in ways the other can note.   (2004 (2001): 142–3)

This triangulation is illustrated in Figure 5. The reason the triangulation is crucial—that is, the interpreter perceiving the speaker as having similar responses to what he (the interpreter) perceives as similar in the environment— is that without this, we could not give enough content to the idea that the speaker had some particular object as the object of his thought. We could not, for example, decide whether the speaker was responding to a proximal or distal stimulus, or which distal stimulus.

Davidson says,

if I am right, the kind of triangulation I have described, while not sufficient to establish that a creature has a concept of a particular object or kind of object, is necessary if there is to be any answer at all to the question what its concepts are concepts of. If we consider a single creature by itself, its responses, no matter how complex, cannot show that it is reacting to, or thinking about, events a certain distance away rather than, say, on its skin.   (2001 (1992): 119)

. . . in addition to being a cause of those thoughts, what makes the particular aspect of the cause of the learner's responses the aspect that gives them the content they have is the

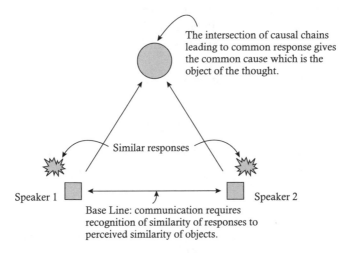

The intersection of causal chains leading to common response gives the common cause which is the object of the thought.

Similar responses

Speaker 1

Speaker 2

Base Line: communication requires recognition of similarity of responses to perceived similarity of objects.

Figure 5

fact that this aspect of the cause is shared by the teacher and the learner. Without such sharing, there would be no grounds for selecting one cause rather than another as the content-fixing cause. A noncommunicating creature may be seen by us as responding to an objective world; but we are not justified in attributing thoughts about our world (or any other) to it.   (2001 (1990): 203)[300]

The central thought is that, without constraints on what a creature is thinking about in addition to those provided by treating it as a rational creature capable of thought and speech, the answer to the question what it is thinking about will be so wildly underdetermined that we can give no clear content to the idea that it is thinking anything at all. This thought echoes a criticism made of the procedure of the radical interpreter in Chapter 13. Seen in this context, the triangulation required for communication to take place offers an additional constraint that promises to narrow down the choices compatible with the evidence to a range that is acceptable.[301]

It has, in addition, a startling new consequence, namely, that language must be public in a surprisingly strong sense. Taken literally, the argument seems to suggest that one must actually be in communication with another for there to be determinate objects of one's thought. But, of course, that is too strong. The idea must rather be that without more or less regular interaction with other speakers, or perhaps interaction with speakers in the past, there could be no question of what the objects of one's thoughts were. For it is only by reference to an actual pattern of interaction with other speakers of the sort exemplified in Figure 5 that there can be a determinate answer to the question what someone is thinking about. Moreover, the appeal here is not *ad hoc*, for the point of language is communication. Without a public object, in the sense of an object which is the common cause of two creatures' speech behavior, there can be no communication.

The argument can be laid out as in (F).

F. The argument from triangulation

(F1)   We can make sense of there being a determinate object of thought for a creature only if we can see it as a speaker triangulating with

---

[300] See also "The Conditions of Thought" (Davidson 1989: 198).

[301] This might be thought to represent a step away from the extremely individualistic stance toward meaning we attributed to Davidson in Part II. However, since the interpreter himself is another speaker, interpretation of another does not require in principle a third person: while interpretation involves essentially a social element, the society involved need be no larger than a pair of individuals.

another speaker in communication about a common object of thought.

(F2) Nothing can have thoughts unless there can be determinate objects of its thoughts.

(F3) Therefore, nothing is a thinker unless it is a speaker which is in communication (or has been in communication) with another speaker.

If the reasoning here is sound, then we apparently have a route to the conclusion that only speakers can have thoughts that is independent of the success of argument (D). At the same time, we have provided a kind of transcendental argument both for the possibility of knowledge of other minds, since the base line of the triangle required for thought requires communication, and for the possibility of knowledge of the external world, since knowledge of other minds must still rely on knowledge of the behavior of other bodies. Moreover, we are assured that the behavior of other bodies is sufficient in principle to extract an account of their thoughts and language, if any. Thus, this seems to provide as well a solution to the problem of showing that psychological and linguistic concepts are theoretical, and that the third person point of view, the interpersonal point of view, is epistemically fundamental.[302] If knowledge of one's own mind can be shown to be presupposed, at least, if not explained, by the possibility of communication, then this would establish that these three varieties of knowledge, of other minds, of the external world, and of one's own mind, are essentially interconnected. The Cartesian picture of our epistemic position, in which knowledge of our own minds is the foundation of knowledge of the world around us and of other minds, would thereby be shown to be fundamentally misconceived.

7. Evaluation of the Argument from Triangulation

Though this picture is appealing (and we will return to it below), it is not clear that it is sustainable.

In the present context, the first, and most important, difficulty is that argument (F) cannot provide a way of supporting what we have called from time to time Davidson's most fundamental assumption, the primacy of the third person point of view. It cannot because it presupposes it. (F) reaches the

[302] This still falls short of showing any speaker is interpretable by any other in any environment: again, at most, we seem to secure that any speaker must have been interpreted correctly by some speaker in some environment on the basis of public evidence.

conclusion that communication is essential to thought by arguing that it is only if a subject is in communication with another that we will be in a position to identify *on third person or objective grounds* what the objects of his thoughts are. If we must be able to identify on third person or objective grounds what his thoughts are, if we are to make sense of his having thoughts at all, then granting the premise, we can conclude communication is necessary for thought. But this argument then *assumes* the primacy of the third person point of view, and cannot be used in support of it. At most, it can be used in defense of the position that assumes the primacy of the third person point of view by showing that it does not lead immediately to absurd results.[303] (F) does not, after all, then, provide us with the a priori argument we were looking for in support of the primacy of the third person point of view. On reflection, this is not surprising.

We turn now to some internal difficulties for the argument.

Our next question is whether appeal to triangulation in solving the problem of the underdetermination of thought content requires seeing two creatures as engaging in linguistic communication. At this point it is especially important to separate the question of what is required for having the concept of objective truth, and the question of what must be so, if we are to identify a unique object of a speaker's thought. Taken together, the two arguments Davidson offers reinforce each other. But our question now is, putting aside the argument for language being essential for the concept of objectivity, can the pattern we have found above be discovered independently of thinking of it as exemplified in communication with one another?

There seems no reason to suppose it cannot. Davidson points out that communication depends on two individuals having common responses to common stimuli: "if someone is the speaker of a language, there must be another sentient being whose innate similarity responses[304] are sufficiently like his own to

---

[303] There is a suggestion, particularly in "Three Varieties of Knowledge" (Davidson 2001*b* (1988): 209–10), that only triangulation can solve Wittgenstein's problem of providing a standard against which to judge the correctness of one's use of words. If this is intended to be distinct from the argument we have just examined that seeks to link having the concept of objective truth with speaking a language, the suggestion is not spelled out enough for it to be clear what is intended.

[304] At some points, Davidson puts this by saying that two individuals *find* the same things similar. "The child finds tables similar; we find tables similar; and we find the child's responses in the presence of tables similar. It now makes sense for us to call the responses of the child responses to tables. Given these three patterns of response we can assign a location to the stimuli that elicit the child's responses. The relevant stimuli are the objects or events we naturally find similar (tables) which are correlated with responses of the child we find similar. It is a form of triangulation: one line goes from the child in the direction of the table, one line goes from us in the direction of the table, and the third line goes between us and the child. Where the lines from child to table and us to table converge "the"

provide an answer to the question, what is the stimulus to which the speaker is responding?" (Davidson 2001 (1992): 120). Creatures who respond to different sorts of things will never be in a position to exemplify the pattern required. But the question arises why the *more* that is required in addition to having the same innate similarity responses is *communication*. Animals fighting over food are responding to the same stimuli in similar ways, and, as we are inclined to say, recognize that they are doing so. Here we have a triangle of causal interaction, and it seems to provide as good a guide to what the common object of thought is as the more sophisticated form of causal interaction provided by linguistic communication. If common cause in the context of mutual interaction is what is important, requiring that the interaction amount to speech is supererogatory. If this is right, even if we grant the primacy of the third person point of view, we fail to secure the necessity of communication for thought, and, hence, we fail to establish the necessity of language for thought.

What we may have secured is a slightly weaker thesis. Namely, if we grant the primacy of the third person point of view, and we grant that there are limits to how much indeterminacy is intelligible, then interaction with others in patterns exemplified by competition or cooperation is required in order to have thoughts.

Even this thesis, however, is predicated on the assumption that such interaction does solve the problem represented by radical underdetermination of thought content by one's causal interactions with the environment. It is far from clear that it succeeds. We raise two objections.

First, Figure 4, with its idealized causal chains, obscures the complexity of the causal factors involved in any actual situation. It is far from clear that there are not many common causes of common responses in speakers in the circumstances in which they interact. Suppose (contrary to fact) that the authors of this book are in the habit of watching television together. One remarks to the other, who concurs ("So much violence on television!"—"Yes, and that's just on the news"). Is it really true that there is only one common cause of their responses? There is the surface of the television screen, events in the stream

stimulus is located. Given our view of child and world, we can pick out "the" cause of the child's responses. It is the common cause of our response and the child's response." (Davidson 2001 (1992): 119). This is already to attribute to the child the ability to think about particular objects (you cannot find one thing to be similar to another unless you can think about each and their features). Were this really a condition for communication, communication would presuppose determinate thought and could not explain it. We take the idea in the text to be that two speakers must be capable of being caused to respond in similar ways by similar things (though the question of course arises by whose standards).

of electrons being projected onto it, events in the cable, at the cable television company's headquarters, in a satellite in geosynchronous orbit around the earth, at CNN in Atlanta, and at distant trouble spots around the globe, and so on. The example, of course, lends itself particularly naturally to tracing out a lengthy causal chain of common causes, but the greater difficulty in mundane cases is apt to be more a matter of ignorance than of the absence of many different common causes. Of course, we know which ones to pay attention to, but that is only because we know what others are apt to notice, namely, what we are apt to notice. But this does not show that such information is extractable solely from information about the common causes of these noticings.

Furthermore, when we consider the sum total of that portion of space–time relevant to our reactions, that is, the distribution of physical magnitudes in the light cone (see n. 197), we can see that conditions in each sub-region, excluding our reactions, can be considered to be a common cause of our reactions, relative to treating the rest as background conditions. Thus, in principle, it seems that there will be many common causes of common responses.

These remarks are not decisive. Perhaps further constraints and enough interaction would significantly narrow down the plausible choices. But they do suggest that the situation is much more complicated than is indicated by the simple diagram above.

If this is right, even this additional constraint will not answer the challenge of radical underdetermination of thought content by causal interaction with the environment. If this challenge must be met for the primacy of the third person point of view to be sustained, then it must be given up.

Davidson's strategy is familiar. We abstract a structural feature from a description of an activity using the resources of the relevant vocabulary. Whenever there is G, there is structural feature H. For example, whenever anyone believes that p, he is in a functional state F. We then suggest that the structural feature is itself sufficient as well as necessary for the presence of the feature describable in the relevant vocabulary: for any x, x believes that p iff x is in functional state F. We hope thereby hope to illuminate what it comes to. In the present case, we notice that a feature of communication is that it involves thoughts about common causes of those thoughts, which evoke the same or similar responses. We then postulate that what suffices for the fact that there is a common object of the thoughts is that they have the same cause and evoke the same responses; and the common cause is then identified with the object of the thought. Yet, here there is a difficulty. For there are many common causes of the thoughts and responses. We were only able to pick out the right one in our original description by identifying it as what the thoughts

410

are about. This resource is lost as soon as we try to characterize what the thoughts are about by reference to a common cause, and so we are left with insufficient resources to pick out the right common cause among the many available. If we fail to notice this initially, it is because we tacitly rely on our originally identifying the right common cause as the object commonly thought about.

The second objection is that the method induces counterintuitive results. In Figure 5, we represented two speakers interacting. Suppose we add a third who is interacting with speaker 1 as exemplified in Figure 6. Is this impossible? No, clearly an actual situation could be constructed with some mirrors and a little ingenuity. If we allow ourselves the fiction of Descartes's malicious demon, or three brains in a vat and enough equipment, we can imagine this carried on endlessly.

The difficulty is immediately apparent. What is speaker 1 really thinking about, the object represented as a small circle, or the object represented as a larger circle? We have equal grounds in this situation to suppose he is thinking about either. If the grounds do not decide, do we bite the bullet and say neither he, nor speakers 2 and 3, since he is the anchor of their base lines, have any thoughts? This is a harsh judgment: and one which does not accord well with

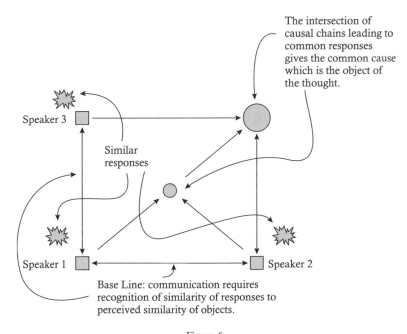

Figure 6

our intuitions about counterfactual situations. For example, how many of us would be willing to grant that we had no thoughts, if we were to (seem to) discover that we had always been in a situation like that presented in Figure 6? (We can imagine how it would go; a visit from a man in a grey suit, the demonstration of the mirrors, a course in optics . . .) Do we know, given that we have thoughts, without any further empirical investigation, that we are not subject to such a trick?

The suspicion that something has gone wrong here can be reinforced with the following thought experiment. Let us imagine a being who is equally adept at paying attention to what is going on at our sensory surfaces and in our environment. He can, we suppose, shift his attention effortlessly between the two. He has a choice, therefore, about whether he treats as the common cause of his and our responses classes of sensory stimulations at our sensory surfaces, or distal events in our environment. What are the objects of our thought? If they are determined by this pattern of triangulation, it looks as if we have to say that what our thoughts are depends on how our interlocutor shifts his attention, whether, for the nonce, he pays attention to familiar objects in the environment, or to the goings on on the surfaces of our skin, and so on. Let us suppose we have been (as we think) in communication with such a creature; he informs us of the trick he has played on us. Do we concur? Do we agree that what our thoughts had been about have been shifting from the proximal to the distal? Not at all.[305]

What these two thought experiments illustrate is the apparent autonomy of our perspective on our own mental lives from that of others. Davidson has attempted to preserve the special access we have to our own thoughts within a framework that makes the third person standpoint primary. This gives rise to paradoxes, however, when multiple third person standpoints give rise to contradictory accounts of an individual's mental life, either at a time, or over time. We must either in such situations deny that it even makes sense to speak of a subject having a mental life, that is, hold that multiple third person standpoints destroy the possibility of thought and language, or give up the primacy of the third person point of view. The apparent coherence of the thought experiments, imagined from the point of view of the agent, counts against the primacy of the third person perspective.

---

[305] It could be objected that we here presuppose that there is a fact of the matter about the other's shifting pattern of attention. The answer is, "yes, we do, but this is part of what seems prima facie intelligible." Apart from this, we could tell the story in purely physical terms.

8. The Problem of Other Minds

Neither reflection on the necessity of triangulation in communication, nor the conditions for having the concept of objective truth have provided an adequate defense of the primacy of the third person point of view. We turn now to a more direct argument, which we have skirted a few times, but not yet addressed directly. This argument can be thought of as resting primarily upon the idea that a certain problem, which it must be possible to solve, if anyone is to be capable of having language in any circumstances, can be solved at all only if we take the third person point of view as primary, that is, only if we suppose that interpretation is possible from the standpoint of the radical interpreter. The problem is the familiar one of how it is possible to have knowledge of other minds. The difficulty is this: if behavior is all we have to go on to justify our beliefs about the existence of other minds and their contents, and the existence of other minds and their contents is logically independent of behavior, we can have knowledge of other minds only if we can establish a contingent correlation between behavior and kinds of mental states in others. But establishing any such correlation presupposes we have knowledge of other minds to begin with, and so knowledge of other minds is impossible if our two assumptions are correct.

The problem also has a semantic analog, which is important, as we will see, in Davidson's conception of it. The semantic analog rests on the assumption of the argument that we know our own minds in a fundamentally different way than we know the minds of others. In the case of others, we go on behavior. In the case of our own minds, by and large, we do not rely on any evidence whatsoever. But if that is so, then what applications of psychological terms to others pay allegiance to is something completely different from what applications of psychological terms to ourselves pay allegiance to. The problem in this guise is to explain how it could be possible that our terms meant the same thing in application to ourselves and others.[306]

The problem of other minds figures in our current discussion in the following way. If to have a language is to be interpretable, at least by someone in suitable circumstances, whether or not by any speaker in any circumstances, then there must in principle be a solution to the problem of other minds, on pain

---

[306] This thought is sometimes said to be developed in Wittgenstein's *Philosophical Investigations* (1950); see e.g. Norman Malcom's (1958) development of it, which clearly looks to Wittgenstein for inspiration.

of admitting that no one is interpretable, and, hence, that no one speaks a language.

We can now lay out the main line of argument in (G).

G. The argument from knowledge of other minds

(G1)   Necessarily, speaking a language is having the capacity to interpret other language speakers and being interpretable by other language speakers [a priori truth].

(G2)   We never have any direct epistemic access to the thoughts of other speakers or to the meanings of their utterances [a priori truth].

(G3)   Therefore, from (G2), the only evidence available for interpretation is third person evidence, that is, evidence equally available to every potential interpreter of a speaker.

(G4)   From (G1) and (G3), any language speaker can be interpreted on the basis of third person evidence in any environment by any other language speaker.

(G5)   From (G4), radical interpretation is possible, or, in other words, question (Q2′) of Chapter 11 admits of answer.

We have put the conclusion in an especially strong form in order to raise the question how much can be established if we grant the premises. Thus, the intermediate conclusion (G4) in fact guarantees what we said Davidson needed to secure simultaneously the impossibility of radically different conceptual schemes and the impossibility of massive error.

We do not think, however, that the argument, even granting the premises, establishes this much. The first premise, to be plausible, must be interpreted as 'Every speaker is interpretable in some environment by some speaker', where for (G4), we need the much stronger 'Every speaker is interpretable in every environment by every speaker on the basis of third person evidence'. At most, we think, the argument can issue in the intermediate conclusion:

(G4′)   Every speaker is interpretable in some environment on the basis of public or third person evidence by some speaker.

This establishes a modified version of the possibility of radical interpretation, namely, every speaker is radically interpretable by some speaker in some environment.[307]

---

[307] This is not the same as logical behaviorism, which requires a reduction of psychological talk to talk of behavior, nor is it equivalent to a general or crude verificationism.

The main question we wish to raise is about the third premise. Davidson recognizes that there is a potential objection to this premise, and has a response. We will consider the response in a moment. The objection is that (G3) is false because we know the contents of our own thoughts independently of observing our behavior. Thus, we can establish correlations between our thoughts and our behavior, and then project these correlations to the case of others. This is a version of what has been called the argument from analogy.

Traditional responses to the argument from analogy, to the effect that it is weak inductive reasoning, are, at least in the standard cases in which we are apt to employ such a procedure, ineffective. The mistake is to represent the reasoning as if it took place in isolation from our broader knowledge of the causal order. Human beings fall within a single biological kind. That biologically based features of one member of a species are found in other members of the species is not a flimsy inductive inference, but central to our inferential practices involving living things. Granting that psychological features of ourselves are biologically based, skepticism about other minds reduces to skepticism about induction in general, but presents no special problems.

Davidson's response to this sort of move is expressed in the following passage:

Do we distinguish between the problems [of skepticism about the external world and skepticism about other minds] because we suppose that while we have no access to the outside world except through experience, we nevertheless can intelligibly extrapolate to the experiences of others, since we have access to experience in our own case? But this supposition begs the question, since it assumes without argument that what we call the mental states of others are similar to what we identify as mental states in ourselves. (2001*b* (1988): 207)

That is, the response is to appeal to what we earlier called the semantic version of the problem.[308]

The charge is that the argument from analogy does not show that what we call mental states in others are the same as what we call mental states in ourselves, but that in the absence of this we cannot consider it to be an adequate solution to the problem.

---

[308] This concern also figures prominently in "First Person Authority" (Davidson 2001*a* (1984)), where Davidson treats the skeptical challenge to knowledge of other minds to be the challenge of showing both that we know that others have mental states, and that the sense in which they do, given the difference in the basis on which they are ascribed (on behavior for them, on nothing for ourselves), is the same as the sense in which we think of ourselves as having mental states. See also "Knowing One's Own Mind" (2001*b* (1987): 16–17) and "The Conditions of Thought" (1989: 194).

415

But is there a problem here? If the worry is that appeal to experience in our own cases could not justify ascription of experience to others on the basis of their behavior, this charge has already been answered. If the worry is that, because we go on the basis of behavior in others, but (need) not in our own cases, we must suppose, *unless we have an argument to the contrary*, that we mean different things by the words we use in each case, then the answer is that this assumes an unappealing operationalist conception of how meaning is determined, which has long been discredited in the philosophy of science. In our own cases, we conceive of our psychological states as causing behavior, indeed, as causally responsible for our behavior. If we blush in embarrassment at a *faux pas* in the presence of the Royal Family, we explain this by appeal to our attitudes to royalty and etiquette. In the case of others, we employ this feature of the concepts we deploy in our own case to infer their passions and beliefs. No question can arise about whether we deploy the same concepts in each case, as long as it is granted that we deploy our concepts correctly in our own cases.

Davidson emphasizes at one point that the difficulty is not just that there are multiple criteria for the application of psychological concepts. He says:

Many concepts can be applied on the basis of multiple criteria, but no others [i.e. non-psychological concepts] are such that ascribers *must*, on particular occasions, use different criteria. If we are to explain this anomaly and avoid an invitation to skepticism [particularly on semantic grounds], the explanation should point to a natural asymmetry between other observers and ourselves, an asymmetry not simply invented to solve the problem.   (2001*a* (1984): 9)

However, this misdescribes the situation. It is not that one *could not* use in one's own case the same criteria as in the case of others, for example, listening to what one says, and seeing how one behaves—clearly one could do that—but that one *need not*. Once we see this, it is not clear why there should be thought to be an important difference. There is a difference, but it just comes down to the fact that we can know in our own case without need to infer from our behavior what our occurrent psychological states are. What is missing in the challenge is some reason to think that this epistemic asymmetry threatens to force us to accept that what we mean when we say *we think* a certain thing is different from what we mean when we say *someone else thinks* the same. But what plausible account of meaning is going to force this view on us? Surely the adequacy of any view that did have this consequence would also be to that extent suspect.

It might be said that we are left with a solution to the problem of other minds on this account at the expense of an explanation of the asymmetry between first and third person knowledge of mental states. It is true that this proposed solution to the problem of knowledge of other minds does not explain, but rather rests on, the asymmetry (which is also of course the source of the difficulty in the first place). But, as we discussed above in Chapter 20, it is not clear that the demand for an explanation of the asymmetry is one which we should accept.

If these considerations are correct, premise (G3) is false. While we must rely *inter alia* on third person evidence in interpreting others, we are not restricted to it. Thus, even granting that to be language speakers one must be interpretable, we need not grant that one must be interpretable by appeal only to objective facts about a speaker's interaction with his environment.

We do not suppose that in casting doubt on premise (G3), we have shown the Cartesian standpoint to be correct. Rather, the point is that it does not self-destruct. The argument we are examining, to establish the primacy of the third person point of view, requires the implosion of the view that the first person perspective is primary; it requires that it make interpretation impossible.

The argument then fails, even granting the first premise. But the first premise should make us suspicious. For if it requires that to be a speaker of a language, one must be justifiably interpretable in some environment by some possible like-minded speaker, then it offers a so far overlooked response to radical skepticism about the external world, that is, the skeptical conclusion that necessarily we can know nothing about the world around us. For this could not be true if it is possible for someone just like us to justifiably interpret us in some environment, for this would, *inter alia*, require that he had justified beliefs about his and our environment. This offers an immediate refutation of radical skepticism.

It is clear why a skeptic would reject this. He would not grant that we cannot understand ourselves to be speakers unless we can be justifiably interpreted in some environment on the basis of broadly empirical evidence. This would require that someone like us be in a position to know something about the external world. He would say that what constitutes our being linguistic beings is that, were we embedded in the world as we suppose we are, then the dispositions we would have would make us interpretable by others. That is, we would then have dispositions that made possible our being correctly interpreted by a like-minded speaker, who proceeded as if his perceptual experiences were correctly representing his environment. He would then be conditionally justified in his interpretations of us, that is, justified in believing that if his beliefs about

417

the world around him (and inductively supported general beliefs) are correct, then his interpretation is correct.

9. Conclusion

We have examined a number of closely interrelated arguments for the necessity of language and, indeed, communication, for thought, and for the concept of objective truth. The aim has been, in the main, to try to find a ground for the central assumption of Davidson's philosophical method, that the third person point of view on others' utterances and psychological states is primary, in the sense that behavioral evidence forms our only evidence for the application of linguistic and psychological concepts and terms, and that their content is to be understood wholly in terms of their role in accounting for the behavioral evidence available to us from this standpoint. The shift of viewpoint is so fundamental that the whole landscape in the philosophy of language and mind looks different when viewed from this position. If Davidson is right, then the central mistake of the philosophical tradition is the assumption of the Cartesian standpoint, and, in particular, the central place in epistemology accorded to the epistemic priority of knowledge of our mental states to knowledge of the world and other minds. If this assumption is given up, then each of these domains in which we have knowledge will be seen to be necessary for the others, but knowledge of the world and, by extension, other minds will turn out to be autonomous from knowledge of our own minds, in the sense that it is inexplicable by appeal to inferences from a basis in knowledge of our own minds.

In light of the alternative, it is an attractive picture. And part of its interest and power lies in its promise to lay to rest what have been perhaps the central problems of the tradition from the beginning of the modern period. For this reason, if for no other, we would be foolish to assume that the picture must be mistaken. Despite the difficulties it faces, it is worth pursuing.

The problems raised here, though, show that there are grave doubts about its tenability. It may be that many of these difficulties could be met with further work and some ingenuity. The central difficulty, we believe, lies in the apparent underdetermination of the content of our thought about meaning and thought content by behavioral evidence, including interactions with objects in our environment. What must be done is to show that the third person standpoint can yield acceptably determinate assignments of contents to beliefs and interpretations to sentences. Perhaps this can yet be done by bringing to bear additional constraints or conceptual resources, without allowing appeal to our knowledge of our own mental states in a way that undermines the idea that the third person point of view is still epistemically and conceptually basic. Yet, at the moment, we have no idea how this could be done.

Summary of Part III

We have been concerned in Part III with a number of important theses which Davidson has sought to ground in reflection on the procedures of the radical interpreter, and with what a priori grounds can be found to support the assumption that radical interpretation is possible for any speaker, in any environment, by any other speaker. In particular, we have examined Davidson's arguments for the impossibility of radically different conceptual schemes, for the impossibility of massive error, and for the relational individuation of thought content, his explanation of first person authority from the standpoint of the radical interpreter, the argument for the inscrutability of reference, and, finally, the arguments for the necessity of language and communication for thought, which, if successful, would establish the primacy of the third person perspective, and underwrite, at least to some extent, the possibility of radical interpretation.

In somewhat more detail, we have examined the following eight theses.

(1) *The rejection of conceptual pluralism*: everyone shares by and large the same conceptual scheme (Chapter 18).

(2) *The impossibility of massive error*: everyone by and large has true beliefs, both general beliefs and particular beliefs about her environment (belief is intrinsically veridical) (Chapter 19).

(3) *The presumption of first person authority in interpretation*: that everyone is an authority over his or her beliefs, etc., is an unavoidable assumption of interpretation (Chapter 20).

(4) *The inscrutability of reference*: any scheme of reference that preserves truth value assignments is equally acceptable (Chapter 21).

(5) *The necessity of language for thought*: every believer has a language (Chapter 22).

(6) *The necessity of the concept of truth for belief*: every believer has the concepts of belief, truth, error and objectivity (Chapter 22).

(7) *The necessity of communication for knowledge*: the possibility of knowledge of one's own mind, the minds of others and the external world requires communication (present or past) with other speakers (Chapter 22).

(8) *The determination of content by common causes of responses of speakers*: what makes someone's thought about a particular object is that it is an object which causes a common response in the person and an interlocutor, where both the person and his interlocutor notice the common responses in the other (Chapter 22).

Thesis (5), the necessity of language for thought, turns out, somewhat surprisingly, perhaps, to play a central role. For arguments to the *nature* of belief from what must be assumed in *interpretation* would be undercut if belief were not essentially tied to being interpretable. Since the arguments for (1), (2), and (3) make this assumption, without (5) they fall apart. Thesis (3) is important, as we have remarked, because without an explanation of first person authority, and related phenomena, from the third person point of view, the claim that the interpreter's standpoint is methodologically basic is thrown into doubt. (5) in turn depends on two lines of argument, one having to do with what is required to make sense of attributions of fine-grained attitudes (the argument from holism), and the other with what is required to have beliefs, namely, the concept of belief (6), and with what is required to have the concept of belief, namely, language. Arguments for (7) and (8) fall out of, or are bound up with, the general line of argument for (6).

The argument against radically different conceptual schemes ultimately relies on assuming that, if our understanding of what it is for a sentence to be true in a language L involves thinking of it as being translatable into a language in which a truth theory can be given for it, then to understand what it could come to for a sentence in a language to be true (or false) requires us to think of it as translatable into our own. But there is no justification for the move *from* requiring for any language that a truth theory be given for it in *some* metalanguage into which the object language can be translated *to* requiring that the metalanguage be translatable into *our* language.

Davidson's argument for the impossibility of massive error in our empirical beliefs rests on the assumptions that (1) charity is required for successful radical interpretation, in particular in application to our beliefs about our environments (the principle of correspondence), and that (2) we are radically interpretable in any environment. Together, these entail that most of our beliefs about our environments are true, and at the same time secure a non-reductive form of externalism about thought content. The difficulty is in securing the second of these assumptions. We saw in Chapter 15 that there are reasons to think that radical interpretation cannot succeed, reasons which emerge from the radical interpreter's perspective. In the absence of an a priori argument for the assumption, we must judge the argument unsuccessful. We returned to this issue in the final chapter of this part.

It is central to the success of Davidson's program that a place be found for the asymmetry of warrant between what we say about our own (occurrent) mental states and those of others. Sincere first person ascriptions are accorded special epistemic weight. When we make them, we apparently do not justify them by appeal to anything else, and certainly not by appeal to behavior. We are credited with non-inferential warrant in theses cases. This threatens the view that psychological concepts are theoretical concepts whose content is exhausted by their role in keeping track of behavior, since the justification for thinking a state falls under a theoretical concept must be inferential. We criticized Davidson's explanation of the asymmetry in warrant between first and third person ascriptions on two primary grounds. First, the explanation he offers, which relies on arguing for an asymmetry in first and third person warrant for believing that we mean a certain thing by our words, fails to establish the explanandum, since it is compatible with the absence of a special warrant, if despite not knowing as well what we mean by our words, someone else knows better what we believe. To establish the asymmetry in warrant, we need also to appeal to an asymmetry in knowledge of our own thoughts, which itself stands in need of explanation. However, we granted that the basic strategy Davidson employs to establish an asymmetry in warrant for knowledge of meanings, namely, to argue that we must assume in interpreting someone that he knows what he means, can be extended to knowledge of one's propositional attitudes. For without supposing that an agent knows by and large what he thinks, which is exhibited in the coherence of his actions in the light of the attitudes we attribute to him, we cannot make sense of him as an agent at all. However, second, we objected that this does not *explain* the asymmetry, since it has the same status as the assumption that the speaker is rational. That we must assume another is rational to interpret him does not constitute an explanation of his rationality. Likewise, that we must assume, as a part of this, that he knows by and large what his occurrent thoughts are to interpret him does not constitute an explanation of his knowledge.

The argument for the inscrutability of reference is also supposed to fall out of reflection on radical interpretation. The thesis is that there are many different reference schemes, assignments of individuals to singular terms, and extensions to predicates, that keep track equally well of the semantic facts about a language. The argument proceeds by showing that, compatibly with keeping fixed the distribution of truth values over sentences (or sentences relativized to contexts), we can systematically reinterpret singular terms and predicates. We argued that this leads to paradoxical results, when we consider its interaction with demonstratives and indexicals. But the main objection is that the aim of the interpreter is to arrive at an interpretive truth theory, and we know in general that preservation of truth value does not in any intuitive sense preserve interpretation. So, an assumption required by the argument is false. As we observed, it does not help to ask that we preserve law-likeness of the axioms either, since this also fails to be sufficient to preserve interpretiveness. The same difficulty arises here that we canvassed in Chapter 15. From the standpoint of the radical interpreter, who can distinguish between the claim that 'George Washington' refers to George Washington, and 'George Washington' refers to George III, it makes no sense to say that different reference schemes employing each do an equally good job in interpreting a speaker's words, except in so far as the speaker's language does not have the expressive resources available to the interpreter: but then the same account will not work for the interpreter's language, and so we cannot conclude that reference is generally inscrutable. We argued that Davidson's appeal to relativization to a language clearly does not avoid this difficulty: for the interpreter must still be able to make distinctions he cannot draw in the speaker's language.

Finally, we examined Davidson's arguments for the necessity of language and communication for thought. The central argument makes appeal to the principle that for a creature to have a certain (basic) concept, there must be scope for its application in its experience, and to the claim that there is scope for the application of the concept of error, or objective truth, and so for that of belief, only in the context of communication. The central difficulty for this style of argument is motivating a strong reading of the principle on which it relies. The principle must be read as requiring that for a creature to possess a basic concept, there must be scope for its correct application in its experience. But it is not clear why this should be required, rather than merely that there be a point to its application from the creature's own point of view. In addition, we argued that Davidson has not provided convincing reasons to think that it is only in the context of communication that there would be scope for the application of the concepts of error and objective truth. We examined also what we called the argument from triangulation, and the argument from knowledge of other minds. The first presupposes, and so cannot support, the assumption of the primacy of the third person perspective. In addition, the assumption it relies on, namely that there is only one common cause of common responses to the environment in communication, is mistaken. Finally, the assumptions of the argument have counterintuitive results in the case of competing triangles of communication. The argument from knowledge of other minds, in the end, rests on the assumption that, without an explanation of the asymmetry in first and third person knowledge of mental states, which can be given only from the third person perspective, we would have to admit that we could not make sense of ourselves attributing the same kinds of state to ourselves and others. We objected that inadequate grounds were advanced to accept that taking the epistemic asymmetry as basic forces us to say that what we mean in our own case when using psychological terms must differ from what we mean in the case of others.

This concludes our defense of the claim that radical interpretation, conceived of as the project of justifying an interpretive truth theory for another solely on the basis of (1) the assumption that he is a rational agent and (2) full information about his physical interactions with his environment, is impossible. The conclusion of Part II, that the radical interpreter himself must see his evidence as underdetermining the correct theory choice, waited for final validation only on the examination of what arguments could be advanced to show a priori that radical interpretation is possible. In the light of our discussion in Chapter 22, we conclude that no convincing case has been made on a priori grounds for the assumption. This central assumption is required, as we have noted, for the defense of all the major theses examined in Part III.

Bibliography

Alston, W. (1964). *Philosophy of Language*. Englewood Cliffs, NJ: Prentice-Hall.

Bar-On, D., and Risjord, M. (1992). Is there Such a Thing as a Language? *Canadian Journal of Philosophy*, 22: 163–90.

Barwise, J., and Perry, J. (1981*a*). Semantic Innocence and Uncompromising Situations. In P. A. French, T. E. Uehling, and H. K. Wettstein (eds.), *Midwest Studies in Philosophy: The Foundations of Analytic Philosophy* (vol. 6, pp. 387–403). Minneapolis: University of Minnesota Press.

—— and —— (1981*b*). Situations and Attitudes. *Journal of Philosophy*, 78: 668–90.

—— and —— (1983). *Situations and Attitudes*. Cambridge, Mass.: MIT Press.

Boghossian, P. (1989). Content and Self-Knowledge. *Philosophical Topics*, 17: 5–26.

Brueckner, A. (1986). Brains in a Vat. *Journal of Philosophy*, 83: 148–67.

Burge, T. (1979). Individualism and the Mental. In P. A. French, T. E. Uehling, and H. K. Wettstein (eds.), *Midwest Studies in Philosophy: Studies in Metaphysics* (vol. 4, pp. 73–121). Minneapolis: University of Minnesota Press.

Carnap, R. (1942). *Introduction to Semantics*. Cambridge: Cambridge University Press.

Chihara, C. S. (1975). Davidson's Extensional Theory of Meaning. *Philosophical Studies*, 28: 1–15.

Chomsky, N. (1969). Quine's Empirical Assumptions. In D. Davidson and J. Hintikka (eds.), *Words and Objections: Essays on the Work of W. V. O. Quine* (pp. 53–68). Dordrecht: Reidel.

Church, A. (1943). Carnap's Introduction to Semantics. *Philosophical Review*, 52: 298–305.

—— (1951). The Need for Abstract Entities in Semantic Analysis. *Proceedings of the American Academy of Arts and Letters*, 80: 100–13.

—— (1956). *Introduction to Mathematical Logic*. Princeton: Princeton University Press.

Cummins, R. (2002). Truth and Meaning. In J. K. Campbell, M. O'Rourke, and D. Shier (eds.), *Meaning and Truth: Investigations in Philosophical Semantics*. New York: Seven Bridges Press.

Davidson, D. (1963). The Method of Extension and Intension. In A. Schilpp (ed.), *The Philosophy of Rudolf Carnap*. La Salle, Ill.: Open Court.

—— (1974). Replies to David Lewis and W. V. Quine. *Synthese*, 27: 345–9.

—— (1985*a*). A New Basis for Decision Theory. *Theory and Decision*, 18: 87–98.

—— (1985*b*). Reply to Quine on Events. In E. Lepore (ed.), *Actions and Events: Perspectives on the Philosophy of Donald Davidson*. Oxford: Blackwell.

Bibliography

Davidson, D. (1986). A Nice Derangement of Epitaphs. In E. Lepore (ed.), *Truth and Interpretation: Perspectives on the Philosophy of Donald Davidson*. Cambridge, Mass.: Blackwell.

——(1989). The Conditions of Thought. In J. Brandl and W. L. Gombocz (eds.), *The Mind of Donald Davidson*. Amsterdam: Rodopi.

——(1990*a*). Meaning, Truth and Evidence. In R. B. Barret and R. F. Gibson (eds.), *Perspectives on Quine*. Cambridge, Mass.: Blackwell.

——(1990*b*). The Structure and Content of Truth. *Journal of Philosophy*, 87: 279–328.

——(1991). Epistemology Externalized. *Dialectica*, 45: 191–202.

——(1993). Reply to Jerry Fodor and Ernest Lepore's 'Is Radical Interpretation Possible?' In R. Stoecker (ed.), *Reflecting Davidson*. Berlin: de Gruyter.

——(1994*a*). Radical Interpretation Interpreted. In J. Tomberlin (ed.), *Philosophical Perspectives: Logic and Language* (vol. 8, pp. 121–8). Atascadero, Calif.: Ridgeview.

——(1994*b*). The Social Aspect of Language. In B. McGuinness and G. Oliveri (eds.), *The Philosophy of Michael Dummett* (pp. 1–16). Dordrecht: Kluwer.

——(1999). Intellectual Autobiography. In L. E. Hahn (ed.), *The Philosophy of Donald Davidson* (pp. 3–70). Chicago, Ill.: Open Court.

——(2000). Truth Rehabilitated. In R. B. Brandom (ed.), *Rorty and His Critics* (pp. 65–73). Cambridge, Mass.: Blackwell.

——(2001 (1963)). Actions, Reasons, and Causes. *Essays on Actions and Events* (2nd edn., pp. 3–20). New York: Clarendon Press. Originally published in *Journal of Philosophy*, 60 (1963), 685–99.

——(2001 (1966)). Theories of Meaning and Learnable Languages. *Inquiries into Truth and Interpretation* (2nd edn., pp. 3–15). New York: Clarendon Press. Originally published in Y. Bar-Hillel (ed.), *Proceedings of the 1964 International Congress for Logic, Methodology and Philosophy of Science*. Amsterdam: North Holland Publishing Co.

——(2001*a* (1967)). Causal Relations. *Essays on Actions and Events* (2nd edn., pp. 149–62). New York: Clarendon Press. Originally published in *Journal of Philosophy*, 64 (1967), 691–703.

——(2001*b* (1967)). The Logical Form of Action Sentences. *Essays on Actions and Events* (2nd edn., pp. 105–21). New York: Clarendon Press. Originally published in N. Rescher (ed.), *The Logic of Decision and Action*. Pittsburgh: University of Pittsburgh Press.

——(2001*c* (1967)). Truth and Meaning. *Inquiries into Truth and Interpretation* (2nd edn., pp. 17–36). New York: Clarendon Press. Originally published in *Synthese*, 17 (1967), 304–23.

——(2001 (1968)). On Saying That. *Inquiries into Truth and Interpretation* (2nd edn., pp. 93–108). New York: Clarendon Press. Originally published in *Synthese*, 19 (1968), 130–46.

——(2001 (1969)). True to the Facts. *Inquiries into Truth and Interpretation* (2nd edn., pp. 37–54). New York: Clarendon Press. Originally published in *Journal of Philosophy*, 66 (1969), 748–64.

——(2001*a* (1970)). How Is Weakness of the Will Possible? *Essays on Actions and Events* (2nd edn., pp. 21–42). New York: Clarendon Press. Originally published in J. Feinberg (ed.), *Moral Concepts*. Oxford: Oxford University Press.

——(2001*b* (1970)). Mental Events. *Essays on Actions and Events* (2nd edn., pp. 207–24). New York: Clarendon Press. Originally published in L. Foster and J. W. Swanson (eds.), *Experience and Theory*. Amherst, Mass.: University of Massachusetts Press.

——(2001*c* (1970)). Reply to Cargile. *Essays on Actions and Events* (2nd edn., pp. 137–46). Oxford: Oxford University Press. Originally published as Action and Reaction. *Inquiry*, 13 (1970), 140–8.

——(2001*d* (1970)). Semantics for Natural Languages. *Inquiries into Truth and Interpretation* (2nd edn., pp. 55–64). New York: Clarendon Press. Originally published in *Linguaggi nella Societa e nella Tecnica*. Milan: Comunita.

——(2001*a* (1973)). In Defence of Convention T. *Inquiries into Truth and Interpretation* (2nd edn., pp. 65–75). New York: Clarendon Press. Originally published in H. Leblanc (ed.), *Truth, Syntax and Modality*. Dordrecht: North-Holland Publishing Company.

——(2001*b* (1973)). The Material Mind. *Essays on Actions and Events* (2nd edn., pp. 245–60). New York: Clarendon Press. Originally published in P. Suppes, L. Henken, G. C. Moisil, and A. Joja (eds.), *Proceedings of he Fourth International Congress for Logic, Methodology, and Philosophy of Science*. Amsterdam: North-Holland Publishing Co.

——(2001*c* (1973)). Radical Interpretation. *Inquiries into Truth and Interpretation* (2nd edn., pp. 125–39). New York: Clarendon Press. Originally published in *Dialectica*, 27 (1973), 314–28.

——(2001*a* (1974)). Belief and the Basis of Meaning. *Inquiries into Truth and Interpretation* (2nd edn., pp. 141–54). New York: Clarendon Press. Originally published in *Synthese*, 27 (1974), 309–23.

——(2001*b* (1974)). Comments and Replies. *Essays on Actions and Events* (2nd edn., pp. 239–44). New York: Clarendon Press. Originally published in S. C. Brown (ed.), *Philosophy of Psychology*. New York: Barnes & Noble.

——(2001*c* (1974)). On the Very Idea of a Conceptual Scheme. *Inquiries into Truth and Interpretation* (2nd edn., pp. 183–98). New York: Clarendon Press. Originally published in *Proceedings and Addresses of the American Philosophical Association*, 47 (1974), 5–20.

——(2001 (1975)). Thought and Talk. *Inquiries into Truth and Interpretation* (2nd edn., pp. 155–70). New York: Clarendon Press. Originally published in S. Guttenplan (ed.), *Mind and Language*. Oxford: Oxford University Press.

Davidson, D. (2001*a* (1976)). Hempel on Explaining Action. *Essays on Actions and Events* (2nd edn., pp. 261–76). New York: Clarendon Press. Originally published in *Erkenntnis*, 10 (1976), 239–53.

——(2001*b* (1976)). Reply to Foster. *Inquiries into Truth and Interpretation* (2nd edn., pp. 171–9). New York: Clarendon Press. Originally published in G. Evans and J. McDowell (eds.), *Truth and Meaning: Essays in Semantics*. Oxford: Oxford University Press.

——(2001*a* (1977)). The Method of Truth in Metaphysics. *Inquiries into Truth and Interpretation* (2nd edn., pp. 199–214). New York: Clarendon Press. Originally published in P. A. French, T. E. Uehling, and H. K. Wettstein (eds.), *Midwest Studies in Philosophy: Studies in the Philosophy of Language*, 2 (1977), 244–54.

——(2001*b* (1977)). Reality without Reference. *Inquiries into Truth and Interpretation* (2nd edn., pp. 215–25). New York: Clarendon Press. Originally published in *Dialectica*, 31 (1977), 247–53.

——(2001*a* (1979)). The Inscrutability of Reference. *Inquiries into Truth and Interpretation* (2nd edn., pp. 227–41). New York: Clarendon Press. Originally published in *Southwest Journal of Philosophy*, 10 (1979), 7–20.

——(2001*b* (1979)). Moods and Performances. *Inquiries into Truth and Interpretation* (2nd edn., pp. 109–21). New York: Clarendon Press. Originally published in A. Margalit (ed.), *Meaning and Use*. Dordrecht: D. Reidel.

——(2001*a* (1982)). Empirical Content. *Subjective, Intersubjective, Objective* (pp. 159–76). New York: Clarendon Press. Originally published in *Grazer Philosophische Studien*, 17 (1982), 471–89.

——(2001*b* (1982)). Rational Animals. *Subjective, Intersubjective, Objective* (pp. 95–106). New York: Clarendon Press. Originally published in *Dialectica*, 36 (1982), 317–28.

——(2001*a* (1983)). A Coherence Theory of Truth and Knowledge. *Subjective, Intersubjective, Objective* (pp. 137–53). New York: Clarendon Press. Originally published in D. Henrich (ed.), *Kant oder Hegel?* Stuttgart: Klett-Cotta.

——(2001*b* (1983)). Communication and Convention. *Inquiries into Truth and Interpretation* (2nd edn., pp. 265–80). New York: Clarendon Press. Originally published in *Journal of the Indian Council of Philosophical Research*, 1 (1983), 13–25.

——(2001 (1984)). First Person Authority. *Subjective, Intersubjective, Objective* (pp. 3–14). New York: Clarendon Press. Originally published in *Dialectica*, 38 (1984), 101–12.

——(2001*a* (1987)). Afterthoughts. *Subjective, Intersubjective, Objective* (pp. 154–8). New York: Clarendon Press. Originally published in A. Malichowski (ed.), *Reading Rorty*. Cambridge: Blackwell.

——(2001*b* (1987)). Knowing One's Own Mind. *Subjective, Intersubjective, Objective* (pp. 15–38). New York: Clarendon Press. Originally published in *Proceedings and Addresses of the American Philosophical Association*, 60 (1987), 441–58.

——(2001*a* (1988)). The Myth of the Subjective. *Subjective, Intersubjective, Objective* (pp. 39–52). New York: Clarendon Press. Originally published in M. Benedikt and R. Berger (eds.), *Bewusstsein, Sprache und die Kunst*. Edition S. Verlag der Österreichischen Staatscruckerei.

—— (2001*b* (1988)). Three Varieties of Knowledge. *Subjective, Intersubjective, Objective* (pp. 205–20). New York: Clarendon Press. Originally published in A. P. Griffiths (ed.), *A. J. Ayer: Memorial Essays*. New York: Cambridge University Press, 1991.

—— (2001 (1989)). What Is Present to the Mind? *Subjective, Intersubjective, Objective* (pp. 53–68). New York: Clarendon Press. Originally published in J. Brandl and W. Gombocz (eds.), *The Mind of Donald Davidson*. Amsterdam: Rodopi.

—— (2001 (1991)). Epistemology Externalized. *Subjective, Intersubjective, Objective* (pp. 193–204). New York: Clarendon Press. Originally published in *Dialectica*, 45 (1991), 191–202.

—— (2001 (1992)). The Second Person. *Subjective, Intersubjective, Objective* (pp. 107–22). New York: Clarendon Press. Originally published in P. A. French, T. E. Uehling, and H. K. Wettstein (eds.), *Midwest Studies in Philosophy: The Wittgenstein Legacy*, 17 (1992), 255–67.

—— (2001*a*). *Essays on Actions and Events* (2nd edn.). Oxford: Clarendon Press.

—— (2001*b*). *Inquiries into Truth and Interpretation* (2nd edn.). Oxford: Clarendon Press.

—— (2001*c*). *Subjective, Intersubjective, Objective*. Oxford: Clarendon Press.

—— (2004 (1980)). A Unified Theory of Thought, Meaning, and Action. *Problems of Rationality* (pp. 151–66). Oxford: Oxford University Press. Originally published as Toward a Unified Theory of Meaning and Action. *Grazer Philosophische Studien*, 11 (1980), 1–12.

—— (2004 (1982)). Paradoxes of Irrationality. *Problems of Rationality* (pp. 169–88). Oxford: Oxford University Press. Originally published in R. Wollheim and J. Hopkins (eds.), *Philosophical Essays on Freud*. London: Cambridge University Press.

—— (2004 (1985)). Incoherence and Irrationality. *Problems of Rationality* (pp. 189–98). Oxford: Oxford University Press. Originally published in *Dialectica*, 39 (1985), 345–54.

—— (2004 (1986)). Deception and Division. *Problems of Rationality* (pp. 199–212). Oxford: Oxford University Press. Originally published in J. Elster (ed.), *The Multiple Self*. Cambridge: Cambridge University Press.

—— (2004 (1990)). Representation and Interpretation. *Problems of Rationality* (pp. 87–100). Oxford: Oxford University Press. Originally published in W. H. Newton-Smith and K. V. Wilkes (eds.), *Modelling the Mind*. Oxford: Oxford University Press.

—— (2004*a* (1995)). Could There Be a Science of Rationality? *Problems of Rationality* (pp. 117–34). Oxford: Oxford University Press. Originally published in *International Journal of Philosophical Studies*, 3 (1995), 1–16.

—— (2004*b* (1995)). The Problem of Objectivity. *Problems of Rationality* (pp. 3–18). Oxford: Oxford University Press. Originally published in *Tijdschr Filosof*, 57 (1995), 203–20.

Bibliography

Davidson, D. (2004 (2001)). What Thought Requires. *Problems of Rationality* (pp. 135–50). Oxford: Oxford University Press. Originally published in J. Branquinho (ed.), *The Foundations of Cognitive Science*. Oxford: Oxford University Press.

——Suppes, P., and Siegel, S. (1957). *Decision Making: An Experimental Approach*. Stanford: Stanford University Press.

Davies, M. (1981*a*). *Meaning, Quantification, Necessity*. London: Routledge & Kegan Paul.

——(1981*b*). Meaning, Structure and Understanding. *Synthese*, 48: 135–62.

Dretske, F. (1988). *Explaining Behavior: Reasons in a World of Causes*. Cambridge, Mass.: MIT Press.

Dummett, M. (1973). *Frege: Philosophy of Language*. London: Duckworth.

——(1975). Wang's Paradox. *Synthese*, 30: 301–24.

——(1986). "A Nice Derangement of Epitaphs": Some Comments on Davidson and Hacking. In E. Lepore (ed.), *Truth and Interpretation: Perspectives on the Philosophy of Donald Davidson*. Cambridge, Mass.: Blackwell.

——(1993). *The Seas of Language*. Oxford: Oxford University Press.

——(1994). Reply to Davidson. In B. McGuinness and G. Oliveri (eds.), *The Philosophy of Michael Dummett* (pp. 257–67). Dordrecht: Kluwer.

Evans, G. (1981). Semantic Theory and Tacit Knowledge. In S. H. Holtzman and C. M. Leich (eds.), *Wittgenstein: To Follow a Rule* (pp. 118–37). London: Routledge & Kegan Paul.

——(1985). Does Tense Logic Rest on a Mistake? *Collected Papers* (pp. 343–63). Oxford: Clarendon Press.

Evans, G., and McDowell, J. (eds.). (1976). *Truth and Meaning: Essays in Semantics*. Oxford: Clarendon Press.

Field, H. (1974). Quine and the Correspondence Theory. *Philosophical Review*, 83: 200–28.

——(1975). Conventionalism and Instrumentalism in Semantics. *Noûs*, 9: 375–405.

——(1977). Logic, Meaning, and Conceptual Role. *Journal of Philosophy*, 7: 379–408.

——(1994). Deflationist Views of Meaning and Content. *Mind*, 103: 249–84.

Fodor, J. A. (1987). *Psychosemantics: The Problem of Meaning in the Philosophy of Mind*. Cambridge, Mass.: MIT Press.

——(1989). Why Should the Mind Be Modular? In A. George (ed.), *Reflections on Chomsky*. Oxford: Blackwell.

——(1990*a*). *A Theory of Content and Other Essays*. Cambridge, Mass.: MIT Press.

——(1990*b*). Psychosemantics or: Where do Truth Conditions Come from? In W. Lycan (ed.), *Mind and Cognition* (pp. 312–38). Cambridge, Mass.: Blackwell.

——and Lepore, E. (1992). *Holism: A Shopper's Guide*. Cambridge, Mass.: Blackwell.

——(1994). Is Radical Interpretation Possible? In J. Tomberlin (ed.), *Philosophical Perspectives: Logic and Language* (vol. 8, pp. 101–19). Atascadero, Calif.: Ridgeview.

Foley, R., and Fumerton, R. (1985). Davidson's Theism? *Philosophical Studies*, 48: 83–90.

Foster, J. A. (1976). Meaning and Truth Theory. In G. Evans and J. McDowell (eds.), *Truth and Meaning: Essays in Semantics* (pp. 1–32). Oxford: Clarendon Press.

Frege, G. (1997 (1892)). On *Sinn* and *Bedeutung*. In M. Beaney (ed.), *The Frege Reader*. Oxford: Blackwell. Originally published as Ueber Sinn und Bedeutung. *Zeitschrift für Philosophie und philosophische Kritik*, 100 (1892), 25–50.

Gödel, K. (1966). Russell's Mathematical Logic. In H. Putnam and P. Benacerraf (eds.), *Philosophy of Mathematics*. Englewood Cliffs: Prentice Hall.

Gopnik, A., and Astington, J. W. (1988). Children's Understanding of Representational Change and Its Relation to the Understanding of False Belief and the Appearance–Reality Distinction. *Child Development*, 59: 26–37.

Grandy, R. (1973). Reference, Meaning, and Belief. *Journal of Philosophy*, 70: 439–52.

Grice, P. (1989). *Studies in the Way of Words*. Cambridge, Mass.: Harvard University Press.

Guttenplan, S. (1985). Review of Inquiries into Truth and Interpretation. *Philosophy*, 60: 408–11.

Haack, R. J. (1978). Davidson on Learnable Languages. *Mind*, 87: 230–49.

Hacking, I. (1975). *Why does Language Matter to Philosophy*. Cambridge: Cambridge University Press.

——(1986). The Parody of Conversation. In E. Lepore (ed.), *Truth and Interpretation: Perspectives on the Philosophy of Donald Davidson*. Cambridge, Mass.: Blackwell.

Hahn, L. E. (1999). *The Philosophy of Donald Davidson*. Chicago, Ill.: Open Court.

Harman, G. (1974). Meaning and Semantics. In M. Munitz and P. Unger (eds.), *Semantics and Philosophy* (pp. 1–16). New York: New York University Press.

Higginbotham, J. (1992). Truth and Understanding. *Philosophical Studies*, 65: 3–16.

Hintikka, J. (1975). A Counterexample to Tarski-Type Truth-Definitions as Applied to Natural Languages. *Philosophia*, 5: 207–12.

Hochberg, H. (1975). Explaining Facts. *Metaphilosophy*, 6: 277–302.

Horwich, P. (1999). The Minimalist Conception of Truth. In S. Blackburn and K. Simmons (eds.), *Truth* (pp. 239–63). New York: Oxford University Press.

Jeffrey, R. (1983). *The Logic of Decision* (2nd edn.). Chicago: University of Chicago Press.

——(1985). Animal Interpretation. In E. Lepore (ed.), *Actions and Events: Perspectives on the Philosophy of Donald Davidson* (pp. 482–7). Oxford: Blackwell.

Kripke, S. A. (1980). *Naming and Necessity*. Cambridge: Harvard University Press.

Kroeber, T. (1961). *Ishi in Two Worlds: A Biography of the Last Wild Indian in North America*. Berkeley, Calif.: University of California Press.

Lepore, E. (1983). Three Trivial Truth Theories. *Canadian Journal of Philosophy*, 13: 433–48.

431

Bibliography

Lepore, E. (1997). Conditions on Understanding Language. *Proceedings of the Aristotelian Society*, 97: 41–60.
—— (2004). An Interview with Donald Davidson. *Problems of Rationality* (pp. 231–65). Oxford: Clarendon Press.
—— and Ludwig, K. (2005). *Donald Davidson: Truth-Theoretic Semantics*. Oxford: Oxford University Press.
Lewis, D. (1969). *Convention*. Cambridge, Mass.: Harvard University Press.
—— (1974). Radical Interpretation. *Synthese*, 27: 331–44.
Loar, B. (1976). Two Theories of Meaning. In G. Evans and J. McDowell (eds.), *Truth and Meaning: Essays in Semantics* (pp. 138–61). Oxford: Clarendon Press.
Ludlow, P., and Martin, N. (1998). *Externalism and Self-Knowledge*. Stanford, Calif.: CSLI Publications.
Ludwig, K. (1990). 'Skepticism and Externalist Theories of Thought Content.' Unpublished Dissertation, University of California, Berkeley.
—— (1992*a*). Brains in a Vat, Subjectivity, and the Causal Theory of Reference. *Journal of Philosophical Research*, 17: 313–45.
—— (1992*b*). Skepticism and Interpretation. *Philosophy and Phenomenological Research*, 52: 317–39.
—— (1994). First Person Knowledge and Authority. In G. Preyer, F. Siebelt, and A. Ulfig (eds.), *Language, Mind, and Epistemology: On Donald Davidson's Philosophy* (pp. 367–98). Dordrecht: Kluwer.
—— (1996*a*). Duplicating Thoughts. *Mind and Language*, 11: 92–102.
—— (1996*b*). Explaining Why Things Look the Way they Do. In K. Akins (ed.), *Perception*. Oxford: Oxford University Press.
—— (1996*c*). Singular Thought and the Cartesian Theory of Mind. *Noûs*, 30: 434–60.
—— (ed.). (2003). *Donald Davidson*. New York: Cambridge University Press.
—— and Ray, G. (2002). Vagueness and the Sorites Paradox. In J. Tomberlin (ed.), *Philosophical Perspectives: Language and Mind* (vol. 16, pp. 419–61). Oxford: Blackwell.
Malcom, N. (1958). Knowledge of Other Minds. *Journal of Philosophy*, 55: 969–78.
Matthews, R. J. (1986). Learnability of Semantic Theory. In E. Lepore (ed.), *Truth and Interpretation: Perspectives on the Philosophy of Donald Davidson* (pp. 49–58). Cambridge, Mass.: Blackwell.
Millikan, R. (1984). *Language, Thought and Other Biological Categories*. Cambridge, Mass.: MIT Press.
Neale, S. (1990). *Descriptions*. Cambridge: MIT Press.
—— (1995). The Philosophical Significance of Gödel's Slingshot. *Mind*, 104: 761–825.
Papineau, D. (1987). *Reality and Representation*. New York: Blackwell.
Perner, J., Leekam, S. R., and Wimmer, H. (1987). Three-Year-Olds' Difficulty with False Belief: The Case for Conceptual Deficit. *British Journal of Developmental Psychology*, 5: 125–37.
Pietroski, P. (1994). A Defense of Derangement. *Canadian Journal of Philosophy*, 24: 95–118.

Putnam, H. (1975). The Meaning of 'Meaning'. *Mind, Language and Reality: Philosophical Papers* (vol. 2, pp. 215–71). Cambridge: Cambridge University Press.

Quine, W. V. O. (1953). Two Dogmas of Empiricism. *From a Logical Point of View* (2nd edn.). Cambridge, Mass.: Harvard University Press.

—— (1960). *Word and Object*. Cambridge, Mass.: MIT Press.

—— (1969a). Epistemology Naturalized. *Ontological Relativity and Other Essays* (pp. 69–90). New York: Columbia University Press.

—— (1969b). *Ontological Relativity and Other Essays*. New York: Columbia University Press.

—— (1974). Comment on Donald Davidson. *Synthese*, 27: 325–9.

Ramberg, B. T. (1989). *Donald Davidson's Philosophy of Language: An Introduction*. Cambridge, Mass.: Blackwell.

Ramsey, F. (1990 (1931)). Truth and Probability. In D. H. Mellor (ed.), *Philosophical Papers*. Cambridge: Cambridge University Press. Originally published in R. B. Braithwaite (ed.), *The Foundations of Mathematics and other Logical Essays*. London: Routledge & Kegan Paul.

Rawling, P. (2002). Radical Interpretation. In K. Ludwig (ed.), *Donald Davidson*. New York: Cambridge University Press.

Richard, M. (1992). Semantic Competence and Disquotational Knowledge. *Philosophical Studies*, 65: 37–52.

Russell, B. (1905). On Denoting. *Mind*, 14: 479–93.

—— (1919). *Introduction to Mathematical Philosophy*. London: George Allen & Unwin.

—— and Whitehead, A. N. (1962). *Principia Mathematica*. Cambridge: Cambridge University Press.

Schiffer, S. (1987). *Remnants of Meaning*. Cambridge, Mass.: MIT Press.

—— (1992). Belief Ascription. *Journal of Philosophy*, 89: 499–521.

Searle, J. R. (1983). *Intentionality: An Essay*. Cambridge: Cambridge University Press.

Soames, S. (1984). Linguistics and Psychology. *Linguistics and Philosophy*, 7: 155–80.

—— (1989). Semantics and Semantic Competence. In J. Tomberlin (ed.), *Philosophy of Mind and Action Theory* (vol. 3). Atascadero, Calif.: Ridgeview.

—— (1992). Truth, Meaning, and Understanding. *Philosophical Studies*, 65: 17–36.

—— (2003). *Philosophical Analysis in the Twentieth Century, II. The Age of Meaning*. Princeton, NJ: Princeton University Press.

Stich, S. (1976). Davidson's Semantic Program. *Canadian Journal of Philosophy*, 6: 201–27.

Strawson, P. F. (1959). *Individuals: An Essay in Descriptive Metaphysics*. London: Methuen.

—— (1984). Hot Pursuit: Inquiries into Truth and Interpretation. *London Review of Books* (19 July–1 Aug.): 17.

Tarski, A. (1944). The Semantic Conception of Truth and the Foundations of Semantics. *Philosophy and Phenomenological Research*, 4: 341–76.

Bibliography

Tarski, A. (1983 (1935)). The Concept of Truth in Formalized Languages. *Logic, Semantics, Metamathematics* (2nd edn., pp. 152–278). Indianapolis: Hackett Publishing Co. Originally published as "De Wahrheitsbegriff in den formalisierten Sprachen." *Studia Philosphica*, I, 261–405.

Tennant, N. (1977). Truth, Meaning and Decidability. *Mind*, 86: 368–87.

Unger, P. (1979). Why there are No People. In P. A. French, T. E. Uehling, and H. K. Wettstein (eds.), *Midwest Studies in Philosophy: Studies in Metaphysics* (vol. 4, pp. 177–222). Minneapolis: University of Minnesota Press.

Wallace, J. (1977). Only in the Context of a Sentence do Words have Any Meaning. In P. A. French, T. E. Uehling, and H. K. Wettstein (eds.), *Midwest Studies in Philosophy: Studies in the Philosophy of Language* (vol. 2, pp. 144–64). Minneapolis: University of Minnesota Press.

——(1978). Logical Form, Meaning, Translation. In M. Guenthener-Reutter (ed.), *Meaning and Translation*. London: Duckworth.

Weinstein, S. (1974). Truth and Demonstratives. *Noûs*, 8: 179–84.

Wiggins, D. (1980). 'Most' and 'All': Some Comments on a Familiar Programme. In M. Platts (ed.), *Reference, Truth and Reality: Essays on the Philosophy of Language* (pp. 318–46). London: Routledge & Kegan Paul.

Wilson, N. L. (1959). Substances without Substrata. *Review of Metaphysics*, 12: 521–39.

Wittgenstein, L. (1950). *Philosophical Investigations*. London: Macmillan.

Wright, C. (1976). Language-Mastery and the Sorites Paradox. In G. Evans and J. McDowell (eds.), *Truth and Meaning* (pp. 223–47). Oxford: Oxford University Press.

——(1987). Further Reflections on the Sorites Paradox. *Philosophical Topics*, 15: 204–50.

Index

Index

Index

Index